THE ZEA
MYTH

And Other Fables about Jesus and the Bible

RON SNYDER

Be ready and prepared to provide a lucid answer to anyone who asks you to explain and defend the hope and faith you have, and respond with gentleness and respect (1 Peter 3:15).

Translations I have used for my research are listed below:

TABLE OF CONTENTS

Introduction...1
Chapter One: Jesus Through an Obscure Lens.........................5
    Assessing the Jesus Seminar...5
    The Reliability of Oral Traditions 10
    The Wrong Methodology 13
    Three Tests for Determining Authenticity and Reliability of the
    Gospels 19
    Erroneous Claims...26
    Marcus Borg and the New Age Jesus 31
    A Critique of Richard Horsley's Views of Jesus, Christianity,
    and Paul 35
    A Brief Look at Islam's View of Jesus............................38
Chapter Two: Unstable Building Blocks..................................41
    The Historical Jesus vs. the Christ-of-Faith 41
    Fixing the Dates...43
    Are the Gospels Unreliable Historical Documents?.........45
    Was Jesus the Leader of a Jewish Movement?.................47
Chapter Three: The Early Years of Jesus 54
    What about Quirinius?...54
    Critical Realism—An Approach for Determining Historicity.59
    Herod's Massacre of the Innocents..................................61
    Explaining the Genealogy of Jesus..................................63
    The Compatibility of the Infancy Stories 65
    Young Jesus at the Temple 66
Chapter Four: The Beginnings of Jesus' Ministry...................68
    Was Jesus Uneducated, Illiterate, and Extremely Poor?........68
    John's Baptism: The Gospels vs. Josephus 71
    Was Jesus Baptized for the Remission of Sins? 76
    Who Is Superior—Jesus or John?....................................81
    The Temptation of Jesus...83
Chapter Five: The Galilean Ministry of Jesus 87
    Seven "Facts" Exposed..87
    Luke's Three "Mistakes"..90
    A Portrait of Jesus...91
    John the Baptizer Beheaded...98
Chapter Six: Jesus as Magician 103
    Magician or Miracle Worker 103
    The Source of Jesus' Power..106
    Refuting Three "Reasons" Why Jesus Might Be a Magician 108
    Four Examples of How Jesus' Miracles Were Unique..........111
    A Misuse of Scripture...112

Celsus and His Attack on Christianity 113
Jesus and the Temple Priests 115
Did the Gospel Writers Ignore Jesus' Being a Magician?.....118
Apollonius vs. Jesus...122
Chapter Seven: The Kingdom of God 125
Did Jesus Know What the Kingdom Was?...........................125
Nine Parables about the Kingdom of God...........................130
The Messiah as "Seed of the Woman" 137
The Transfiguration 145
Chapter Eight: Jesus as Zealot...147
The Beatitudes 147
"I Did Not Come to Bring Peace, but a Sword" 151
The Entry into Jerusalem and the "Cleansing" of the Temple
....156
Pick Up Your Cross—Is this a Call for Revolution?............160
New World Order 165
The Tribute to Caesar 169
Chapter Nine: Was Jesus a Bigot?....................................173
The Canaanite Woman 174
The Good News Taken to all the Nations...........................176
Does "Love Your Neighbor" Have Ethnic Restrictions? 178
Is Jesus Above the Law?...179
A Deplorable View of God..184
God as a "man of war"..184
The "Canaan Conquest" 186
God's "Blood-Stained Clothes".......................................193
"Crushing the Enemies' Heads" 194
Chapter Ten: Jesus as Messiah 198
Did Jesus Reject the Title of Messiah?..............................198
Did the Gospel Writers Reconstruct Jesus?........................201
Jesus as the Redeeming Messiah of the Hebrew Scriptures ..208
Did Jesus Make any Claims about Being God?...................212
What does the title 'Son of Man' Mean?...........................217
Prophecies Regarding the Messianic Kingdom...................223
Three Basic Promises—End Times; Liberation; the Restoration
of Israel 225
Chapter Eleven: A Journey Through the Gospels 236
Mark's Gospel 238
Matthew's Gospel...243
Luke's Gospel..246
John's Gospel...252
Chapter Twelve: Jesus as the Messenger of the Lord.........259

The Messenger of the Lord in the Hebrew Scriptures...........259
Jesus as God Incarnate.....................................262
The Linear Unfolding of History...............................269
Chapter Thirteen: The Arrest, Trial and Execution of Jesus............271
Gethsemane as Jesus' Hideout................................271
Did the Roman Guards Assist in Jesus' Arrest?.................274
Why did Jesus Tell His Disciples to Buy a Sword?.............275
Was Jesus Really Determined to Destroy Those who Opposed
Him?...277
Did the Sanhedrin Trial Break All the Rules?.................282
The Trial before Pilate..285
Sedition or Blasphemy?.......................................291
Three Conclusions...298
Four Ways to make Jesus into a Messiah......................301
The Torn Curtain...302
Chapter Fourteen: The Resurrection of Jesus....................306
What about other Cultures' Resurrection Stories?.............306
Did the Hebrew Scriptures talk about a Resurrection?.........308
Historical Evidence for the Resurrection.......................313
What about Mark's Last Chapter?.............................321
Chapter Fifteen: An Attack on Luke's Book of Acts.............326
What about John the Baptizer's Followers?...................327
Was Peter Illiterate?..328
Questioning Stephen's Knowledge of Jewish History..........330
What Happened to the Disciples of Jesus?...................334
Did Peter, John, and James Hold Strictly to Jewish Laws and
Customs?...335
A Look at the Council Meeting in Acts 15....................336
Did Luke Call Paul an Apostle?...............................338
A Journey Through Acts.......................................339
Chapter Sixteen: Paul as Rogue Apostle.......................346
The Apostles vs. Paul..346
Paul Summoned to Jerusalem?................................347
Is there Evidence from Galatians that Paul was a Rogue
Apostle?...350
Did Paul Suffer from Delusions of Grandeur?.................356
Did Paul Consider Peter, John and James "False Apostles"?357
Jude Agrees with Paul..359
Paul Is Summoned to Jerusalem, Again?......................360
Chapter Seventeen: Paul and the Historical Jesus.............365
Was Paul Disinterested in the Historical Jesus?..............365
Did Paul Really Contradict Jesus?............................369

Paul's Christology 371
Jesus as "Firstborn" 375
Chapter Eighteen: Was the Epistle of James Written as a Polemic against Paul? 383
The Torah and the New Jewish Christian............................383
The "Works of the Law"..387
Faith without Works Is Dead......................................390
No Conflict between James and Paul 392
Comparing Paul and James..393
A Comment by Matthew Henry 394
Chapter Nineteen: Six Questionable Remarks 396
Did Paul Write All the Epistles Attributed to Him? 396
Is Peter the Rock of the Church? 397
Did the Diaspora Jews Write the Gospels?........................400
Two Choices—A False Dilemma.....................................405
The Pseudo-Clementine Documents.................................409
Were the Gospels Written to Support Paul's Christology? ...410
Chapter Twenty: The Last Gasp 416
The Council of Nicaea 416
A Look at "Christian" History 418
Chapter Twenty-one: Postscript—Another Look at Islam 425
Is Allah the same as Yahweh?....................................425
Muhammad and the Beginnings of Islam............................426
The Sunni and Shi'a...428
The Bible vs. the Qur'an..428
Who is the Prophet?...430
The Word of God as a Person.....................................430
No Assurance of Salvation for the Muslim 431
Our Freedom in Jesus 432
Chapter Twenty-two: Why it Matters..............................435
REFERENCE PAGE 438

Introduction

Much has been said about Jesus over the last two thousand years. Scholars have debated his words and deeds for centuries, and some have even questioned his very existence. Those from various cultures, religions and worldviews have also proffered their own opinions and theories about Jesus. Today, the debate centers mostly on what is being called the historical Jesus and the non-historical Jesus (the so-called Christ-of-faith). The goal in this ongoing debate, supposedly, is to discover the "real" Jesus. Where do we begin this odyssey? Has so much been said about Jesus that it is now almost impossible to know the true, historical Jesus? Can we find the real Jesus in the four Gospels—Matthew, Mark, Luke and John—or must we look elsewhere? Some recent books have tried to convince us that the Jesus we think we know is not the Jesus of history. They claim that the Jesus we are familiar with is not the "real" Jesus. They endeavor to "demythologize" Jesus, strip him down to the bare bones, in order to discover the "historical" Jesus. Rudolf Bultmann addresses this modern attempt to "demythologize" Jesus in his books, and many contemporary liberal theologians and biblical scholars have followed in his footsteps.

Throughout my book, I make allusions to liberal theologians and liberal biblical scholars, so let me clarify, for the reader, what I mean by these terms. The liberal theologian/biblical scholar attempts to "demythologize" and "de-dogmatize" the Bible in a number of ways: one, by adopting philosophical expressions popularized by the so-called "freethinkers" of the Enlightenment; two, by making use of literary criticism and form criticism to denigrate the Bible; three, utilizing a form of hermeneutics (biblical exegesis and interpretation) that discounts and/or downplays the supernatural, thereby rejecting the miraculous and removing any and all instances of "superstitious" elements within the Bible. The liberal theologian/biblical scholar often rejects the Bible as a collection of historical, factual statements, and sees it more as a collection of writings that reflect the writers' own feelings and/or beliefs (a postmodern method of interpretation). The liberal theologian/biblical scholar is, therefore, not interested in discovering propositional or objective truth from the Bible, but rather accepts subjective pluralism—"whatever is true for you"—as the normative. The liberal theologian/biblical scholar creates her/his own paradigms and concepts that reflect their own particular view of the Bible and, in doing so, attempts to recreate Jesus by stripping him of all supernatural elements and redefining him in terms that best suits their own particular model—for example, a Cynic, a zealot, a moral teacher, a spiritual guide, etc. The liberal theologian/biblical scholar rejects the Bible as God's Word and denies that Jesus is the Son of God and Messiah (see 1 Jn 2:22). The liberal theologian/biblical scholar often defines faith as an irrational response to reality and, if they do happen to accept God's existence, do not allow him to "interfere" with his creation—i.e., no miraculous "zapping" allowed.

In defining the liberal theologian/biblical scholar as I do, I do not want to disparage the importance of literary criticism or the method of hermeneutics; both are important epistemological tools. But, like most tools, their usefulness and accuracy is determined by the hand that wields the tool. You will find as you read a typical liberal theologian/biblical scholar that they start off making some interesting and, often times, true biblical statements, but as they get deeper into their book you discover that you are now far off the path and are reading things about Jesus, the resurrection, Christianity, biblical doctrine, etc., that are not found within the pages of the Bible but in the imagination of the writer. Some of the modern liberal theologians/biblical scholars that come to mind are John Dominic Crossan and Marcus Borg (both of the Jesus Seminar), Richard Horsley, John Shelby Spong, Bart Ehrman, Elaine Pagels, and Karen Armstrong; they are among the popular writers/scholars who would/could fit this description, having attempted to present a "new" view of Jesus, one that they believe is superior to the portrait of Jesus drawn from the four canonical Gospels—Matthew, Mark, Luke and John. Also included in this list is Dr. Reza Aslan who, in his book *Zealot: The Life and Times of Jesus of Nazareth*, attempts to do his part in helping you find this allusive "real" Jesus. Aslan presents a portrait of Jesus as a mere peasant rebel who had hoped to usher in the "kingdom of God" in Israel, and thereby oppose (and remove) his country's occupied power—namely the Roman Empire. Aslan believes that Jesus had a personal zeal for God that turned him into a zealot, which, of course, got him killed. Is Aslan's portrayal correct? How do we know or determine whether what Aslan says is true or not? Is it possible to recognize and correct erroneous statements about Jesus?

One problem with popular books about Jesus by the likes of Ehrman, Pagels, Crossan, Borg, and Aslan is that the majority of people reading them will probably not do any further research to see if they are correct in what they say. Therefore, let me take this time to thank you for your interest in my treatise; and I hope that you will take the time to truly discover the Jesus of history. So, we must ask ourselves, after reading Aslan's book: Does he help us discover the "real" Jesus? You will have to decide that for yourself. I will attempt to make my case here that he does not.

Why, then, is this project important to me? It is important because I believe that everyone's life, in the here and now and hereafter, hinges on what they believe about Jesus. This can be said of no other human being. What makes Jesus different, and what the four canonical Gospels say about that difference, is, in part, what I will present within these pages. This is my apologetic, written as a reasoned answer to what I think are mistakes (errors) within the worldview and/or mindset of popular authors like Aslan, Crossan, Borg, Pagels, Spong, and others of their ilk, including some of the so-called "new" atheists (I refer to them as such because many, if not most, of their ideas, statements, beliefs, and disclaimers against Christianity are not new, but have been around for centuries and have been refuted). For those of you interested in where I stand regarding Jesus, allow me a brief comment. I became a Christian at the age of eighteen, and what impressed me about Christianity was not only the insistence but the confidence that its claims were historical. Christianity maintained that its doctrines, or belief system, were founded upon historical events, tracing its beginnings to the promises God made to early man, to Abraham, to the nation Israel, and to Moses and the prophets, culminating in the historical life, death and resurrection of Jesus Christ. I found it imperative to my personal growth as a Christian to continue my education, so I spent fifteen years in secular colleges, getting degrees in psychology, philosophy, and history. Most of my forty years as a Christian have been engaged in the study of the Bible, using commentaries and other guides to understand the Scriptures. I have come to the conclusion, based on all that I have learned, that the Jesus of history is the same as the Christ of faith.

No scholarly historian doubts that there was a man named Jesus who lived and died in the first century of our common era. What we see today in many of the books written about Jesus, especially those by liberal theologians/biblical scholars, is that they are purposefully and prejudicially presenting their own worldview, regardless of how reliable that worldview is. Jesus actually warned us that many false teachers would appear and deceive many people (Mt 24:11). It is important to know the truth—and the truth is knowable—in order to identify what is counterfeit. So, how do we know if the things we read about Jesus are true? Especially if those things were written so long ago in what are called the four canonical Gospels? Are there criteria that can be used to determine if what is written about Jesus is correct, whether those books are ancient writings or current ones? Or do we just pick an author with a viewpoint similar to our own and then simply believe what he or she has written? Does it really matter what we believe? Is one belief just as good as the next? In our culture, where opinion often overrides truth, does one even care about the Jesus of history? What is wrong with just creating a portrait of Jesus, one that we are comfortable with, and then believing that? What is wrong with deciding to not care about the whole matter at all? What difference does it make if we believe in Jesus, anyway? Why should we care that Jesus lived and died some two thousand years ago? I hope to bring answers to these questions in my book.

In the first chapter, I will provide an assessment of the ideas and theories of the Jesus Seminar because of their enduring influence on modern views of Jesus. I will show why the Gospels can be accepted as reliable historical documents. I will critique Richard Horsley's ideas about Jesus, Christianity, and Paul because he has also attempted to change the way we see Jesus. Lastly, I will provide a brief look at Islam's view of Jesus because of its influence on Reza Aslan's book, *Zealot*. It is evident after reading *Zealot* that Aslan has adopted many of the conclusions of the Jesus Seminar and follows the Islamic view of Jesus.

Chapter One: Jesus Through an Obscure Lens

Assessing the Jesus Seminar

The Jesus Seminar was started in the mid-1980s by Robert Funk and John Dominic Crossan. Their goal was to thwart fundamentalist ideas of Jesus and present what they considered a more accurate and realistic view. Robert Funk, a New Testament scholar and Greek grammarian, wanted to write a book on the historical Jesus and thought it would be interesting to incorporate in that book different ideas about Jesus from other scholars; in other words, he wanted to gather a consensus of what others thought about who Jesus was. Along with John Dominic Crossan, a Biblical Studies professor, Robert Funk assembled a team of scholars—and others—whose mission it was to vote on each saying of Jesus as recorded in the four Gospels in order to determine how authentic those scholars thought the sayings were. The Jesus Seminar was born, and its task was to find the "real" Jesus. The group decided on four different colored beads that would mark or represent the degree of authenticity of a saying attributed to Jesus. By this method, the JS would create a new kind of red-letter edition of the Gospels. The JS scholars had decided that many of the sayings attributed to Jesus were simply not authentic, and they were going to eliminate all the sayings they believed Jesus did not say, so that what was left were the truly authentic words of Jesus. (The JS would also focus on the deeds attributed to Jesus, such as his healing of diseases, his nature miracles, etc.)

The four colored beads that were chosen to represent what each JS scholar determined were the authentic and inauthentic sayings of Jesus were red, pink, gray, and black. The red bead would mean the voter/scholar believed Jesus said the particular passage, or something very close to it; a pink bead would indicate that the voter believed Jesus probably said something similar to the Gospel passage, but it was not an exact quote; a gray bead meant that the voting scholar believed Jesus did not say the words attributed to him, but that they contained an idea that Jesus would probably agree with; and the "scholar" using the black bead would show that he/she believed Jesus did not say what was attributed to him in the passage. The black bead would therefore indicate that the words attributed to Jesus were, so to speak, put in his mouth; they were added by some later writer who got it from an already developed Christian thought. Typically, the gray and black beads were used to indicate that the JS scholars found the saying attributed to Jesus inconsistent with what they considered was Jesus' original speech. It is interesting to note that they believed they were somehow able to determine what Jesus' original speech was, as if they had some special access to some special documents. And that is, in a sense, what they thought. Those special documents are the Gospel of Thomas and the hypothetical writings known as "Q." Although there are no physical Q documents, this hypothetical artifact is assumed to have existed, its contents being inferred by compiling the verses that Matthew and Luke share in common but are absent from Mark's Gospel. Reza Aslan, as we will see, relies heavily upon the "Q" document.

Since the JS appeared to be interested in the true words of Jesus, they must have had criteria for determining which sayings of Jesus were authentic. Their criteria turned out to be quite simplistic. All the sayings attributed to Jesus in the Gospels that are short, pithy statements, like 'turning the other cheek' (Mt. 5:39) and 'loving your enemies' (Lk 6:27), are considered authentic by the Jesus Seminar. Likewise, those sayings that have a more or less generic moral or philosophical tone are considered authentic by the Jesus Seminar; in other words, statements that were not particularly religious. The sayings that fall out of this criterion, and are therefore rejected, are examples like 'bearing one's cross' (Mk 8:34) and being 'born again' (Jn 3:3); these are not considered authentic by the JS. This includes everything Jesus said from the cross, as well as what he supposedly said about himself. So when Mark says that Jesus alluded to himself as being the Messiah (14:62), or when John had the audacity to have Jesus say that he was "the way, and the truth, and the life," (14:6), the JS simply claims that Jesus did not say these things. And since Jesus did not say them, these passages are not authentic. The reason the JS deems these particular passages or sayings as inauthentic is because the JS views Jesus as a mere peasant sage or a Cynic who roamed the countryside, making pithy statements about the poor, emphasizing hospitality and the importance of communal sharing, and proclaiming the kingdom of God as some kind of egalitarian community. In other words, it is their view of Jesus that determines whether a saying is authentic, or not. So, if Jesus did not say these things, then other people had to have put these words in his mouth, and that makes them inauthentic sayings. The JS scholars' method of reasoning, however, is to first draw their conclusions and then only accept evidence that supports those conclusions, while discarding evidence that does not.

Besides these condensed sayings that the JS accepted as the authentic words of Jesus, they also added a few choice parables to the red list, such as the Good Samaritan (Lk 10:30-35) and the Vineyard Laborers (Mt. 20:1-15). The JS scholars also seem to like Jesus' saying about paying to Caesar what belongs to him and to God what belongs to God. (Maybe they like this particular saying because it appears to sound subversive, which is how Aslan interprets it, as we will see later.) When all was said and done the JS scholars determined that 82 percent of what the Gospels attribute to Jesus was not actually said by him (or done by him), that is, the vast majority of the Gospels were gray and black-beaded. Eighteen percent were given red and pink beads. The Gospel that came out faring the worst was the Gospel of John, where everything Jesus said in it was given a black bead.

The Fellows of the Jesus Seminar (as they like to refer to themselves) have set themselves up as modern arbiters of the Gospels, claiming to have the wherewithal to determine what Jesus did and did not say (and did and did not do). It is, therefore, a legitimate and necessary endeavor to question the reliability of these JS scholars, to discover the criteria they used to determine their conclusions, to know their methodology, and to ascertain how they came to possess the authority to determine what is authentic and what is not. It is certainly justifiable to note that the members of the Jesus Seminar are not a representative body of New Testament scholars. The Jesus Seminar described their process of discovering the historical Jesus in their popular book *The Five Gospels: What Did Jesus Really Say? The Search for the Authentic Words of Jesus*. The book is a record of their attempts to decipher the authenticity of Jesus' sayings recorded in the canonical Gospels. *The Five Gospels* provides the details of how they determined which colored bead to give to a particular passage that recorded what Jesus said. The authors of *The Five Gospels* dedicate their book to Thomas Jefferson who literally cut out (using scissors) passages from the Bible and the Gospels that did not go along with his worldview. Jefferson removed everything that appeared supernatural, thereby creating his own version of the Bible. Like Jefferson, the JS scholars would cut out everything from the Gospels that did not agree with their own worldview. One major complaint about the approach the Fellows take is that they start out by doubting the Gospels as reliable sources of what Jesus said, and then attempt to find the evidence to support their thesis. (Most historians of ancient writings give the document they are studying the benefit of the doubt before finding reasons not to do so.)

So why does the JS make reference to five Gospels in their book's title? You may think there were only four—Matthew, Mark, Luke and John. But the JS have added another one—the Gospel of Thomas, a compilation of 114 sayings attributed to Jesus. The Gospel of Thomas was among some ancient writings found near Nag Hammadi, Egypt, in December 1945. The Gospel of Thomas contains no narration and, in that sense, is similar to Proverbs in the Hebrew Scriptures (Old Testament). Some of the sayings found in the Gospel of Thomas are also found in the four canonical Gospels, with some variation, but there are some sayings that are quite odd. (You can find the Gospel of Thomas on-line; Stephen Patterson and Marvin Meyer's, *The "Scholars' Translation" of the Gospel of Thomas*, is an excellent translation.) The Jesus Seminar places a lot of significance on the Gospel of Thomas and prefers it primarily because there is no narrative; it does not say anything about Jesus. There is nothing about his birth, his miracles, his death and resurrection. Because of this the JS believes the Gospel of Thomas was written before any of the four canonical Gospels, that the four Gospels relied on the Thomas Gospel and not the other way around. They insist that the Gospel of Thomas was an earlier document that provided, along with the hypothetical "Q" document, the foundation for the four canonical Gospels. There is, of course, no evidence for this conclusion, but as seems the case with the JS, presumption is as good as evidence. There is very strong evidence, however, that the Thomas Gospel and many of the other mystical writings, like the Gospel of Peter and the Gospel of Mary, were all written in the second and third centuries A.D., possibly a hundred years or more after all the writings of the New Testament were completed, copied and distributed. (An excellent book on this subject is *Thomas, the Other Gospel* by Nicholas Perrin, who gives convincing evidence as to why the Gospel of Thomas and the other non-canonical "Gospels" were written much later than the New Testament.)

The Gospel of Thomas, rather than being a foundational document, is unable to support the theories and assumptions (and hopes) of the Jesus Seminar. The Gospel of Thomas (and the other mystical "Gospels" of the second and third centuries) was a document that combined authentic sayings of Jesus with inauthentic ones, revealing the extent that some "Christians" had moved away from the truth by the second century. The four canonical Gospels (and other New Testament writings) were the standards the early Church used to determine what was counterfeit and what was not. They were used to discern the false teachings from the legitimate ones. In fact, it did not take long for several false ideas to emerge during the infancy of the Church, which is what most of the New Testament letters addressed. The Jesus Seminar's attempt to switch the foundational stones by asserting that the Gospel of Thomas predates the four canonical Gospels is an assertion without historical evidence.

Beginning in the first century, Christianity had made some uniquely historical claims about its founder; these can be found in the four canonical Gospels and the other New Testament writings. If these claims (especially those surrounding the person of Jesus) can be shown to be non-historical (i.e., they did not happen), then the theological claims of Christianity become foundationless. So it is entirely appropriate to utilize criteria of historical analysis that believers and unbelievers alike can use to determine if the Bible can withstand such scrutiny and be deemed reliable. From the time of the so-called Enlightenment era, the Bible has "gone under the knife" of literary and form criticism, and, I am happy to report, the patient has survived. Many biblical critics (from Voltaire, Thomas Paine, scholars like Friedrich Schleiermacher, Adolf von Harnack, to Rudolf Bultmann) have questioned the reliability, historicity, and authenticity of the Bible, focusing particularly on the Gospels. (The questions arising from their critical methods have been adequately answered in commentaries and books on Christian apologetics.) The JS has merely continued in their footsteps and, therefore, do not really offer anything new; they have merely revived the slumbering ideas of these past biblical critics—ideas that have been sufficiently critiqued. One of the biblical criticisms, then and now, focused on the issue of oral traditions and their reliability.

9

The Reliability of Oral Traditions

It is the consensus of some scholars (especially the liberal theologian/biblical scholar) that the teachings of Jesus were not written down when he first spoke them but were passed along by word of mouth over a period of several decades. During that time the use or practice of oral traditions kept what Jesus said and did from being forgotten until they were eventually placed in the format in which we now find them—the four canonical Gospels. In *The Making of the New Testament*, Patzia shows that oral traditions were referred to in Matthew 15:2 and Galatians 1:14 as acceptable means of remembering the teachings of rabbis. Patzia says that oral traditions served the early Christians well during times when they were asked specific questions about Jesus. Peter, in fact, admonished his readers to always be prepared to provide a defense for the Christian faith (1 Pe 3:15). The early Christians would have been taught the words and deeds of Jesus and would be able to give clear and reasonable explanations for their beliefs. Patzia goes on to claim that oral traditions of Jesus' sayings were being collected in Christian centers established in Judea, Galilee and Syria (Damascus and Antioch), and eventually in Alexandria (Egypt), Asia Minor (modern Turkey), Greece and Rome. The JS and other liberal New Testament scholars, however, do not trust the practice of oral traditions. They say it allowed for too much redaction (editing, revising and embellishing) and, therefore, made the Gospels unreliable as historic documents. But is the practice of oral traditions suspect? If the information we have about Jesus originated from oral traditions, does that dismiss the legitimacy and/or reliability of the four canonical Gospels which are the result of those oral traditions? How legitimate, then, is the practice of oral traditions?

To understand the level of its legitimacy requires a knowledge of how important oral tradition was to the Jews in ancient times. Rabbis were known to memorize entire books of the Hebrew Scriptures. Within the Jewish culture, not only rabbis, but those who came to the synagogue to listen to the reading of Hebrew Scriptures took great care in memorizing what they heard, and were very careful in their recitation to make sure it was correct. This form of oral tradition is quite different from the game of "telephone," where people sit in a circle and someone starts off by saying something and by the time it gets to the last person the original saying is completely changed. (Ehrman attempts to use this "game" in order to question the reliability of ancient oral traditions.) Anyone who compares the game of telephone to the memorization and recitation of the Hebrew Scriptures by rabbis and others throughout Jewish history does not understand the different processes between the two and, furthermore, does not understand and appreciate the capabilities of the mind regarding memorization. Many rabbis spoke in ways that made it easy for the listener to memorize what was being said. The one listening took seriously the task of correctly memorizing what was heard. This was an important part of their culture, going back hundreds (if not thousands) of years. It was a normal practice whereby important information was handed down to each generation so that the idea or concept that needed to be learned would be preserved.

In that typical Jewish tradition, Jesus' words and deeds would be memorized and circulated by his disciples. And in that tradition, his followers would make sure that they were preserved accurately, because that is how oral traditions worked in Jewish culture. When the oral traditions regarding Jesus were first being used (right after Jesus' ascension) the eyewitnesses to these events were both followers of Jesus and non-followers of Jesus (see the second chapter of Acts, Luke's sequel to his Gospel). If the new oral traditions regarding Jesus were false, and the writings that came out of those oral traditions (i.e., the canonical Gospels) were also false, then one would think that this new movement of believers who fabricated a dead person into a Messiah would have been destroyed by the hundreds, if not thousands, of eyewitnesses who would have known it was a fabrication. When we look at the changed behavior of the early disciples (e.g., Peter, Phillip, John, and James—Jesus' brother) that took place in the two-month period between Jesus' crucifixion and his ascension, we have to ask ourselves why would they have started a movement, and died for that movement, when they knew it was based on a lie. Someone might die for a lie that they think is true, but surely no one would die for a lie they knew was a lie.

The JS wants you to believe that is exactly what the early disciples did however do. They claim that the early Christian community simply lacked a genuine interest in correct historical information about Jesus (Aslan makes a similar claim in *Zealot*). The JS offers no real evidence for this claim, only to say that since they were just poor fisherman and other social outcasts and were as uneducated and illiterate as their teacher—Jesus—they just did not get it right. The Jesus Seminar, therefore, takes the practice of oral tradition and then argues that, in the retelling of these stories, the stories were modified and embellished (and even some new stories were created) in order to fit some agenda or belief that the early Christians acquired, beliefs that did not have any roots in historic fact. The JS claims that a lot of these stories, which ended up in the four canonical Gospels that we have today, are myths or legends that had some meaning within the early Christian community, but do not need to be believed today. The JS scholars claim they are simply attempting to separate the historical Jesus from the Christ-of-faith found in the Gospels and other New Testament writings. They want to rid the New Testament of its Christ-of-faith sayings and only retain the Jesus-of-history sayings. In doing so, they remove 82% of the Gospels. The JS boasts that what they are after is historically sound and reliable information about Jesus, but they will not allow the early Christians this same purpose. Did these early Christians really give up their lives for a Jesus of their own imagination? The Jesus Seminar claims that their "scholars" are capable of objectively evaluating the four canonical Gospels, so why could not the writers of those canonical Gospels write objectively? Why would the canonical writers, as the JS scholars said they did, have resorted to manipulating and creating information they knew was wrong? What was their motive? And why were they so willing to die for what they knew was erroneous?

I would, at this point, like to challenge the idea (stated above) that the teachings (sayings) of Jesus were not written down when he first spoke them, but had only been passed along by word of mouth (via oral traditions). We see in the four canonical Gospels that wherever Jesus traveled there were Pharisees, scribes, and teachers of the law that followed him. Although Jesus was sometimes harsh to these groups in pointing out their sins and religious pride, he also seems to have befriended some of them, even accepting invitations into their homes for a meal. Now part of a scribe's job is to write or record what is said, and teachers of the law (the Mosaic Law) were available to make sure what was said about the law was accurate. So, if Jesus had scribes and law teachers around him quite often, it can reasonably be assumed they were writing down what he said, or at least remembering it and writing it down later. We see from ancient days that scribes carried in their belts a writing kit that contained pens and ink (see Eze 9:2). It would not be difficult for the scribes following Jesus to record what he was saying. Also, we know that Matthew, one of Jesus' close disciples, was a taxman or toll collector, and he obviously knew how to keep records. It is possible that he was a recorder, writing down what Jesus said, and he could have done this pretty quickly after the event. Four or five (maybe even half) of the twelve apostles were fishermen. Fishing was their business, and probably a lucrative one. They obviously had to keep records, and were therefore able to read and write. They also could have recorded what Jesus said. Now Luke assuredly implies at the beginning of his Gospel (see 1:1f) that there were written accounts of what he himself was about to write. He used those accounts and a myriad of eyewitnesses (including Jesus' family) as his primary sources. It is quite reasonable to assume that some of these eyewitnesses would include the scribes and law teachers who followed Jesus everywhere, as well as Jesus' disciples. Luke could easily have interviewed these scribes and law teachers and/or been given their written documents to use as sources for his Gospel. Some of those scribes, teachers, and Pharisees actually became believers and followers of Jesus. (We see Pharisaic followers of Jesus at the Jerusalem Council—Acts 15.) Therefore, it is possible and probable that many of Jesus' sayings were written down close to the time of his uttering them, and that these written sayings were used by Luke for his investigative report into the life of Jesus.

The Wrong Methodology

By studying the Jesus Seminar's conclusions, we discover that they used a particular methodology in the use of their four colored beads to determine what is authentic and inauthentic within the four canonical Gospels. For them, a Gospel passage is authentic if it has multiple attestations, which means that more than one Gospel has to have Jesus say the same thing, or nearly the same thing, in order to be considered authentic. If only one Gospel has Jesus say something, then that saying was not authentic; the writer was simply making it up. That is why the JS does not accept any sayings of Jesus in the Gospel of John, because those sayings are particular to that Gospel. Of course, we do not use this criterion for modern-day biographies. Imagine telling a biographer who discovered some new information about their subject (e.g., Abraham Lincoln), as the result of their extensive research, that he was lying because he was the only one who told us this "fact." Another way the JS determines if a Gospel passage is authentic is if it records something embarrassing or negative. For example, the people of Nazareth not accepting Jesus as a bona fide preacher, or his family thinking he had gone off the deep end, so to speak. The JS figures that the writer would not have put something embarrassing in the story if it was not true. According to the JS, a passage is authentic if it showed some kind of irony or even sarcasm. If the saying or parable went against the cultural grain, then it was probably authentic. An example of this would be the admonition to "love your enemies," because this goes against one's normal or natural response. The JS believes these kinds of parables best represented Jesus' lecturing style. The JS will accept a passage as authentic if it admonishes a personal trust in God; for example, where Jesus talked about trusting God to answer one's prayers and needs. This is accepted by the JS because Jews were taught to trust God for their needs. The JS can accept these kinds of passages because they believe Jesus wanted others to experience the same spirit-relationship he had with God. Another way for the JS to tell that a passage is authentic is if it shows double dissimilarity. If a saying is attributed to Jesus and what he says is not something one could imagine a Jewish rabbi or an early Christian would say, then the saying is probably authentic. Otherwise, that saying probably got into one of the Gospels by a Jewish or a Christian writer. The problem with double dissimilarity is that it ignores the fact that Jesus was Jewish and was called a rabbi or teacher, and therefore it would not be odd for him to say something that would sound like what a Jewish person or rabbi would say. Of course, the JS rejects the notion that Jesus was out to create a church, and so they automatically reject any sayings attributed to Jesus that makes a reference to a future community of believers called the church. Again, here is an example of the JS first forming a conclusion and then finding the evidence to fit it, rather than drawing a conclusion based on the evidence itself.

The Jesus Seminar, of course, has decided that there are more inauthentic passages in the Gospels than there are authentic ones. A passage is inauthentic if, in it, Jesus makes a Messianic claim. The "I am" sayings of Jesus in John's Gospel are, therefore, inauthentic. Any passages where Jesus hints at being the Son of God are inauthentic. Any passage that makes a leadership statement, where it alludes to Jesus as some kind of leader or prophet, or Messiah, teacher (rabbi), or the founder of a church, etc., is inauthentic. Any reference to Jesus as the savior of the world is inauthentic and was added on by later writers; it was a fantasy created by the church. The JS insists that Jesus had no interest or intentions in starting a church. For the JS, any passage that contains an apocalyptic theme is definitely inauthentic, which therefore includes those passages that talk about the end of the world, or the end times, or the Second Coming of Christ, or the future resurrection of the dead. The JS rejects any passages that make a reference to a disciple-community; they believe passages that refer to a community of believers were added by later Christian writers. This includes any references to any kind of missionary work where disciples go out into the world to spread the gospel. We can see from what the JS considers authentic and inauthentic passages that their conclusions are based on their own personal bias; it is their own worldview masquerading as "truth." (This worldview was carried over by Aslan, as we will see later.) So the JS works off a preconceived idea of what they believe the historical Jesus was like. They reject major portions of the Gospels because they do not think they represent the real Jesus, but they do so not on the basis of external or internal evidence but merely on their own subjective opinion concerning what he (Jesus) must have been like. It is the JS that creates an imaginary Jesus and then attempts to use their picture of Jesus to measure the biblical portrait. This is not sound work.

Once the JS established their system of authenticating a Gospel passage, what conclusions did they arrive at regarding some of their basic beliefs about Jesus? They believe that Jesus was born in Nazareth during the reign of Herod the Great, and not in Bethlehem. That would put his birth around 4-6 B.C., due to the time period in which Herod died [which most Biblical scholars agree with today and poses no problems for Christianity]. They believe that Jesus was born of two human parents, no supernatural occurrence of parthenogenesis (virgin-birth). They believe that Jesus was an itinerant sage/preacher who ate with and connected with different social outcasts. They believe that Jesus was a faith-healer, but that the diseases and afflictions he healed were mostly psychosomatic. They believe that Jesus did not do nature miracles like walk on water or feed thousands of people from meager supplies or turn water into wine, nor did he raise other people, including Lazarus, from the dead. They believe that Jesus was arrested in Jerusalem for being a public nuisance (and possibly also because he advocated a rebellious movement), and was

15

crucified by the Romans. They believe that Jesus' body was thrown on a heap with other dead bodies and possibly eaten by feral dogs. Jesus was not resurrected and did not ascend into heaven. They believe that people who did not witness the events about Jesus (what he actually said and did), who were removed from those events by at least forty years, radically rewrote whatever authentic information there might have been in circulation about Jesus, and thus compiled a much larger (and false) narrative, adding their own beliefs and renditions into the story. These compilations became what we now know as the four canonical Gospels, drastically edited and embellished.

Therefore, the JS took it upon themselves to strip the Gospels of what they consider inauthentic material and get us back to the basics. To do this the Jesus Seminar have made a number of assumptions regarding first-century Christian writings, assumptions that are designed to cast doubts about the authenticity of those writings. One of their assumptions is that Matthew, Mark, Luke and John are not the authors of the four canonical Gospels; their names were simply attached to the writings, probably in the second century. Now, this idea did not originate with them; the question of Gospel authorship goes back many centuries. It is true that the earliest Gospel manuscripts do not have any authors' names attached to them. How did these names, then, get identified with a particular Gospel? Is there any external evidence that makes claims as to who the Gospel writers were? The answer to that question is a resounding YES! There were Christians in the latter part of the first century and in the second century who attributed authorship of the four Gospels to Matthew, Mark, Luke and John. Who were these people who verified the authors of the four canonical Gospels? One was a man named Papias, who lived from 60-130 A.D. He was a Christian bishop in Hierapolis (a city in what is now modern day Turkey) and happened to be a disciple and friend of John Zebedee, one of Jesus' apostles. Papias, who knew John quite well, tells us that John was the author of the Gospel that bears his name. Papias also claims that John informed him that Mark wrote down what Peter told him about the words and deeds of Jesus, and that those writings became the Gospel that bears Mark's name. Polycarp was another of John's disciples. Polycarp had a disciple named Irenaeus. Irenaeus was a second century bishop in what is today Lyons, France. Irenaeus says that he learned from Polycarp that Matthew published and distributed his Gospel among the Hebrews (i.e., the Jewish population) while

Peter and Paul were preaching the gospel in Rome, which would put its date of origin in the mid-60s. That date would also suggest that Matthew wrote his Gospel before or near the same time Mark was writing his. Irenaeus also agreed with Papias that Mark wrote his Gospel based on what Peter told him, and also stated that Luke got some of his information from what Paul preached about Jesus.

It is quite possible that the synoptic Gospels—Matthew, Mark and Luke—were written and distributed by the mid-60s, before Peter and Paul were executed under Nero's reign. Matthew's Gospel was distributed to a Jewish Christian audience; Mark's Gospel, a more condensed version, was probably sent to Christians in the vicinity of Rome; and Luke's Gospel, more than likely, was sent to those Christians where Paul and he had personally ministered, i.e., Asia Minor and Greece. Irenaeus also reported that John produced his Gospel while he was living in Ephesus, which agrees with what Papias had said. Based on this external evidence, it is possible that Matthew actually wrote his Gospel first, and the reason it was more detailed than Mark's was because it was written specifically to the Jewish population. The JS, Aslan, and others prefer the idea that Mark's Gospel was written first, and they do so because it is the simplest of the four Gospels. They assume that whatever is simpler must come before something more detailed, which is, of course, a false assumption. (Some information regarding Gospel authorship and dating was gleaned from *Tyndale Bible Dictionary* and from *The Apologetics Study Bible*.)

Patzia tells us that Tatian was a Syrian Christian who studied with Justin Martyr (a second century Christian apologist) in Rome. Returning to Syria, Tatian translated his Greek text (the four Gospels) into Syriac, arranging all the Gospel material into a continuous narrative on the life of Jesus, creating the first known "harmony" of the four Gospels. This shows that there was a circulation of all four Gospels by the middle of the second century. Tertullian, who lived in the latter half of the second century, was a native of Carthage in Africa and knew of all four canonical Gospels and claimed that they were written either by the apostles or by associates of the apostles. It seems unlikely that these second-century Christians would assign authorship to Mark and Luke, neither of whom were apostles and/or disciples of Jesus, unless there was evidence that they did, in fact, write the

Gospels that bear their name. Luke was probably a Gentile, and Mark deserted the first missionary journey of Paul and Barnabas (Mark's cousin). Matthew, who was an apostle, was also a former tax-collector, not a real popular job in first-century Jewish culture. One would think the early Christians would have assigned at least the three "synoptic" Gospels to more important figures. In comparison, many of the second and third-century mystical, non-canonical "Gospels" were assigned authorship to Peter, Mary, Thomas, and other important Christian personages in order to make them appear more legitimate.

The JS, of course, believes the four Gospels were all written after the fall of Jerusalem in 70 A.D., which means the first Gospel did not emerge until forty years after Jesus' death, i.e., a whole generation after the events. We have already seen that early Christian fathers have dated the Gospels of Matthew, Mark and Luke in the 60s, with a strong likelihood that Matthew's Gospel was the first to be written. The JS (and other scholars) needs to have Mark's Gospel be the earliest of the four canonical Gospels because they want to use the hypothetical Q document and Mark as the springboard for Matthew and Luke. Although it is difficult to pinpoint exactly when the Gospels were written, the JS (and Aslan) needs later dates to fit in with their agenda. This is not the way most legitimate historians work; you do not set up an agenda and then make the evidence fit that agenda. Luke's Gospel also fits a time frame for being written before 70 A.D. because his second volume (Acts), which was written after his Gospel, ends abruptly with Paul in Rome awaiting his appeal to the Roman emperor. Tradition states that Paul was beheaded in Rome circa 65-67. It is, therefore, quite likely that Luke's Gospel and his Acts were written before Paul's death. (Paul even quotes from the Gospel of Luke in his first pastoral letter to Timothy, which, of course, Aslan and others say Paul did not write; see 1 Tm 5:18.)

Early Christian tradition does, however, place John's Gospel in the late 80s, or early 90s, but this, in itself, does not necessarily throw doubt on his authorship or on the authenticity of what he wrote. (It is fairly probable that John was in his late teens when he joined Jesus with his brother James, and so John would only be in his seventies or early eighties when he wrote his Gospel.) Questioning the authenticity of John's Gospel just on the basis of its later date is no more compelling or legitimate than questioning the authenticity of modern biographies of say Abraham Lincoln or George Washington simply because they are written quite a few years after the fact. Matthew and John personally knew Jesus and so were in a great position to accurately preserve Jesus' teachings. Luke obviously played the consummate historian by talking to eyewitnesses and making use of other primary sources. Mark was with Peter (probably both in Jerusalem and in Rome), and was also reunited with Paul in Rome near the end of Paul's life. Peter and Paul were both executed near 67 A.D, and Luke and Mark's Gospels had obviously been written before then, as was Matthew's. One of the reasons the JS wants the Gospels to be written after the fall of Jerusalem in 70 A.D. is because Jesus had predicted the destruction of the Temple and the JS does not believe that Jesus made such predictions. Again, this is not the way to do history. (Some information for this section was gleaned from the Christian Answers website.) It is worth noting here that the *Didache*, which was composed at the turn of the first century and was used as a kind of teaching manual for Christians, testified to the fact that the written words and deeds of Jesus had been written down; in 8:2 of the *Didache* it admonished believers to "pray ... as the Lord bid us in his gospel" (see Patzia).

Three Tests for Determining Authenticity and Reliability of the Gospels

There are three basic tests historians use to determine the authenticity and reliability of historical documents. These are bibliographical tests, internal evidence tests, and external evidence tests. (Josh McDowell and his son, Sean, show how these tests are used in their book *More Than a Carpenter*, from which I have gleaned some information.) Bibliographical tests attempt to determine the reliability of the copies of a particular manuscript. If the original manuscript is not available, the historian will want to know how many manuscripts have survived and how consistent they are with one another; they would want to know the time interval between the original and the copy. For example, the Dead Sea Scrolls have been able to cast light on the accuracy of the Old Testament copies, showing how they were extremely close to the originals. The scribes, or document copiers, were very precise in their task; they understood the necessity of providing an exact copy of the original. The Scrolls demonstrate how remarkably accurate scribes were in copying the Hebrew Scriptures, showing little textual change over the centuries. Do we have something similar for the New Testament? As a matter of fact, the amount of extant manuscripts for the New Testament is quite impressive. For one thing, there are nearly 5,800 Greek New Testament manuscripts in existence today, with the earliest copy found around 130 A.D., and other copies within a hundred years after the originals. These manuscripts have been estimated to be extremely accurate. If you add these nearly 5,800 Greek manuscripts to the manuscripts that are in Syriac, Latin, Coptic, and Aramaic, there are more than 20,000 New Testament manuscripts that have been discovered since they were first written in the first century A.D. Although there are no originals, this amount of extant manuscripts is unheard of in relation to other ancient writings.

Because of the overabundance of New Testament manuscripts, there is a strong likelihood that there will be some variations between them. In other words, the more manuscripts there are the more chance there will be some (slight) differences among them. Manuscripts were being copied and distributed rather quickly and this did account for the occasional error. Patzia tells us that unintentional errors found in extant manuscripts account for about 95 percent of the variants that are found in the New Testament. These errors typically occurred when copyists simply made natural mistakes when they were copying from one manuscript to another. There were also intentional variations that occurred when copyists copied parallel passages from the Gospels, or similar-sounding phrases from Paul's letters, and deliberately attempted to make all the readings the same. Despite these intentional variations, Patzia heeds that it must be kept in mind that no significant doctrine of the New Testament hinges on any of these variants. Reasons for these variations, Patzia says, are ascribed to the fact that copying centers began to emerge in the fourth century in such places as Rome, Carthage, Alexandria, Caesarea, Antioch and Byzantium. Manuscripts were copied and circulated within a specific geographical area and often "assimilated" the characteristics of that area and thereby developed a "text-type" all their own which differed somewhat from text-types in other areas, even areas that were geographically close to one another. Patzia is confident that with the discoveries of older and superior Greek manuscripts like Sinaiticus and Vaticanus (from the 4th century) and Alexandrinus and Ephraemi (from the 5th century), along with the "criticism" disciplines (which includes textual, form, rhetorical, redaction, historical and source), it is certainly not difficult to conclude that the New Testament we have today is amazingly close in wording to the original manuscripts.

It is a sad fact that many of the professors who teach New Testament studies in our secular universities and colleges (and unfortunately in some of our so-called Christian institutions as well) have an agenda similar to the Jesus Seminar. They contend that the New Testament writers cannot be trusted; that there are too many variations in the extant manuscripts; that Jesus was made into a deity several centuries after he died; that he was not the savior of the world, but only a wandering preacher who wound up getting himself killed by some jealous religious leaders; or that he was some kind of zealot who purposively spoke out against the Roman intrusion and got himself killed for being a subversive rebel. Some liberal New Testament professors (like Ehrman) have written several books trying to prove that the amount of variations in the New Testament manuscripts show that they cannot be trusted. But what kinds of variations have been found? Do these variations reveal the kinds of changes that could upset some major or even minor Christian doctrine? The answer is: No, they do not. The vast majority of these variations are quite insignificant. For example, one manuscript might have a passage that has the word "you," whereas the same passage in another manuscript might have the word "us." One passage might say "one person," and another manuscript might have the same passage say "two people." One manuscript might have a passage that says "the city," and another manuscript has that same passage say "a city." Luke says "blessed are the poor," in his version of the Sermon on the Mount, and Matthew says, "blessed are the poor in spirit" in his. The irony here is that historians, police detectives, psychologists, etc., actually like to see variation. They are suspect of people who say exactly the same thing, as if they are in collusion with one another. Variation is not contradiction, and it is not necessarily an example of error. If an eyewitness says two people went into a store, and another eyewitness says a person went into a store, this is not a contradiction. The fact is one or more persons went into the store. Now these are the kinds of variations we see in the New Testament manuscripts, and they do not amount to any justification to disregard their reliability or their authenticity. The bibliographical testing of the New Testament

21

manuscripts gives us an assurance that the text we have now is as close to the original as possible.

So how does New Testament bibliographical testing stack up against other ancient writings? Let's pick a favorite of the so-called "new" atheists—Lucretius. Lucretius died about 50 years before Jesus was born; he was a Roman poet and philosopher. His only known work is an epic poem (the English translation calls it *On the Nature of Things*), introducing his readers to Epicurean philosophy. Atheists like him because he talks about the principles of atomism and describes the universe as being guided by chance or fortune and not by the divine intervention of the myriad of Roman gods. The historical reliability of *On the Nature of Things* does not seem to concern the so-called "new" atheists since the time span between the original and the two copies that we have is about 1,100 years. Not real good grounds for reliability. What about other ancient writings; how do they fare when it comes to the time span between their original and the earliest copy? What about Plato, the father of philosophy, the one of whom it is said that everything outside of Plato's writings is just footnotes? Well, the earliest copies we have of Plato's *Tetralogies* are about 1,300 years after Plato's death, and of those we have 210. For the most part, Aristotle's works were not copied until around the twelfth century, which makes the gap between his originals and the earliest copy about 1,400 years. Regarding both Herodotus, the father of history, and Thucydides, the Greek historian who wrote *The Peloponnesian Wars*, we have about 1,350 years between their originals and the most recent copies. Regarding Alexander the Great, we find that most historians believe that the Greek king/warrior conquered the cities the ancient documents said he conquered. You would think, then, that there were lots of extant manuscripts regarding Alexander, like we have with the New Testament. There are only about four extant manuscripts that tell us about Alexander, and they supposedly relied on original sources that have been lost, and those four extant manuscripts were written centuries later. Of those four extant manuscripts only two are considered reliable. Now Homer's *Iliad* seems to do real well compared to the other ancient writers (like Pliny, Euripides, Aristophanes, Tacitus, etc.), but, of course, not when you compare it (or all the other ones mentioned above) to the New Testament manuscripts. Homer's time span between his original and the earliest copy of the *Iliad* is about 400 years, but what is nice is that there are over 1,700 of these copies, and the accuracy between the copies is about 95%. Therefore, when you read Homer's *Iliad* you can be pretty sure that you are reading what he wrote. The time difference between the original New Testament manuscripts and the first copy, on the other hand, is less than a hundred years, and the number of manuscript copies that are just in Greek is almost 5,800, with an astounding accuracy rate. As stated earlier, when you add the copies that are in other languages there are more than 20,000 New Testament manuscripts in existence. It is ironic that those who love Lucretius are the first to rant about how unreliable the New Testament is. In fact, if the New Testament can be considered unreliable, then there is no ancient writer who can be said to be reliable, and that includes Josephus, beloved by many liberal scholars. (Some information for this section was gleaned from *Christian Apologetics* and several websites; please see reference page.)

The second test historians use to determine the authenticity and reliability of a historical document is called the internal evidence test. This is evidence that comes from the text itself. The historian uses several methods to discern which copy might be closest to the original, especially if there are copies that have a discrepancy or slight difference in the wording. The New Testament claims to be written by eyewitnesses or by people who were taught by those eyewitnesses. Archeological discoveries continue to show how accurate and precise Luke was despite the confusion regarding a person called Quirinius in the second chapter of his Gospel. (I will talk about this "apparent" error of Luke's later on in the book.) Peter says in his second letter that they were not making up stories about Jesus; that he and others were eyewitnesses of what he was writing about (2 Pe 1:16). The apostle John says in one of his letters that he is talking about what he and others actually saw or witnessed (1 Jn 1:3.) John makes the same claim in his Gospel—that he is giving an accurate account of what he saw or witnessed (Jn 19:35; 20:31). (Ironically, the JS does not accept these writings as authentic although these early Christian writers insist that they are writing about what they have experienced.) The close proximity to the events that Peter and John are talking about gives an authentication to their writings. Their memories are still vivid. The internal evidence shows that the Gospels and letters were written at the time of Jesus' contemporaries and that what was written can be authenticated. If what they wrote was not accurate, there were plenty of people around who could have said so. This is why the Jesus Seminar, Aslan, and today's liberal New Testament professors have attempted to place the dating of the Gospels near the end of the first century and into the second; they are hoping that putting a later date on the Gospels will make them less reliable. This kind of reasoning, if used today for modern biographies, would mean we should not accept any current biographies of George Washington as reliable. The JS (and Aslan) has to ignore the usual way historians use the internal evidence test so that they can justify their own conclusions.

Take, for example, two pieces of internal evidence in Matthew's Gospel that show that Matthew wrote his Gospel before 70 A.D. One is in chapter twenty-four where Jesus talked about the future destruction of the Temple. Jesus' prophetic statement served as a warning for Christians who were living in and around Jerusalem in 66 A.D. (The Fellows of the JS reject this prophetic statement because they do not believe in prophetic statements, which simply reflects a denial based on their worldview and not on historic evidence.) The second example is in chapter twenty-seven when Judas returned the money that he received from the chief priests for betraying Jesus. The priests bought a parcel of land with the blood money and Matthew says in verse eight that "it has been called the Field of Blood to this day" (NIV). At the time of Matthew's writing, the Field of Blood was well-known. (Luke also mentions it in the first chapter of Acts, indicating that it and his Gospel prequel were written before 70 A.D.) If Matthew wrote his Gospel in the 80s A.D., like Aslan and many modern liberal scholars believe, the Temple and Jerusalem and most of Judea would have been destroyed and the Jews dispersed throughout the Roman Empire, and so it is very unlikely that this parcel of ground would have had any significance to Matthew's reading audience. The fact that Matthew says the Field of Blood is still known "to this day" suggests that the Gospel was written before 70 A.D. when Judea was destroyed by the Roman army.

The third test of historicity is external evidence, which seeks to find other historical documents that talk about the events in question. Are there any writings from the first and/or second century that talked about Jesus and the rise of Christianity? I have already mentioned Papias, Polycarp, and Iraneus, but they were Christians. In fact, almost the entire New Testament could be pieced together by going through the writings of the early church fathers during the first three centuries because they included in their writings passages quoted from what would become the New Testament. But are there any non-Christian writings during this time that talk about Jesus and the rise of Christianity? Actually, there are quite a few. For example, there are the writings of Josephus, Tacitus (a Roman historian), Pliny the Younger (aka Gaius Secundus), Lucian of Samosata (who vehemently hated Christianity), and Suetonius (a Roman historian and biographer). These non-Christian writers often mentioned Jesus and his followers in derogatory ways. They complained that the Christians were atheists because they did not worship all the Roman gods, but instead had made their leader—Jesus—into a God. Some of these anti-Christian writers even suggested that the Christians deserved death because they were so different. Now that we have taken a look at the three basic tests historians perform, and how those tests are used in critiquing the New Testament, it is easy to see why the general consensus amongst most historians of ancient writings is that the New Testament, as we have it today, is highly reliable.

There is no hiding the fact that the JS and other liberal theologians have tried their best to discredit the Gospel of John and question its historicity (see Ehrman, Spong, and Aslan). One reason for this is because, if you take John's Gospel at face value, it is a very powerful treatise on the personhood of Jesus, clearly declaring him to be God incarnate, as well as fully human. Now John's Gospel may be different in style and emphasis than the other three canonical Gospels but that does not make his Gospel any less historical. He obviously focused on other episodes of Jesus' life than the other Gospels, and he was able to provide more information about certain individuals since those individuals were now dead and could not be harmed by his disclosure (for example, naming Peter as the one who cut off the person's ear in the Garden of Gethsemane). John's details and specificity should actually reveal his historicity, not be a negative against it. Furthermore, John compliments Matthew's Gospel in that John often fills in information that Matthew left out. That is the beauty of these four Gospels—they compliment one another. (I will come back to this topic later on.)

Erroneous Claims

The JS assumes that the supernatural cannot be the explanation of an event simply because it is difficult to apply historical analysis to a supernatural event. They, therefore, reject any and all predictions or statements that Jesus made regarding his resurrection and his second coming. According to the JS, the early Christians made these sayings up in order to "verify" their claims. This assumption, though, is based on a worldview that says if an event is considered supernatural then it did not happen because there are no supernatural events. (We find this same assumption made by modern anti-God science writers like Victor Stenger, Richard Dawkins, Sam Harris, etc.) Because the JS scholars do not believe in the resurrection, they assume, based on their personal beliefs, that Jesus could not have made post-death statements because there is no resurrection. They are trying to disprove a point by using the point itself, which is a logical fallacy. To deny Jesus' resurrection because one does not believe in the supernatural, or because it violates one's worldview or belief system, is not a sufficient "reason" for rejecting the historicity of the resurrection. The Gospels and other New Testament writings say that there were numerous eyewitnesses to the resurrected Jesus. These eyewitnesses give greater historical authenticity than does the belief that Jesus could not have said anything after his death on the assumption that there was no resurrection.

The JS also says that Jesus actually never did explain his parables and aphorisms to his disciples or anyone else, and so any passages in the Gospels where Jesus explains or interprets his parables has to be made up. I am not quite sure how they could make this assumption. How would the JS even know that Jesus did not do this? It is because they use the Gospel of Thomas as their foundation, and there is no narrative in the Gospel of Thomas. The question arises, of course: Why would Jesus not explain his parables? It was part of rabbinic tradition to provide an explanation to the parables or stories they told, so it makes sense that Jesus would do the same, since he was addressed and/or referred to as a rabbi. The JS claims they want to get back to the historical Jesus, but when Jesus speaks like a real historical teacher from the first century, the JS insists that those sayings are inauthentic. Jesus would not have left his disciples without an explanation of his parables.

The JS also claims that Jesus never directly declared anything about himself, and he certainly did not claim to be God. Therefore, all the "I am" statements, and any other declarations that Jesus supposedly said about himself and his mission, were put there by the Gospel writer. Once again we see how the JS makes an assumption based on their worldview and not on the evidence. The Gospels definitely provide evidence that Jesus made quite specific statements about who he believed he was and what he came to earth to do. But the JS refuses to accept what the Gospels say because they (the JS) do not want to believe what Jesus says about himself. It does not make sense that Jesus would not say anything about himself in the three years of his being with his disciples. It is possible that the Fellows of the JS make this assumption because they do not want to come to terms, on a personal level, with who Jesus is, because if they did do that, then they would have to reevaluate their own lives and beliefs.

The JS even has the audacity to assume that the burden of proof in regards to the sayings of Jesus as recorded in the Gospels does not lie with the skeptic but with the Gospel writers themselves. Now this is not the typical way historians work. If this criterion was used for any other historical inquiry, then we would not be able to make any knowledgeable statement about ancient history, or even about recent history. This is not the approach that the majority of historians use in order to gain knowledge of the past, but this has to be the Fellow's methodology because otherwise they would have to admit the authenticity of what they reject. Historians of ancient writings typically accept what can be tested and then give the benefit of the doubt in areas that cannot be tested until such a time when other evidence arises that gives adequate reasons for its acceptance or rejection. But the JS just flatly rejects the Gospels and then says it is up to the Gospel writers to prove what they have said is true.

Because the JS (and Aslan and other liberal theologians) puts such late dates for the Gospels (70s for Mark; 80s to 90s for Matthew and Luke; into the second century for John), they need someone to have "founded" Christianity. Enter Saul of Tarsus, aka Paul the apostle, a Roman citizen with Jewish ancestry, who studied, as a Pharisee, the Mosaic Law under the eminent Jewish teacher Gamaliel. The JS (Aslan and Horsley do this as well) presents Paul as a fringe or rogue first-century "Christian" preacher, who was out of step with the other

27

apostles. The JS claims that Paul's writings, which make up a large part of the New Testament, display a profound ignorance of any details of Jesus' earthly life. Paul does not mention Jesus' parents, or where he was born, or the parables he recited or the miracles he performed. The JS therefore insists that Paul did not know the Jesus of history; he only wrote about the Christ-of-faith, emphasizing Jesus as resurrected deity. Paul's whole faith, according to the JS, was based on a vision he saw of the resurrected Jesus. So the JS concludes that the Jesus found in Paul's writings was simply a figment of his (Paul's) imagination. The JS proposes that since this imaginary figure—the Christ-of-faith—needed a historic setting, the Gospel writers freely obliged, creating stories and ideas gleaned from the Hebrew Scriptures and the rabbis that would help Paul establish his new religion. The JS asserts that these Gospel writers, especially the one who wrote Matthew's, made sure that Jesus fulfilled any and all prophesies found in the Hebrew Scriptures that implied or suggested a future Messiah. Conjecture, however, is not proof; it is speculation that forms the basis of the Jesus Seminar's conclusions, and this is not sufficient for verifying their worldview. (I will address these issues in Chapters Sixteen and Seventeen.)

We have seen that the Jesus Seminar was formed in order to create a consensus of "critical" scholars who would be able to decipher what is and is not authentic in the four canonical Gospels. In the final analysis, we discovered that these scholars approached their task with predetermined religious and philosophical beliefs that actually got in the way of doing genuine work. The Fellows of the JS are really mere reconstructionists, rewriting history according to their worldview, rather than according to the evidence. Each JS member, in reconstructing Jesus, emphasizes his/her own personal view of him. Some of them see Jesus as an itinerant sage, another might perceive him as a Jewish teacher who was influenced by Greek thought, others focus on Jesus as a healer/magician, and then there are those who claim Jesus was an illiterate preacher whose followers were mostly the marginalized nobodies of their society. Some identify Jesus as a dissenter who spoke out against Jewish tradition and injustice. He supposedly rejected social conventions and teased his audience with paradoxical sayings, talked about the kingdom of God as already arriving and available to anyone who wanted to claim it, and announced that everyone can have a spirit-relationship with God just as he did.

The JS concept of Jesus, however, is far removed from the Judaism of his day. The JS version of Jesus does not speak like other Jewish teachers in first-century Palestine; the JS has created a Jesus who is out of sync with his time. In every occurrence where Jesus appears similar to the teachers of his own time, the JS scholars discount his words as inauthentic. The JS wants Jesus to look more like a Greco-Roman philosopher, like some kind of cynic sage who roams the countryside and, instead of making references to Hebrew Scripture, only speaks in short, rather esoteric parables, and certainly never engages in any arguments with the religious leaders. Since the JS basically wipes out 82 percent of Jesus' sayings, one wonders why he met such a terrible end. It is no wonder that the methods and conclusions of the Jesus Seminar have come under harsh criticism by biblical scholars and historians (see Luke Timothy Johnson's excellent book *The Real Jesus*). It is simply not good practice to first draw a conclusion and then accept only the evidence that fits into that conclusion and reject the evidence that does not fit. This is not a legitimate methodology for authenticating historical documents. This, in fact, is how the JS operates—they dismiss sayings and narratives in the four canonical Gospels that do not match their preconceived ideas. Their use of the colored beads is actually a reflection of their own bias. They begin with an idea of the kind of Jesus they are looking for. They do not draw their conclusions based on the evidence; they start with a conclusion and find evidence for it, and discard any and all evidence against their *a priori* thesis. So instead of following the logical norm of Premise—Premise—Conclusion, the JS flips it on its head and follows their own norm: Conclusion—Premise—Premise.

The JS has created a mythical Jesus—a sage, a Cynic, a zealot, a roving preacher, a community organizer—and then claim that they are searching for the historical Jesus as opposed to a Christ-of-faith. They use their colored beads to accept or discard what is in line with their beliefs. They create a methodology and a criterion for authenticating or inauthenticating passages and arrive at a picture of Jesus that is so thin and weak that it will blow away at the slightest wind. There is no substance to their Jesus; he is a nebulous vapor who strangely entered the Galilean world in the third decade of the first century of the

Common Era, said a few nice words, tried to help the poor, healed some psychosomatic diseases, upset some religious leaders and got himself killed. For some reason, a group of people, about forty or so years later, decided to make up some stories about him and start a new religion and, God knows why, that odd religion is still around today. Unfortunately, the assumptions, deductions and conclusions of the Jesus Seminar are still being promoted, and are still being believed by thousands. It is a sad fact that the likes of a prominent journalist like Peter Jennings would promote the Jesus Seminar agenda. In 2000, Jennings aired a documentary called The Search for Jesus which was nothing more than a vehicle for the Jesus Seminar to propagate their theories to a broader audience. Rather than being a "true" investigative report, Jennings was merely the mouthpiece for the tenets of the Jesus Seminar.

John Dominic Crossan, a co-founder and member of the Jesus Seminar (who contributed to Jennings' documentary), claims in his book *The Historical Jesus: The Life of a Mediterranean Jewish Peasant* that Jesus was a poor peasant, a magician, a Jewish Cynic, and an itinerant egalitarian. He claims that there were two basic views of Jesus in the early (first century) church—one group saw him as a wisdom teacher, the other group saw him as an apocalyptic prophet. Those Christians that regarded Jesus as a wisdom teacher were influenced by the Gospel of Thomas. (Remember, the JS needs to have the Gospel of Thomas be the first Gospel written, the document upon which the four canonical Gospels are based.) Those Christians who regarded Jesus as an apocalyptic preacher were influenced by Paul (Crossan refers to such passages as First Corinthians 7:29-31 and First Thessalonians 5:1-3). Eventually, these views merged and Jesus began to be recognized as a teacher of wise sayings who preached an end-of-the-world message. (Of course, the JS accepts Jesus as a wise teacher, but it denies that he had an apocalyptic message.) Crossan believes that the Jesus image evolved over time and became the deity that saved the world only after several centuries of redevelopment. According to Crossan, Jesus' disciples did not know what happened to him after his crucifixion. They all scattered after his arrest and it was up to those who crucified him (i.e., the Roman executioners) to deal with his body. It was either thrown into a community burial pit or just left out in the open for the roving dogs to devour. According to Crossan, the early Christians had to come up with a storyline where Jesus was buried by his friends. So

Mark created a story about Joseph of Arimathea coming to Pilate to ask for Jesus' body so he could properly bury it. That would then set up the stage for his disciples to know where he was buried so that they could come to the tomb on the day after Sabbath and discover it empty because Jesus rose from the dead. For the JS, the story of Jesus ends with him dying on the cross. The idea of a resurrection was nothing more than his followers continuing to keep his memory alive. This natural part of bereavement, however, then developed into the belief of a "real" resurrection (that for the JS, of course, did not really happen). This belief became so real to Jesus' followers that they actually saw visions and hallucinations of their risen teacher. From this visionary belief came all the doctrine we have come to know as Christianity.

Marcus Borg and the New Age Jesus

Marcus Borg, another member of the Jesus Seminar (who also contributed to Jennings' documentary), has written several books about Jesus that reflect his liberal theological beliefs and the conclusions of the Jesus Seminar. One of his popular books is *Meeting Jesus Again for the First Time*. In it he says that as a child he believed that Jesus was the savior of the world, that Jesus' purpose was to come to earth to die for our sins, and that accepting Jesus as such would give one eternal life. As many teens and early adults do, who have a child's view of Christian doctrine, Borg began to have doubts about his religious beliefs. There is actually nothing wrong with that. Doubts often help us to discover truth. But doubts can also lead us from the truth, so in our searching we need to be careful about what we find, and where we go to find it. The fact of the matter is there are a lot of what the Scriptures call "false teachers." It is easy to point them out when you know what to look for. The Secret Service does not have to study every counterfeit bill, they just need to thoroughly know the real (authentic) one. Once they know the real bill, they are able to compare the fake ones to it. Unfortunately, there are a lot of these "false" teachers teaching New Testament studies in our educational institutions. When Borg went to seminary he tells us that it was there that he learned that what he had been taught about Jesus as a child was a lie. Jesus was not the Son of God, did not come to be the savior of the world, did not die for our sins, did not rise from the dead, and will not come again for his followers. Borg was taught that these were all myths; and he once again, believed what he was told. Borg learned that the Gospels were unreliable documents, that, if anything, they simply recorded the developing traditions of the early Christian movement. These developing traditions had no real historical foundation. Eventually, these traditions were compiled into what we now know as the four canonical Gospels. It was not until some forty, fifty or more years later that these early Christians began to speak of Jesus as some kind of deity, and the idea caught on. So Borg is admitting that just as he accepted what he was taught when a child, he took that same child-like faith with him to the university and believed what he was taught there. Borg remained, in a sense, a child in his theological thinking. He simply swung from one belief to another as a child would, but since he was a young adult at the time, he thinks that the new ideas that he was taught were 'true' and the earlier ideas were 'false.' Now Paul says: "When I was a child, I talked like a child, I thought like a child, I reasoned like a child. When I became a man, I put the ways of childhood behind me" (NIV, 1 Cor 13:11). Borg, it seems, has not followed Paul's example. He accepted what his teachers taught him when he was a child, and then accepted what his teachers taught him when he was a young man in college. The church is to protect itself from false teachings in a very specific, orderly, and reasonable manner. Paul tells us in Ephesians 4:11–16 that Jesus organized the church to have apostles, prophets, evangelists, pastors and teachers so that they can equip each Christian with what is necessary for works of service; the church is to be built up (edified and growing) until they reach unity in their faith and in the knowledge of Jesus (the Son of God), becoming mature, and attaining a likeness of Christ. In that way, Christians will no longer be infants who are tossed around like a little boat on the waves, "blown here and there by every wind of teaching and by the cunning and craftiness of people in their deceitful scheming" (see also James 1:6). Instead, Christians are to speak the truth in love, and grow up (mature) to become more like Jesus. Paul gives us a clear and excellent portrait of how not only the church as a whole but how each Christian is to mature.

For Borg, one of the major tasks of the Jesus Seminar is to drive a wedge between the Jesus-of-history, the pre-Easter Jesus, and the Christ-of-faith, the post-Easter Jesus. Like the other JS members, and most liberal theologians popular today, Borg casts doubt on the historicity of John's Gospel, contrasting it with the synoptic Gospels (Matthew, Mark and Luke). Borg questions its authorship, the proposed date of its composition, and especially its content—because if you take John's Gospel at face value, you have to make some serious decisions about who Jesus is. It is easier to simply discount the whole Gospel rather than accept it as a historical document; if you do the latter, you will have to come to terms with the ultimate realities of life. Borg admitted that he, at first, discounted John's Gospel because it reflected a mythical Christ-of-faith, a distorted image of the Jesus of history. But then Borg was able to see that John was only trying to emphasize how one could, like Jesus, establish a spirit-relationship with God. Borg somehow had an epiphany that John did not write his Gospel to show that Jesus is God incarnate; no, John wrote his Gospel to show how one man developed a spirit-relationship with God so that we can too. John was an ancient New Ager! Borg defines Jesus as a spirit person, not that he was a ghost but that he spoke and taught a spiritual wisdom that is connected to the universal life-power that some people call God.

Borg claims that most mainstream scholars do not believe the Gospels' stories about Jesus' birth or childhood. What does he mean by mainstream? If he means the Fellows of the Jesus Seminar, then, of course, they do not believe those stories are historical. Does he mean contemporary liberal theologians? They pretty much discount the New Testament writings, as well. Are the JS and liberal theologians mainstream? No, they exist on the fringe; they have an agenda to reduce and reconstruct Jesus to where he started out as a typical religious seeker, tutored under John the Baptizer, and then took over the Baptizer's mission when he (the Baptizer) was imprisoned, became an itinerant preacher, said some things that upset the powerful religious leaders of his day, was accused of crimes against the state, and got himself killed. Therefore, Jesus is just one of history's many great religious people who only wanted to show the importance of having a close relationship to God (whatever that may be) by being a conscientiously spiritual person. So the image of Jesus we get from the Gospels is incorrect, for Borg. Borg's Jesus certainly did not think or speak of himself as the Son of God, as God incarnate, who came as a love offering, an atonement for the world's sins. Jesus was a spirit person, a social prophet, inviting any and all into a transforming relationship with the same Spirit that he himself knew. Borg, as one can decipher from his books, actually sees Jesus through the lens of New Age ideology. Borg says he has discovered the historic Jesus, but he has only found a mythical figure emanating from a popular spiritual philosophy.

New Age ideology states that there is no personal god; that god, whatever it is, is within us, and we are moving toward becoming that god. We, as humans, have the potential to become god. So when Gospel/Epistle passages claim that Jesus is the one and only, unique Son of God, Borg cannot accept that because all of us in a sense are a son, or better still, a child of god. After reinterpreting the Gospel of John into a New Age treatise, Borg can now accept it because he realizes that John's Gospel portrays Jesus as a new age spiritualist. The follower of New Age ideology is interested in a variety of "spiritual" experiences, making use of positive thinking, esoteric metaphysical ideas, and self-help and self-actualization methods. There are no borders to one's "spiritual" experiences and no dogma to confine your journey. Grab all the ideas you want and add them to your cognitive salad to create a dish whose nourishment is bottomless. This "salad" can easily include astrology, pantheism, polytheism, and scientism, mixed with toppings (ideas) from a variety of religions like Buddhism, Taoism, Hinduism, and Kabbalah, (even Christianity), with a dressing that envelops it all with hopes of world unity, emphasizing one humanity and one planet. While enjoying this cognitive salad you can engage in such activities as meditation, channeling, and crystal healing as you advance toward a new holistic consciousness (on your journey to becoming god), with a new set of values that do not constrain your voyage. If you want, you can have Jesus show you how, according to Borg. Jesus can be a model, but please do not accept him as your savior. You do not need saving, says Borg; you just need enlightenment.

In presenting the beliefs, methodology and assumptions of the Jesus Seminar, I hope that you can see that their procedures are not the typical way historians do their work. The Jesus Seminar's conclusions are not so much based on sound analysis as they are on personal worldviews. Unfortunately, their ideas are still being taught by many liberal New Testament and Biblical Studies professors in our colleges and universities. These liberal theologians often create scenarios that might look reasonable and logical, and appear to be based on current evidence, but the scenarios are too often based on their own worldview, on how they interpret something, and not necessarily on historical or exegetical accuracy. They often approximate the truth; supplying their suppositions with just enough facts to look as if they are sound and reasonable. Unless you know the real item, it is difficult to decipher the counterfeit. It is therefore a disheartening fact that many of those who read these modern liberal theologians/scholars/religious leaders (like Ehrman, Spong, Crossan, Borg, Horsley and others) do so not in order to find truth, but to find an excuse.

A Critique of Richard Horsley's Views of Jesus, Christianity, and Paul

Another influence on the modern view of Jesus is Richard Horsley. Aslan mentions in his notes that he relies a great deal on the ideas of Richard Horsley and John P. Meier. If you have read their books (and those written by the Fellows of the JS) before reading Aslan's *Zealot*, you can clearly see the influence. I will mention a few things from one of Horsley's books to show the depth of that influence. Richard Horsley and Neil Silberman wrote a book in the late 1990s entitled *The Message and the Kingdom*. In it the authors state that after Jesus was condemned as a threat to civil order and put to death for his preaching, his followers spread a united gospel of resistance throughout the Roman Empire. Horsley and Silberman believe that after being baptized by John the Baptizer, Jesus became active in what they call an anti-Herodian renewal movement. Jesus' mission was to preach and usher in the Renewal of Israel in the towns and villages of Galilee. According to Horsley, Jesus was attempting to establish a non-king Kingdom and was hoping to gain followers who believed in his plan. Horsley believes the synoptic Gospels offer conflicting details, chronological discrepancies, and theological interpretations that greatly complicate any definitive judgment on the historicity of any of the individual incidents, and then goes on to call Crossan—the cofounder of the Jesus Seminar—a leading "historical Jesus" scholar. Horsley rejects the Gospel's rendition of Jesus' trial and claims that the decision to execute Jesus was probably made by a few fairly low-level security officers. Horsley refers to Pilate as a faithful servant of Tiberius Caesar, and we will see later on that that was far from the truth. The authors claim that after Jesus' death little pockets of followers kept the hope alive for the Renewal of Israel and eventually enough ideas merged together, creating a "gradual differentiation"

35

(whatever that means) that would eventually produce a new religion called Christianity. Like Crossan, Horsley believes Jesus' followers had no idea what happened to Jesus' remains after being taken down from the cross.

Horsley is quite convinced that there was an early collection of traditions about Jesus that was kept alive and, although those "traditions" said nothing about Jesus' crucifixion, resurrection, or divine status, they did contain pithy, colorful, and provocatively short speeches about the Kingdom of God. And what is the name of that "collection?" You should be able to venture a guess. It's the famous "Q" Sayings Gospel—that same hypothetical, non-existent, document that the Jesus Seminar and Aslan are so highly dependent upon. The Q Sayings, according to Horsley, offer a set of specific instructions about how people should act and treat each other so that they can usher in the Renewal of Israel. Horsley and Silberman conclude that Jesus was surely a prophet and a vindicated martyr, but not a god. He just simply got himself killed by starting a Renewal of Israel movement in the midst of a Roman occupation. After presenting their views about Jesus (which are very similar to the conclusions of the Jesus Seminar), Horsley and Silberman focus the rest of their book on Paul (Saul of Tarsus). They recount how Paul had a brilliant celestial vision of the Risen Jesus and became convinced that Jesus' earlier incarnation as a poor Galilean peasant was merely a prelude to his revelation as Israel's messianic redeemer. Horsley claims that because Paul believed that time was quickly running out before Jesus would return as the Judge of the world and the Messiah of Israel, he (Paul) needed to get busy and spread the gospel so that Jesus would return even sooner. Horsley believes it was Paul that played a crucial role in the birth of Christianity. While the book of Acts in the New Testament mentions Paul's role in the spread of Christianity, Horsley simply reduces Acts to a powerful montage of vivid anecdotes and evocative biblical images played out on a familiar geographical landscape for the peoples of Syria and Asia Minor. Horsley rejects the historicity of Acts and decides that its value lies in the poetic expression of Luke's faith in the divinely ordained triumph of Christianity.

Horsley says there is a general consensus among some modern scholars that Paul actually only wrote seven of the fourteen letters ascribed to him. For Horsley, Paul's image of Jesus was not only

36

dramatically different from the historical figure, but it appears that Horsley saw everything that Paul did as some form of social/political resistance. Horsley says that Paul's major opponents were Torah-observant members of a different "Christian" sect called the Jesus Movement, headed by James, Jesus' brother, and that these rival apostles were constant thorns in Paul's side. (We will see later that Paul was actually a Torah-observant Pharisee and stayed such throughout his Christian life.) According to Horsley, Paul was out in the field like a lone wolf and had to constantly deal with the "men from James" who came into his territory and challenged his authority and teachings. Of course, Horsley's version of the Jerusalem Council is quite different from the one that we find in Acts 15. Horsley sees the Jerusalem Council as a meeting whereby the apostles ganged up on Paul because they believed Paul's preaching was filled with errors. These Jerusalem Christians, according to Horsley, had little patience for Paul's radical views and saw Paul's attitude as a direct threat to Israel's national struggle against Rome. Of course, Horsley claims that Mark and Matthew were all written in the final decades of the first century, some fifty years or so after Jesus' crucifixion, and are therefore filled with mostly made-up narratives. Horsley says Luke's Gospel and Acts were not written until the beginning of the second century. He also claims that by the closing decades of the first century there was still no single Christian "church" that had emerged and there was no single orthodoxy that had been agreed upon. (It should be obvious to those who have read *Zealot* that Aslan often reiterates Horsley's ideas. I will address these views in forthcoming chapters.)

What so many liberal theologians and scholars do is use a handful of historical facts in order to rewrite history so that it complies with their worldview. This practice can be rightly called spurious reasoning, i.e., reasoning that is superficially plausible, but actually misleading and/or downright wrong. I believe that the liberal theologians and scholars I have mentioned thus far (Crossan, Borg, Pagels, Horsley, Ehrman, Spong, Armstrong, Aslan, etc.) present an alternative history, one that supplies just enough "evidence" to make it look valid. It is doubtful that their readers will take the time to see if they are correct in what they say. The Christian, however, is told to test the words and actions of those who teach them to make sure they are correct (faith is not blind, and the Christian is not to be gullible—see these important passages: Rom 12:2, 16:10; 2 Cor 13:5; Gal 6:4; 1 Thes 5:21; 1 Tim

3:10; 1Jn 4:1). The Christian is to give reasons or evidence for the hope or beliefs he/she has accepted (see 1 Pet 3:15), but many liberal scholars do not think they have to give evidence; they just make statements based on their worldview and repeat them enough times in their books that their readers will soon believe them. They come to the conclusion, as the Jesus Seminar did, that the burden of proof is not with them, but with the ones they are attacking.

A Brief Look at Islam's View of Jesus

Islam's view of Jesus (formulated in the seventh and eighth centuries) has been accepted by many of these liberal theologians/biblical scholars. Islam's holy book, the Qur'an, has made a number of statements about Jesus that are, interestingly, quite similar to what the Jesus Seminar has said, and it these claims that I will cite here. Islam rejects the idea that Jesus is the Son of God, or that Jesus died on the cross (which means he was not resurrected), and it does not believe in a triune God. Of course, these are three standard beliefs within Christian theology. The Qur'an sees Jesus as a very holy prophet, a man who was used by God to preach God's ways to the Jewish people. Jesus is, therefore, considered a Muslim by the Qur'an because he submitted to the will of God. Since Jesus submitted to God's will as a prophet, Muslims believe that God would not have allowed such a great man to have died a horrible death on a Roman cross. Several theories emerged within Islam regarding who actually died on the cross. One is that God may have had someone else look like Jesus and that this person was crucified in Jesus' place; another theory is that it was actually Judas who was crucified as a result of mistaken identity. If Jesus did not die on the cross, then what happened to him? Islam teaches that Jesus was taken up to heaven while still alive, just like Elijah in the Hebrew Scriptures, and will return to judge the world.

Islam believes that each person is able to atone for their own sins. So, when Adam and Eve sinned against God he immediately forgave them, and that was it. Humans are not "fallen," and therefore do not need to be "saved." There is no need of a savior. However, humans are supposed to do good deeds and follow God's will. How good a person is determines if he/she will be with God in the afterlife. It is up to each person to be good enough to get to God. One problem with this idea, of course, is: how do you know when you are good enough? No

Muslim can answer that question; there is no way to know that you have been good enough until you die and face God. Then God will tell you if you were good enough to be with him. If he decides you are not, then you are doomed. If there is no need for salvation, and hence no need for a savior, there is no need for someone to have died for our sins. What God has done instead, according to Islam, is occasionally bring up a prophet in some country to teach the people God's ways. So, Jesus was just a wise man, a prophet for Israel, and nothing more. All the prophets God has sent to teach humans his ways, including Jesus, were sent to specific places. The only exception to this was Muhammad. Islam believes he is the greatest and the last of all prophets, and was therefore sent for the entire world. Muslims believe Islam is the world religion that God wants us all to join. Islam teaches that there is only one God and believes that Christianity teaches that there are three Gods. In fact, some Muslims believe that Christianity teaches that Mary, Jesus' mother, is supposed to be one of those Gods. Muslims disdain the idea that Jesus is referred to as the "only begotten" son of God. They believe that this somehow implies that God had sexual relations with a woman (which is why they may have placed Mary as part of the Trinity) in order to get a son. Islam regards all prophets, including Jesus and Muhammad, to be mortal and without any share in divinity. In fact, Islam believes that allowing any mortal, like Jesus, to have a partnership with God is thereby putting them on an equal plane, and constitutes the only truly unpardonable sin. Islam, therefore, adamantly rejects a Trinitarian view of God, nullifying the idea that Jesus was God incarnate or the Son of God. The Qur'an says that Jesus himself never claimed to be God's Son, and did not come to die for humankind's sins, which, of course is what the Jesus Seminar, Horsley, and Aslan also claim. (Some information was gleaned from *Understanding the Times* by David Noebel and *Answering Islam* by Norman Geisler, et al.)

To correct a few misconceptions, let it be noted that Christians are monotheists, just like Muslims and Jews. Christians, however, believe that God has revealed himself to be three persons in one being, that there is a Trinitarian nature to God disclosed as Father, Son and Holy Spirit. When Jesus is referred to as the "only begotten" and "firstborn" of God this does not imply that God was involved in a physical act with a woman in order to create him. Both phrases—"only begotten" and "firstborn"—suggest a priority in rank or position, not something created at a specific time. The New International Version comes close to the idea of the phrase "only begotten" by saying that Jesus is God's "One and Only" Son. The phrase reveals that Jesus has a unique relation to God as Father to Son, but it does not imply that God created Jesus to be his son. So, for Christians, God is three persons in one essence. This makes sense when we see that the Jewish and Christian Scriptures tell us that God is Love. Before he created any other beings, how could God be seen as having a loving nature? There would be nothing or no one to love, if it was just him and him alone. Love must have an object. The idea that God is love could not be possible if there was no one else to love. Throughout eternity God is Love because there has always been three persons to love within the Godhead—Father, Son and Holy Spirit.

In our extensive look at the tenets of the Jesus Seminar, Horsley's ideas, and Islam's view of Jesus, it will be clear that they have provided a foundation for the theories and ideas Dr. Reza Aslan presents in his book *Zealot: The Life and Times of Jesus of Nazareth.* Aslan's views of Jesus are not unique; they are certainly influenced by the liberal theologians/biblical scholars I have already mentioned. Although I will address specific ideas that Aslan presents in his book, keep in mind that when I refer to Aslan I am not just referring to him, but to the ideas of many other liberal theologians/biblical scholars.

Chapter Two: Unstable Building Blocks

The Historical Jesus vs. the Christ-of-Faith

Aslan tells us in *Zealot* that he spent twenty years researching Christianity and its origins. It is typical for authors to let their readers know that they have studied the subject they will be writing about. (I even did this in the Introduction.) Of course, Aslan wants you to think that this intensive study prompted him to reject Jesus as a Christ-of-faith and simply revere him as a Jewish peasant from Nazareth. This, as we have seen, follows the thoughts of Marcus Borg in his differentiating between the pre-Easter Jesus and the post-Easter Jesus. Like the Jesus Seminar version of Jesus, Aslan's Jesus-of-history is a stripped down model; and it can be transformed into whatever image you choose. Do you see Jesus as just an itinerant preacher who said some interesting things? Then that is what he is for you. You simply remove all the other passages that call him something else—like the Son of God. Do you want to see Jesus as a wise teacher? Then just accept those passages that go along with that idea. Do you see Jesus as a subversive rebel, a zealot who wanted to usher in Israel's independence from Roman rule? Then Horsley and Aslan will show you how to reduce Jesus down to that image. For Aslan, as it is for many other liberal theologians/biblical scholars, there is the Jesus of history and the Jesus after Christianity got hold of him. There are many who believe that the Gospel writers formed Jesus into an image of their own creation. Aslan wants you to believe that the Jesus he has constructed in his book is both accurate and reasonable, and hopes that you will accept his conclusions about Jesus because of the amount of time (twenty years) he has devoted to scholarly research. I hope that you, the reader of this book, make it a practice to look up my Bible references and make sure I am using them correctly, both contextually and exegetically. I hope that you do not blindly accept what I say, but that you make sure that I am being accurate and honest in my conclusions.

Aslan informs us that he will mostly rely on Mark's Gospel and the "Q" Sayings material in creating for us his image of Jesus. Many liberal theologians and scholars rely on the Gospel of Mark because they think it was the first Gospel written, and that it is the "weakest" of the Gospels. The assumption, of course, is that anything in the other Gospels that are not found in Mark's Gospel will have been made up by its author. The assumption itself, however, is in jeopardy; it is not necessarily a logical conclusion. Aslan will also rely on the "Q" document, and one needs to be reminded (quite often it seems) that "Q" is a hypothetical construct; it was created by modern scholars in order to make certain claims about Matthew and Luke's Gospels.

Aslan points out that in first-century Palestine many people were expectantly awaiting a messianic figure to arrive. Many Jews believed God was about to usher in a new apocalyptic phase, and so lots of prophets and so-called messiahs were roaming the cities and the countryside preaching about God's kingdom and his impending judgment. Of course, this expectation of a Messiah had been going on for centuries, so first-century Jews were not unique in that expectation. The Israelites had been hoping for a revolutionary messiah that would bring them independence ever since they returned to Jerusalem after their Babylonian exile and rebuilt the Temple. Aslan makes it seem as if there was a preacher on every corner shouting God's judgment and a zealot/messiah busily searching for followers to assist him in seditious acts of violence. For Aslan, Jesus is just one more of those countless preachers/zealots who claimed that God's kingdom was at hand, just one more person who gave his Jewish listeners false hope.

As the members of the Jesus Seminar have done (and some so-called "new" atheists), Aslan claims that it is difficult to truly identify the Jesus-of-history, believing that if one put aside the Gospels and/or the New Testament, there is nothing much said about him elsewhere. If that is true, then where did Aslan get the information that prompted him to admire Jesus of Nazareth? If he rejects what the New Testament says about Jesus, what compelled him to be so attracted to the Jesus-of-history? What other information did he find, and where? Actually, by ancient standards, there are quite a few references to Jesus in historical sources outside the New Testament. I have already mentioned them in the previous chapter, but I will repeat their names here: Josephus, Tacitus, Secundus, Lucian, and Suetonius; these and other historians and writers of that era made references to Jesus, and the majority of them were not fond of Christianity. These "outside sources" mentioned Jesus as a real historical figure who was crucified at the hands of Pontius Pilate. What needs to be remembered, though, is that there were four "biographical" works being distributed about Jesus before the close of the first century. These biographical works were being read by people all across the Roman Empire. Aslan (and the JS) needs to change the dates of these biographical writings so that they appear to come much later, but this again is an example of fitting the evidence to comply with a preconceived idea. These four biographical writings would become the four canonical Gospels that we find in the New Testament, but before that they were separate documents, copied and distributed across a vast amount of populated territory. As biographers do today, these authors focused on different characteristics of their subject, portraying Jesus from different angles or points-of-view, writing in their own particular style. They each devoted the majority of their writings to the last week of Jesus' life, as if that was the most important part. They all agreed on the significance of that last week.

Fixing the Dates

Like Horsley and others, Aslan must first promote the idea that the canonical Gospels were written late in the first century so that he can then assert that it was Paul, through his epistles, who actually presented us with an initial (and inventive) narrative of Jesus. It is believed by many liberal scholars that Paul "founded" Christianity by creating the Christ-of-faith. The Gospels were then written to give more substance to this Christ, thereby creating Jesus of Nazareth. Aslan complains (much like others in the JS) that Paul shows very little interest in Jesus as a historical figure, and because of this lack Paul can only be considered a good source for someone interested in the early development of Christianity, but a weak one for those interested in the historical Jesus. Since Aslan believes that the Gospels were written to create a "historical" Jesus from Paul's Christology, the Gospels were therefore never meant to be construed as historical documents; they did not depict a real, historical person. Aslan insists that not one of the Gospels was written by someone who knew Jesus personally; the Gospel writers were not able to give an eyewitness account of what Jesus actually said and did. Aslan simply reduces the Gospels to mere "faith" testimonies, arranged and compiled decades after the actual events. Therefore, the Gospels cannot be trusted, according to Aslan, to give us reliable information about the historical Jesus.

43

It is necessary for Aslan, the JS, Horsley, and other liberal scholars to adjust the Gospel dates to fit their theory, and that is why Aslan believes Mark's Gospel was written shortly after 70 A.D., which would be forty years after Jesus' death and around five to seven years after Paul's death. Since Mark's Gospel is a somewhat condensed version, Aslan believes it was left to Matthew and Luke to improve upon Mark's Gospel. According to Aslan, Matthew and Luke (Aslan, the JS, and current liberal theologians do not really believe these are the Gospel writers' real names, but they use them because of their familiarity) worked independently on their accounts somewhere between 90 and 100 A.D. and, since both probably had copies of Mark's Gospel, used it as a kind of guide to update the events by adding their own spin on Jesus' words and deeds. Aslan thinks that the infancy stories found in Matthew and Luke conflict with each other. He also relegates the Gospels' depiction of the resurrection to mere stories that were elaborated to gratify those believers who read their narrative. According to Aslan, the Gospel writers simply rewrote history by taking a few interesting stories about a certain man and then profoundly exercised fictional license to create false narratives and fanciful events. This was done in order to somehow satisfy the Christian community. Aslan believes there was a simple peasant man who gained a few followers by preaching that God's Kingdom was going to replace the Roman occupiers and got himself killed for being too adamant about his beliefs. For some reason, this illiterate peasant was not forgotten even forty years after his death as an insurrectionist. He had now become some kind of folk hero. So someone decided to write a fictional story about him, making up all sorts of fanciful events like healings and walking on water, and even rising from the dead. The hero of the author's fictional story became so popular that over the next forty years three other stories were written about him. The fourth fictional story—John's Gospel—was so enamored with the Christ-of-faith that Aslan says it is simply impossible for it to have been written by someone who actually knew Jesus. This fourth story, says Aslan, had to have been written as late as the first two decades into the second century.

We see then how Aslan's views of Jesus mirror other liberal theologians/biblical scholars; there is not much that is new in Aslan's book. It is important to realize that it does not matter how long a person studies something; what matters is if the study one has done is correct—historically, exegetically, and theologically. Aslan is presenting the worldview he has come to believe based on the sources he has studied. But if the sources you have studied are in error, it does not matter how many years you have studied them; your conclusions will always be wrong. So, Aslan rejects the historical evidence that shows that the three synoptic Gospels—Matthew, Mark and Luke—were written before the fall of Jerusalem in 70 A.D., written before Peter and Paul were executed for their faith. He also discounts any evidence that presents Matthew's Gospel as having been written first. If the synoptic Gospels were written during Paul's lifetime, he would have read at least one of them—Luke's—and he would have known Jesus' story. In fact, Luke tells us that Paul had met with the apostles in Jerusalem several times after his conversion; there is no reason to doubt that he would have been informed about Jesus' life during those meetings. (I will speak more on this in Chapters Sixteen and Seventeen.)

Are the Gospels Unreliable Historical Documents?

Aslan and other liberal theologians/biblical scholars claim that the Gospels were never meant to be construed as historical documents. This claim makes two questionable statements: one is a critique of historical documents, and the other is a declaration about motives or intentions. Taken at face value each Gospel certainly looks like it was written as a historical document; they have all the earmarks of a document that attempts to capture the historical events of a historical person. The Gospels present information the authors think is true. The Gospel writers have placed the events in historical settings. In comparison to other historical biographies and documents of that era, they are quite similar. Today, we want modern biographies to tell us everything about the person we are reading about, down to the minutest of details. Biographies written in ancient times were not as detailed as they are now. They mostly focused on important or major occurrences in the subject's life, like military accomplishments and such. Of course, the content of the Gospels is different than most biographies at that time. The Gospel writers tell of a man—Jesus—who healed peoples' diseases, walked on water, and made some rather bold statements about himself. There is no reason to doubt the historical events of Jesus' life about which the Gospel writers wrote. The doubts mostly come from one's particular worldview. The second reason the idea that the Gospels were never meant to be construed as historical documents is questionable is that it assumes that one can actually determine the Gospel writers' motives and intentions. By making this statement, Aslan is claiming to know the Gospel writers' intentions and that those intentions were to create fictional stories about Jesus. How does Aslan know what their intentions or motives were? How does Aslan know the Gospels were not meant to be historical writings? He doesn't. He assumes it based on his worldview and the theories he holds which are influenced by the Jesus Seminar, Horsley and others.

Does Aslan have any basis for his theory that the Gospels are fictional accounts? Well, people do not walk on water, and the Gospels say Jesus did, so that must be fictional. People do not go around healing others of blindness and skin diseases, so when the Gospels tell us Jesus did that, it must be purposefully lying. People do not go around saying, "I am the resurrection and the life," or "I am going to Jerusalem to suffer and die, but I will rise again on the third day," unless they need to be institutionalized. So Aslan and the Jesus Seminar insist that Jesus did not do or say many of the things that the four canonical Gospels claim that he said and did. All of that mystical, messiah talk was made up by the writers in order to give some spectacular credence to this new Christian movement. What actually sets Christianity apart from most other religions, however, is its reliance on history. From its early days, Christianity has emphasized the historical need for a Messiah, starting with Genesis chapter three and ending with Jesus' substitutionary death. Christianity is firmly based on the historical Jesus. In order to propagate his theory, however, Aslan feels he needs to claim (although he does so erroneously) that the Gospel writers were not concerned with history.

To claim that none of the Gospels were written by an eyewitness is to deny the historical evidence that Matthew and John's Gospels were written by them. They certainly were eyewitnesses, having been Jesus' close followers (apostles) for at least three years. If Mark's Gospel was written under the direction of Peter (and there is no reason to doubt it was not), then Mark's Gospel would certainly be filled with an eyewitness's account, namely Peter's. Luke started off his Gospel letting his readers know that his information was obtained from eyewitnesses. But Aslan says he knows better, and he believes that the

46

Gospels were not written by people who knew Jesus, but were written many years later simply to satisfy some "need" that late first-century Christian readers apparently had. How does Aslan know this? Where is his evidence? Does it merely arise from a worldview not much different from the unstable claims of the Jesus Seminar?

Was Jesus the Leader of a Jewish Movement?

In all of the years that Aslan says he researched Christianity's origins (twenty of them), he can only come up with two solid historical facts about Jesus. The first one is that Jesus was the leader of a Jewish movement; the second one is the Roman authorities crucified him because of it. If this is all that can be truly said about Jesus, one wonders why Aslan (not to mention anyone in the first century) would even care about this person. Why does he say that the Jesus he discovered in his research is so much better than the Jesus found in the Gospels? Is it because the Jesus he prefers was a rebel, a zealot, someone who went against the status quo of Roman society, someone who stood up to the leaders of his day and paid the ultimate price for it? Is it because Aslan's view of Jesus looks a lot like Muhammad who used the sword to further his cause? It certainly looks as if what Aslan is doing is simply presenting an Islamic view of Jesus. What makes Aslan think Jesus was the leader of a Jewish movement? For the most part, Jesus only had his twelve apostles and maybe a scattering of close followers, some of whom were women that helped support him financially. Most people came and went, and only came when he was feeding them or healing them. There were times when it seemed like Jesus was going to have more followers but then he would say something like "give your money to those in need and follow me," or "unless you eat my body and drink my blood, you are not a part of me," and those people would hurry off. When Jesus entered Jerusalem a few days before his death there was a large crowd that sang and shouted and waved palm leaves in the air, but they were not his followers. They were merely admirers and, like most, resembled a typical mob that would stick around when things were going their way and were quickly gone when they were not. They were the kind of admirer who would shout "Hosanna" one day and "Crucify him" the next. Jesus only had his close disciples with him during the Passover meal, and when they followed him to one of his favorite places to pray they quickly scattered when he was arrested there. Aslan is correct to say that Jesus was a Jew and that he was crucified by Rome; but he is mistaken to think that Jesus' intentions were to become the leader of a political movement that would restore Israel's independence. Throughout his book, Aslan reveals his habit of taking a known truth—Jesus was a Jew—and then adding a falsehood—Jesus was the leader of a Jewish mob—and expects you to believe both.

What evidence does Aslan have that Jesus was a subversive leader of a group of zealots? Aslan claims that all we need to do is gather up all we know about the Roman Empire in the first century and we will conclude that this was a time of great political/social tumult in which Jesus lived. Since Jesus lived during a tumultuous time, Jesus must have been a mob leader who was killed by the Romans. So, it was the tumultuous time in which Jesus lived that has convinced Aslan that Jesus was a Jewish zealot; it was the times in which Jesus lived that prompted him to become the leader of a Jewish movement against the Roman occupiers. How do we know that the first century was a tumultuous time? Well, Aslan tells us the Romans wrote about this time period and told us so. Aslan is apparently eager to accept ancient documents that Romans wrote regarding this period of time, but he is not willing to accept the Gospels that were also written around the same time. What makes the Roman authors more reliable or believable? Since the Romans referred to the first century as a tumultuous period—and their view of history is so reliable and non-biased—Aslan concludes that it is possible that his two solid facts about Jesus—i.e., that Jesus started a Jewish movement and was killed because of it—are more accurate than what the Gospels say about Jesus. Now the Gospels do mention that Jesus was a Jew and that he was killed by the Romans, so they agree with Aslan on that. But the Gospels do not say that Jesus was the leader of a Jewish movement that was bent on attacking the Roman occupiers and, while he was at it, the Temple priesthood too. Now we get a glimpse into Aslan's way of thinking. He tells us Jesus must have been a Jewish zealot because the times he lived in were tumultuous, and we know they were tumultuous because the Roman writers, during this time, told us they were. But that is not a very good reason; surely Aslan can come up with something better than that. The only assurance Aslan can give his reader is to say that it is possible that his two hard facts are more accurate historically than the Gospels. If you live in a large city where there is an occasional riot, does that mean that, since you live in that

48

city, you must have joined in on the riot? That is what Aslan wants you to believe about Jesus. He thinks that Jesus lived in a tumultuous time, in a tumultuous city, and that he must have joined in on the tumult. So, Jesus is automatically guilty of being a zealot simply because he lived during a time when there were zealots. Does that appear to you as sound reasoning?

One question I have about Aslan's statement that the first century in Palestine was very tumultuous is: Why then is this period of time known as the Pax Romana? The Pax Romana (Latin for Roman peace) lasted a little over two hundred years, between 27 B.C. and 180 A.D., during which time all nationalities within the Roman Empire, for the most part, existed peacefully. There was only a minimal display of military force during this time. There were, of course, bouts of rebellion scattered across the empire (including Palestine) that the authorities had to occasionally quell. In chapter five of Luke's Acts he references two rebellions that had cropped up in the first decade of the first century. Then there was the great Jewish revolt that began in 66 A.D. between the Jews and Rome, which ended with the destruction of Jerusalem in 70 A.D., causing the dispersal of the Jewish people. For the most part, however, there was peace in the first century; it was not a period of tumultuous activity, and Rome was not constantly stamping out little rebellions throughout Palestine during Jesus' life. In fact, during Jesus' lifetime, Galilee, which is where he had spent most of his time, was a rather peaceful region. Most historians actually see the Pax Romana as an era of relative tranquility.

Now it is true that the teachings of Jesus outraged some of the religious leaders of his day. There were three important groups—the Pharisees, scribes, and the Sadducees—that were often in conflict with Jesus. In that sense, Jesus was similar to many of the prophets throughout Israel's history that spoke truth to a wayward people governed by corrupt religious leaders. These leaders did not like the things Jesus said to them and about them, just like the Hebrew kings did not like what the prophets said to them. There were occasions when large crowds would follow Jesus, but there never appeared to be any rioting or rebellious acts by these people. The religious leaders wanted to get rid of Jesus, but it was mostly because of what he said and not so much because of what he did. But the religious leaders did not want to do the deed themselves. They had to come up with a reason to get Jesus out of the way. The plan was to claim that Jesus threatened to disrupt the fragile political stability in and around Jerusalem that was due in part by the presence of the Roman army. So Jesus was arrested in Jerusalem by the Jewish authorities on a charge of treason and political subversion, but these charges were bogus and Pontius Pilate knew it. However, Pilate was not in good standing with his own superiors because of some prior misdeeds on his part, and so he was not eager to get their attention. Eventually, he gave in to the demands of the Jewish religious leaders, not wanting his refusal to do their bidding to turn into a fiasco, which would not look good to his superiors. So, Jesus was crucified. (I will address this more extensively in Chapter Thirteen.) Pilate and the Jewish religious leaders did not realize, however, (and neither do Aslan, the members of the Jesus Seminar, and many of today's liberal theologians) that this was part of God's plan ever since the great rebellion in the Garden of Eden. Jesus did not die because of some unfortunate event, but he purposefully and freely gave his life to reconcile people back to God. It is unfortunate that this plan—the mystery of reconciliation, as Paul calls it—is rejected by Aslan, Islam and the JS.

Aslan postulates that Jesus was killed simply because he had tried to set up a God-kingdom in the midst of Roman rule with himself as the king. The local Roman authorities, therefore, accused Jesus of treason, and he died for that crime. The plaque nailed to his cross affirms this because it stated his crime as "king of the Jews." Aslan says that every criminal that was crucified had his crime placed on a plaque that would be nailed to the cross beam. Everyone passing by would know why he was being punished in such a hideous manner. We know from the Gospels that on Jesus' cross the plaque read "king of the Jews." Aslan says the plaque proves that Jesus had attempted to set himself up as a king of God's Kingdom here on earth and that the Romans therefore killed him based on the crime of treason. Crucifixion, in fact, was what practically everyone who had aspirations of being Israel's messiah—i.e., one who would bring about Israel's independence—could look forward to experiencing. So, Jesus was just one of many who was killed for treason during that time. There was nothing different or unique about Jesus. Aslan believes that the Gospel writers went to great lengths to downplay and/or remove any revolutionary-like manifestations in Jesus' words and deeds.

Since it was the zealot movement that prompted the beginnings of the Jewish revolt in 66 A.D., and this rebellion resulted in the destruction of Jerusalem and most of Judea by the Romans, the Gospel writers certainly could not have their hero, Jesus, be portrayed as a zealot; after all, those zealots were the cause of the revolt that destroyed everything the Jews loved and which forced them to be dispersed throughout the Empire. Therefore, the Gospel writers, according to Aslan, transformed the zealot Jesus, with his revolutionary zeal and his revolutionary rhetoric, into the spirit-person that Marcus Borg admires. The Gospel writers took an angry Jewish nationalist and made him into a nonviolent spiritual guide. The Gospel writers had to rewrite the events of the historical Jesus in order to recreate the image of Jesus, thereby making him into something different than the zealot Aslan claims he was. So they put words in his mouth that he did not say, and invented deeds that he did not do, in order to entice people to follow the movement that was named after him. This evolving picture of Jesus began with Mark's Gospel, continued with the Gospels of Matthew and Luke, and culminated with a different, highly spiritual rendition of Jesus in the Gospel of John. You have to wonder why anyone would care to keep this Jesus movement going. What would be the purpose? After Jesus was executed for treason, his disciples scattered and supposedly disappeared into obscurity; his dead body, according to Crossan, Aslan and others, was fed to the feral dogs. What motivated these "Christians" to get together sometime later (forty to fifty years later) and recreate a whole new image of Jesus? This did not happen to any other zealot during this time. Once the leader was killed and his followers scattered, that was the end of that group. Did the Gospel writers think the dispersed Jews needed a messiah now that their beautiful city was destroyed, and Jesus—that zealot who got himself killed for treason—was as good as anyone to posthumously lead the cause? Does Aslan really think you are going to agree with his theory? Apparently, he does, and apparently a lot of people have.

Aslan is convinced that Jesus was aware of the political atmosphere of first-century Palestine and that this awareness gradually turned him into a revolutionary. As Jesus travelled throughout Galilee, he assimilated followers into his messianic movement in order to establish God's kingdom in Israel. Jesus was going to, with the help of his followers, restore Israel's independence and set up a theocratic

51

state. But, Aslan says, Jesus failed. The failure was largely due to a terrible blunder—he had entered Jerusalem in a kingly fashion and then attacked the Temple. This apparently prompted the Roman authorities to arrest him, charge him with treason, and execute him. It is true that Jesus rode into Jerusalem in a kingly fashion on a donkey while people joyfully shouted; you can read about it in Mt 21:1-6. But did he attack the Temple as Aslan suggests? (I will address this more extensively in Chapter Eight.) Aslan believes Jesus' followers made him into the long-awaited Messiah predicted in the Hebrew Scriptures. Aslan would have preferred that Jesus' followers would have kept the zealot Jesus alive in their writings because that is the kind of person Aslan would have admired; that is the "historical" Jesus Aslan could revere. Since the Gospels had the audacity to recreate the zealot Jesus of Nazareth into the long-awaited Messiah, Aslan wants to subject the Gospels to the fires of historical analysis. By doing so, Aslan is certain that they can then be purged of all their embellishments and re-creations. Aslan is hoping that the final analysis of this critical examination will result in a more accurate portrait of the "historical" Jesus. If the Gospels are exposed to historical analysis, Aslan is sure that it will reveal how inaccurate the Gospels are. But this historical analysis, this "exposé," has already been done. During the late 19th and early 20th centuries, European and American liberal theologians attempted to use form criticism, literary criticism, and historical analysis to portray the Bible as an unreliable, contradictory, full-of-errors compilation of documents. The Bible survived that test when it was "put under the fire," but modern liberal theologians and scholars like Ehrman, Spong, the members of the Jesus Seminar, and Reza Aslan are trying to fan the flames all over again. These new Disclaimers of Christianity are simply parroting what has already been said and done, and it does not matter that sufficient answers have already been given for their accusations. Their attempt to "raise a dead horse" is ironic, since they do not believe in the idea of a resurrection. Aslan warns us that when the Gospels are exposed to this historical analysis we will discover the "true" Jesus, one that we would not have expected. Aslan is quite certain that modern Christians will not recognize the Jesus that is uncovered by such analysis, but he assures us that this is necessary because this "uncovering" will reveal to us the real Jesus. The process Aslan refers to is not just the former attempts at historical analysis, of course, but the analysis that he presents in his book *Zealot*. Aslan believes the Jesus he reveals in his book is the true

Jesus. Aslan's Jesus, however, is so stripped-down that he (Jesus) would not only be unrecognized by most modern Christians, he would not be recognized by his original followers and the early Christians who came to believe in him as a result of the apostles' preaching the gospel message throughout the Roman Empire. Aslan wants you to believe that the Jesus discovered by the process of historical analysis (which includes his own analysis) will reveal the real Jesus. However, the "real" Jesus that is part of Aslan's worldview is not historical; it is a figment of his imagination. I have titled this chapter Unstable Building Blocks because I am certain that we will see, as I continue my critique, that the ideas Aslan and other liberal theologians/biblical scholars have regarding Jesus are quite unstable, historically and logically.

Chapter Three: The Early Years of Jesus

Aslan provides his reader with a reason that first-century Palestine had so many zealots. It was because of Rome's dominion over Judea, which displayed itself in two major ways: one, the "gentrifying" of Galilee and parts of Judea; and two, a large increase in taxes to pay for this building enterprise. As a result, rural peasants found it difficult to pay taxes to the government and pay their tithes to the Temple. These harsh living conditions would therefore prompt some to occasionally rebel. The members of these peasant gangs were called "bandits" (the Greek word being *lēstēs*); they were vigilantes, insurrectionists, and robbers who often armed themselves against Roman soldiers and anyone, Jew or Gentile, that collaborated with them, like tax collectors. The bandits, of course, could justify their actions by claiming to be "working for God." They were self-proclaimed messiahs bent on dismantling Roman authority in their area. Local authorities mostly saw them as nuisances more than anything else, but they still needed to be stopped. Herod the Great, known for his ruthlessness, did everything he could, with the Roman army behind him, to maintain order in the countryside. Herod would not tolerate even a hint of revolt from the Jews under his reign. When Herod died circa 4 B.C. his death created not only a division within his Judean kingdom (his three sons got pieces of it) but it also revived an outbreak of banditry that had been suppressed during his reign. (Luke mentions two bandit episodes in Acts 5:36.) The Roman army, of course, continued to quell any and all uprisings, which mostly were small and short-lived. Aslan wants us to think that this historical setting was what prompted Jesus to grow up to become one of those zealots.

What about Quirinius?

Aslan uses this historical setting to question the Gospel information regarding the infancy stories of Jesus. Aslan is convinced that Matthew and Luke present contradictory infancy stories about Jesus in their Gospels. Aslan believes it was not until after an interest in Jesus began to increase long after his death (for whatever strange reason) that the early followers of this dead zealot realized that they needed to fill in the gaps of Jesus' early years, and so they created stories about his birth. It apparently did not matter that these stories conflicted with one another. And it did not seem to matter whether or not the stories were true. For example, Aslan tells us that Luke's readers would have realized that Luke's infancy story of Jesus was not historically accurate, including the passage that mentions Quirinius (see Lk 2:2). So, let's take a look at this so-called error that Luke has made. Luke says that "Caesar Augustus issued a decree that a census should be taken of the entire Roman world. (This was the first census that took place while Quirinius was governor of Syria.) And everyone went to their own town to register" (NIV, Lk 2:1-3). Aslan and other Bible critics contend that Luke was factually inaccurate in these verses. John Dominic Crossan, in his aforementioned book, says Augustus never decreed a worldwide census, claiming it was a census just for the Palestinian area and that Quirinius organized it in 6 to 7 A.D. That would make Jesus about ten or twelve years old; too old for the birth narrative found in Luke's first chapter. Crossan further states that the census would have counted the people at their place of residence and not the place of one's ancestry or birth, because this census was for tax purposes. So Aslan, Crossan, and other liberal scholars believe that Luke was mistaken in his "facts." We know from ancient writings, however, that both Rome and Egypt required a census of its people, at various times and for various reasons. The purpose of a census varied: sometimes it was for taxation (as Crossan says); sometimes it was to verify ancestral lineage; sometimes it was to register males fit for military service; and sometimes it was used to determine the labor force for building projects. There were actual instances where a Roman census required a person to return to his/her ancestral home if that person owned property in that district or area. Luke would not have to tell his readers why Joseph had to go to Bethlehem to meet the requirements of this census; they would know since they knew what those requirements were. (See the *New Bible Dictionary* and *What Does the Bible Say About* regarding Quirinius and the Census.)

Many critics of the New Testament—the Jesus Seminar, liberal theologians, so-called "new" atheists, and Aslan—have used this Lukan passage regarding Quirinius being governor of Syria at or near the birth of Jesus to show that Luke cannot be trusted. They believe the story was created in order to fulfill Hebrew Scripture prophecy that stated that the Messiah would be born in Bethlehem. That is why, according to them, the Gospel writer had to get Jesus' family from Nazareth—where the critics claim Jesus was really born—down to

Bethlehem. The critics claim that the timing of the census was off; Quirinius was not governor of Syria at the time of Jesus' birth. Therefore, Luke was wrong. They need him to be wrong on this one thing because if there is anything that can be stated with certainty about Luke it is that he was meticulous in his accuracy, especially when you look at all the cities and places he mentions in Acts. Given his extraordinary accuracy throughout his Gospel and Acts, the typical response most historians would give, which they do for other ancient writings, would be to give Luke the benefit of the doubt. The reason why Aslan and other critics (like Horsley) are unwilling to give Luke the benefit of the doubt in this instance is because Luke's critics want and need to have some example where Luke was mistaken. That would mean that if Luke made one mistake, then it is possible for him to have made others. If Luke made just one mistake, then, for these critics, the entirety of Luke's writings could be discounted. The critics of Luke say that Quirinius was not governor of Syria at this time, but it is certainly possible that Quirinius was acting in a special capacity during this first or initial census/registration, that he began the process of getting the census started, which would have taken considerable organization, requiring quite a length of time, since it was to be a vast endeavor. Acting in a special capacity, it is not unlikely that Quirinius would have been referred to as a governor; people acting in a position, even if for a short period of time, are often given the title of that position for authoritative purposes. Because Quirinius was given the task of handling the census in this part of Palestine, it makes sense for him to be given the title of governor, even though, historically, he was not yet the official governor. This practice occurs even today when a person receives a certain task to perform and is then given an official title while performing that task. Another possibility is that there could have been two different people who served as governors in Syria with the name Quirinius; someone named Quirinius could have served around 11 B.C. until the death of Herod (circa 6-4 B.C.), and a different man also named Quirinius could have served around 6-9 A.D. Another possibility is that Quirinius could have served as governor in two different terms (again, not something unheard of); once around 6-4 B.C. and again around 6-9 A.D. The *Nelson Study Bible* suggests that if Quirinius did serve two different terms, then a census would appear during both terms. (Rome often required a census every fourteen years, or so.) The first term and census would be found in Luke's narrative (chapter two of his Gospel) about Jesus' birth; the second term and census was mentioned in Luke's Acts (5:37) when Gamaliel mentioned the census in 6-9 A.D.

The issue surrounding Quirinius, however, does not have to be as complicated as the three different scenarios (possibilities) I presented above. Let's look again at Luke's wording, this time from a different translation. He says that "a decree went out from Caesar Augustus that all the world should be registered. This was the first registration when Quirinius was governor of Syria" (ESV, Lk 2:1–2). We see by using these two translations that Luke tells us that this was the "first census while" (NIV) or the "first registration when" (ESV) Quirinius was governor of Syria. If you look at the ancient Greek manuscripts, you find that certain words are actually missing within the text; the words are simply assumed or implied by the typical Greek reader. When the Greek sentences are translated into English the translator adds words in order to make the reading flow smoother for us English readers. Now the ancient manuscripts for Luke 2:2 are missing a word that translators have filled in with either the word "when" or "while." So what we have then in some translations of Luke 2:2 is "when Quirinius was governor of Syria" (ESV), and others say "while Quirinius was governor of Syria" (NIV). The words "when" and "while" are assumed. Both the ESV and the NIV acknowledge that the words "when" and "while" could be replaced by the word "before." In other words, Luke could just as easily have been saying "before Quirinius was governor of Syria" a census was held. The *Pulpit Commentary* on this passage in Luke (2:2) points out that if Luke had made an error regarding Quirinius so early on in his Gospel, those "early opponents of Christianity, such as Celsus or Porphyry," would not have wasted any time impugning Luke's record. The fact that they did not shows that Luke's mention of Quirinius in the second chapter of his Gospel was not considered a conspicuous blot. Aslan, the JS, and other liberal theologians are unkindly quick to dismiss Luke on the basis of the words "when" and/or "while," even though they do not even occur in the manuscript, regardless of the accuracy Luke shows throughout both of his books. This is clearly an unprofessional result of bias on their part.

The fact that certain pieces of the puzzle are missing, or not available to us as external evidence, does not mean that we should automatically insist that Luke was in error. Liberal theologians are often quick to point out a so-called biblical error only to have an archaeological find substantiate the biblical passage. It has happened quite often, in fact. For example, the Tel Dan Inscription that archaeologists have discovered gives evidence for King David of Israel, showing that he had established a dynasty in Judah in the eleventh century B.C. Archaeological findings show there was a complex, organized Edomite state as early as the twelfth century B.C., which corresponds to the biblical books of Joshua and Judges. Archaeologists have found evidence of many of the foreign kings listed in the Hebrew Scriptures, including King Sennacherib of Assyria. The water tunnel beneath Jerusalem has also been discovered, which at one time was under dispute. Many other examples can be provided that show that critics like Horsley, who reject biblical passages as non-historical, are often proven wrong by the discoveries of archaeologists. (See the reference page regarding these examples.) So Aslan and other critics of Luke's account are really barking at a shadow. They need Luke to make a mistake and so they picked what is admittedly a difficult passage; but when one puts all the information together, it is not being historically amiss to acknowledge that either Quirinius, in some governmental capacity, was involved in this census that required Joseph, along with Mary, to travel to Bethlehem, or that it happened before he became governor.

Aslan believes that Luke did not intend for his readers to understand his narrative regarding Jesus' birth in Bethlehem as historical fact. The reason Aslan is convinced of this is because he thinks that the majority of those living in ancient times either could not or did not care to distinguish between what was real and what was not; there was no distinction between reality and myth. Therefore, the Gospel writers were not too concerned about historical facts; after all, in those days it was not important to simply uncover facts, it was more important to reveal "truths"—spiritual, esoteric and mystical knowledge that the reader could "take to heart." Aslan claims that for the Gospel writers it did not matter if the events were true or not; it was the message that one wanted to get across that was important. Concern for observable and verifiable events is supposedly a modern idea, and ancient writers (e.g., the Gospel writers) did not see history as a mode for presenting events that could be both observed and verified. For Aslan, it is through the use of critical analysis that we are now able to determine the veracity of past events. The ancients did not have critical analysis and therefore could not distinguish between what was real and what was imagined. So, it is not so much that the Gospel writers were necessarily trying to deceive or lie to their readers, it is just that, according to Aslan, ancient writers did not care that much about the telling of true or factual events; they cared more that their writings presented a message or provided an example than they did about giving factual data. We know that in ancient pagan nations there was a mixture of myth and reality, that their myriad of gods could bless or wreck havoc on individuals and peoples just for fun. Jewish culture, however, had one God—unseen and uncreated—who demanded that they live a righteous life. Jews had a keen sense of reality because they knew what God expected of them, and they knew the consequences of disobedience. The Hebrew Scriptures are filled with historical events; events that the Jews truly believed happened in real space/time. Jews trusted that God was at the helm of their history, and their Scriptures attested to this belief. History, and the factual telling of history, was very important for the Jew. Mixing fact and fiction is not something only an ancient writer was wont to do, however; we find modern writers doing it as well. If Aslan believes ancient writers—which would include the Gospel writers—are not to be trusted, why then does he feel he is able to rely on the Roman writers and Josephus for some of his information? The idea that ancient writers did not care about getting the facts right, but modern writers do, conveys what is known as chronological snobbery, the idea that "non-modern" peoples (including ancients and those living in the Medieval Period) were mostly "backward," non-inventive, superstitious, gullible and uninterested in facts (be they historical or scientific). It is Aslan's worldview that prompts him to conclude that the Gospel writers were not concerned with real facts, real truth, when they wrote about the life of Jesus, that the Gospel writers never meant for their narratives to be understood as historical fact. The Gospel writers, however, were rooted in the Jewish concept of history and were, therefore, very much concerned with historical facts.

Critical Realism—An Approach for Determining Historicity

Aslan thinks the modern use of critical analysis will provide us with the necessary tools to determine the veracity of ancient writings and, for the most part, they are valuable tools for such discovery. The problem with critical analysis as a tool for discovery lies in the hand that holds that tool. Many of those who attempt to use critical analysis already broach the problem they are studying with biased worldviews. They use critical analysis to "prove" their point rather than as a tool to actually search for truth. Many so-called scholars using critical analysis in the late 1800s and early 1900s were using it for one reason: to debunk and demythologize the Bible. There is another technique, however, that can be utilized to study ancient documents (such as biblical narrative) and it is called Critical Realism. It promotes the idea that the text being studied has something "real" in it that can be discovered through "critical" research. The method assumes a connection between reality (what is really there) and human knowledge; therefore, Critical Realism enables the person using it to learn something objectively about what is being studied. Using this method, biblical text can be analyzed by means of critical reflection and, in passing that examination, can be said to speak the truth about reality, i.e., the realness of the subject matter under investigation. Those whose motives are to use critical analysis to debunk and demythologize biblical narratives typically make the assumption that these narratives are not historical; they are seen as fictionalized stories more than they are stories about something that actually happened. For Aslan (and the JS), biblical stories are non-historical; they are viewed as common literature—mere poetry and fiction. The stories are not associated with events that really happened; their purpose is to give a message or moral that affects one's life. But there is nothing intrinsically non-historic in the narratives of the Bible; in other words, the narratives in the Bible that purport to be historical are meant to be taken as historical and not as something written within which one is only supposed to find a hidden meaning or a "spiritual truth" that is only true for the individual reader. This, of course, does not negate the fact that the Holy Spirit can and does apply certain biblical passages to our own lives and makes those passages relevant to the Christian, makes those passages "come alive." However, the historic narratives of the Bible have merit on their own; they are not there just to be read to see how they apply to a person's life. Those who reject the Bible's historical narratives appear to manipulate the evidence in order to justify their own preconceived theory or idea. There is no evidence showing that first century Jews and/or Christians did not understand the real nature of history. There is no evidence showing that they could not tell the difference—or that the difference did not matter—between what really happened and what they wished had happened.

Aslan wants you to believe that the Gospel writers and the early Christians were not concerned with real history, but only with the kernel of truth—a positive message one can take to heart—derived from a non-historical story that is designed to maintain or boost one's faith. The issue at stake is not just determining whether or not there is an historical element in a particular biblical story or text, but also how to discover that historical element and then ascertain its accuracy. This is what critical research really does. It does not start out by doubting the text; it does not start out by stating that all biblical text is non-historical; it does not start out by claiming that the writer was unable to know the difference between truth and exaggeration. Real critical research starts by accepting the statement of the text and then examining it to discover whether it is valid or not. In the Gospel of Luke we are told that the writer carefully investigated everything, using eyewitness testimony and primary sources, so he could write an orderly and truthful account (see Lk 1:1–4). John, in his Gospel, tells the reader that he is a true witness of the events he is writing about (see Jn 19:35; 21:24). Peter tells us in his second epistle that he and the other apostles did not follow cleverly invented stories (see 2 Pe 1:16). There is no reason to doubt their words. The New Testament writers wanted to assure their readers that they were writing about historical events, events that really happened. Critical realism allows us to take the Gospel writers at their word unless or until we find evidence against them. This is what we do with other writings, ancient or modern.

Herod's Massacre of the Innocents

Aslan does not just focus on Luke, though; he also accuses Matthew of writing an imaginary story about Jesus and his family escaping to Egypt. Matthew tells us that Herod has been informed that a king has been born in Bethlehem and, since Herod is the current king, he decides to destroy the child. Aslan is not the only one, of course, to insist that the massacre of young male children that Matthew records in his Gospel (2:16) did not happen; it is often pointed out that the massacre was not recorded in any other document at that time. Only Matthew records it; and it is assumed, upon that basis, that the

61

"massacre of the innocents," as it is called, was simply fabricated. Aslan believes he knows why Matthew made up this horrendous story about the slaughter of young male children. It was not because of Herod's jealousy and fear. Matthew did it so he could use a passage from the Hebrew Scriptures that said, "Out of Egypt I called my son" (NIV, Hosea 11:1), and then apply that passage as messianic prophecy for Jesus. Aslan is sure the Gospel writers created fabled stories about Jesus in order to make him into a more attractive and interesting messiah, despite the fact that he had been dead for forty years. So, the narrative in Matthew about the slaughter of young male children was not intended to be read as real history; it was just a story Matthew made up so he could use a Scriptural passage to "prove" that Jesus was the messiah. The 'out of Egypt' story was invented by Matthew in order to do one thing, Aslan declares (although J.P. Spong had already made the suggestion), and that was to promote the idea that Jesus was the new Moses who would lead Israel to freedom. The problem with this idea, though, is that if Matthew is writing his Gospel in the 80s or 90s as Aslan claims, at a time when the Jews have all been dispersed and Jerusalem destroyed, then why would Matthew's readers care about a man who had been dead for fifty to sixty years, a man who had failed to save Jerusalem? Aslan thinks that Matthew needed to have Jesus fulfill as many prophecies from the Hebrew Scriptures that he could find in order to cover up the fact that Jesus failed to fulfill the most basic messianic prophecy, which was to restore Israel's independence. Of course, Aslan assumes he knows the exact time and date of when Israel was supposed to be restored.

What about Matthew's mention of Herod's killing of the innocents? Why is that event missing in the annals of history; why is it only mentioned in Matthew's Gospel? As I have already noted, Matthew's main audience for his Gospel was his fellow Jews. He made use of a lot of Hebrew Scripture prophecies to convince his readers that Jesus was the long-awaited Messiah. Every Jew knew how ruthless Herod the Great was, how he had killed many of his own people to get the political positions he desired, how he had even killed members of his own family, how he had no qualms about committing any crime that would promote his agenda, and how he saw himself as the king of the Jews. When he learned from the eastern Magi that they travelled to pay homage to a child who was recently born who would be the king of the Jews, there is no doubt, knowing his temper and brutality, that

Herod would do everything he could to destroy the child. Bethlehem was a small village, and it is possible that at that time there were no more than a dozen or two male children two years old and younger who would have been signaled out to be killed in and around that area. The Roman soldiers would be sent to systematically and quickly eliminate the children. Herod's decision would not be recorded; the massacre would take place without fanfare. This massacre of the innocents is not something that would be contrary to Herod's past behavior. No one living at that time would have been surprised that Herod had done such a thing. We should actually be thankful that Matthew recorded it, that the episode is one more thing to show how evil Herod the Great was. The fact that Matthew is the only one to have done so does not mean it did not happen. (Remember, that is one of the assumptions of the Jesus Seminar—if only one Gospel mentions something, and it is therefore not corroborated in another Gospel, then it is not authentic—and it is a wrong assumption.) This was an important event in Jesus' young life, and since Matthew may have been the first Gospel written, no other Gospel writer needed to mention it. Jesus and his family did not have to go to Egypt in order to fulfill a messianic prophecy; they went there to save Jesus' life. But since they had gone to Egypt to keep Jesus from being part of the massacre, Matthew showed his readers how leaving Egypt was similar to when the whole nation of Israel had left it. The fact that the massacre of these male children (two-years-old and younger) was not news-worthy enough to be recorded by Roman historians actually is a good example of how the Romans viewed slaves, Jews, and the poor. Human life was simply not that valuable to Roman soldiers; they would have no qualms about carrying out Herod's order. The killing of these children in an obscure village like Bethlehem would not have even raised an eyebrow in Rome. The fact that this event was not recorded in the annals of Rome's history shows what kinds of people the Romans were; it does not show that Matthew made the story up for the sake of narrative.

Explaining the Genealogy of Jesus

Since we have been discussing Jesus' infancy narratives, it is necessary to look at the so-called discrepancy between Matthew and Luke's list of Jesus' ancestors. The Fellows of the JS and other liberal theologians/biblical scholars try to use the differences between the two lists to show that the Gospel writers were inaccurate. When we look at these two lists, we see that Matthew's genealogy begins with Abraham and moves forward in history to Christ. Luke, on the other hand, moves backward. He begins with Joseph and goes back through David to Abraham, and then all the way to Adam. Even though Luke begins with Joseph, the majority of commentators tell us that Luke is actually using Mary's lineage all the way back to Adam to show that Jesus was the promised "seed of the woman" (see Gen. 3:15). Luke appears to be using a physical lineage to emphasize the humanity of Jesus. Matthew uses Joseph's lineage to show his Hebrew readers that Jesus follows the Messianic line of David. Matthew obviously skips certain people because he wants to organize his list into three groups of fourteen ancestors. The list is still accurate, even if it is missing some people. Matthew's list is not intended to be exhaustive and, for that matter, neither is Luke's. So Matthew presents a royal line, which includes those who actually ruled Israel, like David. Luke presents a legal line of descent, which did not necessarily include those who actually ruled as kings. These genealogies do not contradict one another; they simply emphasize the variation in Jesus' human lineage. The genealogical lists found in Matthew and Luke's Gospels complement each other; they do not contradict each other.

To produce further doubt upon Matthew and Luke's infancy stories, Aslan points out that there are some scholars who suggest that it is possible that Joseph (Jesus' stepfather) is a fabrication, that he never really existed, and that Matthew and Luke had to create him in order to repel the idea that Jesus was simply an illegitimate child. The existence of Joseph supposedly helped soften the odd concept of what is called the virgin birth. These scholars apparently think the people in the first century were so gullible and naïve that they would rather accept or believe a virgin birth before they would accept or believe that Jesus was an illegitimate child. These scholars also like to point out that the Hebrew word that most Bibles translate as 'virgin' really means "young maiden," but what they obviously fail to grasp is that a young maiden or woman in a Jewish community would most likely be a virgin. Since Matthew and Luke are the only ones who mention the virgin birth and mention Joseph, Aslan thinks it is legitimate to reject the virgin birth and question Joseph's existence. Would Aslan have been more apt to accept Joseph's existence if twenty people had mentioned him? Would it really matter to Aslan how many people mentioned Joseph? We see in the Gospels that when Jesus returned to Nazareth during his ministry and spoke in the synagogue, the people were amazed at his wisdom and miraculous power and asked: Isn't this the carpenter's son? (Mt 13:55). They were surprised that Jesus could lecture better than the well-educated scribes because he was just the son of a carpenter named Joseph. In John 6:42, some people were criticizing Jesus because of some things he had said (especially about himself), and they asked among themselves: "Isn't this man Jesus, Joseph's son? Don't we know his father and mother?" ("Scripture is taken from GOD'S WORD®. © 1995 God's Word to the Nations. Used by permission of Baker Publishing Group."). There is no reason to doubt that Joseph existed, and there is no reason to think that the virgin birth was created in order to hide the 'fact' that Jesus was an illegitimate child.

The Compatibility of the Infancy Stories

In order to gain a more comprehensive perspective on the two infancy stories found in Matthew and Luke, let's combine the stories and see how compatible they are. Luke tells us that Zechariah was informed that his wife Elizabeth would give birth to a son whom they were to call John (who would later become the Baptizer). Mary is also told that she will conceive, and so she visits Elizabeth, her relative, who is carrying John. Mary stays with Elizabeth [presumably up to the birth of John] and then returns to Nazareth where she lives. Matthew picks up where Luke leaves off and informs us that Mary's fiancé (Joseph) is concerned about her pregnancy. He is told by an angel that Mary is carrying the Messiah through the power of the Holy Spirit. Luke continues with Joseph and Mary's journey from Nazareth to Bethlehem, explaining why and how the couple got there. Matthew and Luke both record the birth of Jesus, although Luke, possibly because he is writing from Mary's perspective, provides more information. Luke recounts the first few days of Jesus' birth, which include the visit of the shepherds, the circumcision of Jesus at eight days old, and the presentation of Jesus at the Temple on his fortieth day. Joseph and Mary are poor and offer the required sacrifice that poor people give. Then Matthew records the visit of the Magi [which probably occurred when Jesus was around two years old] and the flight to Egypt due to Herod's murderous intent. After Herod dies, the family returns to Nazareth where Jesus grows in strength, wisdom and God's grace (Lk 2:40).

Looking at these two accounts in this way, we see there is no discrepancy; instead, we see great harmony between the two accounts as each writer supplies whatever information is lacking in the other. If the infancy stories found in Matthew and Luke were not meant to be read as historical events, as Aslan claims, then how would they have helped convince those who read them that Jesus was the Messiah?

Young Jesus at the Temple

Aslan not only rejects Matthew and Luke's birth narratives of Jesus, he also rejects Luke's account about Jesus and his family going to Jerusalem on a yearly basis because he (Aslan) believes Jesus' family was too poor to make the annual journey. Luke tells his readers that every year Jesus' parents went to Jerusalem for the Passover festival; he then focuses on the time they went when Jesus was twelve years old (see 2:41f). Fruchtenbaum informs us that Jesus accompanied his parents on this trip because he was at the age when he would need to prepare for his bar mitzvah, which would take place when he turned thirteen. The reason Luke's account is not good enough evidence for Aslan is because it does not fit the scenario that Aslan has created for Jesus. Aslan has built up a narrative of his own within which he has placed Jesus, and any evidence that goes against that narrative is rejected. If Matthew and Luke or any other Gospel writer says something about Jesus that does not fit in the scenario that Aslan has created, it is discarded, rejected, and/or called non-historical. (The JS, as we have seen, have operated this way as well, and the practice is quite common among liberal theologians, like Spong.) Aslan has decided that it is absurd to think that Jesus' poor family made yearly trips to Jerusalem; and it is absurd to think that poor, illiterate, uneducated Jesus, at the age of twelve, could think of any questions to even ask these rabbis and scribes. What Luke was showing in his Gospel about the formative years of Jesus is that he (Jesus) grew up like most normal Jewish boys: he attended synagogue, he visited Jerusalem with his family, and he was proficient enough in his learning as a young boy that he could amaze some of his elders. We have children like that today that simply astound adults with their knowledge, inventiveness, and prodigious activities that seem to go beyond their years. Luke tells us that Jesus "grew and became strong, filled with wisdom" (2:40). That is not too difficult to believe. But Aslan rejects the idea that Jesus, as a twelve-year-old boy, was quite a prodigy. Aslan has to believe that it is nothing but conjecture on Luke's part because it does not fit into Aslan's worldview. Aslan thinks these childhood stories—the virgin birth, the yearly trips to Jerusalem, the smart little twelve-year-old—were all fabricated by the Gospel writers so that they could turn Jesus into a Messiah some forty to fifty years after his death. The evidence for Aslan's conclusions, however, is not so clear. Aslan certainly believes he is approaching truth when he creates his scenarios; why then are the Gospel writers not presenting historical facts when they give us information about Jesus? Certainly Aslan does not think we should believe what he says simply because he has said it? It is easy to see as one reads Aslan's book that his method is to first create a scenario; second, discount events in the Gospel that contradict the scenario he has created; and third, conclude that the Gospel is therefore wrong. I think it is justifiable to reject Aslan's methodology.

Chapter Four: The Beginnings of Jesus' Ministry

Was Jesus Uneducated, Illiterate, and Extremely Poor?

Having dismissed Matthew and Luke's birth narrative, Aslan insists that Jesus was born in a rural area of Galilee. When Aslan and other liberal scholars reject Jesus-as-Messiah they have to then create their own birth narrative. They choose Galilee and reject Bethlehem because the latter is associated with a prophetic declaration. Aslan does not choose Galilee for Jesus' birth because the evidence for it is overwhelming; he chooses it because it agrees with his worldview. Aslan is quite descriptive in what he thinks Nazareth may have been like when Jesus was growing up there, and he (Aslan) assumes that Jesus did not have many opportunities to succeed, or at least do well. In fact, Aslan portrays Jesus as being just a poor, illiterate peasant whose occupation would keep him in extreme poverty. Even Jesus' language—Aramaic—highlighted his lack of education because, according to Aslan, Aramaic was the language of the uneducated; it was the language of peasants, and it would have been very difficult for Jesus to even know Hebrew. The truth is, however, that the Aramaic version of the Scriptures, known as Targums, were used before, during and after Jesus' time to provide traditional synagogue interpretation, as well as being a witness to the Hebrew text (*Holman Illustrated Bible Dictionary*). We see from 2 Kings Chapter 18 that Aramaic was spoken during the time of King Hezekiah and had become the language of international affairs (from a marginal note in Quest Study Bible). It was the common language in Judea in the first-century and was not just a "poor man's" language. The Hebrew Scriptures had also been translated into the Greek language around the third century B.C.; it was known as the Septuagint and was identified with the letters LXX. Most of the scriptural quotations in the New Testament are from the Septuagint. It is quite possible that Jesus knew all three languages—Aramaic, Hebrew and Greek—as we will see later.

If you study ancient Jewish culture, you will find that they held education of the people—especially the males—in high esteem. Part of a Jewish child's education was to teach him/her to understand their special relationship with God, and to teach them to serve him and to be holy (i.e., set apart from pagan customs and culture). Children accompanied their parents to religious services (the synagogue) and festivals where they gained an understanding of the history of their people, learning about all the major events and their significance. Jewish education included character development, studying the Mosaic Law, and memorizing and copying essential passages from the Torah and Prophets. Memorization was extremely important because there were times in their history when they had been exiled to foreign nations and would need to be able to recite their Scriptures from memory. In the second century B.C., Antiochus IV had infiltrated Israel, desecrated the Temple, destroyed religious scrolls, tortured and persecuted Jews, and set himself up as one to be worshipped. It was because of this that every Jewish boy would henceforth not only attend elementary school but continue their education up to their seventeenth year. Children learned to memorize Hebrew Scripture at a very young age, and it was imperative that they repeat the exact words. They also learned to copy and recopy passages in order to learn that skill. Reading aloud was also enforced because it helped in memorization. Along with this basic education, fathers were expected to teach their son their trade. Based on this knowledge of Jewish culture, it is difficult to conclude that Jesus was as unschooled and ignorant as Aslan would like to think. (Some information gleaned from *Tyndale Bible Dictionary* and *Baker Encyclopedia of the Bible*.) There is therefore no reason to doubt that Jesus was educated in the Torah in his local synagogue. Just like every other Galilean Jew, Jesus would have read, memorized and followed the principles of the Torah (see Friedman's *They Loved the Torah*).

The major reason Aslan believes Jesus was poor and uneducated was because there was not much for a woodworker to do in Nazareth. The residents of Nazareth were so impoverished that they would not be able to give Jesus and his family enough work. All Joseph could do was teach his eldest son—Jesus—his trade and hope for the best. So when Jesus grew up, he too became a typical artisan and day laborer and this would have kept him at the lowest rung of peasant class. Aslan believes the Greek word for woodworker was a slang term used by the Romans to indicate that a person was uneducated, which typically would also mean the person was illiterate. The Greek work Aslan has in mind is *tekton*. The *Greek-English Lexicon of the New Testament*, however, states that a person who was regarded as a *tekton* "would be skilled in the use of wood and stone and possibly even metal." But Aslan wants you to think that Jesus' career as a carpenter, a *tekton*, was evidence that he had a lower class job that kept him in poverty. Now, it is true that in ancient Rome carpentry as a menial job was often relegated to the slave class, but non-slaves could also choose that occupation as a skilled laborer and join a local guild. Let's not forget that slaves also worked as physicians, teachers, and accountants, as well as in other professions. Throughout the Roman Empire there existed a huge labor force, constructing bridges, renovating cities, building roads and aqueducts, etc. This labor force consisted of slaves, regular citizens (often poor), certain soldiers, and skilled laborers from local guilds. Carpenters in these guilds worked on specific tasks which called for skilled experience, such as the construction of arches and domes. We are not told what field of carpentry Jesus went into, but just because he lived in Nazareth does not mean that that was the only village where he worked. Nazareth was not very far from other towns, villages and affluent cities. Aslan even suggests that Jesus could have worked on some of the extensive building projects that Antipas (Herod the Great's son) had initiated.

If Jesus was both a carpenter and stone mason, and possibly knew how to work with some metals—which is what the Greek word *tekton* suggests—it is likely that he had plenty of local jobs to keep him busy as he traveled to nearby towns and villages for work. In his occupation, he would certainly know how to read and draw up designs and contracts for the projects he worked on; so there is no reason to assume that Jesus was illiterate. Although it appears he mostly spoke Aramaic, it is also likely that he spoke Greek since that was a common language spoken in that area. Galilee, in the northern territory of Judea, was in close proximity to non-Jewish areas where Greek was spoken. In his occupation and his travels, there is no reason to assume Jesus did not know the Gentile language. He had traveled to Tyre, Caesarea Philippi, and the Decapolis (an area southeast of the Sea of Galilee made up of about ten Hellenistic cities) during his ministry. Those were areas that spoke Greek. Why would Jesus go into these areas if he did not know the language? He said his ministry was to tell the good news about the Kingdom of God, so if he went into areas that spoke mostly Greek, you would think he would know the language so he could tell the good news to those living there. Just because there are several passages in the Gospels showing that Jesus spoke Aramaic does not mean that that was the only language that he knew. In light of his occupation and his travels, there is no reason not to think that Jesus was bilingual (speaking Aramaic and Greek) and maybe even trilingual (adding Hebrew to his linguistic skills). The Jewish Scriptures were available in Hebrew, Aramaic, and Greek before Jesus was born, and it is quite possible that Jesus could speak all three languages. There is no reason to suppose that Jesus was unable to read and write; there is no reason to think that Jesus was not educated as any other Jewish citizen. Claiming that Jesus was illiterate goes against what we know about Jewish culture at the time, i.e., it disagrees with historical fact. Although there is no indication that Jesus was wealthy, there is also no evidence to say that he was as dirt poor and uneducated as Aslan would hope. History disagrees with Aslan's scenario.

John's Baptism: The Gospels vs. Josephus

We see in the Gospels that Jesus leaves Galilee and travels to Judea, near Jerusalem in order to be baptized and begin his ministry. Aslan thinks it odd that Jesus, being thirty years old now, would not have a wife, especially since celibacy was quite rare during this time. If Jesus were married, it would not have caused a problem for one of the Gospel writers to have mentioned it. It would not have taken anything away from Jesus' ministry and his being the Redeeming Messiah. Jesus probably would not have married, though, since he believed he was the Messiah and had a short time to live after he started his ministry. Of course, we know that Peter was married at the time Jesus began his ministry (see Mt 8:14, where Peter's mother-in-law is mentioned), but we are unable to say how many of the other apostles were or not. We know Paul remained single so he could dedicate his time to spreading the gospel (see 1 Cor 7:7). Aslan believes all the Gospels should have started with Jesus' baptism; he believes that everything that was stated in the Gospels that happened before Jesus' baptism was fabrication. But he also thinks that much of what the Gospels say of John the Baptizer is fabrication, too. Like Jesus' early years, Aslan claims that Luke's depiction of John the Baptizer's birth and lineage reads like a fantasy. (Luke's birth narrative of John the Baptizer can be found in the first chapter, verses 5-25.) It seems rather odd that Luke, in his introductory paragraph to his Gospel (1:1-4), would claim that he "carefully investigated everything from the beginning," and then the very first story he tells, beginning in verse

71

five (which is John's birth narrative), is a lie. According to Aslan, Luke had an agenda which he promoted by making up stories to convince others of his theories. That is what I have accused the Jesus Seminar, Aslan, and other liberal theologians/biblical scholars of doing. Did Luke, and the other Gospel writers, do the same thing? How do we know which one is correct? When Luke tells us he has thoroughly investigated what he is writing about, can we trust him? This is where we must rely on the tripartite tests mentioned in chapter one; the tests historians typically apply to historical writings in order to determine their reliability. It is true that Luke is the only one who gives us John the Baptizer's birth narrative, but that, in itself, does not mean it is not true (although that is a criterion the JS use, if you remember).

In Luke's narrative about John the Baptizer's birth, we see that he was quite precise in the information he gave us. We learn that it was during the time of Herod king of Judea, in the Galilean region, so we have the historical time and setting; we learn some things about John's parents: they are in their senior years and his mother was barren and his father (Zechariah) was a local priest; we are told that an angel appeared to Zechariah while he was performing his priestly duties and told him his prayers were going to be answered and his wife, Elizabeth, was going to conceive; Zechariah was not as faithful as he should have been and doubted what he was being told; regardless of his doubts, God was going to bless Zechariah and Elizabeth with a boy and they were to name him John; and that when John grew up he would have an important ministry bringing many of the people of Israel back to the Lord their God. "And he will go on before the Lord, in the spirit and power of Elijah, to turn the hearts of the fathers to their children and the disobedient to the wisdom of the righteous—to make ready a people prepared for the Lord" (NIV, Lk 1:17). Of course, if you do not believe in angels and do not believe that old people can conceive, then this story already sounds fantastic, but this would not seem out of place to a first-century Jew reading this passage. Luke says that Zechariah belonged to the priestly division of Abijah and his wife Elizabeth was a descendant of Aaron, but Aslan claims this lineage is also a fantasy. But there is no reason to believe that these two things— John's parents' lineage and John's birth—are fantastical. Luke provides us with a list of historical facts, and we either believe them or we don't, but to simply relegate them to the realm of "fantasy," as

Aslan does, is not being ingenuous. Are there any historical reasons to disbelieve that Zechariah was a priest and an angel visited him with good news? No, there is not. There might be theological or materialistic reasons to not believe an angel visited him, but we cannot justify calling this account fantastical. What about John's birth? Is that fantastical? Well, it is difficult for a woman in her old age to have a child, but it is not unheard of; it certainly is not fantastical for an elderly man to impregnate a woman. However, if one believes that God can intervene to have an older woman become pregnant, which we see he did do in Old Testament times, then that is not fantastical, either. Today, women past their forties can get pregnant using different medical procedures. Since God created the universe out of nothing, and since he made us and therefore knows what to do, he certainly could have made sure Elizabeth got pregnant through her husband. Aslan uses the typical injunction that most scholars simply reject Luke's narrative about John the Baptizer's birth. But who are these scholars that dismiss John's birth account? They are the members of the JS and liberal theologians/biblical scholars who dismiss most of what the Bible says anyway, and their conclusions are suspect. There is really nothing in John's birth account that justifies it being labeled a fantasy.

Aslan wants to know what exactly John's baptism meant; he wants to know why John was out there in the desert baptizing people. Aslan says we cannot use Mark's Gospel to give us any information because the phrase Mark uses to talk about John's baptism is too "Christian." Because Mark's phrase has a distinctly Christian character, Aslan implores us to doubt it as a historical, authentic, event. Here is what Mark 1:4 says: "John the Baptizer was in the desert telling people about a baptism of repentance for the forgiveness of sins" ("Scripture is taken from GOD'S WORD®. © 1995 God's Word to the Nations. Used by permission of Baker Publishing Group."). Just like the Fellows of the Jesus Seminar, Aslan contends that since this phrase—a baptism of repentance for the forgiveness of sins—is too Christian sounding, it must be rejected as inauthentic. The reasoning behind this rejection, though, is not very sound. Mark was a Christian and it would therefore come as no surprise that he would use a Christian phrase or idea or concept, but in doing so, Aslan and the JS say the passage is suspect. According to Aslan and the JS, it is a fabrication because it promotes a Christian viewpoint. Again, we see that the criteria the JS and Aslan apply to the

Gospels to determine their reliability and historicity is not what they use on their own arguments and/or conclusions. When Mark says that John was preaching a baptism of repentance for the forgiveness of sins, Aslan thinks that Mark is actually saying that John has the power to forgive other people's sin. This, of course, would be a peculiar statement to make for an early Christian. But Mark does not say that John had the power to forgive sins. Notice how Aslan slightly twists things around here. Mark's Gospel says John was preaching that people needed to repent so their sins would be forgiven, and then baptizes them when they did so. What we see happening at the Jordan River is that people were acknowledging and confessing their sin to God, and were then washed with water as a public display of their confession. This practice was done throughout Jewish history. Jews knew they needed to purify themselves with water to properly worship God. The animal sacrifices were set up for people to acknowledge their sins before God, confess them, and be temporarily cleansed by the sprinkled blood and a washing of their bodies and clothes by water. Mark was not just using a 'Christian' phrase; it had its roots in Jewish culture. What John was doing in the desert may have surprised some people because they may have wondered why they could not just do this in the Temple, but it would not have been a foreign idea to them. So, we see that Mark does not say John had the power to forgive sins, like Aslan wants you to think; Mark says John was preaching the forgiveness of sins. Only God has the power to forgive sins. Aslan is trying to make an issue where there is none.

Since Aslan says we cannot use Mark's Gospel to give us any information because the phrase Mark uses to talk about John's baptism is too 'Christian,' then what source are we to use? Aslan says the best source for John the Baptizer is Josephus. What does Josephus say? Josephus says that John the Baptizer commanded the Jews to exercise virtue, both as to righteousness towards one another and piety towards God, and so to come to baptism. Josephus then says that this baptism is "for that the washing [with water] would be acceptable to him, if they made use of it, not in order to the putting away [or the remission] of some sins [only], but for the purification of the body." (The translator of Josephus' *Antiquities* put the words in brackets. The translator believes the word "only" should be there, thinking that it more completes Josephus' thought. So the translator considers that Josephus believes that John the Baptizer baptized for both the remission of sins and for the purification of the body, whereas Aslan only believes that John baptized for the latter.) Aslan, of course, quotes from Josephus without the words in brackets; so that translation would read "not in order to the putting away of some sins, but for the purification of the body." If the translator I used for this quote from Josephus is correct and Josephus did see John's baptism as a twofold ritual—one for the remission of sins, and the second for the purification of the body—then, of course, Aslan is in error. Jewish history will also conclude that Aslan is wrong because the Jews, and that would include John the Baptizer, knew that remission of sins and purification of the body went hand-in-hand with their confession of sin to God. Therefore, as a Jew, John the Baptizer would be doing both. Since Josephus was a Jew, and Mark was a Jew, and John the Baptizer was a Jew, they would all know that remission of sins and purification of the body were typically done at the same time.

Therefore, since the Fellows of the Jesus Seminar, Aslan, and other liberal theologians/biblical scholars reject a passage as authentic simply because it sounds too 'Christian,' we see then that they are not actually rejecting the Bible on sound historical reasons, but rather on the basis of their own worldview or mindset. This allows us to question the legitimacy of that kind of scholarship. Rejecting a passage because it sounds too 'Christian' is not a solid reason for doing so; that is not how real historians decide what is reliable and what is not. After Aslan rejects a passage because it sounds too 'Christian,' he then erroneously assumes that John had the power to forgive sins. The Bible passage does not say that John had the power to forgive sins. John was preaching repentance, and repentance is "a change of mind relative to the previous life an individual lived" (Wuest); to repent is to change the way you think and act, to go from a sinful life to a life that God approves. When a person repents and turns to God that person's sin is forgiven. That is what Mark is stating here. Mark is looking back at John's baptism and saying that when these people came to be baptized, it showed that they were repenting of their sinful lives, and therefore their sins were being forgiven. But they were being forgiven by God, not by John the Baptizer. The next passage in Mark says that the people were confessing their sins as they were being baptized. The process of undergoing the baptism was an outward exclamation of the person's inward rejection of the sin in his/her life, from which they wanted to be washed clean. It was a physical expression of what was going on inside them, i.e., a rejection of a sinful life. These were not people coming out to join a revolution in order fight against Rome's oppression; these were people coming out to show remorse over a sinful life and visibly proclaim that they wanted to get right with God. The *New American Commentary* on Matthew states that these people were showing, by being baptized, that they were repenting and seeking God's forgiveness, and therefore John's baptism is thus distinguished from pagan ritual washings which do not symbolize a turning away from sin. Throughout the Hebrew Scriptures, God calls the Jews to repent and turn to him for forgiveness (see Numbers 14:19; 1 Kings 8:46-51; Nehemiah 9:17; Job 36:10; Psalm 32:5; Isaiah 30:15, 59:20; Ezekiel 14:6, 33:12; Daniel 9:9; and Micah 7:18), and that is what these people coming to John at the Jordan to be baptized were doing. During Paul's first traveling ministry, he spoke at a synagogue in Antioch, a city near Pisidia, and told the congregation, "God had the Savior, Jesus, come to Israel from David's descendants, as he had promised. Before Jesus began his ministry, John [the Baptizer] told everyone in Israel about the baptism of repentance" ("Scripture is taken from GOD'S WORD®. © 1995 God's Word to the Nations. Used by permission of Baker Publishing Group." Acts 13:23f). As people submitted to John's baptism of repentance, Mark reminds us that their sins were forgiven; not because John had the power to do so, but because God saw their repentance was sincere and forgave their sins.

Was Jesus Baptized for the Remission of Sins?

Aslan thinks we have only two choices to make regarding why Jesus came to be baptized by John the Baptizer. The first choice is that Jesus came to be baptized because he had sins from which he needed to be cleansed. The second choice (based on Josephus) is that Jesus was baptized in order to participate in John the Baptizer's initiation rite. Aslan thinks when Josephus says John's baptism was for the "purification of the body" that that meant those who were being baptized were going through a ceremony that then allowed them to join John's clan. Aslan believes Jesus was baptized so that he could join John the Baptizer's clan and be mentored by him. Jesus had simply traveled from Nazareth to the Jordan River so that he could become one of John's disciples. Jesus was just one more disillusioned man who was looking for something to believe in. Aslan actually believes that John's baptism, this initiation rite, allowed a person, like

Jesus, to participate in Israel's renewal. John's baptism, according to Aslan, was a rebel movement that was gathering followers to fight for Israel's independence. John was gathering a group of freedom fighters! Aslan must contend, of course, that John the Baptizer did not know Jesus beforehand. Aslan rejects the biblical passages concerning John's birth, which indicate that John and Jesus were cousins and knew each other. John was certainly baptizing before Jesus started his ministry, but not before John knew him, according to Luke. If Luke is right, and John and Jesus were cousins, it is certainly possible that they visited one another as they were growing up. John would know that his cousin Jesus had been strictly Torah-observant as he grew from child to manhood. That's why the Gospels tell us that John was surprised that Jesus was coming to be baptized. John knew that Jesus did not need to be baptized and repent and confess his sins so that they would be forgiven. In Matthew chapter three, we see Jesus arriving at the Jordan to be baptized, but John tried to stop him. John told Jesus that he (John) actually needed to be baptized by him (Jesus). John wanted to know why Jesus was coming to him. Jesus told him that it was necessary because it was the proper way to do all that God required of both of them. Then John gave in to him and baptized Jesus. Aslan says that if John's baptism was for the forgiveness of sins, as Mark claims, then Jesus' acceptance of it indicated a need to be cleansed of his sins by John. But that certainly is not the only reason why Jesus would be baptized; it merely happens to be the only reason Aslan will accept.

John did not know that his cousin Jesus was the one for whom he (John) was "preparing the way." That was revealed to him when Jesus was baptized. It was, therefore, necessary for Jesus to be baptized by John so that John would know who his savior was. Pharisees and others were sent to the Baptizer in order to question him. They wanted to know if he was the promised Messiah, the prophet Moses had talked about in Deuteronomy 18:15. John told them he was not. They wanted to know who he was and why he was out there baptizing people. John told them that he was the voice crying in the desert to make straight the way for the Lord (Jn 1:22f; Isa 40:3). He told them he only baptized people with water, but there was someone soon to arrive that he (John) was not even worthy enough to untie his sandal straps (Jn 1:26f). John knew he was going to baptize the Messiah because God had told him: "When you see the Spirit come down and stay on someone, you'll know that person is the one who baptizes with the

Holy Spirit" ("Scripture is taken from GOD'S WORD®. © 1995 God's Word to the Nations. Used by permission of Baker Publishing Group." Jn 1:33). John was sent to "prepare the way for the Lord," i.e., to be the Messiah's herald, announcing his arrival. But John did not know who that person was. John would know who the Messiah was when the Holy Spirit descended upon him while being baptized. John was surprised to see Jesus waiting to be baptized and told his cousin that he (Jesus) did not need to be. Jesus told John that it was necessary, and John would soon find out why. When John baptized Jesus he (John) saw the Spirit come down as a dove and rest upon Jesus (Jn 1:32). That confirmed to John that Jesus was the Messiah. Matthew tells us that after Jesus was baptized a voice from heaven said, "This is my Son, whom I love—my Son with whom I am pleased" ("Scripture is taken from GOD'S WORD®. © 1995 God's Word to the Nations. Used by permission of Baker Publishing Group." Mt 3:17).

This was an important event in Jesus' life. He came to be baptized in order to begin his ministry with the power of the Holy Spirit. The proclamation of the Father was to let John and the others know that this man, Jesus, was the Son of God, the Messiah. We have the Trinity involved in this important event because it was the beginning of the ministry that Jesus came to earth to fulfill. That ministry, as John the Baptizer proclaimed in John 1:29, was to be the Lamb of God who takes away the sin of the world. So Jesus' acceptance of baptism was not an indication of a need to be cleansed of his sins by John, as Aslan claims. Jesus' baptism was the commencement of his ministry; it was the visible announcement that he was the Messiah. But Jesus' baptism was also an indication of his desire to identify with the people he was going to minister to. Jesus came in human solidarity to identify himself with the sinners whom he had come to save, says Nolland in his commentary on Matthew. Another commentary says that in submitting to this baptism Matthew does not mean that Jesus was an evildoer who was now reforming his ways; Jesus undergoes John's baptism because he is faithful to Israel (*Reading Matthew*). Boice in his commentary on Matthew tells us that in "Jesus' baptism by John, Jesus identified himself with us in our humanity, thereby taking on himself the obligation to fulfill all righteousness so that he might be a perfect Savior and substitute for us." Jesus identifies with sinners by being baptized, and a believer becomes baptized to identify with Jesus' death and resurrection (Boice). Baptism is now an important act for the

Christian, showing that he/she has died to sin and become a new creation, a new person in Christ. The *Holman New Testament Commentary: Matthew* says that "the need for Jesus to be baptized, and thereby to serve as our representative and model, was not optional for him. It was important to the fulfillment of his mission on earth. It was an identifying step of obedience at the beginning of Jesus' public ministry." *A Handbook on the Gospel of Matthew* says that by this act of baptism, Jesus at once identifies himself with the whole people of God and at the same time does what God demands of him. In the baptism story we see that Jesus identifies with those he has come to save; we see the Holy Spirit descend upon him; and we see God the Father declare his satisfaction with his Son. Jesus has thus far lived a life as a human that is pleasing to God. He is the new Adam, the sinless Adam, who has always done his Father's will, and so at the beginning of his ministry, before he becomes the literal Lamb of God, he has been declared righteous and worthy for his mission.

But Aslan does not assume Jesus' baptism only showed he needed to repent from sin like everyone else, an assumption I believe is wrong, as I have shown above. Aslan also believes John's baptism was an initiation rite, as Josephus supposedly suggests, and that Jesus was being admitted into John's movement when he (Jesus) was baptized. By being baptized, Jesus became just another one of John's disciples. We have looked at what Josephus has said about John the Baptizer and there is no indication there that John was baptizing people as an initiation rite into his political party. Now Herod Antipas may have feared that John was establishing a group of rebels together, but Antipas thought that about lots of people. He was paranoid about rebel groups popping up everywhere, and certainly would not have liked the fact that a large crowd was interested in the Baptizer. That is why the Pharisees and others were sent out to the Jordan to find out about John. There was nothing seditious about what he was doing. Again, let me repeat what Josephus says of John: he was a good man, and commanded the Jews to exercise virtue, both as to righteousness towards one another, and piety towards God. Of course, Aslan thinks that any Jew in the first century A.D. who preached that people should have piety or faithfulness towards God is automatically a rebel, but there is no evidence for such a claim.

Aslan thinks that once John baptized Jesus, thus bringing Jesus into John's secret clan, that John just moved on to the next repentant and baptized him/her. Jesus was nothing, at that moment, to John the Baptizer. From Aslan's point of view, it seems that John the Baptizer was bringing in people left and right to join his clan. Aslan makes it seem that John's purpose for baptizing people was so that he could bring some of them into his rebel forces. John was getting so many disciples and followers that Jesus was just one more unknown person who was upset enough with the Roman infiltration of Israel that he was leaving everything behind in order to join up with John's clan. The question that comes to mind is why would John attempt to build up a rebel force against Antipas and the Roman army right out there in public? Why choose the Jordan River as a place to form his seditious plots? Most of the rebels and bandits during this era hid out in caves and gathered there for meetings—hence the term "den of robbers." The way John was creating his rebel forces is similar to someone going into a police station to announce that he is on his way to rob a bank.

Aslan thinks that up to this point in time, i.e., before Jesus' baptism, Jesus was just a poor peasant working hard up in Galilee with nothing to show for it. After being baptized by John, Jesus then becomes part of a movement, an important movement whose goal is to fight for Israel's freedom. Rejecting all the information from Mathew and Luke regarding the early years of Jesus, Aslan contends that the real Jesus, the historical Jesus, begins when he comes to the Jordan River to be baptized by John the Baptizer. Aslan says the real, historical, Jesus abandoned his hometown, abandoned his family, and abandoned his work obligations; he left Nazareth for some unknown reason when he was around thirty years old and wound up in Judea to be baptized by John. Of course, the Gospels do tell us why Jesus left Nazareth and headed to the Jordan River. It was to begin his ministry, gather his apostles, prepare them for their own ministries, and let them know that he was to die and rise again as the ultimate sacrifice for mankind's sins, which would fulfill the prophecies found in the Hebrew Scriptures. So the Gospels clearly state the reasons Jesus left Nazareth, and there is no indication that Jesus abandoned his family and left them destitute. Aslan is making that up.

Who Is Superior—Jesus or John?

Aslan accuses the Gospel writers of flipping the truth on its head. He claims that John the Baptizer was actually the one who was more important historically than Jesus. Aslan thinks the Gospel writers faced a dilemma when they started to write their Gospels; they realized that John the Baptizer was the teacher and Jesus the student, and so they had to flip the truth to have Jesus come out on top. John the Baptizer's fame was too well known, Aslan says, so the Gospel writers had to come up with something to include him. Aslan contends that the Gospel writers reversed the two men's roles. They made Jesus the one who was superior, the teacher; John became inferior, less important. If the story of John the Baptizer was well known, as Aslan claims, then any role reversal between John and Jesus would have been rejected by those who knew the "real" story. There is no convincing evidence that supports Aslan's theory that John the Baptizer was superior to Jesus, i.e., that John the Baptizer was Jesus' mentor/teacher. But that does not stop Aslan from claiming that the Gospel writers lied and practiced deception in making Jesus superior to John. So when John the Baptizer says, "[Jesus] must increase in importance, but I must decrease in importance," (Jn 3:30), Aslan insists the Gospel writer was lying. When John the Baptizer said he was unworthy to even loosen Jesus' sandals (Jn 1:27), the Gospel writer was lying. Why does Aslan think the Gospel writers were lying regarding the Baptizer's role in launching Jesus' ministry? Because Aslan's theory about the beginnings of Jesus' ministry contradicts what the Gospels say. What seems incongruous, however, is that Aslan is willing to say that John's baptism was too well-known to conceal because lots of people knew about it, but he is not willing to use that same argument when it comes to Jesus' resurrection. Lots of people saw Jesus after his death, so the fact of his resurrection was well-known and difficult to conceal, but Aslan and the JS do not believe in the resurrection of Jesus because it contradicts their worldview. Instead, Aslan is content to assume that it was necessary for the Gospel writers to rewrite history in order to make Jesus come out on top. Aslan accuses the Gospel writers of changing things around in order to make Jesus superior to John, but actually it is Aslan who is changing events in order to propagate his own viewpoint. Aslan is doing what he accuses the Gospel writers of doing, but it does not bother him when he does it. There is no evidence for Aslan to conclude that John was superior to Jesus or that John was Jesus' mentor and teacher. There is no reason to discount the narrative given by the four canonical Gospels regarding Jesus' baptism and the beginnings of his ministry.

Aslan says that Matthew's Gospel records the same basic baptism story as Mark's, but embellishes a little by saying that John the Baptizer realized that "after me comes one who is more powerful than I" (NIV, Mt 3:11). Of course, Aslan takes this moment to reiterate his claim that Matthew wrote his Gospel at least twenty years after Mark wrote his, but we have already addressed that issue, and there is no reason to believe that Matthew and Mark did not write contemporaneously. Aslan wants his reader to think that Matthew had plenty of time to make up lots of information that Mark did not include in his Gospel. There is, however, a big difference between adding information and making up information. Although modern biographers could write about the same person, one of them might add a lot more information about the person they are writing about than the other biographer, but that does not mean they are making it up. Added information does not, in and of itself, imply that that information is fictional. As we have seen, John, in his Gospel, also provided more information than Mark. John the Baptizer declares that: "I am not the Messiah but am sent ahead of him" (Jn 3:28), and then adds, "He must become greater; I must become less" (vs. 30). Aslan says that John the Gospel writer's attempt to make John the Baptizer insignificant only showed how frantic he was; it showed that early Christians felt the need to offset what the real historical evidence shows. What historical evidence is Aslan talking about? Some of it comes from Josephus (and does not appear to be accurately interpreted), but most comes from his own mindset (his own conjectures and theories). There is no historical evidence that clearly suggests Aslan's theories are correct and the Gospel writers are lying.

As we have seen then, Aslan takes the Gospel accounts regarding John the Baptizer and flips them, turning them on their heads. It is as if Aslan's thesis is: whatever the Gospels say, just think the opposite. If the Gospels say black, it is really white; if the Gospels say John the Baptizer was Jesus' herald, it is really Jesus who was the herald or student of John the Baptizer; if the Gospels say Jesus is the Son of God, it is really Jesus who is a zealot. The method of interpretation for Aslan then is to simply turn everything on its head. Aslan's attempt to view the Gospels in this manner denies the real historical evidence. If the Gospels are sound and reliable historical documents (and the evidence is very strong that they are), then Jesus did not begin his ministry as just another one of John's disciples. In fact, it was John who pointed Jesus out to several of his (John's) own disciples and they went and talked with Jesus and decided to become his followers (see Jn 1:35-42). They, and some others, decided to go with Jesus to Galilee when he returned there. Now there is a passage in John's Gospel (3:25f) that says John the Baptizer's disciples were having an argument with someone about purification ceremonies. So John's disciples asked John if he remembered the man that he spoke so favorably about when that man was with John near the Jordan River. They then informed John that that man was now baptizing people, and everyone was going to him. John tells us in his Gospel that Jesus and his disciples were in the Judean countryside, and Jesus' disciples were baptizing those who came to follow Jesus. It appears that John's disciples might have been a little concerned about Jesus horning in on what John was doing, and that is when John told his own disciples that he (John) must decrease while Jesus increases. Now some people, and it appears Aslan is one of them, take the passage where John's disciples say "when he was with you on the other side of the Jordan River" to mean that Jesus was one of John's disciples. This one passage, which can be interpreted several ways, does not necessarily mean, as Aslan would like, that Jesus was John's disciple. It is always important to bear in mind that you do not want to create a theory, or doctrinal belief, upon one passage. When you piece the Gospel stories together, it is obvious that Jesus spent time in that area after he was baptized. He could even have spent time with John the Baptizer, his cousin, but this does not mean that Jesus was John's disciple or that Jesus carried on John's ministry once John was thrown in prison (which Aslan and other liberal theologians/biblical scholars assume had happened).

The Temptation of Jesus

If you reject the Gospels as documents that recorded historical events, then you really have no other option except to recreate the stories of Jesus. These re-creations obviously follow the viewpoint of their authors. When you read books by any of the Fellows of the Jesus Seminar, or by Horsley, Ehrman, Pagels, Spong, (or any other liberal theologian/biblical scholar), and, of course, Aslan, you are reading re-creations. The Gospels are the original accounts of the historical Jesus. When these are rejected, the field is open to make Jesus whatever you want him to be. So, Aslan has chosen to view Jesus as a zealot, a typical "bandit" of the first century, who attempted to fight against the powers that be in order to gain Israel's independence. Jesus' first course was to become John the Baptizer's disciple. He would learn from John what was necessary to begin his campaign. Aslan believes that Jesus stayed in the wilderness amongst John's disciples and learned many spiritual truths from the Baptizer. Aslan rejects the Gospel narratives that record Jesus being tempted by the Deceiver (Satan). He thinks the Gospel writers simply made it up because they did not want to admit that Jesus was actually in the wilderness, learning how to be a zealot from inside John the Baptizer's clan. Since the Gospel writers turned Jesus from a zealot to a Messiah, according to Aslan, they created this story about Jesus being tempted. John the Gospel writer informs us that Jesus remained in Judea for some time after his baptism, and Aslan agrees with him about that. But Aslan claims that while Jesus was there he actually participated as a member of John the Baptizer's clan, being taught by him and then traveling in the vicinity preaching what he had learned, as well as helping John baptize the numerous people coming out for purification. All of this changed, however, says Aslan, when Antipas became frightened and concerned about John's power and popularity and had him arrested and thrown into a dungeon. That is when Jesus left Judea, hoping not to be captured as well, and returned to Galilee, where he would gather in his own followers as he preached about God's Kingdom and God's imminent judgment.

Aslan here is offering an alternative narrative, but it is built upon shifting sand; his re-creation does not have as much of a historical foundation as he would like. He accuses the Gospel writers of lying and rewriting history and embellishing stories and making Jesus look good while diminishing John's importance, but then he does not have any problems being creative in his own assumptions. Aslan dismisses the Gospel accounts of Jesus being tempted by the Deceiver (Satan) in the wilderness and claims what really happened was that Jesus simply joined John's clan. According to Aslan, the Gospel writers had to create a "temptation story" as an alternative to Jesus living in the desert, learning to become a zealot. The significance of this temptation story, however, is founded on Jewish history. There is a historical reason for Jesus to experience temptation. The Deceiver had prompted Adam and Eve to rebel against God and claim their own independence, thinking this to be the way to their own godhood. Adam and Eve's disobedience against God removed them from a wonderful relationship with their Creator, disrupting that relationship not only for all mankind but, in a relative way, for all of creation. Adam's sin resulted in the alienation humans have toward God, each other, the created world, and themselves. Only God could restore the relationship, and he did so by promising to Adam and Eve that there would come a time when the "seed of the woman" would rectify the problem and reconcile humankind back to God (see Gen 3:15). Throughout the Hebrew Scriptures, prophecies were made regarding this Messiah, this "seed of the woman." The Deceiver knew that when the Messiah came as the "seed of the woman," he (the Messiah) would "crush his head." Since Jesus came as that "seed of the woman," the Deceiver was going to do his best to make Jesus sin. He had prompted Adam and Eve to sin; he now had to get the Messiah to sin because that would indeed thwart God's plans. The Messiah, who had to be sinless, could not be the Messiah if he sinned. But it would not be fair to humankind if the Messiah did not experience a temptation to sin, or if he had no chance or opportunity to consciously sin and turn against God, or if he was sheltered from temptation. Just like our first parents had to be open to the possibility of sinning (otherwise we would have had no free will; we would have been more akin to automatons), so too the Messiah had to be tempted as we are (see Heb 2:14; 4:15). Therefore, right after Jesus' baptism, marking the beginning of his Messiah ministry, Jesus entered the desert, alone, and was tempted by the Deceiver. In the forty days Jesus spent there he refused to sin against God and emerged as the one worthy to be the Messiah. This, of course, did not stop the Deceiver from making other attempts to get Jesus to sin throughout the rest of his time on earth (see Lk 4:13; Mt 16:23). The Deceiver could not have the "seed of the woman" crush his head. The temptation scene as recorded in the synoptic Gospels, therefore, has a historic basis for its being there. Aslan has no historic basis for Jesus going out to the desert to join the Baptizer's clan. Jesus came to restore the severed relationship as no one else could; he was to live a sinless life and sacrifice himself to take on the sins of the world as the ultimate offering to God in order to appease God's justice. Jesus was to be the new Adam (see I Cor 15:45-49), the one who would restore the relational separation between God and humans, and bring peace back

85

to that relationship. Aslan dismisses the need for Jesus to be tempted because he, like other Muslims, believes that humans have no need of a savior. According to Aslan, (as we saw with the JS) every Gospel passage that makes Jesus out to be a Messiah, someone who had to die in our place for our sins, is inauthentic and, at worst, a lie.

Chapter Five: The Galilean Ministry of Jesus

Jesus returned to Galilee after John had been imprisoned (Mt 4:12). Aslan, in the eighth chapter of his *Zealot*, claims that Galilee had changed rather drastically since Jesus left there to become one of John the Baptizer's disciples. He says Galilee had morphed into an urbanized province and had become more Hellenized and immoral. The gap between rich and poor had widened drastically. Fact is, however, Antipas, like his father Herod the Great, had been urbanizing Galilee for almost three decades. It was already a Hellenized (Greek-influenced and Greek-speaking) area when Jesus grew up there, which is why it is highly expected that Jesus learned the Greek language as a young boy. Aslan says that Galilee was not the only thing that had changed; Jesus had changed so much that his family and friends hardly recognized him when he arrived on the scene, acting like a typical peripatetic preacher.

Seven "Facts" Exposed

Aslan uses the episode around Mark 3:21 to demonstrate seven "facts" about Jesus and his family. Mark 3:20-21 says: "Then Jesus entered a house, and again a crowd gathered, so that he and his disciples were not even able to eat. When his family heard about this, they went to take charge of him, for they said, "He is out of his mind"" (NIV). The seven "facts" Aslan claims this passage unearths are: One, Jesus' family was worried about him and was offended and appalled by what others were saying about him. Two, in desperation, Jesus' family attempted to come and take control of Jesus to bring him home so he could restart the family business. Three, Jesus refused to go home with his family. Four, Jesus did not respond to his family in such a way that would show there was any animosity or hostility toward them. Five, Jesus' family did not reject Jesus' pedagogical and spiritual message, nor did they reject his identifying himself as a messiah. Aslan believes Jesus' family had no problem seeing him as a messiah or having ambitions to be a messiah because this would only mean that Jesus wanted to become a zealot. Aslan thinks Jesus was confident that his family backed him up regarding his preaching and his desire to be a zealot. Six, Jesus' brothers played important roles in the movement that Jesus had established. Jesus' brother, James, had even become the leader of the Christian community in Jerusalem after Jesus was crucified. Seven, there is historical evidence to support the idea that all of Jesus' brothers had come to accept Jesus' mission. Let's look at Aslan's seven "facts."

Regarding Aslan's first "fact," we actually see from the passage that it was not Jesus' family that was hurt or felt scandalized by what the people were saying about Jesus; it was Jesus' own family that believed he was out of his mind. His family believed he had lost his senses. If anyone was being scandalized, it was Jesus by his own family. Aslan's second "fact" says that Jesus' family came to get him and take him home to get back to the family business. But Mark says Jesus' family came to the house to "take charge of him," to "seize him" (ESV), to take him "by force" (Wuest). The Greek word being used here means "to exercise power or force over someone or something—to have power over, to control" (*Greek-English Lexicon of the New Testament*). Aslan says Jesus' family came to take him home so he could get the family business back up again. The passage does not say that at all; it says Jesus' family came to overpower him because they thought he had lost his mind. Aslan makes it seem as though Jesus' family approached him and urged him to come home for the sake of the family business, but Jesus refused ("fact" three). The passage does not say that Jesus refused. Aslan is adding that. Since Jesus did not return home to the family business, Jesus must have refused, according to Aslan. But Jesus did not refuse a request that was never made; his family did not go to seize him in order for him to return to the family business. Aslan's fourth "fact" states that Jesus did not respond to his family in such a way that would show there was any animosity or hostility toward them. Mark continues with the story: "Jesus' mother and brothers arrived [at the house]. Standing outside, they sent someone in to call him. A crowd was sitting around him, and they told him, "Your mother and brothers are outside looking for you." "Who are my mother and my brothers?" he asked. Then he looked at those seated in a circle around him and said, "Here are my mother and my brothers! Whoever does God's will is my brother and sister and mother"" (NIV, 3:31-35). It is true, Jesus did not respond in hostility to his family, although there was hostility on the part of Jesus' family toward him, but we do see that Jesus told the crowd that his family is those who do God's will. His mother and brothers were coming to stop Jesus from doing God's will, and Jesus would not allow that to happen. Jesus' mother should have known that Jesus saw his life as one who would consistently do what God wanted. When Jesus was twelve years old he had told his mother and stepfather that he had to "be about my Father's business" (see Lk 2:49). Many liberal "scholars" attempt to use this episode in Luke 2:49 and John 2:4 to show that Jesus was disrespectful and unkind to his mother and therefore could not be the sinless man Christians claim that he is. They use John 2:4 to try to show that Jesus was not very nice to his mother by calling her 'Woman.' But the word for 'woman' was spoken as "an address expressive of kindness or respect" (Zodhiates). The same word was used at the cross when Jesus put his mother in the care of his disciple John (see Jn 19:26). One often finds statements in these so-called scholarly, liberal books about Jesus that show the authors either lack knowledge of the language, history, and context of the passage, or they are simply being disingenuous; either way they do this in order to put doubts in their readers' minds about the sinless character of Jesus. In his fifth "fact," Aslan declares that Jesus' family accepted Jesus' message and his desire to be a messiah (another word for zealot, according to Aslan). There is no indication, however, in the Gospels that Jesus' siblings accepted Jesus' ministry. Occasionally, his mother accompanied him, but his siblings did not "believe in him" (see Jn 7:5). Jesus' siblings were not even at his crucifixion, and so Jesus had to put his mother (who was there) into the care of his disciple, John (who was also there; see John 19:26f). In his sixth "fact," Aslan says that Jesus' brothers played important roles in the movement that Jesus had established, and that James (Jesus' brother) had even become the leader of the Christian community in Jerusalem, after Jesus was crucified. But Aslan is missing one critical, historical event. Jesus' family did not believe in him or his mission until after Jesus' resurrection. It was Jesus' resurrection that caused the change in Jesus' disciples and his family. Jesus' followers had scattered and were in hiding after Jesus was arrested. When Jesus appeared to his disciples after his resurrection, and after they were empowered by the Holy Spirit, they were then enabled to boldly preach the good news of Jesus' atoning death, beginning in Jerusalem and expanding across the globe. Jesus' brother James did become a leader in the Jerusalem Christian community, and it was probably this James that wrote the Epistle of James. It is also likely that Jesus' brother Jude wrote the New Testament epistle that bears his name. The transforming change that took place in Jesus' brothers—James and Jude—was the result of seeing the resurrected Jesus. There would be no reason for Jesus' family or disciples to carry on the "good news" that Jesus talked about during his ministry because there would be no good news after Jesus' crucifixion if Jesus had not been raised from the dead. The final, seventh, "fact" Aslan offers is that there is historical evidence to support the idea that all of Jesus' brothers had come to accept Jesus' mission. Aslan's "historical evidence" comes from Josephus' writings where it is mentioned how devoted James (Jesus' brother) was to the Christian community in Jerusalem. James' commitment, however, did not happen until he saw his brother, Jesus, risen from the dead. We see, then, in these seven "facts," Aslan's attempts to tweak (rewrite) the historical documents to say what he wished they would say. His endeavors (weak as they are) mirror the same attempts we find in the Fellows of the JS, Spong, Horsley, and others. They reinterpret the Scriptures to fit their mindset.

Luke's Three "Mistakes"

Aslan tells us that Luke made three blatant mistakes when he (Luke) records Jesus' return to his hometown of Nazareth. Luke's first "mistake" was that Jesus went to a synagogue. It appears that archaeologists have not found an "official" synagogue building in Nazareth, which, of course, does not mean it could not have been in a rabbi's house, or that it just has not yet been discovered. Since one has not been found, Aslan is content to say it did not exist. Luke's second "mistake" was to say that Jesus got up in the synagogue and read a passage from Isaiah. Aslan insists that Jesus was illiterate and could not read. We have already addressed this erroneous idea and found that it would be highly unlikely, due to Jewish culture and Jesus' occupation, that Jesus would be illiterate. Luke's third "mistake," according to Aslan, was that when he claimed the residents of Nazareth had become upset at Jesus' proclamation against them that they "drove him out of the town, and took him to the brow of the hill on which the town was built, in order to throw him off the cliff" (NIV, Lk 4:29). Aslan says this story is fabricated because there is no cliff in Nazareth from which Jesus could be tossed. Now, *The Pulpit Commentary: St. Luke (Vol. 1)* states that there actually is a cliff close to Nazareth that is about forty feet high. (I would think that would be high enough to cause death.) The *New International Greek Testament Commentary* on Luke says that the Greek word for "brow" is used without the article and therefore means a cliff near the village, of which there are in fact suitable cliffs in the neighborhood. M.R. Vincent, in his *Word Studies in the New Testament*, quotes from another scholar who says that most readers will take the words 'the brow of the hill on which the town was built' and imagine that the town was built on the summit of the hill. But this is not what is meant; the passage is saying that Nazareth is built "upon" that is "on the side of" the hill, and so the "brow" or cliff is over the town. This cliff, found in the southwest corner of the town, is made of limestone and is close to forty feet high. So this story, with Luke's so-called "mistakes," is not as suspect as Aslan would hope.

A Portrait of Jesus

Aslan has attempted to create a portrait of Jesus in Galilee, beginning with his establishing a headquarters in Capernaum, a fishing village on the northwest side of the Sea of Galilee. Capernaum, and the surrounding area, had greatly benefited from Antipas' urbanization, and the wealthy were gaining more power, prestige and riches. Aslan thinks Jesus focused his message on four major groups: Gentiles (which included Rome and its military forces), the Judean rulers, the priests of the Temple in Jerusalem, and those enjoying their new wealth. With his "home base" in Capernaum, Jesus began to carefully handpick his disciples as he visited neighboring synagogues, astonishing the crowds with charismatic authority. Jesus' message, according to Aslan, was simply an echo of his mentor/teacher, John the Baptizer. Jesus traveled the countryside warning people that God's kingdom was about to arrive; God was ready to judge the earth, especially the Temple priests who had been usurping their authority. Jesus' message, says Aslan, was to inform the priests that they were no longer God's representatives. Aslan complains that the Gospels tended to show that Jesus' main enemies were the Pharisees, but Aslan reminds us that there were times when Jesus was actually friendly towards the Pharisees. Where does Aslan get the information that Jesus was friendly to the Pharisees? He gets it from the Gospels, of course; they tell us that Jesus occasionally dined with the Pharisees, debated them, and accepted some as his followers. The Gospels actually showed both sides to the Pharisee/Jesus interchange: they show when Jesus was angry at their hypocrisy, and they show when he was friendly toward them. Aslan identifies two groups that he says

91

Jesus did not like: the Temple priests and the scribes (the legal or law scholars). Jesus' foremost antagonist, according to Aslan, wasn't the Roman emperor or his Judean officials; it was Caiaphas, the high priest. Aslan contends that Jesus was so vehemently opposed to Caiaphas that the high priest was eventually compelled to initiate a plot to kill Jesus. The reason Caiaphas wanted Jesus executed was because Jesus posed a threat against the Temple and his (Caiaphas') authority. Aslan provides the passages in Mark 14:1–2, Matthew 26:57–66, and John 11:49–50 as evidence of this. Aslan believes he can prove Jesus' anti-priest attitude through Jesus' own parables. For Aslan, the turning point in Jesus' ministry in Capernaum was when he was at the synagogue, preaching about the Kingdom of God, and healed a man with an impure or unclean spirit (see Mk 1:23). Once that happened, says Aslan, Jesus' fame spread all throughout Galilee. Aslan's portrait is complete. We now need to see how accurate it is.

We see from the Gospels that about a year had passed since Jesus left Nazareth and headed to Judea, where he was baptized by his cousin, John the Baptizer. After the trial by temptation, Jesus acquired several disciples (Andrew, Peter, Philip and Nathaniel); he attended the Passover festival in Jerusalem; performed some miracles, which prompted others to follow him; and spoke with Nicodemus, a Pharisee and member of the Sanhedrin, who came to him at night, probably to prevent being seen by his colleagues. Jesus and his disciples began baptizing not too far from where John the Baptizer was doing the same. Jesus returned to Galilee after John the Baptizer was put in prison and on his way stopped off at a Samaritan well and talked to a woman who then was instrumental in having Jesus stay in the nearby town for a couple of days to deliver his message to the rest of the residents. When Jesus did return to Galilee he went directly to Cana (where he had performed his first miracle—turning water into wine) and was greeted by some of the people who had seen the miraculous things he had done in Jerusalem during Passover. While in Cana a government official asked Jesus to heal his son who lived in Capernaum. Jesus healed the man's son even though he was about 18-20 miles away. (This would be one of three of his long-distance healings.) Jesus continued to stay in Cana for a while and taught at the local synagogues. Then he returned home to Nazareth. It was there that he spoke some rather harsh words to his fellow townspeople because they had rejected him as the Messiah. Jesus escaped from their murderous intent and made his home in Capernaum, where he, as a Torah-observant rabbi/teacher, taught in the synagogues there. He told the people that God's kingdom was near and so they needed to change the way they thought and acted (which is the correct translation of the word 'repent') and believe the good news he was telling them. So we see that a lot actually happened before Jesus settled in Capernaum. The people in that area already knew about Jesus as a healer and a teacher. It did not come as a big surprise when Jesus healed the man with the impure (unclean) spirit in the synagogue. Jesus had healed others before this. After healing the man in the synagogue, Jesus went to Simon Peter's house. Peter's mother-in-law was sick and Jesus healed her. News had spread about Jesus, so by evening time people were bringing their sick to him and he healed them there at Peter's house. Jesus then visited the nearby towns and told them about the Good News. He went to the synagogues in the neighboring towns and cast out demons and healed people of their diseases and pain. People from all over were coming to him for healing. Jesus then sat down with them and taught them how they were to live now that they had heard the Good News about the nearness of God's kingdom and the importance of repentance. The sermon Jesus taught them is referred to as the Sermon on the Mount (Mt 5-7).

Aslan says that when Jesus began preaching in Capernaum his message was a mere echo of the message of his teacher/mentor, John the Baptizer. Just because Jesus told others to repent, as did John the Baptizer, does not mean that the Baptizer was Jesus' mentor and teacher. Matthew says John's message was: "Turn to God and change the way you think and act [i.e., repent], because the kingdom of heaven is near" ("Scripture is taken from GOD'S WORD®. © 1995 God's Word to the Nations. Used by permission of Baker Publishing Group." 3:2). Mark says that when Jesus started preaching in Galilee his message was: "The time has come, and the kingdom of God is near. Change the way you think and act, and believe the Good News" ("Scripture is taken from GOD'S WORD®. © 1995 God's Word to the Nations. Used by permission of Baker Publishing Group." 1:15). Jesus' message was indeed similar to John's; they both were emphasizing the same thing: the need for people to repent and turn to God. The truth in both of their words was quite simple and both men (John and Jesus) were saying it as simply as possible, but that does not mean that Jesus sat at John's feet and learned from him and that when John was imprisoned went out and simply repeated the same simple message he had heard from John. This simple message was the same one God had been saying to humankind ever since our first parents (Adam and Eve) sinned. Aslan does acknowledge that the people were astonished with the charismatic authority with which Jesus spoke. The people apparently heard something different in Jesus' message because it appeared more authoritative than what they typically heard from the scribes who would often teach in the synagogues. Jesus identified with the crowds that came to hear him, but as we see in the Sermon on the Mount and some of his parables, he did not let them "off the hook." Jesus did not offer the poor a list of euphoric and/or sentimental promises that merely looked forward to some heavenly fulfillment. Jesus was offering them an abundant life which only he could offer; they had to accept him as God's true atoning sacrifice in order to receive it. Jesus offered this abundant life to everyone, not just the poor and marginalized.

In his portrait, Aslan says Jesus directly challenged four major groups—Gentiles (including the military), the rulers, the Temple priests (and their associates, like the Pharisees, law teachers and scribes), and the newly rich. Aslan claims that since Jesus had come from a poor background, he (Jesus) was able to identify with the Galilean sentiments that opposed the Judean rulers and priests. While traveling to neighboring villages near and around Capernaum, Aslan says Jesus would speak in the synagogues and his message would contain rhetoric that showed his opposition to these four groups. If Jesus were as opposed to all these groups as Aslan claims, then Jesus would never have been allowed to teach in the synagogues where he traveled; he probably would not have even been allowed inside one. He would have been seen and treated as a pariah. I find it interesting that one of the first people Jesus helped in Cana when he returned from Jerusalem was a government official. The official could have been a Roman, a Greek, or a Jew; it did not matter to Jesus. Jesus healed the official's son. If Jesus was opposed to all the people that Aslan says he (Jesus) was, then Jesus would not have healed this man's boy. Just because Jesus spoke out against the hypocrisy and legalism of the Temple collaborators did not mean that he hated them and hated the Temple. When a doctor tells you that you have cancer and wants to remove it, the doctor does not do it because he hates you; he is trying to save your life. Jesus spoke with and helped Roman soldiers, government officials, Pharisees, and scribes. He even invited a rich man to join him, but it was his love of money that kept him from doing so (see Mk 10:17-31).

We do see that Jesus did have some rough words to say about the religious leaders of his day, but no more than any of the other prophets throughout Israel's history. Throughout the Hebrew Scriptures, God was always trying to get his people to return to him after they had rejected him; and often those who were the first to fall away from him were the religious leaders—the priests and teachers. Jesus was not opposed to the Temple or the priests; but he was not afraid to aim some excellent parables at their arrogance, legalism, and hypocrisy. But Jesus was doing this out of love, hoping they would repent, i.e., turn from the way they thought and acted and return to God. They thought they were serving God, but Jesus let them know that they were not; they were actually more interested in serving their own ambitions. They were following rituals and rites and used them to elevate themselves above everyone else as moral standards, but Jesus pulled back the curtain, so to speak, and revealed their true nature. That is why the religious leaders hated Jesus; but he did not return that hate. Jesus offered them forgiveness and love. Jesus did not speak against certain people, as Aslan claims, but Jesus did speak against the underlying philosophy of those people. He struck at the heart of the matter; he did not just focus on the behavior, he focused on the intent and the evil thoughts that motivated that behavior. Jesus spoke the truth and the truth is sometimes difficult to hear. If the Galileans who listened to Jesus' message did have sentiments or opinions that prompted them to set themselves up against the Temple and the priests, then Jesus was also addressing their sinful attitude in the Sermon on the Mount. This sermon was directed at the common people that Aslan thinks Jesus joined in their contempt for anyone not like them. Jesus was not "anti-establishment," but he was opposed to how the establishment had devolved into mere formality and hypocrisy.

Aslan says Jesus made a strong effort to directly oppose the Temple priests and their religious functions by challenging their power and "right" to act as representatives of God here on earth. Aslan insists that everything and anything that was associated with the Temple was cursed by Jesus; that Jesus opposed and rejected the authority of anyone associated with the Temple, and he did not see these people as God's representatives. On the contrary, Jesus was not opposed to the Pharisees, scribes, teachers of the Law, or the priests as pertained to their office as God's representatives. He did tell them, however, that they were doing a terrible job of being God's representative, and he showed them how it was to be done by his own actions. In fact, Jesus was quite clear in his reminder to his followers that although the Pharisees, scribes and law teachers did not practice what they preached, it was still necessary to follow what they said (see Mt 23:3). We know that Jesus debated and dined with Pharisees on friendly terms, as Aslan also points out, but even when Jesus dined with a Pharisee named Simon he did not fail to point out a customary blunder on the part of his host (see Lk 7). As noted above, Jesus was motivated by love when he spoke against the lifestyle of the Pharisees, scribes and law teachers. He spoke as God had done through the prophets, warning them of the disaster that their attitude was going to bring them. Jesus revealed to them that they were full of greed and neglected justice and the love of God, that they were overly concerned about their status in society, that they loaded people down with unnecessary laws and rituals, and deprived the people of true spiritual knowledge (see Lk 11: 37-53). Jesus was not opposed to the Temple, or the Pharisee, the priests, or even Rome; he was opposed to sin, because sin kept people from a relationship with God. This sin affected both the obvious sinner (the object of the Pharisees' disdain) and the highly religious. This is why Jesus told the parable of the Two Lost Sons to the Pharisees (see Lk 15:11-32, and Timothy Keller's excellent book *The Prodigal God* which discusses this profound parable). For Jesus, sin was a mutation; when sin entered the world it affected all of creation. That is why Islam is mistaken to believe that Adam and Eve were simply forgiven and that there is no need of a savior. God has said otherwise. Jesus came to die for the sins of humankind. He is the Lamb of God who takes away the sins of the world. His resurrection was proof that he accomplished what he had come to do.

Aslan claims that Jesus' real antagonist, the person Jesus really disliked, was the high priest Caiaphas. Aslan thinks Jesus grew increasingly antagonistic toward the high priest, right up to the time of his death. Aslan provides three Gospel passages to prove his point. One passage, Mark 14:1–2, says that "the chief priests and the teachers of the law were scheming to arrest Jesus secretly and kill him" (NIV);

96

so this looks like the priests were actually antagonistic to Jesus. Another passage Aslan uses to "prove" that Jesus was antagonistic toward the high priest is Matthew 26:57–66, where Jesus has been arrested and is being questioned by a rather hostile Caiaphas, who demands that Jesus swear an oath and tell him if he is the Messiah, the Son of God. Jesus answers that he is and then quotes a passage from Daniel in the Hebrew Scriptures identifying himself as that promised Messiah. Caiaphas and the others accuse Jesus of blasphemy and then they spit in his face, strike him with their fists and slap him. Again, this shows hostility on the priest's part, not Jesus'. Aslan gives one more passage to try to show Jesus' antagonism toward the high priest; this one is from John 11:49–50. Here Caiaphas and others hold a meeting and discuss what they are going to do about Jesus. He is healing people of diseases and has just raised his friend Lazarus from the dead, and lots of people are following him. This makes Caiaphas and others frightened because they think the Romans just might come and "take away both our Temple and our nation," in other words, come by force to remove their way of life. Caiaphas makes a prediction that "it is better for you that one man die for the people than that the whole nation perish," and so "from that day on they plotted to take his [Jesus'] life" (NIV). Here again, it is Caiaphas that is hostile to Jesus. What we can conclude, therefore, is that the Gospel passages that Aslan tries to use to show how antagonistic Jesus was toward the high priest actually shows the high priest's hostility to Jesus. Here is another example of Aslan misusing the Gospels.

Not only does Aslan accuse Jesus of developing a deep antagonism toward the high priest and the Judean religious establishment, he also insists that Jesus' parables were often riddled with anticlerical opinions. But it is erroneous to think these parables and statements by Jesus reflected these negative emotions. Jesus was not against the priesthood; he was against the hypocrisy shown by the priests and the scribes. There is a big difference between the two. Jesus clearly spoke parables that angered the Pharisees, scribes and law teachers, but it angered them because he spoke the truth about them. They thought they deserved respect and honor wherever they went regardless of their behavior. Jesus, however, did not afford them what they thought was their expected place of honor; their sin and behavior were too serious. Jesus spoke the truth to them, and that is why they were upset. He did not hate them, but he surely did not condone their behavior. When in

Matthew 23 Jesus says to the scribes and Pharisees, "How horrible it will be for you, scribes and Pharisees! You hypocrites," he was warning them that their social/religious position and status was not going to save them. They needed to repent. Jesus was doing them a favor; he was trying to get them to change the way they thought and acted and to turn to God. He was speaking to them in a manner very similar to the way God spoke to Israel in the Hebrew Scriptures when God told Israel how far they had fallen from him and how they needed to return. Jesus was telling these religious leaders that religion—the following of rituals, traditions, and decrees—could not ultimately save them because salvation based on the Law required the complete fulfillment of the Law. The accumulation of good works would not save them. (Paul would reiterate this same truth in his epistles.)

Only Jesus had been able to fulfill the requirements of the Law (see Jn 8:46; Mt 5:17). Only Jesus was claimed worthy of being the unblemished sacrifice that satisfied God's judgment against sin, once and for all (Heb 7:27). Every religion, except Christianity, believes that one can enter heaven by doing good works. Jesus opposed this idea; we can never be good enough to enter God's presence. It is only by our faith in God's grace (loving kindness) through the death and resurrection of Jesus as the one who took our place, as the one who was sinless and holy enough to take our place, to appease the justice and holiness and righteousness of God. That is why Jesus was able to say: "I am the way and the truth and the life. No one comes to the Father except through me" (NIV, Jn 14:6). The Pharisees, scribes, and law teachers had become complacent and felt that they, as a result of their position, were approved by God; Jesus was telling them otherwise. And it was the kindest thing he could do for them. It is not an easy thing to hear; none of us like to be told where we are going wrong. The Pharisees, scribes, and law teachers did not like it either; and they planned a way to kill Jesus for having the audacity to tell them how far they had fallen from God's approval. We see then that Aslan's portrait of Jesus does not match the historical Jesus.

John the Baptizer Beheaded

While Jesus was traveling throughout Galilee, preaching and healing, John the Baptizer had been in prison. John sent two of his disciples to ask Jesus if he was the Messiah. It was not long after this that John was executed. We have seen how Aslan dismissed John the Baptizer's birth narrative in Luke, and so it is not surprising that Aslan would reject the Gospel accounts of his death. Aslan does so in his seventh chapter and criticizes the Gospels' depiction as implausible, filled with errors, and nothing more than a fabricated story. Aslan asserts that the only place to find an accurate account of John the Baptizer's execution is in Josephus' *Antiquities*. So what does Josephus say about John the Baptizer's execution? Before answering that, it is necessary to present some background information that Josephus gives us about Herod Antipas. Antipas was the son of Herod the Great and ruler of Galilee and the wilderness beyond the Jordan known as Perea. Allow me to paraphrase Josephus' account, which is found in his *Antiquities*, Book 18, Chapter 5. (I do warn you, it sounds like a modern-day soap opera.)

> Antipas visited his brother Philip on his way to Rome, where Antipas was going to do some business. While at his brother's house, he fell in love with Herodias, his brother's wife. He was so head-over-heels with her that he told her he wanted to marry her. Herodias agreed and was looking forward to moving into his palace, but there was one problem. Antipas was also married, and his wife was living with him at the palace; she was the daughter of Aretas, the king of Arabia Petrea. Herodias, of course, demanded that Antipas divorce his wife and force her to leave. He agreed to Herodias's demands. Antipas then continued on to Rome on business and then returned home, not realizing that his wife had already discovered the agreement he made with Herodias. She devised a plan to get back at Antipas and suggested to him that she should take a vacation. Antipas was glad to get rid of her. She went to Macherus, where her husband had a fortress, which also happened to be on the border of both her father's and her husband's territory. She told her dad about her husband's intentions. Her father, Aretas, became very upset with Antipas, and his anger led to war. Antipas lost the war; in fact his army was destroyed because of the treachery of some fugitives. Antipas, being a sore loser, wrote a letter to Tiberius [the emperor] and complained about Aretas. Tiberius becomes so angry at Aretas for destroying Antipas' army that he, in turn, sent a message to Vitellius, the governor of Syria, and ordered him to go to war against Aretas. Vitellius was told he could

either take Aretas alive and bring him to Tiberius in chains, or he could just kill him and send him his head.

I tell this story because Josephus says that a number of Jews thought that Antipas lost the war against Aretas as punishment from God because of what Antipas had done to John the Baptizer. Josephus says that Antipas slew John, "who was a good man." Now that we have some background information about Antipas from Josephus, let's see what he says about John the Baptizer's death. Paraphrasing again, Josephus says: Many people came out to John in the wilderness and were greatly moved by his words. Antipas feared what was happening because he thought John had a great influence over the people and they might convince him to raise a rebellion ("for they seemed ready to do anything he should advise"). Antipas thought it best to put John to death, thus preventing "any mischief he might cause." Antipas sent John off to prison on charges of sedition, to his castle in Macherus, and was "there put to death."

I will now provide a compilation of what the Gospels say about the execution of John the Baptizer:

John spoke out against the ruler Herod Antipas because he had married his own sister-in-law, Herodias. John also spoke out against Antipas for all the evil things he had done. So Antipas added one more evil to all the others; he locked John in prison. Antipas did this for Herodias, the wife of his brother Philip. John had been telling Antipas, "It's not right for you to be married to her." Although Antipas wanted to kill John, he was afraid of the people because they thought John was a prophet. When Antipas celebrated his birthday, Herodias' daughter danced for his guests. Antipas was so delighted with her that he swore he would give her anything she wanted. Urged by her mother, she said, "Give me the head of John the Baptizer on a platter." The king regretted his promise, but because of his oath and his guests being a witness to his promise, he ordered that her wish be granted. He had John's head cut off in prison. So the head was brought on a platter and given to the girl, who took it to her mother. John's disciples came for the body and buried it. Then they went to tell Jesus. (This compilation is taken from passages from God's Word Translation.)

100

Aslan says the Gospel story is too fantastical to be true; it is filled with errors and is historically inaccurate. Aslan believes that Josephus' version is correct because it says John the Baptizer was killed on charges of sedition. Sedition is an easy thing to charge someone with; sedition has been used throughout history to condemn many an innocent person, and it is still being used today. No doubt Antipas was concerned with John the Baptizer, preaching out there in the wilderness. The Gospel narrative does not necessarily disagree with the idea that Antipas would be fearful of someone like John the Baptizer. Antipas, like his father Herod the Great, did not trust very many people. Aslan rejects the Gospel narrative because he does not like the Gospels; his rejection is based on his mindset. He must say it is filled with errors and inaccuracies in order to cast doubts about it on the minds of his readers. But it is similar to charging people with sedition even if they are not seditious. Just saying the Gospels (or the New Testament) are unreliable and filled with inaccuracies does not make it so. There is nothing in the Gospel version of John the Baptizer's execution that shows that it is, or should be seen as, historically inaccurate. The Gospels version certainly sounds typical of Herod Antipas; no one during that time would have been surprised to hear that this had happened. Herodias had reason to hate John, and she found an opportunity to punish him for the things he had said. When Aslan says the Gospel account of John the Baptizer's execution is filled with inaccuracies and errors, it is because he is relying solely on Josephus' account. But it is actually Josephus who is rewriting history here, if it is being done at all. Josephus, who was writing near the end of the first century, did so as a non-Christian Jew who was trying to please the Emperor, and his Roman audience, at a time when Christians were being persecuted and seen as enemies of the state because they would not worship the Emperor as a god. Nero had started the atrocious persecution of Christians, during which time Peter and Paul were executed for their faith, and the persecutions got worse with succeeding emperors. Josephus was thankful to be alive and did not want to make the Roman authorities angry with him since they forgave his crimes against the state when he was an insurrectionist during the Jewish Revolt of 66 A.D. So Aslan is more willing to accept Josephus, who was writing his version of history to please his Roman leaders and protect himself, than he is to accept the Gospel narratives simply because they were written by Christians. But there really is no contradiction here between the Gospel narratives regarding

John the Baptizer's death and the information Josephus supplied. Just as Herod the Great was afraid a child in Bethlehem might be the new Jewish king and so had the male babes killed, so too his son Antipas was afraid that John and his followers were going to cause a riot. Both men (Herod and Antipas) were afraid of insurrectionists, were afraid of rioting, were afraid of the people they governed, and this fear prompted them to label many people seditious, whether they were or not. The Gospel narratives actually give us the reason for Josephus mentioning that Antipas considered John the Baptizer a threat. So, despite Aslan's supposition, the Gospel account of John the Baptizer's execution is not filled with errors and inaccuracies, as he claims.

Chapter Six: Jesus as Magician

Magician or Miracle Worker

We saw in the last chapter that Aslan's portrait of Jesus had many flaws. Aslan makes another attempt to show another side of Jesus in his ninth chapter, claiming that Jesus was a consummate magician who used his skills to not only exorcise demons and heal diseases but to, hopefully, convince like-minded zealots to join him. (This idea of Jesus as magician is, of course, not unique to Aslan; many liberal theologians/biblical scholars promote the idea, as well.) For Aslan, Jesus was certainly not of divine essence, nor was he able to actually heal people of their diseases through god-possessed powers. Jesus had simply learned magic, like so many other people during this time, and had developed a unique method that he could use to his advantage. Aslan informs us that there were many people who traveled throughout Galilee and Judea during the first half of the first century working as professional "miracle" workers—healers, exorcists, and interpreters of dreams—and Jesus was just one of them. These wonder workers had multiple skills that they could apply to any occasion. Being a miracle-worker was a career that was just as customary as being a carpenter or stonemason; it even paid better. Although these wonder workers could make lots of money at their trade, Aslan noted that Jesus provided his services for free, which separated him from the other traveling "miracle" workers. It is no wonder then that Jesus had so many people coming to him for healing, if he was not charging a fee for his services. If Jesus was as dirt poor as Aslan has claimed in his book, you would think Jesus would have put down his hammer and used his magical abilities to support himself. One would also think the other magicians would be quite upset with Jesus for taking over their territory and giving out free services. If Jesus offered his healing services without charge, then it is not unexpected that news about him spread quickly. Wherever Jesus went, the blind, the deaf, the mute, and the paralytic flocked to him. And, of course, Jesus healed each and every one of them. Aslan acknowledges the fact that nearly a third of Mark's Gospel shows Jesus performing healings and exorcisms.

Aslan has depicted the people of the first century as not being too concerned with historical facts; he claims historical facts were not important to ancient peoples, and that they did not bother to distinguish reality from myth. Aslan believes they viewed magic and miracles as just an ordinary feature of their lives. In fact, he uses the words 'magic' and 'miracles' interchangeably. If the practice of magic was so widespread, flourishing from one end of the Roman Empire to the other, which would mean that Jesus would really be nothing special, then why did Jesus get such recognition? Why were all the other magicians and zealots and bandits forgotten and Jesus somehow got to have four "biographies" written about him within fifty years after his death, not to mention a huge religion named after him? Aslan says exorcisms were rather commonplace in Jesus' time because Jews saw illness as a demonstration that either God was punishing them or they were possessed by demons. Aslan tries to back up this either/or statement by claiming that there are lots of exorcists that are mentioned in the Gospels. The passages that Aslan gives us are Matthew 12:27; Luke 11:19; Mark 9:38–40; and Acts 19:11–17. The Matthew and Luke references that Aslan provides were the same episode. The Pharisees had accused Jesus of utilizing satanic power to exorcise demons. In his defense, Jesus acknowledged that others also exorcised demons and wanted to know if they too used satanic powers. Jesus told the Pharisees that it would be illogical for Satan to cast out his own demons from those he controlled; it would destroy his (Satan's) kingdom if he did so. Mark's reference speaks of someone (who was not part of the Twelve) who used the "name of Jesus" to cast demons out of people. Jesus told his followers: "Whoever is not against us is for us." The Acts reference has to do with the seven sons of a high priest who tried to mimic Paul's exorcising power, as if it were a family business. (I will provide an additional comment on Aslan's either/or statement presently.) One must remember that just because the Gospels and Acts mention magicians and/or sorcerers does not mean they are being condoned; every mention of them is negative. The New Testament view of magic and sorcery is equivalent to the one found in the Hebrew Scriptures. If Jesus was a magician, the New Testament would not have been written. (But I am getting ahead of myself.)

Aslan claims that Jesus' opponents never denied the fact that Jesus did do miracles, but did question the source of Jesus' miracles. Aslan says the Jewish intellectuals during this time considered Jesus just another itinerant magician, but they certainly could not deny his skills. As we saw earlier, like most of the prophets in Israel, Jesus did not have the greatest relationship with the current religious leaders. There are good reasons for this animosity, as I already pointed out, but allow me to reiterate that in reading ancient Jewish history we find that religious leaders—priests, priest's assistants, religious advisors to the king or ruler, scribes, teachers of the Mosaic Law, and members of the Jewish court—were often the first to fall away from God. It was always (and still is) much easier to follow one's own inclinations rather than to follow the rules that bring about God's approval, and it was always easier to worship a wooden, stone, or metal god than it was to worship a God one could not see. By Jesus' time, the religious leaders had added so many stipulations to the Mosaic Law that it was impossible for anyone to adhere to them all. The religious leaders had become an elite group who acted very religious and pious on the outside, but in their own thoughts, minds and hearts there was no personal relationship with God. It was a dead religion; they were going through the motions, but did not really believe, and this was a constant problem that the prophets of the Hebrew Scriptures spoke about. This dead religion was the reason so many common people were coming to John's baptism, but not many of the religious leaders were. It was why the religious leaders were constantly hounding Jesus. He revealed to them the depth of their hypocrisy and was not afraid to address the misconceptions they had of God. Like I mentioned earlier, Jesus was not opposed to the Temple, the sacrifices, or the priests; he was opposed to the misconceptions the religious leaders had come to as part of their having fallen away from the important demands of God—mercy, justice, peace, and love. That is why Jesus' opponents turned out to be mostly those from certain Pharisaic groups, the scribes, and the teachers of the Law; these are the ones Aslan refers to as the Jewish intellectuals. The Pharisees were upset with Jesus not only for healing people on a day of worship but also for allowing his disciples to do things they thought violated the Sabbath. They had accused him of associating with sinners and tax collectors and other social misfits. Jesus had healed a man inside a synagogue on a day of worship and this appeared to be the final straw for the Pharisees; Matthew tells us they left and plotted to kill Jesus (12:14).

The Source of Jesus' Power

So, as Aslan says, Jesus' opponents could not question the fact that Jesus was able to do miracles, but they did question the source of his power in doing them. In his book *Every Miracle in the Bible*, Richards states that the reason Jewish leaders did not accuse Jesus of magic was because Jesus did not use typical incantations or materials associated with magic in the ancient world. Jesus clearly did not perform like other magicians. Aslan is incorrect to claim that Jewish intellectuals denounced Jesus as nothing more than just another itinerant magician. They actually accused him of something much worse. Richards goes on to say that the Jewish leaders refused to admit that Jesus was able to do miracles because of his special and unique relationship with God because this would force them to acknowledge his spiritual authority. So these leaders had to devise another tactic. What they did was to accuse Jesus of doing miracles through the use of satanic power. Jesus' opponents claimed that Jesus healed by the power of Beelzebul—Satan. Matthew records an episode where Jesus healed a man with multiple problems—he was blind, mute and possessed by a demon. The Pharisees were outraged when the crowd suggested that this miracle might be proof that Jesus was the Messiah (Mt 12:22f). The crowd asked: "Is this the Son of David?" In asking this question, they were outwardly wondering if Jesus, who had these powers, was the long-awaited Messiah. The Pharisees rejected that suggestion and instead proclaimed, "This man can force demons out of people only with the help of Beelzebul, the ruler of demons." Jesus refuted their accusation and told them, "If I force demons out with the help of God's Spirit, then the kingdom of God has come to you" (vss. 24, 28). On another occasion, Mark says some scribes who had come from Jerusalem said of Jesus, "Beelzebul is in him," and "He forces demons out of people with the help of the ruler of demons" ("Scripture is taken from GOD'S WORD®. © 1995 God's Word to the Nations. Used by permission of Baker Publishing Group." 3:22). Jesus warned them that their statement was actually cursing God the Spirit (the third person of the Trinity) and that such cursing was unforgiveable. The religious leaders rejected Jesus as the Messiah and claimed that he was using satanic powers to heal. They rejected Jesus' claim that he had a special relationship with God and accused him of being in collusion or partnership with Satan. How did Jesus respond to this rejection by the religious leaders? This would have been a good time for Jesus to tell the crowd that he was going to overthrow these religious leaders and free Israel from Rome's tyranny, and then offer a battle cry to see who was with him. If Jesus were a zealot, this, no doubt, is what he would have done. Things could have gotten ugly rather quickly. Jesus could have easily turned this crowd around to attack the religious leaders and thus begin the revolution. But Jesus immediately defused the situation by addressing the accusation given by the Pharisees and showing them, explaining to them, the gravity of their accusation so that they would rethink the conclusions they had formed. (Some information here was gleaned from M.S. Mills' book *The Life of Christ*.)

Who is this Beelzebul (Baal-Zebub) that the Pharisees and scribes said was the source of Jesus' power? We see in the Hebrew Scriptures that Baal-Zebub was the god of the Philistines (2 Ki 1:1–2). Baal was a prominent god in the nations surrounding Israel, and each nation attached different titles and activities to his name. Baal was often worshipped as a god of agriculture and weather, and his devotees performed sexual rites and human sacrifices in order to ensure good crops (*Baker Encyclopedia of the Bible*). Even though the Hebrew Scriptures do not identify Beelzebul (Baal-Zebub) with Satan, it is clear that Satan is the Deceiver who has turned everyone away from the true God in order to worship and follow false gods. The worship of false gods is the worship of Satan. This is what he accomplished with Adam and Eve when he promised that in following him they would become a god (see Gen 3:5). This is why Satan tried to tempt Jesus in this same manner, promising that if Jesus would worship him that he (Satan) would give Jesus worldly kingdoms (see Mt 4:8f). The Pharisees and scribes were accusing Jesus of healing by the power of Satan and not by the power of God. Jesus told them that he was working miracles by the power of the Holy Spirit and not doing magic, which is what Satan uses. Jesus then gave them a terrible warning: if they accused him of exorcising demons by the power of Satan, that is, by magic, and they continued to believe it, they would never be forgiven for their sins. He was warning them that by assigning to Satan what the Holy Spirit was in fact doing, then that mindset would keep them (and anyone else) from ever allowing the Holy Spirit to persuade them to accept God's salvation. Jesus' opponents were not accusing him of performing the typical magic done by other first-century magicians; they were accusing Jesus of performing his exorcisms and healings by the power of Satan. The religious leaders knew the healings were real; they just refused to accept that Jesus healed by

107

God's power. They accused Jesus of healing by the power of Satan. When Aslan, members of the JS, and other liberal theologians/biblical scholars flippantly call Jesus a magician, they are thereby claiming that Jesus makes use of satanic powers in order to influence his potential followers. Jesus told the Pharisees, "If I force demons out with the help of God's Spirit, then the kingdom of God has come to you" (see Mt 12:28). Accepting Jesus as a magician is rejecting the kingdom of God; it is rejecting God's salvation.

Refuting Three "Reasons" Why Jesus Might Be a Magician

Aslan provides three "reasons" why he believes Jesus was a magician. First, there were lots of other magicians in the first century who were making a good living with their art, and so Aslan concludes that Jesus was merely one of them. Second, the literary style that the Gospels used in describing Jesus' miracles was similar to Jewish and pagan writings regarding magic and magicians. The same vocabulary— words and phrases—was used to describe Jesus' miracles and the other magicians "miracles." Third, Jesus' miracles looked very similar to what other magicians were doing at the time. These three reasons, Aslan says, has prompted other biblical scholars to brand Jesus as a magician. Let's look at these three reasons.

Aslan's first reason states that since there were lots of magicians around in Jesus' time, then he must have been one too. Aslan uses this same logic to say that there were lots of bandits and zealots around during Jesus' time, so he was one too. John Dominic Crossan (co-founder of the Jesus Seminar) says there were lots of Cynics around during Jesus' time, so Jesus was a Cynic. (There may have been lots of people who owned horses too, so Jesus must have owned horses.) This kind of reasoning is clearly unsound. The mere fact that there were other magicians in Galilee certainly does not mean that Jesus had to be one of them. Claiming something and providing real proof for it is an entirely different thing. We can make all sorts of claims about Jesus, but if we accept the reliability of the Gospels, and there is no reason not to, we can rely on what Jesus says about himself. He did not own up to being a magician, nor did he concur with others that his power to exorcise and heal came from Satan. He claimed to be the Son of God and that his power to heal proved it; his miracles were manifestations that the Kingdom of God had arrived and that he was the king. And like any good king, he was going to die for his subjects, his kingdom. But unlike other kings, he was going to rise from the dead and rule his kingdom forever. So just because there were other magicians in Jesus' time does not mean Jesus had to be one of them.

Aslan's second reason for accepting Jesus as a magician is that the literary style of other "magical" stories during the time of Jesus is close to the miracle stories found in the Gospels. It makes sense that the literary style would be similar simply due to the common style one uses in writing such a story or narrative. I have read modern biographies where the publisher says in the jacket blurb that it was written so well that the biography reads like a novel, a piece of fiction. That is supposed to entice me to want to read the biography, which is supposed to be a true account of the person's life. The publisher is trying to compare the literary style with the ease of fictional reading while at the same time assuring me that the contents are about real events. Aslan's remark that the Gospel narratives about Jesus' healings are similar to other magical stories is not as odd as Aslan wants it to sound. How would one actually write it differently so as to make it more believable? The same basic vocabulary would have to be used to describe both the fictional miracle and the real miracle. The sentences would all contain a subject, verb, and object. What would the Gospel writers have to put in, or have to remove, in order to make Jesus' healings different from the fictional magic of other contemporary writers? All the magical stories of Jesus' day had a person who needed to be healed and a person who did the healing. The method of healing often included touching the part that needed to be healed, or by telling the person they had to do something like wash the area needing to be healed. So just because the style is similar between fictional magical stories and historical miracle stories does not mean the latter are therefore fictional. Writers of fiction and nonfiction often follow similar literary styles; they use the same words and provide their readers with picturesque writing. Similar literary style does not prove that Jesus was a magician. It does show, however, that Aslan accepts Jesus as a magician because of his worldview, not because there is strong conclusive evidence to suggest it.

The third reason Aslan accepts Jesus as a magician is that Jesus' miracles look very similar to what other magicians were doing at the time. What could Jesus have done differently to show his miracles were not just magic? Let's look at some of his miracles. A government official and a Roman centurion had a son and a servant, respectively, who were healed although they were nowhere near Jesus. These were two of the three long-distance miracles Jesus performed. Jesus was laughed at when he went to heal a young girl because he said she was only sleeping and they knew she was dead. (I am sure the people knew a dead body when they saw one.) He raised the girl from the dead, and he did that also for a woman's son who was in a casket during a funeral march. He did it for a friend of his—Lazarus—who had been dead for four days and everybody knew that when the tomb was opened there was going to be a big, awful smell. I doubt there were other magicians in Galilee and Judea that were raising the dead back to life or healing people from long distances. When Jesus healed people with skin problems he told them to see a priest so that they could be considered "clean" and reenter society. (Aslan says this was a big joke to Jesus, and I will address that later.) Most people that needed to be healed or exorcised came to Jesus; Jesus did not go out looking for miracles to perform, like some sideshow. I am sure the other magicians were busily looking for work since it was their livelihood. There are 35 miracles recorded in the Gospels, including the healing of Peter's mother-in-law from a fever, a woman with hemorrhagic bleeding, a man with dropsy, a man born blind, a paralytic, feeding thousands on very little food, turning water into wine, walking on water, and more. Jesus also refused to do miracles when the Pharisees or scribes demanded he show them some sign that he was who he said he was, i.e., the Messiah. Jesus could have presented some fabulous work of wonder to stun and amaze the crowd to shut the Pharisees up, but he simply said he would perform no miracle as a frivolous "proof." He told them, "The people of an evil and unfaithful era look for a miraculous sign. But the only sign they will get is the sign of the prophet Jonah. Just as Jonah was in the belly of a huge fish for three days and three nights, so the Son of Man will be in the heart of the earth for three days and three nights" ("Scripture is taken from GOD'S WORD®. © 1995 God's Word to the Nations. Used by permission of Baker Publishing Group." Mt 12:39–40). What miracle would he give the Pharisees? His resurrection!

Four Examples of How Jesus' Miracles Were Unique

Although Aslan gave three "reasons" why he believes the miracles of Jesus appeared similar to other magicians, he then offers four examples of how Jesus' miracles were different from other magicians. First, Aslan informs us that magicians, healers, miracle workers, and exorcists were fairly well-paid professionals, and then admits that what set Jesus apart from other exorcists and healers was that he provided his services free of charge. Jesus' compassion and love showed through when he was healing someone. He had legitimate concern for those he healed and for those who would benefit from the healing; for example, Jairus' daughter, the Roman centurion's servant, the government officials' son, and the woman whose son he raised from the dead. Second, Aslan says that exorcisms were commonplace in Jesus' time because the Jews saw illness as a demonstration that either God was punishing them or they were possessed by demons. The problem with this either/or statement is that they are not the only two options. Most Jews knew that most illnesses were simply the result of life. Jesus said of one man's blindness that it was not the result of his or his parents' sins (see Jn 9). James says in his epistle that there are sicknesses that have nothing to do with sin (see Jm 5:13-16). Jesus put sickness into perspective, showing it did not always mean one was being punished by God or possessed by a demon. The book about Job in the Hebrew Scriptures clearly shows that suffering is not based on Aslan's either/or statement. Third, Aslan admitted that Jesus' healings did not always employ a magician's methods. Aslan stated that the Gospel miracle stories are similar to other contemporary magic stories and then admits that the methods used by Jesus to heal people were not like other magician's methods. Fourth, instead of being similar to other magicians, Aslan also admits that Jesus' healings actually served a pedagogical purpose. Jesus' miracles were not done in order to benefit Jesus; his miracles expressed an explicit message to his contemporaries. Jesus' miracles demonstrated that God's kingdom had come to earth. It was God who healed the blind, the deaf, and the mute, and exorcised the demons. We see then that those who claim that Jesus was simply a magician find it difficult holding to that view. They have to hold to that view, however, because the alternative is to accept the fact that Jesus is the Son of God.

A Misuse of Scripture

Aslan believes the impetus for Jesus' desire to heal others came from a passage in Isaiah that says God's messiah would open the eyes of the blind, unstop the ears of the deaf, heal the lame so they leap like a deer, and unleash the tongue of the mute so they can shout for joy (35:5–6). According to Aslan, Jesus took this passage from Isaiah and applied it to himself. Jesus would fulfill Isaiah's prophecy by using his magical skills and convince others that he was the messiah by proclaiming that God's kingdom, God's judgment, and God's vengeance was about to begin. Jesus would exploit his magical skills, take what he learned from his mentor John the Baptizer, and his zeal for a restored Israel, and usher in the Kingdom of God all by himself. Aslan thinks that Jesus believed his miracles were evidence that God's kingdom had arrived on earth; it was God through him that was healing the blind, the deaf and the mute, and exorcizing demons. Jesus believed he was God's instrument. Jesus really had some mental issues, unless, of course, he truly was who he said he was—the Son of God. If he was not the Son of God, then there is absolutely no reason to even want to be concerned about the Jesus whom Aslan says he admires more than the Jesus we find in the Gospels. It is interesting to note that when John the Baptizer was in prison and was probably having doubts about his life, his mission, and who his cousin Jesus was, he had his disciples go ask Jesus if he was really the promised one. Jesus answered John's disciples, "Go back, and tell John what you hear and see: Blind people see again, lame people are walking, those with skin diseases are made clean, deaf people hear again, dead people are brought back to life, and poor people hear the Good News. Whoever doesn't lose his faith in me is indeed blessed" ("Scripture is taken from GOD'S WORD®. © 1995 God's Word to the Nations. Used by permission of Baker Publishing Group." Mt 11:4–6). Jesus was telling John's disciples that the miracles he (Jesus) was performing were authenticating what he had said about himself, that he was the Son of God, the savior of the world, the Messiah. Aslan misuses the passage in Isaiah by claiming that Jesus took this "promise" and simply applied it to himself so that he could use his magical skills to invoke people to join his clan to overthrow the powers that be and restore Israel's independence. It appears the real reason Aslan rejects the truly miraculous healings that Jesus did is because of his own mindset. Aslan, like the JS, denies the supernatural. The syllogism Aslan employs can be shown thusly—Premise: there are no supernatural

112

events; Premise: Jesus did miracles, which are supernatural events; Conclusion: Jesus did not do miracles; Conclusion: Jesus was a magician.

As noted above, the Gospels record 35 miracles that Jesus performed, which compute to one a month in Jesus' three-year ministry. Of course, John says there were lots of other things Jesus did that were not recorded (see Jn 20:30), but these 35 miracles were used to show that Jesus was the Son of God. Jews knew that God was able to act in his creation. His actions could be gradual in that the outcome took some time to occur, or his actions could produce immediate results. The Hebrew Scriptures are filled with miracles that occurred at God's prerogative. For example, the burning bush (Ex 3), ten plagues (Ex 7-12), water from a rock (Ex 17) a withered hand restored (1 Kings 13), a widow's son raised from the dead ((1 Kings 17), a widow's oil multiplied (2 Kings 4), the feeding of one hundred men (2 Kings 4), Naaman healed of leprosy (2 Kings 5), and more. Jesus claimed to be the Son of God, the second Person within Elohim, and performing the miracles ascribed to him would not be difficult because of who he is. If you deny the existence of God, or deny God (if he does exist) the ability to act in his creation, then all you have is a materialistic world wherein no miracle can occur. So, rejecting Jesus' miracles (or accepting them as real) is based on one's mindset.

Celsus and His Attack on Christianity

The claim that Jesus was a magician is an old one; it dates back to at least the second century. It does not appear that Jesus was called a magician by the religious leaders of his day, but they did accuse him of using Satan's power to heal others. After Jesus' resurrection and ascension, thousands of Jews were becoming followers of Jesus, and the message of God's salvation through Jesus' death and resurrection was also going out to the non-Jews—the Gentiles—throughout the Roman Empire. Nero, the Roman Emperor from 54 to 68 A.D., began persecuting the Christians near the end of his reign with a horrible and legendary zeal, a persecution that continued up to the fourth century. Thomas Taylor, in his *Arguments of Celsus*, said that Nero boasted that he had purged the country of Christians, whom he called robbers, accusing them of inculcating their new superstitions upon the world. Taylor further noted that other pagan historians and philosophers often made derogatory remarks against Christianity. For example, Suetonius, who was born around 70 A.D., called Christians "the men of the magical superstition;" Pliny and Tacitus called Christianity a wicked and unreasonable superstition; and Porphyry, from the third century, wrote a scathing book against Christianity, calling it a barbarous, new, and strange religion. (In modern times, we have Karl Marx, Friedrich Nietzsche, Christopher Hitchens and others saying the same thing.) Later, when the Talmud—a compilation of Jewish writings that included the Mishnah—was completed in 500 A.D., it acknowledged that Jesus worked miracles but accused him of practicing magic and leading Israel astray, and also referred to him as a false messiah who was justly condemned to death. But it was a pagan philosopher named Celsus who, in the second century, was the first to write a book—he called it The True Word—that attempted to produce a comprehensive philosophical attack on Christianity. Celsus' book has been lost, but we know of it through the writings of Origen, one of the early church fathers. In the middle of the third century, Origen wrote a point by point refutation of Celsus' anti-Christian claims in his book *Contra Celsum* (Against Celsus), which included fragments from Celsus' book. From Origen's book one can determine Celsus' major claims regarding Jesus: he was brought up as an illegitimate child by his mother; his father was a Roman soldier; he lived and worked in Egypt and became knowledgeable of certain magical powers; he returned to his own country and settled in Galilee where he used these powers to proclaim himself God. So the myth of Jesus as magician began near or at the beginning of the second century in an attempt to denigrate Christianity, and the same sentiment continues to this day by the likes of Morton Smith, John Dominic Crossan, and Reza Aslan. We have seen how modern liberal theologians/biblical scholars, the Fellows of the JS, and Aslan have created or adopted a theory or mindset and then used conjecture as "proof" to back it up. Celsus was one of the first to use this disingenuous approach; he reconstructed the Gospel narrative to fit his theory. It is clear that his negative attitude toward Christianity existed first, and then the rhetoric about magic was used to legitimize his view. Celsus created this new narrative about Jesus, saying he lived a long time in Egypt and learned magic there, in order to circulate his arguments against Christianity. Celsus did not question the truth of the miracle stories, but he questioned the source from which Jesus derived his magical power. Celsus believed that many magicians of his time were "wicked men possessed by an evil demon," and that Jesus was one such sorcerer. Morton Smith, author of *Jesus the Magician*, and Crossan have tried to convince modern readers that Jesus was nothing more than a magician. Crossan devotes a whole chapter called Magic and Meal in his book *The Historical Jesus* to the idea of Jesus as magician. The picture that Celsus and others paint of Jesus makes him into a foremost deceiver, a wicked person who manipulated people with magic, and got people to not only follow him but to patronize him. This is the "historical" Jesus that Aslan admires? If Jesus were a mere magician, then he is to be rejected as an evil person. There would be no reason to even claim him to be a good, moral teacher. (Some information on this section gleaned from Craig L. Blomberg's article in Douglas Groothuis' book *Christian Apologetics*; Choi's article *Christianity, Magic, and Difference*; Cabal's article in *The Apologetics Study Bible*; and Origen's *Contra Celsum*.)

Jesus and the Temple Priests

Aslan not only made the erroneous assertion that Jesus was opposed to the Temple and the priesthood, but he also believes that the Temple in Jerusalem had a specific purpose in its design or role, and that purpose was to keep out certain people. Entrance into the Temple had become progressively restrictive, Aslan says, and the priests had created a kind of monopoly over the people in order to strictly control who could come into the presence of God. This monopoly would make sure that all the undesirables of society did not have access into the Temple. The sick and lame, those with skin diseases (the leper), women who were menstruating or had just given birth—all of these were not allowed entrance into the Temple until they had become clean and been confirmed as clean by the priest. The distinction between "clean" and "unclean" was clearly set forth in Leviticus, where standards were established for approaching God's holy presence. The priests were given the task of declaring when a person was "clean" enough for Temple activity. Could the priests take advantage of their "power," misusing it for their own personal reasons? Of course, but that did not negate the practice itself. Aslan thinks Jesus was working in competition with the Temple priests. He says the people Jesus was healing were those whom the Temple and its priests had discarded as being beyond salvation. But the only ones who are beyond salvation are those who die still rejecting Jesus as their Savior; they are the ones who have sinned against the Holy Spirit (see Mt 12:31). It is true that

115

the Hebrew Scriptures laid down lots of restrictions on who could and could not enter the Temple, but this is because it was a holy place and was not to be contaminated by anything unholy or unclean. If a person had something that was considered unclean, then they had to wait for it to go away and, after being inspected by a priest to determine if it had, then they could reenter the Temple. God was clearly showing his people the difference between being holy and unholy, and that to come into his presence one needed to be holy. That was the purpose of the animal sacrifices—to temporarily make one clean before God so they could enter into his presence. If the animal sacrifices were temporary, then so was the priesthood system. When the Redeeming Messiah arrived and gave his life as an atonement for sin, the animal sacrifices and the priesthood would no longer be necessary. The animal sacrifices started with Adam and Eve as God's way of letting humans know that because of sin the shedding of blood and death was needed to "cover" it. The Temple and the priesthood would serve that purpose. When Jesus healed people of diseases that kept them from the Temple he told them to show themselves to the priest to be classified as clean. Aslan claims that Jesus' healing ministry rendered irrelevant the entire priestly establishment, but Aslan is mistaken; it was Jesus' death and resurrection that made the animal sacrifices no longer necessary. When Jesus offered himself as the Redeeming Messiah (the Suffering Messiah of Isaiah 53) on the cross there was no point in having priests anymore (see Hebrews in the New Testament for a thorough explanation of this).

But Aslan believes that Jesus, through his magic tricks, had found a way to outsmart and ridicule the Temple priests. Aslan contends that every time Jesus cleansed a leper (someone with a skin disease) or healed a paralytic or cast a demon out of someone, he was not just defying the priestly system, he was nullifying the very reason for the purpose of the priesthood's existence. What is Aslan's evidence that Jesus had this in mind when he healed people? Aslan says it can be found in Matthew's Gospel. A leper approached Jesus and asked to be healed. Jesus healed him and told him: "Don't tell anyone about this! Instead, show yourself to the priest. Then offer the sacrifice Moses commanded as proof to people that you are clean" ("Scripture is taken from GOD'S WORD®. © 1995 God's Word to the Nations. Used by permission of Baker Publishing Group." Mt 8:4).This does not appear to be evidence for Aslan's belief that Jesus hated the priesthood, but that is because you

116

do not have the insight Aslan thinks he has. Aslan says Jesus was joking; he was having a good laugh. Jesus did not really want the leper to show himself to the priest; he was merely taking a sarcastic swipe at the priestly system. The obvious question, of course, is: How in the world would Aslan know that Jesus was joking? Is Aslan privy to some inside scoop the rest of us are unaware of? Does Aslan possess a magical motive-reader so he can determine what Jesus' motive was in healing the leper? Or is this another example of Aslan creating a premise and then interpreting Jesus' actions by it? I think it is the latter.

There are two places in the Gospels where Jesus healed someone with skin diseases that required they show themselves to the priests so that they could not only be reinstated into society but enter the Temple to worship God. The first one is the passage from Matthew 8:1-4 that I just referred to above. After healing the leper, Jesus told him not to tell anyone, but to go straight to the priest, then offer the necessary sacrifice as proof that he had been healed. Does this sound like Jesus was joking? Does this sound like he was making a mockery of the Temple and the priest? Of course not. This passage clearly shows Jesus' compassion and willingness to heal a man who was a social pariah. Jesus wanted the man he healed to not stop along the way and tell anyone, not even his family, that he was now healed; Jesus did not want the man to celebrate his healing just yet. Jesus wanted him to go straight to the local priest and offer the proper sacrifice so that he could be reinstated back into society and Temple life. Jesus wanted the healed man to realize that he needed to restore his relationship with God—that is why he needed to go to the priest to be declared 'clean'—and then he could celebrate his healing with his family and friends. Deuteronomy 24:8 states that in cases of skin diseases like leprosy the afflicted person is to "be very careful to do exactly as the Levitical priests instruct you" (NIV). Jesus was following this command. The other instance is in Luke 17:11–19, where ten people with skin diseases asked Jesus to heal them. He told them to show themselves to the local priest and on the way to the priest they were healed. There is no indication here, either, that Jesus was joking or making a mockery of the priesthood or the Temple. Jesus was not rejecting the priestly system, nor was he nullifying the function of the priesthood, as Aslan believes. As a rabbi and a healer, Jesus was careful to adhere to the principles of the Torah in healing the lepers (see *They Loved the Torah*).

Did the Gospel Writers Ignore Jesus' Being a Magician?

Aslan thinks the early Christians were anxious to get rid of the Jesus-as-magician motif, and so they purposely rewrote history so that the Gospels would show Jesus as a miracle worker sent from God. Aslan believes the evidence for this is found in the Hebrew Scriptures where Moses and Aaron faced Pharaoh of Egypt. It was this story that prompted the Gospel writers to change Jesus' magical skills into miracles. The passage Aslan chooses is Exodus 7:1-13. God tells Moses: "When Pharaoh says to you, 'Give me a sign [miracle] to prove that God has sent you,' tell Aaron, 'Take your shepherd's staff and throw it down in front of Pharaoh,' and it will become a large snake" ("Scripture is taken from GOD'S WORD®. © 1995 God's Word to the Nations. Used by permission of Baker Publishing Group." Ex 7:9). Pharaoh's "wise men" do the same trick, but the Scriptures call them "magicians." Aslan believes there is a double-standard being used here. He thinks that a representative of God, like Moses or Elijah, are said to "perform a miracle" whenever they do something "wondrous;" but when Pharaoh's wise men or the priests of Baal do something "wondrous," then they are called false prophets who perform magic. Douglas K. Stuart provides an excellent explanation of this episode in *The New American Commentary* on Exodus, and I would like to share several of his ideas. We see from the text in Exodus 7 that Moses and Aaron were both receptive to allowing God to work through them so that what was done by them was genuine, i.e., it was God who turned a piece of wood into a snake. The text shows that it was not a magical trick performed by Aaron. The text shows that the Egyptians were magicians because they were merely imitating by magical deception what Aaron had done by divine power. It is clear when you read the text that Pharaoh is not eager to be persuaded to believe in a foreigner's God. So he calls in his "wise men" and sorcerers, and they are able to produce snakes from staffs too. The text shows that some time had elapsed before they arrived. This would give the Egyptian magicians time to devise a trick to mimic what Moses and Aaron had done. The text does not go into any details, but Stuart offers the idea that the Egyptians made use of some props that allowed them to perform a typical substitution trick. Pharaoh's magicians accomplished their imitation "by their secret arts," i.e., by the use of "trickery," or slight of hand. Pharaoh's magicians, by the use of trickery, were able to substitute the staffs they held in their hands with real snakes that they tossed to the ground. What happened next completely baffled Pharaoh and his magicians, but not enough for Pharaoh to have a change of heart. Aaron's snake swallowed theirs, a performance the Egyptian magicians could not duplicate. They were at that point trumped because a substitution trick is nothing compared to causing one snake to eat a group of other snakes. Clearly, the power of the God of Moses and Aaron was vastly superior to their ability. This pre-plague miracle performed by Aaron was a warning that God was giving to Pharaoh. Had Pharaoh heeded this warning, the ten plagues would not have happened. This miracle performed by Aaron would test the will of Pharaoh and also show Moses and Aaron what they were up against when Pharaoh rejected God's demands. Egypt's king was not going to be easy to impress, and Pharaoh believed by this simple performance that he now had an excuse for resisting God's demands. He could for the time being content himself with the comforting belief that what Aaron had done was just a magic trick, no different than the magic trick his own magicians had performed. The reality, of course, was that Pharaoh was wrong; Aaron did not perform a magic trick. The Pharaoh's stubbornness and disbelief would be his ruin. In the same manner, to conclude that Jesus is just a magician will result in the same spiritual peril.

Aslan is sure that this passage from Exodus provides the reason why early Christians, especially the Gospel writers, made sure that the idea that Jesus was a magician died on the vine. If Jesus were presented as a magician in the Gospels, then he would have been put on the same level as Pharaoh's false prophets or the priests of Baal. Aslan says that there are certain magical elements that can be found in some of Jesus' miracles, but the Gospels never charge Jesus with having performed any magic. For Aslan, this is proof that the Gospels writers were rewriting history so Jesus would not be seen as a magician, which would have been a rather negative characteristic in the new religion they were creating. The Gospel writers had to come up with some other reason for the priests and other religious leaders to not like Jesus. They had to come up with something that would appeal to their readers. Aslan thinks he has found what the Gospel writers came up with. Instead of admitting that Jesus was a magician, the Gospel

119

writers, according to Aslan, simply had Jesus charged with just about everything else but being a magician. The Gospel writers made sure the authorities—both Jewish and Roman—charged Jesus with sedition and blasphemy, with snubbing the Mosaic Law, refusing to pay taxes, and disrespecting the Temple, but not with being a magician. For Aslan, this appears suspect; he thinks the Gospel writers removed the idea of Jesus being a magician because it just would not look good to acknowledge that as being one of his skills. Of course, the Gospel writers could have easily avoided the whole magician dilemma by not mentioning any of the 35 miracles that Jesus performed. They could have just left them out. They included the miracles of Jesus because the miracles were a part of Jesus' life, and the Gospel writers were being accurate about the historical Jesus. And they included the miracles of Jesus because the miracles backed up what Jesus said about himself—that he was the Son of God, the Messiah. What were some of these magical elements Aslan claims Jesus' miracles contained? Jesus made clay and put it on a man's eyes and told him to wash it off, and when the man did he was able to see. Jesus touched a man with a skin disease, something people strictly avoided doing, when he healed him. Jesus put his fingers in a deaf man's ears when he healed him. We all know the importance of touch, how it represents kindness and acceptance. When Jesus made clay and put it on the man's eyes, it was reminiscent of the time when God formed the first humans from clay. Jesus just got through telling his disciples that he was the light of the world. Then here comes a man who sees only darkness. Jesus makes clay to put it on his eyes and has him wash them in a pool of water, the very source of water that was used for the Temple. The man obeyed Jesus and this was part of his healing process as well. This act of healing kindness was a miracle that showed the grace and power of God; it was not a magical act.

Aslan thinks there is no evidence to support Jesus' miracles as historical events. Aslan simply discards the four "biographies" written in the first century that records these miracles performed by Jesus, even though two of these "biographies" were written by eye-witnesses, his close disciples. There is no clear evidence that can claim these four "biographies" are not reliable documents. Scholars have attempted to judge or discern the authenticity of Jesus' healing miracles and/or exorcisms without success, says Aslan, and therefore none of Jesus' miracles found in the Gospels can be said to have actually happened.

Based on the conclusions of these scholars, Aslan declares that the miracle stories had to have been fabricated by the Gospel writers. Not one miracle, Aslan insists, has any historical validity. As you can see, Aslan just keeps repeating the same idea, but uses different words to say it. Basically, the argument is this: Aslan expresses his belief that the Gospels are not reliable documents; then he finds "scholars" who agree with him; and then he repeats the same thing in a different way. This is the typical method that liberal scholars and theologians use to discount what they personally do not believe in. They do not really offer sound evidence; they just keep repeating the same thing over and over until the reader believes it too. These scholars have not really proven that Jesus' miracles have not been validated; they simply say they have not been. Their worldview does not allow them to accept Jesus' miracles as real historical events. Aslan admits that about one third of Mark's Gospel records Jesus' miracles. Why would Mark spend so much of his Gospel on such fiction? Wouldn't just a couple of miracles have been enough for Mark? Since Mark wrote his Gospel at a time when Christians were being heavily persecuted (mid-60s A.D.), does it make sense that he would write so much about Jesus as a miracle worker when it would just be interpreted as Jesus being a magician? Wouldn't recording Jesus as a miracle worker actually hurt their cause? By using the three tests I have already mentioned that historians use to test the reliability of historical documents—bibliographical, internal and external evidence—one can conclude that the miracles associated with Jesus in the Gospels are authentic. There is no evidence that shows the Gospels embellished the miracle stories. Aslan is simply parroting statements by contemporary liberal theologians/biblical scholars that support his theories. These liberal theologians/biblical scholars consistently use the phrase "many scholars believe," but those scholars they refer to are from within their own circle. They rarely, if ever, provide solid evidence that what they say is true. They rely on each others' authority and offer no real evidence. It is indeed a weak attempt at disqualifying the Gospels.

Maybe you have noticed by now that Aslan's views on the Gospels, Jesus, early Christianity, etc., requires a lot more faith to believe than what one reads in the Gospels themselves. He acts like he is providing lots of evidence, but he is not; and he is also not really saying anything new. He is simply regurgitating the views of many modern liberal theologians/biblical scholars—like Crossan and Borg, Horsley and

Spong, Pagels and Ehrman, etc. And these people got their information from Bultmann and other so-called literary/form/critical analysts of the late 1800s/early 1900s, and they got it from many of the Enlightenment era writers like Voltaire, Diderot, Thomas Paine, etc. The arguments against Jesus and Christianity that Aslan is presenting in his book are not new; they are at least 300-400 years old (some much older) and most of those arguments have been refuted many times over. It is as if each generation of liberal theologians/biblical scholars has to reiterate old arguments to a new generation of young students because they really do not have anything else. And these new young students accept it from their professors because, well, everyone wants a good grade.

Aslan has no real evidence to prove that Jesus was a magician, but Aslan's worldview will not allow him to see Jesus as anything but a magician. Since his view of Jesus contradicts the one found in the Gospels, Aslan must, like all the others who reject the biblical view of Jesus, come up with some explanation for Jesus' ability to perform miracles. Aslan rejects the Gospel declaration that Jesus was able to perform miracles because he was God-in-the-flesh, so he must conclude that Jesus was merely a magician, someone who used slight of hand and trickery. When you reject the true, historical Jesus found in the Gospels, your options are mostly negative—zealot, magician, liar, lunatic, etc. Since Muhammad performed no miracles, Aslan certainly cannot have the Jewish preacher—Jesus—perform the 35 miracles attributed to him. After witnessing Jesus' resurrection and ascension, Peter, along with the other disciples, spoke to a crowd and said: Fellow Israelites. Jesus of Nazareth demonstrated publicly to have come from God by the deeds, miracles and signs that God performed through him, and you are all aware of this (Acts 2:22). Peter based his statement on historical evidence. Aslan rejects the historical evidence and relies on his worldview.

Apollonius vs. Jesus

Several liberal theologians/biblical scholars and even some so-called "new" atheists attempt to compare Apollonius' 'miracles' with Jesus'. Aslan does too, and he even goes so far as to claim that Apollonius of Tyana may have been the most renowned miracle worker of the first two centuries. Apollonius died circa 100 A.D., which makes him a contemporary with Jesus' later first-century followers, but not likely to have been a contemporary with Jesus. It is very unlikely that Jesus and Apollonius knew each other because Jesus was executed some seventy years before Apollonius died. Supposedly, everywhere Apollonius travelled he healed those who were lame, blind and paralyzed, and even raised a dead girl to life. (Sound familiar?) If we objectively examine the historical material, we actually discover that the parallels that some have attempted to make between Jesus and Apollonius are quite weak. There are five basic reasons for rejecting these parallels. The first reason is that Apollonius' biographer, Philostratus, did not write his biography on Apollonius until about one hundred and twenty-five years after Apollonius' death. As already noted, the synoptic Gospels were written within a generation after Jesus' resurrection and had been distributed throughout most if not all of the Roman Empire by the end of the first century, along with John's Gospel. This would be long before Philostratus wrote his biography on Apollonius. If Aslan rejects the Gospels because he thinks they were written forty years after Jesus died, which gave plenty of time for embellishments, then he needs to be consistent and reject Philostratus' 'biography' of Apollonius for the same reason. The second difference is that there are four Gospels of Jesus, plus external evidence like Josephus, Pliny, Tacitus and others. Up to the third century there was only one source regarding Apollonius, and that was Philostratus. (It is said that Apollonius wrote some treatises, but all are lost except for some fragments and possibly one surviving document, which may or may not be genuine.) The third dissimilarity is that the Gospels, regardless of what Aslan, the JS, and other liberal theologians claim, pass the standard tests that are used to assess historical reliability. We cannot say the same about the stories that Philostratus includes in his biography of Apollonius. The fourth non-parallel is that Philostratus was commissioned to write his biography by an empress who was a follower of Apollonius and wanted to dedicate a temple to him. Philostratus would have had a financial reason to embellish his stories to please his empress. The fifth distinction is that Christianity had been present in Cappadocia, where Philostratus was writing, for quite some time, and there is no reason not to think that Philostratus would have heard or known about the miracle stories of Jesus and would have been influenced by them. The miracles that Apollonius performed clearly mimic the ones Jesus performed in the Gospels. (Much of the information on the five non-parallels is from Strobel's interview with

Gregory Boyd in *The Case for Christ*.) In looking at the so-called parallels between Jesus and Apollonius it is clear that Apollonius' biographer intended to show him as a rival to Christ, "including such legendary features as the announcement of his birth by an angel, travels with his disciples during which he taught and healed, his betrayal at Rome by a disciple, his miraculous disappearance during his trial before Domitian, and his subsequent descent to the netherworld and reappearance to his disciples" (see Meyers' article in *The Eerdmans Bible Dictionary*). It is obvious that Philostratus simply took the miracles Jesus performed and transferred them to Apollonius. Try as Aslan might to show that Apollonius rivaled Jesus as a miracle worker, it only reveals the desperation Aslan must feel as we witness the extent that he and others who use Apollonius will go to in order to try to denigrate Jesus and his miracles. How are we to accept someone as a serious scholar who has no problem accepting the writings of Philostratus as valid, but adamantly rejects the four Gospels?

Chapter Seven: The Kingdom of God

Did Jesus Know What the Kingdom Was?

Aslan acknowledges that during Jesus' three-year ministry his (Jesus') most important theme and message was that "the Kingdom of heaven [God] is at hand" (Mt 4:17). Jesus offered the Kingdom of God to his followers and those who listened to his message. Aslan believes that just about everything Jesus said and did served to publicly proclaim the near arrival of the Kingdom, and in that he is not mistaken; the majority of commentaries would agree with him. It needs to be understood that while Matthew uses the phrase "kingdom of heaven," and Mark and Luke use "kingdom of God," both phrases are interchangeable. Matthew's Gospel was primarily addressed to a Jewish audience and so he avoids the direct use of the name of God by using the phrase "kingdom of heaven." Mark and Luke, writing mostly to Gentile readers, use the phrase "kingdom of God" which was probably more intelligible to them. Aslan says that the idea of the Kingdom of God is found in the simple prayer Jesus taught his disciples; the prayer known to us as the Lord's Prayer, wherein it says "your [God's] kingdom come." Without any evidence whatsoever, Aslan then suggests that John the Baptizer taught this prayer (the Lord's Prayer) to Jesus who, in turn, taught it to his disciples. How Aslan could decipher that is beyond me, but he often says things in his book that gives you the idea that he is privy to information the rest of us do not have. It is my assumption that the source of his information is his own mindset. There is no indication anywhere in the Gospels that John the Baptizer taught this prayer to Jesus. The thing that Aslan believes Jesus' disciples were to strive for above anything else was God's Kingdom. Aslan quotes from Matthew 6:33 where Jesus tells his disciples to 'seek first God's kingdom and his righteousness, and all these things will be given to you.' Aslan is correct about that—we are to seek first God's Kingdom, i.e., seek first what God wants before we seek (strive for) anything else. We have already acknowledged that part of Aslan's modus operandi is to state a truth from the Gospel, mix it with his own worldview, and then create a scenario that is mostly fictitious and then call it evidence. We will see him follow that technique throughout this chapter.

The Gospels record the many sermons and parables Jesus gave about the Kingdom of God. But Aslan does not think Jesus was real sure what the Kingdom of God was. Aslan says Jesus often spoke about it, but he did so in an abstract manner, as if he were slightly confused by the idea or concept. Aslan doubts that Jesus even had a cohesive notion or intellectual grasp of what it really meant. One thing Aslan firmly believes and that is that Jesus did not think the Kingdom of God was a spiritual kingdom that existed on some non-terrestrial level. Aslan insists that, for Jesus, the Kingdom of God was to be the restoration of Israel, and the sooner the better. Aslan says that those who claim that the Kingdom of God is an other-worldly kingdom do so because of a passage in John's Gospel where Jesus supposedly tells Pilate: "My kingdom does not belong to this world" (NCV, Jn 18:36). Aslan dismisses this passage by saying it is unreliable and that not many scholars accept it as authentic. (I hope by now that you realize Aslan uses this ploy a lot in exchange for actually giving real evidence). Aslan says that even if Jesus did tell Pilate that his kingdom did not "belong to this world," Jesus would have meant it was not a part of the Roman Empire, that Jesus' kingdom would not be like any other known political system. Again, Aslan wants us to rely on him to interpret (and reinterpret) the meaning of Gospel passages. We also see, yet again, that Aslan considers biblical passages unreliable unless he wants to use them to try to prove his point. And he, once more, dismisses a Gospel passage he does not agree with by saying very few scholars accept it.

In his Gospel, Matthew summarizes the Galilean ministry with these words: "Jesus went throughout Galilee, teaching in their synagogues, proclaiming the good news of the kingdom, and healing every disease and sickness among the people" (NIV, 4:23). The collection of parables in Matthew 13 illustrates the "mystery" of the Kingdom of God (we will look at these parables presently). The key to an understanding of the Kingdom of God lies in the Greek word for kingdom—*basileia*—meaning rule, reign, dominion. W.E. Vine helps us understand this word—*basileia*—when he says the Kingdom of God is the sphere [or realm or domain] of God's rule, the sphere or territory in which His rule is acknowledged. God calls upon people everywhere, regardless of race or nationality (or location), to submit voluntarily to His rule. Vine goes on to say that the phrase "kingdom of God" describes heaven as the place from which God's authority proceeds, while the earth is the place in which it is exercised. The kingdom of God is said to be a mystery (see Mk 4:11) but only because it does not come within the range of the natural powers of observation (see Lk 17:20); it is spiritually discerned (see Jn 3:3 and 1 Cor. 2:14). The fundamental principle of the Kingdom is shown in the words of Jesus who, while standing with a group of Pharisees, told them, "the Kingdom of God is in your midst" (Lk 17:21); in other words, where the King is, there is the Kingdom. ("In your midst" is a better translation than "within you." Jesus was not telling the Pharisees the Kingdom of God was within them in some New Age fashion. The Kingdom of God was right there in the Pharisee's midst, in the person of Jesus, but they were unwilling to see or accept it.) We see the connection between the Kingdom of God and the Tabernacle; Numbers 2:17 says that as the Israelites camped the Tabernacle (God's presence) was in their midst (the middle of camp) and when Jesus came to earth he said the Kingdom of God was in their midst (in the person of Jesus). Jesus told the religious leaders that he (Jesus) was the king inside the Kingdom of God. To show that he was the king of this kingdom, Jesus referred to it both as the Kingdom of the Father (Mt. 26:29) and as his (Jesus') Kingdom (Lk 22:30); they are the same kingdom of which he is the king. Although we are made in God's image, we are far from his kingdom; we are not naturally born into it. One enters the kingdom through a spiritual birthing. To enter the kingdom of God requires a new nature; one must be born from above, i.e., be spiritually born, as Jesus told Nicodemus, a Pharisee who came to talk to Jesus one evening (see Jn 3:1-15). The new nature, received in the new birth, grows by obeying the King. Jesus knew what the Kingdom of God was—he was its King. The kingdom, however, was spiritual, not physical.

Looking back again at Jesus' miracles, we are able to recognize them as proof of the coming of the kingdom. As we saw in the last chapter, Jesus used his miracles as proof to John's disciples that he was the Messiah. Jesus offered the kingdom of heaven as a salvific gift to those who acknowledge their own spiritual poverty, to those who are truly sorrowful about their sinful life, those who hunger and thirst for God's approval, those who show mercy and make peace, and those who are persecuted for doing what God approves of (see Mt. 5:3-10). Jesus reveals to us that the Kingdom of God is open to those who realize their need for God, but it is not a kingdom that we can enter on our own. Forgiveness is needed. Confession of sin is needed. The Jews knew that only God can forgive a person's sins. You can forgive someone who does something against you, but you do not forgive their sin; and you certainly do not forgive someone who does something against someone else. Only God can forgive on a general or across-the-board manner. That is why the Pharisees and other Jews were especially upset whenever Jesus openly forgave the sins of others. By doing so, Jesus was proclaiming that he too had the power to forgive sins. This ability to forgive sins meant that the Kingdom of God had arrived. A good example of this is found in the second chapter of Mark. Jesus was inside a house and some people brought their paralyzed friend to be healed, but the crowd was too thick and they could not get to Jesus. They carried him up to the roof and dug a hole and lowered their friend down to where Jesus was. It is easy to imagine that Jesus watched as the roof was being opened to let down the paralyzed man. He must have smiled at their ingenuity and faithfulness and at the care and concern they had for their friend. Jesus, in fact, called the paralyzed man 'my dear friend,' and then told him "your sins are forgiven." The scribes and Pharisees who were in the house did not like what Jesus said and they started thinking to themselves that Jesus was dishonoring God because only God could forgive sins. Jesus, knowing what they were thinking, asked them, "Why do you have these thoughts? Is it easier to say to this paralyzed man, 'Your sins are forgiven,' or to say, 'Get up, pick up your cot, and walk'? I want you to know that the Son of Man has authority on earth to forgive sins" ("Scripture is taken from GOD'S WORD®. © 1995 God's Word to the Nations. Used by permission of Baker Publishing Group."). Then Jesus told the paralyzed man to pick up his cot and go home, which he did (see Mk 2:1-12). Jesus asked the scribes and Pharisees which is easier, healing someone or forgiving them. He wanted the scribes and Pharisees to know that he had the authority—the ability and power—to forgive other people's sins, and then proved it by healing. Jesus was able (i.e., he had the authority) to forgive sins which, for the Jew, only God could do. Through his ability to heal and forgive sin, Jesus was showing that he was the king of the Kingdom of God, that he was, in fact, God the Son, the Messiah prophesied in the Hebrew Scriptures.

In the Gospels, we often see this authority that Jesus claimed to possess. We learn that unlike the scribes Jesus taught the crowds with authority (Mt 7:29). Jesus had given authority to his disciples to allow them to exorcise demons and heal (Mt 10:1). Jesus had authority over the Sabbath (Mt 12:8). After his resurrection, Jesus met with his eleven disciples before he ascended into heaven, where he had come from. He told them, "All authority in heaven and on earth has been given to me. So wherever you go, make disciples of all nations: Baptize them in the name of the Father, and of the Son, and of the Holy Spirit. Teach them to do everything I have commanded you. And remember that I am always with you until the end of time" ("Scripture is taken from GOD'S WORD®. © 1995 God's Word to the Nations. Used by permission of Baker Publishing Group." Mt 28:18–20). Where did Jesus get this authority that he claimed to possess? He was talking with some people who got upset because the things he told them made him equal to God (Jn 5:18). Jesus told them: "The Father is the source of life, and he has enabled the Son to be the source of life too. He has also given the Son authority to pass judgment because he is the Son of Man" ("Scripture is taken from GOD'S WORD®. © 1995 God's Word to the Nations. Used by permission of Baker Publishing Group." Jn 5:26f). In that same passage Jesus continued: "The tasks that the Father gave me to carry out, these tasks which I perform, testify on my behalf. They prove that the Father has sent me" ("Scripture is taken from GOD'S WORD®. © 1995 God's Word to the Nations. Used by permission of Baker Publishing Group." Jn 5:36). He concluded by saying: "I have come with the authority my Father has given me, but you don't accept me" (Jn 5:43). Regarding his death and resurrection, Jesus said, "I have the authority to give my life, and I have the authority to take my life back again" ("Scripture is taken from GOD'S WORD®. © 1995 God's Word to the Nations. Used by permission of Baker Publishing Group." Jn 10:18).

When Jesus told the crowds that the kingdom was at hand he meant that it was present in and through him; he was the king of that kingdom. Jesus spoke of himself as being the Messiah, the Son of Man, the Servant of the Lord, the Son of God, and the King of the Jews. Jesus is the Messiah in the here and now. He is presented as the One sent by the Father, the One who came to fulfill what the prophets foretold. Jesus came to fulfill the Mosaic Law and the Prophets (Mt. 5:17ff.), to seek and save the lost (Lk. 19:10), to serve others, and to give his life a ransom for many (Mk. 10:45). The secret of belonging to the kingdom lies in belonging to Jesus (Mt. 7:23; 25:41). Jesus, as the Messiah, is the center of all that is announced in the Gospels regarding the kingdom. The kingdom is concentrated in him, in its present and future aspects alike. (As I will show presently, Jesus as

Messiah also has a future aspect.) Jesus proclaimed the Kingdom of God as an event taking place in his own person and mission. Since Jesus persistently talked about the Kingdom of God, you would think he would know what he meant by the phrase. But, as noted above, Aslan thinks Jesus had spoken so abstractly of the kingdom that he questions whether Jesus really knew what it was.

Nine Parables about the Kingdom of God

One would wonder why Jesus made the kingdom of God his central theme, if he did not grasp its meaning. But Jesus, being the king of that kingdom, did have an excellent conception of it. In fact, he provided (among others) nine important parables to give us a clue into his thoughts about the kingdom of heaven. The parables were given soon after the crowd, wondering if Jesus was the Messiah, was told by the Pharisees and scribes that he (Jesus) was not. In order to reveal the nature of God's kingdom (what it is like), Jesus used common scenes or ideas from everyday life in these parables, thus helping to demystify it. Eight of the parables are found in Matthew 13, and the ninth one is from Mark 4:26–29. These parables were an effective tool that Jesus used to reveal truth about the kingdom, but Jesus spoke about the Kingdom of God more than in just these parables. (Regarding these nine parables, I found *The Nelson Study Bible* and Fruchtenbaum's *The Messianic Bible Study Collection* to be helpful resources.)

The first parable is a story about a farmer. This story will explain why Jesus had just been rejected by the religious leaders as the Messiah, and the result of that rejection. In this parable, Jesus told the crowd that the farmer scattered seed over the ground and in doing so some of it landed along the road and was quickly eaten by birds; other seed landed on rocky ground where there was no soil and it was easily scorched by the sun and died; other seed landed in thorn bushes and had no opportunity to be rooted and therefore died; and some seed was planted in good ground and was able to grow and be productive. In explaining the parable to his disciples, Jesus informed them that the seed along the road referred to those people who hear about the Kingdom of God but do not understand it and, instead of making an attempt to understand it, allow the true Deceiver—the real Beelzebul—to influence them and snatch away the chance to enter the kingdom, thereby rejecting the kingdom and the opportunity for salvation. These are the people whose response to the good news of salvation offered through Jesus is unbelief. Then there is the person who is excited to hear about the kingdom, but the excitement does not last very long. The person's joy quickly fades at the slightest trouble and leaves him faithless, which results in his making up various excuses for not accepting entrance into the kingdom. This person is philosophically and spiritually unbalanced, flapping like a flag in the wind, accepting and believing any new idea that comes along, but never coming to the truth. Then there is the person who hears about the kingdom but the worries of life and the deceitful pleasures of riches choke out the word so that it cannot produce anything. This person is so busy with the cares of the world that he or she fails to enter the kingdom at any opportunity. They want the worldly kingdom—the one the Deceiver has to offer—and so they reject the kingdom of heaven, Jesus' kingdom. Then there is the person who hears and understands the message about the kingdom and accepts it. This person will grow and flourish in the kingdom. In this parable, Jesus is the farmer, telling the good news of the kingdom of heaven, and showing the importance of receiving that good news. Hearing the good news requires a response to it. One either accepts or rejects the call to enter the kingdom. One is either offended by or has faith in the king of that kingdom, Jesus Christ. The religious leaders had rejected Jesus' message; they had become blinded to the spiritual nature of Christ's kingdom. Jesus' message as a seed was unable to grow within them. You, dear reader, if you have heard the gospel message, have heard the good news that Jesus voluntarily died in your place for your sins, must also take inventory of yourself and determine which seed in this parable represents you.

With this first parable Jesus hints at the fact that everyone—Jew and Gentile—can be accepted into this kingdom. The Kingdom of God exists on earth within a spiritual realm. The natural and the spiritual realms share the same space. The Kingdom of God is found where one is submitting to God's rule, where one has received God's approval through confession and forgiveness. Noah, Job, Abraham, the prophets God used to bring Israel to repentance, and John the Baptizer—these were all within the Kingdom of God, the spiritual domain where God rules. They were within the Kingdom of God regardless of wherever they were on earth. The Kingdom of God in this parable, and the others, is in the now—the present. But it is not a physical kingdom. It is a spiritual kingdom that Jesus' true followers—the seed planted in good ground—enter while living on earth. The Messianic Kingdom—the physical kingdom—that many of the Jews during Jesus' time were waiting, hoping and praying for would happen sometime in the future. The Kingdom of God that Jesus illustrates in this and the other parables is dwelling in the present here on earth, but in a spiritual realm. Within this Kingdom is the Church—the *ekklesia* or "called out ones." The Church—those who follow Jesus—is not the Kingdom of God, but exists within the Kingdom. The Church is called the "body of Christ" in both a spiritual and physical sense (see Eph 5:30; Ro 12:5; 1 Cor 12:27). The "called out ones" are also "sent out" into the world to be a witness of and for Jesus (see Mt 28:19f). When Jesus spoke about the future Messianic Kingdom (see Mt 24 & 25) he noted that it would begin when he returned to earth to set up his physical kingdom (see the book of Revelation). That return is known as the Second Coming. Between the First and Second Coming—the Church Age—the King is not on earth. In his absence is another "helper." Jesus told his disciples that the Father would give them another Helper, the Spirit of Truth (Jn 14:15–17). The Holy Spirit (the third person of the Triune God) will be our Helper until the King returns to establish his physical kingdom on earth. This eschatological promise of a future Messianic Kingdom is completely rejected by Aslan and the Jesus Seminar. Aslan refuses to accept the dual appearance of the Messiah. The Hebrew Scriptures have shown that the Messiah will appear twice. Once as the "seed of the woman" who would come as the sacrifice for the sins of the world. When that occurred the Church Age—the time of the Gentiles—came into existence. When that time period has been fulfilled the second appearance will take place at the moment the Messiah returns to establish his Messianic Kingdom.

In the following parables Jesus used the phrase "the kingdom of heaven is like." We must bear in mind that Jesus was not saying the kingdom was to be exactly identified with the subject of the story, for instance, the man, or woman, or wheat, or mustard seed, or leaven, etc. What Jesus was doing was revealing some truth about the kingdom in the story or parable that he was telling.

The second parable about the kingdom of God used another common idea—wheat and weeds. Here, Jesus said the kingdom of heaven was similar to someone who planted good seed in his field, but while asleep his enemy planted weeds there. They both grew and because the weeds were similar in appearance to the wheat it would be difficult to pull out the weeds without also pulling up the wheat. Come harvest time, it would be easier to separate the wheat from the weeds. The workers would gather up the weeds at harvest time and toss them in the fire. Here, Jesus was clearly showing how the kingdom of heaven occupied the same space as the natural world. The wheat—those who have accepted Jesus as the Messiah—and the weeds—those who have rejected Jesus—live and work and grow together in the same space— in the world and in the church—but come judgment day God will separate those who are believers from those who are not. These particular weeds resembled wheat in appearance; they had the same stalk and color but they did not produce any fruit, and they were poisonous. Once the wheat and weed matured, it was easy to tell them apart because the wheat stalk produced a head of grain and the weed did not. Jesus also explained this parable to his disciples (Mt. 13:36-43) telling them that he (Jesus) is the one who plants the wheat. The field is the world in which everyone lives. The good seeds are those who have entered the kingdom, but the weeds belong to the Deceiver, Satan. The harvest is the end of the world, and the workers are the angels who will, at that time, separate the wheat—the believer—from the weed—the nonbeliever. There are many who believe that their good behavior and their so-called righteous life will be enough to get into the kingdom. The Pharisees certainly thought that their righteous life was superior to the tax collectors and other sinners, but Jesus was telling them through this parable that they were poisonous weeds that only appear to be what God approved of.

The third parable likens the kingdom of heaven to a tiny mustard seed that when it grows becomes a big, beautiful tree. Jesus was not saying that the kingdom itself is tiny and progresses on and becomes bigger, but he did show that the kingdom grows in the sense of adding more and more people to it. Those entering the kingdom in the first century may not have been significant in the eyes of the world—fishermen, tax collectors, and other "sinners"—and may be small in number, but by their accepting Jesus and witnessing for him more people would be continuously added to it, as we see in the first few chapters of Luke's Acts.

The fourth parable likens the kingdom of heaven to yeast. A small amount of yeast is added to a larger amount of flour and is kneaded until it mixes with the whole lump of dough. Yeast in the Scriptures is usually a symbol of evil or wicked behavior that spoils whatever it gets mixed with, but here the Nelson Study Bible (NSB) sees yeast as being used as a positive illustration, representing an inward power that exists in the Kingdom of God; it is an internal dynamic, where the Holy Spirit is able to help believers discern the truth and reject the teachings of "false teachers" (as we will see, Paul warned his readers often of these false teachers). Fruchtenbaum sees this yeast as the false doctrine and false ideas that can and will creep in to the Church. This parable can easily show us the positive (the transforming of believers into the image of Jesus) and the negative (infiltration of false ideas and doctrines) effects of this 'yeast.' The NSB says the parable of the mustard seed addresses the extent of the kingdom's growth, while this parable concerns the power and process of its growth. Because sin has marred the image of God within humans, the Holy Spirit works with those who are in the kingdom of heaven to grow into the image of Jesus. The marred image of God in humans is replaced by the perfect, sinless image of Jesus.

The next three parables were told just to Jesus' disciples. He wanted them to get a firm handle on the meaning of these parables. The fifth parable says the kingdom of heaven is like a treasure buried in a field. When someone finds it, he or she will sell everything they have in order to purchase that field and gain the treasure. Jesus had just been rejected by the religious leaders; many of the Jews had also rejected Jesus for not using his power to bring in the mighty Davidic or Messianic Kingdom. Jesus told his disciples in this and the next parable that they must count the cost to follow him. They may lose everything, but gaining the treasure of the kingdom will be worth it. The NSB says that the central truth being taught here is the immense value of the kingdom, which far outweighs any sacrifice or inconvenience one might encounter on earth.

The sixth parable likens the kingdom to a merchant who is looking for fine pearls and finding a valuable one, he sells everything he has and buys it. The individual who found the buried treasure (in the fifth parable) may have done so by accident; he was not actually looking for it but when he found it he knew he would give up everything for it.

The merchant appears to have found his "treasure" by diligently searching for it. The kingdom accepts both individuals—those who find it although they were not particularly looking for it, and those who seek it out. In the treasure and pearl parables, Jesus is telling us that the kingdom of heaven will cost us everything; that we must be willing to give up everything to enter it. Earlier, Jesus had told his disciples that anyone who did not take up his/her cross and follow him did not deserve to be his disciple (Mt 10:38). These two parables explain how we are to take up that cross; that we are to give up everything in the sphere controlled by the Deceiver so we can enter the sphere of God's rule—the kingdom of heaven.

The seventh parable likens the kingdom to a fishing net that is thrown into the sea and gathers in all kinds of fish. The fishermen pull it to the shore, sit down and separate the good fish from the bad ones, tossing the bad ones away. This same thing will happen at the Day of Judgment when the angels separate the wicked from the righteous, i.e., those who have rejected Jesus from those who have accepted him. The wicked will not be allowed to be a part of the kingdom, even though for a time they may have pretended to be. This parable is similar to the one about the wheat and weeds growing together. The disciple of Jesus is not to be concerned with the "kind of fish" he or she catches. The disciple of Jesus is responsible for gathering in as many "fish" as possible. It will be up to the angels at the Day of Judgment to toss out the "bad fish." Just as within the twelve disciples there was a traitor, so Jesus warned his disciples that within the Church Age there would be those who were not true followers of Jesus, although they might pretend to be. One is also reminded in light of this parable the terrifying words Jesus spoke during the Sermon on the Mount: "Not everyone who says to me, 'Lord, Lord,' will enter the kingdom of heaven, but only the one who does the will of my Father who is in heaven" (NIV, Mt 7:21; see D. Bonhoeffer's excellent explanation of the "Lord, Lord" statement in *Cost of Discipleship*, Chapter 19). Jesus reiterated this again in Matthew 25:31–46 when he talked about separating the sheep and the goats.

Before giving the eighth parable, Jesus asked his disciples if they understood what he had been talking about, and they answered yes (Mt 13:51). Jesus then told them: "Every teacher of the law who has been taught about the kingdom of heaven is like the owner of a house. He brings out both new things and old things he has saved." (NCV, Mt 13:52). The NSB says that the statement regarding new and old things "refers to truths about the kingdom that were found in the Old Testament and those that were freshly revealed in these parables." The eighth parable is a call for action on the part of the disciples in view of what they have learned from Jesus. The disciples were to be responsible stewards and dispensers of these kingdom treasures. When Jesus ascended he told them "you will be my witnesses in Jerusalem, and in all Judea and Samaria, and to the ends of the earth" (NIV, Acts 1:8).

The ninth parable about the kingdom of heaven is found in Mark 4:26–29 and is also about a farmer. In this parable Jesus says that the kingdom of God is like a man who scatters seeds on the ground. As the days go on the seeds sprout and grow, although the man does not know how. The ground produces the grain by itself. First the green blade appears, and then the head comes into view, and then the head becomes full of grain. When the grain is ready, and it is harvest time, the farmer will cut it with a sickle. Jesus was describing the believer who tells others about the good news of the kingdom but does not know what the outcome is. The power of the gospel message—that Jesus died for our sins and rose on the third day—can result in someone being reborn, regenerated, brought into the kingdom of heaven, without the one who spoke the message knowing the outcome. When a disciple of Jesus tells others about what Jesus has done the Holy Spirit will work to have that 'seed' grow in the individual, resulting, hopefully, in that person accepting and not rejecting Jesus. Just as we may not know all the intricate ways a seed planted in the ground becomes a six-foot stalk of corn, so more and more people are being added to God's kingdom; it is growing in ways we do not always understand. This final parable shows God's kingdom in a succinct way, from the first sowing of the one seed to the final harvest that reaps a multitude.

These nine parables show that Jesus, despite Aslan's belief, did know what the kingdom of heaven is. Jesus knew that the kingdom is a spiritual realm that exists within the physical world, but is also much larger and greater than that physical world. It is a realm in which Jesus is the king. The message about the kingdom is that one can only enter it by accepting the King, Jesus. Those who enter this kingdom are those who hear and understand this message, and then accept it. When they do accept it they still participate in the physical world and live amongst those who may resemble them but are not at all like them. Those who accept the message of the kingdom will grow and resemble the king of that kingdom. When judgment day appears they will be easily identified as those who have entered the kingdom. So, Aslan is mistaken to think that Jesus was not quite sure what the kingdom of God was. Jesus knew quite well what it was, since he was its king. Aslan previously made the assertion that when Jesus talked about the Kingdom of God it was not about a spiritual kingdom that existed on some non-terrestrial level, but Aslan is only sure of that because his theory, his thesis, will not allow it; his theory states that Jesus was a zealot who was trying to bring a physical kingdom of God to Israel by overthrowing Roman rule. Aslan's thesis is wrong. Jesus tells us with these nine parables that the kingdom of God is indeed a spiritual realm that occupies the same space as the physical world. One enters the Kingdom of God by accepting the King, who is Jesus. This King has come, Jesus proclaims throughout his ministry, to die in our place to ransom the world back to himself.

The Messiah as "Seed of the Woman"

Because John the Baptizer was the Messiah's herald, he would be the first to come forward with the announcement that the kingdom of heaven is near (Mt. 3:2). Although Jesus proclaims this same message when he returns to Galilee (Mt. 4:17), it does not imply that Jesus learned this message from John and simply decided to continue saying it. Many Jews during the time period of Jesus were hoping and expecting God to intervene in liberating his people. The first-century Jews wanted a warrior, a zealot, someone who, like Elijah, would call down fire to consume Israel's enemies. But they had become spiritually blind to what their own Scriptures taught, an accusation often told them by Jesus. They were unaware of the meaning of the Messianic prophecies that had been given to them. They only wanted a Messiah that would destroy their enemies and not one who had to die to redeem them from their sins. Their expectation, however, clouded the correct interpretation of Messianic prophesy. So when John the Baptizer and then Jesus began proclaiming that the Kingdom of God was at hand, this proclamation inspired a sentiment in the Jewish people that Jesus had no intentions of fulfilling. Jesus knew what his mission was, what he came to do, and the peoples' expectations, as sincere and devout as they might have been, did not affect Jesus' mission. Jesus was focused on going to Jerusalem to suffer at the hands of the religious leaders and be killed, telling his disciples that he would rise again on the third day (Mt. 16:19). Jesus' miracles and his sermons (which included parables about the kingdom of heaven), were not the main focus of what Jesus was here to do. The healings and the sermons showed his personality; Jesus was a man of power, grace, wisdom and love. But he was also the Messiah prophesied in the Hebrew Scriptures, and his function as the Messiah was to be the "seed of the woman" promised to Adam and Eve (Gen. 3:15). That is why it is ludicrous for Aslan to think that John the Baptizer taught Jesus everything he knew, including the "Lord's Prayer." John the Baptizer was simply the herald of the Messiah; he warned those who were coming out to him to be baptized that the Messiah's "winnowing fork is in his hand, and he will clear his threshing floor, gathering his wheat into the barn and burning up the chaff with unquenchable fire" (NIV, Mt 3:12). John was proclaiming that the Messiah, rather than coming to destroy Israel's enemies, was going to winnow out those who believed in him and those who did not within Israel. The winnowing would begin with the Jew first, and those who rejected him would be the rejected chaff. The Jew and non-Jew would have this same fate, if they rejected him. The Jews knew the Messiah was supposed to arrive soon because of the prophecies in the book of Daniel. John was getting people ready to accept the Messiah when he did arrive. Rather than being Jesus' teacher and mentor, and rather than being the one who taught Jesus the "Lord's Prayer" (an assumption that has no evidence), John the Baptizer expected Jesus to be the one whose hand would be grasping the winnowing fork. The separating of the wheat and chaff, the sheep and the goats, the believer from the nonbeliever, would be a current as well as a future event. (Some information gleaned from Ridderbos's *Kingdom of God, Kingdom of Heaven*.)

The people of Israel were subjects of Rome, and they had been longing and waiting for someone to set them free. When Jesus came speaking about the nearness of the Kingdom of God those who heard hoped and imagined that Jesus was speaking of an earthly kingdom foretold by the prophets. Even after his resurrection, Jesus' disciples asked if he was about to "restore the kingdom to Israel" (Acts 1:6). This

138

restoration had been part of the vision of many of Israel's prophets. The disciples may have been hoping that since Jesus had the power to raise himself from the dead, surely he could now vanquish the Roman army and restore Israel's independence. Jesus let them know that there would come a time when the Kingdom of God would take place on earth as a real physical kingdom. Before that time, however, the Kingdom of God would be manifested in a spiritual manner, during the time period known as the Church Age. Rather than being concerned about the promised earthly kingdom (which was to come later), Jesus told his disciples to wait in Jerusalem for the coming of the Holy Spirit, then they would be enabled to tell others what Jesus had done for humankind (see Acts 1:6-8). Jesus told his disciples that the physical kingdom they had been hoping for was in the future; the present kingdom was a spiritual kingdom, one that would bring a new and unexpected form of God's kingdom here on earth. (Some information gleaned from *Every Teaching of Jesus in the Bible*.)

Aslan believes that since the first-century Jew was expecting a physical Kingdom of God to arrive soon (that would restore Israel as an independent nation), the fact that it had not was due to Jesus' failure to accomplish it. But was their expectation realistic? Did it conform to their Hebrew Scriptures? Messianic prophecy begins as early as the third chapter of Genesis, the very chapter that records the Fall—the moment humans rejected the God who made them in order to become their own god, and in so doing not only created an abyss that separated humans from God but separated them from creation, each other, and themselves. It should come as no surprise that God would provide the first messianic prophecy here and begin the process of healing that aberration. Adam and Eve realized their mistake and obviously wanted it corrected. But it would not be as easy as simply forgiving the wrong. This was a wrong that in a relative sense disrupted all of creation, not just the relationship between humans and God. This great crime demanded a great penalty. Humans could not correct this aberration; only God could. God promised the guilty party that "the seed of the woman" would rectify the problem (Gen 3:15). The "seed of the woman" would be the Redeeming Messiah. After the promise of the "seed of the woman," God provided a temporary solution, a symbolic remedy of what the Messiah would have to do. Adam and Eve had made a pitiful attempt to cover the guilt of their sin with fig leaves, what they had hoped would be a quick and easy fix. God showed them

139

that the shedding of blood and a death was required when he provided them with an animal skin for a covering. The animal skin had a two-fold purpose, albeit a temporary one—it covered the guilt of sin and it showed blood had to be spilt for the forgiveness of sin.

The Messiah, as the "seed of the woman," would shed his blood for the sins of humankind. God told Adam and Eve that the Deceiver whom they had listened to and followed would "bruise the heel" of the Messiah. The price for their rebellion would be the death of the Messiah. They were also given the promise that the Messiah would "crush the head" of the Deceiver, that is, Satan (Gen 3:15), ending sin's destructive power (see Rev. 12:9; 20:2). The error of the first-century Jew was that they saw this promise fulfilled in one event; but it would happen in two. (Many have fallen victim to this error as well, including Aslan.) The bruising of the "seed of the woman" happened when Jesus was executed for the sins of the world. The crushing of the Deceiver's head began at the crucifixion and will have its culmination when that same Messiah—Jesus—returns to establish his physical Messianic Kingdom. (See Hebrews 2:14–18; Rom 16:20; and Rev 20:10.) Because death—both spiritual and physical—occurred for Adam and Eve when they sinned, the penalty to rectify the problem would require a death. It could not be Adam or Eve's; it had to be one without sin. Only God qualified for that. Justice and mercy are shown here in equal measure. The standard was a life for a life; that is what justice demanded. Mercy allowed someone else to pay the penalty; that someone else would be the "seed of the woman." God said it would be the "seed of the woman," not the 'seed of man,' hinting at the virgin birth; but more than that, it also emphasized the humanity of the Messiah. The Messiah, the Redeemer, would not only be a man but would also be God; he would be the God-Man, the only one perfect enough to satisfy the demands of justice. Until the Messiah arrived, animal sacrifice would be the norm for receiving forgiveness from God, but it could only provide a temporary remedy. Islam is incorrect in its belief that God simply forgave Adam and Eve and, therefore, there is no need for a savior. Sin is not that trivial. God would not have needed to promise to remedy their sin by supplying the "seed of the woman" if there was no need of a savior. From God's first promise to humans, it was made known that the "seed of the woman" would suffer and die.

The Hebrew Scriptures are quite clear as to what the Messiah was required to do. This is strikingly expressed in a very tangible and physical way when God told Abraham to sacrifice his "only son," Isaac, as an example of what God the Father would have God the Son do for the sins of the world. When God called Abraham out of the city of Ur he established a list of covenants or promises with Abraham that would lay the groundwork for the Messiah's arrival. After promising Abraham that through his child (his son Isaac) the promised Messiah would be born, Abraham was told to sacrifice that very child (Gen 22). Isaac was called Abraham's "only son" even though we know Abraham fathered Ishmael before Isaac. Jesus was called the "one and only" Son of God. Abraham was asked to sacrifice his son; the very son God promised would be the one to begin a new nation for Abraham. Abraham believed that if he had to kill his son, God would raise him from the dead in order to keep his promise. God was not only testing Abraham's loyalty to him, God was indicating the kind of sacrifice he too was going to make in order to reconcile humans back to himself. Abraham was to be the father of a new nation through a son he was willing to kill as a sacrifice, just as God was going to sacrifice his only Son to create a new nation of believers. Those believers would be both Jews and Gentiles, and they would be allowed access into God's kingdom. God, of course, did not allow Abraham to sacrifice his son; the living metaphor could only go so far. Abraham showed what he was willing to do to please God; and God would show what he was willing to do to bring humans back to himself. He did not allow Abraham to go through with the sacrifice; but he did allow Jesus to go through with it. He had to in order to bring the world back into a state of reconciliation. So God stopped Abraham's sacrificing of his son and promised him in verse 18 that through his "seed" all the nations of the earth would be blessed. Abraham was given the same promise that Eve was given—the 'seed' was going to redeem (and bless) all the peoples on earth. This 'seed' is the Messiah. (You can see Paul's interpretation of the concept of the "seed" in Gal 3:16.) God was confirming his promise again—this time to Abraham—to bring a redeemer to earth to cover everyone's sins. When God gave the promise to Eve animal sacrifices were to be used as a temporary atonement until the Messiah came. When he gave the promise to Abraham God was going to create a human lineage—the Jewish people—through which to bring the Messiah into the world and for the world. We see with the promises made to Adam and Eve, and then to

Abraham, how God was working his plan through history. (This is why historical events are important to both Judaism and Christianity.)

When the Mosaic Law was given to the Jews it was to be a mirror that showed the righteousness that God required. The Law, however, was unable to provide salvation because no one could consistently keep it; it only showed the areas in which one was deficient. The Law showed the necessity of the constant need for forgiveness. Until the Messiah came to fulfill the promise of the "seed of the woman," the Temple and the priesthood—those in charge of the animal sacrifices for the sins of the people—would suffice. The Mosaic Law, the priesthood and the Temple would serve as a means of keeping the people in alignment with God until the Messiah arrived to fulfill the promise. The Kingdom of God would arrive with the Messiah. The Law, the priesthood and the Temple would have then served their purpose. The Psalms and the prophets speak of the suffering Messiah (see especially Psalm 22 and Isaiah 53). The Messiah was to die a substitutionary death on behalf of his people Israel, and for the peoples of every nation. The Messiah was not just for Israel; the promise made to Adam and Eve and to Abraham included everyone. Israel was blessed by being God's conduit through which he would reconcile humans back to himself. The Messiah would come by means of the Jewish nation; the Messiah would be a Jew and would minister to the Jewish people. God had created the Jewish nation for such a purpose. The Hebrew Scriptures show that there were to be two different times the Messiah would arrive; the Messiah had a different task to perform for each arrival. The first arrival was as the "seed of the woman," when he would be the true sacrifice for the world's sins, replacing the animal sacrifices that were just a type or shadow of the real one to come. This would be the time when the Deceiver would "bruise his heal." The Messiah would rise from his execution—his substitutionary death—and would come again sometime in the future as a king to establish a physical, Messianic Kingdom, thereby ultimately "crushing the [Deceiver's] head." (Some information gleaned from Fruchtenbaum's book Messianic Christology.)

Despite the Mosaic Law and the prophets, however, Israel had often rebelled against God. The prophets regularly challenged Israel to get right with God by turning to him in repentance. Israel's rebellion resulted in their being exiled into two different, foreign countries—

Assyria and Babylon. After the Jews returned to Jerusalem from Babylonian exile and rebuilt the city and the Temple (in the sixth century B.C.), the Israelites were obedient to the Law and refrained from their past rebellion. They were certain that by their changed lives surely the Kingdom of God would come, but it did not. Instead, Israel had to succumb to such people as Antiochus IV (Epiphanes), the Hasmoneans, Pompey and Rome. Where was God? Why hadn't he delivered his faithful people? Then a man from Galilee appeared and traveled from town to town, healing the sick and preaching the good news that the Kingdom of God was at hand. Because he had the power to heal, many thought he might also have the power to conquer. For Jesus, the Kingdom of God meant the restoration of communion between God and humans which had been broken by sin. Jesus believed and taught that he was the one to do the restoring, that he was the King of the Kingdom of God, that he was the Messiah of the Hebrew Scriptures. But he was coming as the "seed of the woman." He was the one to be sacrificed for the sins of the world. When the crowd had asked, "Could this be the Son of David?" (Mt 12:23), they were really asking, "Is Jesus the long-awaited Messiah who was promised in our Scriptures?" The first-century Jews were correct to believe that the Messiah was soon to arrive. God had not forgotten his promise of a Messiah. They were just hoping, erroneously, that he would come to restore Israel's independence. He was coming instead to first restore Israel's and the world's relationship with God. This would happen by fulfilling the Mosaic Law and the prophecies concerning the Messiah's first arrival. The only person who could fulfill all that was required in the Hebrew Scriptures was Jesus of Nazareth. When Jesus came to fulfill the first mission of the Messiah—to die a substitutionary death—the Jews were by then longing for the Messiah King who would remove their oppressors and establish Israel's independence. They rejected the promise of the Suffering Messiah, and therefore rejected Jesus. What then did the first-century Jew expect regarding the Messiah? They wanted a king, a zealot, but they had misinterpreted their Scriptures due to their own circumstances. They were an oppressed people, and they wanted freedom. They thought God should grant them that; they thought the Messiah would be the one to do it. But God's time table is not contingent upon our wishes. Jesus did not come to be their king and zealot, despite what Aslan says; he came first to be their Redeemer. (See Fruchtenbaum's *Messianic Christology*.)

143

The Kingdom of God has come to earth, but it is not from the earth. It is a spiritual kingdom, and those who enter it must do so by a spiritual rebirth. The immediate death that occurred as a result of Adam and Eve's having disobeyed God was a spiritual separation (death) from God; physical death would eventually come as a result of their disobedience (sin), as well. Animal sacrifice, as we have seen, offered a temporary remedy; the complete remedy would occur at the death and resurrection of the "seed of the woman," the Messiah. Aslan wants the Kingdom of God to be strictly of-this-world so that he can say Jesus and his followers would therefore be willing to kill and die for that earthly kingdom. That is why Aslan has to pick and choose which Gospel passages he will accept; he only chooses those that he can manipulate to go along with his theories. That is why he rejects the passage in John where Jesus tells Pilate: "My kingdom doesn't belong to this world" (Jn 18:36). Aslan is correct to say that the Kingdom of God is not like any other kingdom or political system found in the world. The Kingdom of God is wherever God rules; it is the sphere or domain where God's will is done. It is not a physical place where you can give it longitudinal and latitudinal positions. You cannot find it in such and such a country, or on top of such and such mountain. Paul tells the Roman Christians: "God's kingdom does not consist of what a person eats or drinks." In other words, it is not physical. "Rather," Paul continues, "God's kingdom consists of righteousness [God's approval], peace and joy that the Holy Spirit gives (Rom 14:17).

Since Aslan believes that the Kingdom of God that Jesus spoke of was a physical kingdom that was soon to happen, he (Aslan) denies any and all futuristic sayings of Jesus; he only allows Jesus to refer to his own time and place. Likewise, the Jesus Seminar also rejects any and all "apocalyptic" and/or "eschatological" messages from Jesus. Aslan and the JS only accept "wisdom" statements from Jesus. They insist that any statements that Jesus made about a future Kingdom, or what is going to happen to unbelievers in the future judgment, are words that the early Christians put on Jesus' lips. All future aspects of the Messianic Kingdom, therefore, are rejected by Aslan. Aslan takes the passage in Mark 13:5-37 where Jesus talks about wars, earthquakes, famines, and false messiahs and claims that these do not refer to or predict future events. Aslan insists that Jesus was talking about the times in which he lived. Wars, earthquakes, famines, false messiahs— they were all happening right then and there. Now it is true that every

144

era can be said to mirror what Jesus said about wars, earthquakes, famines, etc., but it is clear from the Markan passage that Jesus is warning his disciples about the future. When Jesus and his disciples were leaving the Temple area the disciples commented on the beautiful buildings. Jesus told them that the Temple would be destroyed. His disciples were obviously and reasonably horrified by this information and wanted to know more. Jesus warned them to be careful of being deceived. He wanted to make sure his disciples understood what was going to happen during the Church Age, before the Messianic Kingdom would begin; that is part of the information one finds in Mark 13:5-37. Jesus told them about wars, famines, earthquakes, false messiahs, and the persecution those who truly believed in Jesus could expect to receive. Jesus told them that these things did not mean that the end had come. This would just be the beginning. (I will discuss this in more detail later.) As much as Aslan and the JS wish that Jesus made no statements regarding a future kingdom, or a Second Coming, the Gospels are quite clear that he did. Of course, all one has to do is say that those passages are unreliable, that Christians had put those words in Jesus' mouth, but we have seen that by using proper historical testing there is no reason to question the reliability and authenticity of the Gospels. What we can question, however, is the reliability of many of the statements made by Aslan, the JS, and other liberal theologians/biblical scholars.

The Transfiguration

Here is an example where we can question Aslan's reliability in understanding Scripture. Aslan uses Mark 9:1 to insist that Jesus expected God's Kingdom, a physical kingdom, to come soon. In Mark 9:1, Jesus says: "some people standing here will see the kingdom of God come with power before they die" (NCV). Aslan thinks that Jesus was promising his followers, in this passage, that a physical kingdom, complete with a king, was going to happen soon in Israel. Aslan believes that is how those who heard Jesus say this would have interpreted it. The obvious question one would ask is what happened next after Jesus told his disciples this. The very next verse answers that question. In Mark 9:2 we learn that six days later Jesus took three disciples—Peter, James, and John—to a mountain peak. There, Jesus is transformed or transfigured in front of them. The three disciples see the power of God's kingdom when Moses and Elijah appear with

145

Jesus. The spiritual domain of the kingdom becomes visible to the disciples. Moses represents the Law, and Elijah represents the prophetic word of God. Jesus was shown in his spiritual glory, the same glory John will see some fifty to sixty years later when he writes the book of Revelation. Moses and Elijah discuss with Jesus his approaching death and what he was about to fulfill in Jerusalem (Lk. 9:31). God the Father tells the three disciples to be quiet and listen to his Son, Jesus. Jesus was showing his disciples the spiritual kingdom, and God the Father told the disciples to listen to Jesus as he and Moses and Elijah discussed Jesus' sacrificial death. So Aslan is mistaken to assume that what Jesus was proposing in Mark 9:1 was an immediate physical kingdom that would soon be established on earth by an act of insurrection against Rome, an insurrection that would result in the restoration of Israel as an independent nation. Jesus was actually proposing just the opposite. Jesus did not expect a physical kingdom to happen at any moment. He expected to die and rise again on the third day. If Aslan is unable to understand this obvious passage in Mark 9, one should be wary of accepting the other (erroneous) "interpretations" he provides.

I hope you see from this chapter that Jesus did know what the kingdom of God was, and that you realize that Jesus is the King of that kingdom. Jesus came as the "seed of the woman" to provide the way into that kingdom for everyone who accepts him as their Savior. The Transfiguration in Mark 9 showed Jesus as God the Son and the Redeeming Messiah who was to come to take away the sins of the world.

146

Chapter Eight: Jesus as Zealot

Aslan presents six basic examples that he hopes will "prove" Jesus was a zealot. The first one is the Beatitudes in the Sermon on the Mount; the second "proof" is Jesus' statement that he came not "to bring peace, but a sword;" the third one is Jesus' entry into Jerusalem and the "cleansing" of the Temple; the fourth is Jesus' statement that his disciples are to pick up their cross; the fifth is Jesus' new world order concept; and the sixth "proof" regards the paying of the imperial tax.

The Beatitudes

Aslan believes that one of the strongest and best examples of Jesus being a zealot is the Beatitudes (Matthew 5) that began the Sermon on the Mount. Aslan interprets the Beatitudes from a zealot point of view. Aslan asserts that the Beatitudes are Jesus' way of promising his listeners that they can be freed as subjects of Rome and freed from the religious leaders' dominance. But it is up to them. Jesus uses the Beatitudes to show his listeners how to become zealots, like him. Aslan believes the Beatitudes are Jesus' secret and cryptic message of how to establish God's Kingdom in the here and now. Jesus is promising his listeners that God will soon restore Israel and bring about its independence so that it can serve and honor God. And like a proper zealot, Jesus is reminding his listeners that this restoration cannot take place without the current order—Rome and the religious leaders—being destroyed. God cannot set up his kingdom on earth until or unless the current leaders are annihilated. For Aslan, when Jesus says "the kingdom of God has come near" (Mk 1:15) it is the same thing as declaring that the Roman Empire's demise is within reach. When Jesus uses the phrase "kingdom of God" Aslan is firmly convinced that it can mean only one thing—God will replace the Emperor as the ruler of Israel. When Jesus says "the kingdom of God has come near" it can only imply, for Aslan, that Jesus is calling his listeners to revolt. It is important, then, to actually look at the Beatitudes. I will provide two different translations; the first is the ESV, and the second will be the GW. The ESV says:

> Blessed are the poor in spirit, for theirs is the kingdom of heaven.

147

Blessed are those who mourn, for they shall be comforted.

Blessed are the meek, for they shall inherit the earth.

Blessed are those who hunger and thirst for righteousness, for they shall be satisfied.

Blessed are the merciful, for they shall receive mercy.

Blessed are the pure in heart, for they shall see God.

Blessed are the peacemakers, for they shall be called sons of God.

Blessed are those who are persecuted for righteousness' sake, for theirs is the kingdom of heaven.

Blessed are you when others revile you and persecute you and utter all kinds of evil against you falsely on my account. Rejoice and be glad, for your reward is great in heaven, for so they persecuted the prophets who were before you (Mt 5:3–12).

The GW translation says:

Blessed are those who recognize they are spiritually helpless. The kingdom of heaven belongs to them.

Blessed are those who mourn. They will be comforted.

Blessed are those who are gentle. They will inherit the earth.

Blessed are those who hunger and thirst for God's approval. They will be satisfied.

Blessed are those who show mercy. They will be treated mercifully.

Blessed are those whose thoughts are pure. They will see God.

Blessed are those who make peace. They will be called God's children.

Blessed are those who are persecuted for doing what God approves of. The kingdom of heaven belongs to them.

Blessed are you when people insult you, persecute you, lie, and say all kinds of evil things about you because of me. Rejoice and be glad because you have a great reward in heaven! The prophets who lived before you were persecuted in these ways. ("Scripture is taken from GOD'S WORD®. © 1995 God's Word to the Nations. Used by permission of Baker Publishing Group.")

The Jesus Seminar uses "Congratulations" instead of "Blessed." The *Greek-English Lexicon of the New Testament* says the Greek word used here for "blessed" is a word that pertains to the state of being happy with the implication of enjoying favorable circumstances. For example, those who show mercy or compassion are happy because God will be merciful to them. The person who is blessed receives God's favor; they have and experience God's approval. Being blessed is a state of being marked by a fullness or completeness from God. When one is blessed in the fashion Jesus talks about here that person's satisfaction comes from God and not from favorable circumstances (see *The Complete Word Study Dictionary*). *Word Studies in the New Testament* says the Greek word used here for "blessed" gives the idea that one meets with God's approval because one lives a life that pleases God. The Jesus Seminar is in error for using Congratulations instead of Blessed. "Congratulations" is something we say to someone who has accomplished something on their own; we congratulate someone for graduating college, or getting a promotion, or for getting married. The word "Blessed" here gives the idea that despite the negative circumstances one finds themselves in, God will see that person through it. We see an example of this in the first Beatitude— the one who is poor in spirit, or spiritually helpless, belongs to the kingdom because they have put their trust in God. *Word Studies in the New Testament* says the word "poor" here denotes "utter spiritual destitution, the consciousness of which precedes the entrance into the kingdom of God, and which cannot be relieved by one's own efforts, but only by the free mercy of God." Those who are poor in spirit, or spiritually helpless, recognize their state of being spiritually deficient and seek help from God. When one seeks help from God in this state, God responds. Likewise, the person who mourns, who is grieved by their sin, will be comforted. The person who thinks they are doing well, who thinks they are already righteous, who does not think they are spiritually sick and in need of God's grace, they do not belong to the kingdom; they are not comforted by God, they are not satisfied, nor will they see God. Remember, Jesus is giving this sermon to Jews and Gentiles alike. Jews thought that they were already righteous and part of God's kingdom simply because they were the 'sons of Abraham.' Gentiles had multiple gods that they could appease to make them happy. Jesus is telling both groups of people that they need to recognize their spiritual deficiency and turn to the one, true God. Luke has Jesus say "Blessed are the poor" (6:20), and first-century Jews would know this describes pious or humble people. The Aramaic or Hebrew word Jesus would have chosen is the same one he used when he read from the book of Isaiah in Nazareth that said, "The Spirit of the Almighty LORD is with me because the LORD has anointed me to deliver good news to humble people" ("Scripture is taken from GOD'S WORD®. © 1995 God's Word to the Nations. Used by permission of Baker Publishing Group." 61:1). The word "poor" that Jesus used would describe a lowly, humble, afflicted and needy person, one who depended on God for sustenance; in other words, one who is poor in spirit. These were people who were not well off financially and may have been on the fringe of society, but they were not dormant rebels just waiting for the right zealot to come along to lead them in a revolution. These lowly, humble, afflicted and needy people were the ones who belonged to the kingdom because they trusted God to provide for them. James, in his epistle, says of the poor to whom Jesus refers: "has not God chosen those who are poor in the world to be rich in faith and heirs of the kingdom, which he has promised to those who love him" (ESV, 2:5)?

Aslan, however, interprets Jesus' words as though they have no spiritual content; he sees them as words Jesus used to rally the social misfits together for physical battle. Aslan sees the Beatitudes as a rebel cry, dismissing the standard view that understands these beautiful words as coming from someone who desires to see people live in close relationship with God. Through them, Jesus was showing the state of heart and mind people need to be in so they can belong to the kingdom of heaven. Jesus was revealing the simple truth of how to restore the rift between humans and God. But Aslan rejects this idea. For him, Jesus was trying to instigate the poor and oppressed and the marginalized in order to get them to join him in starting an uprising. Aslan sees the Beatitudes as a promise Jesus is making to his listeners that they will soon be delivered from foreign rule and that God's Kingdom will then be established on earth, which will, in turn, restore Israel's preeminence. But this cannot happen, says Aslan, without violent action. Jesus' listeners must join him to destroy the current political and spiritual order. The Kingdom of God cannot occur until the present leaders are annihilated. When people heard the Beatitudes did they really come away with the thought that Jesus hated the Romans so much that he wanted to form an army to destroy them? How deep in one's theory can someone descend in order to twist Jesus' words here to mean or imply that he was looking for followers who were willing to kill for him in order to bring in the kingdom of heaven by getting rid of the Romans, or anyone else who opposed them? What then is the reason Jesus said, "Blessed are those who make peace. They will be called God's children"? *Word Studies in the New Testament* shows that the word for "peacemaker" means one who is a founder and promoter of peace; one who not only keeps the peace, but seeks to bring other people into harmony with each other. Was Jesus just winking at his disciples when he used the word 'peacemaker,' knowing that he actually meant the opposite? Was this a code word that really meant "hater of those Romans"?

Aslan believes Jesus' Beatitudes are Jesus' promise that Israel will be delivered from Roman oppression and the religious leaders' dominance, and this cannot be done without his listeners joining him in destroying the current political and religious order. Jesus did not advocate violence, although he certainly predicted it would happen; but that is something totally different. Twice his followers wanted to do something violent and he rebuked them for it. Once was when they were passing through a town in Samaria and the people there did not give them shelter, so James and John Zebedee wanted Jesus to have them destroyed by calling fire down from heaven (see Lk 9:51-56). They knew Jesus could have, but he refused. The second time was when the priests and soldiers came to arrest Jesus and Peter drew his sword and cut off someone's ear. Jesus rebuked Peter and then healed the man's ear (see Jn 18:10f). Aslan is trying so hard to make Jesus into a zealot that he is willing to manipulate any Gospel passage to have it comply with his theory and agenda. Aslan claims that when Jesus says "the Kingdom of God is near," he (Jesus) is simply and plainly calling for an insurrection. It shows how far Aslan will go to deny the Messiahship of Jesus. Aslan says this view of Jesus as an insurrectionist who wants to raise an army to destroy Rome's oppression of Israel is the historical Jesus he prefers. This idea reveals more about Aslan than it does Jesus. Aslan has failed to prove that Jesus was a zealot by the use of the Beatitudes.

"I Did Not Come to Bring Peace, but a Sword"

Aslan's second "proof" that Jesus was a zealot was when Jesus said, "Do not suppose that I have come to bring peace to the earth. I did not come to bring peace, but a sword" (NIV, Mt 10:34). Again, here is an example of Aslan pulling a passage out of the Gospels when he wants to use it to try to prove his point. I can pull two passages out of the

Gospels to 'prove' that people should commit suicide: one passage says, Judas hanged himself (Mt. 27:5) and another passage has Jesus say, "Go and do likewise" (Lk. 10:37). By pulling these two passages out of context, I can 'prove' that Jesus tells everyone to end their own life. So Aslan uses the 'I came to bring a sword' passage to show that Jesus was not a pacifist. (Aslan likes to quote this particular verse, and does so whenever he can, in order to 'prove' that Jesus had a violent streak.) There are several instances where we see Jesus get angry: he got angry at the stubbornness of unbelieving people (Mk 3:5); and he got angry at the moneychangers using corrupt methods in the Temple courtyard (Mk 11:15), which we will see presently in this chapter. It is possible to be angry, and yet not sin (as Paul informs us; see Ephesians 4:26). What did Jesus mean when he said he "did not come to bring peace, but a sword"?

Let's look at the entire passage Aslan picked to show that Jesus was not averse to violence. We find it in Matthew 10:5–42. What is happening in this passage is Jesus is getting his twelve disciples ready to go off on their own and preach the good news that the kingdom is near. (It is possible that they would be gone for almost a year.) They are given the power to heal others. They are not to take any provisions because they are to rely on God and the kindness of others. If they are not welcomed in a house or town, they are to leave without causing any problems, but they are to shake that town's dust from their sandals as a sign that the people will be punished for rejecting the kingdom. Jesus warns them that they will encounter persecution and may even be dragged into court by people who think they are serving God. Jesus assures them that the Holy Spirit will tell them what to say in situations like that, and so they are not to worry. Jesus alerts them to what they might experience when they tell people about the good news. Some of those who accept the good news—that is, accept Jesus as the Messiah—could be mistreated by their own friends and families. (We see this even today when a Jewish family will disown a member who becomes a Christian. In Islam, it is forbidden for a Muslim to change religions; the penalty for doing so is death.) Jesus warns his disciples that a brother will hand over his own brother to death; that a father will hand over his own child because they have turned to Jesus for salvation. People will hate you because you are committed to me, Jesus tells them. But Jesus also tells his disciples not to fear those who can kill the body, because they cannot kill one's soul. The disciples are to fear God who can destroy both body and soul in hell. Jesus is showing them the huge responsibility they now have and what really is at stake. When they tell others about the kingdom—the domain where God rules through Jesus—those people who reject the message will eventually be judged and punished by God. Whoever believes the message and acknowledges Jesus as the Messiah will be accepted by God the Father. Whoever does not accept the message will not be accepted by God. Rejecting Jesus is rejecting entrance into the Kingdom of God.

It is at this point in the conversation that Jesus then says, "Do not suppose that I have come to bring peace to the earth. I did not come to bring peace, but a sword" (Mt 10:34). Based on the context in which Jesus uses the word 'sword,' it can also connote the idea of 'conflict'. In fact, that is how the GW translates this passage; it says: "Don't think that I came to bring peace to earth. I didn't come to bring peace but conflict. I came to turn a man against his father, a daughter against her mother, a daughter-in-law against her mother-in-law. A person's enemies will be the members of his own family ("Scripture is taken from GOD'S WORD®. © 1995 God's Word to the Nations. Used by permission of Baker Publishing Group." Mt 10:34–36). When a person decides to follow Jesus this can bring conflict in his/her relationship with friends and family. Living for Jesus means being opposed to the worldly system that is under the Deceiver's rule, and therefore conflict can arise. Jesus tells his disciples that he is not yet ushering in the Messianic Kingdom where nations will beat their swords into plowshares and their spears into pruning hooks, where nations will not take up swords against each other, nor will they train for war (see Micah 4:31). The time period Jesus is speaking of here is the Church Age when Jews and Gentiles will come into the kingdom by accepting Jesus as their Redeemer Messiah, the one who came to die for them and then rose again on the third day. In this Church Age, families will turn away from those who have decided to follow Jesus. So, instead of quoting the swords-into-plowshares passage from Micah 4 (which would have referred to the Messianic Kingdom the Jews were looking for), Jesus uses the passage in Micah 7:6 that says a man will turn against his father, a daughter against her mother, a daughter-in-law against her mother-in-law and a person's enemies will be the members of his own family. That is what Jesus means by bringing a sword. Family and friends will turn against the follower of Jesus because of their hatred of God; and, in that sense, there will be conflict, a sword, that drives people apart. Jesus tells his disciples that those who follow him (Jesus) must love him more than they do their own family; Jesus is to be the number one priority in their lives. Jesus clearly believed he had the authority to claim the same kind of honor they were to give to God. Then Jesus told them, "Whoever doesn't take up his cross and follow me doesn't deserve to be my disciple. The person who tries to preserve his life will lose it, but the person who loses his life for me will preserve it" ("Scripture is taken from GOD'S WORD®. © 1995 God's Word to the Nations. Used by permission of Baker Publishing Group." Mt 10:38f). Jesus is saying some powerful things about himself in this passage. But he is not advocating violence against Rome or against the religious leaders. He is telling his disciples that when someone decides to follow Jesus there is going to be adversity in his/her life. One must actually die to their former life of sin—take up his/her cross—and follow Jesus in a reborn state. The first step in entering that new life is to acknowledge that one is poor in spirit, spiritually helpless, and to mourn or be genuinely sorry for one's sinful life, and to turn to God.

So when Aslan pulls that one passage out of the Gospels where Jesus said, "I have not come to bring peace, but a sword," in order to show that Jesus was a zealot and was not averse to violence, Aslan is hoping by that passage to prove that Jesus was advocating the overthrow of the Roman Empire. Nothing could be farther from the truth. Aslan uses Jesus' "kingdom of God" phrase, his Beatitudes, and his warning that becoming a Christian could cause conflict within one's family as plain and simple proofs that Jesus was a zealot. Since zealots advocated violence, Aslan wonders if Jesus felt the same way. He wonders if Jesus agreed with the typical zealot doctrine that believed that God demanded that all foreign influence needed to be "cleansed" from the land. By what Aslan has said in his book, it is obvious that he saw Jesus as a typical zealot. Aslan thinks that accepting Jesus as a typical zealot is what pries the "real" Jesus from the Christian concept of Jesus as Messiah. Aslan accuses some scholars of trying to depict Jesus as an apolitical preacher who had no interest in or knowledge of the political world of his time. Aslan says making Jesus into an apolitical preacher who went around exhorting people to be peacemakers, to love their enemies, and turn the other cheek was an erroneous view. Aslan says this picture of Jesus is nothing but a fabrication. The fact is, of course, that the Gospels do not portray Jesus as being unaware of the political atmosphere that he lived in. Jesus knew enough about Herod Antipas to call him a fox (see Lk 13:32). What Aslan does though is swing the pendulum to the other extreme and claim that if Jesus was not apolitical, then he was a zealot. This idea—that Jesus often acted and spoke like a political zealot—is, of course, exaggerated in order to comply with Aslan's agenda. Jesus was quite aware of his surroundings and the political atmosphere around him. But he knew his mission was to come and die for the sins of the world and he was not going to let anyone interfere with that mission, not even his own disciples (see Mt 16:21-23). Aslan's belief that the Gospel writers tried to hide the zealot nature of Jesus is pure conjecture. In similar mode to the methodology of the Jesus Seminar, Aslan forms assumptions and "new" ways of interpreting Gospel passages in order to portray Jesus in the image that he has created. Aslan accuses the Gospel writers of making Jesus into their own creation, but he does the very thing he accuses them of doing. Aslan justifies this by saying he is actually trying to get back to the real Jesus, the historical Jesus, by removing the sayings of Jesus that he does not like. Aslan wants to remove the Christ-of-faith, which he says the early Christians created, from the historical Jesus that Aslan and the JS have created. Again, what we actually see is that Aslan wants Jesus' phrase—I did not come to bring peace, but a sword—to be about a real sword so that Jesus looks like a zealot, looks more and more like Muhammad. Aslan has again failed to prove that Jesus was a zealot.

Jesus and his disciples leave Capernaum and purposely set out for Jerusalem. Along the way, Jesus continues to heal the sick and cast out demons. Aslan claims that when Jesus arrives in Jerusalem he will inevitably clash with the Temple priests and the Roman authorities that support them. For Aslan, Jesus has been using his magical skills of healing and exorcism to gather together his followers who will be a part of his movement; Jesus has been using the phrase "kingdom of God" to show he is a zealot; and now Jesus is going to Jerusalem to fight against the powers that be. For Aslan, being a zealot and preaching about the kingdom of God went hand in hand. The zealot understood the idea of the kingdom of God as God being the only true sovereign, the only true king, who would reign over the whole world. Of course, every Jew throughout Jewish history believed that God was the true sovereign over Israel and the world. That idea permeates throughout the Hebrew Scriptures (see Zech 14:9 as one example). Every Jew, including Jesus, would be educated during their formative years in the history and Scriptures of the Jewish nation and would accept the idea that God was sovereign over all the earth. It is not much of a stretch, then, for Aslan to say that Jesus' view of God's sovereignty was similar to the bandits and zealots of his own day. Since most all Jews during Jesus' time believed that God was sovereign over all the earth, and since zealots believed it too, this fact does not mean that Jesus is therefore a zealot.

But Aslan is convinced that Jesus was nothing more than a typical zealot whose message was typical of zealots and bandits before him. Jesus was just reiterating what all the other zealots had been saying for years. If the zealots and bandits during Jesus' time had been preaching for an all-encompassing, world-wide Kingdom of God, as Aslan tells us they were, this idea was really nothing new. The Hebrew Scriptures proclaim God as being sovereign over his entire creation, that he is the ultimate king and his kingdom is open to everyone, although not everyone will accept the invitation. Throughout the Hebrew Scriptures, God appealed to his people to come to him and find rest in his presence (see Jer 6:16 as an example); it would be fitting then for Jesus, God's Son, to offer us rest as well—"Come to me, all of you who are tired and have heavy loads, and I will give you rest. Accept my teachings and learn from me, because I am gentle and humble in spirit, and you will find rest for your lives. The burden that I ask you to accept is easy; the load I give you to carry is light" (NCV, Mt 11:28–30). The zealots wanted to actualize God's kingdom into a physical one, but we have seen from Jesus' parables and sermons that the Kingdom of God he referred to was a spiritual kingdom. That was one of the reasons the crowd rejected him; they wanted to make him a physical king but he was unwilling (see Jn 6:15).

The Entry into Jerusalem and the "Cleansing" of the Temple

So, Aslan is hopeful his third 'proof' will fortify his premise that Jesus was a typical first-century zealot. Found in his second prologue, Aslan says Jesus made a provocative and political entry into Jerusalem, which was followed by his "cleansing" of the Temple. Aslan claims that Jesus saw himself as the peasant king. He therefore rode into

Jerusalem on a donkey, thereby showing, that he was going to both usher in the physical Kingdom of God and rule in that kingdom. Again, Aslan interprets events in Jesus' life as though he is privy to some special knowledge, that he is part of some mystery cult that knows the "real" Jesus. The Jews in Jesus' time should have, in fact, been waiting for their king to enter Jerusalem in this manner. When the Jews returned to Israel after the Babylonian exile in the sixth century B.C., Zechariah, a priest and prophet who returned with them, said "Rejoice greatly, Daughter Zion! Shout, Daughter Jerusalem! See, your king comes to you, righteous and victorious, lowly and riding on a donkey" (NIV, Zec 9:9). The Jews, of course, as mentioned before, were hoping for the Messianic Kingdom, missing the many references in their Hebrew Scriptures that their king's first arrival would be as the Redeeming Messiah. Jesus did not ride into Jerusalem as a zealot, ready to do battle. He rode into Jerusalem to be a ransom for many, as he had often said he would (see Mk 10:45). Jesus entered Jerusalem as the Redeeming Messiah. He did not arrive in order to usher in a physical (worldly) Kingdom of God in hopes of ruling that kingdom; he already was the king of that kingdom. He came to Jerusalem to be arrested, killed, and rise again on the third day. His death would buy back those who recognized that they were slaves of sin; his death would provide for their freedom. His resurrection would be proof that he had accomplished that goal. Ridderbos (*Kingdom of God, Kingdom of Heaven*) tells us that Jesus was not going to Jerusalem as a warrior, a zealot, to die on his feet, if necessary, but as a lamb being led to the slaughter (Isa. 53:7). His messianic purpose was to become a ransom for many, to take their place in receiving the punishment for the sin of the world. Who could do that but God? In Jesus, God was visiting his people. The hope of the prophets was being realized in the person of Jesus. He boldly announced that the Kingdom of God had come. The presence of the kingdom was a new event in history, says Ridderbos; it was God becoming man to die for (in place of) humankind. When Jesus said the kingdom is near he was not simply pronouncing judgment, he was issuing a call to repentance that would lead to salvation. Jesus was telling his listeners that the kingdom could be experienced in the present, in the here-and-now. It was a reality manifested in Jesus' own person and ministry. It appeared in Jesus' ability to cast out demons, heal the sick, and forgive peoples' sins.

For Aslan, although Jesus' kingly entrance into Jerusalem was rather provocative, it was nothing compared to what Jesus did the next day. That is when Jesus went into the Temple's public courtyard, where the Gentiles were allowed, and "cleansed" it. Aslan informs us that when Jesus "cleansed" the courtyard he was not only attacking the Temple's business practices but was, in essence, attacking the established priestly system and its hierarchal organization. Aslan goes even further and says that because Caiaphas the high priest and Pilate the governor had a close working relationship, when Jesus attacked the moneychangers and thereby was attacking the priests, he was also attacking Rome. Aslan interprets Jesus' zeal for the Temple as a demonstration that Jesus is a zealot, a bandit, a dangerous subversive. Aslan believes the Temple authorities interpreted Jesus' behavior (his zeal) as an indication that Jesus was a zealot. Aslan invites us to examine Jesus' words and actions when he was at the Temple. Aslan says there is no doubting the fact that it was what he said and did at the Temple that caused Jesus' arrest and his execution. Aslan insists that it would be very difficult to disagree with the obvious fact that Jesus was crucified because he demonstrated strong aspirations to be Israel's messiah and because his zealousness jeopardized the Temple priests' authority. So, let's do what Aslan suggests; let's examine Jesus' words and actions regarding the Temple cleansing. Compiling the text from all the Gospels, we read this:

> Jesus and his disciples came to Jerusalem when the Jewish Passover was near. Jesus rode into Jerusalem on a donkey amidst the joyful shouting of a crowd. The next day Jesus entered the Temple courtyard where the Gentiles were allowed to worship and approached those who were selling cattle, sheep, and pigeons. He made a whip from small ropes and began throwing everyone with their sheep and cattle out of the Temple courtyard, all those who were buying and selling. He overturned the moneychangers' tables, spilling the money across the floor. He told those who sold pigeons, "Pick up this stuff, and get it out of here! Stop making my Father's house [the Temple] a marketplace!" After doing this he told those standing there that, "Scripture says, 'My house will be called a house of prayer for all nations,' (Isaiah 56:7) but you have turned it into a gathering place for thieves" (Jer. 7:11). His disciples remembered the Scripture passage that said,

158

"Devotion for your house will consume me" (Psalms 69:9). Then the blind and lame came to Jesus there in the Temple courtyard, and he healed them. Some Jews reacted to what Jesus had just done and asked him, "What miracle can you show us to justify what you're doing?" Jesus replied, "Tear down this Temple, and I'll rebuild it in three days." The Jews said, "It took forty-six years to build this Temple. Do you really think you're going to rebuild it in three days?" But the Temple Jesus spoke about was his own body. After he came back to life [after his death on the cross], his disciples remembered that he had said this. So they believed the Scripture and this statement that Jesus had made. ["Scripture is taken from GOD'S WORD®. © 1995 God's Word to the Nations. Used by permission of Baker Publishing Group."]

As far as Jesus was concerned the Temple's Gentile courtyard had become a marketplace for robbers (the Greek word the Gospel writers used during the Temple cleansing is a variation of *lēstés*). Jesus did not identify with these robbers, these bandits, these Temple extortionists, who were overcharging the people who came to purchase animals which were to be used for personal sacrifices for sins; in fact, Jesus was outraged that these robbers, these bandits, were making huge profits at the expense of the people. Zodhiates, in his book *The Complete Word Study Dictionary: New Testament*, comments on the word *lēstés* in this context, saying that it is probable that some of these robbers in the Temple were actual zealots in rebellion against the authority of Rome, that the Temple marketplace gave them fancied security in their evildoing, and that there was an element of misplaced patriotism and even religion in their proceedings. What was Jesus so angry about? The area where these "robbers" were selling the sacrificial animals was the courtyard of the Gentiles; it was where God-fearing people of other nations, who were non-Jews, could come and worship God and pray and offer sacrifices for their sins. It was a place for people of all nations to come and get close to God. These moneychangers and high-priced sellers were keeping the people from being able to worship God in a simple and sincere manner. The Temple treasury accepted only one kind of currency (money), and so people from other nations bringing their own currency would have to change their money into the money the Temple treasury accepted. Those who changed the money into the correct currency were charging contemptible prices for their exchange. And then those who sold the sacrificial animals were overcharging for them, as well. So the Gentile worshippers were being charged an enormous amount of money in order to offer a sacrifice to the God they came to worship. This outraged Jesus, and it should have outraged the Pharisees as well. Jesus used this cleansing episode to teach the Pharisees several more parables that exposed their hypocrisy (see Mt 21:28-22:14 and 22:23-23:36). It was the fact that Jesus exposed the religious leaders—the Pharisees and Sadducees—as hypocrites that made them angry enough to want to kill him. He was undermining their authority and power by exposing their sin; this is what made them plot to get rid of him. He was also making claims about himself that they considered blasphemous, claims to be on a par with God, claims that he and God were one. This is why they made arrangements to have him arrested. It was not the cleansing of the Temple that prompted the Temple priests and local Roman authorities to execute Jesus. Aslan once again fails to prove that Jesus was a zealot.

Pick Up Your Cross—Is this a Call for Revolution?

In his fourth 'proof' (found in his tenth chapter), Aslan attempts to show that when Jesus tells us to love our enemies or to turn the other cheek, he (Jesus) is not really advocating a non-violent approach or promoting non-resistance. Aslan believes that Jesus handpicked his twelve disciples so that he could prepare them to help him usher in God's kingdom in Israel. He wanted to prepare them for the inevitable consequences that would result in restoring Israel and fighting against the Roman oppressors and the religious leaders. In other words, Jesus picked these specific men because he wanted to train them to be part of his revolutionary clan that would bring the Kingdom of God to Israel; and it was not going to be a peaceful revolution. Aslan says that Jesus enticed his twelve men with the promise that they would "sit on twelve thrones, judging the twelve tribes of Israel" (NIV, Mt 19:28). Jesus and his band of zealots were going to restore Israel; they were going to fulfill Jeremiah's prophecy, declares Aslan, that promised that God would "break the yoke off their necks and will tear off their bonds; no longer will foreigners enslave them" (NIV, 30:8). Jesus and his disciples would bring in the Kingdom of God that the Baptizer (Jesus' mentor, according to Aslan) preached about; they would restore Israel's independence. John the Baptizer had preached that

God's kingdom was at hand or near, and Jesus and his disciples were going to make that happen. Even if it was not outright war against Rome, Jesus' attempts to restore Israel were not going to be without its danger. That is why Jesus warned his disciples of the consequences of joining with him. Aslan thinks that those consequences were expressed in these words by Jesus in Mark 8:34: "Whoever wants to be my disciple must deny themselves and take up their cross and follow me" (NIV). Aslan believes he has the true interpretation of these words from Jesus; he says that Jesus was telling his disciples that by joining his insurrection it was likely that they would be charged with sedition and be executed on a cross, like all other robbers and bandits. Aslan informs us that Jesus was not telling his disciples that they needed to engage in self-denial; they needed to realize that by joining him they could each die on a cross as punishment for their rebellion.

Aslan thinks Jesus' statement that each of his followers must take up their own cross is not about denying one's self, as is normally thought; it is about dying for the cause of restoring Israel. Why should we accept this "new" interpretation from Aslan? How does he know what Jesus meant by those words. If Jesus is the Son of God, which the evidence in the Gospels clearly indicates, then he has the right to tell us that if we really want to follow him we no longer are to be concerned about ourselves as number one. This self-denial does not mean that we mistreat ourselves or refrain from basic needs; it means that we no longer follow our own desires and whims, but follow God's will instead. Not denying oneself is the major cause of sin and rebellion against God. To deny ourselves is to put God first in our lives. Jesus said that in doing so we will actually receive a better life than we would if we were in charge. By focusing on doing God's will rather than our own will, we paradoxically get real life. This is understandable since it was God who made us and knows what we need. The idea of denying oneself was not new to the Jewish mindset; there were times God told the Israelites "you must deny yourselves" (see Lev 16:29 as an example). When we deny ourselves we are putting our lives back in tune with how we were made. For Aslan, the cross Jesus said the disciples were to carry was simply the realization that their joining him was an act of sedition and they might have to pay the penalty for such sedition, i.e., death on a Roman cross. We have already noted that Jesus had told his disciples that following him could lead to persecution and that even families would turn against those

161

who became his followers (see Mt 10). Carrying your cross means that you do not have control of your life; our lives are to be given back to God so that he can transform us into the people we are supposed to be. When we hold back from carrying our cross we hold back from the gifts God has for us. There is no evidence for accepting Aslan's version of what he thinks carrying one's cross means. Following Jesus by denying ourselves and picking up our own cross is not code words for 'let's start a revolution.' It describes a life that is committed to Jesus.

We see, then, that Aslan not only picks out passages to try to prove that Jesus is a zealot, he also reinterprets Jesus' words to fit his scenario, and he expects his reader to simply assume that he knows the "real" meaning behind Jesus' words, as if he is privy to some inside knowledge. Aslan wants us to believe that when Jesus tells the crowd who had come to be healed by him and to listen to his sermons that they were to love their enemies and turn the other cheek he must have winked at his disciples to let them know he actually meant the opposite. Aslan believes he knows exactly why Jesus picked the men he did to be his twelve disciples—he picked them to train them to become zealots, bandits, who would fight with him against the Roman army and break off the yoke of oppression from the neck of the Jews. Thirteen against thousands are pretty good odds, I guess. Jesus and his Twelve were going to restore Israel's freedom; we know that because Aslan says that is what Jesus meant when he said the kingdom of God was near. When Jesus said that his disciples must deny themselves and take up their own cross, Aslan tells us that Jesus is letting his disciples know that if they join his (Jesus') bandit party they may die as criminals. Aslan thinks his interpretation should be accepted; but why should we accept it? He does not give any evidence for it except to pull certain passages out of the Gospels that he thinks will prove his point. It is simply conjecture, a new way of interpreting the sayings of Jesus based on the theories of the Jesus Seminar and liberal theologians.

If Jesus was creating a group of revolutionaries, then why did the Twelve not begin a revolt after Jesus was killed? Why did they instead stand up in a crowd of Jews days after Jesus was killed with one of them saying such things as: "Fellow Israelites, I want you to know that Jesus of Nazareth was a man who God considered righteous and the proof of that was in the miracles, wonders and signs that God did in your presence through him, which you yourselves know and cannot deny. Jesus was handed over to you by God's deliberate plan and foreknowledge. Aided by wicked men, you put him to death by nailing him to a cross. But God raised him from the dead, and we are all witnesses of it. Therefore, I want you to be sure of this important fact—God has made this Jesus, whom you crucified, both Lord and Messiah" (Ac 2:22–24, 32, 36). When Peter (this was his first sermon) calls Jesus Lord, he uses a word that means Yahweh, the God of Israel, the I AM who encountered Moses at the burning bush. The people who heard this did not accuse Peter and the rest of Jesus' disciples of insurrection; they were mortified and asked what they could do, knowing that they were responsible for putting God's Son to death. Peter told them, "All of you must turn to God and change the way you think and act, and each of you must be baptized in the name of Jesus Christ so that your sins will be forgiven. Then you will receive the Holy Spirit as a gift" ("Scripture is taken from GOD'S WORD®. © 1995 God's Word to the Nations. Used by permission of Baker Publishing Group." Acts 2:38). Instead of continuing the rebellion that Jesus supposedly trained them for, Jesus' disciples went around telling people that Jesus had died for everyone's sins and that the people needed to repent and be drawn into the Kingdom of God. So the way into the Kingdom of God was through repentance, not insurrection. In fact, Peter soon preached his message of repentance to a Gentile family, helping to continue the trek (which Jesus started) into Gentile territory to deliver the message of repentance and salvation through Jesus Christ.

Aslan informs us that Jesus occasionally let his disciples know what lay in store for him when he reached Jerusalem. Aslan provides us with nine Gospel passages: Matthew 16:21, 17:22–23, 20:18–19; Mark 8:31, 9:31, 10:33; Luke 9:22, 44, 18:32–33. In eight of these nine passages Aslan says Jesus told his disciples that four things were going to happen to him; he was going to be rejected, arrested, tortured and executed. The problem here is that Jesus actually said five things were going to happen to him when he reached Jerusalem. Not too surprisingly, Aslan left out the fifth detail. What is that detail? When Jesus said he was going to be rejected, arrested, tortured and executed, he always ended by saying "but on the third day I will rise from the dead." For example, the Matthew 16:21 passage says: "From that time on Jesus began to explain to his disciples that he must go to Jerusalem and suffer many things at the hands of the elders, the chief priests and the teachers of the law, and that he must be killed and on the third day be raised to life" (NIV). In 9:44, Luke says that Jesus told his disciples that they needed to understand that he was going to be betrayed and handed over to a group of people. He did not have to say what was going to happen to him after he was delivered to these men because he had already said it earlier in verse 22. Now, if Aslan accepts the Gospel passages that say Jesus is going to be rejected, arrested, tortured, and executed, why does he not accept the fact that Jesus also said he was going to rise from the dead? It is because Aslan's theory does not include a resurrection. Islam does not believe in Jesus' resurrection. What was Jesus doing when he was preparing his disciples for the fact that he was going to suffer and die? He was showing them that he was the Suffering Messiah of Isaiah 53, that he was the "seed of the woman" promised to Adam and Eve, that he was the fulfillment of the reason for animal sacrifices, and that he was the ultimate sacrifice of which Abraham's "sacrifice" of his son Isaac was only a shadow. Of course, Aslan cannot accept Jesus as the world's Savior because of his own worldview, his own belief system; he must come up with something else, and the best he can do is say that Jesus was a zealot.

Aslan then, for some reason, attempts to be somewhat accommodating by acknowledging the fact that Jesus spoke so often about his arrest and execution that these words recorded in the Gospels were possibly historical, i.e., that Jesus really said this. If Aslan was in a meeting with the Jesus Seminar, he probably would have given these nine passages a pink bead, but only, of course, after removing the part about rising from the dead. Even though Aslan admits that Jesus talked about his arrest and execution, he (Aslan) is quick to claim that Jesus attempted to actually keep the "truth" about God's Kingdom from the general populace; he only talked about it with his disciples. Aslan uses Mark 4:11f to try to prove his point: "The secret of the kingdom of God has been given to you. But to those on the outside everything is said in parables so that, 'they may be ever seeing but never perceiving, and ever hearing but never understanding'" (NIV). But it is not so much that Jesus hid the truth about the Kingdom of God from others; it is that his listeners were unreceptive. His listeners had pre-conceived ideas that were keeping them from hearing the truth of what Jesus was telling them. (We see this same propensity in the JS and Aslan and,

164

sadly, so many more; hopefully, not you, dear reader.) In fact, Jesus was quoting a passage from Isaiah 6 to describe the people that he (Jesus) was talking to. Isaiah was sent to preach to Judah because the nation had turned away from God, and he was about to bring judgment upon them. God warned Isaiah that the people were stubborn and sinful and therefore they see but do not perceive; they hear but do not understand. Jesus was saying the same thing about his own generation; they were just as stubborn and full of sin as their ancestors and, therefore, could not perceive or understand anything about the Kingdom of God. For some reason, though, Aslan did not finish what Mark had said in 4:12; he only referred to the first half of that passage. The full verse tells us that if these people did perceive and understand they would "repent and be forgiven." Earlier, Aslan made the comment that Jesus was not even sure what the kingdom was, that Jesus was kind of making things up as he went along, but here it seems that Aslan acknowledges that Jesus did know after all. This passage that Aslan uses in order to show that Jesus is hiding the Kingdom of God from the populace is in the context of the nine parables that we have already discussed at length. Why does Aslan say Jesus was hiding the kingdom from the populace? It is because Aslan thinks that Jesus did not want the populace to know that he (Jesus) was bringing in a real, physical kingdom where he was going to be the king and his disciples would be his royal rulers. Jesus did not want that grand scenario of his to get out, so he talked in parables. Aslan refers to Jesus' grand scenario as Jesus' messianic secret, which is the subject of Aslan's next 'proof.' What we have seen regarding Aslan's fourth 'proof' is that he has again failed to show that Jesus was a zealot.

New World Order

Aslan offers a fifth 'proof' that Jesus was a zealot with the claim that Jesus was going to bring in a new world order, which, when put into place, would not only be a radical change from the status quo, but would be so dangerous and revolutionary that Rome would have to respond to it by arresting and executing everyone involved in the endeavor. It seems as though Aslan sees Jesus as Genghis Khan, Alexander the Great, and Attila the Hun all wrapped up in one! (Karen Armstrong in *The Case for God* also uses the phrase 'new world order' in reference to Jesus.) If Rome responded to Jesus' new world order with the intensity Aslan claims, then why did the Roman guard that

165

came to Gethsemane to assist in Jesus' arrest not simply (and easily) gather up the eleven disciples who were there with Jesus and arrest and execute them, too? That would have been a good lesson for anyone else stupid enough to think they could do such a thing. If the eleven were party to Jesus' revolutionary purposes, as horrific as Aslan makes them out to be, you can bet that the local Roman army would have searched high and low for any more of Jesus' revolutionaries once they had arrested their leader. Aslan, as we will see, simply rejects the idea that the Roman guard was involved in Jesus' arrest. But that does not make sense; of course the Roman guard would be involved in Jesus' arrest, if he was the kind of revolutionary Aslan says he was. Be that as it may, Aslan's claim that Jesus was instigating a new world order makes it difficult to take him (Aslan) seriously. How did Aslan come to the conclusion that Jesus envisioned a revolution on such a grand scale? We have seen that Aslan and the JS have accused the Gospel writers of making up most of the sayings that they attributed to Jesus in order to make him into a character of their own design. But we can certainly say the same about Aslan and the JS. Isn't that what they have done? Why is Aslan's idea about Jesus as a zealot any truer than the depiction the Gospels have of Jesus? The Gospels have been shown to be reliable documents; I cannot say the same about Aslan's ideas. We see here the adage that when you reject the truth, you will accept just about anything.

Although Aslan sees Jesus as a zealot and revolutionary who is ready to bring in a new world order, Aslan does not think that Jesus has any real plans as to how he (Jesus) is going to do it. Jesus, according to Aslan, does not have a coherent plan or design that will bring in God's Kingdom to Israel. Jesus does not have a comprehensive outline; he does not have any detailed proposals about the kingdom he wants to usher in. Aslan seems to think that Jesus is just going to 'wing it.' According to Aslan, Jesus was not concerned about how God was going to restore Israel's independence and begin his kingdom here on earth; he just allowed himself to be open to whatever God wanted to do through him. God would determine how; Jesus would just be the conduit through which God would operate. Did Aslan imagine that Jesus was going to go out and rampantly and randomly start a revolution with the hope that God would step in to help him? Certainly, if Jesus were a zealot, he would have at least put up a good fight when Judas and the others came to him in the garden to arrest

166

him. He would have known that that would have been his last opportunity to do so. If he was a zealot and was killed and his followers scattered to the wind, what gave them back their courage so that they could stand up a few days later and tell the people who helped in Jesus' execution that they had killed the Messiah but would be forgiven if they turned to Jesus and accepted him as their Savior? And why did Jesus' disciples not continue the fight that Aslan claims Jesus started, instead of going around preaching salvation and healing people?

Aslan claims that Jesus never really thought of himself as a Messiah; he was just waiting until God used him to bring in God's new world order, which would, if successful, free Israel from Rome's occupation. For Aslan, Jesus is nothing more than a zealot who has been made into a messiah. Aslan once more takes the opportunity to tell us that Jesus had followed John the Baptizer into the desert and accepted him as his mentor/teacher; and now two years have passed since Jesus started his own ministry and, although Jesus has carried on the Baptizer's message about the Kingdom of God, he is now going to expand it into a liberation movement for those who are demoralized and marginalized—the poor peasants who are living on the fringe. Aslan (in his eleventh chapter) sees Jesus traveling around the Galilean towns and villages, promising the people that a new world order is coming. Jesus is preparing the people for God's kingdom. He is gathering them together by the use of his magical healing and parables. He is even letting some of them in on his messianic secret. He is forgiving peoples' sins, thereby showing that the priests are no longer necessary. Jesus chooses four villages, Aslan tells us, to preach his new world order to the poor. These four villages are Nazareth, Capernaum, Bethsaida, and Nain. Aslan is happy to announce that the people in these villages received or accepted Jesus' message of a new world order with great excitement. According to Aslan, Jesus gave hints in his sermons that he was going to have his movement blossom into a full-blown insurrection party that would hopefully destroy Rome's oppression. As we have already seen, Aslan believes Jesus sat down on a mountainside and presented his manifesto known as the Beatitudes that gave a secret message to all the oppressed and afflicted to rise up and join his party.

Aslan has Jesus enter the poor village of Nazareth to preach his new world order message, and Aslan says they are eager to accept it. It did not seem to matter to these Nazarenes that Jesus' message was radical, dangerous, and revolutionary enough that Rome would arrest and execute anyone who joined up with Jesus. They had been waiting for a zealot and here was one preaching a new world order that they could eagerly get behind. There is a problem, however, with this idea. This is the same Nazareth that was offended by Jesus when he said that he was the Anointed One and that they (the Nazarenes) had grown so hard-hearted against God that Gentile nations would be forgiven before they would. The Nazarenes became so upset that they attempted to throw Jesus off a cliff (Lk 4:16-30). So, Jesus' new world order message did not go over very well in Nazareth, as Aslan hoped. Maybe Jesus will do better in another city.

Aslan has Jesus take his new world order message to Nain, where he says it was eagerly received. You may never have heard of Nain, but it is there in Luke's Gospel. Jesus went there, but Luke does not say for how long. What did Jesus do there? Just when he was entering Nain, Jesus encountered a funeral procession. What a great opportunity to preach his new world order message! Instead, he was overcome with sorrow for a widow and her only child who had died and so he raised the young man from the dead and gave him back to his mother (Lk 7:11–17). Jesus may have been in Nain when the Baptizer, in prison, sent two of his disciples to Jesus to ask if he really was the Messiah. The Baptizer needed assurance, and Jesus told John's disciples to report back to him what Jesus was doing. Was he preaching a new world order? No, not yet. He was out healing the blind, the lame, those with skin diseases, and the deaf; dead people were being brought back to life; and poor people were hearing the Good News. While still in Nain, Jesus was invited to a Pharisee's house to eat. At the house a woman cried at Jesus' feet and dried his feet with her hair. She was obviously very distraught about her sins. The Pharisee, of course, thought that Jesus should know that this woman was a terrible sinner and should be shunned. But Jesus gave an interesting parable about how grateful a person with a large debt is when that debt is forgiven. Then he graciously turned to the woman and told her that she was forgiven (Lk 7:36-50). After that, Jesus left Nain. No new world order message there.

What about Capernaum or Bethsaida? Did people in those cities eagerly receive the new world order message from Jesus? Well, not exactly. Matthew tells us that Jesus denounced Capernaum and Bethsaida and some of the other cities where he had worked his miracles because they had not repented; that is, they had not turned away from their sins. Jesus said the punishment would be horrible for Bethsaida because, if the miracles that he did there had been done in Tyre and Sidon (Gentile cities), those Gentiles would have repented. Jesus said that judgment day will be better for Tyre and Sidon than for Bethsaida. Then Jesus said the same thing about Capernaum, that they had rejected him and had not turned from their sins, and that they would be worse off on judgment day than Sodom (Mt 11:20–24). Jesus offended the people of Capernaum and Bethsaida, just as he had the people of Nazareth. Only Nain seemed to do okay with Jesus' visit, but it looks like Jesus missed the opportunity to preach his new world order message there. At this rate, Jesus is not going to get anyone to join his insurrection. Aslan has failed to show that Jesus had a new world order that he hoped the marginalized people would accept. Aslan has failed to show that Jesus was a zealot.

The Tribute to Caesar

Aslan's sixth 'proof' that Jesus was a zealot is also found in his second prologue. The evidence, says Aslan, is in the answer Jesus gives when he is asked about the imperial tax paid to Caesar (see Mt 22:17). The imperial tax was a special tax imposed upon Rome's subjects, like the Israelites, and not on its own citizens (NIV note). Aslan believes (and repeats it often in his book) that when Jesus answered this question about paying the tax to Caesar, Jesus was really saying he was a zealot. We will get to Jesus' answer in just a moment. Let's first take a look at the broader context regarding Jesus' statement about paying the imperial tax. Jesus had entered Jerusalem in kingly fashion on a donkey and, on the next day, chased the moneychangers out of the Temple courtyard. He stayed the night outside of Jerusalem in a nearby city called Bethany. When he returned to Jerusalem after the Temple cleansing the religious leaders approached Jesus and wanted to know on what or whose authority he chased out the moneychangers the previous day. Jesus told them he would answer their question if they would answer one of his; they were not willing to answer the question he asked them because in answering it they would entrap themselves (see Mk 11:27-33). Since they were unwilling to answer his question, Jesus gave them several parables that exhibited their hypocrisy (see Mt 21:28-22:14). The Pharisees left in anger and planned ways they could trap Jesus with his own words. They returned and said to Jesus: "Teacher, we know that you are a man of integrity and that you teach the way of God in accordance with the truth. You aren't swayed by others, because you pay no attention to who they are. Tell us then, what is your opinion? Is it right to pay the imperial tax to Caesar or not?" (NIV, Mt 22:16–17). Jesus knew they were trying to trap him, to make him say something for which they could arrest him on the spot. He even called them on their attempts by asking: "Why are you trying to trap me?" He asked for a coin that had the Emperor's image on it, and they handed him one. Jesus answered: "Give the emperor what belongs to the emperor, and give God what belongs to God" ("Scripture is taken from GOD'S WORD®. © 1995 God's Word to the Nations. Used by permission of Baker Publishing Group." Mk 12:17). Aslan declares that when the religious leaders asked Jesus if it was "right to pay the imperial tax to Caesar or not?" that they were really asking Jesus if he was or was not a zealot. Aslan believes Jesus' answer told them he was a zealot. Aslan insists the religious leaders had no doubt that Jesus was a zealot, an insurrectionist, when he told them to give to Caesar what is his, and give God what is God's.

Aslan says that Jesus' answer would be all the authorities would need to label him a *lēstēs*, i.e., a zealot. Aslan would have us believe that the religious leaders really tricked Jesus on that question. It looks like Jesus was so gullible that he did not know his answer about paying taxes was going to get him killed. Let's take a look at the Greek word *lēstēs* that Aslan uses for Jesus. Zodhiates mentions two Greek words for robber—one is *lēstēs* and the other is *kléptēs* (we use this word to form kleptomaniac). *Lēstēs* is the word to describe a common robber who often uses violence to subdue his victim. The *kléptēs* robber uses stealth, he steals secretly so as to not get caught. In this sense, Judas was a *kléptēs*, pilfering from the money pouch, without doing any violence to anyone (see Jn 12:6). Mark in his Gospel (15:7) describes Barabbas (the man exchanged for Jesus when Jesus was standing trial before Pilate) as an insurrectionist, using the Greek word *stasiastēs*, which means a rebel, a revolutionist, someone who stirs up sedition; in other words, a zealot. If Aslan really wanted to identify Jesus with the zealots he should have used the Greek word *stasiastēs*, and not the

170

Greek word *lēstēs*. It is true that there were lots of robbers and bandits in Palestine in the first century, but isn't that true in any century? Did Jesus give any indication that he identified with these robbers? Jesus told a parable that would indicate to his listeners who our neighbor is, who the person is that we should help and/or befriend. That famous parable is called the Good Samaritan (see Lk 10:30-37). It is a parable that even the Jesus Seminar accepts as authentic. It is about a person who is attacked by a robber, a *lēstēs*, who steals his money and beats him up. Now, by speaking this parable, Jesus is telling us not to be a *lēstēs*, but Aslan tells us that this is exactly what Jesus is. Aslan prefers this zealot (*lēstēs*) Jesus to the Christ-of-faith that he thinks the Gospel writers invented. Aslan thinks that by saying "Give the emperor what belongs to the emperor, and give God what belongs to God," Jesus is identifying with the zealots and claiming to be one. I am not sure why Aslan prefers to give such a complex interpretation to Jesus' reply about taxes, rather than simply taking the statement at face value. (Well, actually, I do know why: Aslan needs to find Gospel passages that he can manipulate to help prove his point that Jesus was a zealot, even if those passages are not really good ones to do that.)

To be sure, for the Jew and the Christian, everything belongs to God; God is the one who gives us what we need. Those who trust God know that he is worthy to be trusted. The Jews in Jesus' time clearly did not like living under subjection to the Roman authorities. They did not even like handling the coins that had the emperor's likeness on it. But Jesus took the coin that had the emperor's likeness and used it in his example of how we are to live in society. Many of us find ourselves in situations we would prefer not to be in; how we act in those situations will give or not give glory to God. Jesus is telling his listeners, and those who came to trick him, that the Jews were subjects to Rome, and as such it was their duty to pay taxes, whether they liked it or not. Jesus does not fall for the Pharisee's tricks and, therefore, does not take either side of the issue; he denies that there is an either/or choice between Caesar and God. Jesus claims that Rome has the right to tax its subjects. Jesus does not use this as an opportunity to shout some rebel yell and demand Israel's independence. His reply, therefore, is simple and wise, and if he had meant by his reply what Aslan wishes he meant, then the Pharisees would have arrested him on the spot and taken him to Herod. In his reply, however, Jesus is showing our responsibility as God's children to honor the authority we are under.

Paul echoes Jesus' words here in his epistle to the Roman Christians when he tells them to honor the government and pay their taxes (see Rom 13). Peter says the same thing in the second chapter of his first epistle. As Christians and citizens, we are to fulfill our obligation to the country in which we live. The only conflict that arises is when someone in authority demands that we disobey God. God always comes above worldly kingdoms. Jesus reminded his listeners of that by adding, "Give to God his due," but Jesus did not mean by it that he was a zealot. While Aslan maintains that Jesus shows that he is a zealot and therefore has plans to overthrow Roman authority by making a statement to give Caesar his due and God his due, the conclusion Aslan arrives at is simply not justified. Again, let me make it very plain. Since the religious leaders were trying to trap Jesus with the Caesar tribute question so that they could arrest him, if he had given the answer Aslan thinks he does, revealing that he was a zealot, the Pharisees would have immediately arrested him. Since they did not arrest him on insurrection charges when he gave the "give to Caesar" reply, the reply did not, therefore, reveal that Jesus was an insurrectionist. Aslan is mistaken, and his attempt to try to use it to 'prove' his theory is rather weak. It is also important to note, during this episode, that when the Pharisees approached Jesus they said, "Teacher, we know that you are an honest man and that you teach the truth about God's way" (NCV, Mt 22:16). In other words, they acknowledged that Jesus was Torah-observant; he would not have been called a teacher or rabbi if he was not. Jesus did not reject the Torah; he lived accordingly as any other Jew would have, and he was acknowledged for it.

Aslan has not done a good job in trying to convince us that Jesus was a zealot. It is more reliable to accept the Gospels' portrayal of Jesus as the Messiah, the one who came to die for our sins and rose on the third day, unless, of course, seeing you do not perceive and hearing you do not understand.

Chapter Nine: Was Jesus a Bigot?

Aslan reminds us (in his tenth chapter) that if we really want to uncover what Jesus himself truly believed, then we must not forget one fundamental fact, and that is that Jesus of Nazareth was foremost a Jew. Because Jesus was a Jew, that would mean, according to Aslan, that Jesus was only concerned about his fellow Jews; Israel was all that mattered to Jesus. To prove his point, Aslan quotes from Matthew 15:24 where Jesus said, "I was sent only to the lost sheep of the nation of Israel" ("Scripture is taken from GOD'S WORD®. © 1995 God's Word to the Nations. Used by permission of Baker Publishing Group."). To show that Jesus only cared for his fellow Jews, and that Jesus' attitude toward his fellow Jews was typical of all Jews since the beginnings of Judaism, Aslan attempts to demonstrate that that xenophobic position was commanded in the Hebrew Scriptures. Aslan claims that when the Hebrew Scriptures admonish the Jew to "love your neighbor as you love yourself" (see Lev 19:18), it was treated as a command that was only applied to one's fellow Israelite. It was only how Jews were to treat other Jews. For Aslan, every Jew, including during Jesus' time, believed and acted as though the "neighbor" they were to love was only their fellow Jew. As we have seen, Aslan has a habit of making blatant statements, and then tries to find Gospel passages that 'prove' his point; but when you actually look at the passages in their context or with comparative passages, you find where and how Aslan has greatly erred. I do not think that Jesus being a Jew comes as any surprise to anyone. Yes, Jesus was a Jew. God was not going to use any existing group or race to bring the "seed of the woman" promised to our first parents into the world. He took a righteous man named Abraham who produced a son (Isaac) who would create a race—the Hebrews or Jews—through which the Messiah would enter the world. The Messiah had to be a Jew. Jesus was indeed a Jew, but did he only care about Jews? Was his ministry only to Jews? Aslan says that Jesus was only concerned about his own people, the Jews. Israel was the only nation Jesus cared about. Aslan attempts to portray Jesus as a bigoted Jew, and that is a serious accusation. You may remember that earlier I talked about the religious leaders rejecting Jesus as the "Son of David," the Messiah, and instead accused him of healing through satanic powers rather than by God's power through the Holy Spirit. Jesus had offered the kingdom of heaven to the Jewish people, but

173

many of them had rejected his offer. As we have already seen, God had made a promise to Abraham that through him (Abraham) all the nations (Gentiles) would be blessed (Gen. 12:3). According to many Hebrew Scripture prophecies, it would be through the Jewish nation that the good news would go out to the Gentiles, to bring them into the fold, to bring them into a proper relationship with their Creator when the Messiah arrived. If Jesus was rejected by the Jews as their Messiah, how would the Gentiles enter into the kingdom of heaven? Jesus would take care of that personally by taking the good news to the Gentiles himself (see Fruchtenbaum's *Messianic Christology*). We saw that both Jews and Gentiles were invited to hear the Sermon on the Mount (Mt 5-7). The Gospels show that news about Jesus had spread into Syria and the Decapolis, which were areas of non-Jewish, Greek-speaking people. These Gentiles brought their sick for Jesus to heal and he did not refuse to heal them. Not long after Jesus gave his mountain sermon he traveled over to Gadara, a town in the Decapolis, which was Gentile territory. The miracle he performed there was so intense that the people in that area asked him to leave (see Mt 8:28-34). Since Aslan quoted from Matthew 15:24, we need to look at what is happening in the context of the passage in order to determine if Aslan is correct in his depiction of Jesus. So, let's take a look at Matthew 15.

The Canaanite Woman

Shortly after the religious leaders blatantly rejected Jesus as the Son of David—the Messiah—and relegated his miracles and his kingdom to satanic powers, he left Israel and went into another Gentile area, the region of Tyre and Sidon (Mt 15:21). By going into Gentile territory, Jesus was fulfilling the prophecies of Isaiah 42:1-6 and 49:6. In those passages, Isaiah says that the Messiah would be a light for the nations in order to save people all over the world. Tyre and Sidon were two Phoenician cities on the Mediterranean coastline to the northwest of Galilee, an area under Greek influence. Interestingly, Isaiah 42:4 says, "The coastlands wait for his [the Messiah's] teachings." While in the coastland region of Tyre, a Canaanite woman from that area approached Jesus for the purpose of healing her daughter. Jesus was staying at a house there and it appears that his lineage was well-known, as was his reputation as a miracle worker. The Canaanite woman lost no time in bringing her demon-possessed daughter to

Jesus' attention. Jesus ignored the woman's first appeal to him because that request was made on the wrong basis. She had come to the house where Jesus was staying and asked (basically demanded) Jesus to have mercy on her because her daughter was tormented by a demon. She kept calling Jesus, "Lord, Son of David" (Mt. 15:22). The disciples wanted to send her away, but Jesus was waiting for her to make her appeal correctly. She had referred to him only as Israel's Messiah; "Son of David" was a term a Jew would use, so she was basing her appeal on Jesus' relationship to Israel as the Son of David, a relationship which was founded on God's covenant with David. It is in this context that Jesus responded to her when he said, "I was sent only to the lost sheep of the nation of Israel" (Mt. 15:24). One can imagine the woman standing in the middle of the room where Jesus was relaxing after a long journey, maybe with hands on her hips, demanding that Jesus heal her daughter. She had heard the news about him, and she wanted him to do what she wanted. When Jesus told her he was ministering only to Jews the woman obviously became distraught. The point that Jesus was making to her was that the Messiah's task was primarily to make himself known to the Jews; his first priority was to the Jewish people, not the Gentiles. (Gentiles would also be blessed by the Messiah, but that was to come after his resurrection.) Maybe she momentarily thought all was lost, but then she responded correctly to Jesus. She realized she was not to come to him as if she were a Jew, because she was not. She had to come to him as she was, a Gentile. She bowed before him and said, "Lord, help me." She was now appealing to his mercy and grace; this was the proper approach to God's Messiah. Again, Jesus tested her and said, "It's not right to take the children's food and throw it to the dogs" (Mt 15:26). (By the way, the word for dog here in the Greek is "puppy." Jesus was making a point, but he was being gentle about it.) The woman's answer is just what Jesus wanted to hear: "You're right, Lord. But even the dogs [puppies] eat scraps that fall from their masters' tables" (Mt 15:27). Jesus told the woman that because of her correct response, and her faith, he would heal her daughter. When the woman got home she found her daughter was healed. (This was the third long-distance healing that Jesus performed.) Another interesting thing to note in Jesus' dealings with the Canaanite woman is that Jesus commended her for her "great faith" (Mt 15:28); the other time Jesus noted a person's great faith was to another Gentile, a Roman soldier (Mt 8:5-13). The two people who Jesus said had great faith were

175

Gentiles. (I am grateful to Fruchtenbaum's *Messianic Christology* for information in this section about the Canaanite woman.)

The Good News Taken to all the Nations

We see in Matthew's narrative about the healing of the Canaanite woman's daughter that although the Messiah brings the kingdom of heaven to the Jew first (it is why God created the Jewish people through Abraham), it will ultimately extend to every nation. The disciples got to see, first-hand, the faith that a Gentile woman could display. Peter would remember this when he was called to go to a Gentile's house and speak to the family there about Jesus (see Acts 10). One must bear in mind that Matthew's readers were primarily Jewish. Matthew showed his readers that Jews do not possess the Messiah all to themselves. He is for everyone. Unfortunately, it was this inclusive concept of the Messiah that provoked many of the Jews to completely reject Jesus as their Messiah by the second century. (See M.S. Mills' *The Life of Christ*.) Now Aslan was hoping to use Jesus' statement that he came "only to the lost sheep of Israel" to show how Jesus, the bigoted Jew, wanted nothing to do with Gentiles. But the passage Aslan chooses to 'prove' that Jesus was a bigoted zealot for Israel actually showed Jesus' compassion for a Canaanite woman, a Gentile. The fact that Jesus even paid attention to this Gentile woman and healed her daughter shows that Jesus did not "solely" attend to his fellow Jew. We also see that Jesus had spoken to another woman, a Samaritan, and shared with her the fact that he was the Messiah. He and his disciples stayed in her town for two days, telling them about the good news (see Jn 4). Jews did not actually see the Samaritans as their Jewish brothers. Therefore, Jesus did not attend exclusively to Jews, and Israel was not all that mattered to Jesus, as Aslan would have you believe. Salvation, the kingdom of heaven, started with the Jew; that was God's plan. It had to start somewhere. But Jesus' mission to preach the good news of the kingdom of heaven was not only for Jews. Jesus would always give the Jews the first opportunity to accept Him as their Messiah, but his message extended to all people. The Kingdom of God is open to people of all nations; this was the promise God made to Abraham (Gen 12:3). Paul understood this when he told the Roman Christians that the good news "brings salvation to everyone who believes [in Jesus]: first to the Jew, then to the Gentile" (NIV, Rom 1:16). But he also reminded them that there "will be trouble and distress for every human being who does evil: first for the Jew, then for the Gentile (NIV, Rom 2:9).

Since Aslan wanted to use the passage in Matthew to prove that the bigoted Jesus felt his mission was "only to the lost sheep of Israel," let's look at a few other passages where Jesus uses the word 'sheep.' After healing a blind person, Jesus hinted to the Pharisees that they too were blind—spiritually blind. Then he told them that he was the gate of salvation for the sheep (see Jn 10:7-18). He told them that he was the good shepherd, and they would have immediately thought of King David's poem that said "The LORD is my shepherd, I lack nothing" (NIV, Ps. 23:1). Jesus continued by saying that a good shepherd lays down his life for his sheep, which is what Jesus knew he came to do; that was his mission: to lay down his life for those who would believe in him for salvation. Then he repeated that he was the good shepherd and his sheep knew his voice. He was letting the Pharisees know that since they had rejected him it proved that they had not heard the voice of God; all their outward righteousness was not going to save them. Who are these sheep Jesus referred to? Are they only the lost sheep of Israel? No! Jesus then says, "I have other sheep that are not of this sheep pen. I must bring them also. They too will listen to my voice, and there shall be one flock and one shepherd" (NIV, vs. 16). These "other sheep" are Gentiles, fulfilling the promise that God made to Abraham that the nations would be blessed through him. Jesus then tells the Pharisees that he is going to lay down his life for his sheep and then take it up again; in other words, he will be killed and rise from the dead. (When Jesus was finished saying this, some of the people once again accused Jesus of being demonized.) After Jesus' resurrection, he met with his disciples over a forty-day period in both Jerusalem and Galilee. It was in Jerusalem that Jesus told them that they would receive power from the Holy Spirit to become Jesus' "witnesses in Jerusalem, and in all Judea and Samaria, and to the ends of the earth" (NIV, Acts 1:8). The "ends of the earth" includes Gentiles. In Galilee, Jesus told his disciples that he possessed all authority in heaven and on earth and that they were to go and make disciples of all nations, "baptizing them in the name of the Father and of the Son and of the Holy Spirit, and teaching them to obey everything I have commanded you" (NIV, Mt 28:18–20). These passages show that Jesus, as a Jew, would start with Israel in proclaiming his message of salvation, a message that announced that

177

the Kingdom of God was near at hand. But Jesus did not stop there. We see that he not only ventured into Gentile territory and proclaimed the good news there; he also commissioned his disciples to take the good news to all the nations. The process was: to the Jew first, and then to the Gentile. Aslan is mistaken to think the good news that Jesus proclaimed was solely to be for Israel.

Does "Love Your Neighbor" Have Ethnic Restrictions?

Aslan also tries to prove that, as a Jew, Jesus would adhere to the dictum to "love your neighbor as yourself," as only applying to his fellow Jews. Aslan believes the Scriptural command to love one's neighbor was restricted only to Jews; it was how they were to relate to one another. Of course, we know that an expert in Mosaic Law actually asked Jesus who his neighbor was; the man was looking for a good, clear definition. So Jesus gave the man, and the others standing around, the parable which we call The Good Samaritan (see Lk 10:25-37). In the parable Jesus said a man went from Jerusalem to Jericho and was attacked by robbers and left for dead. Jesus does not identify the nationality of the man; he could have been a foreigner (a Gentile) in Jerusalem on business. Jesus said it was robbers who hurt the man, showing he did not particularly care for that group of people (and yet Aslan keeps trying to put Jesus in with their crowd). A priest sees the half-dead man and passes him by, and so does a Levite. A Samaritan sees him and takes care of him. Jesus told the crowd that one's response to others should be just like the Samaritan's. Why did Jesus use a Samaritan in his parable and not a righteous Jew? Why did Jesus go to the Decapolis—a Gentile territory—to preach and heal there, if he thought he was to show love only to his fellow Jews? Aslan says that to the Israelites, as well as to Jesus' community in first-century Palestine, "neighbor" meant one's fellow Jews. Maybe to first-century Jews the word "neighbor" meant just another Jew, but not to Jesus, and not according to the Hebrew Scriptures either. By his words and deeds, Jesus taught his first-century listeners that everyone is our "neighbor." There are many passages in the Hebrew Scriptures that warn the Israelites to treat foreigners (Gentiles) kindly, and to remember that they too were once foreigners in Egypt. In Numbers 15:15f, God told the Israelites that each community was to have the same laws and regulations apply to both the Israelites and the foreigners (Gentiles) who resided among them. The Israelites could not make one set of laws for themselves and tougher laws for foreigners. God said: "You and the foreigner shall be the same before the Lord" (NIV, Nu 15:15). Foreigners who settled in the land and learned to embrace Israel's ways could gain entry into Israelite social life, which would provide them with greater economic benefits. Serving within Israelite households would also provide a safe haven for any foreigner. It was not to be an oppressive setting, but one that offered economic and social stability. God constantly reminded Israel that they were strangers and aliens in Egypt (Exod. 22:21; 23:9; Lev. 19:34; Deut. 5:15; 10:19; 15:15; 16:12; 24:18, 22), and this memory was to shape Israel's treatment of strangers in their own land. The passage in Deuteronomy 10:18f tells us that God "loves foreigners and gives them food and clothes," and so the Israelites should also love foreigners. According to Israel's civil law, the stranger living in Israel had the same legal rights as the native Israelite. God exhorted Israelites to show concern even for their personal enemies. Instead of hostility, God commanded the Israelites to love and show concern for the foreigners in their midst. "Foreigners living among you will be like your own people. Love them as you love yourself, because you were foreigners living in Egypt" ("Scripture is taken from GOD'S WORD®. © 1995 God's Word to the Nations. Used by permission of Baker Publishing Group." Lev 19:33f). The command to love the foreigner and to treat them the same way as a citizen was rather unique when compared with how other ancient Near East countries treated foreigners. (Some information gleaned from *Christian Apologetics*.) Aslan is mistaken to think that the stipulation to "love one's neighbor" only applied to one's fellow Jew, and that Israel was to care nothing for non-Jews. Aslan cannot, with any honesty, use Jesus' Jewishness or the commandment to love one's neighbor as examples or proofs that Jesus just stuck to his kind and did not care for Gentiles. One final note here: If God did not care for foreigners, then the book of Ruth would not be a part of the Hebrew Scriptures. Metaphorically, Ruth shows how we are all, in a sense, foreigners to God, estranged by sin, and how his love for us redeems us and brings us into his kingdom. God had taken this foreigner, Ruth, and placed her in the lineage of the Messiah.

Is Jesus Above the Law?

Aslan is not finished making comments about Jesus and his Jewishness. He claims that Christians who see Jesus as the literal Son of God ignore the fact that Jesus was Jewish. But that is not true. Christians have no problem accepting Jesus as a Jew and actually point out the fact of Jesus' Jewishness whenever anti-Semitism rears its ugly head. Aslan claims that if Jesus is of divine essence, if he is the Son of God, then Jesus stands above the law, that he does not have to be concerned with a specific custom. One wonders if this is Aslan's definition of being divine—being above the law? Aslan appears to suggest that if Jesus is divine then he does not have to adhere to or obey any laws. In other words, Jesus had no obligation to obey Roman laws or Mosaic laws. Is this how Aslan sees the God of Israel as well? God, being divine, does not have to obey any laws? God could not be a righteous judge who will hold those accountable who have acted wickedly if he himself acted wickedly. He could not demand that we live according to some standard of right if he himself did not. Unlike humans, God has all the facts and can judge justly. The apostle John Zebedee tells us in his first epistle that God is love, and the evidence that God has shown his love to us is the fact that he sent his one and only Son into the world so that we could live (i.e., have real life) through him (1 Jn 4:8–9). God is love. That is his nature. God cannot not love. He proved his love to humankind by sending his Son to die in our place. Murder is not wrong simply because God says it is wrong. God does not whimsically say murder is wrong one day and that it is okay the next. God does not choose which things are moral and which things are immoral. Murder, lying, stealing—these are wrong in themselves, not just because God says they are wrong. David Noebel tells us that the Christian view of law produces a legal system that does not fluctuate according to our whims and preferences; rather, it remains constant and therefore just. Noebel says the source of all divine law is the character and nature of God. The moral order proceeds from and reflects the character of God—His holiness, justice, truth, love, and mercy. In God's legal system, everyone is judged by the same standard of justice (see Noebel's *Understanding the Times*). God is not one to act differently at different times, depending upon his mood at the time, so that we do not know how he is going to react, or how we are supposed to respond. We do not have to worry if he is going to hit us or hug us. He is not sporadic; saying one thing one time and a different thing another. We can trust him, unlike the Greek and Roman gods who acted without consistency. God is the same yesterday, today, and forever (see Heb 13:8). One must keep this in mind in order to understand Jewish history. The God of the Hebrew

180

Scriptures is not any different from the God of the New Testament. God is able to balance mercy, justice, love, peace, compassion, etc.

Jesus said he did not come to abolish the Law, but to fulfill it (Mt 5:17). The Mosaic Law is unable to justify us (i.e., regard us as guiltless); what it does do is show how much we are in need of justification (i.e., how guilty we are). The Law stands as a banner showing that we do not measure up. The Law stands as our accuser because we cannot fulfill it; we cannot do what it tells us to do in order to stand righteous before God. We fail too often at trying to live up to the standard that is the Law. It is a mirror showing us our faults and where we fail. No one living by the Law will be justified by it before God, because at some point we will have broken it. That is why no one can be saved by the good works they do. Along with the good works will be lots of bad works as well. There is no amount of good works that will bring us into God's kingdom. It is recognizing our inability to meet God's standard that is the first step to acknowledging our need for God's grace to come through to help us. The Pharisees and Law teachers during Jesus' time thought they were righteous enough simply because of their position in society and because they did not think of themselves as common sinners. Jesus told them the parable we call The Prodigal Son to show the Pharisees and Law teachers that they were just as far from God as the common sinner. The Pharisees and scribes and Law teachers became angry enough at Jesus, after he told them this parable, that they plotted to kill him because he had revealed to them their hypocrisy and sin and showed them that they could not rely on their own righteousness to enter God's kingdom. Jesus was not concerned about 'rocking the boat.' He did not allow people to become comfortable in their religious state, not the Pharisees and not the common sinner. The Pharisees, scribes and Law Teachers were constantly tyrannizing the so-called common sinner with all kinds of traditions and customs and trivial matters. So Jesus had no problem putting the Pharisees in their place, which they probably had not experienced before. He called them hypocrites, snakes, and whitewashed tombs, and told them they would have a rather rude awakening some day (Mt 23:13-39). The Pharisees had mirrored the problem Isaiah noted in his day—The Lord says: "These people worship me with their mouths, and honor me with their lips, but their hearts are far from me. Their worship is based on nothing but human rules" (NCV; 29:13).

181

Jesus came to fulfill the Law, to live a life that measured up to its standard. The Jews in Jesus' day had tried to live according to the letter of the law, but had forgotten the spirit of the law. Jesus showed them that the way they interpreted the Law was incorrect. Jesus told them they were missing the most important aspect of the Law—the spiritual aspect, the attitude and thoughts that go with the keeping of the Law. That is why we see places in the Gospels where Jesus says, "You have heard it said . . . but I say." Here are some examples: "You have heard that it was said to the people long ago, 'You shall not murder, and anyone who murders will be subject to judgment.' But I tell you that anyone who is angry with a brother or sister will be subject to judgment" (NIV, Mt 5:21f). Jesus said our inner anger is a form of murder; if not controlled it can lead to actual murder; that murder is an outward result of an inner condition. "You have heard that it was said, 'You shall not commit adultery.' But I tell you that anyone who looks at a woman lustfully has already committed adultery with her in his heart" (NIV, Mt 5:27f). Again, Jesus shows that before the act of adultery is committed the person is lusting inside. It is what is happening inside the person's thoughts, mind and heart that prompt the action. The sin does not start at the action; it starts within the person. "You have heard that it was said, 'Love your neighbor and hate your enemy.' But I tell you love your enemies and pray for those who persecute you" (NIV, Mt 5:43f; see also Rom 12:20). Here is an excellent rebuttal to Aslan's using the "love your neighbor" to suggest that Jesus, because he was a Jew, only loved other Jews and wanted to destroy his enemies, the Romans. Jesus taught the crowds to love their enemies—the Romans—and to pray for those who were oppressing them and persecuting them. In fact, Roman soldiers were allowed to "press a person into service," i.e., force someone to assist them, for one mile. Jesus, showing he was no zealot, no revolutionary who would take any opportunity to do harm to the oppressors, tells his listeners to "go an extra mile" (see Mt 5:41).

One other example is necessary. The Pharisees criticized Jesus' disciples for not washing their hands before they ate; in not washing their hands they had violated Jewish traditions and customs. Jesus told the Pharisees that what was needed was not an outward cleansing of the hands, but an inward cleansing of their heart. Jesus told them, "Evil thoughts, murder, adultery [and other] sexual sins, stealing, lying, and cursing come from within. These are the things that make a person unclean" ("Scripture is taken from GOD'S WORD®. © 1995 God's Word to the Nations. Used by permission of Baker Publishing Group." Mt 15:19–20). So we must distinguish between the Law of God and societal customs. Customs are generally devised and created by humans and are not written in stone, so to speak. We must distinguish between laws given us by God, which we are to keep, and customs made by humans, which are not necessarily binding, although one can be ostracized for not following the local customs. Therefore, accepting Jesus as divine—a Person within the Triune God—does not mean he stands above any particular law, as Aslan thinks. Jesus followed the stipulations of the Law; he was able to ask the Pharisees to name a sin that he committed (see Jn 8:46). As the Son of Man, he was able to live like Adam was supposed to: in complete submission to God the Father. Sinless, without blemish, he was able to offer himself as the ultimate and final atonement—sacrifice—for sin. Jesus came to fulfill the Law's requirement for sacrificial atonement, thereby making animal sacrifices no longer necessary.

For the early Christian, the relevant query concerning the 613 Jewish laws in the Hebrew Scriptures was deciding which ones no longer applied to the Christian lifestyle. Would a follower of Jesus still be obligated to practice the Mosaic Law? There were some Christians living in the first century who had decided that since they were saved by God's grace they could outwardly live the way they wanted to, that laws (or the Law) did not apply to them. Paul told the Roman Christians that faith does not abolish or nullify the Mosaic Law; the Law was still to be supported and upheld (3:31). Peter reminded his readers that although they were to live and enjoy the freedom they had in Jesus, they were not to use that freedom to sin (1 Pe 2:16). Certainly, not all the laws contained in the Hebrew legal/ceremonial system were applicable to the Christian life. Jewish Christians no longer had to go to the Temple (before it was destroyed in 70 A.D.) and offer sacrifices for their sins. Jesus had been the ultimate sacrifice and there was no need for continuing that practice (the book of Hebrews explains this). Jewish Christians also had to make a decision about circumcision and its application to their fellow Gentile Christians, which they did do by saying it was no longer necessary. First-century Gentile Christians, however, were given Torah-observant restrictions about what to eat (see Acts 15:29). Friedman shows that there is "ample evidence from the four Gospels that Jesus was a Jewish man who lived his earthly life in absolute loyalty to the sacred covenants that God made with his people, Israel. Jesus was a Torah-observant Jewish man" (see *They Loved the Torah*). For the Christian, faith and obedience goes hand-in-hand (see Bonhoeffer's *Cost of Discipleship*, chapter eight). The Law cannot save us by the doing of it, but it is not to be abolished either. Jesus fulfilled the Law so that his followers can now, with the Holy Spirit's help, fulfill the Law too, i.e., perform what God commands. The ultimate law—the Ten Commandments—is still to be honored and obeyed.

A Deplorable View of God

After accusing Jesus of being a bigoted Jew who only allowed his fellow Jews to be a part of the kingdom he was offering, Aslan then becomes quite vitriolic in describing the God that Jesus served. According to Aslan, the God Jesus served showed that Jesus was not the nice, carefree peasant and charming preacher that we think he was. Aslan claims that we cannot deny the fact that the God Jesus knew, served, and worshipped—the God of the Hebrews—is a horrible God. Aslan envisions the Hebrew God as a hate-filled moral monster akin to the views of popular modern atheists like Dawkins, Hitchens, Stenger, Harris, and others, who pull certain verses out of context to show how terrible God is. Aslan provides us with four examples (in his tenth chapter) that are meant to reveal the kind of God Jesus served and worshipped, a God who was deplorable.

God as a "man of war"

Let's look then at the examples and passages Aslan uses to show the kind of God Jesus supposedly worshipped. The first passage is Exodus 15:3; it says God is a "man of war" (ESV). Now, some translations (NIV, GW, NCV) say God is "a warrior." The word warrior best describes the idea of the Hebrew, rather than the phrase "man of war." What is happening in this passage where God is being referred to as a warrior, or man of war? The nation Israel has been in Egypt for about four hundred years. At first, the relationship between the two nations was a good one; but after a while the Egyptians began to enslave the Israelites. In this slave condition the Israelites called out to God—the God of Abraham, Isaac and Jacob—and prayed for deliverance. When

Moses and Aaron asked the Pharaoh for liberty, the Egyptian king oscillated by agreeing to give the Israelites the freedom to leave and then taking it back. This went on until God sent ten plagues to Egypt—most of which represented a particular god the Egyptians worshipped and/or depended upon. Finally, Pharaoh allowed the Israelites to leave and return to their land. When the Israelites came to a water crossing, the Egyptian army, which had decided to pursue them, arrived with the intent to kill all of the Israelites. God parted the waters and the Israelites crossed over to the other side, but when Pharaoh's army followed, the waters came together and they were drowned. Safe from Pharaoh's army, Moses and the Israelites sang a song to the Lord. You can read the entire song in Exodus 15:1–18. The Israelites sing this song in praise to God for rescuing them. They sing that God is their Savior. They sing, "The Lord is a warrior" (or man of war). This is the passage Aslan quotes (i.e., pulls out of context) to show how terrible God is. The Israelites sing in praise to God for protecting them and rescuing them from Pharaoh's army, and in singing their praise to God they call him a warrior (man of war). The Israelites sing, "With your unlimited majesty, you destroyed those who attacked you." In other words, God protected his people from being attacked and slaughtered. Wouldn't any father do this for his children? In the song, the Israelites remember the hatred of Pharaoh and his army. Pharaoh's army had said, 'I'll pursue them! I'll catch up with them! I'll divide the loot! I'll take all I want! I'll use my sword! I'll take all they have!' Pharaoh was going to utterly destroy the Israelites; God had to protect them. He did to them what they were going to do to his children. In their song, the Israelites sing, "You are glorious because of your holiness and awe-inspiring because of your splendor." They sing, "Lovingly, you will lead the people you have saved. Powerfully, you will guide them to your holy dwelling." ("Scripture is taken from GOD'S WORD®. © 1995 God's Word to the Nations. Used by permission of Baker Publishing Group.") Whenever the Hebrew Scriptures portray God as a warrior (man of war), it does so in relation to God's opposition to evil. God certainly has the right to defend his people from those who mean to do them harm. So we see that Aslan uses Exodus 15:3 to show how terrible God is that he would be referred to as a warrior, or man of war; a passage where we clearly see God's love and protection for his people, Israel.

The "Canaan Conquest"

In Aslan's second example he accuses the Hebrew God of frequently demanding the slaughter of every foreigner—man, woman, and child—who lived in the Promised Land. Aslan does not give any specific Scripture passages for this claim, but it seems obvious that he is making reference to the "Canaan Conquest" found in the books of Deuteronomy and Joshua. The episodes described in these two books, especially Joshua, are very difficult to read and understand for modern readers. In the light of twentieth century wars, we have seen too often the monsters who attempted to eliminate whole groups of peoples and races—Lenin, Stalin, Hitler, Pol Pot, Mao, Rwandan Hutu, and contemporary terrorists. Can Joshua (and God) be compared to these modern monsters? Before looking at the "Canaan Conquest," please allow me a slight digression in order to show how God's mercy was revealed in specific time periods. After the Fall and before the Flood (see Gen 3:1-6:8), there was a time period of immense patience on the part of God. His mercy and forbearance gave humans a lot of leeway. Individual sin was rarely punished. We see an example of this when God protected Cain, the first murderer, so he would not be signaled out for abuse (Gen 4:15). As various cultures and civilizations developed, humans grew more and more wicked, taking advantage of God's mercy. They had so completely turned against God and become such vile creatures that he decided to start over. So the time period between Cain and the Flood was a time when God showed extreme mercy and patience. The more mercy and patience God showed, the more wicked and evil the people became. While Noah was building his boat (the ark), God had given the people 120 years to repent, which they did not do. Those 120 years was a time period of warning, letting the people know that God would punish them for the wicked things they were doing. They ignored this warning. So the cause of the Flood was the immense wickedness of the people. Noah and his family were the only ones righteous enough to be saved. After the Flood, Noah's three sons, Shem, Ham and Japheth, had children of their own. One of Ham's sons was named Canaan and the land he acquired was along the eastern Mediterranean shore. Abraham came from Shem's line—a people who would continue to follow God and his precepts. The promise God had made to Adam and Eve regarding the "seed of the woman"—that is, the Messiah who would reestablish the relationship between humans and God—still needed to be fulfilled. From the land of Ur, in Mesopotamia, God chose Abraham to be the progenitor of a

186

race that would usher in the promised Messiah. He moved Abraham and his family from their home in Ur and brought them to the land of Canaan, promising Abraham that this would be his land. Israel had no inherent right to the land, except as a gift from God; and the Canaanites had no inherent right to remain in it. That is because God owns the earth he has created.

Before Abraham produced a child God told him that his descendants would be enslaved in another land—Egypt—and after 400 years they would return to the land of Canaan and take it for their own. The Canaanites had not yet become evil enough to be driven out of their land, but they would eventually reach that point. However, Sodom and Gomorrah were ready for judgment. Those two cities had become so evil that combined there were not ten righteous persons living there. Only Lot (Abraham's cousin) and his family survived, minus his foolish wife. Jacob, Abraham's grandson, had twelve sons who became the twelve tribes of Israel. Because of a severe famine, Abraham's descendents entered Egypt as God had told Abraham they would. During the time Israel was in Egypt, the Canaanites, instead of turning to God, became more and more evil, engaging in idol worship that included human sacrifices, and engaging in sexual practices that God saw as detestable, like bestiality, incest, and rampant orgies (see Lev 18). The Canaanites had reached a point of no return. They had grown so wicked that there was no saving them. It was now time for their judgment. God gave the Israelites two reasons why he was going to give them the land of Canaan. He wanted the Israelites to know it was not because of them that he was doing this. He told them, "After the LORD your God has forced those nations out ahead of you, don't say to yourself, "The LORD brought me here to take this land because I am so good." No! It is because these nations are evil that the LORD will force them out ahead of you. You are going in to take the land, not because you are good and honest, but because these nations are evil. That is why the LORD your God will force them out ahead of you, to keep his promise to your ancestors, to Abraham, Isaac, and Jacob" (NCV, Dt 9:4–5). The Canaanite's idolatrous practices were not just carried out in the privacy of their homes; they were carried out publicly in the outdoor altars they had built for and to their gods. Their idolatry had become a worldview that profoundly influenced their whole society. Their moral corruption was abundantly evident, and it continued with each passing generation. God considered them ripe for divine judgment, and he used Israel to deliver the Canaanite's punishment. Now, the time period of Canaan lasted over 400 years, giving them plenty of time to repent. Each generation, however, decided to continue in the evil that would bring their destruction. During the time of Canaan, while God was waiting for them to repent, it was the time of Israel's enslavement in Egypt. If the Canaanites had turned to God and repented, the Israelites would not have needed to drive them out. The Canaanites' punishment—being driven out—was due to their wicked lives; they were responsible for the consequences of their behavior. (I am grateful to Paul Copan's book *Is God a Moral Monster?* and *Christian Apologetics* by Douglas Groothius for information regarding these "time periods.")

Many of the so-called "new" atheists today want to use the "Canaan Conquest" as proof that God is immoral, that he is blood-thirsty and cruel. They see this as a form of ethnic cleansing motivated by xenophobia. These so-called "new" atheists apparently do not seem to mind that the Canaanites were involved in incest, bestiality, and human sacrifices, which included burning their children alive to satisfy their many gods. They think God is terrible for ridding the land of these horrible people, but maybe it is simply the case of the wicked mourning the loss of the wicked. It was not xenophobic attitudes that prompted the Israelites to kill the Canaanites. God did not have the Israelites kill the Canaanites because God did not want any foreigners in Israel. Remember, you have already read how God had promised Abraham that all the families of the earth would be blessed through his offspring (Gen. 12:3), and you have seen how the foreigner was to be treated in Israel. God's love fanned out to everyone, especially to those who did his will; and his will was for them to lead a righteous life. God was using the Israelite army as his arm of judgment against the wickedness of the Canaanites. Anyone familiar with ancient Israel's history knows that God also punished Israel for their idolatry and wickedness. God was concerned with sin, not ethnicity. We see, for example, in 2 Chronicles 28:3-5 that King Ahaz of Judah had "sacrificed his children in the fire, engaging in the detestable practices of the nations the LORD had driven out [i.e., the Canaanites] before the Israelites" (NIV). As a result of Israel's "detestable practices," God allowed the Aramean army to conquer Judah as punishment.

When we look at Deuteronomy 7 we see what Joshua's army was instructed to do, and why. They are told: " The LORD your God will hand these nations over to you, and when you defeat them, you must destroy them completely. Do not make a peace treaty with them or show them any mercy. Do not marry any of them, or let your daughters marry their sons, or let your sons marry their daughters. If you do, those people will turn your children away from me, to begin serving other gods. Then the LORD will be very angry with you, and he will quickly destroy you" (NCV, Dt 7:2–4). The Israelite army is to destroy the Canaanites because, if they do not, their wicked influence will seep into their own personal lives and culture. The Israelites are not to marry any of the Canaanites because their influence will cause the Israelites to turn from God and worship idols. If that happens, God says he will destroy Israel. We see in the historical writings of the Hebrew Scriptures that Israel often turned away from God to false idols and God punished them by allowing other nations to come and attack them and even take them away into exile (for example, Assyria and Babylon). The "Canaan Conquest" was a military action that focused on destroying Canaan's strongholds (garrisons and military forts) while removing the Canaanites from the land (mostly by expulsion). The Israelite army was instructed to dismantle and destroy the Canaanite's altars, demolish their sacred stones (where human sacrifices were performed), cut down the Asherah poles (where sexual orgies were performed in dedication to the goddess), and burn their idols (Dt 7:5). God wanted Joshua's army to get rid of the terrible practices of the Canaanites so that they would not influence the Israelites to sin. Unfortunately, the first two chapters of Judges, which follows Joshua's conquests, show there were plenty of Canaanites around in the next generation to lead Israel astray. The Canaanites remained and intermarried with the Israelites, leading them into the same idolatrous lifestyle the Canaanites had been practicing for over four hundred years, which resulted in their (the Israelite's) own punishment. We see in Psalm 106 that because the Israelites had not driven out the Canaanites that they, too, had become like them; the Israelites "mingled with the nations and adopted their customs. They worshiped their idols . . . sacrificed their sons and their daughters . . . shed innocent blood, the blood of their sons and daughters, whom they sacrificed to the idols of Canaan" (NIV, vs. 35-38).

When we look at the biblical text concerning Joshua and the conquest of Canaan we find the typical metaphorical boasting prone to that era; for example, the use of exaggerated assertions that suggested that all the land was captured, and all the kings were defeated, and all the Canaanites destroyed (see Joshua 10:40–42 as an example). When you read the entire context, however, you find that this was not literally the case. Even today, we use similar figurative language when we say our favorite football team slaughtered their opponents. We do not mean that literally. God used Israel to neutralize Canaanite military strongholds and to drive out a people who were morally and spiritually corrupt. They were beyond redemption. When Joshua's army entered the Promised Land the first stronghold they encountered was Jericho. If Israel was xenophobic and God was against foreigners, Rahab and her family would have been killed too. Although Rahab and her family had been immersed in Canaanite culture, they turned to God and God protected them. He would have done the same for anyone else in Canaan. Archaeological evidence shows that Jericho and Ai were probably military forts or garrisons; they were not civilian populations where women and children lived. Jericho was obviously a small settlement of about a hundred or so soldiers, which is why Joshua's army was able to circle it seven times and then do battle against it all on the same day. Most of the population lived out in the countryside and stayed out of Joshua's army's way. Joshua's battles were, therefore, primarily directed at government and military installations, where the local king (the commander or administrator), his army (battalion of soldiers) and the priests (religious officials) resided. Historians of ancient writings know that ancient Middle Eastern culture included women, children, and the aged in their conquest language, even if they were not involved in the battle. It was a way of overstating their victory. This kind of rhetoric is still used today. For an ancient general to make a report that said 'we killed everyone, man, woman and child' was a way of saying that they vanquished their foe; it was not necessarily a literal declaration of the event. Therefore, if you do a careful reading of the first twelve chapters of Joshua, which describes Israel's conquests, you will discover that no specific noncombatants are ever mentioned among the Canaanites (except for Rahab and her family, and they were spared). Noncombatants—non-military—were not the Israelites' target, nor did the Israelite army go out of their way to kill noncombatants. Jericho and Ai, the first two battle locations, were not towns filled with civilians, but forts or military strongholds, and the "king" of those forts was simply the head officials or military administrators. So when it says in Joshua 10:28-42 that "city" after "city" was destroyed it should be understood that the reference was to a fort where the local "king," his army, and the temple priests resided for their own protection. For the most part, civilians fled when their military strongholds were destroyed and soldiers were no longer capable of protecting them. When the biblical text talks about driving out the Canaanites, this was a clearing away of the land for habitation. These wicked people were being expelled from the land; they were not necessarily being annihilated.

Aslan and many of the so-called "new" atheists mistakenly accuse God of frequently demanding the slaughter of foreigners from Israel. What we actually find in the Hebrew Scriptures, however, is that God sent Joshua's army into Canaan to perform their duties in a purposeful and methodical manner. Paul Copan tells us (*Is God a Moral Monster?*) that God gave them detailed and important conditions. First, the maneuvers were limited to a certain window of time in Israel's history. The "Canaan Conquest" was time-specific, not ongoing and constant. This campaign was ordered by God for this specific time and purpose; it was not to be used as a reason or example for future wars. Aslan is therefore incorrect to claim that God frequently demanded that the Jews commit extensive slaughter of all foreigners. It was one command that took several years to accomplish. (There were, of course, other wars recorded in Israel's history, but those were typical wars caused by political disputes with surrounding nations, like we see in our modern times.) Second, these maneuvers were limited to a particular geographical location. Joshua's army rarely, if ever, destroyed villages and towns where noncombatants lived. Third, the maneuvers were limited to a specific group of people. God's ultimate goal was to bring blessing and salvation to all the nations, including the Canaanites, through Abraham (Gen 12:3). Rather than comparing Joshua (and God) to the twentieth-century monsters I mentioned earlier—Lenin, Stalin, Hitler, Pol Pot, etc.—we can actually compare Joshua (and God) to those who fight against such monsters, who fight against such evil.

Throughout the Hebrew Scriptures, God often expressed a willingness to forego punishment on a nation if they repented. We see, for example, in Jeremiah 18:7f where God says, "At one time I may threaten to tear up, break down, and destroy a nation or a kingdom. But suppose the nation that I threatened turns away from doing wrong. Then I will change my plans about the disaster I planned to do to it" ("Scripture is taken from GOD'S WORD®. © 1995 God's Word to the Nations. Used by permission of Baker Publishing Group."). God did exactly that when the evil nation Nineveh repented (see Jonah). We must remember that God expresses his wrath from a position of justice, mercy and love. Only God can righteously manifest these attributes correctly and morally. In looking at the Hebrew Scriptures, it is obvious that God was opposed to Israel's sin just as much as he was opposed to the sins of Israel's neighbors, the Gentiles. We see in the second book of Kings that God used the Assyrians to be the source of punishment against the northern kingdom of Israel because of their wickedness; the ten tribes were then completely immersed in foreign cultures. Several hundred years later, God used Babylon to punish Judah for their wickedness. God did not punish the Canaanites because they were foreigners; they were punished because they had reached a point-of-no-return in their wickedness.

We see, of course, that Aslan does not quote from passages where God talks about his love of all humankind and how he does not want to see any person perish, not even wicked people (see Eze 18:23, 33:11; Isa 30:18; Lam 3:33; 2 Pet 3:9; 1 Tim 2:4). Aslan does not use passages where God mourns the fact that his people have turned away from him, or passages where God is constantly trying to draw them back to him. Like Aslan, we want to make God into an image that fits our theories. We want to control the type of god we are willing to serve or hate. That is why so many have made their god out of wood, stone, bronze and money. We do not want to deal with an actual living being who is so powerful that he spoke the universe into existence. We do not want a God who demands that we live a certain way, a God who keeps reminding us that he made us and we, in that sense, belong to him. We want God to belong to us. We want a grandfather god who exhibits nothing but jolliness and gives us candy. We want a God of love and mercy, but not one that also demands holiness, justice and truth. We cannot pick the attributes or characteristics of the kind of god we want—that is idolatry. The character of God includes love and justice in equal measure. When God shows anger it is because of our sin and his holiness. That anger is the result of justice and truth, but it is not an uncontrolled anger. All of God's attributes are balanced; one

192

is not more powerful than the other. His justice and love and mercy and holiness are in equal proportions. The Hebrew God is a person, with the attributes of a person; but he is far above any human concept.

God's "Blood-Stained Clothes"

The third example Aslan presents to show that Jesus served and worshipped a horrible God is in Isaiah 63:3, where it is said that God boasts that blood has stained his clothes. It can be disturbing, one has to admit, how graphic ancient writers were. When we read passages like this we must remember that we are looking at a culture that described events in a very warlike and vivid manner. We need to be careful not to judge ancient culture with twenty-first century spectacles. Care must be given to how we interpret the rather stunning words that describe something that happened centuries, if not millennia, ago. With that in mind, what is happening in Isaiah 63? Isaiah and all of Israel are concerned with their enemies that surround them. The Edomites, who are offspring of Jacob's brother Esau and, therefore, related ancestrally to Israel, have been long-standing enemies of Israel. Whenever Israel is attacked, the people of Edom help Israel's enemies and never come to the aid of Israel. Symbolically, Edom is referred to in Hebrew Scriptures as those who oppose God and oppose God's children. In this passage from which Aslan quotes the major question being asked is how Israel can be safe while there are enemies out there that are hostile and vicious, like Edom. Isaiah takes on the role of a watchman and sees someone coming from Edom to Israel. Is it a friend or foe? The person coming from Edom is God and he alone has punished Edom for their sins. When it comes to salvation or judgment, God alone is the one who gives both. Edom had caused great harm to Israel. They had rebelled against God, and it was time to judge and punish them. God says, "I trampled them in my anger and trod them down in my wrath; their blood splattered my garments, and I stained all my clothing" (NIV, Is 63:3). This is a graphic word-picture that shows that God exacted out punishment to Edom, a people who constantly attacked or aided in the attack of Israel. In this passage we see God, as a good father, protecting his children from those who would harm and oppress them. God, being God, is right to mete out punishment to those who have been righteously judged.

193

"Crushing the Enemies' Heads"

Aslan's fourth (last) example is from Psalms 68:21-23; it says "God will crush his enemies' heads, the hairy skulls of those who continue to sin. The Lord said, "I will bring the enemy back from Bashan; I will bring them back from the depths of the sea. Then you can stick [wade] your feet in their blood, and your dogs can lick their share" (NCV). Again, this is quite a graphic depiction of God's judgment on sinful people. Let's look more closely at this psalm. We see that it is actually a song of praise to God for once again saving Israel from its enemies. In it the psalmist starts off by saying that when God appears his enemies scatter and those who hate him run away from him (vs. 1). Why do they scatter and flee? Because these people are evil and God's light exposes them for what they are. They flee because God's presence will bring judgment on them. These evil people are like rats that scatter when a light is turned on. Then in verses five and six the psalmist says God is a father to orphans and defends the widows; he puts lonely people into a family's home and helps prisoners lead productive lives. Verse 9 says that it is God who sends the rain that is needed to grow the crops, and in verse ten that God takes care of poor and oppressed people. In verse 19 the psalmist praises God for daily helping his people (he carries our burdens), and in verse twenty he is praised for keeping them safe from a death that comes at the hands of their enemies. What does God do to protect Israel from its enemies? This is where Aslan then uses the verses to show how terrible God is. Verse 21 says God crushes his enemies' heads, those who persist in rebellion and continue to sin. Israel's enemies who scatter when God appears will not find protection in the places where they have run off to hide. (We too pursue criminals who have escaped to other countries to bring them back for trial and justice.) In verse 22, God says he too will go after the enemies and bring them back even if he has to go into the depths of the sea. They will not get away with their crime. Then the psalmist gets rather graphic in verse twenty-three and says, "your feet may stomp in their blood, and your dogs may eat their portion of the enemies' corpses" (NET). This is indeed a powerful and descriptive picture, one that obviously makes us squirmy. Again, we must remember the culture, the times, and the situation. Obviously, the people are not really going to dance in blood and let their dogs eat the corpses; this is rhetoric about rejoicing in God's victory over Israel's enemies. We talk about being happy and relieved that a rapist or child molester has been caught and punished and, although we might not use the gory language found here in verse twenty-three of this psalm, we mean the same as the psalmist does. The rest of the psalm praises God for his help in keeping Israel safe and talks about how other nations will give gifts to Israel because of how God protects them.

So Aslan picked these four examples to try to show us that the God Jesus loved, served, and worshipped was a horrible God. Aslan wants to prove that God is mean and always ready to shed blood, and since this is the God Jesus served, then Jesus must be just like his God, ready to shed his enemies' blood. And that enemy, for Aslan, is the Roman oppressors. By describing Jesus as a bigoted Jew who only cared for his own people and worshipped a God who seemed to enjoy shedding blood, Aslan presents a horribly skewed picture of Jesus and God. This is, of course, typical of the so-called "new" atheists writing today as well. They pull some passages out of context that appear to show God as a horrible moral monster and forget all the other passages that balance that view with how loving and kind and merciful God is. Let's have a look at some.

In Psalm 30:5 we are confidently told that God's "anger lasts only a moment, but his kindness lasts for a lifetime" (NCV). In Psalm 23:6 we see that God's goodness and mercy are always with us. Psalm 145:8 tells us that God shows compassion and patience, and is always ready to forgive. God tells the Israelites: "I take no pleasure in the death of the wicked, but rather that they turn from their ways and live. Turn! Turn from your evil ways!" (NIV, Eze 33:11). In Jeremiah 3:12f, God shows mercy to Israel even though she is unfaithful to him. Lamentations 3:31–33 says that even though God may need to discipline us, he will also show us compassion and bountiful mercy. Just as God is merciful, he requires us to be as well; see Micah 6:8, where we are told that God requires us to live right and be fair, to love mercy (forgiveness), and to walk humbly with God. Micah then reminds us that God forgives sin and overlooks our rebellion because he would rather show us mercy (7:18). Jesus told his disciples that if they forgave others for their failures, then God would also forgive them (Mt 6:14). God wants us to show mercy, just as he shows mercy. Paul reminds us that God's mercy is great because he loves us so much (Eph 2:4). Peter tells us that God "does not want anyone to be lost, but he wants all people to change their hearts and lives," that is, to repent (NCV, 2 Pe 3:9). I could list many more Bible passages that express

195

God's love, forgiveness, kindness, patience, etc., but I hope you get the picture with the few that I have here. Yes, there are passages that show God's anger and judgment for and against sin, but they are more than balanced out by the plethora of references to God's love and mercy. When he does show anger and judgment, it is for a very good reason. Like I said, the ancient language may be more graphic and military sounding than we would prefer, but the language is supposed to move us. It is supposed to shock us, wake us up to the debilitating effects of sin, so that we change the way we think and act (repent). It is because God is love that he has reconciled us back to himself. John tells us that God loves the world so much that he sent his only and unique Son, so that whoever trusts in him will have eternal life (Jn 3:16).

There is no doubt that there are some difficult passages found in the Bible. But looking at the context of the passages, at the historical setting surrounding the passages, the archaeological evidence, and at the original language which includes the idioms, hyperboles, figurative words, etc., we get a clearer understanding of what is meant. Just pulling a Bible verse out of context like Aslan, the JS, liberal theologians, and members of the so-called "new" atheists club do, and then trying to thereby prove that God is not great, shows more about the person doing that than it does the God they are trying to denigrate. Aslan, being a creative writing professor, should be able to appreciate and recognize when hyperbole and figures of speech are being used in order to evoke emotions and a sense of victory. We may not fully comprehend the full extent of what God sometimes asks us to do (for example, asking Abraham to sacrifice Isaac or the killing of Canaanites). What God asks us to do might even bring us some anguish, pain and sorrow. But God is faithful, and we learn over and over again that he can be trusted.

We see, then, that it was necessary for the Israelites to do serious damage to the Canaanite religious infrastructure; if they hadn't, the result would have caused incalculable damage to Israel's integrity and thus to God's entire plan to redeem humanity (see Copan). For anyone who takes the Bible seriously, these war texts found in the Hebrew Scriptures will certainly prove troubling. We can't just shrug them off. But we can't just give them a surface or cursory reading either. We can't take the text out of context. And we need to view that text in the

196

light of the entire Scriptures. Although baffling questions may and do arise with some Hebrew Scripture passages, we should not stop with those passages if we want a clearer revelation of the heart and character of God. In the Hebrew Scriptures, we see how God unfolds his purposes and promises as they reach fulfillment in his Son, Jesus. God's continuing promise of a savior throughout the Hebrew Scriptures finds its fulfillment in the incarnation and atoning death of Jesus Christ. So, when we read difficult passages like the conquest of the Canaanites, we need to keep in mind that God's heart is concerned with redemption. God's concern for humankind shows itself vividly in the fact that he was willing to actually become a human and die naked on a cross (see Copan). You may not believe that, and it is certainly your prerogative, but the cost of that unbelief is too high to pay. The Scriptures show us what God was willing to go through for our salvation. Although God punishes sinful humans, we can also see the patience God has had with us. We also see the love God has for us that while we were still in a state of sin, Christ died for us (Rom. 5:6). God did not wait for us to get better; he died for us in order to make us better. We see in these four examples that Aslan hoped to show that God was a horrible monster and Jesus was quite similar to the God he worshipped. I hope I have given ample evidence to instead show that Aslan is mistaken.

Chapter Ten: Jesus as Messiah

Did Jesus Reject the Title of Messiah?

Aslan tells us in his eleventh chapter that Jesus consistently rejected any and all references to himself as a messiah. Aslan has Jesus doing some kind of dance around the subject in his attempts to avoid the title. Let's look and see if this is true. We do know that Jesus did not want satanic beings who had possessed people shouting that he was the Son of God, which Luke says did occasionally happen (4:41). These satanic beings knew that Jesus was the Messiah. Jesus ordered them not to speak because he refused to allow demonic beings to proclaim his Messiahship; they were not to be his herald. Jesus was not rejecting the title of Messiah by doing this. At the beginning of Jesus' ministry, before he returned to Galilee and was still down in Judea, some of the Baptizer's disciples decided to follow Jesus. One was Philip, who told his friend Nathanael about Jesus. Now Nathanael had been resting in the shade of a fig tree when Philip came up to him. So when Philip and Nathanael approached Jesus he said of Nathanael, "Here is a true Israelite who is sincere." That is a very nice compliment Jesus gave Nathanael. Nathanael asked Jesus, "How do you know anything about me?" They had never met before. Jesus answered him, "I saw you under the fig tree before Philip called you." This must have really rattled Nathanael's cage. He understood that if Jesus could see him resting, then Jesus could see him anywhere at anytime. There was only one person who could do that. Nathanael's reply to Jesus was appropriate: "Rabbi, you are the Son of God! You are the king of Israel!" (Jn 1:49). When Nathanael blurted this declaration out, Jesus did not tell him he went too far, and then just laughed it off. No, Jesus accepted this praise and even told Nathanael that if that impressed him he should see what was yet to come.

Later on, when Jesus and his disciples were in Caesarea Philippi (Gentile territory), Jesus asked them who the people said he was. As it is today, people then had lots of opinions about Jesus and, like today, they were usually wrong. His disciples told him that the people said that Jesus might be John the Baptizer (who had recently been beheaded) or Elijah or maybe Jeremiah or one of the other prophets. Jesus asked them, "But what about you? Who do you say I am?"

Simon Peter answered, "You are the Messiah, the Son of the living God" (NIV, Mt 16:15f). After this confession, Jesus ordered his disciples not to tell anyone that he was the Messiah. The term—messiah—did have some association with the zealot movement and Jesus would clearly want to distance himself from that group of people, so it would not be surprising that he would not want his disciples openly talking about his being the Messiah. It was at this time, when Peter declared that Jesus was the Messiah, that Jesus began to explain to his disciples that he would go to Jerusalem and suffer at the hands of the religious leaders, and that he would be killed and on the third day be raised to life. Jesus was now setting his sights on the real purpose of his ministry; he had come to be the Redeeming Messiah. His ability to heal people's physical and spiritual ailments, including forgiving sins, and to manifest power over nature by turning water into wine, feeding thousands from a few morsels, and walking on water, proved that he not only was able to utilize the power of God, but that he was God in human form. The miracles Jesus performed were his credentials to verify his ministry and his purpose, which was to be the atoning sacrifice for the sins of the world. They were the credentials for his claim to be the Messiah.

Jesus did not shout it from the rooftops that he was the Messiah, but he did not refrain from telling those whom he called friends. When Jesus was passing through Samaria he was resting near a well and a woman came to get water. They started a conversation and eventually she made the statement, "I know that the Messiah is coming. When he comes, he will tell us everything." Jesus told her: "I am he" ("Scripture is taken from GOD'S WORD®. © 1995 God's Word to the Nations. Used by permission of Baker Publishing Group." Jn 4:25–26). As mentioned earlier, Jesus was able to stay in that town for two days and talk to the people about the Kingdom of God. When Jesus was arrested and taken to the high priest and Sanhedrin, the priest charged Jesus under oath and demanded that he tell them if he was the Messiah, the Son of God? Jesus answered him: "Yes, I am" (Mt 26:63f). The chief priest tore his robes in anger and declared that Jesus had dishonored God by his admission. He told the Sanhedrin that they did not need any more witnesses because they all heard him dishonor God. The chief priest asked for their verdict, and they told him that Jesus deserved the death penalty. What is going on here during this questioning is quite revealing. The priests and Sanhedrin have already gathered some people together to testify against Jesus, but they are not doing a good job of implicating Jesus in any crimes of state. Frustrated, the chief priest used the oath law whereby a person must answer truthfully the question set before him. The chief priest put Jesus under the oath law and demanded to know if Jesus was the Messiah, the Son of God. Jesus said, "I am." Then Jesus went even further. He not only acknowledged that he was God's Son, he then quoted a passage in Hebrew Scriptures (Daniel) that he was the one who would come on the clouds of heaven, i.e., in judgment. The chief priest was almost out of his wits with anger and charged Jesus with blasphemy because Jesus had called himself God. As far as the chief priest and the Sanhedrin were concerned, Jesus deserved to die.

One reason Jesus did not announce to the general public that he was the Messiah was because he knew how fickle people were (see Mk 2:8; Lk 6:8; Jn 2:24). He knew they would want him as the Messianic King right then and there, but it was not the time period for the Messianic King; it was the time period of the Redeeming Messiah. He knew the general public could quickly become a mob and easily suspend its moral conscience. Jesus was not avoiding the title of Messiah; he was avoiding being made a physical king before his time. Why does Aslan have Jesus reject the title of the Messiah? Because Aslan believes in something called the messianic secret which entails the idea that the word 'messiah' really meant zealot. As far as Aslan is concerned, the messiah was supposed to be an insurrectionist who was going to bring in a new world order. It had to be kept secret until the right time. Jesus was walking on eggshells, hoping his secret did not get out too soon. He would reject the title of Messiah because he did not want people to realize that he was planning this huge rebellion. Jesus had to keep his real motives secret, and he only let a few people in on what his real plans were. He created a secret code that only his true followers understood. So when Jesus told the crowd, "Blessed are the poor in spirit," his true followers knew it was code words for 'happy are the poor and oppressed who are going to destroy these Romans.' And when Jesus said, "Blessed are the peace makers," he was just being ironic because his true followers knew he meant the opposite—happy are those who kill the ruling oppressors. Once again, we see Aslan creating a scenario based on his worldview; a scenario that he thinks is founded on a more enlightened reinterpretation.

Did the Gospel Writers Reconstruct Jesus?

Aslan believes Jesus failed to jumpstart his insurrection and got himself killed instead, and so the Gospel writers had to do some finagling with Jesus' words. Aslan claims the 'historical' Jesus maintained a messianic secret with his close followers; a simple secret that contained the message of a new world order that would usher in God's kingdom and restore Israel's independence. Jesus could not let this secret get out to the general public because it was so radical that once the Roman authorities got wind of it, they would send their soldiers to kill anyone associated with it. The messianic secret had to stay hush-hush until the right time. Aslan insists that the Gospel writers, especially Matthew and Luke, decided to reconstruct this messianic secret—the zealotry of Jesus—into something else. Aslan argues that the Gospel writers changed all of Jesus' words that pertained to the messianic secret and gave him pretty words to say instead. So rather than Jesus possibly having said, "I am the zealot; I have come to set you free from tyranny," the Gospel writers have him say, "I am the good shepherd and my sheep know my voice." According to Aslan, Mark started changing Jesus' words to make him sound more apolitical and friendly and nice, and then Matthew and Luke simply continued that tradition with more flare and embellishment. Therefore, says Aslan, the Gospels cannot be trusted to give us the real picture of Jesus. We cannot really know the real Jesus from the Gospels because the Gospels changed a lot of Jesus' sayings. We know this because the JS and Aslan and lots of liberal theologians/biblical scholars tell us they did. According to Aslan, it is easy to see that the four Gospels have been enormously embellished because their portrayal of Jesus does not show him to be a zealot, determined to overthrow the Roman Empire. Aslan's Jesus has honed his magical skills and, with the right followers, he just might have a chance at destroying the enemy and getting Israel's independence. Then he can make himself the King of the Jews. Since Aslan believes Jesus is a zealot, and the Gospels do not portray him as such, the Gospels must be wrong.

For Aslan, the Gospel writers reworked Jesus' sayings so he would not look like a zealot, they disregarded Jesus' messianic secret, rejected Jesus' magical skills and turned him into a miracle-worker, and reinterpreted Jesus' death from an execution for sedition into a messianic sacrifice for the sins of the world. Aslan is convinced that

201

the messianic secret holds the key to who Jesus is. He thinks it may be possible to have the messianic secret traced back to the historical Jesus, which would then help us understand what Jesus really thought about himself, and thereby allow us to reject what the early church believed and taught about Jesus. As far as Aslan is concerned the early church's idea or concept of Jesus was quite different than Jesus' own opinion of himself. The Gospels say one thing and the real Jesus says another. The problem, Aslan contends, is that finding the real Jesus will not be easy; it will be next to impossible, in fact, since we will not be able to use the Gospels to give us any clues into Jesus' self-awareness. What Aslan is saying, of course, is if you want to know the real historical Jesus, do not look in the Gospels. Aslan insists that the Gospels are not really about some man named Jesus of Nazareth; they are about a Christ-of-faith, a messiah who entered the physical world, an eternal being who forever sits at God's right hand. Actually, the Gospels do both; they show the human side of Jesus and his divine side. They do not deny either one. That is why in Christian doctrine Jesus is depicted as the God-Man. The Gospels' view of the Messiah matches the one in the Hebrew Scriptures. It is not the fault of the Hebrew Scriptures that the first-century Jews were hoping for the Messianic King instead of the Redeeming Messiah. It is not the fault of the Hebrew Scriptures that the first-century Jew failed to recognize Jesus as the Messiah.

You cannot separate the Jesus of Nazareth from the Messiah (the Christ-of-faith) who is an eternal being sitting at God's right hand. You cannot separate the Jesus of Nazareth from the healings he performed. You cannot separate the Jesus of Nazareth from the power he had over nature—turning water into wine; feeding thousands from a few morsels; walking on water; filling a net full of fish; seeing Nathanael resting under a shade tree; raising several people, including his friend Lazarus, from the dead. You cannot separate the Jesus of Nazareth from the message of the kingdom of heaven—the spiritual realm where he is king, a domain in which those who believe in him are allowed to enter. You cannot separate the Jesus of Nazareth from the death and resurrection of the Messiah. You cannot separate these anymore than you can strip down Abraham Lincoln's accomplishments. If you removed from Lincoln's historical life his presidency, his debates, his being a lawyer, etc., simply because you wanted to believe something totally different about him, a view which you really had no clear evidence to base your belief on, that would not (or should not) make you out to be a serious scholar. Stripping Lincoln of all his accomplishments would leave you with a person who is not significant enough for anyone to care about. That is what Aslan is hoping his readers will do. They will see that this stripped down version of Jesus that Aslan creates merely leaves a skeleton and not a body; they will see that Aslan's Jesus has no substance and reject him as insignificant. Stripping Jesus of what the Gospels say about him would leave you with a person who is not significant enough for anyone to follow.

If Jesus is an eternal being, if Jesus is the Messiah, if Jesus died and rose on the third day, then Muhammad who came after Jesus loses his significance as a religious leader. Joseph Smith loses his significance as a religious leader, as does Brigham Young. The gurus of self-realization lose their significance as religious leaders. Even the religious leaders who came before Jesus, like Buddha or Vishnu, lose their significance as religious leaders. Why? Because they did not die for the sins of the world; they were not the "seed of the woman." They did not rise from the dead to prove they were the Messiah. The resurrection of Jesus puts him far above any other religious leader. If Jesus is the eternal being, the Messiah, then trying to get to heaven by doing a bunch of good deeds is fruitless. How do you know how many good deeds you are supposed to do to qualify for heaven? A thousand, or maybe ten thousand? All the other religions say, "Do all these good things and hopefully it will be enough to get to heaven." Christianity says that God tells us, "All your good works combined are not enough to enter my holiness, my kingdom; you cannot do enough good things to qualify. But have good cheer, I have provided a way for you to enter my kingdom. I sent my Son, Jesus, to provide a way. Trust in him and you will enter my kingdom." But we humans have our pride; we do not want salvation to be that simple. We want to work at it even if we do so blindly and badly. But Jesus said three beautiful things to those who came in contact with him in an attitude of faith: "Your sins are forgiven; your faith has saved you; go in peace" (see Lk 7:36-50). Jesus wants to say these words to you.

Aslan believes Jesus was a zealot; the Gospels claim Jesus was the Messiah. Aslan says the Gospels are wrong. I believe I have, in reviewing Aslan's theories thus far, presented substantial evidence that

Aslan's ideas are not well-founded. The four Gospels, written independently of each other, are historically and textually reliable. The synoptic Gospels—Matthew, Mark, and Luke—were written within a generation of the events they talk about. Very few ancient writings can make that claim. Many people who witnessed those events were still alive when the Gospels were written and distributed, and could have quite easily debunked the whole thing. The Gospels were written so soon after the events that it is highly unlikely that the events they record could have suffered from "legendary" corruption, i.e., embellishments and reconstructions. Each of the Gospels presents a different view or perspective of Jesus. Since Mark was writing mostly to Gentile Christians (possibly those in the western part of the Roman Empire) who had come from a pagan lifestyle that worshiped a myriad of gods, he emphasized Jesus' humanity in his Gospel while also showing that Jesus was the Messiah prophesied in the Hebrew Scriptures. Matthew wrote to a Jewish audience and therefore inserted lots of passages from the Hebrew Scriptures throughout his Gospel in order to prove that Jesus was the Messiah. Luke was writing to a mostly Gentile audience, so he did not have as many scriptural passages in his Gospel as Matthew did. He had no reservations about who Jesus was, however, and there was no question in Luke's mind pertaining to Jesus' Messiahship. In the first chapter of his Gospel, Luke says Jesus is the Son of God (1:35). Throughout his Gospel, Luke builds upon that declaration. The Gospel of John is the one every liberal theologian tries to nullify. They claim it is too spiritual, too esoteric, that Jesus appears too ethereal or other-worldly, that it contains too many nuances, and that it was probably written in the second century by an obscure author. In actuality, John fills in some of the time gaps found in Matthew. John actually records very few miracles and no parables, concentrating more on Jesus' words about himself. John is also able to give greater detail because the people he includes in his Gospel are dead and cannot be harmed by the information. He does emphasize the Godhood of Jesus, but that is because the people he is writing to are falling victim to some erroneous Gnostic ideas and John needs to set his readers straight as to the true nature of Jesus. (This was not necessary when Matthew, Mark and Luke were writing their Gospels in the 60s A.D.) But John also emphasizes the humanity of Jesus by recording events where he was angry, distressed, felt grief at his friend's tomb, felt sorrow, etc. These emotions are not sinful in themselves; they are part of what makes us human. They are part of what made Jesus human. The Gospels did not separate the Jesus of Nazareth—the human side of Jesus—from his being the eternal being, the Messiah. There is no difference between what the Gospels thought Jesus was and who Jesus himself thought he was. They record the historic Jesus accurately. They all pay close attention to the last week of Jesus' life, focusing on his trial, torture, execution and resurrection.

All the synoptic Gospels tell us that Jesus stood before the chief priests and Sanhedrin at his trial and claimed to be God, and it was that declaration that was the reason for his execution. John is brief in his recording the events with the chief priest. John does mention that the chief priest questioned Jesus about his disciples and his teachings. Jesus told him that he had spoken publicly for all to hear, that he had always taught in synagogues or in the Temple courtyard, where all the Jews gathered. "I haven't said anything in secret," Jesus said (Jn 18:20). Aslan says Jesus kept his messianic secret well hidden; but Jesus said his teachings were well known, that he always spoke openly and truthfully. By the time John wrote his Gospel the other three had been circulating for around twenty to thirty years. Not wanting to repeat the same things again, John focused on other details of Jesus' life. Since John's Gospel includes other details not found in the other Gospels, Aslan and the JS discount them, which is not a solid criterion for doing so. (I have already dealt with this propensity for Aslan and the JS to discount something just because it was recorded only once; it is not really a good characteristic—this propensity—to have when attempting to get at the truth.)

Aslan concedes that Jesus' disciples accepted him as messiah, but they did so when he was alive or right after he was executed. We have already seen that Jesus declared that he was the Messiah during his lifetime. His disciples also confessed that he was the Messiah during Jesus' lifetime, but they still had hopes that being the Messiah and having the power over nature that he had that Jesus would help bring relief to Israel from the occupation (see Acts 1:6). Jesus instead told them his mission as Messiah was to go to Jerusalem and suffer many things at the hands of the elders, the chief priests and the teachers of the law, and that he must be killed and on the third day be raised to life (see Mt 16:21f). Peter, like Aslan, did not want to hear this. Aslan might have said to Jesus: 'But what about the messianic secret; didn't you come to start a war against Rome?' Peter said, "Never, Lord! This shall never happen to you!" Peter was telling Jesus what Jesus' mission was supposed to be, just like Aslan has attempted to do in his book. Jesus was angry at Peter's remark and told Peter that he was acting like Satan, like the Deceiver, trying to tempt him not to do what he was sent to do. Jesus said to Peter, "Get behind me, Satan! You are a stumbling block to me; you do not have in mind the concerns of God, but merely human concerns" (NIV, Mt 16:21–23). What were the concerns of God? They were to bring final reconciliation between God and humans; to bring to fulfillment the promise of the "seed of the woman." What were the merely human concerns? They were being an occupied nation, for one. Did the disciples recognize Jesus as Messiah immediately after his death, as Aslan says? Why would they? Why would the disciples scatter off, hear about Jesus being tortured and killed on a cross, be fearful that the chief priest or Herod or Pilate might send Roman guards after them, and then get together and decide to make Jesus a Messiah after all? It does not make sense. The disciples did not recognize Jesus as the Messiah right after he had been executed, as Aslan claims; they recognized Jesus as the Messiah when he rose from the dead on the third day like he said he would.

Aslan thinks the early church had a twofold problem that they had to rectify. The first was that Jesus was unable to match or comply with the Hebrew Scriptures' portrayal of the messiah; and the second problem was that Jesus was unable to fulfill one single requirement that the messiah was expected to do. Where does Aslan get the idea that the early church had a problem to solve because Jesus failed to follow the messianic pattern found in the Hebrew Scriptures? Did he discover a document that hinted at this so-called problem which then also showed how the church solved it? Are there ancient manuscripts showing that the early believers struggled to find a way to squeeze Jesus into a messianic mold so they could create a new religion out of him? Why would they even bother? What would be the purpose in starting a new religion based on a man who was a complete failure? We know that the church held regional (local) synods and councils starting in the first century. These synods and councils were used in order to correct doctrinal errors; errors that disagreed with the Gospels and the early Church's conception of who Jesus is. They were not established, despite what modern liberal theologians might say, in order to create new paradigms about Jesus. There was no evolution of

206

the idea of Jesus, where people kept attaching new attributes to him as the years rolled on until eventually he became some celestial Christ. These synods helped settle ideological and theological conflicts.

One of these conflicting ideas, for example, was Montanism. It was named after Montanus who lived in the second half of the second century. Montanus was a recent convert to Christianity who apparently had a tendency to fall into trances and make predictions regarding the imminent arrival of the heavenly Jerusalem at the village of Pepuza in Phrygia. He urged his followers to assemble there and wait for the New Jerusalem to arrive; while doing so his followers were to fast and give money to a common fund. Synods were organized or established in order to deal with new ideas like Montanism. At the synods, its members could discuss the issues and concerns that were brought to the table, so to speak, and then make resolute decisions based on the foundational truths they already possessed—the truths found in the four canonical Gospels. This process helped maintain the church's unity in expressing the correct belief, and it also gave uniformity to church customs and practices. By the third century these synods became a fixed institution (see *The Encyclopedia of Christianity* on Councils and Montanism).

Around the time of Montanus, other "Christians" were writing fabled stories about Jesus; one of them was the Gospel of Thomas that the JS and Aslan depend on for their erroneous thesis; and there were others like the Gospel of Peter and the Gospel of Mary. The early church used the four Gospels—Matthew, Mark, Luke and John—as well as the writings of Paul and the other apostles as the standard or arbiter to judge any and all writings and ideas emerging from the latter part of the first century on. Jesus, Paul, and the other apostolic writings, warned of false teachers who would attempt to lead others astray. In the first century there were people who said that circumcision was necessary for salvation; or that it was okay to sin once a person was saved; or that the physical realm did not matter, it was only the spiritual domain that mattered; or that Jesus was not fully human or was not God in the flesh (see Mt 7:15, 24:11; Gal 2:4; Col 2:23; 1Tim 1:3; 2Pet 2:1; 1Jn 4:1). Aslan, the JS, and other modern liberal theologians try to use the various Councils that arose—like the ones in Nicaea (325), Constantinople (381), and Ephesus (431)—to promote their theory that the godhood of Jesus and the idea of the Trinity evolved during these councils. But the purpose of the councils was to make sure that any and all ideas about Jesus complied with the four Gospels. The real problem for the early church was not that Jesus did not fit any of the Hebrew Scriptures' portrayal of the Messiah. The problem was combating the false theories and ideas that arose about Jesus, and it continues to be a current problem as so many books, like Aslan's, are being written to deceive people about the real Jesus.

Jesus as the Redeeming Messiah of the Hebrew Scriptures

What do the Hebrew Scriptures say about the Messiah? Studying the Hebrew Scriptures, it becomes obvious that there is a twofold portrayal of the promised Messiah. The Messiah was seen in some passages as one who would actually experience disgrace and shame, that he would be physically harmed and suffer a violent death. The purpose of this death was to act as a substitutionary payment for the sins of not only the Jewish people but for everyone. Other passages regarding the promised Messiah show him as a king who will establish a Messianic Kingdom. The twofold picture of the promised Messiah found in the Hebrew Scriptures emphasized two separate and different appearances by the same Messiah or Person; the passages spoke of one Messiah, two arrivals. Barton Payne's *Encyclopedia of Biblical Prophecy* lists over a hundred Old Testament predictions that were fulfilled at the Messiah's first arrival. It is not surprising that the Jews who had recently become subjects of the Roman Empire would focus on the passages referring to a conquering Messiah rather than a Redeeming Messiah. They wanted peace and prosperity, and they thought it was time for God to fulfill his promises of the Messianic Kingdom. They were tired of suffering, and they certainly did not want a suffering Messiah. They had become complacent in their religion and did not believe they needed a Messiah to redeem them; they needed one to restore Israel's independence. Their independence had been lost because of sin, and now that they considered themselves righteous by strictly obeying the Mosaic Law, there was no need for a Savior. They had fallen into the trap of thinking their good works were enough to save them, but they were mistaken. So any so-called messiah that arrived in and around the first century and promised to fight against Rome was able to gather a quick following; however, they were also able to get the attention of the local Roman authorities and were just as quickly defeated.

When Jesus began his ministry he entered the synagogues and taught the people in ways that surpassed the authority of their own teachers. He was able to heal people of their diseases, and he promised that the Kingdom of God was at hand. People began wondering if he was the Messiah. The only problem is he did not advocate violence. He even healed a Roman soldier's servant, and then told the crowd that he had not seen faith expressed like the soldier's even among his fellow Jews. What a compliment to a Gentile! Jesus told his listeners that it was the peacemaker that was blessed and that they were to love their enemies (who at that time were the Romans). Many people thought he was the Messiah, and they were perplexed as to why he had not started his own army, especially with the powers that he appeared to have. There were others with the fervor of a zealot who claimed to be messiahs and formed little armies. Why hadn't Jesus? The problem they had, and the problem Aslan and other moderns have, is that they wanted to make Jesus into a zealot, but Jesus had no intentions to be one. He knew why he had come at this point in time. He was to be the Redeeming Messiah. The prophet Isaiah clearly mapped this out for the Jewish people in passages such as 42:1–4, where he talked about the Redeeming Messiah's ministry; and in 49:1–13 where God showed the Messiah would be rejected by his own people and would become "a light for the Gentiles;" and in 50:4–9 where Isaiah again talked about the sufferings endured by the Messiah. These passages are firmly connected to the promise of the "seed of the woman" who will have his heal bruised, to the practice of animal sacrifices that foreshadowed the permanent substitutionary death of the Messiah, and to the startling drama of Abraham's "sacrificing" his son Isaac as a vivid enactment of what God was going to have his only Son do for humankind.

Possibly the greatest passage regarding the Redeeming Messiah is found in Isaiah chapter 53. Modern rabbis (as well as Gentiles like Aslan) do their best to try to reduce this chapter in Isaiah to a rather weak symbolic message. But this passage proves to be too powerful for their feeble attempts. Beginning with the last two verses of chapter 52, Isaiah 53 is a powerful statement about the Redeeming Messiah. Here is the essence of what Isaiah 52:13-53:12 says: God's Servant will be respected, praised, and highly honored, but he will soon be so tortured that he will be disfigured and marred beyond human likeness. God's Servant will grow up as an ordinary man, but he will become despised and rejected by his people; he will be someone who is familiar with suffering and pain. He will, in fact, take on our pain and will bear our suffering. He will be punished by God, pierced for our transgressions and wounded for our iniquities; the punishment he endures will bring us peace with God because by his wounds we are healed. We all have sinned and gone astray from God, but God has laid on him the iniquity of us all. He was led like a lamb to the slaughter. He was arrested and no one protested. He was killed and placed in a grave. It was God's will to cause him to suffer, to make his life an offering for sin. After he suffers and dies, he will see the light of life and be satisfied. God's Servant will justify many because he will bear their iniquities. He will give up his life in order to bear our sins and then will rise up from the dead to plead our case before God.

There is no question as to what Isaiah is trying to get across in this passage. The person described in Isaiah 52:13-53:12 is the Redeeming Messiah. He is born and grows up and, after starting his ministry, becomes despised and rejected. He will be killed but it will be a substitutionary death; he will take on our punishment. The penalty for our sinning against God will be placed on him. There will be some who realize that he has suffered and died for them; they will realize that by his wounds they have been healed, i.e., reconciled with God. His death will bring an end to animal sacrifices because he will be the lamb who is slaughtered for our sins. His blood is the offering for our sin. When Isaiah says that after the Messiah has suffered death he will see the light of life, it means that the Redeeming Messiah will rise from the dead. It will give him joy knowing that his righteous death will justify many by bearing their iniquities. It is by his death and resurrection that those who believe in him will be justified, i.e., their sins will not be held against them because of the substitutionary death of the Messiah. Isaiah says that after the Redeeming Messiah takes the penalty for our sins, he then makes intercession for us. Bearing our sins requires a death, and his interceding shows he is still alive because he rose from the dead. There is no other person in history that fulfills this prophecy of the Redeeming Messiah other than Jesus of Nazareth. Paul tells us in Romans 8:34 that now that Jesus died and rose from the dead he is able to intercede for us. The writer of the book of Hebrews (7:25) also says that Jesus intercedes for us. Aslan said Jesus did not comply with even one messianic portrayal found in the Hebrew Scriptures. I think this paradigm of the Redeeming Messiah fits Jesus perfectly.

What else do the Hebrew Scriptures say about the Redeeming Messiah? Besides the magnificent example from Isaiah 52:13-53:12, we have passages like Genesis 3:15 coupled with Isaiah 7:14 regarding the virgin birth (the "seed of the woman"); there is Micah 5:2 that gives the Messiah's birthplace (Bethlehem); Isaiah 11:1 that talks about the Messiah's human lineage; and Psalm 22:1–21 that gives more information about how the Messiah will suffer on the cross. There are Hebrew Scripture passages that tell us God has a Son. In Proverbs 30:4 the writer asks several questions for us to ponder about the majesty of God as shown in his creation. After asking these questions, the writer asks: What is his name or the name of his son? The writer of this proverb is obviously talking about God, and then he asks what God's Son's name is. The author is declaring that God has a Son. The first question the proverb writer wants his reader to ponder is: Who has gone up to heaven and come down? Now, it is interesting to note that when Jesus was talking to a particular Pharisee he said, "No one has gone to heaven except the Son of Man, who came from heaven" ("Scripture is taken from GOD'S WORD®. © 1995 God's Word to the Nations. Used by permission of Baker Publishing Group." Jn 3:13). Are there other passages that show God has a Son? In Isaiah 9:6f we are told that a child will be born and he will be called a Wonderful Counselor, Mighty God, Everlasting Father, and Prince of Peace. Here Isaiah is saying a person will be born who will be God, i.e., God will become human. Zechariah says that God's Shepherd will be attacked and when that happens the sheep will be scattered. God says that this Shepherd is his associate (13:7). Here God calls the coming Shepherd, the Redeeming Messiah, his associate, a Hebrew word that gives the idea of being on equal standing. The only one who is on equal standing with God is God. The Redeeming Messiah is a man who is equal to God; he will be a Shepherd who will be killed and his sheep will be scattered, which is what the disciples did when Jesus was arrested and executed. (Interestingly, in Zechariah 3:8f, God says, "I am going to bring my servant the Branch...and I will remove the sin of this land in a single day." Jesus is the Branch and at his execution (crucifixion) sin was removed on that single day.)

211

Did Jesus Make any Claims about Being God?

Aslan contends that Jesus did not call himself the Son of God, that the title was thrust upon him by others. It is true that others ascribed this title to Jesus. For instance, Mark begins his Gospel by saying he is writing to tell the good news about Jesus Christ, the Son of God (Mk 1:1). Luke starts off his Gospel by telling us that the child developing inside Mary, a young virgin, will be called the Son of God (Lk 1:35). Mark and Luke certainly make more claims that Jesus is the Son of God, but let's do a more comprehensive look at Matthew's Gospel.

Matthew begins his Gospel with a genealogical list showing that Jesus is the Messiah, and then immediately tells us Jesus was born of a virgin, showing that he is the Redeeming Messiah, the "seed of the woman," the one who is called Immanuel—a name that means 'God with us," showing that Jesus is the God-Man, God in human form. In recounting Jesus' birth, Matthew is referring to Isaiah 7:14 as a prophetic text regarding the Redeeming Messiah. Paul expands on that idea by saying that Jesus was in the form of God and equal with God, but he became a human in order to die on the cross, to be the substitutionary death for our sins (see Php 2:6–8). Matthew's first major reference of Jesus as the Son of God is when God called him his Son, a declaration, according to Aslan, that Jesus simply brushed off. At Jesus' baptism, Matthew makes it clear that the Triune God was present when he writes that immediately after Jesus was baptized, the Spirit of God descended upon him like a dove and a voice from heaven said, "This is my Son, whom I love; with him I am well pleased" (NIV, 3:16f). Then Jesus was ushered into the desert by the Spirit of God to undergo a time of temptation (as we saw in Chapter Four). Since Jesus was the "seed of the woman" promised to Adam and Eve as a result of their succumbing to temptation, Jesus, who was to be the new Adam, would need to also undergo a similar temptation. It was only morally fair for someone who was to be the Messiah to be exposed to the same temptations that we are and yet not to fall for them, to arise sinless each time he was tempted. Satan was therefore allowed to tempt Jesus and did so by saying, "If you are the Son of God, tell these stones to become bread" (NIV, 4:3). The Deceiver knew Jesus was God's Son and attempted to provoke Jesus to rely on himself instead of on his Father. In addition, Matthew showed that demon's, spiritual beings under Satan's domain, declared Jesus to be the Son of God (8:29). Jesus also told his followers that "no one knows the Father except the Son and those to whom the Son is willing to reveal him" ("Scripture is taken from GOD'S WORD®. © 1995 God's Word to the Nations. Used by permission of Baker Publishing Group." 11:27).

When the Pharisees demanded that Jesus give them proof that he was the Messiah by providing some kind of sign or miracle, Jesus replied that the only sign they were going to get was the sign of Jonah (12:38-45). He explained that just as Jonah was three days and nights in a huge fish, so he would be three nights in the earth, dead and buried. But then he would rise from the dead, and that would be the sign or proof that he was the Messiah. Then he told them that the people of Nineveh—formidable enemies of Israel—were going to judge the Pharisees because the Ninevites repented when Jonah preached to them. There would be no excuse for the Pharisees because they had someone greater than Jonah preach to them; and that was Jesus. Then Jesus told the Pharisees that even the Queen of the South—another Gentile—would judge and condemn them because she recognized God had given Solomon great wisdom, and she had come to listen to his advice. Jesus told the Pharisees that someone greater than Solomon was in their midst, but they refused to listen to him; and that was Jesus. When Jesus walked on water to get to the disciples' boat, they worshiped him and declared that he was the Son of God (14:33). He did not rebuke them for worshipping him, nor for calling him the Son of God. When Peter told Jesus that he was "the Messiah, the Son of the living God," Jesus did not rebuke him or brush it off or reluctantly accept it. Jesus told Peter that it was his (Jesus') Father who revealed that truth to Peter (16:17). The Pharisees were constantly asking Jesus questions to try to trick him and have him say something false. One day, Jesus asked the Pharisees what they thought about the Messiah (see Mt 22:41–45). "Whose son is he?" Jesus asked. They knew their Scriptures and so they told him the Messiah was David's son, and that he would come from David's lineage. Jesus asked them why David, guided by the Holy Spirit, would call the Messiah Lord, if he were David's son. In Psalm 110:1, David says, 'The Lord said to my Lord, "Take the highest position in heaven until I put your enemies under your control."' Jesus asked the Pharisees, "If David calls him Lord, how can he be his son?" Jesus was letting the Pharisees know that the Messiah is not just a human—coming from David's lineage—but God in human form; and that was Jesus.

213

When Jesus was arrested in Gethsemane he told the arresting party that he was actually submitting to them on his own power. He said to them: "Don't you think that I could call on my Father to send more than twelve legions of angels to help me now? How, then, are the Scriptures to be fulfilled that say this must happen?" ("Scripture is taken from GOD'S WORD®. © 1995 God's Word to the Nations. Used by permission of Baker Publishing Group." 26:53–54). Jesus is referring to the Scriptures that talk about the Redeeming Messiah, like Isaiah 53 and Psalm 22. At his trial before the Sanhedrin, the chief high priest demanded to know, "[A]re you the Messiah, the Son of God?" Jesus answered him, "Yes, I am" (26:63–64). When Jesus was on the cross people passing by mocked him and laughed at him and said, "Come down from the cross, if you are the Son of God!" (NIV, 27:39f). Obviously, they knew that he had called himself this, and they knew that that was the real reason he was hanging there, because he had claimed to be the Son of God. Likewise, the ones who were at his trial with the Sanhedrin, the chief priests and law teachers, mocked him and said, "He trusts in God, so let God save him now, if God really wants him. He himself said, 'I am the Son of God.'" (NCV, 27:43.) They too acknowledged that Jesus had made this claim. After Jesus rose from the dead, like he said he would, he told his disciples to go out into every nation and make disciples and to baptize them in the name of the Father, Son, and Holy Spirit (28:19). Here, Jesus is making a reference to the Triune God and claiming to be a part of that Triune God. We see then that Matthew not only recorded other people calling Jesus the Son of God, without him rebuking them or brushing it off, but we see that Jesus called himself the Son of God.

John, at the beginning of his Gospel, says that Jesus was with God and was God and was the one who created the universe, and that he became human and lived among us (1:1,14a). Nathaniel called Jesus the Son of God and Jesus did not rebuke him for it, nor did he deny it (1:49). Jesus often called God his Father in such a way that showed he was God's equal. At one time some religious leaders were upset at Jesus for healing on the Sabbath and Jesus told them that his Father was busy at work and so was he (5:17). This upset the religious leaders so much that they wanted to kill him. Why? Not only did they think he was breaking the Sabbath by healing people on that holy day, but Jesus had called "God his own Father, making himself equal with God" (vs. 18). Jesus then told them that he, the Son of God, could do nothing by himself; he could only do what he saw his Father doing, because

214

whatever the Father does the Son also does. Jesus is telling the religious leaders about the close and equal relationship he has with God. Jesus tells them that just as the Father has the power to raise the dead and give people life, even so Jesus, the Son, gives life to whomever he wants. In the Hebrew Scriptures, God says he will judge the world for its sin, but Jesus tells these religious leaders that the Father has entrusted all judgment to him, the Son. Not only that, but the Son will get equal honor with the Father. In fact, Jesus makes it clear that whoever does not honor the Son does not honor the Father who sent him. Jesus let these religious leaders know that the time had come when the dead (those poor in spirit, those spiritually dead in their sins) will hear the voice of the Son of God and those who hear (i.e., obey that voice) will live. Jesus concludes his sermon by saying that the Father has given him the authority to judge because he is the Son of Man (5:19, 21, 22f, 25-27). Jesus is clearly calling himself the Son of God throughout this discourse he has with the religious leaders. Jesus links the title—Son of God—with the one he often called himself—the Son of Man.

There was an episode where Jesus was talking to some Jews and suddenly they wanted to pick up stones to kill him. The Jews were relying on the idea that they were good in God's eyes simply because they were children of Abraham. (Similar to people who think they are automatically Christians because they live in the U.S. or go to church.) Jesus told them they were mistaken, that they were not right in God's eyes just because they were Jews. Jesus told them that whoever obeys his (Jesus') words would never see death. They once again accused Jesus of being demon-possessed, complaining that Abraham died and that Jesus could not be greater than Abraham. "Who do you think you are?" they asked Jesus. Jesus replied, "Abraham rejoiced at the thought of seeing my day; he saw it and was glad" (8:56). They mocked him and asked him how he could have seen Abraham when he wasn't even fifty years old yet. Jesus answered, "Before Abraham was born, I am!" (8:58). That is when they picked up stones to kill him. Why would saying "Before Abraham was born, I am!" upset these Jews so much that they would want to murder Jesus. They knew exactly what Jesus was saying when he said, "I am." When God was telling Moses that he was going to help Israel and be God's mouthpiece to the Pharaoh in Egypt, Moses wanted to know what God's name was. God answered Moses, "I Am Who I Am. This is what you must say to the people of

Israel: 'I Am has sent me to you' " ("Scripture is taken from GOD'S WORD®. © 1995 God's Word to the Nations. Used by permission of Baker Publishing Group." Ex 3:14). When Jesus said, "I am," the Jews knew he was using God's holy name to describe himself.

Jesus was walking on Solomon's porch in the Temple courtyard and some Jews came up to him and asked him to plainly tell them if he was the Messiah. He answered that he had already told them but they refused to believe what he said. He told them the miracles he performed, which he did in his Father's name, testified that he was the Messiah. He told them the reason they did not believe was because they were not his followers. His followers believed he was the Messiah and he was going to give them eternal life for believing in him. He told them further that it was actually his Father who gave him these followers and no one would be able to tear his followers away from his Father. Then Jesus told them, "The Father and I are one" (10:30). This really upset the Jews who were talking to Jesus and they picked up some rocks to stone him to death right then and there. Jesus asked them to name one of the good things he did for which they were going to stone him to death. They told him that the reason they wanted to kill him was because he claimed to be God. When he said, "The Father and I are one," the Jews knew he, being a human, was claiming to be God.

Another instance regarding Jesus as the Son of God occurs in the eleventh chapter of John when a good friend of Jesus' had died and Jesus was on his way to his friend's tomb in order to raise him from the dead, which would show his Messianic power. Before arriving, the dead man's sister came to meet Jesus and, of course, was very sad. Jesus promised Lazarus' sister, Martha, that her brother would rise from the dead. Being a devout Jew, she acknowledged that she knew her brother would rise again in the resurrection at the last day. Jesus said to her, "I am the resurrection and the life. Those who believe in me will have life even if they die. And everyone who lives and believes in me will never die. Martha, do you believe this?" Martha answered, "Yes, Lord. I believe that you are the Christ, the Son of God, the One coming to the world" (NCV, Jn 11:25-27). Jesus did not rebuke the title she had given him. One of the disciples (Philip) had asked Jesus to "show us the Father and that will be enough for us," and Jesus responded, "Anyone who has seen me has seen the Father"

216

(14:8f). We have already seen that during Jesus' kangaroo trial before the high priest Jesus was demanded under oath to tell them if he was the Messiah, the Son of God, and Jesus answered them that he was. It was this confession that caused the high priest to condemn Jesus to death. When Jesus faced Pilate the Jewish leaders told him the reason they wanted Jesus crucified: "We have a law, and according to that law he must die, because he claimed to be the Son of God" (NIV, Jn 19:7). John concludes his Gospel by saying that Jesus performed lots more miracles than is recorded in his Gospel but that the purpose of his writing the Gospel was so that you would believe that Jesus is the Messiah, the Son of God, and that by believing you may have life in his name (Jn 20:31).

So, it does look as though Jesus called himself the Son of God. Of course, Aslan's answer is to simply reject any passage where Jesus calls himself or is called the Son of God, claiming it to be inauthentic. But claiming that a passage is inauthentic simply because it does not comply with one's worldview is not the result of sound scholarly work. Aslan and the JS have taken the sayings of Jesus that they do not like—the ones where Jesus says he is God—and removed them from the Gospels, claiming that they were added by later writers who developed that theory. But, in actuality, we see that it is Aslan and the JS who have used their theories as the standards by which they remove sayings or passages that they do not like. They not only remove sayings that do not agree with their theories, they then create a false image of Jesus by making him into something he is not (a zealot or insurrectionist, a Cynic, or an itinerant sage). Jesus was either a lunatic, a liar, or who he said he was—the Son of God.

What does the title 'Son of Man' Mean?

Aslan says that instead of calling himself the Son of God (which we now see Jesus did do), Jesus simply referred to himself as the "Son of Man," a rather enigmatic title that has baffled scholars as to its precise meaning. Aslan notes that the title—Son of Man—is very ambiguous and found infrequently in the Hebrew Scriptures. Aslan concludes that the term "Son of Man" is probably nothing more than a Hebrew and/or Aramaic phrase for "man." Of course, Aslan once again claims that the term "Son of Man" is used as an idiom in the Q document. Now I have provided passages in the discussion above to show that Jesus used the title Son of God and Son of Man to refer to himself. It is true, as Aslan says, that the term Son of Man could be used simply as an idiom for "man," or as a synonym for "I." When Jesus calls himself the Son of God, or calls God his Father, he is showing that he is God, that he is God in human form. When Jesus calls himself the Son of Man he is referring to the fact that he is fully human as well. Son of Man is a reference back to Adam; Jesus is, as a human being, a son of Adam. He is God and Man. Luke made that clear in his genealogy (see Lk 3:38). Since God made the universe and everything in it, including humans, it would not be impossible for him to enter his creation in the form of a human being and still retain his Godhood. Another reason why Jesus called himself the Son of Man is because it identified him with the prophecy found in the book of Daniel, where it says that Daniel had a vision one night and "there before me was one like a son of man, coming with the clouds of heaven" (NIV, 7:13). The phrase 'son of man' means human being in the language (Aramaic) used in Daniel's passage. Jesus quoted this verse during his trial at the Sanhedrin. After the chief priest asked Jesus if he was the Son of God and Jesus answered that he was, Jesus then said, "And you will see the Son of Man sitting at the right hand of the Mighty One and coming on the clouds of heaven" (NIV, Mt 26:64). This was enough for the Sanhedrin to declare that Jesus was deserving of death because he had called himself God. The term "Son of Man" may baffle some scholars as to its precise meaning, but when you see Jesus referring to himself as the Son of God and the Son of Man, it seems clear that he is showing that he is both God and human.

To try to undermine the importance of Daniel's book and prophecies, where the term "Son of Man" clearly refers to someone of a divine nature, Aslan claims that the book of Daniel was actually written in the second century B.C. when Antiochus IV was king of the Seleucid Empire. The book of Daniel in the Hebrew Scriptures records some apocalyptic visions Daniel claims to have had while he served in the Babylonian court during the Judean exile (circa 605-536 B.C.) Aslan believes that these apocalyptic visions actually help explain what was meant by the messianic secret, which, in turn, help us understand what Jesus meant when he called himself the Son of Man. The first thing that needs to be pointed out is that Aslan consistently manipulates the dating of biblical books in order to squeeze them into his mindset. We have already seen Aslan assign late dates to the Gospels so that he can then manipulate their information. He does the same with his dating of the book of Daniel. Aslan accepts what is called the critical, liberal view that 'Daniel' was not written around 536-530 B.C. as traditional scholars believe; i.e., during the time Daniel, the historical person, was actually alive. The critical view actually sees 'Daniel' as a religious novel and not as a record of facts. The critical view believes the book of Daniel was written in the days of the Maccabees to encourage the Jews who were at variance against the Seleucid king Antiochus IV (Epiphanes). Names were changed to reflect Babylonian times but those who read the book would know that it was about Antiochus IV. It is an interesting theory but it does have quite a few drawbacks, which many commentaries will be happy to show you. (One of those commentaries is *The Pulpit Commentary: Daniel*, from which I have gleaned some information for this section.) These drawbacks make it unlikely that Aslan is correct in assuming the book of Daniel was written in the second century B.C. But the dating of the book of Daniel is not the only important issue here. What is also important is to realize that Aslan attempts to use the Son of Man reference in the book of Daniel to promote the idea that Jesus was determined to create a secret society filled with those who accepted his new world order, where the first thing on the agenda would be to fight against the powers that be (the Roman authorities, the Jewish priesthood and other religious leaders). If they succeeded, they would then bring Israel its independence and Jesus would, no doubt, be hailed as its King. To protect his messianic secret, Jesus used the term "Son of Man" as a code phrase for identifying himself as a leader similar to the Maccabees. What becomes obvious in Aslan's attempt to blend the title 'Son of Man' with his theory of the messianic secret is that he is willing to devise any theory, no matter how creative or non-historical, just to keep from accepting the conclusions the Gospels offer about Jesus—that he is the Son of God, the Redeeming Messiah.

Although Aslan does not deny the fact that Jesus called himself the Son of Man, he thinks that Jesus often contradicted himself in the way that he used the phrase. Aslan provides eight passages from Mark's Gospel that he thinks proves that Jesus contradicted himself. In Mark 14:62, Aslan says Jesus used 'Son of Man' to reveal his power; but Mark 13:26 shows Jesus as suffering. In Mark 2:10, Aslan says Jesus used 'Son of Man' to show that he is here on earth, and yet will come sometime in the future (Mark 8:38). In Mark 10:33, Aslan says Jesus

219

used 'Son of Man' to reveal how people will reject him; but in Mark 14:62, Aslan says Jesus used 'Son of Man' to show that he (Jesus) will judge humankind. In Mark 8:38, Aslan says Jesus used 'Son of Man' to reveal that he (Jesus) is a ruler and a servant (Mark 10:45). I hope you have noticed that Aslan uses several passages more than once. Aslan couples Mark 14:62 and 13:26, but it seems he has provided the wrong passages to prove his point; both say pretty much the same thing—Jesus says in Mark 14:62 that "you will see the Son of Man sitting at the right hand of the Mighty One and coming on the clouds of heaven." and Mark 13:26 says, "Then people will see the Son of Man coming in clouds with great power and glory." There is no contradiction here, and there is no reference to Jesus suffering in this passage either, as Aslan claims. Aslan then couples Mark 2:10 and Mark 8:38 where Jesus says, in the former, that he is present on earth and, in the latter, that he will be coming in the future. Now Mark 2:10 says: "I want you to know that the Son of Man has authority on earth to forgive sins." So, yes, Jesus is on earth at a particular place and time making this statement that he has the authority to forgive sins (a statement, of course, that meant Jesus was giving himself a power that only God could have). Mark 8:38, which is supposed to contradict this statement, says this: "If anyone is ashamed of me and my words in this adulterous and sinful generation, the Son of Man will be ashamed of them when he comes in his Father's glory with the holy angels" (NIV). So, Aslan is saying that it is a contradiction to say something now, and then say you are going to do something in the future. I can say that I am here right now at this desk, and in a week I will be back here again; there is no contradiction in that statement. In fact, do we not typically hope that we are here today and tomorrow? It is no contradiction to say that I am here today and will be here some time in the future, which is what Jesus is doing. Another so-called contradiction Aslan gives us is where Jesus says he will be rejected by men and yet will judge men. Aslan uses Mark 10:33 for the rejection part which is where Jesus tells his disciples that they are going to Jerusalem and that he (Jesus) will be arrested by the chief priests, will be condemned to death, will be killed and rise from the dead three days later. So, yes, Jesus is letting his disciples know ahead of time what is going to happen to him. Aslan says this statement of being rejected contradicts the statement in Mark 14:62. This is the second time Aslan uses this passage, in case you had not noticed, to try to prove a contradiction. It did not work the first time, and it does not work now. Mark 14:62

says, "[Y]ou will see the Son of Man sitting at the right hand of the Mighty One and coming on the clouds of heaven." How is it that these two passages contradict each other? They clearly do not. Aslan then couples Mark 8:38 and Mark 10:45 together to try to convince us that Jesus contradicted himself. Mark 8:38 says Jesus is a ruler and Mark 10:45 says he is a servant. Notice Aslan uses the same passage (Mark 8:38) that he used to prove Jesus was coming in the future—Jesus says that when he returns he will be coming in his Father's glory with the holy angels—but now he is using it to show that Jesus is a ruler. Then Aslan uses Mark 10:45 in hopes that it will contradict Jesus being a ruler. Mark 10:45 says: "For even the Son of Man did not come to be served, but to serve, and to give his life as a ransom for many" (NIV). Notice Aslan accepts the first part of the statement from Jesus that he is a servant, but does not accept the part where Jesus says he will give his life as a ransom for many. It is too bad that Aslan is so picky about what sayings of Jesus he accepts. Is there a contradiction here? Of course not! Is it possible for someone to be a ruler, someone to be in a position of power, and yet have a mentality of servanthood? Must a ruler be only harsh, arrogant, and cruel, or can a ruler be also humble and want to serve? Isn't this what we expect of those we put in political office? We want them to be able to rule and at the same time be a civil servant. Again, there is no contradiction here. So, the passages that Aslan offered as proof that Jesus contradicted himself in using the title Son of Man do not, in fact, show any contradictions. Maybe Aslan needs to relearn what the term contradiction means. Generally, it is when a pair of statements is unable to both be true. For example, God exists; God does not exist. This pair of statements cannot both be true. One is false. They contradict each other. Another example: Jesus rose from the dead; Jesus did not rise from the dead. The New Testament claims Jesus rose from the dead; the Qur'an says Jesus did not rise from the dead. One of them is false.

Aslan is not quite finished with the 'Son of Man' concept. He goes on to claim that it is linked to another major idea found in the Gospels—the Kingdom of God. Aslan believes these two ideas—the Son of Man and the Kingdom of God—mean the same thing, that the Gospels actually link them together into one basic concept. Aslan believes that Jesus used these two ideas—the Son of Man and the Kingdom of God—in connection with another idea that was associated with Aslan's concept of the messianic secret. This other idea that Jesus had, which was tied in with his messianic secret, was to create a total about face of the political/religious system Aslan says Jesus hated. This reversal of the political/religious system would mean that the poor would become powerful and the meek would be made mighty. This new social order would flip the current system on its head. The best person to run this new social order, of course, would be Jesus who would act as God's representative. Jesus is the peasant king who rides into Jerusalem on a donkey, thereby showing, Aslan claims, that he is going to both usher in the physical Kingdom of God and rule in that kingdom. In linking these two ideas together—the Son of Man and the Kingdom of God—and then associating them with his concept of the messianic secret, Aslan is, once again, twisting biblical passages into something totally different than what was intended. This practice of reinterpreting and rewriting Gospel passages (something Aslan and the JS consistently do; Spong calls it 'rethinking') follows a postmodern methodology. Because postmodernists do not believe in tangible truth or metanarratives, they allow themselves to twist and turn anything they want into something that meets their own needs or desires. They are not concerned with what the original author meant or was trying to get across; they are concerned with manipulating whatever was said in order to comply with their own interpretation and/or need. Whether it was written thousands of years ago, or in yesterday's newspaper, the postmodern way of accepting any narrative is purely subjective. Aslan often interprets Gospel (and other biblical) passages in the spirit of postmodernistic thought.

Aslan wants you to think that Jesus, with his messianic secret and his new world order and his reversal of the political/religious system he lived under, is setting himself up to be the best choice to be the king to rule over the Kingdom of God on God's behalf. Aslan says Jesus is doing everything he can to embody this new social order he hopes to create. In Jesus' flipped social order the poor will rule, the meek will be mighty, the sinner will be righteous, the marginalized will be important. Aslan believes this social order is a physical one, and that is where he misses the boat, so to speak. Jesus has not been talking about a physical kingdom (that is Aslan's postmodern twisting of the narrative); Jesus is talking about a spiritual realm where those who are oppressed by sin can enter in order to find forgiveness. Since Aslan rejects the supernatural; everything must be interpreted by him in physical terms only. His worldview stifles his thoughts; he is unable to think outside of that worldview. It has, in essence, closed his mind. This unfortunately is true of so many people. It is the Christian who actually exercises an opened mind in accepting a spiritual realm, of accepting more than just the physical. Once the Christian enters the spiritual realm by being open minded, he/she then learns to accept what is true, which, by its nature, limits what one believes. So the Christian is accused of being closed minded simply because he/she does not believe something that is not true. Because a person is willing to believe just about anything, while for the most part denying a spiritual or supernatural realm exists, does not mean they are open minded.

When Jesus used the title 'Son of Man' we see that he was not only identifying himself with humanity, he was also using it as a reference to the One who would come as God to judge the world at the final Day of Judgment. The Jews knew that Jesus was using the title to show that he was God. It was Jesus' reference to Daniel's 'Son of Man' prophecy that upset the religious leaders enough to want him executed.

Prophecies Regarding the Messianic Kingdom

As I mentioned earlier, the Hebrew Scriptures speak of two different time periods for the Messiah. At the Messiah's first arrival, he comes by actually being born, but he is born by the "seed of the woman," i.e., by virgin birth. He lives a normal life until he begins his ministry, which includes healing and preaching. He is executed for the sins of Israel and the world and is resurrected. He returns to heaven, having fulfilled that particular mission, and will come again at some future time to establish his Messianic Kingdom on earth, when he will reign as king. This will be his second arrival. Both arrivals are clearly stated in the Hebrew Scriptures. Between the two arrivals is a time period designated as the time of the Church Age, when the Messiah/King is physically absent, but the Holy Spirit—a Person within the Triune God—works with Jesus' followers as a Helper. The Hebrew Scriptures do not speak of two different Messiahs coming at different times. There is only one Messiah coming at two different times, each time to fulfill something different. When Aslan says Jesus did not complete even one requirement that the Messiah was supposed to fulfill he is only referring to those passages that signify the Messiah's second arrival, when the Messiah will establish the Messianic Kingdom. Of course, Jesus has not yet fulfilled those promises, simply because it has not happened yet. Jesus has, however, fulfilled all the prophecies regarding the Redeemer Messiah. He is yet to fulfill the prophecies regarding the Messianic Kingdom. Aslan has made the error of thinking the Messiah should have accomplished both tasks at the same time. The Hebrew Scriptures do not make that error.

Just as we saw that there are numerous prophecies in the Hebrew Scriptures referring to the Redeeming Messiah, we also find numerous prophecies in the Hebrew Scriptures referring to the King and the Messianic Kingdom. Psalms 15:1-5 and 24:1-6 indicate the type of person/citizen who will live in the Messianic Kingdom. Isaiah 2:2-4 reveals the King as a righteous judge over all the nations during the Messianic Kingdom. He will settle disputes in order to prevent any animosity that may arise among the people that could cause military conflict. The people will beat their swords into plowshares and their spears into pruning hooks, and no one will train for war. Hosea tells us that God will destroy and abolish bows, swords, and other weapons of war, so everyone can live in safety (2:18). In Isaiah 11:6-9 we have the wonderful description of the Messianic Kingdom where the wolf lives in peace with the lamb and the leopard will nap with a goat, and a cow will feed with the bear and a little child will not be afraid to lead them; and best of all, "the earth will be filled with the knowledge of the LORD." Isaiah also tells us that the Messianic King "will reign in righteousness and rulers will rule with justice" (NIV, 32:1). The King will have individual rulers spread throughout his kingdom who will administer justice. Jesus told his twelve disciples that they will "sit on twelve thrones, judging the twelve tribes of Israel" (NIV, Mt 19:28). Other passages in the New Testament identify Jesus as the Messiah king who had been promised in the Hebrew Scriptures; a few will suffice. Matthew records Jesus saying he will reign in power and glory (19:28; 25:31). Luke says Jesus is the Son of the Most High and his kingdom will last forever (1:32f). Paul talks about the Church Age and then refers to the future when the Messianic King will come to rule (Rom 11:25–27). The book of Hebrews says Jesus will return or come a second time to be with those who are waiting for him (9:27f). In Revelation, John talks of Jesus reigning as Messianic King (20:4–6).

Three Basic Promises—End Times; Liberation; the Restoration of Israel

Of course, Aslan, members of the Jesus Seminar, and many liberal theologians reject the futuristic sayings of Jesus. Believing that Jesus was simply a first-century zealot (one among many) who only cared about first-century conditions (Roman occupation and oppression), Aslan insists that the early Christian writers put these futuristic sayings into Jesus' mouth in order to make him more believable to those followers who had suffered through Jerusalem's destruction in 70 A.D. In fact, Aslan claims that Jesus made three basic promises to his followers but failed to bring to fruition what he had promised he would do. The first so-called failure was not bringing about what is called the End Times; the second one was that God did not liberate the Jews; and the third one was Israel had not been restored and so the Kingdom of God did not arrive.

Aslan says Jesus talked about the End Times (see Mt 24; Mk 13; Lk 21), but they did not transpire; what happened instead was that Rome destroyed Jerusalem and the Temple. For Aslan, this shows that Jesus failed and therefore cannot be the Messiah. There is a reason, however, why the End Times did not occur or transpire shortly after Jesus talked about them, and it is quite simple: the End Times did not happen because it was not yet the End Times. If it was not the right time, how then could it have occurred? Why should I be angry that you have not arrived yet for our lunch meeting when it is six o'clock in the morning? It isn't time yet. The Scriptures clearly state that there are two distinct arrival times for the Messiah. It is quite odd that Aslan would discount something that is supposed to happen in the future because it has not happened yet. The reason Aslan makes this error is because he (and the JS) does not believe that Jesus made any futuristic statements. Aslan misses the whole point of Jesus' mission. Since Aslan's thesis is that Jesus was a zealot, and since Jesus did not accomplish the overthrow of Rome like a good zealot should have done, then, for Aslan, Jesus was a failure. But Jesus did not come to fulfill Aslan's thesis. Aslan created a false scenario and then said Jesus did not fulfill it; and since Jesus did not fulfill it, he was not who he said he was. This kind of reasoning is typical of Aslan and the JS, but it is not sound reasoning. The error is not in Jesus' promise; it is in Aslan's mindset. Jesus actually did tell his disciples that the Temple would be destroyed, but he did not say that it would happen in the last days (the End Times). Jesus did not fail to keep his promises, as Aslan says, nor did the early church need to fix Jesus' failure by recreating the messianic prophecies. There are three puzzling things about Aslan's premise: one, Jesus supposedly made some promises he did not keep; two, these so-called failed promises are recorded in the Gospels; and three, the Gospels tried to cover up the failed statements by creating ones that made Jesus look good. The question is: Why would the Gospel writers have included these sayings in the first place? Since Aslan believes the Gospels were written after the destruction of Jerusalem in 70 A.D., there would be no reason for the Gospel writers to make up these promises that had not been kept. Now what we actually do find is that the synoptic Gospels claim that Jesus did make futuristic statements and that most of these statements were about the Messianic Kingdom and the End Times. The passages we will consider in order to answer Aslan's premise that Jesus failed to keep his promise regarding the End Times are found in Matthew 24, Mark 13, and Luke 21:5–36. It is important to look at all three Gospel accounts to understand what Jesus tells his disciples. (I advise you to read these Scripture passages before continuing to read this section, if possible.)

Jesus is leaving the Temple courtyard where he has just pronounced seven final woes upon the Pharisees for their rejection of him as the Messiah. The disciples point out how beautiful the Temple buildings are. Jesus tells his disciples that not one stone will be left on top of another. The Temple will be torn down. Obviously, the disciples want to know more about this. While on their way to Bethany, about a mile and half from Jerusalem, Jesus sits down with his disciples on the western slope of the Mount of Olives, possibly in the garden known as Gethsemane, which gives the disciples the opportunity to ask Jesus the three things that are troubling them. They want to know when the destruction of the Temple will happen. They want to know when Jesus is going to set up the Messianic Kingdom. They want to know when the world will come to an end. Jesus answers the disciples' questions in this penultimate discourse, known as the Olivet Discourse. Jesus will talk about the present, the near future, and the far future as he answers the disciples' questions. He will talk about the fate of Jerusalem, about his return, and about the end or last days. It is certainly appropriate for Jesus to prepare his followers for the destruction of Jerusalem and to let them know about the upcoming dangers they will encounter being Jesus' disciples. Jesus wants them to be in a state of expectation and readiness regarding his return so that his disciples, no matter what year they will be living in, will live in hope and be vigilantly watching. [Each generation of believers is to live as though the king is near and will arrive soon.] Up to that point the disciples had not really experienced any severe, negative repercussions for being Jesus' followers. Jesus now tells them what they can expect will happen to them. Regarding the present, Jesus tells his disciples to be careful not to let anyone deceive them into thinking that he (Jesus) has returned so soon. There will continue to be wars (skirmishes) and insurrections, but they are bound to happen, human nature being what it is. Nations will fight against each other, famines will occur [as one did during Claudius' reign; see Acts 11:28], and there will be the occasional earthquake. All of these things would not indicate that the end was near; these events were only the beginning of the end.

When Jesus sent out his disciples on a missionary journey (see Mt 10) he told them that the people accepting him would suffer rejection even among their own family, that the gospel would bring conflict (a sword) because even family members would hate their brother or sister for being committed to Jesus. Jesus reiterates that warning here. Jesus warns his followers that they will be betrayed and hated, arrested and persecuted. They will be thrown into prison. They will be tortured and killed. [A reading of Luke's book of Acts shows that what Jesus predicted did happen to his followers.] Jesus tells his disciples that false prophets will deceive many people, just like they did all throughout Israel's history. People will grow more lawless, as they did just prior to the Flood. [These false teachers and lawless people are mentioned in the epistles that make up a large portion of the New Testament.] During this time, the gospel—the message about the kingdom of heaven—will continue to be preached throughout the world, even in the midst of persecution. [In his book of Acts, Luke mentions Peter, John and Philip as they venture off to spread the gospel, and then, joining Paul's entourage, he focuses primarily on Paul's ministry as he (Paul) takes the gospel to Asia Minor and parts of Greece. If the other apostles were doing what Paul did, and there is no reason to doubt that they were not, then the gospel was taken throughout the then known world. In fact, Paul informs the believers in Colossae that the good news was producing results and spreading all over the world (Col 1:6).] When all these things Jesus is talking about happen then Jerusalem will soon come to an end; no stone will be left on top of another. This event took place roughly forty years (a generation) after Jesus spoke these words.

So, we see Jesus preparing his disciples for what lies ahead in their near future. Now Jesus will tell his disciples about the destruction of Jerusalem and the Temple. Jesus says a disgusting thing will cause destruction at the Temple. Matthew, since his audience was Jewish, always showed how the Hebrew Scriptures were relative to Jesus and his life and words, and therefore makes a reference to the book of Daniel. Mark leaves out the reference to Daniel because his readers were mostly Gentiles, but he still uses the phrase "disgusting thing that causes destruction." Luke identifies the disgusting thing as armies camped around Jerusalem. Jesus says a disgusting thing will happen to Jerusalem, which will result in the Temple being utterly destroyed. We know that the Jewish Revolt began around 66 A.D., and that the Roman army came in and destroyed Jerusalem and the Temple in 70 A.D. Around 66 A.D., when the Jewish Revolt was just getting underway, Cestius Gallus brought his Roman forces to the walls of Jerusalem and was ready to attack the city, but for some reason decided to abort his plans. The Christians living in Jerusalem took this as a sign to leave, basing their decision on the words of Jesus, and left the city en masse (see *The Pulpit Commentary* on Matthew 24). The carnage and total destruction that Titus would bring to Jerusalem in 70 A.D. would be so complete that it would result in a "kind of misery that has not happened from the beginning of the world until now and will certainly never happen again" ("Scripture is taken from *God's Word*®. © 1995 God's Word to the Nations. Used by permission of Baker Publishing Group." Mt 24:21). The Jews were slaughtered and exiled and would not return until 1948.

Jesus then focuses on the disciples' question regarding his return. Jesus tells them that before he returns there will be numerous people claiming to be the Messiah. This happened during Jesus' lifetime, too. People claimed to be the messiah and promised their followers that they would rescue Israel from Roman rule. Jesus said that in the future, before he returns again, there will be people who will offer salvation to the populace. They will accompany their claims with "spectacular, miraculous signs and do wonderful things," and people will follow them and become deceived. These false messiahs, false ideas, false teachings through false preachers will be so convincing that it will be almost possible for even devout followers of Jesus to be deceived, except that Jesus has warned us ahead of time so that we do not fall for or become enticed by the false saviors' antics. These false messiahs and false teachers are seen today in the myriad of religious cults that have become popular. Pagan ceremonies are abundant. So-called spiritual experiences are inspired by self-help gurus who convince their followers to embark on a journey of personal godhood. Standards have been relaxed so there is nothing to be used in judging the moral quality of a particular experience; it is all based on how it feels. The false messiah is not necessarily a person, but can also be an ideal that assists in so-called human progress. So we have Marxists and Humanists that tell us we can become a greater society, a greater individual, by denouncing traditional values (morals and God, for example) and by working towards our own evolution to become our own God. In this atmosphere of rampant socio-political/religious/spiritual ideas, Jesus tells his followers to stand firm. Jesus warns his followers not to be deceived by people, ideas, and trends that contain a false hope for salvation. He tells them not to go out to the desert to look for the Messiah, because he will not be there. The desert is where armies train; it is where zealots and bandits during Jesus' lifetime were hiding to prepare their followers for combative maneuvers. Aslan wants you to think that Jesus started off in the desert with his teacher John the Baptizer, that he learned about the kingdom of heaven from the Baptizer before heading off to do his own ministry. Do not believe it. Jesus warned us not to believe anyone who says the Messiah is in some secret place. Aslan tells us that Jesus had a messianic secret that he only shared with his close disciples, a secret he could not let the crowd know about; the secret he carried with him was simply that he was a zealot and was going to use his magical skills to fight for Israel's freedom. Do not believe it.

When Jesus returns he will not be hiding out in the desert or in some secret place. He will arrive as visible and clear as lightning flashing across the sky from east to the west. All of today's worldly systems (socio-political/religious/spiritual, with their modern signs and wonders) have humans progressing towards something greater than themselves, to some ideal that is not clearly defined. They are groping in the dark for something to save them, but the Son of Man will come

229

like a lightning flash because he is light and in him there is no darkness (see I Jn 1:5). Jesus will arrive with a glorious declaration that will stretch across the sky. There will be no doubt that he has arrived, and his arrival will be sudden, global, and instantly recognizable. He will return at the time when everything will be restored as God promised (see Acts 3:21). Jesus will send out his angels and they will gather his followers. The Church Age will be finished and the Messianic Kingdom brought in. Then Jesus will reign as king in an earthly Messianic Kingdom.

So we see here in these passages that Jesus answers his disciples' questions about the destruction of Jerusalem's Temple, about his return and the setting up of the Messianic Kingdom. He does this just a few days before he will be arrested, tortured and killed. He knows these three things will happen to him. He knows his disciples will scatter and will fear for their lives. In the midst of the frightening words he has just spoken to them, Jesus offers them hope in letting them know he will return. But he does not give them an exact time as to when he will return. He tells them that it is in his Father's hands. He does tell them to watch and continue to work for the kingdom of heaven, spreading the gospel, and to expect him at any moment. Throughout the years, each generation of Christians is to do the same. We do not know when Jesus will return; we know that he will because he has promised to do so. The invitation to watch and expect his return is privileged to each generation. We see then that Jesus predicted the destruction of Jerusalem, so he knew that Rome would destroy the city and defile God's Temple. Jesus warned his disciples that this would happen. The Christians adhered to Jesus' warnings and in 66 A.D. left Jerusalem to escape the destruction Jesus prophesied would happen. By the way, this is another good indication that the three synoptic Gospels that contained this warning were written and distributed before the destruction of Jerusalem. So, Jesus did not fail to keep his promise about the End Times, as Aslan would have you believe.

The second so-called failure Aslan mentions is that Jesus promised that God would free the Jews from their oppression, but God did not do it, so Jesus misspoke. Now, we have already seen that the religious leaders and many other Jews rejected Jesus as their Messiah during his lifetime. When we read the Hebrew Scriptures we see that God had to punish Israel quite often throughout their history because they rejected him and turned to other idols to worship. They chose a sinful life rather than a God-approved life. In his punishment, God was only able to save a remnant that was willing to follow him. When the Redeeming Messiah arrived—that is, Jesus—the Jews rejected him, just like they had often rejected God. So the kingdom of heaven was going to be given over to the Gentiles until God deemed the time to be ripe for bringing in the promised Messianic Kingdom. Jesus told the religious leaders who had rejected him, "I can guarantee that the kingdom of God will be taken away from you and given to a people who will produce what God wants" ("Scripture is taken from *God's Word®*. © 1995 God's Word to the Nations. Used by permission of Baker Publishing Group." Mt 21:43). In Leviticus 26:14-45, God showed the Israelites what would happen if they rejected him, how they would be captured and exiled and only a remnant would remain. In Matthew 21:43, Jesus told the Pharisees what would happen when they rejected him as the Messiah: the kingdom of heaven would be given to the Gentiles. The Gentiles would be the main participants in the kingdom of heaven during the Church Age, a time Jesus described as "the times of the Gentiles" (Lk 21:24). When this time period is fulfilled Jesus will return and set up his Messianic Kingdom. As he had often done in times past, God will use a small Jewish remnant—the first Jews to accept Jesus as their Messiah—to spread the good news about the kingdom to the rest of the world. Part of the reason Jesus was unable, as Aslan says, to free the Jews from oppression was because they rejected him; in essence, they refused his help. Jesus was not going to violate their free will. But one thing Aslan is unable to understand because of his idea that no one needs a savior is that the bondage Jesus always referred to was the bondage of sin. Jesus came to free humankind from the bondage of sin. Jesus was not referring to the Jewish bondage under Roman rule; he was talking about their bondage to sin. Aslan is unable to understand the difference because of his own mindset.

When Jesus was brought to the Temple when he was just a couple of months old in order to be dedicated to the Lord, an old and devout man named Simeon, who had been waiting for the Messiah, saw Jesus and came over to the family. Luke says the Holy Spirit had told Simeon that he would not die until he had seen the Messiah, whom the Lord would send. Simeon took the child in his arms and, praising God, said that he could now die in peace because the promise of the Messiah had

231

been fulfilled. He had seen the Messiah. Then he told Mary that Jesus, although he was the Messiah, would be rejected by many Israelites which would result in their condemnation, but he would also save many (see Lk 2:26-35). The point here is that this old, devout man who had been waiting for the Messiah like thousands of other Jews at this time knew that the Messiah's arrival did not automatically bring the people out of bondage. Simeon knew that the Messiah would be rejected by many of his people, but that many would also be saved by him. It was a personal choice. There was no blanket salvation that covered every Jew just because they were a Jew. Salvation was offered, and it could be rejected or accepted. Being released from bondage did not automatically apply to everyone, just to those who accepted it. When Jesus was rejected in Nazareth at the beginning of his ministry it was because he told the Jews in the synagogue that God was going to be more lenient on Gentiles than on them because they had rejected him. They got so angry at this that they proceeded to try to kill him, but he escaped their clutches. Again, the promise of release from bondage was not automatic; it was a choice that required acceptance. Jesus' fellow Nazarenes decided to reject him as the Messiah, and so they chose to stay in bondage.

After Jesus was killed and rose on the third day he met two men walking down a country road toward a town outside Jerusalem (see Lk 24:26-35). He asked them what they were talking about. They told him they were discussing the latest news: Jesus of Nazareth, who they thought was a powerful prophet and would be the one to free Israel, had been condemned to death by the religious leaders and crucified. Jesus' followers were still holding to the hope that the Messiah would free Israel from their bondage to Rome, not realizing that the real bondage the Messiah came to free them from was the bondage of sin. Just before Jesus returned to heaven, his disciples asked him if now was the time when he was going to restore the kingdom to Israel (see Acts 1:6). Jesus must have been frustrated that his disciples still did not clearly see God's time table. The fault lay in their acceptance of one group of promises while ignoring the other group. The Hebrew Scriptures affirmed two different arrivals of the Messiah: one to redeem humankind by a substitutionary death, and the other to establish the Messianic Kingdom. Because Aslan does not believe in the necessity of a savior, he rejects the promise of the Redeeming Messiah and only focuses on the Messianic Kingdom, which he says

232

Jesus did not bring in and therefore is a failure. For Aslan, the only conclusion one can come to about Jesus is that he was a zealot who made an abysmal attempt at freeing Israel from Rome and paid for it with his life. That should have been the end of the story, as it was with all the other zealot messiahs during that time. Except that, for some reason, some of Jesus' die-hard followers decided to make up a bunch of stories about him and start a new religion. In answer to the disciples' question about whether Jesus was going to restore the kingdom to Israel, Jesus told them they did not need to know about times or periods, that that was something the Father had determined. Then he told them that they would receive power when the Holy Spirit came to them. With the Holy Spirit's help, the disciples would be Jesus' witnesses, testifying about him, starting in Jerusalem, going throughout Judea and Samaria, and then to the ends of the earth (Acts 1:7f). Jesus had already told them in the Olivet Discourse what they needed to know regarding their question about restoring the kingdom to Israel.

Aslan erroneously thinks the bondage Jesus came to free Israel from was Roman rule. Aslan believes Jesus was setting himself up to be the zealot who would accomplish what none of the other zealots had accomplished before him, but unfortunately was captured and killed before he could bring it to fruition. But Aslan misses the complete picture as seen in both the Hebrew Scriptures and the Gospels. When the announcement was made to Mary that she was going to give birth to the Messiah she was told he would save his people from their sins (Mt 1:21). Jesus explained to his disciples the importance of forgiveness of sins when he told them that if they forgave others when they sinned against them, then God would forgive them; but if they refused to forgive others, then God would not forgive them. Forgiveness of sins was very important to God; it was for the forgiveness of sins that his Son came to earth. Jesus often told those he healed, even before he healed them, that their sins were forgiven. Having their sins forgiven was more important than being healed. Having our sins forgiven means we are made right with God, that we can now enter into a relationship with him. That cannot be done without forgiveness of sins, by having those sins washed away by the blood of Jesus, by his substitutionary death. There are lots of things we can be in bondage to—a job, another person, a country, an ailment—but the worst bondage of all is sin. Without accepting the Redeeming

Messiah, you cannot be released from the bondage of sin. When asked why he ate with tax collectors and sinners, why he hung out with the marginalized and poor and oppressed, Jesus said, "I have not come to call the righteous, but sinners" (Mt 9:13). The Pharisees thought they were too righteous to need a savior, so they rejected Jesus. Jesus did not eat with the sinner because he secretly thought, "I have come to be a zealot and get these people to back me up." No, Jesus came to seek and save the lost (Lk 19:10). Jesus told a group of people that they were going to die in their sins because of their rejection of him. Jesus informed them they were from this world, but he was not from this world. Because they were a part of this world which was affected by sin, Jesus said they would die in those sins if they did not believe that he was the Messiah (Jn 8:23f). Jesus made it abundantly clear that whoever lives a sinful life is a slave to sin and that the only escape from that bondage, that slavery to sin, is being freed from it by Jesus. Jesus said of himself that "if the Son sets you free, you will be absolutely free" (Jn 8:34, 36). Jesus offered freedom to his fellow Jews, but it was not a zealot's freedom, a freedom from socio-political oppression; it was a freedom from sin.

Aslan's third so-called failure was that Israel had not been restored and the Kingdom of God did not become a reality here on earth; in other words, the new world order that Aslan says Jesus promised did not come to fruition. Aslan believes that Jesus promised that Israel would have its independence restored, that the twelve tribes would be reestablished once again, that the twelve apostles would rule over the twelve reestablished tribes, and that this would happen in the third decade of the first century. Aslan says that what happened instead was Rome destroyed Jerusalem and much of Judea, slaughtering numerous Jews and exiling the rest. Therefore, says Aslan, God's kingdom did not arrive in Israel as Jesus had promised; he was unable to bring in the new world order. Since Jesus failed to keep this promise, Aslan believes the early church had to quickly fix Jesus' failure by recreating the messianic prophecies. In presenting his third so-called failure, Aslan again shows that he refuses to accept the future statements of Jesus; he believes that everything Jesus said referred to his lifetime on earth. But Jesus clearly showed in his Olivet Discourse that the Messianic Kingdom will occur some time in the future. As mentioned before, between the first and second arrival of the Messiah, God established a "time of the Gentiles" known as the Church Age. At the end of this time period, Jesus will return and establish the Messianic Kingdom. Jesus promised his disciples that when he returns and assumes his rightful place as King on earth he will have them sit on twelve thrones, judging the twelve tribes of Israel (Mt 19:28). Israel will be restored during the Messianic Kingdom; she will take her place as the ruling nation of the world. An interesting statement is made by Zechariah, a prophet who returned to Jerusalem after the Babylonian exile in the sixth century B.C., five hundred years before the first arrival of the Messiah. Zechariah talks about a future Israel where God will vanquish its enemies and restore Israel's glory. When that happens Zechariah says the Messianic king will appear and the Israelites "will look on me, the one they have pierced" (12:10). What an incredible statement! When Jesus appears in the Messianic Kingdom as the King of Israel the Israelites will see the wounds he endured as the Redeeming Messiah. So, Jesus did not fail to reconstitute the nation as he promised; he just does not operate within Aslan's time frame. Jesus will fulfill this promise, but it will be sometime in the future. Aslan's error was his own failure to realize that when Jesus talked about the kingdom of heaven he was not referring to a physical realm. I have already discussed this at length, so if need be you can refer back to that section. Allow me though to reiterate that it is simply nonsensical to say that Jesus is a failure because the new world order he described never took shape. Jesus did not describe or promise a new world order, especially not the kind that Aslan created—one in which Jesus was going to do something so drastic, perilous, and revolutionary that Rome's response could only be a quick and complete execution of everyone involved. Aslan says that Jesus failed to keep his promises, but what we actually see is that Aslan's list of failures is his own. It is Aslan who fails to show that Jesus failed. Since Jesus did not fail, there was no reason for the early church to see Jesus' assumed failures as a dilemma that they needed to fix.

Chapter Eleven: A Journey Through the Gospels

Since Aslan claims that Mark's Gospel (which he believes was the first Gospel, written in the 70s A.D.) does not contain even one authoritative or reliable statement from Jesus that he is the Messiah, I suggest we take a journey through all the Gospels to see if Aslan is correct. Of course, you might say to yourself: What about Mark 14:61f where the high priest asked Jesus if he was the Messiah, and Jesus said that he was. Aslan says that does not count because when the high priest asked Jesus if he was the Messiah, Jesus was just reflexively accepting the title that everyone kept dumping on him. Aslan wants us to imagine that when Jesus was asked if he was the Messiah at his trial Jesus just shrugged his shoulders and nonchalantly said: 'Yeah, why not.' Aslan thinks that whenever someone in Mark's Gospel tried to call Jesus the Messiah—whether it was a demon, or a person asking for healing, or one of his disciples, or even God—Jesus just shrugged it off or halfheartedly accepted the title. It is certainly absurd for Aslan to claim that even when God told Jesus he was the Messiah at his baptism that Jesus simply brushed it off.

Aslan reminds us that the Q material does not contain one authoritative or reliable statement from Jesus that he is the Messiah. But the Q material is a hypothetical construction that mostly liberal theologians use as a resource for some of the sayings of Jesus. It is not a real historical document. It is a unicorn in the midst of real horses. So, when Aslan says Jesus is not the Messiah because the Q materials do not make a messianic statement about him, you must remember there are no Q materials. You should also realize that Aslan's premise is so weak that he has to constantly refer to a document that does not exist.

Aslan also makes a big deal about the language Mark used in writing his Gospel. It was not written in Aramaic, the so-called 'peasant' language; the language of Jesus. It was not written in the more sophisticated Hebrew language, which Aslan calls God's language. Mark's Gospel was written in Greek, which Aslan calls heathen language, an impure language. It was a language spoken by those who had destroyed Jerusalem and Judea. Aslan attempts to make Mark into some kind of traitor for writing his Gospel in a heathen language— Greek. But, as you already know, the Hebrew Scriptures had been translated into the Greek language in the third century B.C., and Greek was the universal language throughout the Roman Empire. There was no reason for the Gospels not to be written in the Greek language; they could be easily read by Jews and Gentiles alike. The epistles found in the New Testament were written in Greek, as well. Practically all the quotes from the Hebrew Scriptures that are found in the New Testament are from the Greek version called the Septuagint. Greek was not considered an impure or heathen language by first-century Jews or Christians. Aslan is trying to create an issue where there really is none.

Aslan ignores early Christian tradition that says Mark wrote the Gospel in the early 60s when Peter and Paul were still alive, and before Jerusalem had been destroyed. The *Pulpit Commentary* on the Gospel of Mark says that it is very likely that Mark had access to Matthew's Gospel. If he did, Mark is not merely condensing or copying Matthew's Gospel in order to create his own; what he is doing, the *Pulpit Commentary* says, is providing a narrative that gives precise and concise details about facts and events, without repeating information—discourses and parables—that is found in Matthew (and in Luke). (This is also why John's Gospel focuses on other facts and events and sayings of Jesus; it was not necessary for John to simply repeat what had already been said.) What Mark is doing is keeping his narrative simple, almost like a comprehensive abstract, so that we do not lose sight of the narrative's subject, who is Jesus. Mark supplies us with details about incidents that he could only have received from an eyewitness, and that eyewitness was Peter (as early church traditions have suggested). As previously stated, Matthew had in mind a Jewish audience, whereas Mark's Gospel was targeted for a more Gentile readership. We must not make the mistake of thinking that because Mark's Gospel is more "simple" than Matthew's and Luke's that it therefore was written first. We must bear in mind the audience and the purpose of each Gospel and not make broad statements about dates that are more contingent on 'proving' one's theory than on offering true light on the subject. We will see, beginning in Mark's first chapter, that he offers a concise rendering of the events, whereas Matthew and Luke, in contrast, provide more details. Right away we see that Mark is going to give his reader succinct information, not exhaustive information; and we see this pattern throughout Mark's Gospel. Mark pays particular attention to the miracles Jesus performed, using them to show that Jesus is the Messiah. Since Aslan believes that Mark's Gospel was the first one written, and it supposedly does not record one authoritative or reliable statement from Jesus that he is the Messiah, then the Gospels that come after Mark that do have Jesus saying he is the Messiah are just making it up. The thing to do, of course, is look at Mark's Gospel to see if Aslan is correct. So let's do so.

Mark's Gospel

Mark begins his Gospel by saying he is writing about Jesus the Messiah, the Son of God. [There is no question who Mark thinks Jesus is.] Mark immediately offers a passage from Isaiah in the Hebrew Scriptures to show why he believes Jesus is the Messiah, the Son of God. Mark uses the passage to declare that someone is going to announce the arrival of the Messiah, and Mark identifies that someone as John the Baptizer. Mark includes brief (concise) statements about Jesus' baptism and temptation, the beginning of his ministry, the calling of a few disciples, and the performing of some miracles (healings). In the second chapter, Jesus forgives and heals a paralyzed man. Jesus calls Matthew (Levi) to be his follower. Jesus answers questions the Pharisees have directed at him; he makes the claim that he is the Lord of the Sabbath (vs. 28). [This is a significant statement. The Sabbath was a strict law that Jews had to obey; it was listed in the Ten Commandments. Of course, the Pharisees and other religious leaders piled lots of restrictions onto this law, a number of which were rather overly burdensome. But the basic idea of the Sabbath was for God's people to have a day where they could rest, relax, and think about the many blessings God had given them. The Sabbath was to be a joyous occasion, but the Pharisees had made it into a highly restrictive duty. Jesus tells the Pharisees he is the Lord of the Sabbath, that he is the one who instigated it and, therefore, knows what he expects people to do on that day. This was a definitive statement from Jesus that he was God, the promised Messiah. The Pharisees tell Jesus to comply with the Sabbath, and Jesus, in turn, tells them "I created the Sabbath." Jesus has authority to teach the Jewish people about correct Sabbath priorities. Jesus honors the Sabbath and defends it by arguing for its true meaning (see *They Loved the Torah*).]

In chapter three, Jesus heals a disabled man in the synagogue on the Sabbath, which angers the Pharisees. Crowds follow Jesus and he heals those who are demon-possessed, rebuking the impure spirits within them for shouting, "You are the Son of God." [I have already commented on why Jesus did not want demons to profess his Messiahship, but let it be said here that Jesus is not about to let Satan take control of how Jesus' Messiahship is to be pronounced.] Jesus picks the twelve men to be his close followers (disciples). His family accuses him of being insane; Law teachers accuse him of being influenced by Satan. In chapter four, Jesus tells some parables and calms a storm on the sea. [Calming the storm shows that Jesus has power over nature; it is another statement by Mark that he believed Jesus to be God.] In chapter five, Jesus heals a severely demon-possessed man, raises a dead person, and does some more healing. In chapter six, Jesus refers to himself as a prophet, sends out the twelve to preach and heal, miraculously feeds five thousand people, walks on water and heals more people. [So far, Mark is letting his readers know that there definitely is something different and special about Jesus. Mark is talking about a man who had power not only over the Sabbath, but over diseases, Satan, and nature. Mark is undoubtedly declaring that this is no ordinary man. Like the other Gospels, Mark is clearly showing that Jesus is the Messiah.] In chapter seven, Jesus instructs the Pharisees on some important theological issues that the Pharisees should know, but do not. He heals a Gentile woman's daughter [the Canaanite woman, whom I have already discussed], and he heals a deaf and mute person.

In chapter eight, Jesus miraculously feeds four thousand people and heals a blind person. Jesus then specifically asks his disciples an important question. In asking this question, he wants to make sure that his disciples understand the significance of the answer. First, Jesus asks the disciples who the people say he is. [There are multiple answers to this question; this is true even today for those who do not know Jesus as their Messiah—they come up with some odd answers to this question that Jesus posed.] Jesus asks his disciples, "Who do you say I am?" Peter answers, "You are the Messiah." [Jesus wants them to verbally make this announcement. He does not deny it, or accept it reluctantly, as Aslan thinks. But he does not want them making any fanfare about it either. There are four reasons for this: One, there are zealots and bandits combing the countryside, gathering recruits. Jesus does not want to identify with them, nor does he want them or anyone else to take him by force to make him do their bidding. Two, crowds have already been following him because of his healing people of diseases and demon possession. Jesus does not want these crowds to get out of hand due to an early announcement that he is the Messiah. Three, the Pharisees, law teachers, Sadducees, and other religious leaders who are opposed to him have been waiting for the moment to be able to get rid of him. Making an untimely announcement that he is the Messiah would give the religious leaders that opportunity. Fourth, his disciples still have much to learn from him. It suffices that Jesus' disciples know who he is.] Immediately after Peter's declaration, Jesus tells them he will "be rejected by the elders, the chief priests and the teachers of the law, and that he must be killed and after three days rise again" (NIV, 8:31). [Mark has been leading up to this; he clearly announces right from the beginning of his Gospel that Jesus is the Messiah, the Son of God. In the first seven chapters, Mark shows how Jesus is the Messiah by all the healings and miracles he does. Then Mark comes right out and makes it clear in chapter eight that Jesus is the Redeeming Messiah.] Jesus tells the disciples they must deny themselves and take up their cross and follow him. [This is not, as Aslan thinks, a call to join Jesus' new world order where he, in true zealot fashion, will charge the Roman army with his small band of misfits.]

Chapter nine begins with Jesus telling his disciples that some of them are going to see the kingdom of God come with power. Six days later, three of the disciples are invited to go with Jesus to a mountaintop where they see Jesus in his glory. [I have spoken of this episode elsewhere, clarifying Aslan's huge misunderstanding, so there is no need to go into it here.] Jesus heals a boy of demon possession and then, a week after he has already told the disciples, he tells them again that he is going to be killed and will rise from the dead three days later. [Here is another messianic statement from Jesus.] Then Jesus talks about the penalty incurred on those who make people lose their faith in him. [This is why we need to seriously pray for those like Aslan, members of the JS, and other liberal theologians teaching in our colleges and universities, who deny that Jesus is the Messiah and cause people to lose and/or not acquire faith in our Lord.]

In chapter ten, Jesus again has to teach the Pharisees something they should already have known; then he blesses some children, tells a rich person how to enter the kingdom of heaven, and again tells his disciples that he will be killed and rise again on the third day. Jesus tells them, "[T]he Son of Man did not come to be served, but to serve, and to give his life as a ransom for many" (NIV, vs. 45). [Here is another messianic statement from Jesus.] On their way to Jerusalem, Jesus heals a blind person. In chapter eleven, Jesus enters Jerusalem, riding on a donkey. Jesus clears the Temple courtyard of the moneychangers. In chapter twelve, Jesus tells the Pharisees a parable where he announces that God has sent him into the world, that he will be killed, and because the Pharisees have rejected him as their Messiah they will be banished from the kingdom of heaven but the Gentiles will be allowed to enter. The Pharisees are upset at Jesus for this parable and attempt to trap him so they can arrest him as some kind of menace to society. They ask him if they should pay taxes. Jesus tells them to give the Emperor what belongs to him and to give God what belongs to him. (vs. 17.) [Of course, Aslan makes a big deal about this statement, saying it proves that Jesus is a zealot. I have already dealt with this issue, but it is important that you realize that the Pharisees were trying to trap Jesus into saying something so they could arrest him. If Jesus is saying he is a zealot by making this 'pay to Caesar, pay to God' statement, as Aslan believes, the Pharisees would have immediately arrested him.] Jesus has to teach the Sadducees something they should already know. Then a law teacher asks Jesus a question he [the law teacher] should know; he asks, "What is the greatest commandment?" Jesus tells him: "Love the Lord your God with all your heart and with all your soul and with all your mind and with all your strength." Then he quickly adds: "The second is this: 'Love your neighbor as yourself.' There is no commandment greater than these" (NIV, 12:30f). Jesus asks the law teachers why the Messiah was considered David's son when David himself declared: 'The Lord said to my Lord: "Sit at my right hand until I put your enemies under your feet"' (NIV, Psa 110:1). Jesus asks the law teachers, "If David calls him 'Lord' how then can he be his son?" [Jesus is telling them that he is not just in David's lineage, but he is David's Lord, the Messiah; another messianic statement from Jesus.]

In chapter thirteen, Mark records Jesus' discourse from the Mount of Olives regarding the destruction of the Temple and the End Times [something I have already thoroughly discussed]. In chapter fourteen, Mark tells us about the last supper that Jesus has with his disciples. [It is quite possible that this supper was at the home of Mark's parents. Mark may have been a young adolescent when this was taking place.] Peter is told that he will deny knowing Jesus. After supper they go to Gethsemane where some of the religious leaders come to arrest Jesus. Jesus stands before the Jewish Council—the Sanhedrin—to answer the charges against him. People offer false charges and often contradict one another. Some of them say that Jesus said he was going to destroy the Temple and then rebuild it in three days. All this time Jesus speaks not a word. Then the high priest asks him directly if he is the "Messiah, the Son of the Blessed One." Jesus says, "I am." Jesus adds, "And you will see the Son of Man sitting at the right hand of the Mighty One and coming on the clouds of heaven." [Here, I would say, is another distinct and profound statement from Jesus that he is the Messiah.] The high priest is extremely upset at this reply and rips his clothes in anger, declaring that Jesus has made a statement worthy of death. And to show he meant it, the high priest sends him off to Pilate to be crucified. In chapter fifteen, Jesus is tried before Pilate; he is mocked, beaten almost to the point of death, crucified, dies, and is buried. In the final chapter (sixteen), Mark tells his reader that Jesus rose on the third day just as he said he would. [Lots of controversy surrounds verses 9–20 of this chapter, as we will see in the Chapter Fourteen.]

Based on what we have discovered by going through Mark's entire Gospel, I would say that Aslan is in error in his declaration that Jesus did not make one authoritative or reliable statement that he is the Messiah.

Since Aslan also insists that the Gospels of Matthew and Luke (which he believes were written in the last decade of the first century) never claim that Jesus is the Son of God, we will now take a look at those Gospels. Then we will take a journey through John's Gospel as well. One thing to bear in mind as we look at Matthew and Luke's Gospels is that they would rather show than just tell that Jesus is the Son of God. Any creative writing professor should appreciate that; I am sure they often tell their students to show and not merely tell when they have a story to write. As we look at Matthew's narrative, it is important to remember that he is writing his Gospel to a Jewish audience with the purpose of giving evidence that Jesus is the Messiah that has been promised in the Hebrew Scriptures.

Matthew's Gospel

Matthew immediately begins with Jesus' genealogy to show that Jesus is the Son of David and the Messiah. Matthew makes it clear that Jesus' lineage follows the Messianic line of David. Matthew records Jesus' birth, claiming that Jesus was born miraculously [by virgin birth], and then sets the stage to demonstrate how Jesus is the Messiah by stating that Jesus was born in Bethlehem, fulfilling a messianic prophecy. Matthew mentions Herod [showing the historical setting], and the Magi from the east [probably when Jesus is around two years old] who supply the family with the money they will need to return to Nazareth. However, that return will be delayed because of Herod's anger and instructions to have Jesus killed. Jesus' family escapes to Egypt until Herod dies, and then his family settles in Nazareth in Galilee. Jesus begins his ministry by being baptized by John the Baptizer. Matthew sees John as the herald who was prophesied to announce the arrival of the Messiah. Matthew says that at the baptism of Jesus the Holy Spirit visibly descends upon him and God claims, in an audible voice, that Jesus is his Son. [Matthew is showing that Elohim, who created the universe, is present at the beginning of Jesus' ministry.]

The temptation occurs soon after the baptism. The Deceiver attempts to have Jesus disobey God [as he had gotten the first humans to do. The Deceiver will have his head crushed by the "seed of the woman," that is, by Jesus, unless he (the Deceiver) can get Jesus to sin.] The Deceiver calls Jesus the Son of God and attempts to have Jesus use his divine power in an ungodly way, thereby sinning and not being able to be the world's Messiah. Jesus [unlike Adam and Eve] does not fall for the Deceiver's lies and is able to continue his ministry as the Messiah. Jesus returns to Galilee and begins preaching. He develops a close following of twelve men who will be his disciples. He travels throughout the region, healing people, preaching, and continuing to fulfill messianic prophesies. Matthew shows how Jesus is able to control nature (calm the sea waves). [We see in the Hebrew Scriptures how God controlled nature.] Matthew records how, when Jesus heals demon-possessed people, they shout out that he is the Son of God.

Jesus forgives the sins of others [something Jews knew only God could do], which offends some Jews who were with Jesus. Matthew shows that Jesus has the power to forgive sins when Jesus heals a man from chronic paralysis after he forgives him. [Throughout his Gospel, Matthew attributes to Jesus actions that only God can do: heal leprosy and other diseases, calm storms, forgive sins, and raise the dead.]

Jesus calls God "My Father," not something a Jew would do. [By referring to God as his Father, Jesus is acknowledging that he is God's Son, and that he is on an equal par with God.] When John the Baptizer sends two disciples to ask Jesus if he is the Messiah, Jesus uses what he has been doing (healing and preaching) as proof that he is. Jesus tells the crowd that a person is blessed who puts his faith in him (Jesus). [Jews knew they were only to put their faith in God, but Jesus claims that those who put their faith in him will be blessed.] Then, Jesus casts a powerful warning upon the cities where he has preached and healed because they have not believed in him. After this warning, Jesus prays for his followers and thanks his Father for them, referring to himself as the Father's Son, that is, the Son of God, and then tells his followers that if they want rest, the kind of rest that God alone can give, they need to trust him (Jesus). Next, Jesus claims he is greater— of more significance—than the Temple and that he has authority over the Sabbath. When people begin to wonder aloud if Jesus is the Messiah, the Pharisees reject Jesus as the Messiah. Jesus rebukes them for their lack of faith and rejection and tells them that he will be killed and rise from the dead, just as Jonah had been three days inside the fish. He tells them that he is greater than Jonah, greater than Solomon, and that only those who do his Father's will are his true brothers and sisters. At the time that the Pharisees are rejecting him as the Messiah, Jesus refers to God as his Father, once again showing that he saw himself as the Son of God. After being rejected as the Messiah, Jesus begins to recite important, memorable parables, showing the danger of such rejection. He says he is the one who will send his angels at the Day of Judgment to gather the wicked for punishment. Jesus says the angels are at his disposal. [God had said the same thing in the Hebrew Scriptures.] Matthew shows again that Jesus has control over nature by feeding thousands from a few morsels and by walking on water. His followers, seeing the power that Jesus has over nature, worship him and call him the Son of God. A little while later, Jesus asks the disciples who they think he is. Peter answers for them and declares that he is the Messiah, the Son of the living God. Jesus then predicts his death and resurrection, showing that his purpose on earth is to die for the sins of the world. Jesus takes three of his disciples to a mountain top where Jesus meets with Moses and Elijah. Once again, God audibly states that Jesus is his Son. Later, Jesus tells his followers that to be truly perfect and right in God's eyes, it is imperative that they follow him (Jesus). Jesus claims that he will, in the future, sit on a throne of glory when he returns as the Messianic King.

Jesus again announces that he will be killed, but will rise on the third day. He comes to Jerusalem and purposefully fulfills a prophecy related to the coming King by riding into the city on a donkey. [Although this may have excited many who thought he was coming as the Messianic King], Matthew tells us that Jesus let his followers know that he was actually coming as the Redeeming Messiah. By riding into Jerusalem as a king, Jesus is announcing his kingship, that he is the one worthy to come as Israel's king. [He is the King—God—coming to redeem humankind.] Because of his love for the Temple and its function throughout Jewish history, he throws out the moneychangers who are using the selling of sacrificial animals for extreme profit. He begins teaching in the courtyard and tells an important parable about how he is God's Son and how he will be killed when he arrives at the vineyard (i.e., earth). Jesus calls himself the cornerstone, the one prophesied to be rejected by the religious leaders. He warns them that the kingdom will be taken away from them (the religious leaders and disbelieving Jews) and given to others—the Gentiles. He then shows, by quoting Hebrew Scriptures, that the Messiah, although the son of David—which is what people had been calling Jesus—was actually David's Lord, and not merely his son or offspring. Jesus then comments on the hypocrisy of the religious leaders in similar fashion to how God had done throughout the Scriptures. Jesus laments the unbelief Jerusalem has shown throughout its history and says that he "often wanted to gather them together" like a protective hen would do for its chicks. [This lament suggests that Jesus believed he had experienced their rejection for many centuries, not just the thirty years he had been on earth.] He tells his listeners that in the future they will acknowledge him as being the one who comes in the name of the Lord. Jesus then meets with just his disciples and tells them about the coming destruction of Jerusalem—the Olivet Discourse. He talks about a future time when he will return as the Messianic King. Right after the Passover meal, Jesus tells his disciples about his death and resurrection. When Jesus is arrested he says that it is part of the plan that was spoken of in the Hebrew Scriptures. He stands trial before the Sanhedrin and is commanded under oath by the chief priest to state if he is the Messiah, the Son of God. Jesus admits that he is. He is condemned to die based on this confession. In front of Pilate, Jesus announces that he is the king of the Jews. Jesus is crucified and buried. As he said would happen, he rises from the dead on the third day. He appears to the eleven disciples as the risen Lord and commissions them to make disciples of all nations and to baptize believers in the name of the Father, Son, and Holy Spirit.

Because Matthew is writing to a Jewish audience, he uses Hebrew Scriptures to show that Jesus fulfilled the Messianic promises, quoting from about eighteen passages. He also recorded Jesus quoting numerous times from the Hebrew Scriptures to show that he was the Messiah. Of course, Aslan will say that Jesus did not really say these things about himself, that it was Matthew who put these words in his (Jesus') mouth. This is the same argument used by the Jesus Seminar. This is a typical "escape clause" Aslan and other liberal theologians/biblical scholars use whenever they have no solid historical evidence for their claims. Aslan cannot prove his statement that Jesus did not really say these things, but he believes that if he says it enough times in his book, then people will believe him. It does appear from looking at Matthew's Gospel that Matthew considered Jesus to be the literal Son of God, and claimed that Jesus said so too. Now, let's look at Luke's Gospel to see if it views Jesus as the literal Son of God.

Luke's Gospel

Luke begins by acknowledging that others have written and spoken about what he is going to write about, and that they were, unlike him, eyewitnesses of the events. Luke has followed the historical events closely and is providing an orderly account of his investigation into these historical events. Luke gives details about John the Baptizer's birth because John played an important role in Jesus' life—the role of herald. He also shows the relationship between the two—they are cousins. Luke provides information about Mary and the conception of Jesus. This takes place in Galilee. Because of a census, Joseph—

246

Mary's fiancé—and the pregnant Mary go to Bethlehem and register. Luke shows that the conception of both John and Jesus are significant by the fact that God has sent angels to their parents. [By the end of Luke's first chapter the reader knows that John and Jesus are going to be special.] In the second chapter, Luke records Jesus' birth in Bethlehem, stating that angels announce it to insignificant shepherds. Jesus is circumcised when he is eight days old, and his parents offer sacrifices indicating their poverty. When the baby Jesus is taken to the Temple for dedication two godly people—Simeon and Anna—announce that Jesus is the Messiah they have been waiting for. Luke has the family—Jesus, Mary and Joseph—return to Nazareth without relating the details that Matthew has already given in his Gospel. [Each of the Gospel writers emphasizes events that are part of the reason behind which they have written their narratives.] Luke gives one more episode of the young Jesus—he travels with his family to Jerusalem when he is twelve, something they have done every year [which indicates that Joseph had enough work to provide for his family]. Luke shows that the twelve-year-old Jesus knows that he is different—he calls God "My Father" and says it is reasonable for him to be in the Temple.

Luke provides a timeline—the fifteenth year in the reign of Tiberius—and then talks about John's ministry and his preaching as preparation for the Messiah. At Jesus' baptism, Luke states that God declared Jesus to be his Son. It is at this point that Luke discloses Jesus' genealogy in order to show that Jesus not only has a divine nature—he is God's Son—but he is human, too. Luke mentions Jesus' temptation and shows that Jesus is able to resist the Deceiver and not sin. [This allows Jesus to continue his ministry; otherwise, he would not have been able to fulfill the duties of the Messiah.] Luke says that Jesus was about thirty years old when he began his ministry. [Jews considered this to be the age when a person reached full maturity; it was the age when a scribe or teacher could lawfully teach (see Pulpit Commentary on Luke 3:23a).] Jesus returns to Galilee and in Nazareth, his hometown, reads a passage from Isaiah regarding the promised Messiah, claiming that he has come to fulfill those promises. Jesus begins to travel and heal others; demon-possessed people proclaim him to be the Son of God. He tells his followers that he has been sent to proclaim the good news about the Kingdom of God. [Of course, the Jews already thought they were in the kingdom of God, but they were

247

wrong. To be in the kingdom one must accept the King (Jesus), but not all of them did so.] Jesus then begins to call certain men to be his special disciples, those he is going to train and get ready to spread the Good News of God's salvation. Jesus continues to cure diseases and forgive sins, and even associates with "sinners and tax-collectors," showing not only his Messianic powers, but his concerns for the poor, oppressed and marginalized [the very people God was always concerned about as seen throughout the Hebrew Scriptures]. Jesus, as Messiah, has authority over the Sabbath and can therefore heal on the Sabbath. After choosing the twelve men who will be his close followers, he continues to heal others and preach. The people come from the coast lands, parts of Gentile regions, and all Judea to be healed by Jesus. [This clearly shows how compassionate God is; when he came to earth to die for our sins, he did not just come and get that done, he spent three years healing and caring for others.] Luke records a shortened version of Matthew's Sermon on the Mount, highlighting specific issues he wants his readers to comprehend. Jesus warns his listeners to not just hear or listen to his words; they must obey them. [God constantly said this same thing in the Hebrew Scriptures.]

Jesus heals the personal servant of a Roman army officer (a centurion) [showing, as did Matthew, that Jesus is no zealot; if Jesus were a zealot, he would have had nothing to do with this Roman]. Jesus is, in fact, so impressed by the officer's faith that he says that it (the centurion's faith) is greater than the faith displayed by his fellow Jews. [This is a great statement to make about a Gentile, and a Roman officer at that. The only other person Jesus said this about was another Gentile, a woman.] Jesus then raises a widow's son back to life. He tells two disciples whom John has sent that his miracles show that he is the Messiah. Jesus forgives a marginalized woman who was looked down upon by a religious leader. Luke records some of Jesus' sermons, spoken in parabolic format. Jesus asserts that his true family are those who do God's will. Jesus then shows he has the power to calm the seas from a violent storm. Jesus heals a demon-possessed man who claims Jesus is the Son of God. Jesus raises another person— a girl—from the dead. Jesus sends out his twelve disciples on a missionary journey. Jesus feeds thousands from a few morsels of food, a miracle that clearly shows Jesus' power. Now that the disciples have been with Jesus for a couple of years, Jesus wants to know what conclusion they have formed about him. Peter announces that Jesus is the Messiah. Jesus then tells his disciples that he will be rejected and killed, but that he will rise from the dead. Jesus lists the requirements for following him: they must obey his will and die daily to their own desires. [This is something God required of the Jew; Jesus is telling them they are to give their lives over to him. Luke is showing here that Jesus is to receive the same worship and devotion that God demands.] Jesus says he will arrive sometime in the future and will judge people based on their acceptance or rejection of him. Jesus is transfigured, showing his glory as the Son of God. Luke says that God, at this time, calls Jesus his Son. Jesus announces that he will be betrayed. He sends seventy disciples out to prepare people to accept him when he comes to their villages. Jesus voices his praise to God, his Father, and says that only he—the Son—knows God fully and that he—as the Son—is the one who chooses to reveal God to others.

Jesus is accused of having satanic power, but he refutes that by saying his power shows that God's kingdom has appeared. He uses Jonah's three days in the fish as an example that he will be buried for three days and will rise from the dead. He then calls himself greater than Jonah, and greater than Solomon. He criticizes the hypocrisy of the religious leaders and continues to preach using parables. Jesus talks about his second coming, when he will return as the Messianic King. Jesus warns his disciples that his coming to die for the sins of the world—the good news they will preach—will cause divisions among family and friends because of the fact that people will either accept him or reject him. Jesus heals a disabled woman on the Sabbath, irritating some religious leaders. Jesus continues to preach about the Kingdom of God. When someone asks Jesus how to get eternal life he tells the man to follow him. Jesus then tells his disciples, for the third time, that he will be rejected and killed, but will rise from the dead. At a person's house, where Jesus is having dinner, Jesus says that he came to the world to seek and save people who are lost [i.e., everyone]. Jesus approaches Jerusalem and enters riding a donkey as a prophetic declaration that he is King. He throws out the moneychangers because of the way they manipulate payments, hurting the poor. The Pharisees try to trick and trap Jesus into saying something whereby they can arrest him, but they are unable. Jesus uses Scripture to show that the Messiah is more than human, that he is also divine. Jesus talks about the near future and also far-off future events with his disciples, giving them warnings about what is to come. Judas betrays Jesus and, after the Passover meal, leads the arresting party to Gethsemane where Jesus is arrested. Jesus claims to be the Son of God at his trial. Jesus is questioned by Pilate and Herod, and then is crucified. While on the cross, some people ridicule Jesus, throwing his own words back at him, saying that he called himself the Messiah so he should be able to save himself. Jesus dies and is buried. Female disciples of Jesus come to his tomb on Sunday to perfume it and are surprised that the tomb is empty. Jesus begins to make appearances to his followers after he rises from the dead. Jesus shows his disciples how the Hebrew Scriptures talked about the necessity of the Redeeming Messiah. He promises to send the Holy Spirit to help each of them as they spread the good news. He blesses them and then ascends back to heaven. From that day on, they worship Jesus as God and preach about him in the Temple courtyard.

Luke certainly considered Jesus to be the literal Son of God. Luke also recorded Jesus speaking in a tone and manner that we find in John's Gospel. Many liberal theologians/biblical scholars, including Aslan, attempt to denigrate John's Gospel because of its powerful presentation of the historical Jesus. It is, for that reason, attacked severely by enemies of Christianity. They figure if they can raise doubts about John's Gospel, they can then keep people from seriously seeking its truth. It is not that they have proven that John's Gospel is unreliable and nonhistorical; what they have shown is the extent they will go to in order to deny its veracity. That is why Aslan and others assign an extremely late date to John's Gospel, perhaps to suggest that the later the date the less historical it is, which in itself is not a valid conclusion. Aslan believes the Gospel of John was written in the first two decades of the second century (100 to 120 A.D.) and rejects John Zebedee, Jesus' apostle, as its author. Aslan claims John's Gospel was written to promote Paul's image of Jesus as the eternal logos, a view that does not comply with the other apostles (more on this in Chapters Seventeen and Nineteen). There is, of course, no evidence that John's Gospel was written in the second century. There is evidence, however, that it was John Zebedee who wrote the Gospel, and that he did so in the 80s or early 90s. Aslan believes only John's Gospel presents Jesus as the Messiah, but we have seen that the other three Gospels make that same declaration. What John's Gospel does, mostly, is to fill in some events that Matthew had left out. John's Gospel is, therefore, a great complement to Matthew's, and should be read as such. As already noted, Matthew was writing to a Jewish audience some thirty years after Jesus ascended (within a generation, so that many of those who witnessed the events were still alive) John was writing to the next generation, to those who were not eyewitnesses to the events, and was adding (not making up) vital information that the first-generation writers (Matthew, Mark and Luke) did not need to put in their narratives. John did not create a new image of Jesus, or redesign the peasant magician into an eternal Logos that supposedly went along with Paul's supposedly divergent views.

When John wrote his Gospel he was probably the only living apostle left. He was the bishop at Ephesus and, if he were a young adult (17-20 years old) when Jesus called him and his brother to be his disciples, John would be near or in his eighties when he wrote his Gospel. It would not have been unusual for him to have lived that long, especially if he had lived a rather quiet and pedagogical life. There is no reason to doubt that John, the son of Zebedee, the apostle of Jesus, wrote the Gospel, the Revelation, and the three epistles that are all assigned to him. He would be writing to a new generation of believers, a generation that had not physically seen Jesus. There were many different philosophies that had infiltrated society and the church in the latter half of the first century, and one of the worst was Gnosticism. John had a new audience and different problems and issues to address. Since he was the last of the Twelve, and there was a new generation of believers and skeptics, John felt it was necessary to show how Jesus is both God and human. There were also time gaps in the synoptic Gospels due to the events they emphasized that John felt compelled to address. For example, Matthew had Jesus go right up to Galilee after his baptism and temptation because he wanted to start off with Jesus' Galilean ministry. John shows us that Jesus was actually in the Jerusalem area for quite a while before and after his baptism and temptation, before he returned to Galilee. John is also able to mention people's names, knowing that they cannot be injured by his naming them because they are dead. So, he is able to inform us that it was Peter who chopped off the person's ear in Gethsemane and that Nicodemus, a member of the Sanhedrin, came to talk to Jesus one night. John is not, as many modern liberal theologians believe, presenting a Jesus that is totally foreign to the synoptic Gospels. He is not creating a cosmic being as Aslan would like you to believe. He is not creating a non-historic Jesus in his own image. If God were to

251

become human, he would look exactly like the Jesus we find in John's Gospel. The author of John's Gospel knew Jesus personally; he was an eye-witness to the deeds and sayings of Jesus of Nazareth. As we journey through this beautiful Gospel, notice the wonderful "I am" statements that Jesus makes.

John's Gospel

John begins his first chapter by saying exactly who Jesus is. In the first verse, John says: "In the beginning was the Word, and the Word was with God, and the Word was God" (NIV). [John clearly believes that as long as God has been in existence, Jesus, the Son of God, the Messiah, has been in existence. Just as in the beginning God created the universe (Gen 1:1), so too, in the beginning the Word was God. Jesus is not a created being; he has always been with God, always has been God. He is the Messenger (Word) of the Lord. He is Life itself, and he is the one who created the universe.] John tells us that John the Baptizer is the Word's herald [just like the other Gospel writers do]. Jesus, the eternal Word, is rejected by the Jews, but anyone who believes in Jesus will become a child of God's. Jesus is God's Son and he is full of grace and truth, and he has shown us God because he is God in human form. John says he is an eyewitness to the historical events he is writing about. He tells us more about John the Baptizer, emphasizing the fact that the Baptizer is not the Messiah, only the herald of the Messiah. The Baptizer, in fact, calls Jesus the Lamb of God, making a sacrificial reference, showing that Jesus is the one "who takes away the sin of the world!" (vs. 29). The Baptizer declares that Jesus is God's Chosen One. While in Jerusalem, Jesus has several disciples, including Peter and his brother, come and join him. In chapter two, John mentions two events that may or may not fit chronologically but are placed there to emphasize Jesus' divine character. The first event is at a wedding in Cana of Galilee where Jesus turns water into wine. [John is showing that Jesus is the master of nature. (The other Gospel writers did the same.) Just as in the beginning Jesus was God who created the universe (1:1-3), so he is able to perform miracles as a human.] The second event is the clearing of the Temple of the moneychangers [which shows that Jesus is master of the Temple. John used these two events at the beginning of his Gospel to reveal important attributes about Jesus. He wanted his readers to know that Jesus was God and could control nature and that the Temple was his.]

In the third chapter, John continues with Jesus still in Jerusalem. A Pharisee named Nicodemus, who is also a member of the Sanhedrin, visits Jesus in the cover of night. [Since Nicodemus is himself from Galilee, it is possible that he knew about Jesus.] Jesus lets him know that he (Nicodemus) must experience a second birth—a spiritual birth—in order to please God. [Nicodemus may have thought he already pleased God by being a Pharisee, but Jesus informs him that he is mistaken.] Jesus tells Nicodemus that he must allow the Holy Spirit to make him into a new creation. Jesus tells him that he (Jesus) has come to earth from heaven in order to be lifted up on a cross so that everyone who believes in him (Jesus) will have eternal life. John then states that wonderful verse that "God so loved the world that he gave his one and only Son, that whoever believes in him shall not perish but have eternal life" (NIV, 3:16). Whoever believes in Jesus will not be condemned for their sins. [This must have had some effect on Nicodemus because he will later join Joseph, his colleague, in taking Jesus' body down from the cross that Jesus told him he would die upon.] John gives us another episode of John the Baptizer testifying about Jesus. In chapter four, Jesus leaves Jerusalem and heads toward Galilee, but first passes through Samaria. Jesus is tired and thirsty and rests at Jacob's well in Sychar while his disciples go off to get some food. [Throughout John's Gospel, he is quick to point out the humanity of Jesus in order to counter erroneous Gnostic ideas, which also dispels Aslan's idea that John's Jesus is just some cosmic, mystical being.] It was around noon and a woman, who would be considered unclean by Jewish standards, comes to get some water for herself. Jesus strikes up a conversation with her and lets her know that he is the Messiah. The townspeople invite him to stay, and so he stays with them for a couple of days, and many people believe in him. [Just as Matthew showed his Jewish audience that Jesus cared for Gentiles by healing the Canaanite woman's daughter, so John shows his readers that Jesus loved the outcast—the Samaritans.] Jesus returns to Galilee and heals a royal official's son. [John shows that Jesus can heal from a distance, just like God can.] In chapter five, John focuses on Jesus' return to Jerusalem since the other Gospels have already gone into details about what Jesus did in and around Galilee. In Jerusalem, Jesus heals a man on the Sabbath. The religious leaders are upset that Jesus has "worked" on the Sabbath and demand that he tell them why he is doing this. Jesus tells them that God, his Father, is always working and so he must work too. The religious leaders want to kill him because Jesus has called "God his own Father, making himself equal with God" (NIV, vs. 18). Jesus then tells the religious leaders the unique relationship he has with God, the Father. He tells them that the works that he does [for example, the healings and other miracles] "testify that the Father has sent me" (NIV, vs. 36). Jesus tells them that they study the Hebrew Scriptures in order to find eternal life in their teachings, and yet the Scriptures "testify about me." Jesus scolds them for refusing to come to him so that they can have true life.

In chapter six, John shows his readers that Jesus is the master over nature by recording two events that the other Gospel writers have mentioned: the feeding of the five thousand and walking on water. [In his Gospel, Matthew told us that Jesus healed many of the people on the other side of the lake, and then challenged the Pharisees about their traditions before going off to the Tyre and Sidon region.] John [filling in some information that Matthew left out] tells us that when Jesus is back in Capernaum and teaching at the synagogue he is confronted by some of those whom Jesus had recently and miraculously fed. [They realize the power Jesus has and think that if they can make him their ruler or leader, he will be obligated to take care of them. They think Jesus' power can work toward their advantage.] Jesus tells them that the only reason they are interested in him is because they saw the miracle he had done in feeding them. He advises them to not be so concerned about physical food, but the spiritual food that lasts an eternity. He tells them he can give them this eternal food. They want to know what they have to do to get it, what God requires of them. Jesus tells them that what God requires of them is "to believe in the one [Jesus] he has sent." They want to know what Jesus will do so they can believe him. [He had recently fed more than five thousand of them with a handful of morsels, but they wanted further proof.] They tell Jesus that God had given their ancestors manna to eat. They want to know what food Jesus is going to be able to give them. Jesus tells them that the bread God wants to give them will bring life to the world. They ask Jesus for that bread. Jesus tells them: "I am the bread of life." He said he had come down from heaven to do God's will and to offer this bread (himself) to those who would believe in him. When the people heard this they grumbled, complaining that they knew Jesus' family and there was no way that Jesus came down from heaven. Jesus told them: "I am the living bread that came down from heaven. Whoever eats this bread will live forever. This bread is my flesh, which I will give for the life of the world" (NIV, vs. 51). Many of the Jews were disgusted with what Jesus just said. [Of course, the idea of human sacrifice and cannibalism was anathema to Jews. But Jesus was talking about how he was going to die for the sins of the world, that his crucified body would be the sacrifice for their sins.] Many of Jesus' followers left him, but his close disciples stayed. Peter spoke up for the rest of the Twelve and said, "You have the words of eternal life. We have come to believe and to know that you are the Holy One of God" (NIV, vs. 68f). [Faith and knowledge are important for Christians; it is not unreasonable faith.] Then Jesus predicts that one of them will betray him [referring to Judas Iscariot].

In chapter seven Jesus travels throughout Galilee. He avoids Judea because there are some people there who want to kill him for the things he has said and done. [This is, of course, in agreement with the synoptic Gospels.] An important Jewish festival is on hand, and Jesus' brothers decide to go to Jerusalem to celebrate. They think Jesus should go with them. Jesus declines the invitation and stays in Galilee. After they leave, Jesus goes to the festival alone. [It turns out that Jesus' brothers wanted him to prove himself by doing miracles at the festival, but, in agreement with the other Gospels, John shows that Jesus did not perform magic tricks to get people to follow him.] Many of the Jews look for Jesus, wondering where he is and why he is not at the festival. Some say he is a good man; others say he is a deceiver. After the festival has been going on for several days, Jesus arrives at the Temple courtyard and begins teaching there. Some people come and argue with him about Moses' Law and breaking the Sabbath. They wonder if he is the Messiah. Some are convinced that he is because of the miracles he has done. They think he must be the Prophet Moses prophesied about [see Deuteronomy 18:18]. People are divided about who Jesus is. Even the Temple guards who have been sent by the chief priest and Pharisees to arrest Jesus do not arrest him because they are impressed with his teachings. Nicodemus stands up for Jesus and is rebuked for it. In chapter eight, Jesus, again in the Temple courtyard, announces: "I am the light of the world" (vs. 12). Jesus tells the Pharisees that knowing God the Father is to know Jesus his Son. He tells them that he has come from heaven, that he is not from this world [something he will later tell Pilate at his trial]. He tells them they will die in their sins, regardless of having strictly followed the Law, if they fail to believe in him as their Messiah. He tells them about his death and how following him will make them truly free. [They are enslaved to sin despite their good works; only Jesus can truly set them free.] They claim to know God and yet they have rejected his Son. Jesus tells them it is impossible to know God and yet reject him (Jesus.) Jesus tells them that if they truly love God, they will love him because he is God's Son. Jesus tells the Pharisees that he is greater than Abraham. [In the synoptic Gospels, Jesus said he was greater than Jonah and Solomon.] Then Jesus said: "Before Abraham was ever born, I am." ["I am" is God's name. Jesus was identifying himself as God. What was the response of the Pharisees when Jesus said this?] The Pharisees attempt to murder Jesus for blasphemy.

In chapter nine, Jesus heals a blind man and an interesting discussion arises because of this miracle. In chapter ten, Jesus said: "I am the gate. Those who enter the sheep pen through me will be saved" ("Scripture is taken from *God's Word*®. © 1995 God's Word to the Nations. Used by permission of Baker Publishing Group." vs. 9). Jesus tells them: "I am the good shepherd. The good shepherd lays down his life for the sheep" (NIV, vs. 11). Jesus tells his listeners that he is the good shepherd [a profession that clearly referred to God in the Hebrew Scriptures (see Psalm 23)]. Jesus continues: "No one takes it [Jesus' life] from me, but I lay it down of my own accord" (NIV, vs. 18). Jesus will voluntarily give his life as a ransom in order to reconcile humans back to God. [That is the only way the reconciliation can be done. Of course, the synoptic Gospels also state that Jesus would go to Jerusalem and turn himself over to the religious leaders in order to be tried, executed, and then rise from the dead on the third day.] Jesus said he will freely giving his life for those who believe in him. Then, again at the Temple courtyard, Jesus claims to be the Messiah and, more than that, he claims that he and God are one. The religious leaders once again pick up stones in order to murder him because he, being a human, claims to also be God. In chapter eleven, John once more shows the humanity and divine nature of Jesus when he learns that a close friend, Lazarus, has died. Lazarus' sister tells Jesus that if he had come before her brother died that Jesus may have been able to heal him, but now that he is dead her brother will not be alive until the resurrection at judgment day. Jesus tells her: "I am the resurrection and the life" (vs.

25). [Jesus is the one who will bring people to life to be judged, and he will be the one doing the judging.] Jesus is deeply moved by the sorrow of those who mourn Lazarus' death, and he cries with them. Then he raises Lazarus from the dead. This miracle is too much for the Sanhedrin. They decide to execute Jesus. Knowing this, Jesus avoids Jerusalem for the time being. In chapter twelve, Mary, Lazarus' sister, anoints Jesus with perfume while he and his disciples are having dinner at a friend's house in Bethany. Jesus is the guest of honor because of what he has done for Lazarus and his family. When Mary anoints Jesus with the perfume Jesus remarks that it is in preparation of his death. It is soon after that, at the beginning of Passover week, that Jesus rides into Jerusalem on a donkey. He tells the crowd that he is the Redeeming Messiah, claiming also that seeing Jesus is the same as seeing God (vs. 45). Then he announces that he has come as light into the world (vs. 46), and then warns the crowd that those who reject him and do not accept what he says will have the words that he has spoken to them be their accuser come Judgment Day (vs. 48).

Starting with chapter thirteen (and ending at the beginning of chapter eighteen), John gives us more information about what happened while Jesus and his twelve disciples participate in the Passover meal in the upper room of a friend's house. [The synoptic Gospels focused more on the arrest, trial, execution and resurrection for their readers because they already knew, through the early oral traditions, what Jesus said and did during this time. John's audience is a generation removed, and so John provides more information about what Jesus said and did during the Passover meal.] During the meal, Jesus washes his disciples' feet [a task usually relegated to a household servant or slave], showing that he wants them to exemplify the same by serving others. He predicts Judas will betray him and that Peter will deny knowing him in order to protect himself. In the next chapter, Jesus tells them: "I am the way and the truth and the life. No one comes to the Father except through me" (NIV, vs. 6). [This is not an odd statement that John records. In Matthew and Luke's Gospels, Jesus said: "No one knows the Father except the Son and those to whom the Son chooses to reveal him" (NIV, Mt 11:27; Lk 10:22).] Jesus promises to send the Holy Spirit to be their Advocate and Helper; the Holy Spirit will "remind you of everything I have said to you." The Holy Spirit will give them the power to obey his (Jesus') commandments [true obedience without the Holy Spirit is impossible]. Continuing on in the next chapter, Jesus tells his disciples: "I am the true vine" and "apart from me you can do nothing." Jesus tells his disciples that Love is what fulfills God's commandments. Jesus loves them enough to die for them, and they in turn must love one another. Jesus warns his disciples that they will encounter hatred and contempt from others. [Matthew also recorded this warning.] In chapter sixteen, Jesus talks about returning to God the Father after he has been killed and resurrected. He again tells them that they will be receiving the Holy Spirit. In the next chapter, John records the beautiful prayer that Jesus prays for his followers.

In chapter eighteen, Jesus and his disciples go to Gethsemane where Judas arrives with soldiers and Temple guards to arrest Jesus. Peter denies knowing Jesus when he is questioned about being one of Jesus' disciples. Jesus is questioned by the chief priest. He is then sent to Pilate. In the next chapter, Jesus is crucified and buried. In chapter twenty, Jesus is raised from the dead and makes several appearances while his disciples are still in Jerusalem. In the final chapter, Jesus joins some of his disciples for breakfast when they return to Galilee. [Jesus specifically wants to comfort Peter who must have been emotionally and mentally distraught because he had denied knowing Jesus at Jesus' darkest hour.] John verifies what he has written about Jesus in his Gospel by reminding his readers that he is an eyewitness to the things Jesus said and did.

As we can see, the same Jesus we find in the synoptic Gospels is found in John's. The Jesus we find in all four canonical Gospels is the Jesus Peter, James, Paul and all the other apostles preached.

Chapter Twelve: Jesus as the Messenger of the Lord

The Messenger of the Lord in the Hebrew Scriptures

We learn from the Hebrew Scriptures that God is a spiritual or nonmaterial, non-corporeal, being. Since he is a spiritual being, it is difficult for many to worship and obey only him; they prefer physical objects to worship, ones they can see and touch and make with their own hands. Although God is a spiritual being, the Scriptures do, however, record times when God actually appeared in human form; these appearances are called a theophany, and they have been accepted within Jewish thought and theology. It is possible that the first theophany of God is found in Genesis 3:8, where it is said God walked in the garden in which he had placed Adam and Eve. He was there to fellowship with Adam and Eve, but the couple had sinned against God and they were hiding from him. There really is no reason to doubt that when God made the earth and a special garden in which to place the man and woman whom he had made in his image that he would not physically visit them. If he did, he would take on a human form. It certainly is possible for God to do so. We know from Scripture that the spiritual world can become manifested in the physical. The Deceiver, Satan, became visible to Adam and Eve. God sent angels to aid humans at times, and they took on human form. According to Scripture, it is not difficult for spiritual beings to enter the physical world. Jews do not have, or at least non-modern Jews did not have, a problem believing this. Throughout the Hebrew Scriptures, there are many references to a being called the Angel or Messenger of the Lord (măl·'ăk yhwh). This Messenger of the Lord appears to be different from the other angels God sent to do his will.

The first appearance of the Messenger of the Lord is found in Genesis 16. He appeared to Hagar who had been forced to leave Abraham's clan. She was pregnant and the Messenger of the Lord helped and comforted her. Hagar said to the Messenger of the Lord, "You are the God who watches over me" (vs.13). The Messenger of the Lord did not rebuke her for calling him God as we see angels do when someone attempted to worship them or speak too highly of them. In the title

Messenger of the Lord, the word for Lord is YHWH or Yahweh. In Genesis 18, the Messenger of the Lord appeared to Abraham in human form and told him that his wife would bear a son. The Messenger is identified as YHWH. In Genesis 21 the Messenger of the Lord again appeared to Hagar to help her. In Genesis 22, God tells Abraham to sacrifice his son Isaac. At the right moment the Messenger of the Lord stepped in and prevented him from killing his son, and then provided Abraham with a ram to take his son's place. In Genesis 31 the Messenger of the Lord appeared to Jacob and called himself God. Jacob, in blessing his sons, said, "May the Messenger who has delivered me from all harm bless my sons" (Gen 48:16). In Exodus 3, Moses, who had been living as a shepherd, saw flames of fire coming out of a bush and went to investigate it. The Messenger of the Lord appeared to him in those flames and commanded Moses to remove his sandals because he was standing on holy ground. The Messenger of the Lord told Moses his name was "I am that I am." That would be the name God would use for himself—I AM. In Exodus 14, the Messenger of the Lord traveled with Israel as they left Egypt and wandered in the desert. Here the Messenger of the Lord appeared like a column of smoke or fire. In Numbers 22, the Messenger of the Lord appeared to Balaam and chastised him for the wrong he was about to do. Joshua encountered the Commander of the army of the Lord, who came as the Messenger, and was told to remove his sandals because he was standing on holy ground. The Commander/Messenger was called Yahweh (see Jos 5:13-6:5). In Judges 2:1, the Messenger of the Lord told the Israelites, "I brought you out of Egypt into the land that I swore to give to your ancestors," and thereby identified himself with God. In Judges 6, the Messenger of the Lord appeared to Gideon and Gideon called him God. In Judges 13, the Messenger of the Lord appeared to Samson's parents and he was referred to as God. In 2 Samuel 24, the Messenger of the Lord came with judgment against David and David referred to him as God. In Psalm 34, David identified the Messenger of the Lord as God. In Zechariah 1, 3, and 12, the Messenger of the Lord was referred to as God. In Malachi 3:1, the Messenger of the Lord was called the Messenger of Promise; it was said of him: "The Lord you are looking for will suddenly come to his Temple. The messenger of the promise will come" ("Scripture is taken from *God's Word*®. © 1995 God's Word to the Nations. Used by permission of Baker Publishing Group.").

Looking at these passages we see that there are times when God took on a human form and affected history in some way by doing so. God taking on a human form was therefore not a concept that would contradict Jewish Scripture, Jewish thought, or Jewish theology.

We see from these passages that the Messenger of the Lord was referred to as Yahweh (YHWH), and we learn that Yahweh is a title that is used exclusively of God in the Hebrew Scriptures. God is quite adamant that no one else is allowed to use that name; it is God's alone. He says, "I am the LORD (YHWH), and there is no other" (Isa. 45:18). Even though the Messenger of the Lord is identified as YHWH, he is sometimes referred to as his own person. We see this in the first chapter of Zechariah where the Messenger of the Lord talks to someone other than himself and says, "LORD Almighty, how long will you withhold mercy from Jerusalem and from the towns of Judah, which you have been angry with these seventy years?" (NIV, vs. 12). So the Messenger of the Lord who is YHWH talks to someone else who is YHWH, but we are told that there is no other YHWH, so these two individual persons must be the same God. Jesus also used Psalm 110:1 to show the Pharisees that the Messiah was more than just a human; the Messiah was God (see Mt 22:41-46). There is another instance where God is talking to the Messiah and calls him God; it is in Psalm 45:6f, and the writer of Hebrews (a New Testament epistle) quotes this passage to show that God was saying this to his Son, the Messiah.

The early Christians realized the continuity between the Hebrew Scriptures' Messianic prophecies and the New Testament's claim of fulfilling those prophecies. We notice that the Messenger of the Lord and the role of the Messiah are very similar; both are sent to do the will of the Father. It is clear that YHWH in the Hebrew Scriptures is often seen as a Father. The Messenger of the Lord is sent by the Father, or is issued from the Father, and yet is also referred to as YHWH. The Messenger of the Lord is the Messiah that God often sent to redeem Israel at particular times in her history; and he is the one who will also redeem humankind. In Isaiah 63:7-10, the prophet shows how the Triune God is at work in this act of redemption. Isaiah announces how kind and compassionate the Lord (YHWH, the Father) is because he became Israel's Savior by sending the Messenger (also YHWH) to save them; it was the Father's love and mercy that prompted him to redeem them; but alas, they reject the Messenger and offend (blaspheme) the Holy Spirit. The Messenger (YHWH) is sent by the Lord (YHWH) for the purpose of redemption and is rejected, which offends the Holy Spirit (YHWH). These three separate persons are referred to as God. The Messenger comes as one who speaks the word of God. Jesus told a group of religious leaders: "For the works that the Father has given me to finish—the very works that I am doing—testify that the Father has sent me" (NIV, Jn 5:36). But the word of God is not just language; the word of God is also a person. John tells us: "In the beginning was the Word, and the Word was with God, and the Word was God. He was with God in the beginning" (NIV, 1:1). The Messenger, the Word, has existed from the very beginning; this Word is always with God, that is, the Word has always been in the presence of God; the Word is God. Then John tells us: "The Word became flesh and made his dwelling among us. We have seen his glory, the glory of the one and only Son, who came from the Father, full of grace and truth" (NIV, vs.14). We saw in the Hebrew Scriptures how the Messenger (Word) of the Lord appeared for a specific purpose, that he did what he came to do and then left; his appearance was usually just for a few moments. But when the Messenger (the Word) came to redeem humankind, he dwelt among us; he stayed for about thirty-three years. John says this Word (the Son) came from the Father. This is similar language to what we find in the Hebrew Scriptures regarding the Messenger of the Lord being sent out from God.

Jesus as God Incarnate

Now Aslan thinks that although most modern Christians believe Jesus is God incarnate, Jews would never have conceived of their Messiah as being such. Aslan claims that Jews would never think of the Messiah as God incarnate; it would go against 5,000 years of their history, their Scriptures, and their theology. Of course, it is not just modern Christians that consider Jesus as God incarnate; first-century Christians (many of whom were Jewish) believed it too. The idea of Jesus-as-God-incarnate was not a later development; it did not become a "doctrine" some centuries later. Many modern liberal theologians/biblical scholars are convinced that Jesus was not considered God incarnate until the fourth century, especially during important Councils like the one at Nicaea; but they are mistaken. First-century Christians not only accepted Jesus as their Messiah and

Savior, but also believed he was the Son of God. The gospel message that spread throughout the Roman Empire and beyond was based on the authority of those who knew the historical Jesus; they carried on the message of Jesus, and their message was consistent. All of the apostles proclaimed the same thing—Jesus was the Messiah; he was the Son of God; he came to die in our place, paying the penalty for our sins; he rose from the dead; ascended into heaven; and will return in power and glory to set up the Messianic Kingdom and pronounce the final judgment on all humankind. Peter, in his first sermon less than two months after Jesus' death, told the Jews in Jerusalem that the Messiah they were looking for had arrived. Peter quoted some Hebrew Scriptures regarding the Messiah and then concluded his sermon by telling his listeners that Jesus, whom they helped put to death, had risen from the dead and was both Lord and Christ (see Acts 2:14-36). The title Peter gave Jesus was highly significant—Lord referred to the God of the Hebrew Scriptures (YHWH—Yahweh); Christ referred to the Anointed One, the Messiah who was promised to take away the sin of the world. These first believers, outside the circle of Jesus' original disciples, were all Jews. Peter told these Jews that the man they helped crucify was the Lord and Christ. Luke tells us these Jews were terribly upset when they heard this and asked what they could do now that they had become aware of what they had done. Peter told them to repent and be baptized in the name of Jesus Christ and their sins would be forgiven.

The Christian Jews, recognizing the Hebrew Scriptures that made reference to a Redeeming Messiah, took this same message that Peter preached to them in Jerusalem to their own hometowns. These new believers, numbering about 3,000, were both Jews and Gentile converts to Judaism who had arrived in Jerusalem for the Passover festival. They were Parthians, Medes, and Elamites; they had come from Mesopotamia, Judea, Cappadocia, Pontus, the province of Asia, Phrygia, Pamphylia, Egypt, Libya near Cyrene, Rome, Crete, and Arabia (Ac 2:9–11). The gospel message quickly traveled to the Samaritans, into Galilee, and further north to Antioch, Syria. Luke tells us that Philip talked to an Ethiopian (a Gentile) and told him about Jesus the Messiah; not long after that Peter told an entire Gentile family about Jesus (see Acts 8 & 10, respectively). When a prominent, intelligent, young Jew (Saul qua Paul) became a Christian after spending some time persecuting Christians, he then spent the rest of his life spreading the good news of Jesus as Messiah to a large part of the Gentile region known as Asia Minor and Greece. Many of the Jews who lived in the Gentile regions where Paul went to preach also accepted Jesus as their long awaited Messiah, although many did not. In some areas, Jews and Christians utilized the same local synagogue since Jews used it on Sabbath and Christians used it on Sunday. Although the first Christians had been Jews in and around Jerusalem, the admission of Gentiles was quickly instigated and church communities began to spring up throughout the Levant. These communities upset the social structure within both Jewish and pagan society by allowing men and women, people of different races and nationalities, and people from different social rankings to all worship and commune together.

What became a great thorn in the side for many non-Christian Jews during the first century was the idea that the Messiah was to die and that his death was a sacrifice for all of humankind. They wanted a Messiah who was to come as a king and successfully conquer Israel's enemies and gain Israel's independence forever. The Messiah's death, the Christians taught, would end the need for sacrifices; it would end the need for a Temple in which to do those sacrifices; and it would end the priesthood since every believer and follower of Jesus would now be their own priest—everyone who accepted Jesus could approach God for forgiveness and blessings directly because of what Jesus had done for them. For many non-Christian Jews this was unacceptable. After the destruction of Jerusalem and the Temple in 70 A.D., any good relations between Jew and Christian began to dwindle quickly. By the time the Mishnah had been compiled in the late second century, the growing animosity between Jews and Christians had reached a high point. In fact, it was the aftermath of the Bar Kokhba Revolt, around 132 A.D., that created a permanent schism between Judaism and Christianity. Nearly four hundred years later, when the Talmud was formed, it declared a total rejection of Jesus as the Jewish Messiah, a rejection that had already started when the Pharisees rejected Jesus (see Mt 12). Christians today still await Jesus' return, believing he will set up a Messianic Kingdom for Israel and all Jews, and they look forward to having that happen.

Based on the Hebrew Scriptures regarding the Messenger of the Lord, we see that Aslan is mistaken to think that the Messiah as God incarnate would go against 5,000 years of their history, their Scriptures, and their theology. The ancient Jews, from Abraham to the second century A.D., did not have a problem in Jewish scripture, thought, and theology with identifying God and the Messiah together. They did not have a problem with the idea that God could take on a human form. The problem came with the claim that Jesus of Nazareth was that Messenger of the Lord, the Word who became human, the Messiah. The Jews rejected Jesus, the Messenger of the Lord, just as Isaiah predicted they would, and this rejection offended and grieved the Holy Spirit. The Gospel writers believed they were continuing, or actually fulfilling, the "Messiah promise" that was first given by God to Adam and Eve. This "Messiah promise" was the main thread throughout the Hebrew Scriptures. It was the reason for God creating the Jewish nation from Abraham; it was the reason for the animal sacrifices; it was the reason for the prophetic messages God sent his people. Although the modern Jew may perhaps reject Jesus as God incarnate, they surely would not deny the fact that God could become human if he wanted to. It is certainly not beyond his power to do so. The question is: Did he? Was Jesus the God who became human? Let's look.

In Isaiah, the Lord (YHWH) is described as Israel's King and Redeemer or Defender. The Lord says, "I am the first and the last [the beginning and the end]. I am the only God; there is no other" (44:6). In Revelation 1:17, Jesus declared, "I am the First and the Last," and in 22:13 he says, "I am the Alpha and the Omega, the First and the Last, the Beginning and the End" (NIV). Jesus is lying, deceived, blaspheming, or telling the truth. The decision is yours. Also in Isaiah, God says, "I am the LORD [YHWH]; that is my name. I will not give my glory to anyone else or the praise I deserve to idols" ("Scripture is taken from *God's Word®*. © 1995 God's Word to the Nations. Used by permission of Baker Publishing Group." 42:8). Jesus, in a wonderful prayer recorded in John 17:1-26, prays to his Father that he give him (Jesus) glory so that he, in turn, could give his Father glory. Jesus says that the Father has given him the authority to give eternal life to everyone his Father has given to him. Jesus then explains that eternal life is to know God the Father and Jesus the Messiah, whom the Father has sent. Jesus declared that he had given his Father glory by accomplishing the work or task that the Father gave him to do. [That task was to be the Redeeming Messiah.] Jesus then stated that he had been with the

Father and participated in the Father's glory before the world (the universe) was created. Jesus told his Father that he had given his disciples the message that his Father had given him to tell. [Here Jesus identifies himself with the Messenger of the Lord.] By accepting Jesus' message Jesus says his disciples know for sure that he came from God, that God had sent him. Jesus affirms that everything he has belongs to God, and everything God has is his. Jesus prays that the unity his disciples have with one another is like the unity that he (Jesus) has with his Father (God). Jesus tells his Father that he is coming home and that he is sending his disciples out into the world, just like the Father sent Jesus into the world. Jesus prays that his disciples will see his glory, the glory God gave him because God loved him before the world was made. Jesus ends the prayer by asking that his disciples will know and share the same love that he (Jesus) and his Father have. We see in these two passages that God will not share his glory with anyone else and yet Jesus talks with God about the wonderful glory that they share together. Jesus is lying, deceived, blaspheming, or telling the truth. The decision is yours.

We have already seen other Gospel passages where Jesus talks about God as his Father and that the Father had sent him into the world (see Jn 3:16 & 6:57), and that he and his Father are one (Jn 10:30). Sometimes when Jesus made these comments the crowd got angry enough at him to want to stone him for blasphemy. One of those times was recorded in John 8:58 when Jesus said, "Before Abraham was born, I am!" Jesus knew what he was saying; he was using the very name God called himself. We have seen that it was the Messenger of the Lord who had called himself 'I AM' when he spoke with Moses at the burning bush. The Israelites would henceforward know that God's name was 'I AM' (LORD). Jesus called himself 'I AM' and it so angered those he was speaking to that they wanted to murder him for blasphemy. In John's Gospel, he records quite a few instances where Jesus used the phrase "I am" to describe himself. For example, Jesus said, "I am the good shepherd," (10:11), which his listeners would immediately think of Psalm 23 where David said, "The Lord is my shepherd" (vs. 1). Jesus said, "I am the bread of life" (6:35), and his listeners would think of the manna God gave the Jews in the desert; "I am the light of the world" (8:10); "I am from above" (8:23); "I am the resurrection and the life" (11:25); "I am the way, the truth, and the life" (14:6); "I am in my Father and my Father is in me" (14:11); "I am the true vine" (15:1). Jesus is lying, deceived, blaspheming, or telling the truth. The decision is yours.

There are other things Jesus did, said or allowed that showed that he believed he was the Messenger of the Lord, the Word of God, the Son of God, the Son of Man, the great I Am. He said he was going to judge everyone at the final Day of Judgment, something God said he was going to do. Jesus allowed others to worship him, something that was only allowed for God. Jesus told his disciples to pray in his name and that he would answer their prayers, something that only God can do. In Jesus' parables he often implied that he was God. He gave himself titles—like Redeemer and Savior—that God said applied to him (God gave himself these titles in the Hebrew Scriptures). Jesus showed his power by calming the sea, walking on water, feeding thousands from a few morsels—activities attributed to God. Jesus showed he knew what was happening out of his visual and physical range—he knew where Nathaniel was sitting, he knew who would betray him, he knew Lazarus was dead, he knew the private life of the Samaritan woman, he knew the immediate thoughts of people who were judging him negatively. (See Geisler's *Systematic Theology, Volume Two*.)

We see then that the ancient Jews did not think God becoming human was anathema or impossible, as Aslan claims. There are many occurrences in the Hebrew Scriptures where God did exactly that. The issue, of course, is whether or not Jesus is God incarnate. I believe I have offered evidence to show that Jesus is God-in-the-flesh, but the ultimate decision is left to you, the reader. Aslan thinks first-century Jews did not have an integrated idea or concept of the phrase "son of man," but whether the "common" Jew did or did not, we know that the religious leaders certainly knew what the title meant. When Jesus called himself the "son of man" at his trial he was condemned to death because of it. The reason he was condemned to death by the religious leaders is because Jesus was claiming to be God.

Aslan tells us (in his sixth chapter) that it was not long after Jerusalem had been destroyed in 70 A.D., the Temple in ruins, the rebels crushed, and the Jews scattered, that a Jew with half a Roman name called John Mark began to write the first Gospel about a man named Jesus of Nazareth. Mark would attempt to convince his readers that this Jesus was the Jewish Messiah. For some obscure reason, Mark had chosen one of the rebels that had died roughly forty years before Jerusalem's destruction. It was a rather weak narrative because of its concise depiction of the rebel leader. This short "biography" showed this Jesus performing some magical healings, but it mostly emphasized the rebel's last week of life. Mark could not imagine that his story would become so popular. It became so popular, in fact, that within about twenty years a couple more "biographies" were written, but they were filled with lots of embellishments and made-up stories about this Jesus. Then about fifteen years after that another one was written and this simply went over the top. There was no doubt about it, this new author had definitely made that rebel woodworker from Nazareth—Jesus—into a deity, a god who was going to come back and seek revenge on everyone who opposed him and his followers. And that, according to Aslan, is how we got our four Gospels—Mark, Matthew, Luke and John. Aslan hopes to convince us in his book that Jesus' followers decided to make him the Messiah of the Hebrew Scriptures, possibly to bring hope to the Jews and God-fearing Gentiles after the destruction of their city, Jerusalem, in 70 A.D. The Gospel writers would have to change lots of Jesus' sayings so they would comply with the Gospel writers' new theories. Aslan says the Gospel writers' theory or viewpoint of Jesus as the Messiah promised in the Hebrew Scriptures was wrong. Aslan says his viewpoint of Jesus as a common zealot is correct. They both cannot, of course, be right. One of them (or possibly both) is wrong. Maybe there is another viewpoint that is correct. Jesus could have come from another planet, or he could have been a time traveler. As mentioned before, lots of people have lots of different ideas about Jesus, and in this postmodern world where any viewpoint is correct, no matter how absurd, it is not surprising to find people calling Jesus a zealot, a Cynic, a sage, a good man, a madman, a phony, a manipulator, a spirit-guide, a guru, or a liar. In this postmodern world any answer to Jesus' question, "Who do you say that I am?" will do. Important questions pertaining to life—why are we here; what is expected of me; does death end it all; what are my obligations to others and the world we live in; etc.—are not taken seriously in a postmodern framework. There are no answers to those questions; you simply make it up as you go.

The Linear Unfolding of History

The Jews, however, have from their inception seen life and history as purposeful and meaningful. The Jewish view of history rejects the idea that it is cyclical; that it is bound to a wheel from which it cannot escape, simply repeating the same episodes over and over; or that it is at the whim and control of a myriad of gods that might be benign one day and simply horrible the next. The Jews see history as linear, starting at one point and moving or unfolding from there to a specific end. This linear view of history is rooted in a God who is at the helm of history. It begins with a belief that there is a God and that he created the universe. It did not appear by chance; there was a reason for its beginning. When God created the universe he had a plan that involved this particular, somewhat insignificant sphere we call Earth. He would make beings on this earth with whom he could enjoy a special relationship. Not that he was lonely. From all eternity, God had enjoyed the relationship of the three persons that are God. When God made humans in his image it was so they would have the privilege and opportunity of forming a relational, personal, bond with God. This bond was a daily choice; each day the humans God created had to choose to remain in that fellowship, or to depart from it. Each day, humans stood at the crossroads, open to the choice of choosing the Tree of Life—God—or the tree that represented good and evil. Once the first humans chose the path of good and evil, once they had that option, their tendency would be to choose evil. This was shown in the fact that their relationship with God had immediately changed. Now they were hiding and lying to him. Now their firstborn after sin had entered the world committed murder.

When sin—the now ingrained tendency in humans to avoid God's will and break the universal moral code—was committed by Adam and Eve, God began his work in history to prepare the way for the Messiah by promising a Redeemer, the "seed of the woman." History unfolded in a linear path towards that goal. God determined the right time for the Messiah to arrive. He chose the period of time when Rome ruled the world because it was a relative time of peace. The Greek language was familiar to the known world; roads were built throughout the empire; cities were built; laws were established. It was the right time for the Redeeming Messiah to appear. The linear unfolding of history, pointing to and moving toward the arrival of the Redeeming Messiah, was recorded in the Hebrew Scriptures. The Gospel writers were believers in this linear view of history and continued that idea within their writings. The Gospel writers saw Jesus as the fulfillment of the Hebrew Scriptures regarding the Redeeming Messiah. They also saw Jesus as the fulfillment of the Hebrew Scriptures regarding the Messianic King. The Redeeming Messiah would restore the relationship forever between humans and God; that was the first and most imperative action that had to be done. This restored relationship would involve a daily choice to choose God or one's own way; to choose God requires denying yourself, but that is simply because we do not always know what is best for us. By denying ourselves we then rely on the God who made us and wants the best for us. Just as the Redeeming Messiah had to pick up his cross in order to buy us back from the evil one, who had had us in his clutches since Adam and Eve chose to side with him, so each day the Messiah's followers must choose to pick up their cross to follow him. But the Redeeming Messiah is not the last promise of God. In this linear view of history is a final phase—the restoration of the universe. It is when the evil one and those who follow him are finally judged and can no longer influence history or the lives of God's children. Jesus as Messianic King will rule at this time, and forever.

For Aslan, there is no plan, there is no purpose, and there is no need for restoration. So, in rejecting Jesus as the Messiah in his role as both the Redeeming Messiah and the Messianic King, all that Aslan has left is to create some other role for Jesus. As I have said, there are lots of other roles to choose from. Aslan picked Jesus-as-zealot; he thought that he could pull some passages out of the Gospels—documents that he claims are historically unreliable—that would prove his point. Why do Aslan, the members of the JS, and many modern liberal New Testament professors and theologians not believe Jesus is the Son of God, the Messiah? They hear the message, and some may have even believed it for a while, but they reach a point (maybe they feel God abandoned them at some time in their lives, or they accepted the teachings of an agnostic/atheistic professor in college, or they determined that it was just too difficult to live for God in this self-absorbed world) when they reject it and then spend their lives writing books so that other people will reject it too. They are the seeds in the parable of the farmer that unfortunately have not been buried deep enough in solid ground in order to grow and blossom (see Mt 13:3-8).

270

Chapter Thirteen: The Arrest, Trial and Execution of Jesus

Gethsemane as Jesus' Hideout

As we have often seen, Aslan's version of Jesus' life is quite different from the one found in the Gospels. Aslan looks at Jesus' life through the lens or theory that he was a zealot; therefore, Jesus was baptized in order to submit to the discipleship training of John the Baptizer, he preached a physical Kingdom of God that would create a new world order, he healed people by means of magic, and died under charges of sedition just like the myriad of other zealots at that time. Since Aslan believes that Jesus is a zealot and is ready to unleash his messianic secret—his new world order—in Jerusalem, then Jesus needs to have a hideout. Aslan says Jesus picked Gethsemane, the garden near the Mount of Olives, to be that lair. There, Jesus and his disciples could hide in the darkness of the grove trees, having armed themselves with swords for protection. Aslan reminds us that Jesus had actually commanded his disciples to buy these swords for this purpose. Jesus is determined to fight if there are any attempts to arrest him by the powers that be. That is why when Jesus is about to be arrested one of his disciples used his sword to injure the high priest's servant, who was part of the arresting party. That is Aslan's portrayal of Jesus' arrest. For comparison, let's look at how the Gospels portray it. (The rendition I offer below is my own compilation based on all four Gospels.)

Jesus entered Jerusalem on a donkey and accepted the adulation of the crowd who appeared to accept him as a kingly figure. The next day, he chased away the moneychangers in the Temple because they had dishonored God by their manipulation of prices. He then taught in the Temple courtyard and continued to use parables that addressed the religious leaders' hypocrisies. This, of course, made them angry and they stalked away, determined to find a way to get rid of Jesus, permanently. Two days before the Passover, the chief priests, scribes, and other leaders gathered in the palace of the chief priest Caiaphas for the express purpose of making plans to arrest Jesus and then kill him. They knew they could not arrest him during the festival because they feared the people might riot. Satan motivated Judas Iscariot, one of the twelve apostles, to visit the chief priests and the Temple guards to discuss with them how he could betray Jesus to them. They were very pleased with this turn of events and agreed to give him some money. So Judas looked for an opportunity to betray Jesus to them when there wasn't a crowd around. While Jesus was eating the Passover meal with his disciples he quoted from the Hebrew Scriptures that one of them would turn against him and betray him. He knew that it would be Judas. He told Judas to go and do what he had to do. Judas left and told the chief priests the opportunity was now. They had to make some quick decisions and preparations. They had already put the right people on notice. Even if they had to break traditions or customs, they were going to arrest Jesus and put him on trial that same evening, before anyone could protest. Meanwhile, Jesus talked with his disciples, reminding them of the first time he sent them out to the different Galilean villages to tell people about the kingdom of heaven. At that time the disciples did not take a traveling bag or wallet or even sandals. They relied on God and the kindness of the people they talked with to supply their needs. Now, Jesus told them that they were going to need to take a wallet and a traveling bag. The person who did not have a sword should sell his coat and buy one. Jesus then quoted a Hebrew Scripture passage that said, 'He was counted with criminals,' and told his disciples that he would be fulfilling that passage, adding that the things that were written about him in the Scriptures would come true. The disciples did an inventory and told Jesus they had two swords among them. Jesus told them that was enough. Then they sang a hymn and walked over to Gethsemane. Judas, who betrayed him, knew the place because Jesus and his disciples had often gone there. When they arrived at Gethsemane Jesus took Peter, James and John and went to a quiet place to pray. Soon, the peacefulness of the garden was interrupted with the noise of Judas arriving with a troop of soldiers, some Temple guards, priests and Pharisees. The crowd was carrying lighted torches, swords and clubs. Judas had told the soldiers and Temple guards that the person he kissed would be the man they wanted. Judas walked up to Jesus and kissed him. Jesus asked those who came out to arrest him who they wanted. They told him they were looking for Jesus of Nazareth. Jesus said "I am," as he stepped toward them. The crowd stepped back and fell to the ground. Jesus' disciples realized what was happening and they asked Jesus if they should use their swords to fight. Without waiting for a reply from Jesus, Peter used his sword to cut off the ear of a priest's servant. Jesus shouted at Peter to stop and to put his sword away, letting him and the rest of his disciples know that they who live by the sword will die by it. That is not what he wanted his disciples to do. Jesus was willing to drink the cup of suffering that his Father had given him to drink. Jesus healed the servant's ear and then told the crowd that had come out to arrest him that if he wanted to he could have his Father send more than twelve legions of angels to help him. But then, Jesus added, the Scriptures would not be fulfilled that says this event must happen. Jesus asked why they had come out with swords and clubs to arrest him as if he were a revolutionary. He reminded them that he used to sit in the Temple courtyard teaching the people. He wondered why they hadn't arrested him then, in the daytime, instead of coming out here like this at night. So they arrested Jesus, tied him up, and all the disciples abandoned him and ran away.

We see then that the Gospels do not have Jesus using Gethsemane as a hideout, where he and his disciples can hunker down, hiding behind trees, swords in hand, to do their zealot best to protect themselves and fight to the death. Most zealots and bandits during this time hid out in the desert and in the surrounding caves where they could make their plans and gather weapons, and store other necessities like food and clothing. I would like to also point out that when the arresting party asked for Jesus of Nazareth, Jesus stepped forward and said, "I am." (The "he" that many translations include is not in the original Greek; it is implied.) Jesus had said this before when he told his listeners, "Before Abraham was born, I am" (Jn 8:58). Jesus was telling those who came to arrest him that he was God and that is why they stumbled and fell backwards to the ground. Jesus asked the arresting party: "Have you come out as against a robber, with swords and clubs to capture me? Day after day I sat in the temple teaching, and you did not seize me." (ESV, Mt 26:55). Those who came to arrest Jesus knew he was not a zealot, a bandit, an insurrectionist. But they needed to accuse him of something that was greater than just mere complaints that he was not always nice to the Pharisees, scribes and Law Teachers. He had made some self-declarations that made it seem that he was putting himself on an equal plane with God. They could certainly charge him with blasphemy, but they were not allowed to execute blasphemers or anyone else, for that matter; execution was to be done by Roman authorities. The only real option open for them was to charge him with sedition and have the Romans crucify him. Jesus knew they had no real charges against him, and he let them know that what would soon follow—his arrest and execution—had been foretold by the prophets and needed to be fulfilled (see Mt 26:56).

Did the Roman Guards Assist in Jesus' Arrest?

Aslan, of course, questions the likelihood that Roman troops accompanied the Temple guards and priests to Gethsemane to arrest Jesus. He says that the only way a Roman soldier would arrest a criminal and then take that criminal to stand trial before the Sanhedrin was if he had been ordered by Pilate to do that. Aslan cannot imagine that Pilate would do so. The Pharisees and Temple priests had been planning Jesus' arrest and had gathered the necessary witnesses and made sure everything was prepared for a quick and non-public trial. They were waiting for the right moment. Joseph Caiaphas, who had been the high priest the entire ten years Pilate ruled as governor of Judea, would have informed Pilate of their plans to arrest Jesus, which is why they were able to send Jesus over to him at such an early hour. Caiaphas would have also asked for and gotten permission from Pilate to use the soldiers that were assigned to the Temple area. There was a fortress near the northwest corner of the Temple called the Antonia. The Roman government kept a number of soldiers there to be called in on emergencies and to be especially ready for action during the Jewish festivals when Jerusalem was overfilling with celebrants. The Pharisees and Temple priests were making sure that if a mob did get wind of what was happening, the soldiers would be there to disperse them. There is no reason to think that Caiaphas, the chief priest, (even Aslan says Pilate and Caiaphas had a good working relationship) would have any trouble securing the soldiers to help his Temple guards in order to prevent a riot during the Passover festival. When Jesus saw the large crowd that came to arrest him he said he could call down twelve legions of angels to help him, which indicated that there was quite a huge group that came to arrest him. (See a list of eight commentaries in the reference page that I consulted for this section.)

When we journeyed through the Gospel of Mark we saw that on three separate occasions Mark recorded that Jesus told his disciples ahead of time that when they got to Jerusalem he would be arrested, killed, and rise the third day. Jesus knew what was going to happen to him in

Jerusalem, just as he knew Nathanael was sitting under a fig tree, and just as he knew what the Pharisees were thinking when they thought he wasn't much of a prophet because he associated with "sinners." Jesus also knew ahead of time that Judas would betray him. Jesus would know that Judas knew they were going to Gethsemane after dinner. Jesus had not gone to Gethsemane to hide out with drawn swords. He went to Gethsemane to pray and to wait for his arrest, which he knew beforehand was going to happen. Not because he was a zealot and it was only a matter of time that he would be caught; but because he believed he was the Redeeming Messiah prophesied in the Hebrew Scriptures. Of course, you the reader must decide whether Aslan's version of the Gethsemane episode is correct, or whether the Gospels are correct.

Why did Jesus Tell His Disciples to Buy a Sword?

Aslan says Jesus commanded his disciples to arm themselves with swords; it was time for them to no longer be pacifists. It was time to fight. After all, the religious leaders were coming after him. And they would be coming after his disciples too. In Luke 22:36, Jesus told his disciples to sell their cloak, if need be, and buy a sword. The Greek word that Luke used for "sword" referred to a short, sharp dagger, similar to the knives Peter, Andrew, James and John would be familiar with as fishermen. These "swords" were not really weapons for war. Many people carried these daggers for work and for protection (many of the roads throughout the Levant, during this time, were dangerous to walk on because of the robbers and bandits who took advantage of singular travelers, as we see in Jesus' parable of the Good Samaritan (Lk 10:25-37). Let's look more closely at the context where Jesus told his disciples to buy a sword.

After the Passover meal, Jesus shared with them what would become known as Communion or the Eucharist. He told his disciples that he deeply appreciated how they had stayed with him the three years or so of his ministry. He told them that they would participate in the Messianic Kingdom when it arrived; they would be established as judges. Jesus told them how concerned he was for them because Satan was not satisfied with just getting one of them (Judas); he (Satan) wanted to ruin all of them. But Jesus had prayed for his disciples and especially for Peter so that his faith would not fail him. Jesus hinted that Peter would do something for which he would need to recover, and when he did recover he was to then help strengthen his fellow disciples. Peter, of course, blurted out that he was ready to go to prison or even die for Jesus. This time, Jesus did not hint; he told Peter quite succinctly that Peter would actually deny that he even knew Jesus. It was then that Jesus told them that things were going to be different from then on. He reminded them when he first had them go on their missionary journey that they went without a wallet, traveling bag, or even sandals and they did not lack anything. But from then on, they would not be treated as kindly as they were before. This time, in contrast, they were to take a wallet and a traveling bag and, if need be, they should sell their coat and buy a sword. Jesus was attempting to show them the different responses they were going to be experiencing soon; things were not going to be as they were. Jesus was preparing them for the occasional violent response they would receive for being his followers. They would now need to carry provisions and means of protection because they would soon be experiencing conflict and persecution because of him. Then Jesus quickly changed the subject and told them he was about to fulfill some Hebrew Scriptures regarding the Redeeming Messiah. As if not hearing or paying attention to the fact that Jesus was talking about his death, the disciples blurted out, "Look, we've got two swords." Jesus told them: "That's enough."

It would seem odd that Jesus would tell the eleven disciples (Judas had left to do Satan's bidding) to buy swords, and then be told they already had two among them and say that was enough. Aslan wants you to believe Jesus is actually telling his disciples to go out and buy swords and then to use them to do violence. And the only way Aslan can get you to believe that Jesus would do this is to come up with something he calls Jesus' messianic secret about a new world order. As we saw earlier, Aslan tried to make another obviously figurative phrase into a literal one when Jesus said that he came to bring a sword and not peace (see Mt 10:34). We saw how the word 'conflict' easily replaced the word 'sword' because that fits better in the context and reveals the intent of what Jesus was saying. His message brought conflict among people, including family members, because of how they will often turn against those who become followers of Jesus. If "sword" meant conflict in that context, it is easy to see how "sword" means courage in this one. This was no zealot's call to arms. Looking at the context of the text, it is reasonable to conclude that Jesus was not commanding his disciples to go out and buy swords, as Aslan suggests, in order to continue his (Jesus') zealot mission after he was killed. Jesus was telling his disciples that the time had come when they were going to need courage. If the religious leaders were coming after Jesus, they no doubt would be coming after the disciples; and we see this occurring in the book of Acts. The disciples did not fight back when they were attacked and persecuted for preaching the gospel after Jesus' resurrection. They understood that the gospel message was to be accompanied with agape love (the love God has for humankind that would compel him to send his Son to die in our place—John 3:16). Of course, in Gethsemane we see Peter impulsively use his dagger to cut off someone's ear. But Jesus was quick to stop that kind of nonsense, showing that violence was not the answer. If you use a real sword, says Jesus, you will die by that real sword. He showed Peter and the rest of his disciples that he did not mean for them to use violence. He showed it by his words and he showed it by his actions—he healed the man that Peter injured. In fact, he even questioned those who came to arrest him. Jesus wanted to know why they had come out with swords and clubs to arrest him as if he were a criminal, a *lēstēs*. He reminded them that he used to sit in the Temple courtyard everyday and teach, and they could have easily arrested him in the daytime. Instead, they came out there like that at night to arrest a peaceful man.

Was Jesus Really Determined to Destroy Those who Opposed Him?

After Jesus was arrested, the Gospels tell us that Jesus stood trial before the Sanhedrin. Aslan claims that Jesus refused to answer any charges brought against him; Jesus remained silent, says Aslan, because there was nothing more to say. Jesus had spent his three-year ministry raging against the Temple, the priest system and the religious leaders, threatening their authority and condemning their office. He even called some of them "a brood of vipers" (see Mt 23:33). Aslan is sure that Jesus was going to set up God's Kingdom by getting rid of these priests and religious leaders, by destroying the current political/religious system and overthrowing everyone who stood in his way. Aslan thinks that since Jesus was then in the hands of his enemies there was nothing else for him to say. It was as if Jesus threw up his hands and said, "You caught me." But the fact is he did answer relevant questions; he simply did not reply to any of the false testimony given by the so-called witnesses when he was in front of the Sanhedrin. There is no reason to try to argue your case when people are bringing false testimony against you. It is best to keep silent until that façade is over, which is what Jesus did. Of course, Jesus' silent reaction to this kangaroo court upset the chief priest; he wanted to watch Jesus bury himself by his own words. If things continued as they were going, they would have to release Jesus. The religious leaders could not let that happen. It was already getting near dawn and they wanted this over with soon, before the people started their day. Aslan says Jesus was silent because he had already spent three years raging against everything and everyone he disliked—the Temple, the priests, the Pharisees, scribes and law teachers—so there was no reason for him to rage now. He had already said what he wanted to say. Aslan chooses violent, potent words to describe what he thinks Jesus had been doing during his three-year ministry. Aslan says Jesus had been raging, threatening, condemning, and hoping to destroy and remove anyone who opposed him. The word rage denotes angry fury, a violent or intense anger; it can express zealous enthusiasm or strong devotion or violent passion. We talk of a battle or fierce storm raging, or a fire that is raging out of control. This is the image Aslan wants you to think of when he talks about Jesus raging, like some madman, against the priests and the whole establishment of the priesthood. One, of course, must wonder where Aslan gets the notion that Jesus did this. Do the Gospels reflect Aslan's view of Jesus? No, they do not. They do show Jesus speaking out against the religious leaders for their hypocrisy. The religious leaders were doing a very poor job of representing God to his people. They had created a powerful religious system that stifled individual worship, manipulated the Mosaic Law, established a taxation system that overburdened the poor; and co-conspired with Roman authority to maintain the upper hand, by force if necessary. These and other actions by the religious leaders upset Jesus, and they should have done. If Jesus was who he said he was— the Son of God—then he should have been very upset indeed. So Jesus spoke out against the actions of the religious leaders, but the records show that Jesus had control over his emotions and did not rage at them in the way Aslan would like you to believe.

Speaking out against the actions of the religious leaders does not necessarily imply that Jesus was opposed to the system or practice itself. If you speak out against the injustice of a political system, it does not mean you are opposed to the political system per se; you are opposed to the injustice that is found within the political system that should not be there. Only an anarchist opposes the whole concept of a political system. One can identify the moral and legal wrong inside a system and work to change it, without destroying the system itself. When you speak the truth against a wrong you often upset the status quo. The prophets of old did this; Jesus did this. Jesus was not threatening to remove the priests' authority and power in a violent or destructive manner; he was casting judgment on them because they needed to be told how they had gone wrong. Jesus was not just taking on the role of a prophet; he was speaking as the Son of God against those who had corrupted the religious system that he had created as a temporary system until he arrived. As mentioned earlier, the purpose of the animal sacrifices, the Temple, and the priesthood were coming to a close; they had been established as temporary substitutes for the promised Redeeming Messiah. God was bringing in a new time period just as he had done throughout history. With the arrival of the Redeeming Messiah, the priests knew their role would end, and they did not want this to happen. The priesthood had served its purpose; it was coming to a close. Jesus' death would end the requirements of the Temple, priests, and animal sacrifices; these were part of a temporary system that was put in place until the Redeeming Messiah—the "seed of the woman"—would die for humankind.

We have seen how Jesus spoke to the religious leaders as a typical Jewish prophet; he spoke out against their injustice, their oppression, and their hypocrisy. Isaiah had referred to the Israelites as "a brood of evildoers" (1:4), and it was appropriate for Jesus to call some of the religious leaders a "brood of vipers." In Matthew 23, just before his Olivet Discourse (which we have already looked at), Jesus pronounced seven "woes" upon the religious leaders in Jerusalem as a final warning to the Pharisees and scribes who had been following him those past three years. Earlier, the religious leaders had rejected Jesus as the Messiah, leading him to illustrate the Kingdom of God with nine important parables, which addressed their rejection (this has been discussed in a previous chapter). Jesus told the crowd at the Temple courtyard that because the scribes and Pharisees taught the Mosaic Law, they were to be careful to do what the scribes and Pharisees told them. Jesus did not negate the Mosaic Law just because those who taught it might not be following it, and so he told the crowd to follow the laws of God even if they were taught by arrogant, oppressive teachers. The reason Jesus said they were not to follow the Pharisee's example was because the Pharisees did not practice what they preached. Jesus then gave some details about how the Pharisees acted and how his disciples were not to be like them. The one who followed the Messiah was to have an attitude of service to others. So Jesus presented a powerful case against the Pharisees and scribes by charging them with seven "Woe unto you" indictments. Jesus here was being the compassionate, but realistic, surgeon who must tell his patient what needs to be done to make the person well again. In very strong words, Jesus was taking on the role of a prophet for the last time. Jesus called the religious leaders standing nearby hypocrites, i.e., actors or pretenders, because they did not practice what they preached. Let's take a look at the seven Woes Jesus delivered to the religious leaders.

In the first woe, Jesus accused the religious leaders of keeping people out of the kingdom of heaven. They were like the birds in the parable of the farmer who came and snatched the seed away from the ground so that it could not grow. In the second woe, Jesus accused the religious leaders of recruiting a follower and then, once they had him, not doing anything to educate him. They left the new recruit in ignorance. In the third woe, Jesus said the Pharisees were blind guides; they put more importance on the gold in the Temple than the Temple itself. Jesus gave several examples where the Pharisees put importance on the wrong thing. In the fourth woe, Jesus accused them of being so tied to their traditions that they had forgotten and/or neglected what God really demanded—justice, mercy, and faithfulness. These three were the most important things in Moses' Teachings, Jesus told them. This was an echo of what Micah had said—that God requires us to be just, love mercy, and live humbly with (in faithfulness to) God" (6:8). In the fifth woe, Jesus accused them of looking good on the outside, but in their thoughts, mind and heart they were filthy, full of greed and uncontrolled desires. The religious leaders pretended to be religious by doing good works that people would see and thereby conclude that they must be good. But Jesus said that God looks on the heart and sees us for what we are. Jesus told the Pharisees they better clean up their thoughts and minds because instead of actually following the Law they were full of lawlessness. Jesus was telling the Pharisees that no matter how good they thought they were, they were in need of repentance—a change in the way they acted and thought. In the sixth woe, Jesus expanded on the idea that the Pharisees looked good on the outside but not on the inside by comparing them to whitewashed graves. You might look good on the outside, Jesus told them, but inside you are full of dead people's bones and every kind of impurity. People might look at the Pharisees and say they must be righteous because of all the good things they do, but Jesus looked on the heart and told them they were full of hypocrisy and lawlessness. In Jesus' final woe to the religious leaders, he told them that they pretended to build tombs for former prophets as if they were honoring them. Jesus told the religious leaders that it was their ancestors who killed the prophets who testified against their sinful lifestyles, and that the religious leaders were just like their ancestors because they were going to kill the greatest prophet of all—God in human form, the Redeeming Messiah. It was at this point that Jesus called them poisonous snakes, or a brood of vipers, and informed them of their punishment—eternal separation from God.

Can you imagine standing there listening to someone criticize you in such a manner? No wonder these religious leaders had had enough of Jesus. They were going to make sure he paid for the things he had just said about them. After speaking these seven woes to the religious leaders, Jesus was overwhelmed with sorrow at how Israel had, throughout its history, rejected and killed the prophets that God (that Jesus) had sent to them. Mournfully, Jesus uttered this heartbreaking lament: "Jerusalem, Jerusalem, you kill the prophets and stone to death those sent to you! How often I wanted to gather your children together the way a hen gathers her chicks under her wings! But you were not willing! Your house will be abandoned, deserted" ("Scripture is taken from GOD'S WORD®. © 1995 God's Word to the Nations. Used by permission of Baker Publishing Group." Mt 23:37f). These words echo the heartfelt desire God expressed regarding the Israelites before they were about to enter the land God had promised them: Oh, that they would be inclined to respect me and keep my commandments, so that it might go well with them and their children forever! (Dt 5:29). The Pharisees stormed off after hearing Jesus' indictments against them and conspired to get him arrested and killed. They wanted him to suffer; they wanted him crucified. They were going to kill the final Prophet that God would send them (and the world).

Aslan says that Jesus promised that the new world order Jesus was going to establish—the kingdom of God on earth—would end the priesthood. But the priesthood was designed to come to an end; it was only a temporary system created by God to serve a particular time period. When the Redeeming Messiah appeared and fulfilled his mission, the priesthood would no longer be necessary. So Aslan is correct in saying the priestly class would end; but it would not be swept away in the way Aslan proposes. Aslan's way of having the priestly class end is for Jesus to violently overthrow the religious leaders by killing them off. Aslan claims that Jesus' ministry was established on the premise that he would destroy the current political/religious system and depose everyone who stood against him. Aslan thinks Jesus had been keeping score of everyone who mistreated him or had done him wrong, and he was going to pay them back for their treatment. The very foundation of Jesus' ministry, Aslan tells us, was to do violence to those who mistreated him. This is the Jesus Aslan says he prefers to the supposedly made up Jesus of the Gospels. Aslan's Jesus was going to annihilate the present order—the priesthood, the religious system, the Temple, and the Roman oppressors—and create a new world order. Once again, Aslan attempts to have Jesus look like Muhammad. But now Jesus has been arrested and is standing trial. He has nothing to say, says Aslan, and so says nothing.

Did the Sanhedrin Trial Break All the Rules?

Aslan doubts that there actually was a Sanhedrin trial; he thinks it was all made up by the Gospel writers. Aslan contends that if Jesus had been tried before the Sanhedrin it would have violated just about every condition for a legal proceeding that had been established by Jewish law. According to Aslan, the Sanhedrin was not allowed to hold night court; it was not allowed to convene on Sabbath or during the Passover festival; it could not assemble in the high priest's courtyard; and it was required to commence the "trial" with a detailed list explaining why the accused person is actually innocent. Aslan accuses the Gospel writers of misrepresenting the Sanhedrin and suggests that their obvious errors show that they had a very inaccurate understanding of how the Sanhedrin worked. Aslan thinks that the Gospel writers' inaccurate understanding of legal procedures should be all that one needs to conclude that the trial of Jesus before the Sanhedrin and

Caiaphas the high priest was fabricated; this trial should cause us to doubt the historicity of the Gospels.

Now *The Bible Knowledge Commentary* on Mark reminds us that even though trials were to be done in daytime, Jesus' pre-dawn trial was "informal" and only "required a 'formal' ratification after dawn." This hasty trial was necessary because Jewish law stipulated that a person was to be tried immediately after being arrested. Now, there is a considerable problem with the list of conditions Aslan says the Sanhedrin were supposed to follow. These conditions were not in complete written format until the Mishnah was compiled around the fourth decade of the second century, about a hundred years after Jesus' trial. These "rules" or conditions were not as legally binding in the 30s A.D. when Jesus was tried, as Aslan wants you to believe. So, when Aslan says the Gospel record of the trial of Jesus is a lie because it breaks the rules of the Sanhedrin court, you must bear in mind that those rules had not been in firm force when Jesus was tried. But that does not matter to Aslan. It is just like when Aslan says Jesus did not fulfill the promise of the End Times, even though the End Times had not arrived yet. It is like punishing someone for breaking a rule or law that has not been created yet. Aslan says the Sanhedrin broke a handful of rules when they put Jesus on trial, rules that had not been firmly set down yet. Aslan attempts to dismiss the fact that the Mishnah was not compiled until the second century, by saying that the Gospels were not written in the 30s A.D. either. But this is not a good argument. Of course, no one has proposed the Gospels were written in the 30s A.D. I have proposed that there is evidence to show that the three synoptic Gospels were written in the 60s A.D., before Peter and Paul were executed. Even if the Gospels were written after 70 A.D. but before the end of the first century, they still would have recorded the trial of Jesus before the Mishnah had been compiled and completed. There is simply no argument here; worse, it is a terrible attempt at an argument. Aslan makes a feeble attempt to use rules not yet established as rules that had been broken during Jesus' trial. Even if there were some rules of how the Sanhedrin was supposed to operate, it does not mean that the Sanhedrin followed them when they arrested Jesus. It might surprise Aslan that a legal system does not always follow its own rules (just as people do not), but hopefully it does not surprise you, my reader. There are lots of innocent people who are serving prison terms throughout the world who have had the so-called "legal system" misuse the law.

The Sanhedrin trial of Jesus was a quickly put together kangaroo court for the express purpose of getting rid of Jesus. Even if the Sanhedrin did break some rules that had not yet been fully established in written format, it shows how desperate they were to get rid of Jesus. Aslan accused the Gospel writers of having an inaccurate knowledge of Jewish legal proceedings, and that we should thereby doubt the Gospels' historicity. But we have found that Aslan has created a false scenario in order to try to prove his point, and this should prompt us to doubt the reliability of his theories about Jesus. There is no reason to doubt that the Sanhedrin formed a quick trial to condemn Jesus. He had earlier presented seven Woes on the religious leaders; they were now going to condemn him to death because of it. This quick trial was meant to establish a formal complaint against Jesus so they could send him to Pilate. The Jewish authorities were not able to legally execute a person; that was for the Romans to do. Therefore, the Sanhedrin needed to get a quick consensus together so they could transfer Jesus over to the Romans for execution. This hasty attempt to gather charges is exactly what the Gospels record. Let's look at how the Gospels portray the trial of Jesus before the Sanhedrin. (The rendition I offer below is my own compilation based on all four Gospels.)

Jesus was first taken to Annas, Caiaphas' father-in-law. Annas questioned Jesus about his disciples and his teachings. Jesus told Annas what he had told the Temple guards and priests who came out to arrest him. He said that he had spoken publicly and taught in the synagogues and in the Temple courtyard and had not said anything in secret. Peter and John followed the crowd and came into the courtyard, where John left Peter. Peter was warming himself by a fire and was questioned by some people who accused him of being one of Jesus' followers. Peter quickly and vehemently denied knowing Jesus. When the Sanhedrin was ready, having gathered together the scribes, religious leaders, and the witnesses who had been called in to testify, Annas sent Jesus to Caiaphas. Many of the witnesses came forward with false testimony, and then two men stated that they had heard Jesus say that he was going to tear down the man-made Temple and in three days have one built without needing builders to do it. Even their testimony was contradictory; they could not get their story straight.

The chief priest was angry that Jesus just stood there silent, making no attempt to argue his case. So the chief priest made Jesus swear an oath and answer the question he (the priest) was going to set before Jesus. The chief priest asked Jesus, "Are you the Messiah, the Son of God?" Jesus answered, "Yes, I am." Then he added that they will see the Son of Man coming on the clouds of heaven. The chief priest was outraged at this declaration and said that they needed no more testimony because Jesus had just incriminated himself by dishonoring God. He dishonored God by calling himself God. The verdict handed down was that Jesus deserved the death penalty. Then those near Jesus began to spit on him and hit him with their fists and mock him.

We see that the Sanhedrin's verdict involved capital punishment, but this was beyond the jurisdiction of the Sanhedrin; it had to go before a Roman court. That is why they hastily sent Jesus to Pilate, early in the morning. The charge against Jesus could not be blasphemy against the Jewish God; the Roman court would have dismissed that as religious squabble. The charge had to be serious; it had to be sedition. So Aslan is mistaken in his attempts to show that the Gospel writers recorded blatant and deliberate errors regarding Jesus' trial before the Sanhedrin. Aslan says Jesus' trial before the Sanhedrin is all the evidence we really need to reject the Gospel record, but instead we see that Aslan is the one who stands accused of the very thing he accuses the Gospel writers of—unreliability and blatant errors.

The Trial before Pilate

Aslan attempts to denigrate the Gospel narratives even more by claiming that the Gospel writers fabricated Jesus' trial before Pilate. Aslan accuses the Gospel writers of creating a theatrical atmosphere with their narrative concerning Jesus' trial before Pilate. Is the trial before Pilate a fabrication? Let's take a look at the Gospel passages regarding Jesus' trial before Pilate, and then you can decide if the event appears to be fabricated. Remember, Jesus has already been arrested and brought before the Sanhedrin in order to devise charges against him to justify bringing him to Pilate for condemnation. Here is the Gospel rendering of Jesus' trial before Pilate (again, the rendition I offer is my own compilation based on all four Gospels):

285

Having decided that Jesus was to be executed, the chief priests and other religious leaders restrained Jesus and took him to Pilate, the governor, around six o'clock in the morning. Pilate came out to the accusers because they would not go into the palace for fear of becoming unclean for the festival at hand. Pilate, of course, wanted to know what the charges were against the man they had brought to him. The religious leaders were quite vague as to the charges, so Pilate told them to try him by Jewish law. This would not do because they were not allowed to execute anyone. The religious leaders had to have a formidable charge, one that violated Roman not Jewish law, so they told Pilate that the man they brought before him had stirred up trouble, telling people not to pay their taxes and claiming to be a king. Once Pilate heard this accusation, he took the matter more seriously. He went inside the palace and asked Jesus if he were king of the Jews. Jesus wanted to know if Pilate had come to that conclusion on his own, or if someone had told him. Pilate told Jesus it was his own people— the Jewish leaders—who had made the accusation. He wanted to hear it from Jesus what he had done wrong. Jesus admitted that he was a king but that his kingdom was a spiritual kingdom, not a physical or earthly kingdom. He told Pilate that if his kingdom were of this world, his followers would have at least done something to prevent the religious leaders from handing him over to Pilate. Pilate narrows it down and plainly asks Jesus, "You are a king then?" to which Jesus replied, "Yes, I am." Then Jesus told him that he was born into this world in order to testify to the truth, to which Pilate skeptically asked, "What is truth?" After this conversation Pilate went back out to Jesus' accusers, the religious leaders, and said he did not find anything wrong with Jesus that would merit death. The religious leaders continued to hurl accusations against Jesus, but Jesus remained silent. During this time, Pilate's wife sent him a message warning him to have nothing to do with Jesus, implying that he should let Jesus go free. But the religious leaders kept on with their accusations. They said he started in Galilee with his trouble-making and brought it to Jerusalem. When Pilate learned that Jesus was a Galilean he sent him over to Herod Antipas, who ruled Galilee. Herod was in Jerusalem and had wanted to meet Jesus for quite some time. Although he asked Jesus many questions, Jesus did not reply to any of them. So Herod and his soldiers mocked Jesus and sent him back to Pilate. Pilate hoped to quickly conclude the trial. He publically announced the charge that had been brought against Jesus by the religious leaders: Jesus had attempted to turn people against the government. Then Pilate offered his verdict: I have questioned him, and so did Herod, and we do not find this man guilty of the crimes you accuse him of. Pilate informed the crowd that he would have Jesus whipped, and then set him free. Since it was customary during Passover to release a prisoner, Pilate would honor this custom hoping the religious leaders would come to their senses and release Jesus. Instead, they chose an insurrectionist named Barabbas. Pilate was surprised and wanted to know what he was supposed to do with Jesus. "Crucify him," they shouted. He asked why and they kept shouting to crucify him. Pilate realized he was getting nowhere and, in order to prevent a riot, he gave in to their demand to crucify Jesus. To show he wanted no part in this decision, he dipped his hands in a bowl of water and told the religious leaders that he would not be guilty of killing Jesus; that guilt would rest on them. In a state of emotional fervor, they agreed to accept the responsibility of Jesus' death. Jesus was taken away to be flogged, and then he was brought out one more time to meet his accusers. Perhaps the flogging would be enough, and they would be satisfied and let Jesus go. When the religious leaders saw Jesus they shouted that they wanted him crucified. Pilate was at a loss and again told the religious leaders he found that Jesus had done nothing wrong. The religious leaders now told Pilate why they really wanted Jesus executed. They told Pilate that their law insisted that Jesus must die because he called himself the Son of God. For the first time during the trial, Pilate was now afraid. He confronted Jesus again and asked where he was from. Jesus did not answer him. Pilate, no doubt very concerned, reminded Jesus that he (Pilate) had the authority to set him (Jesus) free. Jesus told him that actually Pilate did not have any authority over Jesus except what had been given to him from above. Pilate then told the religious leaders that he wanted to free Jesus. They told him that if he did, he would not be a friend of the Emperor's. Pilate brought Jesus back out to them and, sitting on his judge's chair, pointed at Jesus and said "here is your king," but the crowd shouted that they wanted him killed; they wanted him crucified. Pilate shouted back, "Am I to crucify your king?" Then the religious leaders said that their only king was the emperor. At that, Pilate turned Jesus over to his soldiers to be crucified.

One main reason Aslan believes Jesus' trial before Pilate is a fabrication is because he (Aslan) thinks that Jesus was just an unimportant, unknown Jewish peasant whom Pilate would never consider trying in a court of law. Pilate would not have given any time to the likes of Jesus. Aslan assumes Pilate had simply put his signature to lots of execution orders on that particular day and would not have taken any notice of the peasant from Galilee. (We saw in Chapter One that Horsley believes that the decision to execute Jesus was probably made by a few fairly low-level security officers.) Aslan concludes that the Gospel accounts of Jesus' trial before Pilate is too preposterous to be taken seriously. There are, however, several reasons why such a thing would not be preposterous or outlandish; I will mention six of them. First, during Jesus' three-year ministry he traveled several times to Jerusalem, through Samaria, around Galilee and to some Gentile areas, like the Decapolis, Caesarea Philippi, and Tyre and Sidon. Herod Antipas knew about him and desired to meet with him; the chief priest in Jerusalem knew about him; and there is no reason why Pilate would not have known about him. He would certainly have been informed about someone like Jesus who attracted such a large crowd wherever he went. Therefore, Jesus was not some unimportant, unknown Jewish peasant, as Aslan thinks. Second, Jesus stood trial before Pilate early in the morning, sometime around six. I doubt that Pilate would have already signed off on lots of execution orders at that time, as Aslan suggests. Jesus' trial would probably have been the first case Pilate encountered that morning. Third, according to *Harper's Bible Dictionary*, Jesus' trial before Pilate followed the logistics and procedures for the Roman trial of a noncitizen; an individual had the legal right to bring charges of misdeeds against another person and, in turn, the Roman governor could use his own discretion in deciding how to respond to each case, to either dismiss it or hear it. The procedure in which Jesus is brought before Pilate's tribunal is therefore historically legitimate and should not be seen as a remarkable or unlikely event. Just because Aslan says the idea that Jesus stood trial before Pilate is preposterous does not mean it is. What Aslan does here is use a literary ploy or technique to attempt to show something is absurd by simply stating that it is absurd. But simply saying something is absurd does not make it so. The fourth reason why Jesus' trial before Pilate is not outlandish is that one of Jesus' accusers is none other than the chief priest, Caiaphas, with whom, as Aslan admitted, Pilate had a working relationship. Pilate would honor his relationship with Caiaphas by participating in Jesus' trial. Fifth, there is no reason to doubt that Pilate was informed beforehand of Jesus' arrest and allowed his Roman soldiers to accompany the religious leaders and Temple guards when they arrested Jesus. Sixth, besides the Gospels, Tacitus and other Roman historians mention Pilate's connection with Jesus' trial and crucifixion, although the noncanonical writings do not go into any details. Based on all these factors, it is not difficult to see why Pilate would hear this case. There is no reason to conclude, as Aslan does, that Jesus' trial before Pilate was preposterous.

Aslan had made an earlier comment in his fifth chapter that the Gospels presented an inaccurate portrayal of Pilate, showing him to be a rather cowardly man. Aslan claims the Gospels depicted Pilate as doubting Jesus' guilt and then doing what he could to save Jesus' life. When that did not work, Pilate just washed his hands to show he wanted nothing to do with their demand to execute Jesus. Aslan dismisses this portrayal of Pilate as complete fabrication. The reason Aslan believes it is fiction is because Pilate was known for being corrupt and uncaring; he disliked the Jews and held their traditions, laws, and customs with disdain. Philo and Josephus described Pilate as a detached administrator who had no problem exercising his power over those he ruled (he served in his capacity as prefect of Judea from A.D. 26 to 36). Philo, a first-century Jewish writer, was not kind to Pilate in his writings, describing him as corrupt, insolent, insulting, cruel, and apt to murder people who had not been tried and/or condemned. Josephus also painted Pilate with unfavorable colors. Luke shows the character of Pilate when he (Luke) recorded that Pilate had ordered some Galileans to be executed while they were in the process of offering sacrificial animals in the Temple in Jerusalem (see Lk 13:1). Historical sources show that Pilate was no real friend to the Jewish community, and that he had little or no respect for those he governed. Aslan concludes that the Gospel accounts of Jesus' trial before Pilate portray a contradictory view of Pilate in comparison to these historical sources. He thinks the Gospels portray Pilate as weak, irresolute and indecisive, allowing the crowd to manipulate him as if he were the one that was submissive to them. Remember, Aslan believes Mark wrote his Gospel in early 70s A.D., and Matthew and Luke wrote theirs in late 80s to 90s A.D., and John wrote his in the first two decades of the second century. Based on these dates, Aslan thinks that the further each Gospel writer was from 70 A.D., when Jerusalem was destroyed, the more fabricated and obscure the rendition of Jesus' trial before Pilate became. For Aslan, each consecutive Gospel, starting with Mark, added more fictitious details to Jesus' trial, not to mention Jesus' whole life. As the years went by the Gospel writers just piled on more erroneous material until John finally added the deathblow that catapulted anti-Semitism into the next two thousand years. It is Aslan's worldview, his belief system, which compels him to place late dates on the Gospels and to then conclude that those Gospels present a fabricated view of Pilate.

Rather than portraying Pilate in a fabricated manner, the Gospels show that Pilate offered a courtesy to Caiaphas to hear the case. As the trial unraveled, the Gospels then reveal Pilate's contempt and lack of patience with the religious leaders. The Gospels reveal Pilate's total frustration at the manner in which the trial was taking shape. He was fed up with these religious leaders and was relieved to find that Jesus was a Galilean so he could send him off to Herod and get a reprieve from the trial. He may have thought that that was the end of that morning's terrible debacle of a trial. When Jesus appeared before Herod Antipas he was totally silent. Herod had wanted to meet Jesus ever since he had heard about him, but never did. He was probably excited that he was finally going to meet him. But Jesus said nothing to him, although Herod and his advisors pounded him with questions. Jesus refused to satisfy Herod's curiosity. In order to save face, Herod spent some time mocking Jesus before sending him back to Pilate. Pilate was probably a bit upset that he now had to continue this charade. Pilate had Jesus brutally whipped and then presented him to the crowd once again. And again the crowd shouted that they wanted him crucified, and this time they gave the real reason they wanted Jesus dead. They told Pilate that their law insisted that Jesus must die because he called himself the Son of God. This accusation may have truly frightened Pilate. Being a Roman pagan who believed in many gods, Pilate may have been concerned about this allegation. Pilate did not want to take a chance that this man—Jesus—was the son of a god. Pilate confronted Jesus again and asked where he was from. Jesus did not answer him. Pilate, no doubt very anxious and apprehensive, reminded Jesus that he (Pilate) had the authority to set him (Jesus) free. Jesus told him that actually Pilate did not have any authority over Jesus except what had been given to him from above. That was the kind of response Pilate knew a god would make, so when he heard this he wanted desperately to free Jesus. He went out to the religious leaders and told them he wanted to free Jesus. The religious leaders had another trump up their sleeve. They told Pilate that if he released Jesus then Pilate was no friend of the Emperor. The religious leaders knew that Pilate was not in good standing with the Emperor. (In Chapter One, we saw that Horsley incorrectly referred to Pilate as a faithful servant of Tiberius.) Tiberius had recently come out of retirement and assumed the role of emperor again. During Tiberius' retirement, the commander of his Praetorian Guard, a man named Sejanus, had pretty much run the empire. Tiberius had grown suspicious of Sejanus and had him executed. Tiberius not only had Sejanus killed but decided to murder some of the officials that Sejanus had put in power. Pilate was one of those officials who received his position from Sejanus. Being far away from Rome, in Judea, had so far been beneficial for Pilate, but when the religious leaders told Pilate that if he released Jesus he would show he was no friend of the Emperor's, that pretty much sealed Jesus' fate. Pilate had no desire, especially with his reputation, to arouse the attention of the emperor. So even though Philo and Josephus portray Pilate as a horribly ruthless man, which he was, during this time of Jesus' trial, Pilate had to make sure he was not being noticed by Tiberius. This threat by the religious leaders showed that they too understood Pilate's tottering political position. Pilate had no advocate in Rome, and he did not have many friends in Jerusalem. There was no way to cross over the bridges he had burned. So Pilate turned Jesus over to his soldiers to be crucified. (Some information in this section has been gleaned from *Tyndale Bible Dictionary* and *Every Man in the Bible*.) Based on the above, I do not believe Jesus' trial before Pilate was fabricated; but you must decide for yourself.

Sedition or Blasphemy?

Let's return to the charges against Jesus for more elucidation. The religious leaders had to make sure the charges against Jesus would stick. The trial before the Sanhedrin had been a disaster because the so-called witnesses against Jesus were contradicting themselves and nothing substantial had been offered. Jesus' accusers were not able to provide evidence that Jesus had broken any particular Jewish law. The religious leaders certainly could not use the same charges that had been part of the Sanhedrin trial to convince Pilate to have Jesus executed. The religious leaders needed charges that appeared seditious; otherwise Pilate would have dismissed their case against

Jesus as no more than religious squabble. There were two charges they thought they could present to Pilate that would force him to take them seriously. The first charge was that Jesus told people they did not have to pay taxes. Where would they have gotten that idea? Just a couple of days prior to the trial, some religious leaders had approached Jesus with a question in order to trap him so they could arrest him on charges of sedition. The question was: Is it right to pay taxes to the emperor or not? Jesus told them to give the emperor what belongs to the emperor, and give God what belongs to God. With that answer they were unable to arrest him. I have already discussed this episode and showed that Aslan was mistaken to use it as an example or proof that Jesus was a zealot. Aslan, of course, was not the first one to use Jesus' answer to try to prove he was a zealot. The religious leaders at Jesus' trial tried to use it. It was a false accusation then, and the religious leaders knew that, and it is a false accusation now. In fact, Pilate did not seem to be interested in that charge; he was more concerned about the second one, which was that Jesus said he was king of the Jews. Pilate asked Jesus if that charge was true. Did Jesus see himself as king of the Jews? Jesus replied that he was, but then clarified his answer by saying his kingship differed from the one implied in Pilate's question. His kingship was spiritual, not physical. He told Pilate that if his kingdom were of this world, his followers would have at least done something to prevent the religious leaders from handing him over to Pilate. In other words, Jesus is saying if he were a zealot, an insurrectionist, his followers would have put up a fight. Peter tried to in Gethsemane but Jesus had quickly stopped it. Jesus' reply to Pilate did not give solid ground for the death penalty.

But Aslan says that Jesus was declared guilty because he admitted, by saying "Give Caesar his due and God his," that he was a zealot, a bandit, a lēstēs. It was for that reason Aslan claims that Jesus was declared guilty and executed. Aslan uses the plaque that was nailed to Jesus' cross—the plaque that stated his "crime"—as evidence that Jesus was determined to usher in God's kingdom and be its kingly ruler, which would be seen as an act of sedition. That plaque said that Jesus was the King of the Jews. That plaque prompts Aslan to declare that Jesus was killed for no other reason except that he claimed he was both king and messiah. The Gospels claim that Jesus was arrested for one reason: he had made claims of being the God of the Hebrew Scriptures who came to present himself as the sacrifice for the world's sins. When Jesus was arrested the chief priest asked him if he was the Messiah, the Son of God, because this is what Jesus had claimed about himself throughout his ministry. Jesus answered, "Yes, I am." (See Mk14:62, Mt 26:64, Lk 22:70.) Jesus' accusers had heard his parables; they had heard the statements he made against their hypocrisy; they had heard the claims he made about being the Messiah; and they had heard the declaration from his mouth that he was the Son of God. For this they wanted him crucified. Why did the cross Jesus was nailed to have the plaque that said King of the Jews? Because Pilate asked him straight out if Jesus was the king of the Jews, and Jesus answered him, "Yes, I am." (See Lk 23:3.) But then Jesus added, "My kingdom doesn't belong to this world. If my kingdom belonged to this world, my followers would fight to keep me from being handed over to the Jews. My kingdom doesn't have its origin on earth" ("Scripture is taken from GOD'S WORD®. © 1995 God's Word to the Nations. Used by permission of Baker Publishing Group." Jn 18:36). He lets Pilate know that he is no insurrectionist; he is no zealot. Of course, Aslan does not believe Jesus had an audience with Pilate; he believes the Gospel writers made that up. But Aslan does believe that Jesus was a zealot, plotting to overthrow Roman rule in Israel, and so he dismisses any and all biblical passages that disagree with him.

Another reason Aslan (and other liberal theologian/scholars) dismisses the Gospel account regarding Jesus' trial before Pilate is because of the reference of a customary ritual to try to get Jesus released (see Mt 27:15). The Gospels state that it was customary for the Roman governor—in this case, Pilate—to release a Jewish criminal during Passover week. Aslan says that such a custom did not exist because there is nothing about this custom in other (noncanonical) historical writings during this time. Therefore, when the Gospels say that Pilate gave the religious leaders an opportunity to come to their senses and free Jesus as part of a ritual during Passover, it was a fabricated story. The *Bible Knowledge Commentary* says that though it is true that this particular event (Pilate offering the release of a prisoner) is not recorded in noncanonical sources, the releasing of a prisoner was consistent with the way Rome responded to its subjects in goodwill fashion regarding local customs. In other words, Rome was known to honor the local customs of its subjects throughout the Empire and these occurrences would not always be recorded. (This habit of honoring local customs was one way that Rome was able to maintain its Pax Romana for some 200 years.) If Rome honored local customs, it would stand to reason that in doing so there was no necessity of recording something that was just business as usual. So Pilate chose to grant this custom to appease the religious leaders, assuming they would come to their senses and request Jesus' release. Instead, the religious leaders demanded the release of a real insurrectionist, and this, of course, was rather perplexing for Pilate. He demanded to know what the religious leaders wanted him to do with Jesus. Their reply: Crucify him. Frustrated by their inability to concede, Pilate ceremoniously washed his hands of the whole mess. He told the crowd he did not find Jesus guilty. In a state of emotional fervor, the religious leaders agreed to accept the responsibility of Jesus' death. The Gospels said the people responded by saying: "The responsibility for killing him will rest on us and our children." A lot of biblical critics say that this is one of the major reasons that many Christians through the centuries have been anti-Semitic. There is, of course, no denying that there have been terrible episodes throughout history where so-called Christians have persecuted and murdered Jews simply for being Jews. This is a horrible tragedy and is totally uncharacteristic of what Christianity stands for. Christians value love, justice, forgiveness, and mercy, among others, and there is no justification for the mistreatment of anyone based on race, ethnicity, sex, or religion. What was said in the heat of this emotional trial is no justification for future mistreatment. In fact, we have already seen the real Christian attitude in Peter's first sermon toward the Jews who helped kill Jesus. It was one of forgiveness and acceptance (see Acts 2:38).

Aslan, making full use of hyperbole, claims that John the Gospel writer made a permanent insult upon all Jews by stating that they had performed the worst deed a Jew in the first century could ever do. What was this horrible thing John the Gospel writer accused the Jews of doing? When Pilate asked them what he should do with their king, Jesus, John has the Jews reply: "We have no king but Caesar!" (Jn 19:15). Aslan claims this statement became the reason or justification for Christians to then commit anti-Semitic actions against Jews for the next two thousand years. But anti-Semitism is actually a non-Christian attitude. There are no passages in the New Testament that condone anti-Semitism. Becoming a Christian is a mature, individual, conscious decision; it is the result of recognizing and accepting the responsibility of your own sin and separation from God, with the realization that you

294

cannot make yourself good enough to satisfy God's holiness, and acknowledging that God the Father has provided a remedy for our lack by sending God the Son, Jesus, to take the penalty for our sins upon himself. Once a person accepts Jesus' act of atonement for themselves, God the Holy Spirit begins to work in that person's life to transform them into the image of the Son, while still retaining the individual's personality. The individual, of course, must decide on a daily basis whether to live according to his/her own plan or to freely allow the Spirit to work in their lives. The Christian now has a dual nature—the sinful nature that keeps him/her from God, and the renewed spiritual nature that is the result of the Spirit working in his/her life. Unfortunately, the sinful nature is not yet totally destroyed in the Christian; that will happen at the final resurrection. Therefore, we still see lots of instances where a Christian will allow the sinful nature to be manifested in his/her life. When that happens, the Christian is actually acting with the same sinful nature that the non-Christian has submitted to on a continual basis. There is no denying the fact that some Christians have been anti-Semitic; and there is no justifying it. But I doubt that when the Jews replied, "We have no king but Caesar!" that that particular statement recorded by John was the impetus or basis for two thousand years of Christian anti-Semitism, as Aslan claims. There are lots of other factors, events and issues that helped create an occasional anti-Semitic outburst. It was not like the next two thousand years saw nothing but bloody wars between Christians and Jews. One must also realize that when Christianity became a recognized and national religion in the fourth century (a very sad thing to have happened, by the way), the erroneous idea developed that everyone now, by simply being born in a certain area, was a Christian. One became a Christian by default. Being a Christian now simply meant you were born in Rome, or in France, or in Great Britain. That is not, however, how one becomes a Christian. One is not a Christian by simply being born in a particular location. Lots of people may think they are a Christian simply because they were born in the USA or England or Germany, or because they attend a particular church, but they are sadly mistaken. And they will be sadly mistaken when Jesus returns to make a final judgment on all mankind (see Mt 7:21-23).

Aslan insists there is an essential fact we should not forget and that is that Jesus did not die by being stoned to death on charges of blasphemy. Aslan insists that Jesus was crucified at the hands of Rome on charges of sedition. Jesus simply met the same fate as all the other 'messiahs' or insurrectionists of the first century. The only big difference is that, for some reason, Jesus would be remembered enough that some forty years later someone would write a brief 'biography' about him. Aslan is unable to tell us why anyone would even care to have made anything of Jesus, this so-called unimportant, unknown Jewish peasant who contrived an outlandish new world order paradigm that went totally awry. Instead, Aslan simply dismisses Jesus' crucifixion story that is found in the Gospels based on the fact that criminals were crucified by the Romans in order to not only punish them for their crimes, but to humiliate them and have them be an example to others who might think of doing something stupid. Aslan also agrees with the JS, Horsley, and others that Jesus' corpse, like everyone else's, would either be left on the cross to be eaten by birds or thrown to the ground to be eaten by dogs. Jesus' bones would then be tossed on the huge pile of bones that the area was named for— Golgotha, the place of skulls. Aslan, of course, insists that Jesus was chiefly executed for sedition and that this charge against Jesus— sedition—is the only way we can interpret everything that happened to Jesus during his final days. Aslan says this charge against Jesus is an undeniable, inflexible fact. Again, let it be recognized that the charge of sedition was prompted by the religious leaders because that charge would guarantee that Jesus would be executed, which is what the religious leaders wanted. We see this happen throughout history. Lots of people have been imprisoned on trumped up charges. Just because Jesus was charged with sedition does not mean he was seditious. Aslan cannot be that naïve to think that one must be automatically guilty of the charges made against them. And just because many people who were crucified ended up being eaten by birds and dogs or thrown onto a killing floor, does not mean Jesus was. There is no reason to doubt that two men, Joseph and Nicodemus, both who served as religious leaders, requested Jesus' body and gave him a proper burial (see Jn 19:38-42). Deuteronomy 21:22f makes it clear that God required that when a convicted person was put to death his/her body was not to be left hanging overnight on a pole; they were to bury the person that same day. Leaving the body overnight would make the land unclean. Since Jesus died near the end of Passover week, it was not unusual that these two men (obviously quiet followers of Jesus) would want to remove Jesus' body and entomb it. (Thanks to *New Testament Commentary* on Mark for this insight.)

As I mentioned before, the reason why the religious leaders did not stone Jesus to death on charges of blasphemy was because Jews were not really allowed to execute people during this time. That was for Romans to do. Whenever Jews did stone someone to death during this time it was basically a lynch job; it was done very quickly before Roman guards could step in. They also did not want to stone Jesus to death because they feared a riot if they would have done so (Mt 26:5). The religious leaders did charge Jesus with blasphemy and did announce that he deserved to die because of it. But they wanted him to be crucified, and that required a Roman trial. Charging him with sedition would guarantee that Jesus would be executed. Another reason why Jesus was crucified is because the Hebrew Scriptures said the Redeeming Messiah would be executed by crucifixion. Psalm 22:16 says the Redeeming Messiah would have his hands and feet pierced. Zechariah 12:10 says that in the Messianic Kingdom people will look at the King and realize he is the one they had pierced. Isaiah 53 talks about the Messiah who will be killed for our iniquities. The death of the Messiah was not a foreign idea for the Jew; they had simply chosen to ignore this aspect of the Messiah's role and focus exclusively, at their peril, on the Messianic King. Aslan wants to believe, and wants you to believe, that since Jesus was not stoned to death it proves he was a zealot. Just because the charge of sedition was brought against Jesus does not mean that he was guilty of it. Aslan should know, as all of us should, that many innocent people are in prison because of false charges. Aslan does not seem concerned that Jesus was an innocent man killed on trumped up charges; Aslan wants to accuse an innocent man of being a zealot and getting what he deserved. But Aslan cannot deny the fact that unlike all the other zealots, bandits, and 'messiahs' of the first century, Jesus did not become an obscure insurrectionist like all the rest of them. Why not? Could it be that Jesus rose from the dead on the third day like he said he was going to do? Could it be that the risen Jesus revealed the wounds from his flogging and crucifixion and this sparked a newfound faith in his followers? His horrible death surely was not the impetus for his followers to keep his memory alive by creating a brand new religion where they made up a bunch of sayings and attributed them to him. If Jesus was just another zealot along with the myriad of zealots in the first century, then why would these followers of an executed zealot be any different from the followers of other executed zealot

297

leaders? Why did they not just disappear from history? Unless Jesus, their Messiah, rose from the dead.

Three Conclusions

Aslan insists that he and other scholars have trouble with Jesus' trial because of the various traditions (including oral) that mention it. Aslan thinks these traditions are too obscure to offer any solid historical facts. Of course, Aslan is referring to the Gospel accounts of Jesus' trial, which were written for the express purpose of showing that Jesus was the messiah promised in the Hebrew Scriptures. Once again, Aslan takes the opportunity to make the erroneous claim that historical accuracy did not matter to the Gospel writers. Facts were not relevant. Aslan says what really mattered to the Gospel writers and the early believers was not history, but Christology; that is, creating a doctrine, religion, or dogma around the person of Jesus, linking him with the concept of the Messiah found in the Hebrew Scriptures. So Aslan concludes that Jesus' trial and crucifixion, just like everything else the Gospel writers wrote about Jesus, was obscured by embellishments and outright lies. Were the Gospel writers concerned with history? I have shown that the Hebrew Scriptures predicted the coming of the Redeeming Messiah and that the Gospels recorded the fulfillment of that hope. Aslan thinks that having four "biographical" accounts of Jesus' trial and crucifixion (the four canonical Gospels) makes the story harder to understand; it is less clear and difficult to grasp because there are four versions. I am sure that if there was only one Gospel, Aslan would have said it was too unreliable because there would not be another one to compare it with. And I am sure if there were two Gospels, Aslan would have said they were unreliable because they probably collaborated with one another. The fact is the Gospel record is not fuzzy because there are four 'traditions' upon which to rely. These four Gospel accounts are reliable as historical documents. The fact that there are four Gospels does not negate the value of their work. It is not the number of Gospels that is important; it is whether or not what those Gospels say is correct. Aslan says the Gospels cannot be trusted; but I can truthfully say that the Gospels (and the entire Bible) have undergone more scrutiny, more criticism, and more investigations than any other piece of historical work, and they have proven their reliability and authenticity.

So Aslan arrives at three conclusions regarding the arrest, trial and execution of Jesus: one, the Gospel writers only wanted to prove that Jesus was the promised messiah; two, historical accuracy was irrelevant to the Gospel writers; and three, all that mattered to the Gospel writers was formulating a Christology based on Jesus' life. In stating these three things, Aslan is right about one, wrong about the other, and half-correct about the third. Yes, the Gospel writers did write in order to prove that Jesus was the promised Messiah. As I said before, the Gospel writers believed in a linear history; they believed in the continuity of history; and they believed God was at the helm of history. The Gospel writers were convinced that God had raised up the Jewish nation, had established the priesthood and the animal sacrifices as temporary modes of atonement, had provided prophets to keep the Israelites from rejecting the Lord God and turning to idols, provided prophesies regarding both the Redeeming Messiah and the Messianic King, and then brought the "seed of the woman," Jesus Christ—God in human form—into the world to live and die for us. The Gospel writers firmly believed this because Jesus' resurrection confirmed that belief. The Gospel writers would not have written a thing about Jesus if he had not risen from the dead and thereby proved that he was the Messiah. So, yes, Aslan is correct to say that the Gospel writers wrote their Gospels in order to prove that Jesus was the Messiah. But Aslan is wrong to think that historical accuracy was not relevant to the Gospel writers. Factual accuracy was extremely important to the Gospel writers. When Aslan says that historical accuracy was not relevant to the Gospel writers it actually shows his own bias; he has come to that conclusion, not because he has strong evidence to prove it, but because that statement fits in with his theory, with his belief system. He accepts the findings of the Jesus Seminar; he accepts the conclusions of Horsley; and he accepts the ideas of the liberal scholars and professors. How does Aslan know that factual accuracy did not matter to the Gospel writers? Did the Gospel writers hint somewhere in their writings that facts did not matter to them, that they were content with making stuff up in order to fashion a messiah in their own image so that they could then create a new religion to replace the old traditional and dying Judaism? What do the Gospel writers say outright or by implication about their intentions or reasons for writing? Matthew says that Mary was pregnant by the Holy Spirit, that she would give birth to a son and he would be named Jesus, which means God saves, because he will save his people from their sins (1:20f).

Matthew believes there is evidence to prove that Jesus is the Messiah spoken of in the Hebrew Scriptures, and so he writes his Gospel to offer that proof to his Jewish audience. But Aslan says Matthew is a liar; Aslan thinks Matthew has made most of it up. Mark says he is writing the Good News about Jesus Christ, the Son of God (1:1). You would think if Mark was writing about the Son of God he would do his best to get it right; but Aslan says Mark is a liar. At the beginning of Luke's Gospel, he says: I have "followed everything closely from the beginning. So I thought it would be a good idea to write an orderly account for Your Excellency, Theophilus. In this way you will know that what you've been told is true" ("Scripture is taken from GOD'S WORD®. © 1995 God's Word to the Nations. Used by permission of Baker Publishing Group." 1:3–4). Luke clearly says what his intent in writing his Gospel was; but Aslan says Luke is a liar. John says at the end of his Gospel that he wrote it so that "you will believe that Jesus is the Messiah, the Son of God, and so that you will have life by believing in him" ("Scripture is taken from GOD'S WORD®. © 1995 God's Word to the Nations. Used by permission of Baker Publishing Group." 20:31). Then in verse 24 of the next chapter John lets his reader know that he "was an eyewitness of these things and wrote them down." But Aslan says John is a liar. Based on the historical evidence, it is safe to conclude that the Gospel writers were not lying, that they were not trying to deceive their readers, but that they were recording the actual events of Jesus of Nazareth, the promised Messiah. Two of the Gospel writers were constant companions of Jesus during his three-year ministry; they knew and understood what they were writing about, and they made sure what they had written was historically accurate. Peter, one of Jesus' disciples, said in an epistle to other believers: "For we did not follow cleverly devised stories when we told you about the coming of our Lord Jesus Christ in power, but we were eyewitnesses of his majesty" (NIV, 2 Pe 1:16). But Aslan says Peter is a liar. Regarding Aslan's third conclusion, we see he is half-correct in stating that all that mattered to the Gospel writers was formulating a Christology. It is true that the Gospel writers were interested in Jesus-as-Christ; but they were also interested in him as Jesus of Nazareth. They saw Jesus as human and as God in human form. Their Christology, if you want to call it that, was quite simple: Jesus was God in human form; he dwelt among us in order to be the fulfillment of God's promise to restore the broken relationship between God and humans, to heal the wounds that sin had caused. This was the early Christians' Christology. It was firmly rooted in history. History was important to the Gospel writers because God was at the helm of history.

Four Ways to make Jesus into a Messiah

Based on his three conclusions, Aslan believes the Gospel writers had to do at least four things to make Jesus into the Messiah. One, they had to remove Jesus from the restoration of Israel movement. That is why, according to Aslan, the Gospels do not mention Jesus forming an insurrection party to fight against Rome's oppression of the people. Two, the Gospel writers had to remove any and all clues or suggestions that Jesus had a radical streak, that he had a "zealous" nature. According to Aslan, the Gospel writers, for some reason, chose a nondescript zealot and decided to do a total makeover on his story. They removed the violent nature from the real Jesus and changed him into a pleasant, though sometimes self-righteous, preacher. Third, the Gospel writers had to change all of Jesus' words and deeds to reflect their new image of Jesus and to go along with the new situation they were in. In other words, now that the Jews had lost the war against the Romans and their country and capital (Jerusalem) were destroyed, the Gospel writers needed to exchange Jesus' zealot words and actions with peaceful words and actions. What purpose would this serve? If the Jews were now scattered throughout the Roman Empire, why would four people, some twenty to forty years removed from each other, decide to make some long-dead zealot into the Messiah? What would be their reason? Fourth, the Gospel writers needed to remove themselves from any and all identification with Judaism and modify the zealot Jesus from an insurrectionist into a nice, peaceful preacher who taught that God's kingdom was "not of this world." Does Aslan have any solid evidence that the Gospel writers did these four things, or does he simply assert this based on his non-evidential theory that Jesus was a zealot? It is the latter. Aslan has accepted the theory that the historical Jesus was a zealot, so he has to denigrate the Gospel narrative; but he has no actual proof.

Of course, three of the Gospel writers were Jewish and wrote to show that Jesus fulfilled the Hebrew Scriptures regarding the Redeeming Messiah. The Gospel writers saw Jesus as the promised Messiah based on the promises God had given to the Jewish people. The Gospel writers did not take a zealot and turn him into the Jewish Messiah; the

301

Jews who rejected Jesus as Messiah turned him into a zealot. Once the Jews firmly rejected Jesus as their Messiah, they had to make something else of him. So we see in the Jewish writings of the second to the sixth century, culminating in the Talmud, that they turned their Messiah—Jesus—into a magician, zealot and insignificant preacher. The question begs to be answered: Why would the meager followers of a dead zealot decide to make him into something he was not forty years after he was dead? What was their motivation? Was it because they wanted to create a new religion, a religion that the Romans spent three centuries trying to wipe off the face of the earth by heavily persecuting its followers? Aslan's proposal does not make sense. In essence, Aslan rejects the historic facts about Jesus recorded in the Gospels solely based on his personal worldview. But this is not solid criteria for rejecting or accepting historical documents. We should not reject or accept the reliability of historical documents based on whether or not they agree with our worldview. This, however, is what Aslan does; he rejects the Gospels simply because they disagree with his worldview. He reinvents a new "history" of Jesus based on his worldview, and then has the audacity to accuse the Gospel writers of doing the same. Aslan (as well as the JS and other liberal theologians) wants us to believe that the four Gospel writers, sitting independently in their own rooms, decided to choose the same zealot that had died some fifty or sixty years earlier to be the main character of their new book. Each writer was going to have this zealot preach some of the most wonderful sermons, perform some of the most marvelous deeds, and create some of the most interesting sayings. These four pieces of fiction were going to use Jewish Scriptures to show how this dead and almost forgotten zealot fulfilled prophesies of a promised Messiah. These four writers were all going to insist that although this zealot died horribly on a cross he rose from the dead on the third day, thereby proving that he was the Messiah. Aslan's premise is incorrect. The reason the four Gospels were written was because their authors wanted to tell the world that the promised "seed of a woman" had finally arrived and restored our relationship with God.

The Torn Curtain

One final event that occurred at the time of Jesus' death which Aslan hopes to dismiss was the Temple curtain being torn in half. Matthew (27:51) and Mark (15:38) both claim that when Jesus died on the cross the Temple curtain separating the Holy of Holies was torn in two. Aslan, in his thirteenth chapter, misunderstands and rejects the historical significance of this event and merely states that it was a fabrication that later first-century Christians could reflect upon as a symbolic relic. The torn curtain showed that the Temple and the animal sacrifices were no longer relevant; it showed that Jesus had reconciled humans and God by his death; it showed that God was no longer hidden. If the Temple had been destroyed at the time that Matthew and Mark wrote their Gospels, as Aslan believes, then why would they have even mentioned the torn curtain? They mention the torn curtain because the Temple had not yet been destroyed; they were writing their Gospels prior to the Jewish Revolt in 66 A.D. that resulted in the Temple's destruction. They mentioned the torn curtain because it had historic significance. At the moment Jesus died, Matthew tells us that the curtain in the Temple split in two from top to bottom. This would have particular meaning to the Jewish audience Matthew is writing to. Before a permanent Temple was made in Jerusalem, a tent was set up where priests performed animal sacrifices as a temporary cleansing for the sins of the people. Pagan nations built their own altars and performed not only animal but human sacrifices to the many gods they believed in. Although pagan cultures and rituals went far off the mark of what God required, they retained in their belief system the promise of the "seed of the woman." This vital promise (the "seed of the woman)" that God made to the human race can be seen, even if horribly distorted and misrepresented, in most ancient cultures. As mentioned before, God would use Abraham, a righteous man who believed in the one true God, to create a nation whereby God himself would fulfill the promise of the "seed of the woman." Through the Mosaic Law and Levitical practices, God established a system whereby his people, the Jews, would be able to maintain a relationship with God through the atoning of their sins. This system would include a Temple, a priest system, and animal sacrifices. This triumvirate system would be temporary; it was established only as a provisional method of gaining favor with God until the "seed of the woman" arrived. Since priests also sinned and did not meet the requirements of God for a holy life, they would need to offer sacrifices for their own sins. The "seed of the woman" would need to be sinless, however, because he would be the one to bear the sins of humankind, just like the animals to be sacrificed needed to be without blemish so they could be a temporary bearer of sin. Since the "seed of the

303

woman" could only be sinless, the "seed" had to be God. When God, compelled by justice, demanded that death was required as penalty for sin, then God, compelled by immeasurable love, took on that penalty. Who else could have done it? When God died for our sins, being God he would not stay dead; he would rise on the third day.

Before the Temple was made, a tent would suffice for the temporary "Presence" of God; it would be his dwelling place. It was where the priest would offer sacrifices for the people's (and his own) sins. There was a section of the tent, and later in the Temple, that was called the Holy of Holies. This is where the priest would go in once a year and offer the grand sacrifice for atonement. The Holy of Holies was separated from the rest of the tent, and later the Temple, by a curtain. Only the high priest could enter beyond the veil or curtain. They were entering the Kingdom of God on earth. Once the "seed of the woman" arrived and offered the ultimate sacrifice, the Temple, the priesthood and the animal sacrifices would no longer be necessary. They would have served their purpose. Since Matthew is writing his Gospel to a mostly Jewish audience, they would understand the meaning and the relevance of the Temple curtain being torn in half. It would mean that it would no longer be necessary for the priest to go into a forbidden area once a year to offer an atoning sacrifice for the people. The torn curtain would mean the "seed of the woman" had arrived and the ultimate sacrifice had been given. That is why Matthew describes the curtain being torn from top to bottom. Because God is the one tearing it. Humans would have cut it at the bottom and worked their way up. The writer of the book of Hebrews (an excellent New Testament epistle that shows exactly how Jesus was the archetypal sacrifice that the Temple, the priesthood and the animal sacrifices pointed to) says: "because of the blood of Jesus we can now confidently go into the holy place. Jesus has opened a new and living way for us to go through the curtain" ("Scripture is taken from *GOD'S WORD*®. © 1995 God's Word to the Nations. Used by permission of Baker Publishing Group." 10:19–20).

The tearing of the Temple curtain was not symbolic, nor was it fabricated; it demonstrated that God could now be approached by everyone, freely, through the sacrificial death of the "seed of the woman." God is no longer unapproachable because of our sin; we can now come to the throne of grace and find mercy on an individual basis (see Heb 4:16) because of the sacrificial death of Jesus. This idea did

304

not occur to Jesus' followers many decades later, as Aslan would have you believe.

Chapter Fourteen: The Resurrection of Jesus

When you look at the death and resurrection of Jesus on a historical basis it is quite difficult to dismiss the Gospel accounts of both events. Some have attempted to research the resurrection of Jesus for the purpose of showing it did not happen only to discover that their research confirmed the resurrection. Many have invented theories to dismiss the resurrection—the swoon theory, the misplaced grave site, mass hypnotism, etc.—but they do not hold up to proper scrutiny. You may deny the resurrection of Jesus because it does not fit into your worldview, but one cannot easily reject the resurrection of Jesus on historical grounds.

What about other Cultures' Resurrection Stories?

Many liberal theologians/biblical scholars, along with the so-called "new" atheists, assume one can disregard Jesus' resurrection by showing that other cultures—like the ancient Egyptians, Greeks, Babylonians, and Persians—had some idea or belief regarding the resurrection of the dead. The gods in these religions were said to have died and risen again. An example of this is found in the Egyptian stories of Osiris, where he was worshipped as the god of the Underworld and was associated with nature's cyclical seasons. In comparing the death and resurrection stories of these ancient cultures, we see that their gods were quite similar to one another; only the names had changed. These stories were often centered on a god and goddess. So, in the Egyptian cult we see Osiris and Isis; in Canaan we see Baal and Asherah; in Greek culture we see Cybele and Attis. The male gods were mostly agricultural gods who also controlled the weather, and therefore we find these gods caught up in the cycle or rhythm of the seasons (dying in the winter, resurrecting in the spring). Worship of these gods included bacchanal orgies and human sacrifices. These worshippers developed the hope that they would enjoy life after death in order to continue their corrupt lifestyles. The Greeks believed in the immortality of the soul and thought that souls were cast into Hades or the Underworld where they, as ethereal beings, wandered around aimlessly. Because the Greeks believed in a cyclical view of history the soul that wandered aimlessly in the Underworld could enter another body through a form of reincarnation. There was, therefore, no real sense of the idea of a resurrection in early Greek thought. For the Greek the most meaningful idea of immortality would be the kind a person might receive by simply being remembered for his/her accomplishments while alive. Eventually, the idea of an after-life system of reward and punishment found its way into Greek thought, and so we see Virgil's *Aeneid* talk about souls that cross the river Styx and either go to receive punishment or go to the Elysian Fields where they are rewarded with a somewhat happy existence. In Hinduism and Buddhism we see resurrection in the form of reincarnation, a constant rebirthing based on one's karma, until eventually one does enough good deeds to reach either oneness with the universe—which is similar to nonexistence—or Nirvana. (Some information gleaned from *Myths and Legends*.)

Of course, Aslan offers nothing new by citing these ancient 'resurrection' stories; these stories have been used for centuries to try to prove that Christianity's concept of resurrection is similar. If you have read any books on Christian apologetics, you will know that these so-called resurrection stories—like the myth of Osiris—cannot be compared to the concept found in the New Testament. Just because other cultures maintained a belief in some kind of resurrection does not negate the concept itself. It would actually be surprising to find no other cultures having this concept, more than it is surprising that they do. The fact that many ancient, pagan cultures contained ideas of a dying and rising god shows that they, at one time, knew the truth as God revealed it to humankind; but they perverted that truth and created their own beliefs and rituals. That is why God was so meticulous with the Jews regarding the proper method for meeting the requirements of a holy life. They were to present the true God, the true rituals, the true beliefs regarding the "seed of the woman" as a gift to the world. The Israelites believed in one, true God, and they knew that God revealed himself as Elohim (a plurality)—Lord Almighty (Father), Messenger (Son), and Spirit. These three persons are God; each a distinct Person within God. If God the Son, the Redeeming Messiah, was to die to redeem humankind back to himself, then, as a logical matter of course, he would rise from the dead because he is God. The Redeeming Messiah could not stay dead because he is, in essence, one Person within the triune Godhead. That is why Isaiah (chapter 53) says that after the Redeeming Messiah dies he would nevertheless be able to intercede for us because it was understood that after having died the

Redeeming Messiah, God the Son, would rise from the dead. But Aslan contends that a bodily resurrection that leads to an eternal life is essentially absent in Judaic thought and theology and, therefore, the claim by early Christians that Jesus rose from the dead, which was supposed to prove he was the Messiah, has no foundation in Judaism. Aslan is sure that the Hebrew Scriptures do not have one solitary passage that shows the Messiah is going to die, or any that shows he will rise from the dead. We have seen, however, that Aslan is mistaken; there are many passages in the Hebrew Scriptures that talk about the Redeeming Messiah.

Did the Hebrew Scriptures talk about a Resurrection?

The Gospel narratives, in contrast to other cultures' resurrection stories, show Jesus' resurrection as a rather simple and uncomplicated event; there are no symbolic notions or any need to acquire insightful knowledge, like you find in mystery religions. The Gospel writers provide no decisive references to Hebrew Scriptures regarding Jesus' resurrection, as one would think Matthew at least would do. This has led some to think there were no Hebrew Scripture passages available for the Gospel writers to use as a reference for the Messiah's resurrection; while some theologians and scholars do admit there are some, but they are quite subtle. Drane, in his *Introducing the New Testament*, says there was no consistent expectation of life after death in the Hebrew tradition, let alone any preconceived notion of what it might be like. Now it is true, the Hebrew Scriptures do not advance a comprehensive idea of resurrection, whereas the New Testament does develop the concept more fully and completely. The *Tyndale Concise Bible Commentary* says that the disciples were convinced of the resurrection first (because they actually saw Jesus alive after he had been killed) and then later came to an understanding of the prophetic passages in the Hebrew Scriptures, and this suggests they did not manufacture a resurrection story in order to agree with their interpretation of prophecy. In the book of Acts, Peter and Paul, at separate occasions, referred to Psalm 16:10 that rejoices that one is not abandoned in death and allowed to decay as a reference to the resurrection in general and also, specifically, of the Messiah (see Acts 2:27; 13:35). John in his Gospel (see 20:9) says that when he and Peter saw the empty tomb he believed that Jesus had been raised from the dead just as he had often told his disciples he would be. Then John says parenthetically that at that time the disciples had not understood from Scripture that Jesus had to rise from the dead. This indicates that after the resurrection John and the others may have searched the Hebrew Scriptures to see if there were any passages relating to the Messiah's resurrection. They would have obviously understood Isaiah 53 in a different light now that they had witnessed Jesus' death and resurrection. They would understand the significance of Zechariah 12:10 that says when the Messiah comes to set up his physical kingdom, the people will look at him, the one they have pierced. After Jesus rose from the dead, his disciples certainly saw the Scripture passages and God's working in Jewish history in a new light. We often say that hindsight is 20/20 because we are able to look back at an event with clearer vision than when we actually experienced it. Jesus' disciples, having seen the risen Lord, now had a fresher, more accurate understanding of the Hebrew Scriptures than they did when they traveled with Jesus during his ministry.

Aslan says Jesus never mentioned a Scripture passage that supported his claim that he would rise on the third day, but actually Jesus did use the story of Jonah (which is found in the Hebrew Scriptures). We see in Matthew 12 that the Pharisees had just rejected Jesus as the Messiah, and then they demanded that Jesus perform a miracle or wondrous sign to prove he was the Messiah. Jesus told them that the only wondrous sign they were going to get was the sign of Jonah. Just as Jonah was in the fish for three days and nights, so he too would be in the ground—dead and buried—for three days and nights, and then he would rise from the dead. Jesus then told the Pharisees that when Jonah emerged from the fish that swallowed him and preached to the people of Nineveh, they repented of their sins and turned to God. Jesus told the Pharisees that something greater than Jonah had arrived— himself. Jesus was using Jonah's experience as a sign that he (Jesus) would rise from the dead.

We know there were at least two opposing views regarding the resurrection, during Jesus' time. There was the Pharisaic view, which was held by the majority of Jews, that there was a resurrection which took place at the Day of Judgment, and then there were the Sadducees who did not believe in a resurrection or survival of the individual after death. There is an episode in Matthew (22:23–32) where some Sadducees presented Jesus with a scenario that they hoped would challenge the concept of the resurrection. Jesus showed the Sadducees that they had made three errors: one, they lacked proper knowledge of the Scriptures and God's power; two, their idea of connecting marriage and the resurrection was wrong; three, God made it clear that a person goes on after death by stating 'I am the God of Abraham, Isaac, and Jacob,' and not 'I was the God of Abraham, Isaac, and Jacob.' God was still their God because they still existed, even though they had died long ago, a point that the Sadducees had missed. Jesus concluded by saying, "He's not the God of the dead but of the living." The phrase "gathered to his people" (beginning in Gen 25:8 and used throughout the Hebrew Scriptures) had a significant meaning for the Jew. The phrase alludes not only to the death of the person mentioned but also to the idea that the person has now joined his/her ancestors in Sheol (a temporary place of the dead). Jesus appears, in his discussion with the Sadducees, to confirm this ancient Jewish idea. It is true that although the teachings of the Hebrew Scriptures do not give a clear idea of what life after death is like, it does contain a belief in resurrection. But it is to be an event that occurs at the end of history, when all will be judged according to their deeds. Job, who probably lived around the time of Abraham, believed that when he was dead and buried and his body decayed that he would one day rise from the dead and see God (see Job 19:25f). In fact, when Abraham, the father of the Jews, was promised a son and then was told to sacrifice that son, he reasoned that God could raise the dead (see (Heb 11:19; Gen 22:1-19). The Psalmist knew he would see a resurrection and stated such: "God will redeem me from the realm of the dead; he will surely take me to himself" (NIV; 49:15).

We see a pattern in the Hebrew Scriptures regarding the method God used to disclose or reveal what he wanted humans to know and learn about him. God did not simply reveal everything to humans and then expect them to deal with the vast quantity of knowledge and requirements. God gradually revealed what he wanted, distributing knowledge as the people progressed and showed a capacity to learn more. As humans matured and grew in knowledge and experience, God was able to reveal more of himself and more of his requirements. God is not concerned with time; if it takes a person a hundred times to learn something, God has the patience for that, knowing that the hundred and first time the person will get it right. When Adam and Eve broke the one negative requirement God had given them, he then gave them a simple promise—the "seed of the woman." Throughout human history, God continued to reveal to humans what that "seed" would do. As people traveled across the land, creating their own cultures and civilizations, the promises of God went with them. But the people rejected God and began to make their own gods, fashioned after their own needs and desires, and the promises of God were reinterpreted to comply with the gods of their own making. So people invented religion and with it invented ways to protect their culture. But God had nothing to do with the religions humans made. He called Abram out from paganism and changed his name to Abraham to indicate his turning from false gods to serve and trust in the one true God. From Abraham, God created a people who would bring forth the promised "seed of the woman." God created the Jewish nation to keep the promises pure and to reveal additions to these promises as time went on. This was a gradual process because humans continuously turned away from God, but God would wait for them to return so he could continue. God was at the helm of history, and no matter how many times humans went off course, God was able to bring things back to his purpose and goal. His purpose and goal was to restore the relationship between humans and God. He had set up a temporary system so people could fellowship with him; this system was animal sacrifices (which would include a priesthood), and we see this practice in cultures throughout history where people sacrificed to their own gods, which unfortunately also included human sacrifices. The Israelites were to be a special people, developed by God to be his conduit of blessings upon humankind.

All of this, of course, was because our first parents, Adam and Eve, had decided to turn against God and choose their own way. In doing so, death entered into human life. God had made humans to live forever. When sin entered into God's creation, it first created a spiritual death for humans; a separation from God. It was of primary importance that it be quickly addressed. That is why God established the practice of animal sacrifice; we see that when God made animal skins for Adam and Eve (see Gen 3:21). The second type of death that occurred for humans was physical death; we would now physically die. But that too will be cured at the final resurrection. God was more concerned with the first death—spiritual death; the death that removed the fellowship we had with God. He made promises throughout history that spiritual death would be conquered. Spiritual death was first, and it would be that one that the Redeeming Messiah would heal first. Physical death would be conquered later at the time of the final judgment and resurrection. Just prior to this final judgment the Messianic King will set up his kingdom for Israel's Renewal, a promise God had made to the Jews and he has not forgotten. The Messiah comes twice, just like death comes twice—a spiritual death followed by a physical death. Life on earth was important to the Israelites because it was the only one they had. As God revealed more about the afterlife to Israel, they were able to develop a greater sense of God's plan, but God never did reveal enough about the resurrection of the body for them to create a substantial doctrine about it. God did not want that to be their major concern. What God wanted them to develop was a sense of his faithfulness to them and their faithfulness to him in this life. (See *Baker Encyclopedia of the Bible* on Resurrection.) So we see passages like Job 19:25–27 that hint at a resurrection; and Psalms 139:8 where God does not abandon us even when we are in the grave; and Isaiah 43 that talks about a final resurrection when all of God's people will be gathered together (see especially vs. 5-7). There is a passage in Daniel that certainly gives the clearest declaration in the Hebrew Scriptures regarding the final resurrection: "Many sleeping in the ground will wake up. Some will wake up to live forever, but others will wake up to be ashamed and disgraced forever" ("Scripture is taken from GOD'S WORD®. © 1995 God's Word to the Nations. Used by permission of Baker Publishing Group." 12:2). This passage claims that there will be a resurrection of the righteous and the wicked, each receiving the eternal consequences they deserve. Jewish tradition asserts that everyone will be resurrected, but the resurrection will not occur until the Messiah arrives and ushers in the Messianic Era. This, too, the Gospels teach. Since the Messiah rose from the dead, God has guaranteed that all of us will rise from the dead, as well. So, Aslan is mistaken in his declaration that there are no passages in the Hebrew Scriptures that hint at the idea or concept of the resurrection.

Although there are not many passages that hint at the idea that the Messiah would be raised from the dead, one must bear in mind that the Messiah is God the Son, that he came to die for our sins, and therefore the grave could not keep him. He is, after all, an eternal being. He would rise from the dead, just as he raised others from the dead while he was on earth—a little girl, a widow's son, his friend Lazarus—and when he returns for the Messianic Era they will look at him who has been pierced and wounded for our sins. It may be true that the Jews during Jesus' time did not believe in the idea that their Messiah was supposed to suffer and die; it may be true that they were expecting a Messiah that would restore Israel's independence. Aslan attempts to use their misconception of what the Messiah was supposed to do during his first arrival as proof that the Messiah was supposed to come as a triumphant king. The best way to prove something, however, is not by relying on or referring to someone's ignorance. Just because someone is ignorant of something that they should not be ignorant of does not mean that the thing they should know is not true. If the Jews during Jesus' time had rejected the promises of the Redeeming Messiah (and I have shown in this book that they had done so), and were only looking forward to an avenging Messiah who would take care of the Roman occupiers, that does not mean they were correct in their thinking. Aslan has not provided any evidence that Jesus is not the Redeeming Messiah, sent here to die for our sins, to remove the first death—the spiritual death—that separated us from God. Aslan has not shown any evidence that Jesus did not rise from the dead. The only evidence he gives is to simply say that Jesus did not rise from the dead, and that is not evidence. Again, it all depends on the kind of god you believe in. If you believe in the God who made the universe and sustains it, it is not difficult to believe that he can have his Son be born of a virgin and raise him from the dead.

Historical Evidence for the Resurrection

Aslan argues that the historian views Jesus' resurrection as a complicated subject because it prevents a clear assessment of the historical Jesus. How would the historian approach the resurrection? It is true that Jesus' resurrection happened only once, and it cannot be replicated; there are no bones or other artifacts that can be used to show that someone has risen from the dead. The fact that it happened only once does not nullify it, however. The moment of creation happened only once, your birth happened only once; there are lots of things that have happened only once. That, in itself, is not a basis for rejecting something. The resurrection of Jesus is within the scope of history because there are historical artifacts—pieces of evidence—that attest to it. There is no reason to think, as Aslan does, that some people in the first century, for whatever reason, took the name of some dead zealot and years later wrote some extraordinary things about him, including having him rise up from the dead, and then "sold" their idea to a bunch of people who would then be willing to die for the lie. Of course, Aslan would not apply his criterion of events being outside the scope of history on anything else but the resurrection and maybe some other claims by early Christians. But you cannot pick and choose how you are going to apply a method of determining whether something is authentic or not. The same criterion historians use to determine the historicity or authenticity of Plato or Julius Caesar or any other historical figure can be and has been used to authenticate the Gospels. The criterion and methodology that is used by historians demonstrate that the Gospels—including the resurrection of Jesus—are historical and authentic.

The historian could, therefore, broach the topic of the resurrection by utilizing the three types of evidence that were discussed in the section on the Jesus Seminar. These three types again are bibliographical evidence, internal evidence, and external evidence. The historian deciphers the reliability of a document or past event by using these three tests; although the historian is not limited to just these three. If a document makes a particular statement, the historian can conclude whether the statement is accurate (or acceptable within given parameters) based on the established criteria used for drawing such conclusions. As for bibliographical evidence, we have four accounts or biographies of Jesus—the four canonical Gospels—and they all state that Jesus rose from the dead. The question of the reliability of the four Gospels cannot be determined on one's viewpoint or theory or belief system. The reliability of the four Gospels is to be judged using the same criteria historians use for all other ancient documents. As we have already seen, the four Gospels show remarkably well that they are reliable documents. Besides the four Gospels, we have other first century documents that report that Jesus had risen from the dead; these documents are the majority of epistles written to the early Christians by Paul, Peter, James, Jude and John. All of them had seen the risen Jesus. There were twenty-seven documents written during the first century that all attested to Jesus' resurrection. These documents were eventually compiled into what we know as the New Testament. One cannot easily dismiss these twenty-seven documents; the majority written within a forty-year period.

314

Many deny the resurrection of Jesus simply because they deny the possibility of the supernatural. The supernatural is not in their worldview and therefore does not and cannot exist for them. Now the Bible simply states that God is; it offers no "proofs." People have devised reasonable arguments for and against the existence of God, but in the final analysis both groups have to utilize faith as their method of reaching a conclusion, one way or the other. Now if God exists, and he made the universe and all that is in it, by his own methods and in his own time, then he could, if he wanted to, enter the universe he made. He is not a part of his creation, but he could enter it if he so desired. Just like a person who builds a house can enter the house he built. God could have made humans special, above all the other animals—special in the sense that he desired a personal relationship with humans. The relationship went sour because of personal choices on the humans' part, but God decided the relationship was worth mending. Humans had purposefully broken a moral code which entailed death as punishment—first, a spiritual death, and then a physical death. God still loved his creation, but that love did not nullify the need for justice. God would show his love for the humans he created by becoming human and taking the punishment in our place. God would satisfy the demands of justice by this act of love. God became human and paid the price for the disruption with his own life; but being God he was able to raise himself from the dead. The raising of a dead body is not something that would be impossible for God to do, especially his own. To believe this requires faith; but not a denial of reality. There is historic evidence to base this faith upon.

The internal evidence reveals that Jesus had at least fourteen post-death appearances: he appeared to Mary Magdalene; to a group of other women; to Peter; to two disciples on the road to Emmaus; to ten apostles without Thomas; to the apostles with Thomas present; to seven apostles up in Galilee; to 500 people, either in Jerusalem or in Galilee; to the apostles again; to James, Jesus' earthly brother; with the apostles at the Mount of Olives before his ascension; to Stephen at his murder; to Paul on the road to Damascus; and to John exiled on Patmos. At the time of the writing of the Gospels, especially if you have three of them written before Peter and Paul were executed in the late 60s A.D., many of the people who witnessed the risen Jesus would still be alive. Now, Paul, who never got over the fact that he had been involved in Stephen's murder and the persecution of the early church, made it clear that if the resurrection of Jesus did not happen, then Christians are to be pitied for believing that it had because their faith in Jesus would be useless, worthless, and meaningless (see 1 Cor 15:14, 19). Paul stakes everything on the objective truth of Jesus' resurrection. Also in 1 Corinthians 15, Paul appears to quote an early creed of the church: Christ died for our sins according to the Scriptures; he was buried; he was raised on the third day according to the Scriptures (see vs. 3f). (The Scriptures Paul refers to could be both the Hebrew Scriptures and one or all three of the Gospels that had been written during his lifetime.) Paul then provides a list of people that had seen Jesus after his resurrection (some of those people are in the list I already provided above). This list of persons who had seen Jesus after his resurrection is not easily denied, although there have been some (modern liberal theologians/biblicalscholars, for instance) who have tried to come up with all sorts of reasons against it. If the resurrection did not happen, and yet Paul had created this list of so-called eyewitnesses, he would have lost any integrity he had established with the Corinthian Christians by lying in so blatant a manner. We see, then, that the internal evidence of the New Testament documents attests to Jesus' death and resurrection in a clear and reliable manner.

The early Christians believed Jesus died and rose from the dead; this was central to their beliefs. It was not something that came much later in their thinking. The resurrection was the impetus for the apostles to spread the message of Jesus as Savior, and it was the crowning point for those who believed that message. The resurrection was the proof. There would be no Christianity if there were no resurrection. For Paul, the resurrection was the only proof one needed for Jesus being the Messiah promised in the Hebrew Scriptures. Why? Take a look at his background. He was educated by Gamaliel, a highly respected teacher of the Mosaic Law; he was an Israelite, from the tribe of Benjamin; and he was a Pharisee when it came to living according to the standards and traditions of Jewish life. Paul was so committed to Judaism that he fervently and violently persecuted Jewish Christians. He was on his way to Syria to arrest any and all Christians that he could find. On the road to Damascus, something happened. Just as the Messenger of the Lord (Jesus) had appeared to Abraham, Jacob, Hagar, Balaam, and others in the Hebrew Scriptures, Jesus appeared to Paul. Paul came face to face with the resurrected Jesus, the eternal Son of God. Paul had waged his own personal war against the people who were preaching Christ crucified and risen, and now he was confronted by the risen Christ. This is what accounted for Paul's dramatic change, just as it accounted for the apostles' dramatic change, and what accounted for the dramatic change in those who believed (and continue to believe) in Jesus as the risen Lord and Christ. This change was dramatic for the Jew who became a Christian because it meant a total change in his/her social structure.

The Jewish Christian no longer needed to go to the Temple to offer animal sacrifices for their sins; Jesus was the ultimate sacrifice and, for the Christian, there was no need for the temporary system of animal sacrifices any longer. The Mosaic Law was to be rigidly adhered to if you were a Jew and wanted to please God, but Jewish Christians realized that it was not simply obeying the Mosaic Law that mattered, that no one entered heaven by being good or by trying to follow the Law, but by believing in the Redeeming Messiah. The Jewish Christian learned a freedom that they had never had before; they did not have to rigidly follow a set of laws in hopes of becoming good enough for God. They could now live in the freedom of forgiveness and allow God's Spirit to transform them into the image of their Savior. They did not deny or reject the commandments of God—the commandments were still true and binding—but the Jewish Christian found freedom in the forgiveness of the ultimate sacrifice, Jesus Christ. The commandments that were most important to follow for the Jewish Christian were to love God with all one's heart, strength, soul, and mind; and to love one's neighbor—that is, everyone. Jews had been following the Sabbath laws for hundreds of years, but now Jewish Christians were meeting on Sundays and considering that the holy day. It was on Sunday, the first day of the week, that Jesus rose from the dead, and it would be that day that Christians would meet to eat, pray, and read Scriptures. Jewish Christians began to worship Jesus as God; this was total heresy for the typical Jew. The Jewish Christian believed that Jesus was God in the flesh, that he was the "seed of the woman." This worship of Jesus as God began early in the church and not several centuries later as some modern theologians and professors would have us believe. Most first-century Jews were waiting for a Messiah who would free Israel from its oppressors; but Jewish Christians accepted Jesus as the Redeeming Messiah, the one who was to come and suffer and die for the sins of the world, the

Messiah of Isaiah 53. The freedom that God first offers to those who believe is a freedom from the bondage of sin—a rebirth from the spiritual death that has kept us estranged from God. (The second freedom will take place at the Day of Judgment when God will restore his creation.) Thousands of Jews were willing to give up their social structure and former beliefs when Peter preached his first sermon to them shortly after Jesus ascended back into heaven. Why? It was because of the resurrection. The resurrection was proof that Jesus was the Messiah. All that the Jews or the Romans needed to do to destroy the inception of Christianity was to present Jesus' dead body; they could not do so, because he had risen from the dead. (Some information gleaned from *The Case for Christ*.)

The external evidence for the resurrection of Jesus would include the writings of those mentioned earlier—like Tacitus and Pliny. Did they say anything about the resurrection of Jesus? Tacitus, the Roman historian and senator, made reference to Christ and his execution by Pontius Pilate in his final work called *Annals*, written around 116 A.D. He knew enough about Christianity to distinguish it from the religion of the Jews. Tacitus was no friend of this so-called new religion that had arisen from Judea and had made its way across the Roman Empire. By the second century there were Jews and Gentiles alike who accused Christians of cannibalism because of the practice of Communion, in which Christians engaged in a breaking of bread and drinking of wine that commemorated the death of Jesus. Because the early Christians believed in Jesus' resurrection, they considered him an eternal being who was God and with God; in other words, a distinct person (one of three) within the one God. While Christians believed Jesus was God in the flesh and that they were remembering his death in Communion (Eucharist), this all made sense only within the historical fact of the resurrection. Tacitus believed Communion was a ritual where Christians ate the body and drank the blood of their God; this would seem to imply, since Christians believed their God to be alive, that Tacitus is making an indirect reference to the resurrection because Christians were doing this every week, and their God had to be alive for this to happen. (See reference page for source information on Tacitus.) Of course, Tacitus made no reference to Jesus' resurrection, but the fact that he knew Christians celebrated Communion each week does imply that the Christians believed in Jesus' resurrection, and is therefore an indirect reference to the resurrection. This idea can also be applied to Pliny the Younger, who was a Roman governor inside Asia Minor (now a part of modern Turkey). Around 112 A.D., he wrote a letter to Emperor Trajan seeking advice in dealing with Christians under his rule. Pliny was concerned with the Christian practice of early morning meetings where they sang hymns to Jesus the Christ and revered him as God, rejecting the worship of Roman gods (which included the Emperor). Again, if Pliny refers to the fact that Christians saw Jesus as their God, it was not a dead god they were singing hymns to. Pliny would know that Jesus was executed and is therefore indirectly acknowledging Jesus' resurrection, or at least indirectly acknowledging that Christians believed Jesus was resurrected. (See reference page for source information on Pliny.)

Aslan acknowledges the fact that many of the disciples who said they saw the risen Jesus had died in some horrible ways without renouncing their beliefs. Even those who had not seen the risen Jesus personally were willing to die because they believed Jesus was the risen Messiah. What would make their beliefs so strong that they would die for them? The book of Acts provides a couple reasons: One, Paul made it a habit to preach in the synagogues wherever he traveled, and there he used the Hebrew Scriptures to prove that Jesus was the Son of God, the Messiah (see Acts 9:20; 13:5, 14-38; 14:1; 17:2f, and more). The second reason is that many others, like the Berean Jews, examined the Scriptures for themselves to see if what Paul said was true (Ac 17:11). Was each of the 520 or so people who saw the risen Jesus, individually or in groups, suffering from a bad case of food poisoning and seeing things that were not there? Were they all deluded? Had they based their faith on an hallucination? Was it just wish-fulfillment? Are we to believe that Peter, who some forty days after he saw the risen Jesus told his fellow Jews gathering in the Temple courtyard that they had murdered the Lord and Messiah, but that he rose on the third day and was willing to forgive them if they put their trust in him, had gone mad with grief at the execution of his master? Had Peter gone so insane that he saw the risen Jesus in an hallucinatory vision, and then, based on that vision, went out and started preaching that he saw the risen Jesus and eventually got himself killed for it?

Aslan asserts that it was not until the 90s A.D. that the Christians actually received their first resurrection stories. Aslan, of course, has to remind us once again that the "Q" document does not contain any resurrection appearances of Jesus. Aslan relies on a hypothetical document to 'prove' Jesus did not rise from the dead; he also provides us with a date (around 59 A.D.) as to when he thinks the "Q" document was compiled. It is amazing that Aslan actually gives an historical date to a hypothetical document! He really is desperate for his reader to believe that the "Q" document exists. For Aslan to say there are no resurrection appearances found within a hypothetical document is the same as me saying that I am holding a hypothetical document in my hands and it does not say anything about you in it; therefore, you do not exist. In fact, I am not reading anything in this hypothetical document; therefore, nothing exists. Do you want to know why there are no resurrection appearances in the "Q" document? Because there is no "Q" document. Aslan and lots of other scholars, mostly of the liberal sect, rely on the non-existent "Q" document more than they rely on actual and reliable documents, like the four canonical Gospels. To see how drastically they cling to a hypothetical document in order to denigrate four historical documents—the Gospels— certainly reveals their methodology and bias. Besides the "Q" document not recording any resurrection appearances of Jesus, Aslan says there are no resurrection appearances in Mark's Gospel, which, of course, he contends was written a little after 70 A.D. Aslan believes (along with other liberal theologians) that by the time the oral traditions regarding Jesus' words and deeds were eventually compiled into Mark's Gospel they had been enormously embellished. For Aslan, the first Gospels that actually provide resurrection appearances of Jesus were Matthew and Luke, and they were not written until sixty years after Jesus' execution, giving them plenty of time to fabricate lots of different stories. Matthew and Luke, if they had written their Gospels in the 90s A.D., would have had enough time, Aslan says, to have heard all the different objections to Jesus' resurrection and to then answer each one. That again, is why Aslan needs to have the late dates for the Gospels. It is not that he has sufficient evidence for the late dates; he simply needs them for his scenario to work.

Aslan, the Fellows of the JS, and other liberal theologians, have such a hatred for Christianity that they are willing to rewrite history themselves and reject the real historical events in order to prove to you that Christianity is based on a pack of lies. They are willing to ignore the importance oral traditions had for Jews and others, and how the oral traditions were carefully guarded and memorized (see Chapter One). They are willing to boast that historical facts are important to them, but not for first-century Gospel writers. For Aslan, there is no reason to believe in the resurrection because nothing was written about the resurrection until the 90s A.D. By then, Christianity was fortified by one big lie after another. It seems that people would believe anything to be a part of this religion that ostracized them from society and almost guaranteed persecution and/or death by local authorities. As I have mentioned before, there is no clear evidence that Aslan's late dating of the Gospels is correct. The late dating is needed for his theories to sound more reliable. Of course, simply placing a late date on a historical document does not necessarily negate the reliability of that document. Just because someone writes about an event decades after the event occurred does not mean we have solid grounds for rejecting what that person has written; that alone cannot be the reason the document must be rejected. There are other factors that must be considered before we reject the document. Aslan wants you to think that the Gospels were written from forty to almost a hundred years after Jesus' execution and should therefore be considered unreliable. That, however, is not a sufficient reason.

What about Mark's Last Chapter?

Aslan believes Mark's Gospel was the first Gospel written, and that the others used Mark's Gospel and the "Q" document as a springboard. So Aslan's theory is that since there are no resurrection appearances in Mark's Gospel, and Matthew and Luke (and John) do have resurrection appearances, then Matthew and Luke (and John) made them up. Aslan rejects the idea that the three synoptic Gospels— Matthew, Mark and Luke—were written before the destruction of Jerusalem in 70 A.D. Aslan also rejects the idea that Matthew's Gospel may have been written before or near the same time as Mark's Gospel. Now, we have first and second century sources that claim the Gospels were written by those whose names are attached to them— that is, Matthew, Mark, Luke and John. We have first and second century sources that say the three synoptic Gospels—Matthew, Mark and Luke—were written in the 60s A.D., while Peter and Paul were still alive. Does Aslan have first and second century sources to verify the things he rejects about the Gospels, including their content and dating? I do not believe he does. What he does have are modern scholars who reject the Bible and God's existence because of their personal worldview, which he has adopted. He rejects the Gospels—their historicity and reliability—because of his worldview and then tries to find evidence to back it up. But his evidence is simply to repeat the same theories that modern liberal scholars have been chanting for the last hundred or so years, especially relying on the humanistic ideas of the likes of Rudolf Bultmann.

If Mark was actually using Matthew's Gospel, or at least was aware of it, that would account for why they often talk about the same things but in different degrees. Matthew is writing to Jews and will therefore include lots of details and lots of Hebrew Scripture passages. Mark wrote his Gospel in a succinct, to-the-point fashion. His style was to simply mention an event and then go on to the next; he did this with Jesus' baptism, the calling of the disciples, the sending out of the Twelve for missionary work, the Passover meal, Jesus' trial and execution; and he did the same with Jesus' resurrection. Mark remained consistent throughout the writing of his Gospel in accordance with his style. Mark obviously decided he did not need to go into any details about the resurrection except to simply state that it had happened. What Mark's Gospel does say about the resurrection of Jesus is that on Sunday at least three women came to the tomb where Jesus was buried in order to follow the Jewish rituals of anointing Jesus' body with spices; in other words, the women came to the tomb expecting Jesus to be dead. When they arrived at the tomb the entrance stone was rolled away, so they went inside. They encountered an angel and were alarmed, but the angel told them not to be frightened. The angel told them that Jesus was not there; he was risen from the dead, and that he would meet them in Galilee, just like he said he would (see Mk 16:1–7). Now, did Mark ever make any previous references to Jesus' resurrection in his Gospel? Yes, he did. Mark provided three instances where Jesus predicted his death and resurrection (8:31; 9:9, 31; 10:33f). Jesus also told his disciples that after he rose from the dead he would meet them in Galilee (14:28). In Mark's penultimate verse, the angel reminds the women to tell the disciples that Jesus will meet them in Galilee (16:7). Mark was consistent throughout his Gospel in showing that Jesus was the Messiah who came to die for our sins and who would rise from the dead three days after his execution. So, Mark tells us in several places in his Gospel that Jesus says he will rise from the dead, and then later records that Jesus did indeed rise from the dead.

Now, it is true that Mark does not record any appearances made by Jesus after his resurrection. What Mark does have is the empty tomb, the angel announcing Jesus is risen, and the reminder that Jesus had told them he would rise from the dead and meet them in Galilee. The majority of modern translations have a note after verse eight in chapter sixteen letting the reader know that verses 9-20 are questionable. Many scholars, both conservative and liberal, believe that Mark ends his Gospel at verse eight (remember, there were no chapter and verse divisions in the original). They suggest that ending in verse eight with the words "because they were afraid" was simply emblematic of Mark's style and was his intentional ending. Some scholars think it odd for Mark to end with a conjunction; the last word of Mark's Gospel (when you look at it in the Greek) ends with the word "for" or "because." It is possible that Mark ended the Gospel with fear ("because they were afraid") because the Christians in the 60s—when Mark wrote his Gospel—were experiencing persecution and were often afraid for their own and their loved ones' lives. Mark may have ended his Gospel with the women at Jesus' empty tomb being afraid, knowing that his readers would realize that the women actually had nothing to fear because they would soon be seeing the resurrected Christ. Likewise, the persecuted Christians reading Mark's Gospel in the 60s would know that they too had nothing to fear because they would be seeing Jesus as well, whether they were killed for their beliefs or they died of natural causes. A few scholars insist that Mark did not end with verse eight but that somehow whatever final verses he may have ended with had been accidently destroyed, and so a later copyist added the last twelve verses (9-20), using information found in Matthew and Luke's Gospels. In looking at verses 9-20, it does appear that the grammar and style do not match the rest of Mark's writing. One major reason the last twelve verses in Mark's Gospel are questionable is because two important ancient manuscripts of Mark's Gospel do not have the final twelve verses (9–20). Now, we do not know why these two manuscripts do not contain the twelve verses, but we do know that the vast majority of all the other Greek manuscripts of Mark do contain these twelve verses. As far as the early church fathers are concerned, we know that Clement, Origen, and Jerome accepted Mark's ending at verse eight; whereas Justin, Irenaeus, and

Tertullian accepted verses 9–20. One thing is certainly clear: Mark's ending has puzzled scholars for years and many have devised all kinds of reasons for it. There is no doubt that these final twelve verses will continue to be debated, and it is doubtful whether there will be any conclusive results. (See the reference page for books from which I gleaned some information for this section on the last twelve verses of Mark's Gospel.)

If Mark ends his Gospel at 16:8, and therefore does not record any actual resurrection appearances of Jesus, Aslan thinks he has fodder for his theory. (Aslan even tries to dispute the eight verses of chapter sixteen, but he is not successful.) Was it necessary for Mark to add resurrection appearances? Would that have made the resurrection more plausible and believable for the initial readers of Mark's Gospel? The resurrection of Jesus was the impetus that changed the disciples from frightened, scattered followers into dynamic and courageous leaders. The eleven disciples were changed when they saw the risen Jesus. The resurrection was the driving force behind the disciples' preaching, and their lifestyle change. If there was no resurrection, there would have been no Christianity. Since Mark wrote his Gospel in the 60s, about the same period of time that Paul and Peter were writing some of their epistles, the resurrection was already the foundation of Christian belief, and the resurrection appearances were already well known. If Mark had included three or four resurrection appearances would that have convinced Aslan that Jesus rose from the dead? I do not think so. It does not matter if Mark simply stated that Jesus had risen from the dead, or if he had given a hundred resurrection appearances, Aslan would not have believed it. When a person clings to their worldview, it does not matter how much evidence you give them, they will not accept it. There are, however, some (and I hope, dear reader, you will be one) who will look into the historical fact of the resurrection and, in doing so, will change their way of thinking and acting and accept Jesus as their Savior, as the risen Lord.

Aslan is therefore mistaken to conclude that the resurrection is an event that has no historical basis. It is true that after Jesus' ascension, we no longer see the risen Jesus—except for those rare and personal occurrences where Jesus appeared; for example, to Stephen, Paul and John—and therefore he is outside the realm of history today and must be accepted by faith. But it is not a faith that has no historical backing;

it is a faith based on evidence, historical evidence. The major difference between Christianity and other religions is that the doctrines and beliefs within Christianity are backed up historically. Christianity offers historical evidence upon which one bases one's faith—it is not a faith opposed to reason or objectivity. From the ascension on, Christians accepted Jesus as their Savior by faith; it had to be by faith because they could no longer "see" Jesus. All of the apostles made it known that faith in Jesus as the Redeeming Messiah is how a person gains God's approval; we cannot obtain salvation by following a set of standards, although they are still important to follow. Jesus has done all that is necessary for us to receive God's approval. We accept what Jesus has done for us by believing—having faith—that he has done all that is necessary. There are four basic "reasons" why many people reject Jesus' substitutionary death: one, they do not believe in sin and thus reject the idea that they are sinful; two, they do not believe they are sinful enough to not meet God's standard; three, they believe they can do good things that will force God to see how good they are, and that their own goodness will get them into heaven; and four, they do not believe in God. If you believe—have put your faith in—any of the above four and have therefore refused to accept God's remedy for your sins—Jesus' substitutionary death—then, according to Christian doctrine, you will not receive God's approval, and you will not get multiple chances after you die—through reincarnation—to receive it, either.

Chapter Fifteen: An Attack on Luke's Book of Acts

Aslan made numerous attacks on the Gospels in his book and so, in his third and final prologue and parts of his thirteenth chapter, he focuses his assault on Acts, the sequel to Luke's Gospel. Jesus has been executed and his disciples have remained in Jerusalem; they have apparently mustered up enough courage to show themselves in public. Aslan describes the disciples as a gang of farmers and fishermen from Galilee who meander in the vicinity of the Temple courtyard where their leader—Jesus—used to preach. This time they are declaring their leader, this carpenter from Nazareth, to be the Messiah. They claim that Jesus was executed but brought back to life three days after he was buried. I have already mentioned Peter's first sermon and how he had told the Jews that they had killed their Messiah—the Lord and Christ—but that he had risen from the grave. Peter did not condemn them to hell for killing the Messiah, or tell them that God hated them for killing the Messiah, or that Jews would now experience ceaseless anti-Semitic persecution because they had killed the Messiah. No, Peter told them that although they were instrumental in killing the Messiah they could repent and be baptized in the name of Jesus and be forgiven. Luke says that about three thousand people believed Peter's message and accepted Jesus as their Messiah that day (read about it in Acts 2:14b-39). Again, one must ask why Jesus' followers, some forty days after Jesus was executed in a horrific manner, suddenly wandered around the Gentile courtyard preaching that Jesus was the Messiah. What had happened to them? Why did they not abandon Jesus after he was killed like all the other followers of all the other zealot leaders who had been killed at that time? If they saw what happened to Jesus, would they not be worried that the same fate awaited them? The Temple guards and the Roman soldiers were not too far away. What happened that gave them such courage? Peter told the crowd that although they were instrumental in killing Jesus, God raised him from the dead. It was the resurrection that changed them.

What about John the Baptizer's Followers?

Aslan appears to be concerned that John the Baptizer's followers were still baptizing Jews long after the Baptizer had been executed. When John the Baptizer was murdered his disciples buried him and then told Jesus what had happened (see Mt 14:12). They may have joined Jesus at that time; we do not know. John's followers would have seen John as a martyr, like many of the other Hebrew prophets of old; but Jesus would have been a condemned criminal, and anyone still preaching him would have been seen as the same. The courage it took Jesus' followers to go to the Temple and preach that Jesus was the Messiah was enormous. If John the Baptizer's followers were still baptizing and preaching after Jesus rose from the dead, we do know they were not baptizing in John's name, as Aslan would have you think. The people who came out to confess their sins and be baptized were baptized by John, but not in his name. On the other hand, Jesus told his followers to go out to the world and baptize people in the name of the Father, Son [Jesus] and Holy Spirit—the triune God (see Mt 28:19). Jesus also told his followers to pray in his name, which is a blasphemous thing for a Jew (or anyone) to do, unless Jesus is God (see Jn 15:16). During Paul's first missionary journey, when he and Barnabas came to Pisidian Antioch, in Asia Minor, Paul was preaching in a synagogue and told his listeners that before Jesus started his ministry, John had been preaching repentance and baptism. Then Paul added, "As John was completing his work, he said: 'Who do you suppose I am? I am not the one you are looking for. But there is one coming after me whose sandals I am not worthy to untie'" (NIV, (Acts 13:25). Let it be known that Paul is quoting from Matthew's Gospel, which, according to Aslan, was not supposed to be written until Paul was dead for about twenty some years. Also note that Paul was saying that John was completing his work right around the time that Jesus was beginning his. After Jesus was killed, buried and rose from the dead, baptism was incorporated into the Way (the name for those who had accepted Jesus as their Savior; see Acts 9:2; 19:9, 23; 22:4; 24:14, 22) so that Christians identified with Jesus' death in a symbolic manner. Peter, in his first sermon, told the Jews he was preaching to that they needed to repent and be baptized in the Name of Jesus Christ so their sins could be forgiven (Ac 2:38). Baptism itself does not save anyone; it is a symbol that a person has given themselves to Jesus, that they have died with him symbolically in order to rise up (from the water) as a new creation. As we see in the book of Acts (18:24–28; 19:1–7), there were people who knew about John's baptism, but did not know about Jesus and the importance of accepting him as their Messiah. So John's baptism was known, but it is difficult to know if it was still being practiced by this time.

Aslan feels the need to remind his readers that Jesus had failed to bring about God's Kingdom, but, as I have already made clear, Aslan's mistake was in not realizing that the Kingdom of God is a spiritual realm and that Jesus' substitutionary death allowed anyone who accepted him as the Messiah to enter into that kingdom. Aslan says that since Jesus was killed like every other messiah or zealot by the Roman authorities, the only thing left for his disciples to do was to give up their own zealot ways and go back home to their villages and farms. The apostles who followed Jesus throughout his three-year ministry did run off and hide when Jesus was arrested and executed. Out of the eleven apostles, only John Zebedee had accompanied Jesus' mother to Golgotha. Although the apostles stayed out of sight, they still remained in Jerusalem. When they witnessed the risen Messiah (Jesus) they began to openly preach the good news, which was very dangerous for them to do. The authorities, in fact, continued to threaten Peter and John and the others with imprisonment and death, but they continued to preach about Jesus. John's older brother, James, was killed for preaching. Peter was arrested and faced execution. He was released miraculously and left Jerusalem for a time. In fact, almost all of the apostles were executed for their belief that Jesus was the Messiah. John Zebedee may have been the only one who lived a long life and died of natural causes, although there was a time when he was exiled to the small island of Patmos for his beliefs. What changed the apostles and others was the fact that they had seen the risen Christ.

Was Peter Illiterate?

Aslan claims that Peter, being a fisherman, was uneducated, illiterate, and ignorant about the Hebrew Scriptures, but was so unfettered in his zealous fervor that his lack of education and knowledge did not stop him from exhibiting a careless assurance in what he was preaching. Aslan seems to be appalled that Peter would even recite a Psalm written by David and say that the Psalm prophesied about Jesus' crucifixion and resurrection. Aslan forgot to mention that just before Peter quoted from the Hebrew Scriptures regarding David's Psalm he had also quoted from the book of Joel, which is also in the Hebrew Scriptures. It is amazing that Peter who was, according to Aslan, ignorant of the Hebrew Scriptures could so easily quote from them during an impromptu sermon. But Aslan does not just denigrate Peter; he claims the other apostles were just a bunch of overjoyed ignoramuses. He reviles them for peddling an inventive and completely unorthodox understanding of the Hebrew Scriptures' concept of the messiah. Aslan accuses Peter and the other disciples of taking passages from the Scriptures and completely twisting them around to "prove" that Jesus is the Messiah. Of course, Aslan has made a habit of taking biblical passages out of context and manipulating them to try to prove his theories, but it is okay when he does it. Just as Aslan was mistaken when he attempted to show that Jesus was illiterate (see Chapter Four), so he is here in trying to show that Peter and the other apostles were also. We know that during the first century the Jews held education in high esteem and there is, therefore, no reason to doubt that Peter and all the other apostles were educated and knew how to read and write. Now, in Acts chapter 4, we see that some religious leaders were quite upset that Peter and John were teaching the people the doctrine of resurrection from the dead and offering Jesus' resurrection as proof (vs. 2). The religious leaders saw Peter and John's courage and realized that "they were unschooled, ordinary men" who had been with Jesus (vs. 13). In other words, the religious leaders knew that Peter and John had not studied in rabbinic schools; they lacked formal theological schooling and were, therefore, not professional men but laymen (Wuest). The *Greek-English Lexicon of the New Testament* tells us that the Greek word for 'unschooled' should not be taken to mean 'illiterate' in the sense of not being able to read or write; the reason being that it is highly unlikely in view of the fact that Israel enjoyed almost universal literacy during the first century, mostly due to the extensive system of local synagogue schools. To call the disciples a bunch of overjoyed ignoramuses is certainly unfair. Aslan might think that Peter exhibited a careless assurance, but what the Greek actually shows is that Peter manifested free and fearless confidence, boldness, and courage. Peter and the other disciples had "purchased the sword" that Jesus told them to acquire during their last Passover meal; they had gained courage to meet the requirements of being Jesus' disciples. As Jews, schooled in the memorization of Scriptures, Peter and the rest of Jesus' disciples would have been genuinely opposed to making up stories by manipulating Scriptures in order to present some inventive and completely unorthodox understanding of the messiah. As I mentioned in the previous chapter, the apostles, having seen Jesus risen from the dead, revisited the Scriptures in a new light and understanding of what the Messiah was coming to do. Aslan feels free to negate the enlightenment that Jesus' disciples received when they saw the Scriptures in the light of the risen Christ. Now the irony is that Aslan believes his eyes were opened by the things he learned from the liberal theologians and scholars at university. If he can easily negate the disciples' "enlightenment," what makes his own enlightenment that caused him to write his book *Zealot* valid? Why is Aslan's experience any more legitimate than Jesus' disciples' experience?

Questioning Stephen's Knowledge of Jewish History

Aslan then attempts to cast doubts on Luke's account of Stephen's murder. Luke tells us that Stephen was preaching about Jesus and the changing times and how some traditional Jews, offended by his speech, had him arrested and brought before the Sanhedrin. While standing accused in front of the Sanhedrin, Stephen provided them with a summary of Jewish history, which of course would begin with Abraham. Stephen would end his discourse by mentioning Jesus. Aslan says Stephen's speech was an obvious and complete fabrication; Luke made it all up. How is it obvious that Stephen's speech is fabricated by Luke? It is only obvious in Aslan's mind, as are his other scenarios. There is nothing in this account to indicate that Luke created this speech for whatever reason he may have had. Aslan asserts that Stephen's speech is filled with errors, but then only provides us with two. Stephen's first error was in getting Jacob's burial site wrong; and the second error was in claiming that it was an angel that gave Moses the law. Aslan is quick to let us know that any Jew, even an uneducated one, would know that it was God who gave the law to Moses. Another reason Aslan downgrades Luke's account as fabrication is because Stephen had a vision of Jesus—the Son of Man—while he was being murdered. Luke says Stephen was filled with the Holy Spirit, gazed into heaven and saw the glory of God and Jesus standing at God's right hand (Acts 7:55). For Aslan, Stephen committed the greatest kind of blasphemy a Jew could do; he declared that Jesus, a mere man, was an eternal being who was equal to God, that he was God-in-the-flesh. Of course, we have seen that Jesus made that same declaration of himself.

I am sure you have noticed by now that whenever Aslan, the JS, or other liberal theologians do not like a particular saying or event recorded in the Gospels or other New Testament writings, they simply say it was made up. Do they actually have any real evidence for their claim that it was made up? Simply saying it was made up does not make it so. Stephen, who would have been educated in Jewish history and Scripture like all Jewish people were, was arrested on trumped up charges and was allowed to defend himself. Stephen does so by recounting Jewish history. This would have been appropriate for Stephen to do, especially if he was, by doing so, attempting to show how the Jewish people—like those who had him arrested—had often turned against God. Let's now look at the errors Aslan says Stephen's speech was full of.

Aslan says Stephen misidentifies Jacob's burial site. In his speech, Stephen says Jacob "and our ancestors" died in Egypt and "were taken to Shechem for burial in the tomb that Abraham purchased in Shechem from Hamor's sons" (Acts 7:15f). When Jacob and his family went to Egypt to avoid a terrible famine his son Joseph was already there, working as a high-ranking official. When Jacob was dying he made Joseph promise that he would bury him where his ancestors were buried (Gen 47:30), in the cave Abraham bought (Gen 49:30). After Jacob died Joseph and his brothers buried their father according to his wishes (Gen 50:12). Joseph requested that he too be buried in Israel, and not in Egypt (Gen 50:25). Joshua tells us that Joseph's bones were carried out of Egypt, as he requested, and were buried at Shechem, a plot Jacob had purchased from Hamor's sons (Josh 24:32; compare with Gen 33:18–19). Abraham bought land from Ephron at Machpelah, east of Mamre, which included a cave to bury his wife in (Gen 23:1–20). So the discrepancy that Aslan points out is that Stephen got Abraham and Jacob mixed up. Now, it might be true that Stephen got the two mixed up; it is easy when one is under trial and duress as he was to make a mistake like this. Regardless of the mistake, if it was one, Luke would have recorded it just as Stephen said it. This does not make the account wrong, which is what Aslan is trying to say it does do; Luke is simply recording the episode correctly, even if Stephen might have made a mistake. The Bible often records the lies spoken by false prophets, but that does not mean the Bible is lying; it is simply recording the lie. Journalists and newspapers do this all the time. But, was Stephen mistaken? Is there a real discrepancy? We know from the book of Genesis that Abraham spent time in Shechem, and it is possible that he bought some land there, especially since he settled in the vicinity (see Gen 12:6–7). In Genesis 33:19, we see that Jacob also purchased land in Shechem where Abraham had settled. In looking at Stephen's speech, it is easy to see that he was quite knowledgeable about Jewish history, so how could he make this mistake, if it was one? In the *New Testament Commentary* on Acts, the authors suggest that since Stephen and his accusers knew the Scriptures well, a brief mention of that point in their history would be sufficient for all of them to recall the entire account. In other words, it would not be necessary for Stephen to present the entire episode, detail for detail; he would only need to make a brief reference that everyone listening would know what he meant, or would know what time in Jewish history he was referring to. When Stephen says "their bodies," his accusers would know he is referring to both Jacob and Joseph, and they would know that both men were buried in different places—Jacob would be buried in the cave Abraham purchased from Ephron, and Joseph would be buried on the land in Shechem that Jacob purchased. The authors of the commentary say that Stephen is merely combining both Genesis accounts into one short sentence. Stephen's accusers would not be worried or upset that he had condensed the two events in this way; they would understand the gist of what he was trying to get across. Aslan's attempt to make this into a vital mistake that should cause us to disregard the entire speech is overdramatic.

The other mistake Aslan says Stephen makes is regarding the Mosaic Law. Aslan rejects the idea that an angel gave Moses the law. When one encounters something in the Bible that appears contradictory or confusing it is certainly appropriate to consult several different resources in order to understand the passage, and this includes looking at different translations. Stephen tells his accusers and the Sanhedrin that they are stubborn, heartless and disobedient, just like their ancestors who opposed the Holy Spirit. Their ancestors persecuted the prophets God sent to them, and killed the prophets who predicted the Righteous One would come, [i.e., Jesus, the Redeeming Messiah]. Stephen accuses the Sanhedrin of betraying and murdering the

Righteous One. He tells them they have failed to obey the laws which were given to Moses through or by God's angels. Aslan has a problem with the idea that God used his angels to deliver the laws to Moses. Aslan's mistake is in thinking that Stephen's reference to the law here is to only the Ten Commandments; Stephen is referring to the entirety of the law, which would be all that is contained in the Pentateuch. Later on, Paul, who witnessed and approved Stephen's lynching before he (Paul) became a Christian, told the believers in Galatia that Moses' law was put into effect through angels (Gal 3:19). Moses gave a blessing to the Israelites just before his death and told them that the Lord came from Sinai (this would be a reference to the Ten Commandments) and from Seir and from Mount Paran and when he did he came with myriads of holy ones, i.e., angels (see Dt 33:1–2). It was understood in Jewish tradition that God appointed the Law, but the angels helped bring it to humankind. The angels were instrumental in delivering it to the Jewish nation. So, it appears that it is actually Aslan who has made a couple of general errors (mistakes) in his interpretation of Stephen's speech.

Aslan has a problem with Stephen's Christology, too. Aslan does not like the idea that early Christians already viewed Jesus as God-in-the-flesh. Stephen, having been taught by the apostles of Jesus, would correctly see Jesus as an eternal being who spoke about God's kingdom as a spiritual entity. Stephen would have believed that Jesus was equal to God, and that he shared the same glory and honor with his Father. Stephen would have believed that Jesus was God in human form. This belief would have been blasphemous to the Sanhedrin; it was certainly blasphemous to them when Jesus himself claimed to be God. I have already shown how the Hebrew Scriptures revealed that God often "assumed" human form (a theophany), how the Messenger of the Lord was actually YHWH, and that the three persons of the Godhead are mentioned throughout the Scriptures. This concept was not anathema to the Jewish mind. What many Jews considered blasphemous, and the Sanhedrin certainly did, was that Jesus claimed to be God-in-the-flesh, and his disciples claimed he was, too. John, a Jew, says Jesus was with God and was God and became human and lived among us (1:1, 14). Paul, a Pharisaic Jew, says Jesus was in the form of God and equal with God but did not take advantage of this equality. Instead, Jesus became like other humans (Php 2:6–7). Peter, a Jew, says that Christ went to heaven where he has the highest position that God gives. Angels, rulers, and powers have been placed under his authority (1 Pe 3:22). Peter goes on to say that "Glory and power belong to Jesus Christ forever and ever!" (4:11). Peter also calls the kingdom of heaven "the eternal kingdom of our Lord and Savior Jesus Christ" (2 Pe 1:11). To say that God could become human was not blasphemy for a Jew, as Aslan would have you believe. It is not difficult for God, who made humans, to become human for specific purposes as we have seen in the Hebrew Scriptures, any more than it is for him to arrive on earth through a virgin, to die and be resurrected. These are not difficult tasks for God to perform. The question that one must ask for themselves is: Is Jesus God in the flesh? Isaiah had no problem with God becoming human. He wrote that a virgin would conceive and give birth to a son, and he would be called Immanuel (7:14), which means God with us, showing that he will be God in human form. Isaiah continues that thought by saying a child would be born whose name would be Wonderful Counselor, Mighty God, Everlasting Father, Prince of Peace (9:6). Then Isaiah adds that the Messiah would come from David's lineage and the "Spirit of the Lord will rest on him—the Spirit of wisdom and understanding, the Spirit of advice and power, the Spirit of knowledge and fear of the Lord. He will gladly bear the fear of the Lord" ("Scripture is taken from GOD'S WORD®. © 1995 God's Word to the Nations. Used by permission of Baker Publishing Group." 11:1–3). Jesus bore the fear of the Lord when he bore our sins on the cross (see Isa 53). Of course, Jews and Gentiles alike have rejected Jesus as God in the flesh, but they do not do so because it is blasphemous, or because of a lack of evidence, or because it is impossible for God to take on human flesh. They do so because of their own sinful nature that rebels against God and rebels against his provision of salvation. They do so because they have accepted a worldview that prevents them from seeing the truth.

What Happened to the Disciples of Jesus?

Aslan believes the majority of those who had actually followed Jesus while he was alive simply drifted out of sight, returning back home to their farms and villages. A few may have worked in an insignificant way in the newly established Jesus movement. Of course, Luke tells us, in Acts, that Jesus' foremost disciples—Peter, James, and John—did play significant roles in the beginnings of Christianity. As people began to believe the message of Jesus in the neighboring towns, Peter and John were sent to them in order to make sure that everything was proper and right (see Acts 8:14). The disciples of Jesus did not want people believing just anything they wanted about Jesus. The early church was extremely organized and knew what it believed. They did not make things up as they went along. When John's brother James was killed it did not take long for Jesus' brother, also named James, to become a pillar of the church and become the head overseer in Jerusalem. When Paul, a strict, devout Pharisaic Jew, became a follower of Jesus he made sure that his gospel message was the same as the message taught by Jesus' original followers. We see, despite Aslan's claims, that Jesus' original disciples actually played a significantly large role in the so-called Jesus movement. They were the pillars that upheld the growing church, with Jesus as the foundation. What was happening out in the churches as they developed from town to town was closely watched in order to make sure they were teaching the truth. Leaders were put into place that would keep the message and the beliefs on target, not allowing for different opinions to infiltrate. The epistles to the churches were filled with exhortations and warnings against false teachers and others coming in to lead the people astray. The beliefs of the early church were not left to those who did not know Jesus and simply made up some interesting stories about him based on the oral traditions. The beliefs of the early church were set down by Jesus' disciples and were strictly maintained.

Did Peter, John, and James Hold Strictly to Jewish Laws and Customs?

Although Aslan is sure that most of Jesus' disciples returned to their farms and villages and resumed their lives after Jesus was executed, Aslan does accept the fact that Peter and John, along with James (Jesus' brother), became the Jesus movement's main leaders in Jerusalem. Aslan contends that these three leaders, however, continued to stay loyal to Jewish customs and the Mosaic Law for the rest of their lives. He makes this assertion because he will soon proffer the idea that these three leaders—the pillars of the church—were antagonistically hostile towards Paul. David Friedman (*They Loved the Torah*) demonstrated not only how Peter, John and James but also Paul continued to be somewhat Torah-observant; they did so, however, not in a confining, legalistic manner but within the realm of a freedom from the bondage of law. How far did Peter, John and James continue their loyalty to Jewish customs after they became 'Christians'? We find in Acts chapter 10 that Peter was told in a vision to eat all sorts of animals that were forbidden by Jewish custom and law. He was told that what once was regarded as "unclean" was now to be recognized or accepted as "clean." Now the Jews had viewed Gentiles who had not adopted Judaism as unclean, and so we see from the context of Acts 10 that God was telling Peter not to consider the Gentiles as "unclean." Why did God give Peter this vision? God was preparing Peter to accept an invitation to go to a Gentile's house, which was against Jewish customs, and deliver to them the good news about Jesus. Gentiles were now to become part of the new dispensation that was unfolding; it was a new covenant that now included Gentiles (Paul, in agreement with Peter's experience, speaks of this in Romans 10). Paul was not the first who went to the Gentiles; it was Peter. When Peter returned to Jerusalem he explained why he had gone to this Gentile family and preached the good news. The leaders in Jerusalem accepted his explanation and realized that God was opening the gospel to the Gentiles. We see in this passage that God was bringing greater freedom from Jewish customs to Jewish Christians. The Jewish church in Jerusalem accepted this change (see Acts 11).

A Look at the Council Meeting in Acts 15

Allowing all Gentiles into God's new dispensation brought another matter to the forefront—circumcision. There were some Jewish Christians that would simply not give up the idea of the "necessity" of circumcision, insisting that Gentile Christians needed to be circumcised. This was a big issue in the early church because circumcision was such an important covenant that God had made with the Jewish nation. In fact, Gentiles who were willing to adopt Judaism as their religion could become circumcised and be recognized by the Jewish community as children of God and Abraham. Therefore, some Jewish Christians in the early church insisted that when Gentiles became Christians, the Gentiles should also be circumcised. An important council meeting was held in Jerusalem to discuss this issue regarding circumcision, which you will find in Acts 15. The Jewish Christians at the Council (which Peter, John, and James attended) debated whether or not to maintain this very important Jewish custom. The question regarding circumcision was widespread in the Christian community, and so Barnabas and Paul and a few others were sent to

336

Jerusalem from the Antioch church in Syria to discuss this issue at the Council. When they arrived in Jerusalem Barnabas and Paul were welcomed by the apostles and elders, including Peter, John, and James. Barnabas and Paul told them everything that God had been doing in Antioch and the surrounding towns. Some Jewish believers who belonged to the Pharisaic party stood up at the council meeting and demanded that the Gentiles be circumcised. After discussing the issue for a while, Peter got up and recounted how he had gone into a Gentile house and preached the good news; Gentiles were now able to receive God's salvation and there was no need to make them try to conform to Jewish laws and customs. Peter then rather humorously said that even Jews were finding the laws very hard to do, so why should they make Gentiles try to follow them. Peter concluded by saying, "we believe that we and they too will be saved by the grace of the Lord Jesus" (NCV, Acts 15:11). After Peter spoke, the whole assembly listened to Barnabas and Paul, who told them about what they were doing in spreading the gospel to the Gentiles. Then James, the Lord's brother, who was the bishop or overseer of the church in Jerusalem (and possibly the author of the epistle that bears his name), stood up and stated the final decision of the Council. That decision was to not make it burdensome for Gentile Christians by insisting on circumcision. The church leaders did, however, think it was necessary to suggest that Gentile Christians should avoid anything polluted by idols/false gods, and refrain from sexual immorality, the meat of strangled animals, and from eating bloody meat (Acts 15:20). These four are, of course, Torah-observant stipulations, which everyone (including Paul) agreed with. A letter that contained the Council's decision was written and distributed among the churches. Barnabas and Paul returned to Antioch with the letter. We see then a very important Jewish custom—circumcision—being removed as a necessity for both Jewish and Gentile Christians. Although Jewish Christians did not dismiss the Mosaic Law (the Ten Commandments have always been an important moral code for Christians), they also did not strictly maintain a die-hard loyalty to Jewish customs, as Aslan thinks. As I noted earlier, many Jewish Christians gave up the social structure they had been born into, thereby diminishing their loyalty to Jewish customs.

Did Luke Call Paul an Apostle?

Aslan believes Luke was being overdramatic and exercising unnecessary flare with his story of how Paul was converted to Christianity on the road to Damascus. Luke, it appears, needed some creative narrative to make Paul stand out, and what better way than to include a rather stunning resurrection appearance of Jesus. Aslan thinks Luke was writing Acts as a tribute to Paul some forty or so years after Paul's death, and so he added this fabricated story to make his deceased teacher appear in a good light to and for a new generation of Christians. Aslan alleges that Luke is guilty of writing a purposeful and calculated, but completely non-historical, portrayal of Paul in hopes that others will accept Luke's idea that Paul was instrumental in the founding of Christianity. Aslan thinks it is important to notice that Luke never indicated that Paul was an apostle. Aslan believes, as we will see presently, that Paul and the other apostles were enemies, so maybe Aslan thinks Luke does not call Paul an apostle because Luke would know that Paul would not want to be associated with the other apostles in Jerusalem. But is it true that Luke never called Paul an apostle? Well, when Paul and Barnabas were in Iconium they preached in a synagogue per their customary practice. Luke tells us (Acts 14:4) that some Jews did not believe the message Paul and Barnabas preached, while others sided "with the apostles." Luke calls Paul and Barnabas apostles. So, Luke did call Paul an apostle, despite Aslan's claim. Aslan also thinks it is important to note that Paul never told the story in his epistles about how he was blinded when he saw the risen Jesus on his way to Damascus. We see that Paul talked about people being blinded and not accepting the truth, that they were so blind they "cannot see the light of the gospel that displays the glory of Christ, who is the image of God" (NIV, 2 Cor 4:4). The fact is Paul would not need to tell his epistle readers that he had been blinded when he saw the risen Jesus because most of them would already have known his history. The majority of Paul's letters were to people who knew him; he would not need to go into the details about his life. When he did do that, for instance in the letter to the Galatian Christians, he did so in order to make a powerful point. We do find Luke recording a sermon that Paul gave to a crowd of Jews where he talked about his being blinded on the road to Damascus and that he had to be led into the city (see Acts 22:11); it is not difficult to imagine that Paul repeated that sermon whenever he could. Aslan, of course, thinks Luke was lying when he wrote about that event, that Luke was putting words into

Paul's mouth. But that is the typical "escape clause" Aslan and other liberal theologians/biblical scholars use whenever they have no solid historical evidence for their claims.

Aslan, Horsley, and others have often questioned the reliability of Luke's works (his Gospel and Acts). They boast that Luke is not historically accurate and use as an example the Quirinius passage (a topic I devoted some space to in Chapter Three), or point out where a particular local leader may not be mentioned in other Roman writings (Horsley does this with Sergius Paulus), and then suggest Luke was wrong because of the absent notifications in those Roman writings. In fact, archaeology has confirmed over and over again the accuracy of Luke's writings. In his Acts alone, Luke has over eighty references to cities and ports and mountain ranges and local rulers and none of them have been shown to be in error. The book of Acts is an ancient, historical document that clearly stands on its own. If Luke records a local ruler, but other Roman documents do not mention that ruler by name, it does not mean that Luke is wrong; it simply means the ruler's name, for whatever reason, did not appear in other documents. To simply say because a person's name or an event does not appear in other documents that the document it does appear in is necessarily wrong is not using proper historical methodology.

A Journey Through Acts

In closing this chapter, I will have us (as we have done with the Gospels) proceed with a journey through the book of Acts. We will see the beginnings of the early church and the spreading of the Good News throughout the Roman Empire. It is quite possible that Luke was already finished with his Gospel before he met Paul for the first time in Troas, during Paul's second missionary trip. He may have been doing research into the spread of the gospel and had already compiled information that would later become the first twelve or so chapters of Acts.

Beginning in Luke's first chapter of Acts we see Jesus giving his disciples some final last words before ascending back to heaven. The disciples choose someone to replace Judas and wait in Jerusalem for the promised Helper that Jesus said he would send. The promised Helper would be the Holy Spirit and would give the disciples power and courage to be Jesus' witnesses "to the ends of the earth." The disciples received the Holy Spirit on Pentecost and immediately began preaching the Good News in Jerusalem, with Peter as their main spokesperson. After Peter's sermon in Acts 2 (which has already been referenced), about three thousand believers were added to the group of disciples. These people had come from surrounding regions; Luke mentions about thirteen cities and/or provinces. [With so many people receiving Jesus as their Savior, who would then return home, it was imperative that the apostles, who had followed Jesus throughout his ministry, quickly establish order. Paul tells us that God is not a God of disorder or confusion, but a God of peace (see 1 Cor 14:33). Therefore, it was extremely important that everyone accept and follow the same beliefs and procedures.] The chapter ends showing how the early church (people, not a building) quickly began to share their personal goods with one another and formed, in a sense, a subculture within Jerusalem and the surrounding area. They met in groups and supported one another, supplying both physical and spiritual needs. In chapter three we see Peter and John working together to heal and preach; in the next chapter they are arrested. Believers continue to share possessions with their less fortunate brothers and sisters. Healings, preaching and persecutions are spoken of in chapter five and, in chapter six, the office of deacons (helpers to the apostles for the people) is established. Stephen, one of the deacons, gives a powerful speech before the Sanhedrin and is murdered (chapter seven). Saul (who becomes the apostle Paul) approves of the murder. Chapter eight informs us that Saul orchestrated a great persecution against the church in Jerusalem, scattering the Christians into Samaria and throughout Judea. Philip, one of the deacons, had also gone there and preached the Good News in a Samaritan city. When the apostles learned that people were accepting the gospel in Samaria, Peter and John were sent there in order to make sure everything was done properly. [Why? Because God is not a God of confusion but of peace, and therefore it was extremely important that everyone accept and follow the same beliefs and procedures. The early Christians made sure that the same gospel was being preached as it went out to the world.] Persecution prompted Christians further north, into Syria, and so, in chapter nine, Saul was given the authorization to go and arrest any and all Christians he found there and bring them back as prisoners to Jerusalem. As Saul was coming into Damascus, he was confronted by the risen Jesus and the experience led him to become a Christian.

Ananias, who obviously was a leader in the assembly of Christians in Damascus, was sent by God to take care of Saul. [Now Saul had been educated by one of the best teachers in Jerusalem—Gamaliel—and he was very knowledgeable about the Hebrew Scriptures. After meeting the risen Jesus, he was able to revisit those passages in the Scriptures that talked about the Redeeming Messiah and became firmly convinced that Jesus was that Messiah.] Saul began visiting the synagogues in Damascus and proving that Jesus was the Messiah, using the Hebrew Scriptures. Eventually, some non-believing Jews became so angry at Saul that they plotted to murder him, so Saul left Damascus. [We learn from his epistle to the Galatians that he did not return to Jerusalem—the people that sent him to Syria to arrest Christians would not be happy with the fact that he had become one—but went into the Arabian desert (perhaps to think about what had just happened to him) and then returned to Damascus.] When Saul did finally arrive in Jerusalem a prominent Christian in Jerusalem named Barnabas took Saul under his wing and introduced him to other Christians. Saul traveled throughout Jerusalem with other believers and he spoke boldly about Jesus. Once again, some non-believing Jews tried to murder him, so his fellow believers, in order to protect him, took Saul to Caesarea on the coast and had him board a ship to Tarsus, which was where he was from. In chapter ten, we learn that Peter has been traveling around Lydda and Joppa (cities near the coast) and is told in a vision to go to Caesarea. He is to enter a Gentile house and preach the gospel. [Jews did not enter the house of Gentiles; nor had a group of Gentiles been preached to yet like that.] Peter returns to Jerusalem in chapter eleven and has to explain why he, a Jew, went into a Gentile's home. Peter explained—point by point—the reasons for what he had done. When they heard Peter's explanation, no one had any further objections, but instead they praised God saying that God was now allowing Gentiles to repent and have eternal life.

Meanwhile, the church in Antioch, Syria, was growing and diversifying. [The Antioch church was a cultural anomaly. Here was a group of people that included men and women worshipping together. It was a group of people from different races and cultures who had come from different religious backgrounds. They were all congregating (having meals together), worshipping and singing about Jesus. This was definitely unheard of in Roman, Greek, and Jewish society. (Although the church at Antioch was socially diverse, the church in Jerusalem was not. It took time for some hearts to change; for others, the change came swiftly.)] When the news about what was happening in Antioch reached the leaders in Jerusalem, they sent Barnabas to Antioch to check it out. [Why? Because God is not a God of confusion but of peace, and therefore it was extremely important that everyone accept and follow the same beliefs and procedures.] Barnabas was quite pleased to see what God was doing in the Antioch church, and he encouraged them all to stay solidly committed to the Lord. He also decided to stay there and help them, but he knew he could not do it on his own. So he went to Tarsus to look for Saul and, finding him, brought him back to Antioch. Barnabas and Saul stayed in Antioch for a whole year and taught the new Christians. A famine occurred while Claudius was emperor, so the Christians in Antioch decided to contribute whatever they could afford to help the believers living in Judea, and sent their contribution with Barnabas and Saul to the leaders in Jerusalem. [This would become a practice that Paul would keep throughout his ministry.] In chapter twelve, we learn that Herod had James—John's brother—executed and Peter arrested. Peter miraculously escaped the prison cell and left Jerusalem. Barnabas and Saul returned to Antioch and chapter thirteen tells us that they, along with John Mark, are sent off on their first missionary journey. During this trip, we learn that Saul changed his name to Paul [possibly after the conversion of Sergius Paulus, a Roman proconsul on Cyprus.] Barnabas and Paul traveled on to Asia Minor, bringing the Good News to the Gentiles, and made it their continual practice to enter synagogues wherever they went so they could also bring the Good News to their fellow Jews. In chapter fourteen, Barnabas and Paul returned to Antioch and reported everything God had done through them, letting them know that Gentiles were receptive to the gospel. Barnabas and Paul stayed with the Christians at Antioch for quite a long time.

Luke tells us in chapter fifteen, that certain people arrived in Antioch from Jerusalem and insisted that the Gentile believers be circumcised as part of their salvation. This became a great controversy, and Paul and Barnabas sharply disputed the idea and debated with those who were insisting on circumcision. Since the believers in Antioch were determined to maintain order and correct teaching on the subject, they appointed Paul and Barnabas, along with some other believers, to go up to Jerusalem to see the apostles and elders about this question regarding circumcision. On their way to Jerusalem, they traveled through Phoenicia and Samaria and told the Christians there how the Gentiles had accepted Jesus, and this news made all the believers very happy. When they arrived in Jerusalem they were welcomed by the church and the apostles and elders, to whom they reported everything God was doing in the Gentile regions. During the Council meeting some believers who belonged to the party of the Pharisees maintained that Gentiles must be circumcised and required to keep the Law of Moses. The apostles and elders considered this issue and, after much discussion, Peter got up and reminded everyone how God had told him to enter a Gentile house and bring them the Good News about Jesus. Peter said that this was a clear indication that God had accepted the Gentiles by giving the Holy Spirit to them, just as God had done for the Jewish believers at Pentecost. Peter told them that God does not discriminate between Jews and Gentiles, but purifies every heart by faith. Peter then, with bold insight, told his fellow Jewish believers that it actually amounted to testing God by requiring Gentiles to try to live according to the Law that even Jews were not able to follow. Peter concluded by saying: "We believe it is through the grace of our Lord Jesus that we are saved." Then Barnabas and Paul (a Pharisee himself) stood up in the Council meeting and told about the great things God had done among the Gentiles in Asia Minor. When they finished, James—Jesus' brother—spoke up. He told the assembly that the prophets in the Hebrew Scriptures agreed with Peter and the rest regarding how God had also chosen the Gentiles. James told them that it was his verdict that Jews should not make it difficult for Gentiles who were turning to God. He proposed that they put their decision in writing and distribute it to the Gentile Christians. In the letter, they asked that Gentile Christians abstain from eating food that had been part of pagan sacrificial worship, from sexual immorality, from eating bloody meat, and the flesh of strangled animals. Also in the letter, James acknowledged that some individuals from Jerusalem had gone to Antioch and confused the Christians there with statements regarding the supposed necessity of circumcision. James told them: We did not authorize these men. Near the end of the letter, James also praised Barnabas and Paul for having dedicated their lives to the Lord Jesus Christ.

After Barnabas and Paul return to Antioch with the letter from James, Paul soon wanted to revisit the places that he and Barnabas had traveled as they spread the Good News. There was a disagreement among them (Luke, as a true historian, records this conflict) and so Paul left with another believer named Silas and they traveled through Syria and Cilicia, strengthening the churches. In chapter sixteen, Timothy joins Paul's entourage [Silas and Timothy played important roles in Paul's life and ministry] and soon they traveled to Troas [where it is obvious that Luke joined them at this time because he uses the word 'we,' to include himself] to set sail for Macedonia. They arrived in Philippi, where Paul and Silas were thrown into prison for preaching the Good News. After being released, they went on to Thessalonica (chapter seventeen) and, as per their custom, preached the Good News in the synagogue and, of course, some conflicts arose. They stopped in Berea, then Paul preached a somewhat philosophical sermon in Athens, and finally they arrived in Corinth (chapter eighteen), where Paul remained for a year and a half. Paul and his entourage went back to Asia Minor, dropped Priscilla and Aquila off in Ephesus, and then came to Jerusalem to greet the church [and obviously report what he had done on his second missionary journey]. After that, he returned to Antioch, his home church. After being home for a while, Paul decided to travel once again throughout Galatia and Phrygia in order to visit and help the disciples there. He returned to Ephesus (chapter nineteen) and a riot broke out. Paul set out for Macedonia (chapter twenty), and after traveling in that region, spreading the gospel and helping the believers, he went on to Greece, circled back to Macedonia, and then on to Troas. They sailed along the coast and only stopped at a few places because Paul was determined to get to Jerusalem before Pentecost. In chapter twenty-one, Paul and his entourage arrive in Jerusalem and visited James and the other elders. Paul reported in detail what God had done among the Gentiles through his ministry, and everyone praised God. The elders were concerned that some Jewish believers in Jerusalem would cause some conflict because they had believed some erroneous reports about Paul. The elders wanted to clear up the confusion (because God is a God of peace) and asked Paul to accompany some men take part in a purification rite. He agreed and some non-believing Jews made false accusations against Paul and he was arrested. Paul appeared before the Sanhedrin (chapter twenty-two) and, because of a plot to kill him, was transferred to Caesarea, to hold trial before Governor Felix (chapter twenty-four). Two years passed and Paul was still under house arrest. He was tried before Festus who succeeded Felix (chapter twenty-five).

King Agrippa was visiting and so Paul was able to preach the Good News to both Festus and Agrippa. Because Paul had made an appeal to be tried by Caesar, he was sent to Rome (chapter twenty-seven). After encountering some rough seas and shipwreck, Paul and his close friends arrived in Rome (chapter twenty-eight). Luke ends the book by saying that Paul stayed in Rome at his own rented house for two years.

Aslan thinks it odd that Luke did not mention that Peter was in Rome when Paul arrived there at the end of Acts. There is, however, nothing to make out of this. It is quite possible that Peter was not in Rome yet. There is really nothing here for Aslan to be worried about. Because Luke does not mention Peter being in Rome does not mean Luke cannot be trusted with his narrative, which is why I think Aslan mentions it. We see, in going through the book of Acts that the early Christians believed one gospel message; that they were committed to Jesus and each other; that Paul was accepted as a legitimate Christian; that he spread the same gospel message as the apostles; that he went to Jerusalem after each of his missionary journeys to report to the apostles what he had done; and that he was falsely accused by non-believing Jews of violating Mosaic Law and was arrested and eventually sent off to Rome. Aslan will attempt to twist and manipulate passages in Acts and Galatians to show that Paul was a rogue apostle. It is to that scenario we now turn.

Chapter Sixteen: Paul as Rogue Apostle

The Apostles vs. Paul

Aslan joins other liberal theologians/biblical scholars in trying to prove that Paul was a rogue preacher spreading his own theory of Jesus, one that was quite different from the apostles who had actually traveled with Jesus. We saw in Chapter One that Horsley created his own narrative concerning Paul, which is similar to what Aslan advances in his book. Aslan contends that Paul regarded the "esteemed pillars" of the Jerusalem church—Peter, John, and James (Jesus' brother)—as enemies, and vice-versa. As we saw in the previous chapter, Aslan thinks that Luke wrote his Acts as a kind of eulogy to his teacher, Paul, in order to show that it was Paul who was the 'founder' of the Christianity we know today. Aslan and other liberal theologians/biblical scholars view Paul as a "lone wolf" who lashed out against the church leaders in Jerusalem and then created a different kind of Christianity from the one they were forming. They want you to think that there were two Christianities in the decades following Jesus' death: one that was based on the Mosaic Law and was spread by the eleven apostles in and around Jerusalem; and the other based on faith spread by Paul to non-Jewish people. When Jerusalem was destroyed in 70 A.D., it was Paul's "Christianity" that survived. But there were not two Christianities, and there were not two gospel messages—one for Jews and one for Gentiles. Nonetheless, Aslan believes Paul went to great lengths to break away from the "esteemed pillars" of the Jerusalem church because he (Paul) wanted to be free to create his own religion, a Christianity totally different from the apostles' Christianity. Aslan claims that Paul created a Jesus that was so radical that it went far beyond what most Jews (especially orthodox Jews) would accept. Therefore, the only way Paul could get away with his version of Jesus was to convince others that it came from Jesus personally. But Aslan is making that scenario up. When you compare what Paul says about Jesus in his epistles with what is said about Jesus in the Gospels, you can easily see that there is no evidence that shows Paul was preaching a completely different, made-up version of Jesus. Paul believed the same thing about Jesus that Peter, James, and John taught. If what Paul and the other apostles taught about Jesus was not accepted by many Jews at that time, it is only because those Jews had rejected Jesus as their Messiah. If many of the Jews of the first century ignored or outright rejected the Hebrew Scripture passages regarding the Redeeming Messiah, that does not mean the Gospels and Paul's view of Jesus were excessive or radical; it means those Jews were wrong. The Jews who rejected Jesus as Messiah cannot be used as a standard to judge Paul's views of Jesus. If I reject something that is true, then my opinion about what I reject or deny should not be used as the standard for judgment. Aslan is trying to use the first-century Jews who denied that Jesus was the Messiah as the standard to judge Paul's views of Jesus. That is an illogical approach.

What Aslan hopes to demonstrate, however, is that Paul's epistle to the Galatians will prove that he (Paul) held a strong disdain (almost hatred) toward the "esteemed pillars" of the Jerusalem church—Peter, John, and James. Now, it is true, that Paul was not one to get star-struck; he was confident enough in his own self and position not to be enchanted by the apostles. Paul does recognize that James, Peter and John were esteemed as pillars, or had the reputation of being seen as pillars of the church. But Paul is not deriding these men as Aslan wants you to think. Paul is simply acknowledging that these three men were known by the early church as substantial pillars of the faith; in other words, these three men, who represented the rest of the apostles, supported and maintained the truth of the gospel message. The apostles were the support team for the early church; they had heard the words of Jesus and had seen the works of Jesus. They had followed Jesus for some three years during his ministry and were, as a result, excellent resources for the maintenance of the gospel message. The apostles were very protective of the gospel message; to be considered a follower of Jesus and a member of the church that he established, one needed to believe and preach one gospel. But Aslan insists that the epistle to the Galatian Christians is Paul's defense against and answer to the terrible treatment he received from the apostles. Before looking at the epistle to the Galatians, let's look at the episode where Aslan says Paul received this terrible treatment.

Paul Summoned to Jerusalem?

Aslan says Paul was summoned to appear before the apostles because of his shocking and heretical teachings about Jesus, and this meeting was known as the Council at Jerusalem, found in Acts 15. According to Aslan, Paul was called to appear at this Council in order to present his reasons for assigning himself the role of being the missionary to the uncircumcised (the Gentiles). Aslan imagines that Paul had to stand like an accused person in front of James, Peter, John, and the other elders in Jerusalem so that he could justify what he had been preaching. Now we have already looked at Acts 15 in the previous chapter, but I will give a brief rendition of the Council meeting. We know circumcision was important for the Jew; it was deeply embedded in their culture. But so were animal sacrifices and the priesthood. So was the custom that Jews did not enter a Gentile's house. When Jews became Christians (i.e., accepted Jesus as their Messiah) their social structure changed drastically (some more quickly than others) because they no longer had to go to the Temple to offer animal sacrifices for their sins. It is not difficult to imagine that the Jerusalem church had held council meetings to discuss the important issues affecting the early Jewish Christians. So, when the topic of circumcision became too controversial to ignore the Jerusalem leaders called for a council meeting. Luke gives us a clear insight into how the early church dealt with debates, disagreements, and various conflicting ideas among the early Christians. Luke demonstrates the reason for the meeting, how the meeting progressed, what the issues were, who the major personnel were, and how it concluded. The topic under discussion was whether or not circumcision was necessary for Gentile Christians. James, the bishop in Jerusalem, had sent some Jewish Christians to the church in Antioch, Syria, because its congregation was one of the first to accept believers from different socio/religious/economic backgrounds. These Jewish Christians had insisted that the Gentile Christians become circumcised. Barnabas and Paul disagreed with this requirement and they debated this issue with the Jewish Christians. The Antioch church decided to send Barnabas and Paul to Jerusalem to meet with the elders there. At the Council meeting, some Pharisaic believers insisted that Gentile Christians had to be circumcised in order to be recognized by the Christian community. Remember, God-fearing Gentiles had been receiving circumcision for years so that they could adopt Judaism as their religion. Some of these Jewish Christians felt that all Gentiles should be circumcised to be fully "saved," and/or accepted. What this implied was that a person needed to do something, some kind of task, for salvation to take full effect. The gospel message that Peter, John, James and all the other original apostles preached was that one became saved by accepting the free gift of salvation from God through the death of Jesus Christ. There was no task to perform. Therefore, following the Mosaic Law in order to be saved, and being circumcised in order to be saved, was not a part of the Christian gospel. That is exactly how Paul had understood the gospel as well. After discussing the issue for a while, James, the Lord's brother and bishop of the church in Jerusalem, stated the final decision of the Council. That decision was to not make it burdensome for Gentile Christians by insisting on circumcision. An official letter was written, copied, and given to all the delegates. Barnabas and Paul returned to their church in Antioch, Syria, with the letter.

When one reads Acts 15 one has to wonder where Aslan came up with the idea that Paul was summoned to appear before the apostles because of his shocking and heretical teachings about Jesus. Of course, Aslan accuses Luke, who wrote about this Council meeting, of writing about it in such a way that it revealed Luke's obvious motive, which was to validate Paul's ministry to the Gentiles. But that is Aslan's typical "escape clause," and it simply reflects his habit of taking passages from the New Testament and then twisting and manipulating them so he can have them coincide with his theories (something he does throughout his book). So, Aslan readily accepts the passages in Acts 15 that mention the Jerusalem Council, but then he acts as if he has a motive-reader that helps him determine that Luke lies about the "true" purpose of the meeting; he accuses Luke of twisting the narrative so that Paul, his teacher, is able to validate his ministry to the Gentiles. Where then does Aslan get his information? Many of his theories appear to be influenced by the hypothetical (non-existent) "Q" document. His fabricated story about Paul being summoned to Jerusalem by the "esteemed pillars," however, matches Horsley's version of the Jerusalem Council. As noted above, Horsley sees the Jerusalem Council as a meeting whereby the apostles ganged up on Paul because they believed Paul's preaching was filled with errors. These Jerusalem Christians, according to Horsley, had little patience for Paul's radical views. So, let's look at the epistle to the Galatians to see if Aslan, Horsley, and other liberal scholars are correct.

Is there Evidence from Galatians that Paul was a Rogue Apostle?

Aslan (like Horsley) insists that the epistle to the Galatian Christians is Paul's defense against and answer to the terrible treatment he received from the apostles at the Jerusalem Council. In his letter to the Galatians, Paul warns the believers not to accept a different gospel than the one they had already accepted; they were to reject any message that included the necessity of circumcision for complete salvation. The entire epistle was written to show that circumcision was not necessary for salvation. This had been the definitive decision by the Jerusalem Council, and Paul was reiterating it here. The only requirement for salvation was to believe that "Christ paid the price to free us from the curse that God's laws bring by becoming cursed instead of us" ("Scripture is taken from GOD'S WORD®. © 1995 God's Word to the Nations. Used by permission of Baker Publishing Group." Gal 3:13). Paul taught, as all the apostles taught, that Jesus' crucifixion—the shedding of his blood—was the only source of salvation (see 1 Pe 1:19; 1 Jn 1:7). Paul was rightfully angry at those who were misleading the Galatians into thinking they needed to be circumcised in order to complete their salvation. Why? Because it was not true. Paul was concerned with the truth, and the truth was that nothing needed to be added to the gospel. No one needed to be circumcised in order to complete their salvation. No one needed to gather up enough "good" points in order to gain salvation. Salvation is a gift, paid for by Christ's blood, and available to anyone who believes it (see Rom 3:25; Eph 1:7).

Aslan and Horsley believe that Paul had been ambushed at the Council meeting by some "false believers" and, as a consequence, used his letter to the Galatians to complain about it, expressing his rage at how he was treated at the meeting. But is it the apostles and elders—especially Peter, John, and James—that Paul calls "false believers"? When we actually look at the passage Aslan uses within its context, we clearly see Aslan's error. In Galatians 2:4, Paul says that some false believers had arrived at the Council meeting "to spy on the freedom we have in Christ Jesus." Paul says in the next verse that no one at the meeting gave in to them for a moment, "so that the truth of the gospel might be preserved for you." Paul does not say he was personally ambushed, but simply states that some false believers were at the meeting and tried to push their ideas on everyone else, but that no one gave them the time of day. The whole Council meeting was ambushed by these "false believers," not just Paul. The word Paul uses for 'false believer' is pseudadelphous; the *Greek-English Lexicon of the New Testament* says it refers to an individual who pretends to be a close member of a socio-religious group, but is not. This is someone who pretends to be a Christian, but is not. (This is similar to Jesus' parable of the sower (Mt 13), where some people hear the word but do not really accept it; they only pretend to for a time.) Paul uses the same Greek word in 2 Corinthians 11:26 when he says that in his travels he had been in danger from rivers, bandits, non-believing Jews, Gentiles, and false believers (pseudadelphous). In 2 Corinthians 11:13, Paul identifies other "false believers" as dishonest workers who masquerade as Christ's apostles. He calls them "false-apostles," but he is not referring to the other twelve apostles, which would include the "esteemed pillars" in Jerusalem (I will address this presently). Paul did not think the twelve apostles were illegitimate (false) and he was the only true or legitimate one out there. We find that others in the early church were referred to as apostles; the word had a rather wide usage beyond the original twelve disciples of Jesus. In Acts 14:4, 14, we see it being used of Barnabas as well as of Paul. In Romans 16:7, Paul numbers Andronicus and Junia (a woman) among the apostles. In 2 Corinthians 8:23, there are some unnamed brothers who are called apostles. In Philippians 2:25, Epaphroditus is referred to as an apostle. Paul includes himself, Silas and Timothy as apostles in 1 Thessalonians 2:6. The term "apostles" was, therefore, often used as a reference to a leader or head teacher/bishop in a local church. It defined their relation to Christ and to the people. In Corinth, some false teachers had wrecked havoc in the church, teaching things that were opposed not only to the gospel but to the moral code Christians are compelled to follow. Aslan wants you to think that Paul is calling the twelve apostles "false-apostles" or "false believers," but he is not.

Paul does not use the epistle to the Galatians to express his rage at how he was treated at the Council meeting, as Aslan wants you to believe. Paul had no animosity towards James, Peter and John. In Galatians 2:2, Paul says that he met with the apostles in Jerusalem privately and revealed to them the gospel message that he preached to the Gentiles because he wanted to make sure his work was not in vain. In other words, Paul wanted to verify that he was preaching the gospel correctly, and this verification would come from the "pillars" of the

Jerusalem church, i.e., James, Peter, and John. This does not sound like a person who is outraged at how he was treated. This does not sound like a person who had been practically dragged into a meeting against his will in order to stand before the leaders of the church to defend his ministry and/or his teachings. It sounds like a person who humbly wants to make sure that he is preaching the right thing. And what do these "esteemed pillars"—James, Peter, and John—do when Paul shares with them what he has been preaching to the Gentiles? Did they mark him an apostate? Did they chuck him out in the streets and brand him an infidel? No! Paul says: "they recognized that I had been entrusted with the task of preaching the gospel to the uncircumcised, just as Peter had been to the circumcised" (NIV, Gal 2:7). What did these "esteemed pillars" of the church do then? They gave Paul and Barnabas the right hand of fellowship (2:9). Once again, we see Aslan creating a scenario that did not exist. Why does Aslan do this? He has an agenda, and he wants you to believe that agenda. His agenda is to dissuade you from acknowledging your need to accept Jesus as your Savior. He will, however, have to answer to God as to why he has so misrepresented the New Testament, and he will be responsible for the disbelief he causes through his writings. See what Jesus says about those who lead people astray from the truth (see Mt 18:6).

Aslan claims that Paul was hurt and surprised by the fact that the Galatian Christians had abandoned him, using the passage in 1:6 as evidence. It says: "I am astonished that you are so quickly deserting the one who called you to live in the grace of Christ and are turning to a different gospel" (NIV). Further on in the letter, Paul repeats this thought: Whatever means of persuasion the person who is trying to wrongly influence you used, it is not from the One who chose and calls you. (5:8). Paul is telling the Galatians that he is amazed or surprised that they are so quickly deserting Jesus; it is Jesus who is "the one who called you." Aslan is clearly mistaken as to the subject of Paul's reference. Aslan then claims that Paul insisted that the Galatian Christians ignore everyone else and follow only what he tells them, and uses as "proof" of this the passage in Galatians 1:9. Here is what that passage says: "If anybody is preaching to you a gospel other than what you accepted, let them be under God's curse" (NIV). (Paul told the Roman Christians the same thing: "I urge you, brothers and sisters, to watch out for those who cause divisions and put obstacles in your way that are contrary to the teaching you have learned. Keep away from them" (NIV, Rom 16:17).) What is the gospel that Paul does not want the Galatians to stray from? It is this: Christ died for our sins according to the Scriptures; he was buried; he was raised on the third day according to the Scriptures (1 Cor 15:3). This was the same gospel all the apostles preached. Today, we have all sorts of people preaching all sorts of different gospels. For Paul, the only gospel message he preached was about Jesus and his death on the cross (1 Cor 2:2). To the Galatians, Paul says, "It's unthinkable that I could ever brag about anything except the cross of our Lord Jesus Christ" ("Scripture is taken from GOD'S WORD®. © 1995 God's Word to the Nations. Used by permission of Baker Publishing Group." 6:14).

Aslan thinks Paul was hounded by James' men everywhere he (Paul) went. Aslan says James' men began showing up in Galatia and in Corinth—everywhere Paul preached he was sure to find someone who had been sent from James to counter whatever Paul said. James was purposefully trying to thwart every move Paul made, using his (James') own teachers to travel to all the churches Paul founded and then correct all of Paul's heretical teachings. Aslan uses Galatians 2:12 where Paul says Peter was visiting the church in Antioch and then "certain men came from James . . . who belonged to the circumcision group." We know from Acts 11:2 that after Peter left the Gentile house where the family had accepted the Good News he returned to Jerusalem and some believers there who still insisted on circumcision criticized him for what he had done. After Peter explained what had happened, they had no further objections and praised God. We see from Acts 11:2 and Galatians 2:12 that there were Jewish Christians that still insisted on circumcision, and both Peter and Paul had encounters with them. We learn from the letter James wrote to the churches that the Council had come to a decision regarding circumcision. In that letter, James said: "We have heard that some went out from us without our authorization and disturbed you, troubling your minds by what they said" (NIV, Acts 15:24). James wants to make it very clear that these 'trouble-makers' were not authorized by him to insist that the Gentile believers had to be circumcised. Then, James called Paul and Barnabas "our dear friends," and added that they "have risked their lives for the name of our Lord Jesus Christ" (NIV, Acts 15:25f). The Council's final decision validated what Paul had been preaching. Aslan takes this one episode where James sends some representatives to the Antioch church, and then embellishes it to make it seem as if James was constantly sending out his own people to travel to all the churches Paul founded so that they could correct all of Paul's heretical teachings. This is completely made up. There is no indication that James did this, especially when we see from James himself that those people did not have James' authorization. The letter James wrote also included four Torah-observant stipulations (see Acts 15:20), which Paul also accepted and clearly mentioned in his epistles. We see in Paul's first letter to the Corinthians that he instructed them not to eat food sacrificed to idols (8:1-13; see also 10:18–21), or to engage in sexual immorality (see 6:13). So, far from disagreeing with the leaders in Jerusalem, Paul emphasized the teachings of the Jerusalem leaders in his epistles.

Rather than Paul using his epistle to Galatians to express his contempt toward Peter, John, and James, as Aslan imagines, we see Paul actually expressing the opposite. Paul says in Galatians 2:9 that James, Peter and John "gave me and Barnabas the right hand of fellowship, agreeing to be our partners." The "esteemed pillars" acknowledged Paul's ministry to the Gentiles, just as their ministry was to the Jews. The word 'fellowship' that Paul uses refers to "an association involving close mutual relations and involvement" (*Greek-English Lexicon of the New Testament*). It is the Greek word used for the kind of fellowship a Christian has with Jesus. The word reveals that people in that fellowship have something in common. Paul is telling the Galatians that when he met with Peter, James and John, they all had one thing in common: the gospel message. They all preached the same gospel, although some preached primarily to Jews and others preached primarily to Gentiles. Paul says this same thing in 1 Corinthians 15:11—that the gospel message Paul preached was the same as the ones "they" (the other apostles) preached. Paul did not hold Peter, John and James in contempt; on the contrary, he saw them as fellow-workers spreading the same gospel, but to different groups of people. So Paul was not some hot-head who told the apostles that he was going to preach whatever he wanted; he showed that he was to be included in the undertaking of the spreading of the gospel. Paul lets his readers know that the "esteemed pillars" of the church acknowledged that he was not preaching a different gospel, that he had not added his own thoughts and ideas into the gospel message. That is why Paul was so upset with the Galatian believers. Paul asked them why they had so readily accepted a different gospel (see Gal 1:6), one that had added the stipulation of circumcision as a part of salvation. Paul was not deriding the "pillars" of the church; he was using them as further proof that he was in agreement with them regarding the gospel message. Aslan's attempt to show animosity and even hostility between Paul and the other apostles is simply unfounded.

In Aslan's scenario, he wants you to think Paul was not only a zealous outsider who cared nothing for the Christian leaders in Jerusalem, forging his own path and doctrines with no concern for the original gospel that Peter and the other apostles preached, but that Paul also felt encouraged to do so because, in Galatians 1:15f, he says that God had chosen him before he was born in order to reveal his Son to him, so that he could then preach Jesus to the Gentiles. Aslan takes this mean that Paul thought that while he was in his "mother's womb" Jesus commissioned him to preach the Good News, and therefore no one else could tell him what to preach. Aslan thinks this prompted Paul to reject the notion that he was the thirteenth apostle; this made Paul believe he was the first and foremost apostle. Paul must have thought himself the best of all the apostles because Jesus picked him from the womb. Actually, the idea that God was an important part of one's life, from birth on, is prevalent in Jewish tradition. David, in Psalm 22, declares that God had been with him since he was in his mother's womb (vs. 10), and in Psalm 71:6 David says God brought him out of his mother's womb. Jeremiah writes that before he was formed in his mother's womb, God had set him apart to be a prophet (1:5). Isaiah says that before he was born the Lord chose him (49:1). This was a common and beautiful belief that Jews held—that they were no accident, that their lives had a purpose, a meaning, because God was there at their birth and would be there when they took their last breath. Paul is simply acknowledging that God had been with him his whole life; helping him, directing him, and making him into the person God wanted him to be. Aslan takes a wonderful concept and uses it to make something ugly. Paul was not telling the Galatian believers that he was the most important apostle or that he considered himself the first or even the best apostle. In fact, as you read his epistles (e.g., 1 Corinthians 15:9), Paul often talks about how he was the least of the apostles and did not even deserve to be called an apostle, because of how he had persecuted the church. The image of Stephen being stoned to death in front of him never left him, and it was something he had to deal with all of his life. In Ephesians 3:8, Paul says he was the least of

355

all Jewish people, but God was kind enough to allow him to spread the Good News (the gospel message) about Jesus. This was not a fake humility; in various passages in his epistles Paul reveals how heartbroken he was that he had persecuted the church that he now belonged to. He loved the church that now accepted him; and he loved to preach the one true gospel about Jesus, the gospel that all the church leaders preached. In his writings, Paul shows that his gospel is the same as the other apostles who gave him the right hand of fellowship. We see then that Aslan's attempt to try to make Paul at contemptible odds with the other apostles, trying to make him into someone who preached a gospel contrary to the other apostles, and trying to make Paul an egotistical preacher who obstinately creates a savior from his own imagination, falls flat on its face. But that does not matter to Aslan; he has his agenda to promote and he will not allow truth to stand in his way.

Did Paul Suffer from Delusions of Grandeur?

Aslan attempts to use Acts 13 to show that Paul was having some kind of delusion of grandeur. It was in Acts 13 that Luke recorded a sermon Paul gave in a synagogue in Pisidian Antioch in Asia Minor (vs. 13-48). A week after the sermon, Paul and Barnabas were back at the synagogue and preaching about Jesus. A discussion arose and some Jews began to verbally attack Paul. Aslan claims that Paul then used a quote from Isaiah to prove that the Hebrew prophet had predicted Paul's ministry; therefore, if the Jews rejected Paul, they were, in essence, rejecting God. The passage Paul used was from Isaiah 49:6, which said: I have made you a light for the Gentiles (nations) to bring salvation throughout the world. Aslan thinks Paul was applying this only to himself, but the context shows Barnabas was included too; in fact, anyone who preaches the Good News is included. Paul did not use this verse to say that Isaiah actually predicted his (Paul's) ministry to create a new Christianity. He used it to tell the disbelieving Jews that they did not have a monopoly on God, that God was concerned about the Gentiles also. God had promised Abraham that through him (Abraham) God would bless all other nations or peoples (i.e., Gentiles). God had promised Israel, through Moses and the prophets, that he (God) would use the Jews as a conduit to bless all other nations. This promise to bless all other nations had to do with fulfilling the promise of the "seed of the woman," the Messiah who would bring

356

salvation to redeem humankind. This was the Good News (gospel) that God proclaimed throughout human history. The Jewish nation was established in order to keep this message of salvation pure because many other cultures had distorted and/or rejected the promises God had made to our first parents (Adam and Eve). The Jews were, in essence, a light to the Gentiles because they had God's Law and God's Promises. They were to keep both in a trust, so to speak, until the Laws and the Promises were to be fulfilled by the Redeeming Messiah. The Redeeming Messiah, the root of Jesse in whom the Gentiles would put their hope (Isa 11:10) would be the Servant of the Lord who would be a light to the Gentiles (Isa 49:6). Jesus said, "I am the light of the world. Whoever follows me will have a life filled with light and will never live in the dark" (Jn 8:12). But he also told his followers, "You are the light of the world" (Matt 5: 14). He told them to make disciples of all nations (Matt 28:19), and he told them just before he ascended that they were to be his witnesses and to testify about him, starting in Jerusalem and going out to all the world (Acts 1:8). Every follower of Jesus is, therefore, a "light to the Gentiles." Paul is not making some grandiose claim that the prophets were talking about him as being *the* light to the Gentiles. Edward J. Young, in his commentary on Isaiah, shows that when "His people labor in His Name as Paul and Barnabas were doing, He works through them." Paul uses this Isaiah verse regarding the 'light to the Gentiles,' to show that he and Barnabas, and any other follower of Jesus, is a light to the Gentiles. If you look at the context of the verse Aslan is using to try to prove Paul believed Isaiah was talking about him, and compare it with other relevant Scripture passages, you will discover that Aslan is mistaken.

Did Paul Consider Peter, John and James "False Apostles"?

Just as Aslan attempted to use Galatians 2:4 to say that Paul thought the "esteemed pillars"—Paul, John, and James—were "false believers" (a truly erroneous idea), Aslan is convinced that these Jerusalem leaders are the ones Paul is talking about in 2 Corinthians 11:13-15, where Paul speaks of some people as "false apostles, deceitful workers, masquerading as apostles of Christ. And no wonder, for Satan himself masquerades as an angel of light" (NIV). Aslan wants to convince you that Paul is actually calling the Jerusalem leaders Satan's servants. Aslan says Paul makes this comment partly because of his need to constantly defend his apostleship. Why do we often find Paul defending his apostleship in his epistles? For one thing, as noted above, Paul believed he did not deserve to be called an apostle because of how he had persecuted the church (1 Cor 15:9). Secondly, there were people who decided that since Paul was not consistently present at the churches he had founded (because he was either traveling or in prison), he did not have the authority to tell them what to do. Paul challenged this idea and reminded them that he did have apostolic authority, and that it had been given him by God (which, by the way, the apostles in Jerusalem concurred). Thirdly, Paul says that the reputation of all the apostles was sometimes looked upon with contempt. Paul says that "it seems to me that God has put us apostles on display at the end of the procession, like those condemned to die in the arena" (NIV, 1 Cor 4:9). He says the apostles "have been made a spectacle to the whole universe." The apostles are fools for Christ, they are dishonored; they go hungry, are brutally treated, and homeless. The apostles are often cursed, persecuted, and slandered. Paul does not just single himself out here; he says this is how lots of the apostles were being treated. There were those who attempted to thwart the authority of the apostles and Paul is defending, not only himself, but all of his apostolic colleagues.

If Paul is not referring to the apostles in Jerusalem—Jesus' original followers—as Satan's servants, as Aslan claims, then who is Paul talking about in 2 Corinthians 11:13-15? In the Corinthian church, the believers were dividing themselves into cliques; some were saying they followed Paul, others said they followed Peter, or Apollos, and those who were really spiritually proud boasted that they followed Christ. Each of these groups or cliques was being led by someone who had set themselves up, in the Corinthian church, as apostles, leaders, and teachers. They were boasting that they were not timid like Paul, and that they had as much authority as Paul and the apostles in Jerusalem. These are the "false" apostles that Paul is referring to; all you need to do is read the passage in its context and you will see that. Paul reprimands the Corinthian believers for listening to others preach a Jesus other than the Jesus that Paul (and the real apostles) preached, for accepting a different spirit from the Spirit they had received, and for believing a different gospel from the one they had first accepted. Because these false apostles—teachers at the Corinthian assemblies—were boasting that they were the ones the believers there should be

358

listening to, Paul says, "I do not think I am in the least inferior to those "super-apostles" (vs. 5). These super-apostles were trying to denigrate Paul's authority while advancing their own. Paul tried to appeal to the Corinthians by showing how much he cared for them, how much he had done for them, and how much he loved them. He was perplexed by their rejection of him, and he knew it was because of these "super-apostles" that they had turned against him. Paul called these divisive teachers false apostles because they were deceitful workers, masquerading as apostles of Christ (vs. 13), just as Satan masquerades as an angel of light (vs. 14). These false apostles are clearly not Christians or, if they are, have become so deceived and arrogant that they are preaching a false gospel in order to be recognized as highly enlightened. Paul says these false teachers are servants of Satan, because Satan is the great Deceiver, and these false teachers masquerade as servants of righteousness (vs. 15). Paul wants the Corinthian believers to know that as far as these false apostles are concerned "their end will be what their actions deserve." Paul is trying to protect the Corinthian believers from non-Christian influence. (This is also why John had written his Gospel and epistles—to protect the believers from erroneous Gnostic beliefs that had crept into the church.) We see this same problem affecting the church today. There are a lot of phony preachers working in churches, pretending to know Jesus as their Savior but doing more harm to the cause of Christ than they do to promote it. There are many professors who teach Religious Studies at colleges and universities who would fall under the nomenclature of a "false apostle." Practically every epistle in the New Testament has warnings against false teachers. So, Paul is not referring to Peter, James, John, and the other apostles in this passage; he is referring to false teachers in the Corinthian church who have set themselves up as those assuming apostolic authority.

Jude Agrees with Paul

Like Paul, Jude (Jesus' brother) wrote an epistle expressing his concern about false (heretical) teachings going around the church. In his short, but powerful letter Jude encouraged his friends (his readers) to continue in their fight for the Christian faith. This was a spiritual, not a physical, battle. Jude warned his readers that some "people have slipped in among you unnoticed." They were false teachers. Jude says that God means nothing to them; he says this because it was apparent by what they were teaching. What were they teaching or doing? They denied "our only Master and Lord, Jesus Christ." Now, remember Jude was a Jew and knew the Hebrew Scriptures condemned worshipping anyone other than the one true God. Every Jew knew the Shema: Hear, O Israel: The LORD our God, the LORD is one (Deut 6:4). Jude had come to believe that Jesus was the unique, one and only, Son of God because of the resurrection. And he was warning his readers that there were false teachers who denied that Jesus was God and to have nothing to do with them. Jude tells his dear friends to use their holy faith to grow; he reminds them to pray with the Holy Spirit's help. Jude encourages them to remain "in God's love as you look for the mercy of our Lord Jesus Christ to give you eternal life." He reminds them to show mercy to those who have doubts and to those whose lives are stained with sin. He ends by saying that "glory, majesty, power, and authority belong to the only God, our Savior, through Jesus Christ our Lord." Jude was writing to warn his readers against those who denied the uniqueness of Jesus Christ. That, too, is part of the reason I am writing this response to Aslan. Jesus is unique. He is not just a man who one day decided to walk around Galilee, creating a secret society of rebels with the designs to go to Jerusalem and somehow dismantle the priesthood and destroy the Roman army. Jesus is the Son of God, the second Person of the Triune Godhead, the Redeeming Messiah, the "seed of the woman," the Messenger of the Lord, the Word of God, God in the flesh. Jesus is the promised Savior, who can be none other than God himself.

Paul Is Summoned to Jerusalem, Again?

Aslan is unrelenting in his attempts to show that Paul was a rogue apostle by claiming that Paul had to be summoned a second time to Jerusalem. Aslan says that while Paul was preaching and writing some of his epistles in the 50s A.D., more and more people were becoming especially concerned with Paul's depictions and views of Jesus. Therefore, around 57 A.D., the apostles in Jerusalem were compelled to insist that Paul come and defend his teachings. There is nothing in the book of Acts, of course, that makes this kind of accusation. This whole scenario is made up by Aslan (but not only by him; it can also be seen in the writings of others, like Horsley). Despite Aslan's proposal, Paul did not create a different Jesus than the one the apostles in Jerusalem (Jesus' original followers) believed in. That is obvious when you read Paul's letters. In Peter's first sermon, he calls Jesus Lord (Yahweh) and Messiah. He told his listeners that Jesus died and rose from the dead and that they needed to accept Jesus Christ for the forgiveness of their sins. Paul preached this same message. In 1 Corinthians 1:3, Paul gives the full title for Jesus—Lord Jesus Christ—agreeing with Peter. In 1 Corinthians 15, Paul says his gospel consisted of this message: Christ died for our sins according to the Scriptures; he was buried; he was raised on the third day according to the Scriptures. Paul was not preaching some shocking and heretical message. He was preaching the same message that all the other apostles who knew Jesus were preaching. So where does Aslan get his theory that Paul was preaching a shocking and heretical gospel? He is making it up. Just like he makes up the zealot image of Jesus. If James and the apostles did not demand that Paul come to Jerusalem to explain to them his unusual and non-apostolic views, then why did he go to Jerusalem? He went there to bring gifts for the poor (Acts 24:17). Paul had made a habit of collecting contributions from Gentile churches in Asia Minor, Macedonia, and Greece to send to the Jewish Christians in Jerusalem who were in need (see 2 Cor 8-9). He believed the Gentile Christians had somewhat of an obligation to the Jewish Christians in Jerusalem because it was through the Jews that the Messiah blessed all the nations (Gentiles). Paul cared deeply for the Christians (Jewish and Gentile) in Jerusalem, and this included the apostles, the "esteemed pillars."

One can see from Paul's letters that he was deeply concerned about the poor, the marginalized, and the widows, and this attitude was quite typical of Jewish culture. The Hebrew Scriptures were frequently reminding the Jews to care for the poor and widows, and those who could not care for themselves. Jesus was adamant that his followers continue this tradition (see Mt 25:31-46). Paul made it a practice to gather contributions from the Gentile churches and send them to the needy Jewish believers in Jerusalem. Aslan wants to turn this great Christian tradition into something ugly. Aslan wants to take Paul's generosity and use it to try to prove his (Aslan's) theory of how James and Paul hated each other. Aslan tells us that Paul was summoned to come to Jerusalem for the second time in order to answer for his behavior and teachings. Aslan creates a scenario where James directly confronts Paul and demands to know why he (Paul) is teaching others to reject the Mosaic Law, circumcision, and Jewish customs (see Acts

361

21:21). (It is ironic that Stephen, an early deacon and martyr for the Way, was charged with similar accusations (see Acts 6:14) and was stoned to death while Paul (known then as Saul) stood approvingly by.) The fact is Paul was not summoned by a frustrated church leader to prove to the "esteemed pillars" that he was not a rogue preacher. Paul arrived in Jerusalem, carrying a monetary contribution that the Gentile churches collected to give to the needy Jewish believers. When Paul and his entourage arrived in Jerusalem Luke says they were warmly received by the church, the brothers and sisters (Acts 21:17). On the following day Paul and everyone who had travelled with him met with James and all the elders. Paul gave them a detailed report about what God had been doing among the Gentiles through his ministry. When they heard what Paul had been doing, they all praised God (Acts 21:20). Now, does this episode in any way mirror what Aslan wants you to believe? Of course not. But Aslan's defense, of course, is to simply assert (without any evidence) that Luke was just trying to sugar-coat the volatile situation. Unfortunately, for Aslan, there was no confrontation between Paul and James, or any of the other apostles.

There was a matter, however, that James wanted to rectify; and he had every right to do so. Some rumors were spreading that Paul was teaching Jews who lived out in the Gentile regions that they could turn away from the Mosaic Law, that they did not have to circumcise their children or live according to Jewish customs. Now, one thing you must know and remember, Paul did not nullify the Mosaic Law, nor did he teach against circumcision per se, nor did he tell others they were no longer allowed to follow their cultural traditions. What Paul taught, and is entirely true, is that the Mosaic Law and circumcision and following traditions is not going to save you. Only Jesus can save you. Paul did not go around saying now that you are saved you no longer have to follow the laws. Friedman (*They Loved the Torah*) shows how Paul continued his Torah observance after he became a believer in Jesus. Throughout the book of Acts, we see Paul observing the Sabbath. Since Paul was always allowed to speak in synagogues wherever he traveled, he would not have had that opportunity if everyone knew he had rejected the Mosaic Law. Before leaving Corinth, Paul had his hair cut off because of a vow he had made, in accordance with Mosaic Law (Acts 18:18). Paul had deemed it necessary that Timothy be circumcised when the young man joined him on his missionary journeys so that Timothy would not be a stumbling-block to the Jews they would encounter on their missionary trips (see Acts 16:3). We know by looking at Acts 23:6 that Paul still considered himself a Pharisee. When he did arrive in Rome at the end of Acts he tells his fellow Jewish Christians, "I have done nothing against our people or against the customs of our ancestors" (NIV, 28:17). Paul says in 1 Corinthians 7:18 that if a man was already circumcised when he became a Christian, then he should not become uncircumcised; and if he was uncircumcised when he became a Christian, then he should not consider becoming circumcised. In Galatians 5:6 Paul says: "As far as our relationship to Christ Jesus is concerned, it doesn't matter whether we are circumcised or not. But what matters is a faith that expresses itself through love" ("Scripture is taken from GOD'S WORD®. © 1995 God's Word to the Nations. Used by permission of Baker Publishing Group.").

So, James and the elders were concerned that when some Jewish Christians, who happened to believe the erroneous rumors about Paul, found out that Paul was in town, there might be some trouble. Four men in the church had made plans to go through a purification rite. The elders of the church suggested that Paul take these four men who had made the vow and go with them to their purification ceremony and pay their expenses, thereby showing that he (Paul) had no animosity about these Jewish traditions. Paul had no problem with that; as we have seen, Paul was not averse to following Jewish customs. So Paul went with the men and went through the purification rite, along with them. Afterwards, Paul went to the Temple and notified the officials of when the purification would end and when the offering would be made for each of the men. The plan to avoid a confrontation with certain Jewish Christians appeared to have worked. However, when Paul returned to the Temple seven days later to make the offering some non-Christian Jews from Asia Minor noticed him, made false accusations against him, and began to cause a riot. Paul was arrested and eventually sent to Rome to appeal his case before Caesar.

This episode certainly does not show any animosity between Paul and James, nor does it show that Paul was opposed to Jewish traditions. There is no reason not to take Luke at his word and read and accept this episode as it was written. But Aslan has another interpretation, and he demands that his interpretation be the only way to understand why

363

Paul would participate in this purification ceremony. Aslan believes that Paul was being forced by James and the elders to completely renounce his ministry to the Gentiles and make a public acknowledgment of subservience to James' authority. Once again, we see Aslan rewriting history so that it conforms to his agenda. He accuses Luke of fabricating episodes in order to validate Paul and his ministry, and insists that Luke cannot be trusted because he nonchalantly suggests that Paul simply went along with this ritual without complaining. But, as we have seen often enough, it is Aslan that manufactures false scenarios in order to justify his theories.

We certainly cannot deny the fact that there were debates, disagreements, and varying ideas among the early Christians. That was one of the reasons for the Jerusalem Council (Acts 15), and the many councils and synods that followed in the next three centuries. We saw how warmly Paul was received at the Jerusalem Council meeting. We also saw how warmly Paul was received when he met with James, Peter, and the others when he brought the monetary contribution to Jerusalem around 57 A.D. Aslan wants you to believe that the apostles ganged up on Paul at both of these events, but that did not happen. Paul was not out on the fringe, teaching a deviant message that sent shock waves all the way back to Jerusalem, culminating in his being reined in by the "esteemed pillars" that he supposedly openly defied. There were no demands that Paul come to Jerusalem in humble contrition. Aslan, as he does throughout his book, makes up these stories knowing that the majority of his readers will not take the time to see if he is correct. Aslan knows his readers will simply accept what he says. Although Aslan would have you think that Paul was just a rogue apostle, he does not offer substantial evidence; it is nothing more than an unverifiable exaggeration. Aslan then makes another blatant allegation against Paul, accusing him of demonstrating not one bit of interest in the historical Jesus. It is that subject we address in the next chapter.

Chapter Seventeen: Paul and the Historical Jesus

Was Paul Disinterested in the Historical Jesus?

Aslan is firmly convinced that Paul manifested a disinterest in the historical Jesus—a real live human being—and believes his proof is that Paul hardly says anything about Jesus of Nazareth in his epistles nor does he recount any events taken from Jesus' life and ministry. Aslan not only thinks Paul has no clue as to the "real" Jesus but that Paul does not even care to know. We learn from Paul's letters that he does mention the Last Supper and Jesus' crucifixion, but Aslan claims Paul is simply transforming these two events into a kind of ritual rather than simply accepting them at face value. Of course, there is one very obvious reason why Paul did not enumerate or describe the events of Jesus' life in his epistles. Paul was writing to people who already knew about the historical Jesus. If I am writing to a friend about a mutual friend, I do not have to spend any time going into details about that person's life because we both know him. If I do not include a lot of details about our mutual friend in my letter, that does not mean (nor should anyone imply that it means) I have no interest in him as a real historical person. Aslan assumes that because Paul does not go into any details about Jesus' life in his epistles that that means Paul is not interested in the historical Jesus; but that is a wrong assumption. Paul is writing to people who already know about the historical Jesus; it is, therefore, not necessary for Paul to go into any details about Jesus' life.

When we compare Acts to Paul's epistles we see that Paul often spent quite a bit of time in the cities where he had preached the gospel. There is no reason to doubt that Paul did not talk about the historical Jesus to those who had accepted the Good News. If the Good News was about what Jesus did in reconciling humankind back to God, it certainly seems logical that those believing the Good News would want to know about Jesus. It would also seem logical that Paul, being who he was, would be interested in Jesus as a person. Paul was a student of Gamaliel's, one of the top rabbis and experts of the Mosaic Law. Paul was well versed in the Messianic passages of the Hebrew Scriptures. When he came face to face with the risen Jesus it had to completely disrupt his theology. Here he was persecuting the followers of Jesus because they were spreading Jesus' words and deeds around and convincing their fellow Jews that Jesus was the awaited Messiah. Paul hated these Christians because they were contradicting everything he believed about the Messiah. Then, Paul came in contact with Jesus, the risen Messiah, and he became an ardent follower of Jesus. Knowing the kind of person Paul was—studious and knowledgeable concerning the Scriptures—you can bet that he made every effort to learn about Jesus, the man. Is there any indication in his epistles that he did, in fact, make an effort to learn about Jesus, the man?

We saw in the previous chapter how Aslan tried to use Paul's letter to the Galatian Christians to show that Paul did not get along with the other apostles, an idea that was shown to be untrue. In his letter to the Galatian Christians, Paul actually revealed how interested he was in the historical Jesus. All we need to do is look at Galatians 1:18f. Paul says he visited Peter for fifteen days and got acquainted with him. Paul used the Greek word *historēsai* to describe this visit. The word *historēsai* is where we get the word history. Paul used it to show he was very interested in the historical Jesus. Paul used the word to indicate that he went to see Peter in order to gain knowledge; it was a fact-finding mission. Zodhiates tells us Paul visited Peter to "ascertain by inquiry and personal examination" information about Jesus. This visit was no casual meeting. Paul knew that Peter was an excellent source because of how close he was to Jesus. Aslan will have you think that Paul did not care about the historical Jesus. But Paul did not just meet with Peter on this visit to learn about the real Jesus; he also met with James, Jesus' brother. In this Galatians passage, Paul clearly shows that he was interested in the historical Jesus. Paul had sought out two prominent sources so he could learn about the man Jesus— James and Peter. Patzia verifies this with the claim that when Paul became a Christian he had contact with believers in Damascus, Tarsus, Antioch and Jerusalem, all of whom exposed him to the ideas and practices of early Christianity. Those ideas and practices made their way into Paul's letters. Aslan is, therefore, way off the mark in claiming that Paul did not know, nor care to know, about the historical Jesus. It is obvious, however, from reading Aslan's *Zealot*, that he does not know, nor does he really care to know, the historical Jesus.

Regarding Aslan's false claim that Paul did not care about the historical Jesus, allow me to make another observation. As noted above, in Acts 13:13-41 Luke records a sermon that Paul gave on his first missionary journey. Paul and Barnabas were in a synagogue in Pisidian Antioch. As it was per Jewish custom, the new visitors were asked if they wanted to speak. Paul got up and, like Stephen whom he watched being murdered, gave a little history lesson. Paul shows he is interested in history. He told those in the synagogue about how God had chosen the Israelites, had made them prosper in Egypt, and led them out of that country and into their own. How God gave them judges and kings to lead them; how from David's lineage God would bring the Messiah; and how this Messiah was the Savior Jesus. Paul talked about John the Baptizer being the herald of the promised Messiah, Jesus. Paul asserted that the religious leaders and other Jews did not recognize Jesus as the Messiah and condemned him to death, which, Paul claimed, fulfilled what the prophets had said would happen. Paul stated that Jesus stood before Pilate and was sentenced to death. Jesus was buried, but God raised him from the dead. Paul then claimed that Jesus was seen by many of his followers and that they were witnesses that the resurrection was true. Paul concluded his sermon by telling the people in the synagogue that the Mosaic Law could not free them from their sins; it was only through Jesus that their sins would be forgiven. (Acts 13:38f). This certainly sounds like Paul knew about and cared about the historical Jesus, just as he cared about the history of his people, the Jews. The rebuttal, of course, is that Luke put those words in Paul's mouth, just like the Gospel writers put words in Jesus' mouth; but that is a cop-out and not a valid argument. We could say that about anything. Anytime someone quotes another person, I could just say, "You're putting words in their mouth; I don't believe they said that," and that is supposed to be enough evidence that I am right. We have come to the point in our postmodern epistemology where we do not need evidence anymore; if we hear someone say something and we like what is said, we simply say it is 'true for me.' There is no longer truth "out there;" there is only "my truth" or "your truth." What happens then is what Kierkegaard warned us of: When everything is true, then nothing is.

We saw in our walk through the book of Acts that when Paul visited the church leaders in Jerusalem they all acknowledged they were preaching the same gospel. We saw how Paul returned to Jerusalem after his missionary journeys to, in a sense, check in with the apostles and let them know what he had been doing. He was no lone-wolf rogue, out there on the circuit, preaching whatever he wanted. While he was establishing churches, there is no reason to doubt that he did not teach about the historical Jesus. We see, in fact, in his famous and beautiful passage on Love (1 Cor 13) that Paul makes several references to events in Jesus' life that were recorded in all three synoptic Gospels (suggesting, of course, that they were known to Paul). In 1 Corinthians 13:1, Paul says: "I may speak in different languages of people or even angels. But if I do not have love, I am only a noisy bell or a crashing cymbal" (NCV). In Mark's Gospel (16:15–17), Jesus told his disciples to go everywhere and tell everyone the Good News. Those who believe and are baptized will be saved, but those who do not believe will be condemned. The disciples will be able to perform miracles and cast out demons in the power and authority of Jesus' name. They will speak new languages. In 1 Corinthians 13:2, Paul says: "If I have enough faith to move mountains, but do not have love, I am nothing." In a private conversation with his disciples, Jesus told them: "Truly I tell you, if you have faith as small as a mustard seed, you can say to this mountain, 'Move from here to there,' and it will move" (NIV, Mt 17:20). In 1 Corinthians 13:3, Paul says that he could give away everything that he owned, but if he didn't have love, he would not gain a thing. Paul probably has in mind the story of Zacchaeus who, in Luke 19:8, told Jesus that he would give half of his property to the poor.

What Paul does in his epistles is emphasize the two most important events in Jesus' life. For Paul, they were the crucifixion and resurrection. Paul was convinced that the death of Jesus was the fulfillment of the promised "seed of the woman." As a Jew, Paul must have thoroughly searched the Hebrew Scriptures after becoming a follower of Jesus and discovered, through the revelation provided by the Holy Spirit, all the passages that referred to the Redeeming Messiah. But the crucifixion would not mean anything without the resurrection. Paul shows how both the death and resurrection of Jesus are the cornerstones of Christianity. This is no different from Peter's first sermon to the Jews that we find in the second chapter of Acts (which has already been discussed). Preaching about the Savior of the world would not make sense unless there was some historical foundation supporting it. It is difficult to imagine that Paul went into Gentile territory and simply told people that a Jew had died and rose from the dead and that, in doing so, removed their sins if they only just believed. Paul's habit was to enter a Jewish synagogue wherever he went and to use the Hebrew Scriptures to show that Jesus was the Messiah (see Acts 13:14). He would obviously talk about the historical Jesus and show how the Scriptures prophesied about him. The assumption that Paul did not care about the historical Jesus simply because he does not include events in Jesus' life in his epistles is absurd.

Did Paul Really Contradict Jesus?

But Aslan does not just assume that Paul manifested a disinterest in the historical Jesus, he (Aslan) also claims that Paul actually contradicted Jesus. What evidence does Aslan give for this statement? He tells us to compare two different New Testament passages. One is in Paul's letter to the Romans where he says: "Everyone who calls on the name of the Lord will be saved" (NIV, 10:13). Aslan says we need to compare that with what Jesus said in Matthew's Gospel: "Not everyone who says to me, 'Lord, Lord,' will enter the kingdom of heaven" (NIV, 7:21). You will discover by reading the context of both of these passages that Aslan is clearly misinterpreting, misrepresenting and misunderstanding both of them. Remember earlier how Aslan tried to show in Mark's Gospel how Jesus contradicted himself (see Chapter Ten), but ended up not doing a good job of proving it? Well, Aslan does not do a good job here, either. Paul is clearly not contradicting Jesus. In the passage Aslan uses from Romans, Paul has been talking about how the Jews have rejected their Messiah and how God has given the gift of salvation to all the nations—Gentiles—(Paul is quoting from Matthew 21:43), and then he reminds his readers that God has not forgotten his promises to the Jewish nation. Paul says the gospel message he preaches is for the Jew and the Gentile; there is not one gospel for the Jew and a different one for the Gentile. The gospel message that Paul proclaims is: "If you declare with your mouth, "Jesus is Lord," and believe in your heart that God raised him from the dead, you will be saved" (NIV, Rom 10:9). Paul says this salvation is for everyone—"the same Lord is Lord of all and richly blesses all who call on him, for, "Everyone who calls on the name of the Lord will be saved"" (NIV, 10:12f). There are some interesting things Paul tells us in this passage. We are to declare with our mouths that Jesus is Lord. In Matthew 10:32, Jesus says that he will acknowledge to his Father anyone who acknowledges him to others. Paul obviously was aware that the historical Jesus said this and is telling his readers of the importance of making a declaration that Jesus is Lord. Now the phrase "Jesus is Lord" is very important. Paul is calling Jesus Yahweh, which is the name God called himself throughout the Hebrew Scriptures. In calling Jesus Lord, Paul is acknowledging that Jesus is the God of Abraham, Isaac, and Jacob (Peter concurred with Paul; see Acts 2:36). Paul continues in this Roman passage by saying you also must believe that God raised Jesus from the dead. Here we have Jesus as Yahweh, the one who visited Abraham, Moses and others as the Messenger of the Lord, and we have God the Father who raised his Son from the dead. When Paul says that Jesus is Lord he must be recalling how the historical Jesus had called himself Lord; for example, during the last Passover meal, Jesus told his disciples that they were right to call him rabbi (teacher) and Lord (Jn 13:13). So Paul says that if we acknowledge the historical Jesus as God in the flesh and believe that he rose from the dead, we will be saved. Paul then reminds his readers that Jesus is the same Lord for the Jew and the Gentile, and then he quotes a Hebrew Scripture that says "Everyone who calls on the name of the Lord will be saved" (see Joel 2:32; Peter quotes this same passage in Acts 2:21).

So, what does Jesus say that makes Aslan believe that Paul is contradicting Jesus? Aslan quotes the passage in Matthew where Jesus is giving the Sermon on the Mount. Jesus has told his listeners that they can ask and seek and knock, and God is gracious to answer them. Jesus told them to do to others what they would like others to do to them. Jesus told them that the gate and road to true life is narrow and only a few find it. Jesus warned them about false prophets and teachers who will come in sheep's clothing but will be wolves, leading the people astray. Then Jesus says: "Not everyone who says to me 'Lord, Lord' shall enter the kingdom of heaven." That is where Aslan says Paul contradicts Jesus. But Aslan does not finish the entire quote (it is a habit of his not to do so). Here is what Jesus said: "Not everyone who says to me, 'Lord, Lord!' will enter the kingdom of heaven, but only the person who does what my Father in heaven wants. Many will say to me on that day, 'Lord, Lord, didn't we prophesy in your name? Didn't we force out demons and do many miracles by the power and authority of your name?' Then I will tell them publicly, 'I've never known you. Get away from me, you evil people'" ("Scripture is taken from

Mt 7:21–23). Jesus is distinguishing between those who do lip-service—those "who say to me"—and those who actually do what God wants. Jesus said that those who do the will of his Father are his brothers and sisters (see Mt. 12:50). We see God rejecting others for mere lip-service in Hosea 8. God knows what is in our heart; he is not fooled or mocked. Just because someone says "Lord, Lord" does not mean they are acknowledging Jesus as their Savior. When Paul quotes from Joel 2:32 that "everyone who calls on the name of the LORD will be saved," he is speaking about people who sincerely call on Jesus to save them; and when Jesus says "Not everyone who says to me, 'Lord, Lord!' will enter the kingdom of heaven," he is referring to people who are not sincere but only pretending. They are the "false believers" that Paul often talks about in his epistles. As we can see, there is no contradiction between Paul and Jesus, as Aslan had hoped.

Paul's Christology

Aslan claims that Paul had a different idea about Jesus than the other disciples. Aslan, along with many liberal theologians/biblical scholars, adopts Rudolf Bultmann's (*Faith and Understanding*) view that Paul created a new religion—a Jesus-as-Christ religion—as opposed to the Christianity promoted by the apostles in Jerusalem. Aslan says Paul's Jesus is not human; he only seems to be. Aslan uses Philippians 2:7 to prove that Paul's Jesus is only an other-worldly, eternal being who only seemed to be human; that passage says that Jesus "emptied himself, by taking the form of a servant, being born in the likeness of men" (ESV). We have noticed throughout Aslan's book that he likes to take passages out of context and then reinterpret them to "prove" his theory. We need to, therefore, look at the whole passage. At the beginning of chapter two, Paul asked his Philippian readers to be united with Christ, to be comforted by Christ's love, to be sharing and tender and compassionate so that they could be like-minded, manifesting the same love and being one in spirit and mind. He tells them to make sure they behave without selfish ambitions and vain conceit, but to humbly value other people above themselves so that they can look out for the interests of others and not just their own interests. Paul wants them to have the same mindset that Jesus has; in verses six through eleven he tells his readers that the mindset Jesus has is this: "though he was in the form of God, did not count equality with God a thing to be grasped [did not take advantage of this equality (GW)], but emptied himself, by taking the form of a servant, being born in the likeness of men. And being found in human form, he humbled himself by becoming obedient to the point of death, even death on a cross. Therefore God has highly exalted him and bestowed on him the name that is above every name, so that at the name of Jesus every knee should bow, in heaven and on earth and under the earth, and every tongue confess that Jesus Christ is Lord, to the glory of God the Father" (ESV). There are several things that need to be pointed out from this wonderful passage. First, Paul says that Jesus existed in the form of God, that Jesus was equal with God. He shares this view with the Gospel writers and all the apostles. Second, Jesus emptied himself of his position as the second person of the Godhead. This phrase 'emptied himself' is pregnant with meaning, but Zodhiates tells us that after his incarnation Jesus was still in the form of God despite this 'being emptied.' Although Jesus took on the form of a servant he did not displace his deity. The word 'form' in the phrases "form of God" and "form of a servant" is the Greek word *morphe*, which Vine says (quoting another scholar) refers to the nature or essence of the subject, in this case God and a servant. Jesus is God in his nature and essence, and when he became human he was, in nature and essence, a servant. Third, this 'being emptied' began with the incarnation and ended at the crucifixion. "In His resurrection, He laid aside His form of a servant" (Zodhiates). Fourth, Jesus was found in human form; the Greek word here for 'form' is *schēmati* (where we get the word schematic from) and not *morphe*. Zodhiates suggests Paul used *morphe* and *schēmati* to distinguish Jesus' pre-incarnate glory (his being God the Son) from his humanity. "Servanthood was the mode of existence which the Son of God assumed and humanity was the receptacle, as it were, into which He poured Himself" (Zodhiates). Fifth, everyone at the Day of Judgment will bow their knee to Jesus, because he is God, their maker. Every person will confess or acknowledge that Jesus Christ is Lord (Yahweh).

Like the apostles, Paul believed Jesus was God-in-the-flesh, that he always existed, that he and only he could be the promised "seed of the woman." Paul's Christology was the same as the apostles—Jesus was God and he became human; he was an eternal being who came into the temporal space and time that he created. Paul did not create a different

372

Christianity; Paul did not preach a different gospel. After meeting the risen Jesus, he was not about to go off and preach some meaningless tale so that he could establish his own religion. After meeting the risen Jesus, he wanted to know about the historical Jesus. His training and education would have prompted him to do so. He would also want to study the Hebrew Scriptures, to go back over all of the passages that made reference to the Messiah. When he did that he would realize there were two appearances of the Messiah. The first appearance would be the Redeeming Messiah with the first biblical reference being the promise to Adam and Eve of the "seed of the woman." The second appearance would be as the Messianic King. Paul's Christ is fully human, but he is more than human. When Paul wrote to the Romans he told them that the gospel message he preached was about the Lord Jesus Christ, who in his human nature (i.e., as a human male) was a descendant of David and in his spiritual, holy nature was the Son of God. The human Jesus was shown to be God's Son when he rose from the dead (Rom 1:3–4). Jesus-as-human was just as important to Paul as the Christ-of-faith (Jesus as the Son of God). For Paul, Jesus is God in the flesh. But this is not just Paul's idea. The other apostles made this claim as well. When Thomas saw the risen Jesus he could do nothing other than to exclaim, "My Lord and my God" (Jn 20:28). The Gospel writers declared Jesus to be God in the flesh. John, one of Jesus' close disciples, said of Jesus that he was with God and was God and that through Jesus all things were made; that Jesus was the light of all humankind, and that he became flesh and lived among us (Jn 1:1-3, 14). For Paul, Jesus was very human, but he, like the others who saw the risen Jesus, knew that Jesus was more—that he was the Messenger of the Lord, God in human flesh. Jesus did not "become" God after the second century, and after some querulous council meeting discussions, as modern liberal scholars profess. Early Christians believed Jesus was God in the flesh, that he came to die for the world's sins and reconcile us back to God, and then rose from the dead to prove who he was. Only God could reconcile us back to himself. No amount of "good works" on our part would qualify us for self-redemption (saving ourselves).

For Paul, Jesus was not a cosmic being in some New Age sense. We have seen how Borg (see Chapter One) has relegated Jesus to some New Age Spirit-person who seemingly ushered in a type of first-century Aquarius Age (Spong does this too), but this is total nonsense.

373

John tells us that Jesus is the one through whom "all things were made," that nothing was made without his making it (Jn 1:3). Paul says the same thing: "There is only one God, the Father. Everything came from him, and we live for him. There is only one Lord, Jesus Christ. Everything came into being through him, and we live because of him" ("Scripture is taken from *GOD'S WORD*®. © 1995 God's Word to the Nations. Used by permission of Baker Publishing Group." 1 Cor 8:6). It is possible that Paul was quoting an early Christian creed when he said in Colossians (1:15-20): Jesus "is the image of the invisible God, the firstborn of all creation. For by him all things were created, in heaven and on earth, visible and invisible, whether thrones or dominions or rulers or authorities—all things were created through him and for him. And he is before all things, and in him all things hold together. And he is the head of the body, the church. He is the beginning, the firstborn from the dead, that in everything he might be preeminent. For in him all the fullness of God was pleased to dwell, and through him to reconcile to himself all things, whether on earth or in heaven, making peace by the blood of his cross" (ESV). The writer of the book of Hebrews says Jesus is the "one through whom God made the universe." Jesus is "the reflection of God's glory and the exact likeness of God's being. He holds everything together through his powerful words ("Scripture is taken from GOD'S WORD®. © 1995 God's Word to the Nations. Used by permission of Baker Publishing Group." Heb 1:2–3). The New Testament writers believed Jesus was God the Son, that he participated in the creation of the universe. In fact, when you look at the creation narrative in the first chapter of Genesis, you see the name for God is Elohim, which is plural and could be translated "the Gods." The word 'Elohim' is plural intensive with a singular meaning; it suggests the idea that the Person referred to has a multiple nature. That is the reason why Elohim, when he is about to make humans, says, "Let us . . ." (Gen 1:26). God is one in essence, but in that one essence are three Persons: the Father, Son, and Holy Spirit. The doctrine of the Trinity does not contradict the God who is revealed in the Hebrew Scriptures. So, yes, Paul believed Jesus existed before time; he believed that Jesus was God, the Son, who created everything, including time. The other apostles and early Christians believed this, too.

Jesus as "Firstborn"

Aslan thinks he can prove that Jesus was a created being and uses Colossians 1:15f to do this. Aslan is certainly not the first to declare that Jesus was the initial thing God created, and then had Jesus assist him in creating all the rest. There is really nothing unique about Jesus, says Aslan; he was simply "the firstborn of many brothers and sisters" (Rom 8.29). When Aslan says that Jesus is the first of God's creation he is actually stating a basic Muslim belief. Islam sees Jesus as the first of all created beings, who then helped God create the rest of the universe. Do Muslims think God needed help in creating the universe? The idea that God had to create some other being to assist him in creating the universe is erroneous for at least two reasons: it would mean that God is not all-powerful since he would need to have someone help him; and secondly, God would have given the "being" who helped him the power to help him, which would mean that God would already have the power to finish the creation without the need of anyone else's help. Do Muslims think God was lonely and just simply wanted someone to assist him in the creation of the universe? If so, and if this is why Muslims think God created Jesus, then God has a deficiency, which would be a profound blemish on his nature. The Scriptural doctrine of the Trinity answers the question of how God can know and experience Love without another created being since there are three Persons within God who love each other. None of these three Persons were created. They are who God is. I briefly addressed the use of the word 'firstborn' in connection with Jesus in Chapter One, in the section regarding Islam. It was there I said: When Jesus is referred to as the "only begotten" and "firstborn" of God this does not imply that God was involved in a physical act with a woman in order to create him, which Islam purports to imply. Both phrases—"only begotten" and "firstborn"—suggest a priority in rank or position, not something created at a specific time. The New International Version reveals the idea behind the phrase "only begotten" by saying that Jesus is God's "One and Only" Son, which brings to light the fact that Jesus has a unique relationship to God as Father to Son, but it does not imply that God created Jesus to be his son. Nowhere in the New Testament does it say that Jesus was created by God.

So, let's look at the passages where the word 'firstborn' is applied to Jesus. Zodhiates (from whom I glean some information in this section) tells us in his *Word Study Dictionary* that Prōtótokos (firstborn) is a theologically significant title used of Jesus in five New Testament passages: Romans 8:29; Colossians 1:15; Colossians 1:18; Hebrews 1:6; and Revelation 1:5.

In Romans 8:29 (from which Aslan partially quotes), we see that those whom God has saved are to be conformed to the image of his Son, Jesus, "that he [Jesus] might be the firstborn among many brothers and sisters" (NIV). The word Prōtótokos (firstborn) presents Jesus as the preeminent or ranking member of this group of believers, known as the Church, the body of Christ. Among Christians—Jesus' followers—Jesus is the preeminent one, he is the one we are to imitate. The conformity of sinners into the glorious image of God's Son places Jesus in a position of preeminence and glory among them. One of the purposes of salvation, then, is for the believer to become like Jesus. Humans were made in the image of God (Gen 1:26), but sin marred that image. Jesus is the new image to which we are to be conformed. Adam failed to be the image of God on earth; Jesus became the new Adam (as Paul says in 1 Corinthians 15), living a sinless life, a life pleasing to his Father, so that he would be the firstborn of his followers. Jesus is the preeminent Model to which all believers are to conform in their words, deeds, and thoughts. What Paul is not saying in Romans 8:29 is that Jesus is the first one of this "new creation" that God has established. This passage shows that Jesus is the firstborn—the preeminent one, the Lord and Head—in his relationship to his followers. Salvation through Jesus Christ is the restoration of humans to God's original purpose. Christ can be exalted and made preeminent among his followers now that salvation has restored the divine image in humans. Jesus is the firstborn, the Model, for his followers.

The second passage where Jesus is called 'firstborn' is Colossians 1:15; it says: "The Son is the image of the invisible God, the firstborn over all creation" (NIV). Here, Zodhiates says Prōtótokos is used in reference to God's creation, showing Christ's supremacy over it. Vine, in his *Expository Dictionary of New Testament Words*, agrees with Zodhiates when he says that the term 'firstborn' when applied to Jesus expresses Jesus' priority to and preeminence over creation; that it does not mean the "first" to be born. Paul explains what he means by 'firstborn' in the very next verse: "Through his power all things were made—things in heaven and on earth, things seen and unseen, all powers, authorities, lords, and rulers. All things were made through

Christ and for Christ" (NCV). Paul places Jesus above his creation; he shows that the phrase 'firstborn of all creation' is to be understood to mean that Jesus has preeminence over all creation. The Jewish New Testament translates 'firstborn over all creation' as: "He is supreme over all creation"; this is the idea Paul is conveying. *The Pulpit Commentary*, regarding Colossians 1:15, says that the word 'firstborn' was used as a title of sovereignty and that rabbis had even referred to God as "Firstborn of the world." Jesus has existed before everything (the universe), and he holds everything together (Col 1:17). How can Jesus be the first one created and yet also exist before everything was created? If Jesus existed before everything was created, then he could not be created, otherwise he would be part of the creation that he was supposed to have created. The *Greek-English Lexicon of the New Testament* concurs; it says that 'firstborn of all creation' (Col 1:15) could be interpreted as 'existing before all creation' or 'existing superior to all creation.' Prōtótokos, in the way Paul is using it here, refers to Jesus as the source or cause of the creation, not a product of it. We see in Revelation 3:14 that Jesus calls himself the ruler (source, origin, beginning) of all creation. So, 'firstborn of all creation' does not mean Jesus was created; it means he is the one who created all that exists.

The third passage where Jesus is called 'firstborn' is in Colossians 1:18; it says: Jesus "is the head of the body, the church; he is the beginning and the firstborn from among the dead, so that in everything he might have the supremacy" (NIV). During a court proceeding before governor Festus, Paul declared that the Hebrew prophets and Moses all claimed that the Messiah would suffer and be the first one to come back to life and never die (Acts 26:22–23). In Revelation 1:5, John also calls Jesus the firstborn from the dead. Now we know that Jesus was not the first one to be raised from the dead; others in both Testaments were raised from the dead. Jesus, however, is the first to be raised and not die again; he remained alive and, in fact, ascended alive and will return to set up his Messianic Kingdom. In this passage, Paul says Christ is the head of the church—Jesus' true followers. Jesus is the beginning, that is, the source or principal cause. In Revelation, Jesus says, "I am the Alpha and the Omega, the Beginning and the End" (NIV, 21:6). When Jesus is referred to as the 'head of the church,' the 'beginning,' and/or the 'firstborn of all creation,' these phrases are all used to show or assert that Jesus has supremacy or preeminence over his church, over creation, and over death (since he rose from the dead, never to die again). Since Paul has stated that Jesus is the firstborn over the creation of the universe, that is, he is the one who created it, he (Paul) then says Jesus is the firstborn of the dead, to show that Jesus' resurrection brings in a new creation. Paul talks about this new creation in 2 Corinthians 5:17: "Whoever is a believer in Christ is a new creation. The old way of living has disappeared. A new way of living has come into existence" ("Scripture is taken from GOD'S WORD®. © 1995 God's Word to the Nations. Used by permission of Baker Publishing Group."). Zodhiates tells us that what Paul is doing by using the words 'head,' 'beginning,' and 'firstborn' is to show that Jesus is supreme in redemption as well as in creation. Zodhiates makes it clear that Paul is not saying that Jesus has an acquired right to be preeminent, but an inherent right by virtue of his nature, that is by being the creator.

The fourth passage where Jesus is called 'firstborn' is in Hebrews 1:6; it says: "When God brings his firstborn Son into the world, he says, "Let all God's angels worship him""" (NCV). Zodhiates believes this passage refers to the Second Coming of the Lord Jesus. Just as angels were present at Jesus' birth, resurrection and ascension, so will they be at his return and they will worship him not only for all he has done in redeeming humankind back to God but also as the Messianic King. Some commentaries on this passage believe it refers to Jesus' first arrival, as the Redeeming Messiah. When Jesus 'emptied himself' and became a human in order to reconcile us back to God, the "angels appear only as attendant worshippers"; they are not "sharers of the throne" as Jesus is, but only worshippers (*The Pulpit Commentary*). What does it mean that Jesus is the 'firstborn,' the begotten of God? John says it rather beautifully: "No one has ever seen God, but the one and only Son, who is himself God and is in closest relationship with the Father, has made him known" (NIV, 1:18). Jesus is God's preeminent Son, his One and Only Son, in contrast to God's created children to whom he refers as 'sons and daughters.' The fifth passage where Jesus is called 'firstborn' is in Revelation 1:5; it says that Jesus is "the faithful witness, the firstborn from the dead [i.e., the first to come back to life to never die again], and the ruler of the kings of the earth" (NIV). This passage coincides with Paul's statement in Colossians 1:18.

We must not forget that Paul and John, whom we have referenced in the use of the word 'firstborn,' understood that the word had its roots in the Hebrew Scriptures. The firstborn son in a Jewish family typically received twice or double what his siblings were given (see Deut. 21:17). The firstborn received a special blessing from his father (see Gen 27). The firstborn became the head of the family, gaining control of land and material goods. (There were, of course, occasions when the practice of primogeniture was not followed: Isaac, Abraham's, second son, and Jacob, Isaac's second-born.) The Septuagint (Greek) Jewish Scriptures use *prōtotokos* to express the idea of preeminence. That is how it should be understood in the context of Colossians 1:15 where it says Jesus is the firstborn of all creation. It is how it should be understood in Romans 8:29 where it says Jesus is the "firstborn among many brothers," giving us the understanding that it is through Jesus that those who accept him as their Savior are to be blessed by God who will then allow them to become transformed into the image of Jesus. By being accepted by God through the redemptive work of Jesus, a person then becomes Jesus' brother or sister. Jesus told his listeners that those who do the will of his Father—and that "will" was to believe in his Son, Jesus— were his brothers and sisters (Mt 12:50). Beginning with the promise of the "seed of the woman" in Genesis 3:15, God has shown his plan for reconciling humans back to himself. He instigated the Mosaic Law, the priesthood, and the Temple as a temporary solution and, when the time was right, God sent his only Son—Jesus—to be the "seed of the woman." By being the Redeeming Messiah, Jesus became the "firstborn of many brothers and sisters." By his death and resurrection, people from all nations could now approach the throne of grace and find mercy (Heb 4:16). By entering the world he had made, Jesus was able to create a new creation—a body of believers that, by the help of the Holy Spirit (Jn 14:16f) would be transformed into his image (see Richards' *Every Name of God in the Bible*).

When we do an analysis of the word Prōtótokos we see it can be divided into *prŏtos* and *tíktō*. Protos indicates 'first' or 'before.' The word proto-history, for example, can be used to signify either first in time or first in place (preeminence). The word proto can also be used to indicate something that comes before something else; for example, the word proto-planet refers to conditions that arise before a planet's complete formation, or proto-Gnosticism identifies ideas that arose just prior to the full development of the basic concept. *Tíktō* means to bear or bring forth. Paul, in using the word Prótótokos, is saying that Jesus as human, as the Son of Man, is the "chiefborn" or "firstborn" in relation to what has been created; he is the foremost of all creation. When Paul, in these verses we've been looking at, talks of Jesus as the firstborn he is referring to Jesus' humanity, the historical Jesus, the God in human flesh. Paul makes it clear that by calling Jesus the "firstborn of all creation" he does not mean that Jesus is the first creature created by God because he then quickly clarifies what he means by stating in the very next verse that all things were created in, through, and for Jesus (see Col. 1:15–17). Paul and John saw Jesus as a co-participant in the creation of all things, but they did not see Jesus as a created being. They saw him as the Son of God, the Second Person of the Godhead, who has existed from eternity. Just as Jesus is the firstborn of all creation and therefore has priority over creation, so he is the firstborn of his brothers and sisters and is therefore head (ruler) of the Church. As the firstborn of the dead, Jesus guarantees that his followers will rise from the dead and be with him. The ultimate idea that Paul is trying to get across is that Jesus has first place in everything (Col 1:18). (Some information in this section gleaned from *Holman Treasury of Key Bible Words*.)

Just as there were false teachers in Galatia insisting that Gentile Christians be circumcised (as we saw in the previous chapter), there were also false teachers in Colossae who were "challenging Christ's preeminence and distracting the Colossians from the power of the gospel" (Myers). Paul, like the other apostles, was concerned that the gospel message was being added to and/or rejected. Throughout Colossians, Paul emphasized the preeminence of Jesus and the central role he played in creation and redemption (see 1:16, 22; 2:13–15). Just as Paul, Peter, James, Jude and John wrote their epistles to Christians who were dealing with persecution and false teachers, so the church has had to deal with false ideas and false teachers through the centuries. The four canonical Gospels and the letters found in the New Testament are foundations of Christian belief, and all ideas and theories are to be held up to their light in order to discern the truth. Gnostic ideas attempted to permeate the early church as did other heretical teachings and writings. We see in the second century that people were writing pseudo-gospels, like the Gospel of Thomas (the one the Jesus Seminar is so enamored with) and the Gospel of Mary and the Gospel of Peter. These were considered either "uninspired" or heretical because they attempted to portray Jesus contrary to the historical Jesus of Matthew, Mark, Luke and John. The church has battled heretical doctrine and ideas from within and without: Docetism (which taught that Christ did not have a real physical body); Arianism (which denied the full divinity of Christ and held that Jesus was not eternal but was created); Armenianism (denying Christ's two distinct natures); the Roman Catholic Church (which added pagan beliefs and rituals); Islam (denying the divinity of Jesus and rejecting the need of a Savior, thereby attempting to nullify the redemptive power of Christ's death and resurrection); and the Jehovah Witnesses (who have also used "the firstborn of creation" to teach that Christ was a creation of God and not coequal with God). These and other heretical ideas are refuted when you look at the context and historical background of the New Testament text. (Some information in this section gleaned from *Nelson's New Christian Dictionary* and Shedd's *Dogmatic Theology*.)

Aslan is mistaken to think that Paul's version of Jesus-as-Christ was his own invention, that no one else during this time (30s A.D. to late 60s A.D.) had written the things Paul had written about Jesus. Aslan claims that none of Paul's contemporaries believed what he believed about Jesus, but Aslan is mistaken. Paul did not make Jesus of Nazareth, a man who Aslan thinks died as a Jewish nationalist (a zealot), into an other-worldly, preexistent, Son of God so he could make a new religion, and thereby reject the Jesus of the apostles. Aslan, like many other liberal theologians/biblical scholars, has allowed his worldview (more than the evidence) determine his methodology and his conclusions. We have seen how Paul had engaged in a fact-finding meeting with Peter and James for the purpose of learning about the historical Jesus. We have seen how Paul was given the right hand of fellowship by all the apostles, and how he was sent off with a blessing as he went to preach to the Gentiles. We have seen how Paul was involved in the important Jerusalem Council that determined that Gentile Christians did not need to be circumcised to be saved (see Acts 15). We have seen how Paul had his home base in the Antioch church in Syria, where he had submitted himself to the leaders there. We have seen how there was no need for Paul to give an account of Jesus' life in the epistles he wrote because the Christians in the established churches throughout the Roman Empire already knew about Jesus, either through strictly-held oral tradition or from the

Gospels that had been written and distributed. We see, then, how Aslan is mistaken to think that Jesus-as-Christ is Paul's own invention. Having no other evidence, Aslan once more has to rely on the 'Q' document, insisting that it does not contain anything close to Paul's vision of Jesus. Aslan needs to be reminded, once more, that the 'Q' document does not really exist. In fact, he finally admits, in the Epilogue of his book, that the 'Q' document is a hypothetical text. But Aslan is not finished yet. He still wants to prove that Paul and James were engaged in a theological (and personal) struggle.

Chapter Eighteen: Was the Epistle of James Written as a Polemic against Paul?

Debates and questions linger around the Epistle of James in the New Testament regarding its author, the date it was written, and its content. If the author of this epistle was James, Jesus' brother, then it had to be written before 62 A.D., which is the year James died. Aslan, however, attaches an extremely late date for the epistle, suggesting that it was written in the 80s A.D. as a polemic against Paul and his theology. Many scholars actually place an early date on James' epistle, somewhere in the 40s or 50s. Some have suggested he was writing to the Jews who had come to Jerusalem during the Passover festival when Jesus was killed, and who then heard Peter's first sermon (Acts 2) before returning to their homes as Christians. Others suggest the letter could have been sent out to Jewish Christians after the Council meeting (Acts 15). Aslan (and others, like Crossan) puts a late date on the Epistle of James in order to rationalize his belief that there were two Christianities—Paul's version, and then the eleven apostles' version. So, for Aslan, who thinks the author considered Paul an enemy of early Christianity, this epistle was written as a final attempt to try to show that Paul was wrong.

The Torah and the New Jewish Christian

Of course, Aslan believes it is obvious that James, one of the "esteemed pillars" of the Jerusalem church, could not have written the epistle ascribed to him because he, just like Jesus and the majority of apostles, was illiterate. As we have already observed (see Chapters Four and Fifteen), there is no reason, knowing Jewish culture, to propose that Jesus, his brothers, and his apostles did not know how to read and write. Aslan has no real evidence to back up this claim, but even if James could not write, he could certainly think; and someone else could have written down his spoken thoughts. (In fact, the formally educated Paul sometimes used scribes to write the words he dictated; see Rom 16:22 as an example.) Aslan thinks we can determine what Jesus believed by what James said he believes; in fact, Aslan thinks that is the best way to know what Jesus believed. The implication is that Jesus believed the same things his brother James believed and, since Paul did not believe what James did, then Paul did not teach or believe what Jesus did. Aslan thinks he has tied all the loose ends together with that kind of logic. Aslan must be unaware of the fact that siblings can be total opposites of each other. Mark, in fact, shows us that James and the rest of his family thought that Jesus might have gone somewhat crazy because of some of the things he taught and believed about himself (3:21). The Gospels make it clear that Jesus' siblings did not believe in him until he rose from the dead. We have seen from the last two chapters that the "esteemed pillars" in Jerusalem and Paul preached the same gospel message and taught others about the same Jesus. Paul was not spreading heretical teachings that shocked the apostles to such an extent that they had to demand that he come to Jerusalem to defend himself and make amends. Aslan thinks that what was of utmost significance to James was balancing one's commitment to the Mosaic Law with one's faith in Jesus as the Messiah; and that is why, according to Aslan, James wrote his epistle. James' epistle, says Aslan, was written to Jewish Christians in order to remind them not to wander from the Torah and to warn them to stay away from Paul's ideas. Aslan is convinced that James wrote his epistle in such a way that there is no mistaking James' enmity toward Paul and his theology. We will soon see if Aslan's premise holds up.

Now, as I have already said, there is no denying that there were disputes among the early Christians, and there is certainly no denying the fact that it did not take long for "false teachers" to infiltrate the church. Practically every epistle in the New Testament warns believers of the false teachers in their congregations. That is why the early church quickly set up strong leaders in Jerusalem (the hub for the spreading of the gospel), established order, set down doctrinal beliefs, and held council meetings to discuss relevant issues. Aslan has tried, without success, to have Paul be at odds with the leaders in Jerusalem, to have created his own doctrinal beliefs (that differed from those leaders), and to snub council decisions. Paul, of course, did none of these things, but Aslan wants you to think he did so that he (Aslan) can further his agenda. You must remember that Christianity began as the Jewish fulfillment of the prophecies and promises in the Hebrew Scriptures regarding the Redeeming Messiah (who would later arrive as the Messianic King). Those Jews in the first century who were the first to believe the message that Jesus was the Messiah they had been waiting for had a long history of Laws, traditions, prophecies, promises, and worship. They believed they were God's chosen people and that circumcision, animal sacrifices, the priesthood, the Temple, and their Scriptures proved that they were. Jews had allowed an area at the Temple for Gentiles to worship and had allowed God-fearing Gentiles into the synagogue. However, what upset many of the early Jewish Christians was the idea that Gentiles could actually be on an equal footing with them without being circumcised. The very idea that Gentiles could now come directly to God by faith in Jesus Christ was offensive to many of the Jewish believers (see *The Nelson Study Bible*). Because circumcision was part of a covenant or contract God established with Abraham, and the Mosaic Law was given to the Jews to make them holy or set apart from other nations, it is easy to understand why, for first-century Jewish believers, it would be extremely difficult to say circumcision did not matter anymore or that one need not concern themselves with following parts of the Mosaic Law. Not long after Paul (a Pharisee and rabbi) became a Christian, he and others (see Acts 15:2) were convinced that it was not necessary for Gentile believers to be circumcised as a required step for their salvation; this, in fact, was the decisive conclusion of the Jerusalem Council, of which James was the leader. Paul also believed that the Mosaic Law itself did not lead to salvation, but that it instead showed or revealed how much a person needed salvation. The Mosaic Law was like a mirror, revealing the horrible stain of sin; but it could not permanently remove that stain. The animal sacrifices contained in the Law, as I have noted elsewhere, were only a temporary remedy. The Mosaic Law, therefore, simply pointed to one's need for God's mercy. Paul believed, as did all the other apostles, that that mercy was shown in the death and resurrection of Jesus Christ.

We know from Acts 2 that thousands of Jews became believers in Jesus-as-Messiah after Peter preached his first sermon. Many of these new believers, being Jewish, would be devoted to the Torah (the first five books of the Bible, which includes the Mosaic Law). Now that they accepted Jesus as their Messiah, the imperative query would be how to balance their new belief with the Torah. The essential question on everyone's mind would be: Is the Torah still valid? It certainly stands to reason that Jewish Christians would grapple with this issue and wonder about the relevance of all 613 Jewish laws in the Hebrew Scriptures. How many of these laws now applied to the Jewish

Christian? Gentile Christians questioned whether they were even obligated to follow the Mosaic Law. Some Gentile Christians in the first century had decided that since they were saved by God's grace they could outwardly live the way they wanted to, that laws (or the Law) did not apply to them. Regarding the Law, Paul was adamant about two things: one, the Law cannot save a person, it can only reveal the person's desperate need for salvation; and two, once a person accepts Jesus as their Messiah (Savior), the commandments are to be obeyed. Paul says to the Roman Christians: No one can receive God's approval by following the Mosaic Law; the Law can only show that we are sinners. The way to receive God's approval is through faith in Jesus Christ. This holds true for the Jew and the Gentile. Everyone has sinned; everyone has fallen short of what God's Law demands. We can only receive God's approval through the price Christ Jesus paid on the cross to set us free from sin. God's approval is given to those who believe in Jesus. So, we do not have anything to brag about. Salvation does not come from our own efforts. A person has God's approval because of faith, not because of his/her own efforts. In saying this, are we abolishing the Mosaic Law? That's unthinkable! Rather, we are supporting the Mosaic Law (see Rom 3:20–31). Paul did not reject the Mosaic Law *in toto* and declare that one no longer needed to follow the moral codes within it. Many of the laws within the Mosaic Law had to do specifically with how God wanted the Jews to live, and many of these laws had to do with sacrificial worship. Since sacrificial worship—which involved the Temple, animal sacrifices, and the priesthood—was no longer necessary once one became a Christian, these laws no longer needed to be enforced. However, the moral code that existed within the Mosaic Law was not to be rejected, and Paul never taught that it should be. He believed, like all the leaders of Jerusalem believed, that Love was the fulfillment of the law (see Rom 13:10; James 2:8; 1 Pe 1:22; 1 Jn 3:23). The greatest expression of love was God offering himself to pay the penalty our sins accrued. Love expresses itself in good works. Paul was adamant about that; but he was just as adamant to point out that the good works themselves are impotent for salvation. They must, however, follow salvation.

The Law cannot save us by the doing of it, but it is not to be abolished either. Jesus fulfilled the Law so that his followers can now, with the Holy Spirit's help, fulfill the Law, i.e., perform what God commands. The ultimate law—the Ten Commandments—was still to be honored and obeyed. Friedman has shown how both Paul and Peter continued to remain Torah-observant after they became Christians (see his *They Loved the Torah*). However, not all the laws contained in the Hebrew legal/ceremonial system are applicable to the Christian life. As stated earlier, Jewish Christians no longer had to go to the Temple (before it was destroyed in 70 A.D.) and offer sacrifices for their sins. Jesus had been the ultimate sacrifice and there was no need for continuing that practice. Jewish Christians also had to make a decision about circumcision and its application to their fellow Gentile Christians, which they did do by saying it was no longer necessary. First-century Gentile Christians were given Torah-observant restrictions about what to eat and how to behave (see Acts 15:29). Paul was in total agreement with those stipulations, having mentioned them in his epistles. The Hebrew Scriptures were certainly not abandoned by Paul, who constantly quoted from them to confirm his position. Paul understood and appreciated the "tension" between obeying the Torah and the freedom one enjoys "in Christ." In his epistles, Paul stressed the freedom a Christian has while also cautioning that that freedom not be used to consciously and dismissively sin (Peter agrees with Paul; see 1 Pe 2:16). For Paul, freedom in Christ meant that he could adjust himself to different circumstances so that he could win others to Christ. Paul saw freedom not as an opportunity to sin but as a means to become transformed into the image of Jesus. He says in his first letter to the Corinthian Christians that although he was a free man and a slave to no one, he chose to become a servant to humankind so he could help win some to Jesus. This attitude allowed Paul to enter synagogues wherever he traveled, so he could share the gospel with his fellow Torah-observant Jews. It also allowed him to share the gospel with Gentiles who lived outside the Mosaic Law. He did this so he could win both groups to the Lord. Paul was quick to add that although he was a free man in Christ he was not free from God's law (1 Co 9:19–21).

The "Works of the Law"

Aslan promotes the idea that James and Paul were enemies, that each one taught a different Christology and preached a different gospel. Aslan is sure that Paul was a constant thorn in James' side, and that James retaliated by sending his own men out to hound Paul at every step. Aslan believes there is a difference between Paul's concept of "works of the law" (Rom 3:20) and James'. The difference is that Paul sees these "works of the law" as unnecessary for salvation, and James sees the "works of the law" as a necessary condition for belief in Jesus as one's Savior. Aslan believes that Romans 3-4 and Galatians 2-3 are at odds with James' epistle and provides the "proof" that Paul and James were advancing different views regarding Christianity. Aslan thinks Paul and James were on opposite sides of the fence, but he does not realize there was not even a fence. Paul and James were not preaching opposing ideas in their epistle(s); they were addressing different issues altogether. What Paul is discussing in Romans 3-4 and Galatians 2-3 is a totally different issue from what James is discussing in his epistle. Paul is concerned with the Gentiles being admitted into the family of God, of obtaining God's approval. Now the Jews thought that since they had the Law and the Prophets, they, in a sense, automatically had found God's favor, but Gentiles had to work really hard to get God's approval; the Gentiles had to completely change their ways and adopt the Jewish lifestyle. What Paul was pointing out in Romans 3-4 and Galatians 2-3 (and Jesus pointed out to the Pharisees in the Gospels) was that the Jew and Gentile alike had fallen short of what God wanted, that all of them were guilty of sin, and all of them needed to be redeemed by somebody other than themselves, i.e., Jesus. It is not circumcision or following the Mosaic Law that makes a person righteous before God; it is accepting his gift of salvation through Jesus Christ by faith, not by any "works" that we do. Paul was saying in these passages that circumcision and following the food laws found in the Hebrew Scriptures was not what was going to save anyone. (Peter learned this same lesson when he was given the vision that so-called "unclean" food was now acceptable to eat, and that entering a Gentile house was now acceptable to do, and that preaching to a Gentile family resulted in them receiving the same Holy Spirit that all the apostles and disciples did on Pentecost (see Acts 10).) Paul is opposed to the idea that any so-called good works could lead to salvation. For Paul, and the other apostles, salvation comes by believing in Jesus Christ as one's Lord and Messiah (see Peter's first sermon in Acts 2). Paul did not have a problem with someone who wanted to follow the Mosaic Law; Paul followed many of its commandments throughout his life. The problem arose when someone thought that by following the Law one could be saved, could receive God's approval.

In Paul's epistles, he was constantly reminding his readers that good works followed faith, and that faith did not nullify the Law. Paul had made it a practice to gather monetary contributions from the churches he had established in Asia Minor and Greece and distribute it to the needy believers in Jerusalem (these are the people Aslan says Paul hated). He wrote to the Corinthians letting them know that he was on his way there and would pick up the contribution they had set aside for Jerusalem believers. Paul told the Corinthians that this service of good works that they were doing would be a "proof of your faith" (NCV; compare with James 2:18). The NIV says that this contribution was an act of obedience that accompanied their confession of the gospel of Christ. That is, they were putting their faith to work; they were practicing what they preached. This is exactly the point James makes when he asks the rhetorical question: "What good is it, my brothers and sisters, if someone claims to have faith but has no deeds? Can such faith save them?" (NIV, James 2:14; I will speak more on this passage later). Paul made it clear that he was not preaching a Law-free gospel; he made it clear in his epistles that good deeds play a large part in a Christian's life. In fact, the majority of his epistles included a section where he talked specifically about how a Christian should live now that he/she had been saved. Romans 12–14 shows a striking resemblance to the Sermon on the Mount, found in Matthew's Gospel (chapters 5-7), as Paul lists the kinds of behavior and the type of character he expected to see in those who follow Jesus. (See J.W. Drane's *Introducing the New Testament* for other examples where Paul's writings show that traditions related to Jesus' life and teachings were familiar to the early Gentile churches.) In his letters, Paul regularly informed his readers that now that they were Christians, they were to live "in Christ Jesus," that is, they were to live lives filled with good works (Eph 2:10). Paul insisted that Christians should be enthusiastic about doing good things (Titus 2:14). A Christian is to manifest the fruit of the Spirit, which Paul enumerated in Galatians 5:22f—love, joy, peace, forbearance, kindness, goodness, faithfulness, gentleness and self-control. Paul often talked about our being transformed into the image of Jesus (2 Cor 3:18), and that this transformation included the performing of good deeds. Several times Paul talked about everyone appearing before God's throne on the day of judgment and being judged for the good works they have done (see Rom 2:6). In Romans 14:12, Paul tells us that "each of us will give an account of ourselves to God" (NIV). This concurs with Jesus' warning that we will all give an account on the Day of Judgment for every careless word we've spoken (Mt 12:36). Our words and deeds (and thoughts) are to be God-approved. In 1 Thessalonians 1:3, Paul talks about how the Christians there manifested a "work produced by faith, labor prompted by love, and an endurance inspired by hope in Jesus."

What we find, under no uncertain terms, in Paul's epistles is that no amount of good works was going to lead to a complete restorative reconciliation with God. Attempting to follow one's conscience for the Gentile, or trying to obey the commandments of the Law for the Jew, was not going to lead to salvation. Why? Because everyone falls short of the full requirement; everyone misses the mark (Rom 3:23). No one can stand before God and justify themselves by the good works they have done. For Paul, and the other apostles, salvation comes only by believing in Jesus Christ as one's Lord and Messiah (Peter—one of the "esteemed pillars" of the church—concurs with Paul; see his first sermon in Acts 2). For Paul and the other apostles a person is justified (a legal term) as a free gift from God through the redemption that came by Jesus' death. God presented his Son, Jesus, as a sacrifice of atonement, through the shedding of his blood. This gift of salvation is to be received by faith (see Rom 3:24f). This is the gospel that Paul preached, and it was not shocking or heretical to the other apostles; it was the same gospel they preached. (This is why Islam, Buddhism, Hinduism, and all other religions (including atheism) are opposed to Christianity. It is because Christianity says that a person's good works will not save them; only Jesus Christ can save a person and make them right with God. Following the Eight-fold Path of Buddhism or the Sharia law of Islam might be a nice thing to do, but it will not make you right with God.)

Faith without Works Is Dead

Now, it is true that if you do a mere cursory reading of the Epistle of James, and neglect to do a proper exegetical study of the context of the epistle, that it may appear to put a great, or greater, emphasis on works in comparison to faith and, in doing so, contradict Paul's writings about the subject. For example, James asks the rhetorical question: What good is it, or what benefit is it, if someone claims to have faith but has no deeds or good works to show for it? Can such faith save them? (2:14). James is talking about someone who "claims" to have

390

faith, but there is an absence of good works in that person's life; that person's faith, then, is just a matter of words, not 'works' (see Ellsworth). James shows us that faith without deeds is useless or dead. He demonstrates that Abraham was considered righteous when he offered his son Isaac on the altar. Abraham's faith was tested, and Abraham passed that test, showing that his faith was genuine; it was not mere talk. James concludes that Abraham's faith and his actions were working together, and his "faith was made complete by what he did" (James 2:22). Abraham's faith was genuine enough to show results; it was not just a verbal declaration without a foundation; it was a real faith that showed itself in action. Therefore, what James is addressing in his epistle is how someone's words and deeds, now that they are saved, should be manifested in a believer's life. James is concerned about how a Christian lives his/her life now that they have received the free gift of salvation through Jesus Christ. (Paul, as we have seen, was concerned about that, too.) James shows that faith and the good works that flow from that faith are closely connected. For James, there is no such thing as faith by itself, with nothing to show for it. James does not want his readers—Jewish believers—to think that since they have been saved by faith they no longer have to do good deeds, that somehow the moral code of the Law no longer applies to them.

Even though James and Paul both use Genesis 15:6—Abraham believed God, and God accepted Abraham's faith; it was that faith that made him right with God—they do so for different purposes or reasons. Paul uses Abraham's faith to show that the promises made to Abraham as a result of his faith included Gentiles. Paul uses the Genesis passage to show that following the Mosaic Law, which came some 400 years after this event, does not make one righteous before God. James, on the other hand, uses Genesis 15:6 to make a totally different point—saving faith will be expressed by good deeds (an idea that Paul would also agree with). Those good deeds do not save a person, but they will be expressed in a person who has been saved. Paul and James both understood the relationship between faith and works, and both knew they were not antithetical. So Abraham could be used as an example of both faith (Paul) and good deeds (James). Faith is not contrasted with works; they both operate together. Although Paul and James use the same words—justify, righteous, etc.—they are using the words differently in order to focus on their own particular issues. Paul uses the word "justify" to show that God has pronounced a person as forgiven by their faith in the redemption of Jesus Christ. James uses the word "justify" to mean that a Christian is now to demonstrate that he/she has been changed as a result of their faith. (Some information gleaned from the *Pulpit Commentary* on James and from *Reading Hebrews and James*.)

No Conflict between James and Paul

If James happened to have written his epistle after Paul had been executed, the readers of James's epistle would not think it a new concept that faith and good deeds worked together. Paul had been saying that same thing in his epistles. The so-called conflict between Paul and James is imaginary. James was not trying to thwart or circumvent or nullify what Paul had written. There is nothing in the Epistle of James to show that he was involved in some doctrinal debate with Paul. James and Paul were not preaching opposing ideas in their epistle(s). One is not writing in order to nullify the other; both are writing to focus on particular issues concerning their audience. James is clearly writing to a Jewish Christian audience and therefore makes references to Abraham, Job and Elijah. When James warns his readers that faith without works is dead, he is not writing in order to destroy Paul's thesis, but to show his own readers that they cannot relax in a Pharisaic spirit and live a fruitless life. James reminds us to not merely listen to what the Word tells us, but to do it; he tells us to look intently into the perfect law that gives freedom, and continue in it (1:22, 25). For James, faith is manifested by one's deeds, and those deeds are to be ones of which God would approve. Throughout Paul's epistles, he clearly and consistently admonishes his readers to do good works, thereby agreeing with James.

It is, therefore, of utmost importance to understand that when Paul talks about faith versus works he is talking about one's life before salvation; he is showing that no amount of works can save us, that all the good works we do when added up are not going to be enough. Paul says we all fall short of what God requires (Rom 3:23); we all have sinned and are unable to save ourselves by our own deeds and are therefore in need of a savior. God in his mercy sent his Son, Jesus, to die in our place for our sins so that we can be reconciled to God. We accept God's gift by faith. James, on the other hand, focuses on faith and works after one is saved. James is letting his Christian readers know that now that they are saved they need to have their faith (something inward) manifest itself in good deeds (something outward). We do not place our faith in our works; we place our faith in the redemption of Jesus Christ. But we have a faith that includes good works. Salvation does not come by good works, but good works are produced by the person who is saved. In reading both Paul and James in their context and completeness, we can, with confidence, come to the conclusion that they are in agreement with each other regarding the natural flow of good works from one who is saved. They both agree that once one is a Christian good deeds become a part of his/her life. (Even Luther, who reputedly did not like the Epistle of James, agreed with that; see his excellent little book *A Treatise on Good Works*.) So, Paul emphasized grace and faith, and James emphasized action and works; but they were not at variance with one another. James wanted to see good works follow one's proclamation of faith as evidence, and Paul would not disagree. Anyone can proclaim faith (even demons believe in God—James 2:19); James and Paul both wanted to see evidence of that faith. (See *Opening up James*.)

Comparing Paul and James

To show that Paul wrote in agreement with James, I will provide some passages from several of his epistles that reflect James' views. The first passage is Romans 2:13: "Hearing the law does not make people right with God. It is those who obey the law who will be right with him" (NCV). James tells us: "Do what God's teaching says; when you only listen and do nothing, you are fooling yourselves" (NCV, 1:22). The second passage is Romans 12:2: "Don't become like the people of this world. Instead, change the way you think. Then you will always be able to determine what God really wants—what is good, pleasing, and perfect" ("Scripture is taken from *GOD'S WORD*®. © 1995 God's Word to the Nations. Used by permission of Baker Publishing Group."). James tells us: "Don't you know that friendship with the world means enmity against God?" (NIV, 4:4). A third passage is Romans 14:22f: "Blessed is the one who does not condemn himself by what he approves. But whoever has doubts is condemned if they eat [certain foods], because their eating is not from faith; and everything that does not come from faith is sin" (NIV). James says: "But when you ask, you must believe and not doubt, because the one who doubts is like a wave of the sea, blown and tossed by the wind. That person should not expect to receive anything from the Lord" (NIV, 1:6–7). The fourth passage is 1 Timothy 5:21 where Paul tells Timothy "to do nothing out of favoritism" (NIV). James tells his readers: "believers in our glorious Lord Jesus Christ must not show favoritism" (NIV 2:1). The fifth passage is Titus 3:8 where Paul says those who believe in God should be careful to "devote themselves to doing what is good" (NIV). James says we are to show our wisdom by the good deeds we do (3:13), and, "If anyone, then, knows the good they ought to do and doesn't do it, it is sin for them" (NIV, 4:17). Many more passages could be used, but I hope you see that Paul and James agreed with the kind of life Christians were to lead and both offered similar admonitions regarding proper conduct and thoughts.

A Comment by Matthew Henry

In concluding my remarks on this subject, I would like to include what Matthew Henry, in his commentary on James, says about this supposed disagreement between James and Paul. Henry says that when Paul states that a person is justified by faith, without the deeds of the law (Rom. 3:28), he plainly speaks of another sort of work than James does, but not of another sort of faith. That is clearly important. The works that Paul talks about are those that come in obedience to the Mosaic Law before one accepts the grace of the gospel. The works that James focuses on are those done in obedience to the gospel; they are works that flow as a proper and necessary effect of the Christian's faith. When Paul speaks about justification he uses the word in reference to our being justified before God; when James uses the word he speaks of a person's faith being justified before others. When James says, "Show me your faith without deeds," he is stating the difficulty of demonstrating one's faith without doing good deeds. A Christian's faith is justified in the eyes of those who actually see that faith demonstrated by good works. Paul speaks about a different kind of justification; one that is in the sight of God, who justifies those who believe in the redemption that is in Christ Jesus (Rom 3:24). So, we see that we are justified before God by faith (Paul), and our faith is justified before others by good works (James). Works, therefore, are evidence of faith. Good deeds show the faith is genuine. When James says, "I will show you my faith by my deeds," he is revealing how we can determine whether one has just a verbal declaration of faith or has an actual faith that works. We will know a true follower of Jesus by the fruit (the good works) he/she bears, just as we will know false teachers from the fruit they bear (see Mt 7:15-20). Matthew Henry aptly concludes that "faith is the root, good works are the fruits, and we must see to it that we have both."

We see then that Aslan is mistaken to think that the Epistle of James was written specifically to denigrate Paul's ministry and theology. There is nothing in James' epistle that can be seen as an outright attack on Paul. What we do see, however, is that they agreed faith and works go hand-in-hand, after salvation. One must not overlook Paul's insistence that "God saved you through faith as an act of kindness. You had nothing to do with it. Being saved is a gift from God" ("Scripture is taken from GOD'S WORD®. © 1995 God's Word to the Nations. Used by permission of Baker Publishing Group." Eph 2:8). Nor do we overlook James' insistence that once we are saved faith is to be accompanied by action or else it will be considered a dead faith (Jm 2:17). Paul succinctly declares that our relationship with Jesus is not based on whether we are circumcised or not. What matters is that our faith is expressed through love (Ga 5:6). James concurs by saying: "If you really keep the royal law found in Scripture, "Love your neighbor as yourself," you are doing right" (NIV, 2:8). Both Paul and James follow what Jesus said when a person asked him what the greatest commandment was. Jesus answered him, "'Love the Lord your God with all your heart, with all your soul, and with all your mind.' This is the greatest and most important commandment. The second is like it: 'Love your neighbor as you love yourself.' All of Moses' Teachings and the Prophets depend on these two commandments" ("Scripture is taken from GOD'S WORD®. © 1995 God's Word to the Nations. Used by permission of Baker Publishing Group." Mt 22:37–40).

Chapter Nineteen: Six Questionable Remarks

Aslan, Horsley, the Fellows of the Jesus Seminar, and other liberal theologians/biblical scholars (like Spong, Pagels, Ehrman) have made questionable remarks about the Bible and Christianity, and so I will address them here.

Did Paul Write All the Epistles Attributed to Him?

Aslan says, along with many other liberal theologians (like Horsley), that of the thirteen letters attributed to Paul the apostle had actually written only six or seven of them. These liberal theologians/biblical scholars maintain that Colossians, both epistles to Timothy, Titus, 2 Thessalonians, and a few others were composed years after Paul died in circa 67 A.D. In *The Making of the New Testament*, Patzia gives us two good reasons to question this idea: For one thing, there is no conclusive evidence that any pseudepigraphic epistles or letters were accepted by the early church; and secondly, it would be unethical, dishonest, and deceptive to pass off these forged documents as if they were written by Paul. *The Pulpit Commentary* on 1 Timothy says that if these epistles were not written by Paul, then they "are artful forgeries, written for the express purpose of deceiving . . . written with a pen steeped in lies and falsehood." Aslan, Horsley, and other liberal scholars want us to believe there were non-Pauline epistles being distributed throughout Christian communities in the first century as though they had been written by Paul. If these non-Pauline epistles had been written long after Paul had died, as Aslan claims, the reader would certainly know that Paul was dead and would therefore reject these letters with Paul's name falsely attached to them. Why would the reader allow himself to be fooled? Since truth, honesty, practicing goodness, avoiding hypocrisy, etc., were behaviors that the early Christians were told to adhere to, why would a Christian or a group of Christians be involved in an attempt to deceive the reader into thinking what he/she was reading was from Paul? In fact, 2 Thessalonians, which Aslan asserts was not written by Paul, has Paul warning his readers to reject any false letter that claims to be written by him (2:2). Later on in the letter (3:17), Paul tells his readers that they can tell the letter was from him because of the way he writes (something he also said to his Corinthian readers—1 Cor 16:21). There is no reason for

Paul not to have written to his two protégés—Timothy and Titus—near the end of his life. We meet Timothy in Acts 16, and he so impressed Paul that the apostle took Timothy with him on his missionary journeys. Paul mentions Timothy in Romans, 1 & 2 Corinthians, Philippians, Colossians, 1 & 2 Thessalonians, and Philemon. Titus is mentioned in 2 Corinthians, Galatians, and 2 Timothy. Both men had become bishops in different areas—Timothy in Ephesus, and Titus on Crete—and Paul would certainly have written them letters of encouragement. *The Pulpit Commentary* on 1 Timothy mentions several examples of external evidence that attests to the fact that Paul wrote all the letters (epistles) ascribed to him, of which I will cite four. One, Eusebius, born in the third century, was the first major church historian and wrote that Paul's fourteen epistles (the book of Hebrews included) were "among the universally acknowledged books of Holy Scripture." Two, the "Muratorian Canon (about A.D. 170) includes thirteen Epistles of St. Paul, excluding the Epistle to the Hebrews." Three, the "Peschito Canon (of about the same date) reckons fourteen Epistles of St. Paul, including the Epistle to the Hebrews." (As one can see, there were some debates about the authorship of Hebrews, but the language and content certainly matches Paul's other epistles.) Fourth, early church fathers, like Clement, quote from the epistles of Timothy and Titus and attribute them to Paul. We also see that Colossians and Philemon are closely associated, with Onesimus (a possible convert of Paul's) personally connected to both. Epaphras, a good friend of Paul's, appears to be the one who founded the church in Colossae, and it makes sense that Paul would write a letter to them, probably at Epaphras' request (see Col 4:12). Aslan offers no convincing historical evidence to conclude that Paul did not write/dictate the epistles that bear his name.

Is Peter the Rock of the Church?

After making several references to James, Jesus' brother, as being the principal leader of the church in Jerusalem—the hub of the expanding church—Aslan then reminds us of an episode from the Gospels where Jesus says to Peter: "I tell you that you are Peter, and on this rock I will build my church" (NIV, Mt 16:18). Aslan alleges that there are two problems with this verse: one, this passage in Matthew is the only place where Peter is referred to as the head of the church; and, two, a large number of scholars reject this passage as nonhistorical. Since

Matthew is the only one who records this episode, Aslan says this passage is to be disputed, basing his claim upon the fact that lots of scholars reject this passage. Of course, the scholars who dispute it are the Fellows of the JS and a few other liberal theologians/biblical scholars who reject any and all passages if they are not repeated in another Gospel. Their methodology, as we saw in Chapter One, is heavily disputed and should be rejected. In order to understand this episode, we need to see it in its context, and we need to look at a couple of Greek words. Clearly, the Gospels see Peter, as well as James and John Zebedee, as important disciples of Jesus. The Gospels also clearly show the character flaws in each of them. In bringing up this episode, Aslan is obviously pointing out what he thinks is a discrepancy; in other words, if Jesus said Peter is the head of the church, then why was James the principal leader in Jerusalem. The thing to determine, of course, is: Was Jesus actually saying, in this passage, that Peter was the head of the church? Let's look at the context of this passage.

Jesus had earlier fed more than five thousand people from a few morsels. Jesus had walked on water during which time Peter had displayed a lack of faith. Jesus explained the spirit of the Law to Pharisees who should not have needed it explained to them. Jesus entered Gentile territory and healed a Gentile woman's daughter. Jesus fed more than four thousand people who came to have him heal their loved ones from diseases and disabilities. Jesus rebuked the Pharisees for their constant demand of a sign and told them the only sign he would give them was his resurrection (cloaking it within the story of Jonah, which the Pharisees knew well and should have understood what Jesus was hinting at). Then Jesus and his apostles arrived at another Gentile territory, Caesarea Philippi. The city was about 1,150 feet above sea level and sat in a plain at the foothills of Mount Hermon. Nearby were tall rocky bluffs and rugged mountain peaks (see *Holman Illustrated Bible Dictionary*). One of the main sources for the Jordan River was there, along with some nice tree groves, and it was a very beautiful area where Jesus and his apostles could relax for a while. But it was also a religious/political site. Baal had been worshipped there in ancient times; the Greek god Pan had been worshipped there; and decisive battles had been fought there. Herod the Great, the killer of innocent male babes, had built a marble temple there to Augustus Caesar. Philip the tetrarch had made improvements to the city and, in honor of Augustus and himself, gave it the name Caesarea Philippi (see *New Bible Dictionary*).

It was in this setting, where other gods had been worshipped and battles fought, that Jesus asked his disciples: Who do people say I am? The disciples said that some thought he was John the Baptizer, while others said Elijah, Jeremiah or one of the prophets. Jesus then asked his disciples: Who do you say I am? It was Peter who answered for everyone, saying: You are the Messiah, the Son of the living God. Jesus told Peter that he (Peter) was blessed to know this great truth. Jesus told Peter that he had not discovered it on his own, but it was Jesus' Father in heaven who had made it known to him. Then Jesus said to Peter, whose common name was Simon: I tell you that you are Peter, and on this rock I will build my church, and the gates of Hell will not overcome it. Now Jesus was being quite clever here; he had picked a great setting to teach his disciples something very important, and it centered upon the words "Peter" and "rock." The Greek word for Peter is *Petros*, and the Greek word for "rock" is *Petra*. Now, that does not seem like a big difference, but *Petros* means a stone or pebble that you can throw (that was Peter); and *Petra* is a huge rock, like the rocky cliffs that soared above them. *Petra* is a massive rock, something unmovable and fixed; *Petros* is a pebble, easily thrown. Jesus is making a huge contrast to reveal the powerful foundation that his church was going to be built upon. (One of the reasons the Fellows of the Jesus Seminar reject this passage is because they do not believe Jesus ever made reference to a future church that would be established in his name.) Peter has just proclaimed that Jesus was the Messiah, the Son of God. The situation could have looked like this: Jesus points at Peter and says, "You are a little pebble who has made this grand and truthful declaration," and then points at the huge cliffs above them and says, "It is on the foundation of my being the Messiah, the Son of God, this massive rock, that my church will be built." Jesus was not putting his future church on Peter's shoulders; Jesus was saying that his future church would have its foundation in him (Jesus). Jesus as the Messiah, the Son of God, would be the rock that the church would be built upon. (The Romish Church misinterpreted this passage, possibly deliberately, and established their papal system upon it, bringing centuries of misery upon the peoples of the Medieval Period.)

Later on in Matthew, Jesus will refer to himself as the cornerstone (see 21:42). A cornerstone is the capstone of a building and is considered an essential part of its construction (see the *Greek-English Lexicon of the New Testament*); the cornerstone is the keystone of the upper corner which not only unites and strengthens the whole building but is also at the very summit of it (see *The Complete Word Study Dictionary*). Jesus is both the foundation and the upper capstone of the church, the spiritual body of believers. Not Peter. In fact, Peter agrees that Jesus is the cornerstone; he also believed that Jesus was the Petra (the solid, foundational rock) and stated such in his first epistle (see 1 Pet 2:4–8). Paul understood this as well and told the Corinthian believers that the only true foundation for the church is Jesus Christ (see (1 Cor 3:11). When Jesus told Peter, "I will give you the keys of the kingdom of heaven," we see that taking place at Pentecost when Peter became the spokesperson and gave his first sermon telling his listeners that although they had been instrumental in killing Jesus that Jesus rose from the dead and is the Lord and Messiah (see Acts 2). All of the apostles, not just Peter, had the "keys of the kingdom of heaven." Soon after Jesus had said this to Peter and the other apostles, Jesus told them that when he arrived in Jerusalem he would be killed, but on the third day would rise from the dead. Peter, in an emotional fit, actually rebuked Jesus for saying this. Jesus had to use forceful words to show Peter how he was being influenced by Satan. This entire passage in Matthew shows that it is not Peter who was designated as the head of the church; he is not the foundation upon which it is built. Jesus is. Aslan is severely mistaken to think that this passage in Matthew is the only place in the New Testament that appoints Peter to be the head of the church. There is no passage in the New Testament that declares Peter to be the head of the church!

Did the Diaspora Jews Write the Gospels?

As we have seen, Aslan devised at least ten schemes based on his major theory that Jesus was just a Jewish nationalist, an extreme zealot. Those schemes are: One, Jesus of Nazareth was a Jewish peasant from Galilee who gathered some followers in an attempt to restore Israel's independence. Two, Jesus preached that God's kingdom was a physical entity that could not happen without the restoration of Israel. Three, Jesus created a new world order paradigm for his restored Israel. Four, Jesus campaigned against the Temple, the priests and scribes, and the Roman army. Five, Jesus was a bigoted Jew who cared only for the Jewish people. Six, Jesus made no claim that he was the promised Messiah of the Hebrew Scriptures. Seven, Jesus' attempt to restore Israel's independence led to his arrest as a zealot, and he was convicted and executed for sedition. Eight, since Jesus' mission ended in his death, no one needed to believe in his cause anymore. Nine, someone, for some reason, decided his story should continue, and so this failed zealot needed to rise from the dead as the Messiah. A new beginning would occur with an empty tomb. Ten, the Gospel writers, in creating this "new" story about Jesus, rejected the peasant, rejected the zealot, rejected the person concerned about overthrowing the priesthood and Roman oppression, and suggested instead that Jesus was not just the Messiah but that he was God incarnate. I have addressed these ten schemes in this book and have shown how and why Aslan was mistaken about each one.

For Aslan, Jesus should have been less than a footnote in the annals of history, like all the other forgotten zealots of his time. Aslan wants to know how this failed messiah/zealot who died a criminal's death on a cross could have been turned into the creator of the universe, God incarnate, in a matter of a few years. Actually, it took less than two months. As we have seen, Peter, in his first sermon forty days after Jesus was executed, preached a sermon at or near the Temple courtyard, and told thousands of Jews that Jesus was Yahweh (the Lord Almighty, the creator of all things) and Messiah (Acts 2). The Gospels even declare that Jesus' followers became convinced that Jesus was the Messiah, the Son of God, during the three years they were with Jesus. His miracles and sermons, his compassion and love, attested to that fact. Their belief in Jesus as the Son of God was affirmed three days after Jesus was executed when he rose from the dead. It was the resurrection, the empty tomb, the appearances of Jesus to individuals and groups as large as five hundred people that caused his followers to see him as God in the flesh. If you read modern books on Jesus, like Aslan's, Horsley's, Borg's, Crossan's, Ehrman's, Spong's, or any of the others that deny that Jesus is God, you see that they flippantly and simply deny the resurrection of Jesus, but they do not really offer considerable "proof" that the resurrection did not happen; they simply deny that it happened. They try to make it into some spiritual phenomenon that is only to be accepted as a motivator towards becoming a better person.

There was no process that took place over a number of years whereby Jesus gradually went from a peasant and zealot to a miracle worker, then a Messiah, and then God. The church was quickly established in Jerusalem as the epicenter and spread out like spokes on a wheel. It went eastward to the Jews and Gentiles in Babylon, and beyond; it went southward to Arabia, to Alexandria and Ethiopia and other North African nations; it went northward to Damascus and Antioch in Syria; and it traveled westward into Asia Minor, Greece, and Rome. Within a generation the message that Jesus was the Redeeming Messiah, the long awaited "seed of the woman" (a promise that had found its way into a vast majority of pagan nations), had spread throughout the Roman Empire, and beyond. Although it began by the use of oral traditions, within that first generation of followers three Gospels had been written. The Hebrew Scriptures declared that the Messiah would arrive in order to break the curse of the first death (the spiritual death) by providing the ultimate sacrifice (his life) in order to restore humans back to God. The only one worthy of doing this would be God himself. The Gospel writers believed that Jesus fulfilled that promise. No other person in history has or could have fulfilled that promise. The Gospel writers and early Christians believed they were interpreting the Hebrew Scripture passages regarding the Redeeming Messiah accurately. It was the false teachers that arose that began to reinterpret the Scriptures (the false teachers spoken against in the majority of the New Testament epistles), and the Church has continued throughout its history to contend with the ideas and "rethinking" of these false teachers (see Jude).

What reason does Aslan give for people believing that a failed zealot eventually evolved into God-in-the-flesh? What would compel them to believe this? Aslan says the answer lies in a significant fact that he and others have discovered. This fact is that just about everything written down in the four canonical Gospels was written by people who did not personally know the historical Jesus of Nazareth. According to Aslan, Jesus became God due to the evolving beliefs of those who did not know Jesus. Aslan knows him, though. Aslan knows that Jesus was just a peasant and magician. Aslan knows that Jesus was just a zealot who said a few condemnatory things about the priests and the Roman oppressors, and then was killed for doing so. Aslan is certain that those who did not know the historical Jesus made up a bunch of lies about him, some forty to eighty years after his death. Now, the reason they would do this is still not totally clear. Why did they pick Jesus and not some other person? Maybe Jesus is just a compilation of several zealots. So, who were these Gospel writers? If the Gospels were not written by anyone who knew Jesus, as Aslan claims, who then wrote them? Aslan thinks that a group of Greek-speaking, educated Jews living in the major cities throughout the Roman Empire (due to the Diaspora after 70 A.D.) had been the real impetus that helped expand the new faith known as the Jesus movement. These Diaspora Jews would be the influence and/or writers of the Gospels we have today. These scattered Jews, who did not personally know Jesus, created a new Jesus forty or more years after Jesus was executed. According to Aslan, the Diaspora Jews had reached a point in their theology where they were more open to new and exotic interpretations of the Hebrew Scriptures, especially those suggested by Jesus' followers. Of course, the idea that the Gospels present a new and exotic interpretation of the Hebrew Scriptures is an old, but false, criticism from liberal theologians, and Aslan is simply reiterating their worldview.

Aslan thinks that Hellenistic Jews (i.e., Jews who had become entrenched in Greek culture, customs and language) were responsible for gradually adding different doctrines to their belief system, so that little by little, over the years, seminal Christianity (which was more rural-based) evolved into an urbanized, Greek-inspired religion. So, Aslan (as well as Horsley and others) creates a whole new history of the beginnings of Christianity, but his innovative re-creation is simply based on the ideas and writings of modern liberal theologians who follow in the footsteps of the false teachers that Jesus and the New Testament epistles warned us about. It is odd that these Diaspora Jews would do this since Christianity, at this time, was a movement whose followers were being heavily persecuted. Aslan wants you to believe that while people were compiling the Gospels—people who had never known Jesus personally—they must have brainstormed all the different scenarios that might make the story more interesting. They would have Jesus say all sorts of nice things and have him do all kinds of neat tricks (miracles); he would be a type of marionette in their hands. They would find passages—no matter how obscure—in the Hebrew Scriptures to use to "prove" that Jesus was the promised Messiah. Certainly the poor Jews who had lost their Temple and their city could use a Messiah right now. While they were at it, they could write several versions, each one emphasizing a different aspect of the zealot qua Messiah. There would be one for the Jews; one for Greek Christians; one for Roman (Latin) Christians; and maybe one that was kind of mystical to satisfy those kinds of people.

If the Gospel writers were creating this Jesus near the end of the first century, as Aslan claims, who was it for? Who was the audience? Who would have read and followed these Gospels? Who would have cared about a zealot that had been dead for sixty years? Gentiles did not need a savior figure; they had lots of gods they could pray to. They certainly did not need a Jewish god. Were the Jews who had been scattered after the destruction of Jerusalem in A.D. 70 looking for a messiah who would come, once for all, and beat the Romans up? If so, it certainly would not be the Christian's messiah. Aslan claims that by the second century Christians had abandoned the Jews, but, of course, it is not that simple. Jews were not abandoned. Many Jews, even before the destruction of Jerusalem in 70 A.D., had rejected Jesus as their Messiah. Jews had distanced themselves further from Christians by the end of the first century. In the third decade of the second century, Simon bar Kokhba led the final Jewish revolt against Rome; the Jews had seen him as their messiah. The Bar Kokhba Revolt, the Mishnah, and eventually the Talmud would solidify Jews' rejection of Jesus as their Messiah. It appears that Aslan chooses a date for the Gospels during a time when both Jews and Gentiles could really not care less.

Aslan must dismiss the fact that there are historical reasons to conclude that Matthew and John—close followers of Jesus—wrote the Gospels that bear their names; that Matthew wrote his Gospel in the early to mid-60s, and John wrote his in the 80s or early 90s. Aslan must dismiss the fact that it is historically reasonable to conclude that Mark's Gospel was based on the eye-witness account of Peter, a close follower of Jesus, and was written in the early to mid-60s. Aslan must dismiss the fact that it is historically reasonable to conclude that Luke, a physician and historian, wrote his Gospel after considerable research; and that it too, like Matthew and Mark, was written in the early to mid-60s. Aslan dismisses all of this because it does not fit his worldview, his mindset. Christianity is deeply concerned with historical evidence; it does not ask you to believe in something ethereal, unintelligible, or fabricated. That is why Aslan is so completely mistaken to think that early Christians cared nothing for history, cared nothing for truth, cared nothing for reliable statements about God and Jesus. That is why Aslan is mistaken to think that some Diaspora Jews, who did not know

Jesus personally, wrote some fabricated stories about Jesus at the end of the first century which would later be turned into what is known as the four canonical Gospels.

Two Choices—A False Dilemma

Aslan believes Jesus' death left the early church with only two choices. Either Jesus was a failed messiah, like so many other zealots. Or the Jews were mistaken about their expected messiah, and so their expectations or ideas had to be adjusted. What Aslan is doing here is setting up a scenario called the false dilemma. He offers two options, but in reality there is only one to choose from; and the one option he is really offering comes with some stipulations attached to it that make it an undesirable choice as well. The first option is to declare that Jesus was a failed messiah, which of course is an option the early church would reject. This is really not a true option for them. The second option is to declare that the Jews were wrong concerning what they expected the messiah to do and be, and so their expectations had to be readjusted. Now, on the surface, this second option is the one that I have been suggesting in this book. I have shown that the Hebrew Scriptures, beginning with the promise of the "seed of the woman," talk about one Messiah and two arrivals. In the first arrival, he comes as a Redeeming Messiah, as a once-for-all sacrifice for the sins of the world, opening the door for all who accept him as their savior to enter the Kingdom of God, a spiritual realm in which the believer is restored to a proper relationship with God; a relationship that had been broken by sin and repaired by Jesus' blood. Just as God had used Abraham and his descendants to bring in the promised "seed of the woman," God is now using the time period known as the Church Age—the fullness of the Gentiles—to bring people from all nations (another promise God had made to Abraham) into his Kingdom. When the Church Age has run its course the Messiah will return a second time to establish the Messianic Kingdom.

We see throughout the Hebrew Scriptures that God's time table is different from our own. It is understandable, knowing what the Jews had experienced from the Babylonian exile to Herod Antipas, that the Jews would want a Messiah King to release them from the oppression they had been under for so long. It is understandable that they would rally behind every zealot that stood up to their oppressors. It is

405

understandable that they would want Jesus, who had the power to heal diseases and raise the dead, to be their King and attack the Roman Empire. But though their desire and hope and anger were understandable, their plan was not God's plan. God's plan was to first deal with the problem of sin, to heal the terrible wound created by our rebellion. The problem was (and is) our sin; the solution was (and is) the Redeeming Messiah. The Jews during Jesus' time did not want their Messiah going around telling them that they were sinners and needed salvation; that they were like whitewashed tombs, all pretty on the outside but dead inside; that they needed to recognize their spiritual poverty more than they concentrated on their physical poverty. That is what Jesus did, and that is why they rejected him. They had in mind a different kind of Messiah. They were not willing to accept God's plan, and that had been their problem throughout their history—their own Scriptures attested to that. So, Aslan's second option that what the Jews of Jesus' time expected of the messiah was wrong and had to be adjusted is correct, but Aslan does not stop there. He adds some stipulations to his second option that makes it just as meaningless and unacceptable as his first option. Aslan claims that the early church was forced to find a reason to reject the first option, while verifying the second one, and found it in two apocalyptic books called 1 Enoch and 4 Ezra, two books that he says were written long after Jesus' death. Aslan thinks that when the church accepted 1 Enoch and 4 Ezra to explain their views that Jesus was the Messiah it actually dismissed Jesus' own self-understanding and made him into something he would have rejected. Aslan claims that after the destruction of Jerusalem in 70 A.D. the Christians turned the man Jesus of Nazareth into a messiah who was preexistent, divine, lived in a heavenly world, and would be coming again to judge those who rejected him. Since Christians accepted the second option—that the Jews were mistaken about their messiah—they had to justify it. Aslan says the only way they could justify this belief was to accept the apocalyptic imagery of 1 Enoch and 4 Ezra. Now, remember, Aslan (and the JS) does not accept the apocalyptic sayings of Jesus, and so he is not going to accept those found in 1 Enoch or 4 Ezra either. Aslan simply says this is your only choice: if you think the Jews were wrong about the Messiah's first arrival being the establishment of the Kingdom of God as the political and physical restoration of Israel, then all you can use to prove your point are these two books that are not even in the canonical Hebrew Scriptures. Aslan says the early church used these two apocalyptic books—1 Enoch and 4 Ezra—to change Jesus' image of himself into something else.

According to Aslan, Jesus had a messianic secret about a new world order where he and his followers were going to subdue the religious leaders and the Roman army and free Israel. It did not work out that way. So, what Jesus' followers did, says Aslan, is announce that Jesus is coming a second time and then he will undoubtedly bring in the Messianic Kingdom. Aslan says the early church came up with this idea of a second arrival of the messiah by using the apocalyptic imagery found in 1 Enoch and 4 Ezra, which were written, Aslan claims, long after Jesus' death. Aslan needs them to be long after Jesus' death because he has the Gospels written long after Jesus' death—Mark in the 70s; Matthew and Luke in the 80s to 90s; John in the first two decades of the second century. Aslan also needs them to be long after Jesus' death because that way he can "prove" that the early Christians did not believe Jesus would come a second time; that it was a belief developed many years later, prompted by 1 Enoch and 4 Ezra. Is Aslan correct about the dating of 1 Enoch and 4 Ezra? Not exactly. The Book of Enoch is a compilation of stories, written by a variety of writers, beginning in the first two centuries B.C.; it was, in a sense, a work in progress, finished by the first century A.D. It is considered an important piece of Jewish writing containing strong religious content, but it has not been fully accepted as worthy to be included in with the prophets of the Hebrew Scriptures. Catholic Bibles (and some Protestant ones) do include these books, and other pseudepigraphs like them, as appendixes. The Book of Enoch is divided into five sections with a total of 108 chapters. Aslan mentions 1 Enoch, which would be the first thirty-six chapters. The Book of Enoch was a valuable resource for Jews and early Christians alike, in the first century. In fact, Jude, one of the epistle writers in the New Testament, quotes from Enoch (vs.14f). Just about every religious idea or subject important to its Jewish readers is addressed in the Book of Enoch—the future destiny of the wicked and the righteous, the demoralization of humankind, the messianic kingdom, some parables on the judgment of the wicked, writings about the Son of Man, the resurrection of the dead, praise for the Messiah and God, judgment of earthly rulers, and more. They, therefore, address many of the themes already found in the Hebrew Scriptures. The other apocalyptic book Aslan mentions is 4 Ezra, which was probably written in the second or first century B.C. as well, although the final editing of the book is assumed to have been in the early part of the second century A.D. 4 Ezra contains twelve chapters, numbered 3-14; they consist of seven visions by Ezra the scribe. In each vision Ezra asks different questions of God and receives answers from him. Many of these questions that Ezra asks God are found throughout the Hebrew Scriptures, so there is nothing really new here either. Since 4 Ezra had its final editing in the early part of the second century it is easy to see that it was just as likely that Christianity had an influence on it as it had on Christianity. (Some information gleaned from *Pseudepigrapha of the Old Testament*.)

In Aslan's attempts to use 1 Enoch and 4 Ezra to "prove" his theory about Jesus going from zealot to messiah to God incarnate, we get a glimpse into his methodology. He first rejects any and all apocalyptic sayings of Jesus found in the Gospel narratives. Then, he asserts that Jesus failed as a messiah because he got himself killed before the revolution even began. Next, he claims that Jesus' followers, for some reason, decided to keep his memory alive and therefore had to come up with something that would entice other people to join their new religion. They found their answer in the apocalyptic writings of 1 Enoch and 4 Ezra. With these two apocalyptic writings, the church now had some material they could use to turn Jesus of Nazareth into a preexistent, divine being called the "Son of Man." After the destruction of Jerusalem in 70 A.D., the church had to make Jesus into something other than the zealot Aslan says he was. The problem, of course, with Aslan's theory is that the initial Christians had already believed Jesus to be the preexistent, heavenly, and divine Son of Man, one whose "kingdom" was not of this world. There was no need for a new messianic paradigm. Jesus' followers did not need to use 1 Enoch and 4 Ezra to come up with information to compensate for a failed messiah. The early Christians already had Matthew, Mark, and Luke's Gospels before the Revolt began in 66 A.D. The false dilemma that Aslan created to try to prove that Jesus failed and that his followers therefore had to come up with a quick remedy (which they found in two popular apocalyptic writings that allowed them to fashion a new messianic paradigm) has itself failed and fallen flat. There was no reason to come up with a new messianic paradigm because the first one still worked quite well.

The Pseudo-Clementine Documents

The fifth questionable remark demonstrates Aslan's desperation by his use of the Pseudo-Clementine documents to try to prove his theory. Aslan says these documents confirm his (Aslan's) belief that the "esteemed pillars"—James, Peter, John—along with the other apostles considered Paul to be a rogue apostle. Aslan believes the other apostles mistrusted and disliked Paul so much that they went to great lengths to refute his teachings, warn others about him, and send out people to the churches he founded so they could correct Paul's deviant ideas. As we have seen from Chapters Sixteen, Seventeen, and Eighteen, Aslan is clearly mistaken. The fabricated scenario that Aslan has created is so blatantly ridiculous that it would be laughable except for the sad fact that many will believe it simply because Aslan has written it. He routinely accuses the Gospel writers of embellishment and fabrication, but we have seen throughout Aslan's *Zealot* that he is the one who stands to be legitimately accused of such an offense. To show to what extent Aslan will try to convince you that his theories should be believed, he turns to the Pseudo-Clementine documents for help. Aslan makes a reference to an Ante-Nicene document called *Recognitions* and assumes that James' "enemy" in the document was Paul. The Pseudo-Clementine writings are referred to as "Clementina;" they are a compilation of fictional writings that appear to be written for a Jewish Christian audience. Surprisingly, there is no mention of Paul in them, although he was a Jewish Christian. The writings within the Clementina are considered literature and are therefore classified as fictitious writing. There is no definitive evidence regarding the authors of the stories, nor of the exact date of their composition. The initial writings could be as early as the latter half of the second century, or sometime in the first half of the third century. The writer of the *Recognitions* chose Jesus' disciples and their followers as his main characters in the fictitious stories; since this is fiction, the author(s) is not presenting his ideas as facts. What he has done is put his own ideas and beliefs into the mouths of his characters (this, of course, is what the Jesus Seminar accuse the Gospel writers of doing with Jesus). Since Paul is not named in the Clementina, it is, of course, odd to suggest, as Aslan does, that one of the stories contains anti-Pauline sentiment.

Here is a summary of the story that Aslan thinks indicates that the apostles, and especially James, considered Paul's teachings to be heretical: The fictitious narrator of the story says that he was present at a meeting where it was said that Satan had sent out his own apostles to deceive the Christian church. Therefore, since Satan's apostles had infiltrated the church, it was important to shun or reject any person, whether they be an apostle, teacher or prophet, who did not accurately align his/her teachings or preaching with that of James, Jesus' brother. One of the apostles or teachers whom Satan had sent to deceive the church was named Simon who, under pretence, claimed to preach in the name of the Lord but was actually sowing error. (See *Pseudo-Clement of Rome*.) So, Aslan uses a piece of fiction (a novel) as "proof" that Paul was considered an outcast; a piece of fiction that was written one hundred to two hundred years after Paul was executed. And in that piece of fiction, Paul was not even named. Aslan is assuming the person called Simon is a reference to Paul. This is how far Aslan will go to try to propagate his agenda.

Were the Gospels Written to Support Paul's Christology?

Aslan thinks that the church's belief in Jesus as God incarnate is purely the result of Paul's letters, which, of course, mirrored his Christology. The only information many Christians received about Jesus, especially Gentile Christians, was from Paul, and Aslan says Paul was uninterested in the historical Jesus (a claim I believe I refuted in Chapter Seventeen). Aslan is sure that the only Jesus Gentile Christians outside of Jerusalem knew was a cosmic, preexistent Messiah that Paul manufactured in defiance of the apostles who actually knew Jesus. Aslan wants you to think that the only information and knowledge that Gentile Christians had of Jesus came from the writings of Paul, before 70 A.D. All other information about Jesus—the four Gospels, and the epistles of James, Jude and John—were all written after Paul's death and were written (except for James' epistle) to validate Paul's Christology. According to Aslan, Horsley, and others, it was Paul's Christology that survived the Revolt, not the seminal Christianity of the apostles. Aslan has to, of course, once again claim that if there were any writings about Jesus before Paul wrote his epistles, then they would be found in the 'Q' document. As I have said many times within these pages, there is ample evidence to show that three of the Gospels—Matthew, Mark and Luke—were written within Paul's lifetime, as were the epistles of James, Peter, and

Jude. It has already been established that Aslan, the Jesus Seminar, and other liberal theologians need to put late dates on the Gospels because that is the only way they can try to give some credence to their theories and agenda. That is why Aslan must contend, for the sake of his agenda, that Paul's letters influenced the Gospel writers. The Gospel writers, according to Aslan, took the ideas that Paul had about Jesus and created a huge, fabricated story around them. Aslan claims that Mark and Matthew's Gospels reveal only a silhouette or outline of Paul's theology and Christology. Luke's Gospel, since he was a disciple of Paul's, is more fundamental about Paul's views about Jesus. But if you really want to know what Paul thought about Jesus, you will find it, says Aslan, in the Gospel of John; it is John's Gospel that clearly presents Paul's Christology in story format. By claiming that Paul's letters are our only true source of knowing anything about Jesus (pre-Revolt), and that the Gospels were written as fabricated stories about Jesus based on Paul's letters, Aslan is summing up a major point of his thesis: Christianity was invented by Paul, who knew nothing of the historical Jesus. Aslan's assumption, however, does not agree with history.

In Peter's first letter, he wrote to Christians living in the provinces of Pontus, Galatia, Cappadocia, Asia and Bithynia (1 Pet 1:1). There is no evidence in Acts or in Paul's epistles that Paul established any churches in Pontus, Cappadocia, and Bithynia. We also know that Paul did not "found" the church in Rome, Colossae or Laodicea. John mentioned some churches in Smyrna, Pergamum, Thyatira, Sardis, and Philadelphia (Rev 2–3), and none of them seem to have been established by Paul. Even though John may have written the Revelation in the 80s or 90s, these churches had obviously been around long enough to have developed a deficiency in their spiritual condition (Melick). Paul had seen the risen Jesus about five years after Jesus' ascension. Paul was on his way to arrest Christians in Syria. Obviously, Paul had not "founded" the "churches" there, which would include at least the cities of Damascus and Antioch (the diverse congregation where believers were first given the nomenclature "Christian"). Paul did not invent Christianity. Paul did not invent the risen Jesus; he saw the risen Jesus and it totally changed his life. His whole life took a completely different turn. He was being groomed to be one of the most intelligent, young rabbis in Jerusalem. He had a solid future ahead of him. He was becoming well established in the

Pharisaic movement that was determinedly focused on wiping out the followers of Jesus. But Paul, en route to arresting some of those followers, met the one they were following; and he became a follower too. No wonder there were so many Jews who thereafter tried to thwart Paul at every step. Instead of holding a lucrative teaching position in Jerusalem, or possibly becoming a member of the Sanhedrin, Paul instead lived a life devoted to Jesus Christ, a life where he was frequently imprisoned, flogged, pelted with stones, shipwrecked, in danger crossing rivers, endangered by bandits while traveling on the roads, imperiled by his own countrymen (Jews), by Gentiles, and false believers. He had gone without food, water, proper clothes, and sleep (see 2 Cor 11:23–28). Why would he do this? Because he had seen the risen Jesus and understood, for the first time, the meaning of the wonderful promises and prophecies within the Hebrew Scriptures that he loved and continued to quote from in his epistles. The early church, long before Paul began writing his letters in the 50s and 60s, had already arrived at the conclusion that Jesus was the Lord (Yahweh) and Messiah (see Acts 2:36). There were quite a few churches that Paul had not established during his three missionary journeys, and those believers already believed that Jesus was the Son of God who died to reconcile humans back to God. It is interesting to see that Peter and Paul used the same phrase in their letters to describe Jesus: "Praise be to the God and Father of our Lord Jesus Christ!" (NIV, 1 Pet 1:3; 2 Cor 1:3; Eph 1:3). Paul and the other apostles were all in agreement as to whom Jesus was. Paul did not invent the Christianity that we know today; he was proclaiming the truth about Jesus that Christians had been teaching since seeing the risen Christ.

Aslan thinks that because the Gospels mirror Paul's Christology that they were fabricated based on Paul's teachings. But it is not that one can trace Pauline theology in the Gospels, as if they were written to promote Paul's ideas of Jesus. The fact that one can trace Paul's theology in the Gospels shows that they were all in sync with their conception of Jesus. There was no contradiction between the synoptic Gospel writers and Paul as they wrote contemporaneously with one another. The fact that Mark and Matthew's Gospels reveal Paul's Christology is actually a good testimony to the fact that Paul was aware of those Gospels when he was writing his letters. We know from Galatians 1:18 that Paul met with Peter and James (Jesus' brother) to learn more about Jesus the man, showing how interested

412

Paul was in Jesus of Nazareth. Aslan believes Luke's Gospel provides a more fundamental or basic rendering of Paul's views about Jesus, but it is quite possible that Luke wrote his Gospel before he even met Paul. When we meet Luke in Acts he is in Troas and travels with Paul, who is on his second missionary journey, for a short while before going back to Troas, and then joins Paul later on a more permanent basis. It is possible Luke was busy researching either for his Gospel as he said he had done (Lk 1:3), or he was already finished with his Gospel and was busy writing the first half of his sequel—Acts. Aslan has no evidence that Luke wrote his Gospel specifically to promote Paul's view of Jesus. The facts actually show that the Gospel writers and the apostles, including Paul, were all on the same page regarding their view of Jesus. It was not that Paul had influenced the Gospel writers; the fact was, they were all influenced by the risen Jesus and wrote in harmony with one another about him (Jesus). If there is conformity between what John's Gospel says about Jesus and what Paul says in his letters about Jesus, that is because they were in agreement with the historical facts, not that John wrote in order to verify Paul. They were not writing to verify each other's theories (not like what the liberal theologians/biblical scholars do today); they were writing about the historical Jesus they knew. John's Gospel is a powerful narrative about the life and ministry of Jesus, and that is why so many liberal theologians attack it and attempt to discredit it. Aslan is compelled to maintain that the Gospels were not written by anyone who knew Jesus because the Gospels comply with Paul's doctrinal ideas, and Aslan believes that Paul and all the other apostles hated each other. That is also why Aslan and other liberal theologians/biblical scholars claim that Peter did not write 2 Peter, because in it Peter calls Paul "our dear brother" (3:15). Aslan has to dismiss any evidence that shows that Paul and the other apostles were on friendly terms, but in dismissing the evidence Aslan shows that he is more interested in maintaining his erroneous theories than he is with historical facts.

Aslan believes that Paul created Jesus-as-Christ and in doing so completely consumed (eliminated) Jesus of Nazareth, the historical Jesus. In other words, Paul's Christ-of-faith ideology—which is the Christianity of today—has completely rid itself of the historical Jesus, the real Jesus that Aslan calls the zealot. Aslan thinks the Christ we know today is based on Paul's own creation and vision, and not based on those who knew Jesus—the eleven apostles. Aslan thinks we should be grateful to him and the other liberal theologians/biblical scholars that the Jesus-as-zealot was not utterly lost, stricken from history. Aslan claims that there is very little in the Gospels or the rest of the New Testament that is true. For Aslan, the New Testament is a collection of fables, fabricated stories that turned an unknown zealot into a messiah. Again, we have to wonder why the New Testament writers would do this. What would be their reason for making this up? Why would the original followers of Jesus melt into oblivion, as Aslan wants us to believe, only to have a young rabbi, five years after Jesus' horrific death, turn away from his lucrative future and make things up about a person he did not know personally? Aslan thinks he has reintroduced us to the Jesus-of-history. Where did Aslan get his information? How does he know that Jesus was just an illiterate Jewish zealot who decided to form a mob that would challenge the Roman occupation and, while he was at it, get rid of the Temple priesthood too? Did Aslan get his information from historical documents? No, he learned it from the liberal theologians and non-believing Religious Studies professors that have come into popularity since the early part of the 20th century. The writings of Bultmann, Ehrman, Spong, Crossan, Borg, Horsley, Pagels, and others have all attempted to make Jesus into a mere man and to discredit the reliability and historicity of the New Testament. Is it because they have found the truth and want all of us to know it? Or is it because they, for whatever reason, are similar to the false teachers the early Christians had to contend with?

Aslan thinks it is a shame that we have believed Paul's version of Jesus because the version that Aslan believes in is much better. Aslan likes the Jesus he has fabricated and believes that his Jesus is much more gripping, exciting, captivating and laudable than Paul's Jesus-as-Christ. Aslan says that if we engage in an extensive analysis of the "real" historical Jesus, we will discover Aslan's Jesus. Where does Aslan propose we go to obtain this extensive analysis of the "real" historical Jesus? He rejects the Gospels and the rest of the New Testament as reliable evidence of the historical Jesus. For Aslan, you would have to read and believe the liberal theologians that he believes in. So it is not really a study of the historical Jesus; it is the study of the Jesus that these liberal theologians believe in. How do we know they are accurate? We have to take it on their authority that they are telling us the truth. They reject the historical reliability of the New Testament; they say we are not to trust the authority of the Gospels.

But they insist that we rely on their authority as they debunk the historical documents. Aslan rejects the Jesus of the New Testament, what he calls the Christ-of-faith, and says that when you strip Jesus of all that is said about him in the New Testament and only see him as a poor peasant zealot who attempted to put down the Roman army with a small band of followers, then you will realize that this new view of Jesus is much better. But there is nothing gripping, exciting, captivating and laudable about the Jesus that has been created in the mind of Aslan. Aslan's Jesus has been so stripped of humanity that he is not even a caricature; he is a ghost. What Aslan has attempted to do is make Jesus into a revolutionary man like Muhammad. Aslan thinks his vision of Jesus is someone worthy of our belief, but he is not. What is the point of believing in someone who was just one of many zealots in the first century that stupidly believed that with a small band of followers they could take on the Roman army? Why would anyone think such a person is gripping, exciting, captivating and laudable? The Christianity of the New Testament emphasizes love and forgiveness because those were the very ideals that Jesus portrayed in his life. He healed the sick, cared for the oppressed, sought out the sinner and, through love and forgiveness, gave himself as the substitutionary sacrifice for the sins of the world. Aslan's Jesus is not worth thinking about, or writing about. And that is exactly the conclusion Aslan wants you to come to. He wants you to dismiss Jesus as a nobody, a fable existing in the minds of several first-century writers. Rejecting Jesus has its consequences. The writer of Hebrews asked: "how shall we escape if we ignore so great a salvation?" (NIV, 2:3.)

We see by these six questionable remarks that Aslan has fabricated stories about Jesus, Peter, and Paul that are not true. Aslan's theories have no foundation, and when you look at the entirety of his book, *Zealot*, one finds that he has merely built a house of cards, which the winds of truth easily collapse. But Aslan is still not finished. In his Epilogue, he attempted to paint Christianity as an almost diabolical force in the world.

Chapter Twenty: The Last Gasp

Aslan contends that Constantine, Rome's emperor in the fourth century, brought some church leaders (all men) together and commanded them to come to a consensus regarding the religion (Christianity) that he had recently adopted. This meeting became known as the Council of Nicaea. Aslan claims that the Council's decisions produced more than a thousand years of horrible killings in the name of Christ and the teachings of the Church.

The Council of Nicaea

The Council of Nicaea was attended by around three hundred bishops, many of whom showed physical scars they had received from the rampant persecution during Diocletian's reign. Considered the first major ecumenical council, the bishops met in 325 A.D. to mostly resolve the controversy surrounding Arianism (see *The Moody Handbook of Theology*). Arius, a presbyter of Alexandria, denied the divinity of Christ and claimed that Jesus was created and not eternal, that Jesus was the first creature created by God the Father. (Aslan, Islam, the Jehovah Witnesses, and many others also make this same mistake.) The Council upheld the deity of Christ, which the church had believed in since its inception (based on seeing the risen Jesus which compelled Thomas to proclaim, "My Lord and my God"), affirming that Jesus is "true God from true God." (Even though the Council had condemned Arianism, the idea continued to influence the church until the Council of Constantinople in 381.) Emperor Constantine, who had called for the meeting in order to unite the church and solidify his empire, approved the conclusions of the Council. As a result, a creed was created and adopted by the Council known as The Nicene Creed; it affirms:

> We believe in one God, the Father Almighty, maker of all things visible and invisible, and in one Lord, Jesus Christ, the Son of God, the only-begotten of the Father, that is, of the substance of the Father, God from God, light from light, true God from true God, begotten, not made, of one substance with the Father, through whom all things came to be, those things that are in heaven and those things that are on earth, who for us

men and for our salvation came down and was made flesh, and was made man, suffered, rose the third day, ascended into the heavens, and will come to judge the living and the dead.

The phrases "begotten, not made" and "came down" emphasize Jesus' eternality. The Council of Nicaea did not create Jesus into God, as some modern liberal theologians suggest (like Ehrman); the New Testament clearly affirms—in the Gospels and the epistles—that Jesus is both divine and human. The early church had already determined that Jesus was the Son of God who had come to earth to redeem humankind, believing that by his (Jesus') sacrificial death humans are reconciled back to God. One of the earliest church creeds appears to be:

> Jesus Christ, although he was in the form of God, did not consider equality with God as something to cling to, or something to be used for his own benefit, but set aside his Godhood by becoming a servant, born as a human male. Being a human, he humbled himself and became obedient to death on a cross. God raised Jesus from the dead and brought him back to his exalted state, where he has the name honored above every name, so that at the name of Jesus everyone will bow, whether in heaven or on earth or under the earth, and every person will confess that Jesus Christ is Lord, which will bring glory to God the Father. (Php 2:6–11).

False teachers and new philosophical ideas (like Gnosticism) began to influence the church in the first century, and it was imperative that true doctrinal beliefs be firmly established. It is why John was compelled to write his Gospel. It is also why, even before the Council of Nicaea, there had been numerous local councils and synods that dealt with different issues that arose within the budding church (Luke gave us insight into one of the Councils in Acts 15). Near the end of the first century, for example, Docetists focused so much on Jesus' divinity that they taught that Christ only appeared to have a human body and that his earthly life, including his suffering and death, was an illusion. The Ebionites denied Jesus' divinity and claimed that Jesus was merely a human being who had acquired divine power at his baptism. There were some Jewish Christians who put too much of an emphasis on the observance of the Mosaic Law. The church had to contend with these and other various ideas/beliefs. Besides these, there were fictional writings emerging in the second century, like the Gospel of Thomas, the Gospel of Peter and the Gospel of Mary, etc., each of them presenting diverse (and often incorrect) views of Jesus. The early church had a strong belief in Truth, and the epistles of Paul, Peter, James, Jude and John showed no tolerance for something not true, warning their readers of the constant threat of false teachers spreading false ideas. The early Christians were not concerned about erroneous ideas out in the world; they were concerned about erroneous ideas inside the church—the body of Christ. The strict policy on truth should not, however, have resulted in physical persecution and torture, which are horrible stains upon the Church, going against the edicts in the New Testament regarding love, humility, kindness, patience, etc. Although Aslan points out that there have been horrible deeds done in the name of Christ, one should realize that just because something is done in the name of Christ does not mean the action is actually in agreement with the doctrines set down by Jesus or the New Testament. That being said, please allow a somewhat lengthy explanation of what Aslan accuses Christianity of doing throughout the entire Medieval Period and beyond. (I will glean some information in this section from *Church History in Plain Language*.)

A Look at "Christian" History

Beginning in the second half of the first century, Christians began to be persecuted in a variety of ways because they rejected pagan forms of worship and lifestyles and considered Jesus to be God and not just one of the gods pagans worshipped. This persecution continued, sometimes quite heavily, into the beginning of the fourth century. During the first eighty years of the third century, many emperors served for very short periods of time, slain by rivals almost as quickly as they donned the royal garb. Chaos and anarchy ran amok. Rome's political power was crumbling. Then Diocletian became emperor in the latter half of the third century and was able to reestablish order and power during his twenty-year reign. Although a pagan, he had allowed Christians to serve in his court; even his wife and daughter were known to have accepted Christianity as their religion. Near the end of his reign, for reasons still not completely known, he began to ruthlessly and savagely persecute Christians. He ordered a complete purging of Christians from the land. The brutal killing of Christians, the destruction of churches, the burning of Scriptures, and the imprisonment of bishops began in earnest. Emperors that followed Diocletian continued the persecution of Christians, until the reign of Constantine. After Constantine's supposed conversion to Christianity, believers were then able to move from the "underground" and enjoy a somewhat non-persecuted existence. Christianity was now to be treated as just another religion to be tolerated. Unfortunately, by the end of the fourth century Christianity had become the established religion of the empire. Many, myself included, think this was one of the worst things that could have happened to the Christian faith. The Christian Church now became associated with the power of the state and the result was a secularization of the faith. The body of Christ— the universal collection of believers—had joined itself with the political state—the ungodly prostitute (see 1 Cor 6:15) The Roman Empire was now able to interfere in the affairs of the church. The politicalization of Christianity led to its being exploited and weakened throughout the Medieval Period. Christianity had become so infiltrated with paganism that it became almost unrecognizable at times. What was referred to as Christianity was actually a caricature; it was paganism with just enough Christian ideology to fool the masses. The majority of peasants, being illiterate and uneducated, were able to be fooled and controlled by the religious leaders. When literacy became more prevalent, individual reading of the Bible, especially the New Testament, was forbidden because then it would be clearly seen that much of what passed as "Christian," under Roman Catholic rule, was actually closer to pagan religious beliefs. (See *The Two Babylons* for more detailed information regarding paganism's influence in "Christianity.")

It is possible that Constantine's "conversion" was a purely political maneuver because paganism still remained not only in his personal life but throughout his empire. He continued in conspiracies against others, engaged in murder, and kept the title *Pontifex Maximus*, which indicated his desire to continue as head of the state religious cult. What Constantine had done was simply to make Christianity one of the religions tolerated within the empire, so now a professing Christian could openly practice his/her religion without fear of persecution, just as those who had been practicing pagan religions had been able to do. Although Constantine's mother appeared to be a devout Christian, and it appeared that he had raised his family with Christian principles,

Constantine did not receive baptism until shortly before his death. He may have waited so long simply because he was hoping to cover all the bases before he died. Many ancient kings accepted and prayed to different gods just in case one of them was willing to answer his prayers and help him conquer his foes. Constantine could have been engaging in that age-old practice of trying to please any god out there just before he died.

Since Christians could now preach and worship openly and rebuild their churches, it is understandable that they saw Constantine as a great Christian emperor, but one must not confuse the good one does with what is really in one's heart. Only God can see what is in one's heart; and only God can say whether Constantine truly believed in his Son, Jesus, for salvation. Be that as it may, Christians were now tolerated in the empire and permitted to freely practice their religion. However, Constantine still ruled the Christian bishops just like any other political subject. Now that there was no more persecution, many people became "Christian" in order to obtain religious and political occupations. Masses of people now streamed into the church so that they could benefit from political and lucrative posts they desired. These people, infiltrating the church, brought along their various views about Jesus and their pagan teachings and lifestyle. During the period when Christians were being heavily persecuted, it is pretty safe to say that the vast majority of those who identified themselves as Christians, as followers of Jesus, were truly Christian. When Christianity became a tolerated religion, and it was beneficial to be a "Christian" in order to hold desirable religious and political positions, lots of people were now becoming "Christian." Holding the office of a bishop was seen as a great occupation; it did not matter if one was a true Christian or not. Many became "Christian" only to satisfy their political/social ambitions, even if they were disinterested in Christianity as a practicing religion. They could profess to be Christian to get the position they desired and still adhere privately and personally to their pagan beliefs and practices.

Around 380 A.D., when the emperor Theodosius, as a matter of imperial command, established Christianity as the empire's religion, a complete turn-around occurred, so that now Christians were being rewarded and non-Christians were being punished. This, again, was another terrible blow for Christianity. Typical of a ruler's pride of position, Theodosius took for granted that there was a 'natural' relationship between his own will and God's. Whatever the emperor wanted, surely it was what God wanted, too. More and more pagan ideas infiltrated the church, so that even buildings where the church met were being designed according to the architecture found in Persia and ancient Babylon. Ancient gods were beginning to be worshipped with new Christianized names. Statues would soon be made and prayed to in complete disobedience to Judeo/Christian thought. The interior of churches became more and more pagan, following the Babylonian cult, and this overflowed into the beliefs and lives of worshipers. Bishops began to exercise extreme power over their congregations. Excommunication became a handy tool for the bishops to use against local parishioners, and even the pope was known to use it against emperors and local political powers. Soon, the bishop of Rome (the pope) became the ruler of the western church, and the bishop of Constantinople became the ruler of the eastern church. These bishops wielded not only religious power but political power as well.

Beginning with Constantine, and certainly during and after Theodosius, there was a huge decline in Christian commitment despite the growing membership in local churches. The church that had suffered persecution under Diocletian was now infiltrated with a growing mixture of half-converted pagans. Before Constantine, Christians had laid down their lives for the truth, and regretfully new "Christians" were now persecuting each other in order to gain religious and political positions. Soon, men, who had no personal relationship with or concerns about Jesus, were being awarded positions as local bishops and abbots and priests, and as popes. One now was simply a "Christian" because one happened to be born in a certain locale. True Christianity was rarely to be seen, in the church and throughout the land. Many church leaders (bishops and such) had purchased their positions from the pope or local king; many, if not most, had no real, personal convictions about Jesus and did not recognize or confess him as their Savior. A purchased bishopric was desirable because it had the potential to be a very comfortably lucrative position. These bishops, and other powerful church leaders, found it imperative to control their district, and often resorted to persecuting those who differed doctrinally from them. They may have done this in the name of Christ but they were really doing it in the name of their own pocketbook.

When the Visigoths, led by Alaric who claimed to be a Christian, forced their way into Rome and devastated everything in it except the churches, they were able to rid Rome of its paganism, but only for a time. Since the pope erroneously declared that Peter was the first bishop/pope of Rome, and that each pope followed Peter in succession, the pope was able to maintain extreme power over his people. No matter how ungodly, irreligious and/or pagan a pope might be, he was to have honor attached to him as a rightful heir of Peter. The basis for belief in Petran succession is nowhere to be found in the New Testament. It was not long before the Roman church (and the Byzantine church as well) blended Roman law, Christianity, Hellenistic (Greek) philosophy, Babylonian mystery cults, and local pagan thought and lifestyle together. What you see throughout the Medieval Period is this blended religion. It is not, strictly speaking, Christianity. Icons and statues, to worship and pray to, became important, but were unchristian. Sainthood was established and parishioners were prompted to pray to them, while offering money; again a non-Christian concept. Confessional practice was established, which became another form of control over the congregation. Anyone differing from the edicts brought down by the pope and/or local bishops were to be labeled as heretics and punished. Christianity, which teaches love, joy, peace, forbearance, kindness, goodness, faithfulness, gentleness and self-control (see Gal 5:23), was not the impetus for the terrible crimes done in the name of Jesus; it was paganism in the guise of Christianity that had done so.

During the Medieval Period, true Christianity was seen in the preaching of Jesus and his crucifixion and resurrection; it was seen in the believer's moral lifestyle; it was seen in the way a Christian treated others, especially those who did not know Jesus personally; it was seen in the building of hospitals, orphanages and universities; in the communities working together to help one another in bad times and celebrating with each other in good times; in the care of the poor and marginalized; in the protection of the Jews when other so-called Christians were persecuting them; in the Renaissance that Charlemagne had instigated; in the attempts to lessen the confinements of feudalism; to control the enjoyment of war; and to reform the papacy and monasticism.

False Christianity became more and more associated with the state, thereby becoming more infiltrated with paganism. Christianity became lost in the mire of popular paganistic lifestyles. Was it because Christianity was not strong enough to conquer paganism? No, it was powerful enough to overcome the world; it is just that people will typically believe and accept a lie over the truth. They did so then; they do so now. Popular liberal theologians, the so-called "new" atheists, and Aslan are counting on it. The atrocities made in the name of Christ during the Medieval Period were contrary to Christian doctrine. Early Christians were reluctant to go to war because they believed this world was not their true home. There was no reason to war against another group of people because Christianity taught that it was imperative to love one another. The Christian's warfare was spiritual; it was against Satan and his followers. Nowhere in the New Testament do we see an admonition to physically fight against someone else. Aslan's attempts to show that Jesus told his followers to take up a sword to physically fight against those that opposed him are clearly unfounded.

When we look at the terrible activities the Romish Church engaged in—indulgences, excommunications, inquisitions, etc.—we can easily see they were not endorsed by New Testament values and ethics. It is imperative that you understand the difference between those who "claim" to have faith, "claim" to know Jesus, "claim" to be the authoritative head of the church, and those who actually follow Jesus and are being transformed into his image. Do not use the excuse that "Christianity" has done so many horrible things through the centuries. Look at the true Christianity as found in the New Testament and compare that to the actions of people who "claim" to know Jesus. Jesus warned us: "Be careful of false prophets. They come to you looking gentle like sheep, but they are really dangerous like wolves. You will know these people by what they do" (NCV, Mt 7:15). John tells us that we are not to simply believe someone who "claims" to be a Christian, "claims" to have the Spirit of Jesus; but we are to test them to see whether they truly have the Spirit of Jesus because lots of false teachers are out in the world (1 Jn 4:1). Paul says we should examine and test ourselves to see if we are living according to the Christian faith (2 Co 13:5) In Galatians 6:4 Paul says: "Each one should test their own actions" (NIV). In 1 Thessalonians 5:20-22, Paul admonishes us to not despise or scorn what God has revealed through others, but to test everything. We are to hold on to what is good or true and reject what is wrong. John tells us to test and reject anyone who denies that Jesus Christ has come in the flesh, i.e., that Jesus is God incarnate (see 1 Jn 4:2).

Chapter Twenty-one: Postscript—Another Look at Islam

Throughout his book, Aslan claimed that Jesus was nothing more than a zealot, a nationalist, who only cared for the Jews and believed in a warrior God. I hope I have shown that Aslan's portrayal of Jesus is wrong. We can, however, acknowledge that Muhammad was a radical Arab nationalist, and it is possible that Aslan's whole premise was to try to make Jesus into a Jewish type of Muhammad so that he (Aslan) could dismiss everything the Gospels and the rest of the New Testament says about him. Muslims have, in the past, made futile attempts to try to present Jesus as a follower of Islam, and Aslan seems to be engaged in that same futility in his book *Zealot*.

Is Allah the same as Yahweh?

Christianity considers itself the fulfillment of Judaism; it honors the Hebrew Scriptures and sees them as God's progressive revelation of his plan to humankind. That plan was to redeem humans and reconcile them back to him. This was to be done through the sacrificial death of the Redeeming Messiah, Jesus Christ. Now, Islam arose from a pagan society that was aware of Judaism and Christianity. The Arab people were polytheists, and had been for millennia, adopting the cultic beliefs of Persians, Babylonians, Egyptians, and those among the Levant. Arabian merchants traveling throughout the then known world were in constant contact with other belief systems. The Kaaba, the black cubic structure at the mosque in Mecca, which Arab tradition claims was built by Abraham and Ishmael, once housed some 360 idols that the Arab tribes had collected over the years. Each tribe had their own special or patron idol to worship. The idols were made to conform to the image the worshipper desired; so some idols were in human form, others looked like a lion or a horse or some kind of bird. Blood sacrifices were offered to the gods at the Kaaba, including human sacrifice. Besides worshipping these man-made idols, they also worshipped celestial images—sun, stars and moon. One of the many gods that was worshipped by the Arabs was Allah, long before Muhammad was born. The word 'Allah' is a contraction of two words; 'al' meaning "the," and 'ila' meaning "god"—hence Allah means "the god." When Muhammad chose Allah to be the god for his religion, out of the 360 available, was it the same one who identified himself as Yahweh in the Hebrew Scriptures? No, it was not. Islam's god should not be associated with the Judeo/Christian Lord God.

Muhammad and the Beginnings of Islam

Before Muhammad was born, his tribe—the Quraysh tribe—worshipped the god Allah. The Quarysh tribe was in control of Mecca and therefore their god—Allah—was the chief god. Muhammad was born around 570 A.D. in Mecca and was apparently orphaned by the time he was six and was cared for by his grandfather and then his uncle, who was a merchant trader. Muhammad travelled with his uncle along the merchant trade routes. When Muhammad was around twenty-five he worked for a wealthy widow named Khadija who, eventually, became his wife (one of many). To help relieve his bouts of depression, Muhammad often ventured off to the mountains to be alone. He preferred one particular cave to meditate in and one day, while meditating in that cave, Muhammad thought he received a prophetic call from God through the angel Gabriel. (Here, of course, we see some Christian influence in Muhammad's biography concerning the angel Gabriel.) Muhammad, being illiterate, never read the Hebrew Scriptures or the New Testament books. He did know about Judaism and Christianity because both religions were prevalent in Arabia long before he was born, but his knowledge of them was second-hand at best; whoever taught him about these two religions probably was not well versed in them either because Muhammad had quite a few misconceptions of what Christianity taught. Muhammad was forty years old (610 A.D.) when he was visited by the "cave angel," and he was so frightened by this angelic appearance that he believed it was an evil spirit. He thought he must be possessed by a demon and even contemplated suicide. Khadija convinced him it was no evil spirit, and that he was not possessed, suggesting that it was a sign that he, like Moses, would be a prophet for his people. (Now, Muslims believe that Satan is real and refer to him as a great deceiver in the Qur'an. Norman Geisler, from whom I glean some information in this section, wonders if it is not possible that Muhammad was correct in thinking he was possessed and being deceived by Satan.)

But Muhammad continued to go to the cave and was told by the angel visiting him to "recite." Muhammad, being illiterate, did not write

426

down the revelations he received, but recited them orally. (Maybe it was Muhammad's own illiteracy and lack of education that prompted Aslan to insist the same of Jesus, although such illiteracy actually went against Jewish custom.) About three years passed before Muhammad began to "recite" the words he had been given to others. (Aslan has denigrated the oral traditions of early Christianity, saying they were too easily exposed to embellishment and redaction, and therefore Christian oral traditions could not be trusted once put in written form, so surely he must denigrate the oral traditions of Islam—his own religion. The Qur'an, which became the written form of the recited words Muhammad heard from the angel, cannot be trusted as a reliable document on the same grounds Aslan uses to reject the Gospels.) Having been rejected in Mecca, Muhammad left there in 622 and went to Medina with about seventy men and their families. This marked the beginning of the Islamic era, becoming year one in the Islamic calendar. There were Jewish clans living in and around Medina. Because the Jews had rejected their Messiah, they were therefore still looking for a Messiah to arrive. Many non-Jews who lived in Medina may have been more ready to accept Muhammad as a prophet because they had heard about the expectations of the Jewish Messiah. Nearly all the Jews in Medina, however, dismissed Muhammad as a Messiah and/or prophet, rejected his "recited" words (which would become the Qur'an), and actively opposed his followers, the Muslims. Muhammad, in retaliation, expelled some Jewish clans from Medina and executed others. By 630 Muhammad had compiled an army strong enough to take Mecca. It did not take long for people in Mecca to become Muslims and soon many tribes all over Arabia were joining his religion. By 632, Muhammad was dead, and he had named no successor. Within twelve years of Muhammad's death, the Muslims had occupied Egypt, Syria and Iraq, and were advancing into Libya and Persia (Iran). By the eighth century, they had crossed into Spain. Muhammad became the example for all Muslims, and his sayings and deeds were compiled into two collections known as the Hadith and the Sunna. These sayings and deeds of Muhammad were compiled generations after his death, and it took several centuries after Muhammad's death for them to be placed in complete written form. (It seems that since the Qur'an did not record any miracles performed by Muhammad, Aslan must have felt compelled to conclude that Jesus was a magician simply because Aslan does not want Jesus being able to do miracles while Muhammad could not.)

427

The Sunni and Shi'a

Because Muhammad did not choose a successor, two basic groups arose within Islam—the Sunni and Shi'a. According to the Sunni, Muhammad could not be replaced because he was the ultimate prophet, the last one God needed to give to humankind. The leader who succeeded Muhammad could therefore only be a caliph who exercised a subordinate authority to Muhammad, but would still be the leader of the Muslims. The second group, the Shi'a Muslims, selected Muhammad's cousin, Ali, to succeed their prophet, and subsequently elected an imam as their main religious authority, believing he was given the ability to interpret the Qur'an with inspiration and infallibility. Both sects adhere to a comprehensive social structure, a system of community law, called the Sharia, which is based on the teachings of the Qur'an and the Sunna. For Muslims, the Qur'an is God's final revelation and therefore contains perfect truth. It replaces all earlier revelations that God sent to humankind. Muhammad was the last messenger and prophet of God. On Judgment Day everyone will be judged according to their sincere repentance (which means becoming a Muslim) and good deeds, which will be measured by how well they obeyed the Sharia, God's perfect law. If a person earns favor from God on Judgment Day, based on their good deeds, then they will get heaven as their reward. (Some information in this paragraph gleaned from *Introduction to World Religions*.)

The Bible vs. the Qur'an

Of course, Jews and Christians reject many of the passages (and ideas) that are found in the Qur'an. According to the Bible, the Qur'an is incorrect in some of its statements about Jesus. A case in point: there is internal and external evidence that Jesus was crucified, but the Qur'an denies this historical event. According to the Bible, the Qur'an is incorrect in some of its statements about God. It teaches that whatever happens, God willed it. The Qur'an dispenses with human's free will and responsibility and resorts to a fatalistic view of life. The Qur'an does not differentiate between the concepts that God allows something to happen and God wills it to happen. For Muslims, whatever happens, God willed it. So if an "infidel" gets beheaded by a Muslim, then God willed it simply because it happened. For the Muslim, God is unknowable and one cannot have a personal relationship with him. God is only a lawgiver who demands, from an infinite distance, that we obey him. For the Jew and Christian, God is knowable. In fact, God wants us to know him. He does not expect us to just follow his laws; he wants us to experientially know his love, mercy and compassion; to know him on a personal level as we do a friend. Muslims know about God, but they do not know him personally. According to the Bible, the Qur'an is incorrect in its statements about salvation and sin. The Qur'an promotes righteousness-by-works as a means of salvation, informing the Muslim how she/he must live in order to merit Allah's favor. Although the Qur'an bases salvation on good works, it yet sees every action as something that God wills. The person doing the good works is not really doing them if they are being done because God wills it. Why should that person get the credit? A Muslim can never know until he/she dies if they have accumulated enough good works to get to heaven. But Islam (and any other religion) is inadequate to make you good enough to enter God's Kingdom.

Muslims have a very weak idea of sin and do not realize how God views sin, and how it keeps us from God. Their weak view of sin allows Allah to be so great that he can do what he likes, even break his own laws. God hates sin; it destroys his creation. Islam, however, treats sin as if it were a mere mistake that is easily forgiven and forgotten. This attitude makes a mockery of God. Evil has a source other than the will of God; one is right in fighting moral evil because it does not come from God. Islam portrays a false image of humans, not recognizing the sinful nature that lives within us, a nature that keeps us from God. Their denial of the sinful nature in humans is a detriment to their doctrine of man. When one acknowledges their cancer and comes to terms with it, they can then fight against it. To ignore or deny the cancer increases one's chances of death. Islam ignores and denies the cancer of sin and is therefore unable to ever know God, in this life and in the next, because they are unwilling to accept his remedy. They are, therefore, unable to please God with the salvific system they have created. There is a clear and dangerous naïveté that Islam has regarding sin. The Bible, on the other hand, offers a realistic view of humans and, as such, offers the only remedy for the human condition (the cancer of sin). That remedy is atonement—God's plan of redemption through the substitutionary death of Jesus. According to the Bible, the Qur'an is incorrect in its statements about heaven. For Muslims, heaven is a place where every wish is fulfilled as if God were now at their beck and call since one has proven to be so good as to get there. One gets to heaven by having their good deeds be more than their bad deeds, which is confusing since every event is what God willed anyway. Again, the only way to get to heaven, according to Christianity, is by accepting God's Redeeming Messiah—Jesus. (Some information gleaned from Geisler's *Answering Islam*.)

Who is the Prophet?

As the Jews had done in the first century, Muhammad rejected the Messiah and made himself to be the final, ultimate Prophet, claiming (erroneously) that he was the one prophesied in Deuteronomy 18:15: "The LORD your God will raise up for you a prophet like me [Moses] from among you, from your fellow Israelites. You must listen to him" (NIV). Jesus fulfilled this passage from the Hebrew Scriptures and all the other prophecies regarding the Redeeming Messiah. Notice that the Prophet from God would be an Israelite, not an Arab like Muhammad. Muhammad rejected God's final Prophet—Jesus—and claimed that position for himself. The Qur'an and the Bible cannot both be true since they contradict each other. Aslan sides with the Qur'an and wants you, his reader, to doubt the reliability and historicity of the Bible so that the only option left is to believe the Qur'an.

The Word of God as a Person

Geisler informs us that Muslims see the Qur'an as the eternal Word of God recited to Muhammad to bring final guidance to humans. Therefore, Muslims believe that the Qur'an supersedes all previous revelations. Christians, however, see Jesus as the eternal Word of God. If the Qur'an is the eternal Word of God, then why does it contain historical and doctrinal errors, like saying Jesus was not crucified and Mary is the third person of the Trinity. Again, this is why Aslan has to be so disparaging of the Bible—he has to show that the Bible is historically unreliable because the Qur'an is. Muslims claim the Bible is historically unreliable because it has changed too much over the years. But the Dead Sea Scrolls have shown the reliability of the Hebrew Scriptures, and the more than 5,700 extant Greek manuscripts have shown the reliability of the New Testament writings. The most ancient manuscripts show that our modern translations of the New Testament are extremely accurate. There is absolutely no evidence to

430

indicate that the New Testament has been distorted over the years, as Muslims and Aslan claim. They make this claim in order to rationalize and justify their rejection of the Bible, but the evidence is against them. Muslims are also in the habit of selecting Bible passages that seem to support their own doctrines and affirm those particular passages as authentic, but then dismiss the many other Bible passages that clearly contradict the Qur'an. This, of course, is what Aslan does throughout *Zealot*. Aslan needs to show that the Bible is wrong because if it is correct, then Islam, his religion, is wrong. Aslan demonstrates that he responds to Jesus and the Bible in typical Muslim fashion. Despite the many years he says he researched and studied Jesus and early Christianity, he really is only presenting the Muslim view of both.

No Assurance of Salvation for the Muslim

Although Islam teaches that you can earn your way into heaven by doing good works, the Muslim has no real assurance that he/she will be saved; they have no promises to rely upon. They must be careful to fulfill all the religious requirements and obligations of Islam and to make up for any shortcomings they have by balancing them out by doing good deeds, like giving alms. The Muslim must strictly adhere to the teachings of the Qur'an in order to have any chance at getting into heaven; their system is built on salvation-by-works. Their system is also built on the idea of jihad—a Muslim's duty to maintain their edicts, which includes a personal struggle to not sin and a resistance (violent, if necessary) against the 'infidel' (a person who does not follow Islam). Only a Judeo/Christian worldview realistically acknowledges the fact that humans are not as righteous as they would like to think, nor can they ever truly be. Humans are in need of a Savior due to their inability to perform the amount of good works it would take to be acquitted at the judgment bench of a truly righteous and holy God. Islam, like most other religions, says humans can be good enough to enter heaven on their own, but it does not know when one is good enough. The Hindu realizes it cannot be done in one lifetime and therefore multiple lives are required to finally be good enough to enter heaven. The Buddhist believes it may be possible, but very unlikely, to be good enough in one lifetime to reach Nirvana, so it too relies on reincarnation. Islam does not know how many good works are required to reach heaven so it teaches that you must follow the strict Shari'a, and if you do that, hopefully God will be merciful enough to let you into heaven. Salvation, for the Muslim, is a crap shoot; a throw of the dice and hope you win. Paul tells us in Galatians 3:24f that before the Messiah appeared the Law served as our guardian. It could not save us, but it could guide us. The purpose of the Law was to lead people to the Messiah; it revealed how unrighteous we are in comparison to God's righteousness. The Law showed our need for a Savior, one who would stand with us at God's judgment bench and declare us righteous. We are declared righteous when we accept what Jesus did in our place. We receive God's approval because of faith in Jesus. Unfortunately, Muslims, in rejecting the Messiah, can only rely on the Law to save them, which it cannot nor was it meant to do. The only way to try to justify themselves is by creating this strict law (Shari'a) and then demand that everyone follow it in order to be saved. But neither the Shari'a nor the Mosaic Law has the power to save.

Our Freedom in Jesus

Christianity offers freedom from the tyranny of good works. By recognizing that you can never be good enough to get to heaven on your own, you simply place your faith in the Redeeming Messiah who stepped in and took your rightful punishment so that your sins, which blocked you from a personal relationship with God, can be forgiven and removed, allowing you to be reconciled to God. Once you are saved, then God expects you to do the good works he designed you to do. The commandments of God are still to be obeyed by the children of God, i.e., Christians. But, in Christianity, the good works do not save; only faith in the Redeeming Messiah can do that. Jews and Christians are allowed to enjoy life. In the Hebrew Scriptures the Jews were allowed joyous festivals that included wine and other fermented drinks (Dt 14:26), simply for enjoyment, so that families and communities could get together and eat, drink, dance and have fun. But it was to be done in self-control and moderation. God did not allow drunkenness, gluttony, and such, because these were harmful to oneself and the community. But he did allow people to enjoy themselves. Christians continued this tradition. A Christian is not forbidden to enjoy a beer at dinner, or to enjoy a cigar at the end of the day. A Christian is not enslaved by customs, traditions and legalistic notions. There is a freedom in Christianity that prompts one to enjoy life, without sinning. But it is important to maintain self-control. In Islam, one's behavior is strictly controlled so that many things are restricted and forbidden. When you rely on good works for salvation you must create all sorts of restrictions that keep you from enjoying the life God gave you. Other religions, like Buddhism, Mormonism, the Jehovah Witnesses, etc., do this too. The Pharisees in Jesus' time had attached so many restrictions onto the Law that they had forgotten the spirit of the Law. This is what Jesus was trying to point out to them, but they were not able to understand because of their spiritual blindness.

In Islam, God does not have a knowable essence, except for the idea that he is absolute will, which means he acts according to his will at the moment. He has no nature or essence that compels him to act a certain way, so if he chooses to be loving or hateful he will act accordingly. When John says that God is, according to his nature, Love (see Wuest, 1 Jn 4:8), the Muslim would deny this because, for them, God does not have a nature or essence. For the Muslim, God is called good because he causes good things to happen, but not because goodness itself is part of his nature or essence. There is no nature or essence in God according to which he must act. It would seem as if the Muslim God acts immorally when it suits him, but they find a way out of this dilemma by saying that evil cannot be attributed to God because evil implies an imperfection, and God is perfect. Of course, this seems contradictory since Muslims believe that God does not have a knowable essence. So how can a Muslim worship or love God when he/she does not really know anything about him? (Some information in this section gleaned from Geisler's *Answering Islam*.)

Aslan is wrong to think that the "real" Jesus has been lost, and that he has helped us find him again. The four canonical Gospels give us a clear picture of the Jesus of history and the Messiah who saves us (Jesus-as-Christ). The Gospels are reliable, historic documents. We have seen that Islam bases its beginnings on words that Muhammad received from an angel in a cave that he was to recite to others. But how reliable are these oral traditions that were the beginnings of Islam? We know how important it was to the Jewish culture that the message of their oral traditions not get lost in the retelling of the events. We cannot, however, be as sure of the oral traditions of Islam. When we see a particular pagan god chosen from among many others

433

to be the god of Islam we can assuredly assert that Islam's Allah is not the same as Yahweh, the God of Judeo/Christian Scriptures. When we see the historical errors in the Qur'an we cannot say that it is the eternal Word of God. When we see that Muhammad took the promise of a Prophet that was to come to Israel and claimed it referred to himself we cannot say with any candor that Muhammad is the final prophet that God has sent to guide humankind. When the Bible clearly shows us God's plan for reconciling humans back to him, when we see the extent of God's love for humankind that he would come to earth himself to be pierced for our transgressions and crushed for our iniquities (Is 53:5), why would there be the need for another religion that says that you must live according to some strict law in order to collect all these points for good works that you really do not know is going to save you anyway? There is no need for a man-made plan for salvation—which is what Islam is—when you have God's wonderful plan already. It is clear that Muhammad took a pagan god and made it the god that Muslims pray to and worship. Allah, the god of the Muslims, is clearly not the same as the God of the Bible. May any Muslim reading this heed the words of Moses: "Acknowledge and take to heart this day that the Lord [Yahweh] is God in heaven above and on the earth below. There is no other" (NIV, Dt 4:39).

Chapter Twenty-two: Why it Matters

We hear in the news about some wonderful thing someone did to help a stranger. How someone would risk their own life to go into a burning building to save someone, or to jump into a river to rescue someone from drowning, or volunteer to help search for someone who is lost. We are encouraged by these stories, and we should be. It would be tragic to go through life and not know or experience the greatest story of rescue ever told. Which is why I hope that you, dear reader, will, if you have not yet, take the time to find out who Jesus is and what he did for you.

Christians believe that Adam and Eve's original disobedience resulted in a fundamental change in the relationship between humans and God, as well as disrupting the relationship between humans and the created world, others, and themselves. Theirs was an act of rebellion against God that had vast moral repercussions. It created a chasm, a terrible abyss, that completely separated us from the kind of relationship that God had wanted to have with humans. This act of rebellion, the result of a free-will choice, became engrained in our nature, causing humans to be repelled against God and his love. Down through the ages, humans have created religions to try to get back to that original state, but no amount of human effort can do that. Justice demanded a penalty for the wrongs committed. God, who has a Trinitarian nature and who, by that nature, is Love, endured the penalty for this act of rebellion so that the relationship between God and humans could be restored. The Son of that triune God, referred to as the second person of the Trinity, became a human in order to die in our place for the crimes (sins) we committed against him. It would be the greatest act of love ever known. Imagine that you have committed the most heinous of crimes and are set to be executed for them, when the person most effected by those crimes steps forward and, out of love for you, dies for those crimes instead. It's unthinkable! But that is what Jesus did. "At the right time," he entered history the same way all humans enter it, so that he could redeem humans after living a pure and holy life. After he took the punishment for our sins, satisfying justice's demands, he rose from the dead. The Spirit of the Lord (the Holy Spirit) then began to grow the church into the image of Jesus, transforming each believer to reflect the character of our Lord.

When you look at all other religions, other than Christianity, you find that their basis for salvation is the feeble attempt to do good works in order to please their god, to get some kind of pass to enter into oneness with their god, or Nirvana, or heaven. They think their occasional good behavior should remove the penalty they deserve. Some attempt to remove as many obstacles as possible from their lives in order to avoid doing wrong so that it will be easier to get to heaven; Buddhist monks do this, as do lots of other religious people. But if you are hanging from a cliff and holding onto a chain with ten links in it, it only takes the breaking of one link to send you to your death. You must realize the breaking of one law makes you a law-breaker. You must pay the penalty. If you reject the person who has already paid the ultimate penalty for you—that is, Jesus—you will have to pay the penalty yourself. That is why it matters—if you attempt to pay the penalty yourself, you will be forever estranged from God. If you accept on faith that Jesus paid your penalty in full on the cross, then you will be reconciled with God. I do hope that you will consider Jesus; that you will realize that God has brought salvation to you through the death and resurrection of the Redeeming Messiah—Jesus—so that you can be reconciled with God. The reason it matters is that, in rejecting Jesus as your Savior, you doom yourself to take on the penalty you deserve.

In conclusion, I hope that I have successfully and satisfactorily answered the allegations, declarations, conjectures, misrepresentations and conclusions Aslan has proposed in his *Zealot*. I hope that I have clearly explained and given evidence for my position—that Jesus is God-in-the-flesh, who came to redeem humankind and reconcile us back to God (himself). I hope I have successfully debunked the idea that Jesus was a mere lowly, uneducated peasant who was influenced by a zealot (John the Baptizer), and that he too became one and used his magical skills to gather followers in order to disrupt and destroy the religious/political system of the first century so that he could restore Israel's independence and set himself up as a king in God's kingdom here on earth.

It is now up to you to decide if Aslan's point of view is the correct one, or if the four canonical Gospels portray the real historical Jesus. Jesus asked his disciples: What current theory is being said about me? (See Mt 16:13-19). Then he asked his disciples: What do you say about me? Their answer: You are the Messiah, the Son of the living God. May that be your answer as well.

REFERENCE PAGE

Introduction

Aslan, Reza. *Zealot: The Life and Times of Jesus of Nazareth*. Random House (2013)

Chapter One: Jesus Through an Obscure Lens

Funk, Robert W; Roy W. Hoover and the Jesus Seminar. *The Five Gospels: What Did Jesus Really Say? The Search for the Authentic Words of Jesus*. HarperOne; Reprint edition (December 19, 1996)

Patterson, Stephen and Marvin Meyer. *The "Scholars' Translation" of the Gospel of Thomas.*
Website: http://earlychristianwritings.com/text/thomas-scholars.html

Perrin, Nicholas. *Thomas, the Other Gospel*. Publisher: SPCK. 2007

Patzia, Arthur G. *The Making of the New Testament: Origin, Collection, Text & Canon*. 2nd Edition. Intervarsity Press. 2011.

Elwell, W. A. and P. W. Comfort. (2001). *Tyndale Bible Dictionary*. Wheaton, IL: Tyndale House Publishers.

Cabal, T. (Ed.) (2007). *The Apologetics Study Bible: Real Questions, Straight Answers, Stronger Faith*. Nashville, TN: Holman Bible Publishers.

http://www.christiananswers.net. (Although not used as material for this section, I suggest reading Luke Timothy Johnson's *The Real Jesus* (an excellent critique of the Jesus Seminar), and the excellent online article by Dr. Mark D. Roberts entitled *Unmasking the Jesus Seminar: A Critique of Its Methods and Conclusions*.)

Patzia. *The Making of the New Testament.*

McDowell, Josh and Sean McDowell. *More Than a Carpenter*. Tyndale Momentum; Revised edition (May 20, 2009)

Patzia. *The Making of the New Testament*.

Groothuis, Douglas. *Christian Apologetics: A Comprehensive Case for Biblical Faith*. IVP Academic. 2011.

http://carm.org/manuscript-evidence;
http://www.knowwhatyoubelieve.com;
http://www.equip.org/articles/the-bibliographical-test-updated/

Crossan, John Dominic. *The Historical Jesus: The Life of a Mediterranean Jewish Peasant*. HarperOne; Reprint edition (February 26, 1993).

Borg, Marcus. *Meeting Jesus Again for the First Time*. HarperOne.1994.

Horsley, Richard A. and Neil Asher Silberman. *The Message and the Kingdom*. 1997. Augsburg Fortress Publishers.

Noebel, David. *Understanding the Times*: The Collision of Today's Competing Worldviews. Summit Press; 2nd edition. 2006

Geisler, Norman L. and Abdul Saleeb. *Answering Islam: The Crescent in Light of the Cross*. 2002. Baker.

Chapter Three: The Early Years of Jesus

Bruce, F. F. (1996). **Quirinius**. In D. R. W. Wood, I. H. Marshall, A. R. Millard, J. I. Packer and D. J. Wiseman (Eds.). *New Bible Dictionary*. (3rd ed.). Leicester, England; Downers Grove, IL: InterVarsity Press.

Bruce, F. F. (1996). **Census**. In D. R. W. Wood, I. H. Marshall, A. R. Millard, J. I. Packer and D. J. Wiseman (Eds.). *New Bible dictionary*. (3rd ed.). Leicester, England; Downers Grove, IL: InterVarsity Press.

What Does the Bible Say About... The Ultimate A to Z Resource Fully Illustrated. Nelson's A to Z series. **Census**. Thomas Nelson Publishers. (2001). Nashville, TN.

Radmacher, E. D., R. B. Allen and H. W. House. (1997). *The Nelson Study Bible: New King James Version.* Nashville: T. Nelson Publishers.

Spence, H. D. M. (Ed.). The Pulpit Commentary. London; New York: Funk & Wagnalls Company. 1909. *St. Luke Vol. I.*

http://evidenceforchristianity.org/two-recent-archaeological-discoveries-support-the-bible;
http://en.wikipedia.org/wiki/Tel_Dan_Stele;
http://www.bibleuniverse.com/articles/bible-universe-blog/articletype/articleview/articleid/1584/pageid/1715.

Fruchtenbaum, A. G. (1983). *Vol. 127*: *The Messianic Bible Study Collection.* Tustin, CA: Ariel Ministries.

Chapter Four: The Beginnings of Jesus' Ministry

Fuller, Russell and C. W. Draper. (2003). *Holman Illustrated Bible Dictionary* (C. Brand, C. Draper, A. England, S. Bond, E. R. Clendenen and T. C. Butler, Ed.) Nashville, TN: Holman Bible Publishers.

Quest Study Bible. Zondervan. Grand Rapids, MI. 1994, 2003. Marginal note for 2 Kings 18:26-28.

Hughes, R. B. and J. C. Laney. (2001). *Tyndale Concise Bible Commentary.* Wheaton, IL: Tyndale House Publishers.

Elwell, W. A., and B. J. Beitzel. (1988). *Baker Encyclopedia of the Bible.* Grand Rapids, MI: Baker Book House.

Friedman, David. (2001). *They Loved the Torah: What Jesus's First Followers Really Thought About the Law*. Baltimore, MD: Messianic Jewish Publishers.

Louw, J. P. and E. A. Nida. (1996). *Vol. 1: Greek-English Lexicon of the New Testament: Based on Semantic Domains*. New York: United Bible Societies.

Josephus, F. and W. Whiston. (1987). *The Works of Josephus: Complete and Unabridged*. Peabody: Hendrickson. *Antiquities*.

Blomberg, C. (1992). *Vol. 22: Matthew*. The New American Commentary. Nashville: Broadman & Holman Publishers.

Nolland John. (2005). *The Gospel of Matthew: A Commentary on the Greek Text*. New International Greek Testament Commentary. Grand Rapids, MI; Carlisle: W.B. Eerdmans; Paternoster Press.

Garland, D. E. (2001). *Reading Matthew: A Literary and Theological Commentary on the First Gospel*. Reading the New Testament Series. Macon, GA: Smyth & Helwys Publishing.

Boice, J. M. (2001). *The Gospel of Matthew*. Grand Rapids, MI: Baker Books.

Weber, S. K. (2000). *Vol. 1: Matthew*. Holman New Testament Commentary. Nashville, TN: Broadman & Holman Publishers.

Newman, B. M. and P. C. Stine. (1992). *A Handbook on the Gospel of Matthew*. UBS Handbook Series. New York: United Bible Societies.

Chapter Five: The Galilean Ministry of Jesus

Louw. *Greek-English Lexicon of the New Testament*.

Spence, *St. Luke Vol. I*.

Marshall, I. H. (1978). *The Gospel of Luke: A Commentary on the Greek Text*. New International Greek Testament Commentary. Exeter: Paternoster Press.

Vincent, M. R. (1887). *Word Studies in the New Testament*. New York: Charles Scribner's Sons.

Chapter Six: Jesus as Magician

Richards, Larry. *Every Miracle in the Bible*. Thomas Nelson Publishers. Nashville. 1998.

Mills, M.S. *The Life of Christ: A Study Guide to the Gospel Record*. 1999. Dallas, TX: 3E Ministries.

Elwell, W. A., and B. J. Beitzel. (1988). *Baker Encyclopedia of the Bible* (**Baal-zebub**). Grand Rapids, MI: Baker Book House.

Taylor, Thomas. *Arguments of Celsus, Porphyry, and the Emperor Julian, Against the Christians*. Public Domain

Crossan, *The Historical Jesus*

Blomberg, Craig L., *Jesus of Nazareth: How Historians Can Know Him and Why It Matters*. In Douglas Groothuis' *Christian Apologetics: A Comprehensive Case for Biblical Faith*. IVP Academic. 2011.

Choi, Mihwa. (1997). *Christianity, Magic, and Difference: Name-Calling and Resistance between the Lines in Contra Celsum*. Semeia, 79, 75.

Cabal, *Notable Christian Apologist: Origen*. In *The Apologetics Study Bible*.

Origen. *Contra Celsum*. (1885). Origen against Celsus, translated by F. Crombie; In A. Roberts, J. Donaldson & A. C. Coxe (Eds.) *Vol. 4: Fathers of the Third Century: Tertullian, Part Fourth; Minucius Felix;*

Commodian; Origen, Parts First and Second. The Ante-Nicene Fathers. Buffalo, NY: Christian Literature Company. Origen, *Against Celsus.*

Stuart, D. K. (2006). *Vol. 2: Exodus.* The New American Commentary. Nashville: Broadman & Holman Publishers.

Strobel, Lee. *The Case for Christ.* Interview with Gregory Boyd. Zondervan Publishing (1988)

Myers, A. C. *The Eerdmans Bible Dictionary.* (1987). William B. Eerdmans Publishing Company. Grand Rapids, MI.

Chapter Seven: The Kingdom of God

Vine, W. E., M. F. Unger and W. White, Jr. (1996). *Vol. 2: Vine's Complete Expository Dictionary of Old and New Testament Words.* Nashville, TN: T. Nelson.

Radmacher, E. D., et al. (1997). *The Nelson Study Bible: New King James Version.* Nashville: T. Nelson Publishers.

Fruchtenbaum. *The Messianic Bible Study Collection.*

Bonhoeffer, Dietrich. *Cost of Discipleship.* Chapter 19. SCM Press (2011).

Ridderbos, H. N. (1996). *Kingdom of God, Kingdom of Heaven.* In D. R. W. Wood, I. H. Marshall, A. R. Millard, J. I. Packer, and D. J. Wiseman (Eds.), *New Bible Dictionary* (3rd ed.). Leicester, England; Downers Grove, IL: InterVarsity Press.

Richards, Larry. *Every Teaching of Jesus in the Bible.* (2001). Thomas Nelson Publishers. Nashville.

Fruchtenbaum, Arnold G. (1998). *Messianic Christology: A Study of Old Testament Prophecy Concerning the First Coming of the Messiah.* Tustin, CA: Ariel Ministries.

Josephus' *Antiquities*.

Chapter Eight: Jesus as Zealot

Louw, *The Greek-English Lexicon of the New Testament*.

Zodhiates, S. (2000). *The Complete Word Study Dictionary: New Testament*. (electronic ed.). Chattanooga, TN: AMG Publishers.

Vincent, *Word Studies in the New Testament*.

Ridderbos. *Kingdom of God, Kingdom of Heaven*

Zodhiates. *The Complete Word Study Dictionary: New Testament*

Armstrong, Karen. *The Case for God*. Anchor Books, 2009.

Chapter Nine: Was Jesus a Bigot?

Fruchtenbaum, *Messianic Christology*.

Mills, *The Life of Christ*.

Groothuis. *Christian Apologetics*.

Noebel. *Understanding the Times*.

Friedman. *They Loved the Torah*.

Bonhoeffer. *Cost of Discipleship*, chapter eight

Copan, Paul. *Is God a Moral Monster? Making Sense of the Old Testament God*. Baker Publishing Group Grand Rapids, MI. 2010.

Groothuis. *Christian Apologetics*.

Chapter Ten: Jesus as Messiah

Fahlbusch, E. (Ed.). (1999-2003). *Vol. 1: The Encyclopedia of Christianity*. (**Councils. Synods.**) Grand Rapids, MI; Leiden, Netherlands: Wm. B. Eerdmans.

Fahlbusch, E. (Ed.). (1999-2003). *Vol. 3: The Encyclopedia of Christianity*. (**Monatanism.**) Grand Rapids, MI; Leiden, Netherlands: Wm. B. Eerdmans.

Payne, J. Barton. *Encyclopedia of Biblical Prophecy*. Baker Book House.1980.

Spence, H. D. M (Ed.). *St. Matthew Vol. II, Chapter 24*.1909. The Pulpit Commentary. London; New York: Funk & Wagnalls Company.

Chapter Eleven: A Journey Through the Gospels

Spence, H. D. M (Ed.). *St. Mark Vol. 1*. 1909. The Pulpit Commentary. London; New York: Funk & Wagnalls Company.

Friedman, *They Loved the Torah*.

Spence, H. D. M (Ed.). *Daniel*. 1909. The Friedman. London; New York: Funk & Wagnalls Company.

Spence, Luke 3:23a.

Chapter Twelve: Jesus as the Messenger of the Lord

Geisler, N. L. (2003). *Systematic Theology, Volume Two: God, Creation*. Minneapolis, MN: Bethany House Publishers.

Chapter Thirteen: The Arrest, Trial and Execution of Jesus

The eight commentaries I used to investigate Aslan's idea that Roman soldiers would not have been used in the arrest of Jesus are:

Cabal, T. (Ed.). (2007). *The Apologetics Study Bible: Real Questions, Straight Answers, Stronger Faith.* Nashville, TN: Holman Bible Publishers;

Spence, H. D. M (Ed.). *St. John Vol. II.* 1909. The Pulpit Commentary. London; New York: Funk & Wagnalls Company;

Borchert, G. L. (2002). *Vol. 25B: John 12–21.* The New American Commentary. Nashville: Broadman & Holman Publishers;

Boice, J. M. (2005). *The Gospel of John: An Expositional Commentary.* Grand Rapids, MI: Baker Books;

Radmacher, E. D., et al. (1997). *The Nelson Study Bible: New King James Version.* Nashville: T. Nelson Publishers;

Talbert, C. H. (2005). *Reading John: A Literary and Theological Commentary on the Fourth Gospel and the Johannine Epistles* (Rev. ed.). Reading the New Testament Series. Macon, GA: Smyth & Helwys Publishing;

Hendriksen, W. and S. J. Kistemaker. (1953-2001). *Vol. 1-2: Exposition of the Gospel According to John.* New Testament Commentary. Grand Rapids: Baker Book House;

Gangel, K. O. (2000). *Vol. 4: John.* Holman New Testament Commentary. Nashville, TN: Broadman & Holman Publishers.

Achtemeier, P. J. Harper & Row, & Society of Biblical Literature. (1985). *Harper's Bible Dictionary* (1st ed.) San Francisco: Harper & Row.

Elwell, W. A. and P. W. Comfort. (2001). *Tyndale Bible Dictionary.* Wheaton, IL: Tyndale House Publishers.

Richards, L. (1999). *Every Man in the Bible.* Nashville: T. Nelson.

Grassmick, J. D. (1985). Mark. J. F. Walvoord and R. B. Zuck (Eds.). *The Bible Knowledge Commentary: An Exposition of the Scriptures.* Wheaton, IL: Victor Books.

Hendriksen, W., & S. J. Kistemaker. (1953-2001). *Vol. 10: Exposition of the Gospel According to Mark.* New Testament Commentary. Grand Rapids: Baker Book House.

Chapter Fourteen: The Resurrection of Jesus

Berens, E.M. *The Myths and Legends of Ancient Greece and Rome.* Maynard, Merrill, & Co; New York. Public Domain.

Drane, J. W. (2000). *Introducing the New Testament* (Completely rev. and updated.) Oxford: Lion Publishing.

Hughes. *Tyndale Concise Bible Commentary*

Elwell. *Baker Encyclopedia of the Bible* on **Resurrection**

Strobel. *The Case for Christ.*

http://en.wikipedia.org/wiki/Tacitus_on_Jesus

http://en.wikipedia.org/wiki/Pliny_the_Younger_on_Christians

I reviewed five books regarding Mark's last 12 verses:
Brooks, J. A. (1991). *Vol. 23: Mark.* The New American Commentary. Nashville: Broadman & Holman Publishers;

Bratcher, R. G., & Nida, E. A. (1993). *A Handbook on the Gospel of Mark.* UBS Handbook Series. New York: United Bible Societies;

France, R. T. (2002). *The Gospel of Mark: A Commentary on the Greek Text.* New International Greek Testament Commentary. Grand Rapids, MI; Carlisle: W.B. Eerdmans; Paternoster Press;

Cooper, R. L. (2000). *Vol. 2: Mark*. Holman New Testament Commentary. Nashville, TN: Broadman & Holman Publishers;

Warren, B. (2007). Textual Issues in the Gospels. *Holman Christian Standard Bible: Harmony of the Gospels*. Nashville, TN: Holman Bible Publishers.

Chapter Fifteen: An Attack on Luke's Book of Acts

Louw. *Greek-English Lexicon of the New Testament.*

Kistemaker, S. J. and W. Hendriksen. (1953-2001). *Vol. 17: Exposition of the Acts of the Apostles*. New Testament Commentary. Grand Rapids: Baker Book House.

Friedman. *They Loved the Torah*

Chapter Sixteen: Paul as Rogue Apostle

Louw. *Greek-English Lexicon of the New Testament.*

Young, E. (1972). *The Book of Isaiah: Volume 3, Chapters 40–66.* Grand Rapids, MI
Wm. B. Eerdmans Publishing Co.

Friedman. *They Loved the Torah*

Chapter Seventeen: Paul and the Historical Jesus

Zodhiates. *The Complete Word Study Dictionary: New Testament.*

Patzia. *The Making of the New Testament*

Bultmann, Rudolf. *Faith and Understanding*. Library of Philosophy and Theology Series. Publisher: Hymns Ancient & Modern Ltd (June 18, 2012)

Zodhiates. *The Complete Word Study Dictionary: New Testament.*

Vine. *Expository Dictionary of New Testament Words.*

Spence. *Colossians.* The Pulpit Commentary.

Louw. *Greek-English Lexicon of the New Testament.*

Zodhiates. *The Complete Word Study Dictionary: New Testament.*

Spence. *Hebrews.* The Pulpit Commentary.

Richards, L. (2001). *Every Name of God in the Bible.* Everything in the Bible series. Nashville, TN: Thomas Nelson.

Carpenter, E. E. and P. W. Comfort. (2000). *Holman Treasury of Key Bible Words: 200 Greek and 200 Hebrew Words Defined and Explained.* Nashville, TN: Broadman & Holman Publishers.

Myers, A. C. (1987). *The Eerdmans Bible Dictionary.* Grand Rapids, MI: Eerdmans.

Kurian, G. T. (2001). *Nelson's New Christian Dictionary: The Authoritative Resource on the Christian World.* Nashville, TN: Thomas Nelson Publishers.

Shedd, W. G. T. (2003). *Dogmatic Theology* (A. W. Gomes, Ed.) (3rd ed.) Phillipsburg, NJ: P & R Pub.

Chapter Eighteen: Was the Epistle of James Written as a Polemic against Paul?

Radmacher, E. D., R. B. Allen and H. W. House. (1997). *The Nelson Study Bible: New King James Version.* Nashville: T. Nelson Publishers.

Friedman. *They Loved the Torah.*

Drane. *Introducing the New Testament*

Ellsworth, R. (2009). *Opening up James*. Opening Up Commentary. Leominster: Day One Publications.

Spence, *James*. The Pulpit Commentary.

Isaacs, M. E. (2002). *Reading Hebrews and James: A Literary and Theological Commentary*. Reading the New Testament Series. Macon, GA: Smyth & Helwys Publishing.

Luther, Martin. (1520) *A Treatise on Good Works*. (Public domain).

Ellsworth. *Opening up James*.

Henry, Matthew. (1994). *Matthew Henry's Commentary on the Whole Bible: Complete and Unabridged in One Volume* (Commentary on James). Peabody: Hendrickson.

Chapter Nineteen: Six Questionable Remarks

Patzia. *The Making of the New Testament*

Spence. *1 Timothy*. The Pulpit Commentary.

Fuller. *Holman Illustrated Bible Dictionary*, **Caesarea Philippi**.

Wood. *New Bible Dictionary* **Caesarea Philippi**.

Louw. *Greek-English Lexicon of the New Testament*

Zodhiates. *The Complete Word Study Dictionary*

Charles, R. H. (Ed.) *Pseudepigrapha of the Old Testament*. 2004 (1 Enoch; 4 Ezra). Bellingham, WA: Logos Bible Software.

Pseudo-Clement of Rome. (1886). (The Clementine Homilies, T. Smith, Trans.). In A. Roberts, J. Donaldson and A. C. Coxe (Eds.), *Vol. 8: Fathers of the Third and Fourth Centuries: The Twelve Patriarchs, Excerpts and Epistles, the Clementina, Apocrypha,*

Decretals, Memoirs of Edessa and Syriac Documents, Remains of the First Ages. The Ante-Nicene Fathers. Buffalo, NY: Christian Literature Company.

Chapter Twenty: The Last Gasp

Enns, P. P. (1989). *The Moody Handbook of Theology.* Chicago, IL: Moody Press.

Shelley, B. L. (1995). *Church History in Plain Language* (Updated 2nd ed.). Dallas, TX: Word Pub.

Hislop, Alexander (2012-07-01). The Two Babylons. E-Life Publishing. Kindle Edition.

Melick, R. R. (1991). *Vol. 32: Philippians, Colossians, Philemon.* The New American Commentary. Nashville: Broadman & Holman Publishers.

Chapter Twenty-one: Another Look at Islam

Geisler. *Answering Islam.*

Partridge, C., *Introduction to World Religions.* 2005. Minneapolis, MN: Fortress Press.

Geisler. *Answering Islam.*

19603212R00258

Printed in Poland
by Amazon Fulfillment
Poland Sp. z o.o., Wrocław